W9-BDL-354

# THE PAPER OFFICE, THIRD EDITION

# THE CLINICIAN'S TOOLBOX™

A Guilford Series

EDWARD L. ZUCKERMAN, *Series Editor*

# The Paper Office

**THIRD EDITION**

Forms, Guidelines, and Resources
to Make Your Practice Work Ethically, Legally, and Profitably

Edward L. Zuckerman, PhD

THE GUILFORD PRESS
New York    London

© 2003 Edward L. Zuckerman
Published by The Guilford Press
A Division of Guilford Publications, Inc.
72 Spring Street, New York, NY 10012

All rights reserved

The Clinician's ToolBox™ and the toolbox logo are registered trademarks and may not be used without permission from the Publisher.

Except as indicated, no part of this book may be reproduced, stored in a retrieval system, or transmitted, in any form or by any means, electronic, mechanical, photocopying, microfilming, recording, or otherwise, without written permission from the Publisher.

Printed in the United States of America

This book is printed on acid-free paper.

Last digit is print number:  9  8  7  6  5  4  3  2  1

LIMITED PHOTOCOPY LICENSE

These materials are intended for use only by qualified mental health professionals.

The Publisher grants to individual purchasers of this book nonassignable permission to reproduce the handouts and forms in this book and CD-ROM for use with their own clients and patients. This license is limited to the individual purchaser and does not extend to additional clinicians or practice settings. The license does not grant the right to reproduce these materials for resale, redistribution, or any other purposes (including but not limited to research, books, pamphlets, articles, video- or audiotapes, and handouts or slides for lectures or workshops). Permission to reproduce these materials for these and any other purposes must be obtained in writing from the Permissions Department at Guilford Publications.

**Library of Congress Cataloging-in-Publication Data**

Zuckerman, Edward L.
    The paper office: forms, guidelines, and resources to make your practice work ethically, legally, and profitably / Edward L. Zuckerman. — 3rd ed.
        p. cm. — (The clinician's toolbox)
    Includes bibliographical references and index.
    ISBN 1-57230-769-2
    1. Psychiatric records—Forms.   2. Psychiatric records—Handbooks, manuals, etc.     I. Title.   II. Series.
RC455.2.M38 Z828   2003
616.89'14'068-dc21

                                                                2002005597

*To my beloved daughter, Lilly Charlotte Lawrence Zuckerman.*
*This book is for the education you richly deserve.*

# About the Author

Born in New York City, Ed Zuckerman found his life's passion while working as a psychiatric aide at New York's Bellevue Hospital in the 1960s. He earned his PhD in clinical psychology at the University of Pittsburgh and worked in community mental health while gaining his license. He has worked with adults with developmental disabilities as well as those with severe alcohol addiction, acted as liaison with state hospitals, taught undergraduates, and been in the independent practice of general clinical psychology for many years. He now lives with his family in rural western Pennsylvania with horses, ducks, geese, chickens, and lots of mud and trees. There he consults and creates worthwhile practice tools for clinicians.

# Acknowledgments

Many of my professional colleagues have generously taken the time to offer their advice, suggestions, and creations (and I hope that you, the present reader, will do the same; see p. 7). In most cases their names appear next to their contributions throughout this book, and I must restate my gratitude for their assistance in making this book as useful to our professions as it has become. Thank you all.

Joan Anderson, PhD, Houston, TX
Marc Andrews, ACSW, Pittsburgh, PA
Bruce Barrett, MA, CPT, Duxbury, MA
Mitchell Berk, CSW, MA, Island Park, NY
Ginger E. Blume, PhD, Middletown, CT
Margaret A. Bogie, Chantilly, VA
Sheila Carluccio, MA, Dickson City, PA
David Clovard, MD, Raleigh, NC
Allan J. Comeau, PhD, West Los Angeles, CA
Harry Corsover, PhD, Evergreen, CO
Estelle Disch, PhD, Cambridge, MA
Constance Fisher, PhD, Pittsburgh, PA
Donald J. Franklin, PhD, Bridgewater, NJ
Muriel L. Golub, PhD, Tustin, CA
Irvin P. R. Guyett, PhD, Pittsburgh, PA
Gordon Herz, PhD, Madison, WI
Ronnie M. Hirsch, PhD, New York, NY
Russ Holstein, PhD, Long Branch, NJ
Glenn W. Humphrey, OFM, PhD, New York, NY
Susan Hutchinson, DSW, LCSW, Irvine, CA
Richard E. Jensen, PhD, St. Charles, IL
Sam Knapp, EdD, Harrisburg, PA
Susan Lentulay, MA, Erie, PA
Don-David Lusterman, PhD, Baldwin, NY
Robert E. McCarthy, PhD, Myrtle Beach, SC

David A. Miller, PhD, Kansas City, MO
Ivan J. Miller, PhD, Boulder, CO
Kathleen Quinn, EdD, Cheyenne, WY
Jackson Rainer, PhD, Norcross, GA
George F. Rhoades, Jr., PhD, Aiea, HI
John Roraback, PhD, Moline, IL (deceased)
Mickie Rosen, MS, ATR, Huntington Valley, PA
Joseph Rosenfeld, PhD, Southampton, PA
Mason B. Scott, EdD, Pittsburgh, PA
John M. Smothers, PhD, ABPP, Bethesda, MD
Eugene Snellings, CsW, ACP, Baton Rouge, LA
Ruth H. Sosis, PhD, Cincinnati, OH
Charles H. Steinmeyer, PhD, Warren, PA

I also wish to express my appreciation to Bob Matloff and Seymour Weingarten of The Guilford Press for their continuing support and trust in the value of this project, as well as for their honesty and openness as friends and associates. The best thing they did for me was to provide me with an ideal editor, Barbara Watkins. She has been consistently smart, articulate, patient, enthusiastic, and a damn quick learner. I must also express my great appreciation for the tireless efforts of editorial project manager Anna Brackett and copyeditor Marie Sprayberry, whose superb sense of style, proportion, and language have greatly increased this book's readability, clarity, and value.

# Contents

*Note:* All figures, forms, and handouts are shown in ***bold italic***.

# List of Figures, Forms, and Handouts

# Introduction

## Ways This Book Can Help You

This book is designed for both the novice independent therapist and the experienced practitioner.

If you are a clinician just entering independent practice, who wishes to start up a practice properly, this book will help you get organized and develop good professional habits. It will make you

- less vulnerable (and therefore less anxious) when doing clinical work,

- more efficient, and

- more profitable and stable as a business.

All of this should result in giving you more satisfaction with the career of therapist. This book cannot contain everything you should know to be in independent practice; it does contain all you need to make the correct initial decisions about office practices and paperwork, and so it will help you start out right.

If you have been in private practice for a few years, this book offers the means to update your practice to conform to current legal and ethical developments. We live in a world that has become more litigious. Standards of professional practice and conduct have evolved rapidly, becoming ever more complex and subtle. Private practice has become more difficult because of the anxieties raised by malpractice cases and ethics complaints. For all of us, the remedies for this anxiety lie in increasing our coping skills (such as by acquiring particular expertise), developing fuller and more realistic understanding of the issues, and taking preventative actions. As therapists, our best defenses against malpractice are to offer high-quality and thoughtful care, use rational and effective procedures, and document our reasons and decisions thoroughly.

The resources in this book are specifically and carefully tailored to meet each of these needs. *The Paper Office* provides the basic operational "tools" needed by psychotherapists of any orientation, training level, or discipline. It should be emphasized that they are designed for the solo practitioner and the small-group practice, and may not meet the needs of a large or diverse group, agency, prison, school, or military practice. In addition, *The Paper Office's* forms and other materials are designed only for outpatient settings—not hospitals of any kind, and not university or teaching settings.

## What This Book Contains

This book provides both practical information and ready-to-use resources:

- Brief, highly informative guidelines and checklists provide the facts needed to alert you to the most important legal and ethical issues, and to direct you in developing solid working procedures.

- Paper resources—sample documents and photocopiable forms—offer effective ways to meet specific challenges to your practice.

- This book is designed to function as "a malpractice risk reduction kit."

The forms and other materials offered are administrative and procedural. They organize information to support the delivery of clinical services and to protect both clients and therapists. These materials will enable you to do the following:

- Collect identifying and personal data.

- Guide the taking of relevant histories.

- Clarify a client's financial and insurance resources.

- Document the client's mental status and suicide risk.

- Organize the results of the intake evaluations (e.g., diagnoses, prognoses, treatment plans).

- Assure informed consent (to evaluation, treatment, release of records, etc.).

- Partially socialize clients into the way therapy unfolds.

**This book assumes that you, the reader, are already a trained, practicing clinician.** It assumes that you know how to do evaluations and therapy, and that you deal with clients and families. Therefore, the forms offered in this book are not forms for collecting data on symptoms or dynamics. For example, although you are offered a way of summarizing a client's mental status (Form 34), you are not given any tests or protocol of questions to collect the data the form summarizes. If you need questions to assess a client's presentation, history, symptoms, and mental status, and the words to describe these, the *Clinician's Thesaurus* (Zuckerman, 2000) contains the entire language of mental health.

## Unique Features

**The professions' ethical standards, principles, and guidelines have been incorporated into each form and sample document.** This avoids the remoteness of reading about abstract principles, the narrowness of individual case studies, and the possibility of overlooking the necessary application of an important principle in your practice's procedures and paperwork. After the principles are learned through these applications, they can be more easily applied to new situations through your sensitized and enhanced ethical reasoning.

**The forms and other materials have been designed and updated to meet current legal and ethical standards for the practice of psychotherapy by the several disciplines.**[1] As you know, there are significant differences in these standards by state, discipline, and population. To be comprehensive, this book tries to include any point or issue raised in any jurisdiction. It is very likely that concerns now raised in only a few places will eventually be applied in every location, and so these should be addressed now. The courts, the mass media, and the public have generally not paid attention to the differences among the professions, and so the book is inclusive in this respect as well.

**However, you must know your local rules.** Although I have made sincere and extensive efforts to be inclusive, I cannot guarantee that these materials will meet *all* the ethical and legal rules of *all* professions and jurisdictions. Your best sources of current and localized information are your state's and discipline's organizations. Join them, contribute to them, and participate in them; doing so will make you more aware and sophisticated, and will keep your practice up to date. This knowledge is necessary for continuing to use the best practices and for reducing your risks.

In a similar vein, some readers have asked whether this book has been read and reviewed by lawyers. It has not, both because of the problem stated above of local and discipline differences, and because there would be some conflicting opinions that could not be resolved. Instead, I have relied heavily on published articles that have had the benefit of peer review, and on books by authorities who represent the consensus or vanguard in the field.

## How to Use This Book in Your Practice

If you are an experienced clinician, read the table of contents for the forms and other materials you think are most important to the way you currently practice. Some will be ones you know you should implement to meet ethical and legal standards; others will make you more efficient and help you be better organized.

If you are a beginning practitioner, I recommend that you start with the materials offered in "Quick Start," below.

The sections of this book are generally organized as follows:

[1]The ethics code for psychologists has undergone a major revision from the 1992 version, and a new code was approved in August 2002. The features of this newer code have been incorporated into this edition of *The Paper Office*. The current version can be seen at the APA's Web site (http://www.apa.org/ethics).

■ The background you need to make use of the forms or other materials is offered first. Much of this information is displayed for rapid learning in the form of guidelines and checklists.

■ The legal and ethical aspects and options for each element of the forms or sample documents, and any areas where these can be modified for your own practice, are described next.

■ The model forms or other materials are then presented. (Note that the in-text discussion of each form or handout is indicated in the left margin with the form or handout number itself in a box; e.g., **FORM 1** .)

# Quick Start: Recommended Core Materials

| | |
|---|---|
| Form 20 | First-contact record |
| Form 23 | Client demographic information form |
| Form 24 | Client clinical information form |
| Form 25 | Brief health information form |
| Form 26 | Chemical use survey |
| Form 27 | Financial information form |
| Form 29 | Adult checklist of concerns |
| Form 30 | Child checklist of characteristics |
| Form 32 | Intake interview questions and guide |
| Form 33 | Mental status evaluation and report |
| Form 36 | Suicide risk assessment summary and recommendations |
| Form 37 | Intake summary and case formulation |
| Form 38 | Individualized treatment plan for managed care organizations |
| Form 41 | Structured progress note form |
| Form 47 | Briefer form for requesting/releasing confidential records and information |
| Form 49 | Release-of-records cover letter |

This collection of materials can be produced for your practice in just a few minutes for a few cents, and more can be made as needed. The forms will photocopy clearly and look quite professional. On these forms, a space at the top is allowed for your own letterhead. If you anticipate using a small label on your paperwork to identify the client by name, ID number, barcode, or something similar, you can offset your "letterhead" information to the left and leave room for the label on the right side. If you want to modify them or use ones that must be tailored to your practice, you can use the CD-ROM that contains the text of all the forms and sample documents you will need (see below). The Health Insurance Portability and Accountability Act (HIPAA) of 1996 requires that after April 14, 2003, you use a Notice of Privacy Practices form, use a simple consent form, and make some other small changes to your paperwork. See Section 7.8 (in Chapter 7 of this book) for more information.

Use the forms for 3 months with every new (and some old) clients. Mark the end of the 3-month period in your appointment book when you start. Then relax and focus on doing a fine job as a therapist. After 3 months, review how the forms are working for you. Decide which additional forms you want to incorporate into your practice or what changes you need to make to fit them better into your practice. Make any modifications or additions, and write to me with your suggestions and criticisms. If you make changes, please see the section below on sharing your changes.

## Availability of Materials on CD-ROM

To save you time and effort, all the forms and handouts you might use in your practice are available on the CD-ROM inside the back cover. The materials are word-processed documents in several formats, so any computer can open and display them. Instructions for using the CD-ROM are on the last page of this book.

## A Cautionary Note and Disclaimer

Although the publisher and I have made reasonable efforts to assure that the contents of this book are both accurate and up to date, we cannot be responsible for matters beyond its scope or level of detail, local variations, or future developments. For example, the laws and regulations that apply to your work as a clinician may be federal, state, or local, or they may pertain specifically to drug and alcohol clients, clients of mental health/mental retardation programs, clients of specific government programs, or AIDS patients. In addition, special rules may govern practitioners working in schools, health facilities, outpatient clinics, or the like. Your local professional societies and experts on the scene are the best sources for information about current and applicable rules, both ethical and legal.

All of my comments about HIPAA and its regulations are my own interpretation from reading the Act and other resources and have not been reviewed by lawyers. My recommendations are designed to address the needs of therapists in typical solo or small group practices.

Neither the publisher nor I assume responsibility for any loss incurred as a result of the application of any of the information contained in this book, or for any incidental or consequential damages in connection with or arising out of the furnishing of the materials in this book. No representation is made that they are the only or best ways to practice as a professional psychotherapist. This book is intended to assist an informed intermediary in the treatment of clients and patients—that is, the professional psychotherapist. It is neither recommended nor appropriate for use by amateurs or for self-help.

This book is sold with the understanding that the publisher, distributors, and I are not attorneys, accountants, or ethicists; nor are we engaged in rendering legal, financial, ethical, or other professional consulting services. If materials other than those presented here are needed to manage the purchaser's professional practice or a specific clinical case in any respect, we advise you to engage the services of a competent professional. Any forms that create a contract between the practitioner and the client should be reviewed by your legal counsel and should be modified to conform to local law and practice.

No warranty is expressed or implied, and in no event shall the publisher, author, or any reseller be liable for consequential or incidental damages.

# About Reproducing Materials in This Book

One of the main advantages of this book over other books on ethics or practice is the high quality of the materials—the forms, checklists, patient education handouts, and so forth—and it was probably for these materials that you purchased it. However, before you begin using these materials to enhance your practice, I must remind you of the legal context of copyright in which they exist. **I have legal copyright to many of the forms and handouts in this book,** but I want you to be able to use them in your practice. Thus, I ask the following:

1. You, the individual professional who purchased this book, may photocopy or print from the CD-ROM any of the forms and handouts in the book for which photocopying rights are expressly granted in the form's or handout's caption, but only for use in your individual clinical practice and with your own patients.

    This means you cannot give copies to your associates, supervisees, friends, or other professionals for their own use. A professional should not use these forms without understanding fully their ethical and legal underpinnings, context, and implications, and not owning the book will significantly limit that understanding and expose him or her to increased malpractice risk. If others want to use these materials, they must purchase a copy of *The Paper Office* themselves.

2. You may modify the reproducible forms and figures to suit your practice or your needs. In fact, **you should modify them** for the specific legal or other conditions that apply to your practice, and in any way that will further your clients' understanding. However, modification does not invalidate my copyright.

    - Again, the modified version can only be used in your individual clinical practice with your own patients.

    - If you do modify them and feel that you've made a significant improvement, please send me a copy so that I can see if your changes should be incorporated into the next edition of *The Paper Office*. If they are, you will receive full credit in that edition and a free copy of it.

3. If you work in a group practice and want to use these materials in that setting, you must buy a copy of this book for each individual who will use the materials. Multiple-copy discounts are available.

4. If you are leading a class, workshop, or other educational program and want to distribute copies of some of these materials, you should do the following:

    - Review the law regarding copyright restrictions on what is and is not "fair use." For example, decide whether providing copies of the materials in this book would in any way reduce the sales of the book, which would then make your distribution illegal.

    - Consider requiring students to purchase copies of this book, because the use of these materials without the legal and ethical guidance contained in this book may get them into trouble.

5. Some materials in this book are copyrighted by individuals who did not grant reproduction rights beyond their publication in *The Paper Office*. Therefore, such materials may not be reproduced without the written permission of the copyright holder indicated on the form itself.

6. In addition, all materials for which photocopying rights are not given in a caption, and that are not copyrighted by other individuals, are copyrighted by Edward L. Zuckerman. Their reproduction is forbidden without prior written permission from Guilford Publications.

## Your Forms and Other Contributions: A Nice Offer

- If you're disappointed with any part of this book, don't keep it a secret. Be a good customer, citizen, and therapist: Complain. Send in your criticisms and improvements.

- If you need forms or materials not offered here, let me know.

- If you design or find better or additional forms that you think should be included here, please send them to me for the next revision of this book or for specialized versions of *The Paper Office*. You will receive full credit for your contributions and comments if they are used, and you will receive **a free copy of the next version or edition** if your valuable contributions have been included.

Send your contributions to me at this address:

Edward L. Zuckerman, PhD
P.O. Box 222
Armbrust, PA 15616
http://www.thepaperoffice.com

## Future Developments

As this field develops, this book will be revised to meet the needs of practicing clinicians. The publishers and I will be very grateful for your comments, suggestions, and criticisms. There is a feedback form at the back of the book to make your contributing easier.

It is my hope that by sharing the best efforts and ideas I have been able to borrow, modify, and devise, this book will make your professional life easier and more productive, and will further the professional development of all practitioners of the craft of therapy. Ideally, it will help therapists of all disciplines to strive for the goals expressed in the following oath, which the graduate program in psychology at Adelphi University requires of all entering students:[2]

---

[2]This oath is reprinted by permission of the Chair, Derner Institute of Advanced Psychological Studies, Adelphi University, Garden City, NY.

As I embark on a career as a psychologist, I vow to respect the dignity and worth of the individual and honor the preservation and protection of fundamental human rights. I will be committed to increasing knowledge of human behavior and of people's understanding of themselves and others, and to utilizing such knowledge for the promotion of human welfare. While I pursue these endeavors, I will make every effort to protect the welfare of those who seek my services or of any human being or animal that may be the object of my study. I will use my skills only for purposes consistent with these values, and will not knowingly permit their misuse by others. While demanding for myself freedom of inquiry and communication, I accept the responsibility this freedom requires: competence, objectivity in the application of skills, and concern for the best interests of clients, patients, colleagues, and society in general. I accept with pride these commitments I have made and will cherish this day of entry into the profession of psychology.

# CHAPTER 1

# Basic Paperwork and Communication Tools

## 1.1 Basic Paperwork Tools: An Overview

*I must create a System or be enslaved by another man's.*
—WILLIAM BLAKE

**Your psychotherapeutic skills and personal resources are the basis of your effectiveness as a therapist.** But practice also requires the effective operation of your professional office, and this is based on specialized paperwork. This book presents the essential paperwork tools to help you operate a solo or small-group psychotherapy practice ethically, legally, and profitably.

**Therapeutic practice has ethical dimensions.** Mental health clinicians have been in the forefront of the development of professional ethical guidelines. Concepts such as confidentiality, informed consent, and boundary issues have been articulated through careful deliberations. Professional ethics safeguard patients, enhance therapists' trustworthiness, and improve the climates of communities.

**Therapeutic practice also has legal dimensions.** Therapists live and work in a complex and rapidly developing legal context designed to protect the individual and reinforce socially approved behaviors. The United States is a nation under laws, and social policies are incorporated into laws.

**Finally, therapeutic practice has financial dimensions.** The delivery of U.S. health care services is inescapably intertwined with commerce, and mental health services are no exception. Therapists must be paid for services, and so financial functions such as income, expenses, fees, billing, and taxes must be attended to. Therapists operate in offices and meet for appointments, and so they use standard business resources and office equipment.

Thus there are four aspects of a psychotherapy practice: the therapeutic, the ethical, the legal, and the financial. These four dimensions interact, intertwine, and may compete with one another. We, as professional therapists, need to take account of all of them. We must also respond effectively to their continually evolving interactions. Sometimes the demands of doing so seem burdensome, but we cannot ignore them. This book is one carefully reasoned response to this burden and obligation.

Each tool in *The Paper Office* has a primary function in one of these four areas, but each tool also has ramifications in the other areas. For example, stationery and business cards are important business tools. But the professions have important legal and ethical rules about how therapists present themselves. Similarly, the making and keeping of financial and treatment records are basic administrative office tasks. But rules of confidentiality mean that treatment records cannot be handled and copied like documents in other kinds of business. Also, ensuring payment for services is essential, but the way this is done can affect treatment in many ways that are unique to the practice of psychotherapy. **This book's photocopiable forms and sample documents, guidelines and checklists, and step-by-step procedures will help you integrate the relevant legal and ethical principles and current practices into your ordinary paperwork, thus lightening both your worry and your administrative burdens.** The adoption of just those tools and procedures appropriate for your practices will reduce your malpractice and ethics violation risks substantially. Review the materials described in the following chapters, and evaluate for yourself how much they will lower your anxiety over your practices.

This first chapter begins (at the beginning) with an overview of some office administration basics: What needs to go on a letterhead and in a resume, and what should not? What records do you need to keep? Where and how should you keep them, and for how long? Chapter 2 takes a detailed look at financial tools and procedures, from tracking income and expenses to procedures for billing and to methods for getting paid. Chapters 3 and 4 explore practical ways to meet the ethical and legal requirements of practice, including methods for reducing malpractice risk, and a range of specific tools for obtaining informed consent. Chapters 5 and 6 offer detailed forms and procedures for recording treatment from intake through termination. Chapter 7 offers methods for ensuring confidentiality and offers many forms and form letters for releasing and obtaining client records. Appendices are guides to further resources.

# 1.2   Presenting Yourself on Paper

## Ethical Aspects of Self-Presentation

In choosing the wording that presents you and your practice to the public, it is important to recognize that there are legal, ethical, and rational differences between competence, credentials, and titles. The American Psychological Association's (APA, 2002, Standard 5.01b) code of ethics states that a psychologist must not misrepresent himself or herself in regard to training, skills, or credentials. Furthermore, it is solely the professional's responsibility to assure the absence of confusion, ambiguity, or falsity. **Be certain that your credentials are stated accurately and precisely every time.**

## Guidelines for Clear and Accurate Self-Presentations

- Always use your highest degree. Earlier ones are unnecessary, and their use suggests pomposity (always inappropriate in a therapist) rather than extra training. However, it *is* appropriate to use two degrees if the degrees are in different but relevant fields (e.g., a forensic psychologist's possession of a PhD and a JD). Use the exact degree's abbreviation rather than "Dr."; this lessens confusion. Do not use both "Dr." and "PhD" or "EdD"; this is redundant. "Ph.D." and "PhD" are both acceptable styles because they do not mislead. "PhD" is a more modern style.

- The use of "Doctor" for nonphysicians is acceptable in casual conversations and nonmedical settings, where it is not misleading. Those having a doctorate from a nonpsychological program (such as biochemistry) should not use "Doctor" in psychological settings.

- A professional title is optional but often clarifying. However, depending on the state, some titles have legal definitions. Check your state's definition of the following to ensure legitimacy: "consultant," "evaluator," "clinical psychologist," "counselor," "therapist," "psychoanalyst," and "psychotherapist."

- No one can use the title "psychologist" in any state unless he or she is licensed or similarly credentialed. "Licensed psychologist" (or "certified psychologist") is now considered acceptable, but this was not always the case. Using both words together was seen as redundant. It was also seen as misleading, in that it seemed to suggest that a *"licensed* psychologist" was somehow better than just a "psychologist," or even that there were *unlicensed* psychologists. "Licensed psychologist" is currently permissible, however, and you could include your license number for clarity.

- Specialties of practice (e.g., "practice confined to children" or specialty in "forensic evaluations") are useful to introduce yourself to other professionals or possible referrers, and to convey your areas of competence. However, beware of creating false impressions, because you will have to deliver what you advertise at a high level of expertise. When clinicians present themselves to clients as having certain areas of competence, the courts have generally held them to the standards that professional organizations set, even if the clinician is not a member of such organizations or qualified for membership. Evidence of competence differs by specialty (e.g., certification by the Academy of Certified Social Workers or the National Register of Health Service Providers in Psychology), so know and use only the ones appropriate for your profession, and be scrupulous about your qualifications. There are "boards" whose only requirement for membership is paying a fee. Do not bother to join such boards, because other professionals know which are real credentials and which aren't. They will think less of you and your real credentials if you indicate membership in such "vanity boards" (Dattilio, 2002).

- "Member/Fellow [as appropriate] of the American Psychological Association" is now acceptable. For years it was frowned on because it suggested a credential where there was none; there is no special training or particular skill required for APA membership. However, it does represent conformance to the APA's ethical code, and so is quite important.

## The Name of Your Practice

Your practice's name is up to you. The simplest option is to be yourself: "First name Last name, Degree," or, more traditionally, "John Doe, PhD."

You may also create a name for your practice, such as the professional-sounding "Associated Associates" or the grandiose "The American Research Foundation for Interpersonal Therapeutics." This is called "doing business as" (D/B/A). Descriptive terms such as "Therapy" or "Counseling" may be useful pegs to keep you in others' memories, but some have been used so often that they offer no identity. Check phone books for examples, and try for some uniqueness. Location names are assumed to stick in memory (e.g., Allegheny, Gateway, and Three Rivers are popular in Pittsburgh), and they may be helpful, as patients (or at least referrers) seem to prefer a local therapist.

If you are going to operate your practice under anything other than your real name, you need to register this D/B/A name with your state government for legal reasons. Usually the appropriate government office is called something like the Corporation Bureau of the Department of State. You can call your practice anything except a name someone else has already taken or something a government official finds improper. You will need to fill out a simple form that identifies you as the person behind the facade, pay a small fee, and publish the name in your local newspaper of record. The newspaper's classified ad department will help you with the procedure, and the fee for this is modest.

## Your Stationery and Cards

*Checklist for Necessary Information for Letterheads*

- ❏ Use your legal name without nicknames (unless you live in the South, in a small community, or in some other locality where nicknames are acceptable). If there is a similarly named professional in your area, add initials or, better yet, a distinguishing subtitle or practice name.

- ❏ Include your highest clinical degree, specializations, and other credentials.

- ❏ Include your complete address with zip codes. Use all nine digits these days. (Remember, the referral or check lost in the mail is worse than worthless; it's a hassle.) If you have multiple addresses, indicate them, but make it clear to which address mail (especially payments to you) is to be sent. Do not use abbreviations (e.g., Bldg.), as they are tacky and do not save space on a letterhead. In particular, avoid using erroneous or outmoded abbreviations (e.g., Penna. is archaic for Pennsylvania).

- ❏ An e-mail address on all your forms is no longer an affectation. I recommend its inclusion, both for its convenience and for the image it conveys of someone who is in the *avant garde* or at least *au courant*. If you have developed a Web site, indicate it as well.

- ❏ Your telephone number should always include your area code. You can add a note like "24-Hour Answering Service," if it's true and you want to encourage after-hours calls (see below). If you will be getting a separate fax line, and are getting new phone numbers, order both numbers at the same time and you can get them in sequence for simplicity.

❑ There is no consensus on putting your home number (or address) on your stationery or making it available to your clients. Some report that calls are rare, are almost always justified by a true emergency, and when not are grist for the therapy mill. Others do not want to involve their family members inside the boundaries of therapy and are concerned about violent or harassing patients. An unlisted number may be worth the added cost. If you ever make calls from home to clients, you should consider arranging for blocking of your caller ID, because without this a client will be able to discover the number from which you called.

❑ You should also decide whether you want to be available on a 24-hour basis (is that part of your responsibility to your patients, or is your privacy part of maintaining boundaries?), and then make your rules clear in your client information brochure (see Section 4.2).

❑ List your Social Security *or* tax identification number (the latter is preferable) and license number (with type and state) on anything that will become a bill or accompany a bill, because insurers need these to pay you.

❑ Check and recheck the accuracy of *every word and number* before you print hundreds of any card or paper. I once had to rewrite my area code on 1,000 cards.

### Logos

Logos are popular but not yet standardized. Orthopedists are using a braced-tree design, podiatrists a foot in a winged serpent (Aesculapius) design, and psychologists and psychotherapists the Greek letter "psi" ($\Psi$), but these devices have no meaning for the uninitiated. Most stationery printers offer at least one other logo you might consider, or you could use a simple letter monogram. You may want to design a logo suitable for the name of your practice (tree motifs are nonthreatening). You could have the printer do it for a small charge, or actually hire a professional who has done this before and have a really good job done. (Therapists are notorious for their resistance to using other professionals.) If you can't find an experienced artist, call the owners of a funeral home that has a nice text/logo and ask who did theirs. (This is a good tip—really!)

Phrases such as "We care for you" are tacky. You don't really care for the people who may see your card until they become patients, and we should presume that all therapists care for their patients (as noted by Constance Fisher, PhD, of Pittsburgh, PA).

### Type Style and Size

You cannot go wrong with a typeface from one of the large medical stationery printers. Roman is preferable to *italic*. **Bold** in small sizes is not sharp and uses more space. Serif and sans serif faces are equally acceptable these days for professionals. Larger type is easier to read for seniors (over 40 and also your likely referrers) and for anyone struggling with a seventh-generation photocopy: This is 10 point, this is 12 point, this is 14 point.

## Paper and Envelopes

When I receive it, I always notice crisp, heavy, linen-textured, laid, 100% cotton rag, water-marked, ivory-colored bond paper. I fiddle with it and admire it, but am not impressed by the professional behind it—only curious about how much extra this person has to charge me or my clients for this affectation. Are there any documents created by therapists that deserve or need anything but ordinary 20-pound white paper? If the client's records are to be destroyed in a few years to prevent misinterpretation, why use archival acid-free paper that will last 200 years?

If you use a word processor, you may not need printed stationery at all. You can print the letterhead on each page as it comes out of your laser or inkjet printer (minimum 300-dot-per-inch resolution).

You need envelopes with your name and address, because if a letter is undeliverable it will be returned to you only if the return address is on the envelope. Your computer's printer may be able to print a return address on blank envelopes. Although this is not cheaper, it allows you to select a format to suit each letter and addressee.

For sending out bills, you will need envelopes imprinted with your name and address, or you can use a "two-window envelope" that shows your address through the upper window and the patient's address through the lower window. Save a tree: If you decide on imprinted envelopes, you need buy only a year's supply of #10 window envelopes for billing and regular imprinted envelopes for correspondence (a box of each, usually 500). No business occasion requires fancier stationery, so spend your money on your well-earned pleasures.

## Business Cards

**Business cards are essential.** Carry a few in your wallet and in your datebook, because they have many purposes. You can offer a card to introduce yourself tactfully; the recipient can easily make conversation by inquiring about your location or what you have listed as your specialties. When you make presentations, always bring some cards to give to audience members so that they may call on you for professional services. You can also use them for small notes to others, or can use others' cards to note your promises to call or send something to them.

Plain black ink, slightly raised, roman lettering on a firm (but not too stiff), very white card is always acceptable. The catalogs of the major medical printers offer dozens of designs, typefaces, and colors. After you have made some contacts in your practice area, you can discover the local standards of good taste by examining the cards for which you have traded and then follow these examples. Even so, wait until you have been in practice a few years before ordering 5,000, baby blue, translucent smoky plastic, gold-foil-lettered cards with a logo of doughboy figures hugging each other. (Yes, I received these from a therapist.) Remember the old rule about dressing for a party: You can always dress down from formal attire, but you can't dress up from jeans.

Some business cards incorporate an appointment card on the back. These can provide for single or multiple appointments and different formats; these features make the card even more useful and not much more expensive. Medical Arts Press offers a card that has "Questions to ask my doctor" or "Special instructions" printed on the back. Local printers could do the same for you if this makes sense for your way of practicing. If you have two related positions (e.g., a clinic staff job and a private practice), you can have each printed on one side of a card. If you do business in another language or country, you can have cards printed with translations or addresses on each side.

### Announcement Cards

Announcement cards are usually heavy cardboard ("pasteboard"), paneled cards about 4" high and 5" wide, which you are supposed to send to anyone who might conceivably refer a patient to you. They simply announce the opening of your office, your specialties, and your location, or the fact that you have taken on a partner or moved. All the medical stationers' catalogs show sample designs from which to choose. I have 2,000 of them that I never sent. I don't keep the ones I receive because they do not fit into any filing system. The addresses are more easily found in the phone book, anyway. A better method might be to send a letter, which allows a fuller description of your work with some personalized elements, and include a few business cards (which *can* be filed) or perhaps a preprinted Rolodex™ card (see your local printer or run them off on your photocopier).

## Your Resume and Curriculum Vitae

A resume usually presents your current job functions or future goals, the strongest of your educational and vocational accomplishments, or other relevant experiences. It is generally required if you are seeking to change jobs. Two pages is the maximum length, and one page is often all that others expect to read. A curriculum vitae (Latin for "course of life," usually abbreviated as CV) is more formal and professional in orientation. It is usually sequential and emphasizes any activities that bear on your career development (education, honors, scholarships, professional experiences, grants received, publications, memberships, licenses, etc.). The distinctions between a resume and a CV are often blurred these days.

Any bookstore will provide several books of samples and guidelines for writing a resume or CV and for phrasing one's accomplishments attractively. There are several from a small publisher called Ten Speed Press, which I like for their simplicity and efficiency, but which are not as polished and professional as some others.

Keeping your resume or CV on a word processor permits you to add new information easily and to reorganize and tailor information to the recipient's needs. For example, you might emphasize your teaching experience for a school consulting job, your clinical work and training for a hospital, or your publications for a research position. Always date it currently. As an effective alternative that will get more attention when many people apply to the same job, you can write up your resume as a letter, describing your skills and history together.

Many professionals keep a file folder labeled "Resume" (or "CV" or "Professional Development") in which they place any paper that documents activities to be added to the resume or CV, such as presentations made, publications, all training received, continuing education unit credits, or anything that mentions them by name. Periodically, they then update the resume or CV from this folder. (Such a file will also serve as a defense if a complaint alleges that you are untrained or unqualified to practice some technique or procedure.)

Keep copies of your resume or CV available and up to date, so you can give it to potential consultees, other professionals, referrers, credentialing groups, hospital medical staffs, and potential employers. It should function as an expanded business card. In particular, if you do any public speaking, bring a full resume or CV (as a resource for those who hired you) and a one-paragraph narrative presentation of your relevant credentials and experiences, printed or typed in large letters. Ask the person introducing you to read it to the group. Remember, your peers (and an ethics committee) will hold you alone fully responsible for assuring that the media present you correctly.

### Checklist for Your Resume or CV

❑ Plain white paper is sufficient unless you are applying for a job where your sense of style matters.

❑ More than two pages may seem like bragging, so unless you are applying for an academic position where your history of publications and presentations matter, keep it skimmably short.

❑ Use one typeface, and only a few **boldfaced** words. Boldface is a tasteful emphasizer if used with discretion. Use underlining instead of italics only if you are typewriting. Using ALL CAPITALS is like shouting, so be judicious. Do not use fancy layout or display typefaces.

❑ Your resume or CV must be scrupulously accurate—no lies, distortions, exaggerations, or other misrepresentations. These are ethical violations and reportable as such, which might cut short your promising career. Careful readers who find inappropriate statements will lose faith in your competence.

❑ Both resumes and CVs are business forms, and so there is no room for your sex, marital status, age, children, hobbies, musical interests, charitable or religious activities, or the like. If in doubt, leave it out. However, many people offer both a work and home address and phone, because professional contacts often overlap social ones these days.

### Creating a Different Version of Your Resume or CV

It is helpful to have at least two versions of your resume or CV. The "maximum version" should have every heading and entry, name and date. New material can be added, and selections from it can be tailored to specific audiences. A single-page "synoptic version" can be used for others less fascinated with *all* of your accomplishments.

Figure 1 shows a partially filled-in sample CV, to illustrate the headings and layout for a maximum version.

## 1.3    Your Appointment Book

We all need a simple way to keep track of our obligations. Call it an "appointment book," "datebook," "calendar," "schedule," "little black book," or *"vade mecum,"* but it is a necessity of every practitioner. I have found it practical to operate by the rule "If it is not in my

# Curriculum Vitae

## SIGMUND J. THERAPIST
1001 Spectacular View Lane
Terrific City, Supreme State 12345
(900) 555-1212

January 15, 2003

### EDUCATION

| | |
|---|---|
| 1995 | PhD in Clinical Psychology—Distinguished University, Sovereign State |
| 1991–1992 | Internship in Clinical Psychology (American Psychological Association-approved)—Psychology Department, Splendid Health Center, Altered State University, Altered State |

### ADDITIONAL EDUCATIONAL EXPERIENCES

### HONORS

### CREDENTIALS

| | |
|---|---|
| 1995 | Licensed as a Psychologist in Supreme State, Number 12345 |
| 1997 | National Register of Health Service Providers in Psychology, Number 12345 |
| 1998 | Fellow, American Psychological Association, Number 1234-5678 |

### TEACHING EXPERIENCE

| | |
|---|---|
| 1990–1999 | Superb University, Department of Psychology, Terrific City, Supreme State 12345 Adjunct Associate Professor since 1993 |

### CLINICAL PRACTICE

| | |
|---|---|
| 1995–2002 | Independent Practice of General Clinical Psychology at Excellent Hospital, Terrific City, Supreme State 12345 |

### RESEARCH/CONSULTATION EXPERIENCE

| | |
|---|---|
| 1990–1991 | Research Assistant (half-time)—Project Champion, Psychology Department, Magnificent University, Marvelous City, Ecstatic State 54321 |

### PUBLICATIONS

### TRAINING PROGRAMS PRESENTED

### REFERENCES

Professional, business, and personal recommendations are available.

FIGURE 1. Sample curriculum vitae, partially filled in.

book, it does not exist," and so I write down all plans and appointments, both personal and professional. However, it appears to be a universal law that anything written in your datebook in ink will have to be changed.

Your appointment book is a record of your business; thus, it should be kept indefinitely. It not only documents your activities, but also records the services you rendered. It can be of value with the tax people or in court, and can be used to reconstruct your day even years later, so keep your old ones.

### What an Appointment Book Should Include

Look for a book that covers an 8 A.M. to 9 P.M. schedule. The diary should also include a phone/ address book (removable for transfer to the next year's book), an area code map, and spaces for daily notes. With all this, it should still be small enough to fit into a shirt pocket or purse.

Ohio Psychology Publications, Inc. sells an appointment calendar that has a: 13-hour-per-day, 6-day-per-week schedule, with 15-minute intervals to meet the needs of even the most "workaholic" clinician. It also includes DSM codes, a listing of psychotropic medications, and other useful sections. It is 8½" × 11" and lies flat when open. If you write, ask for the company's catalog, as it has many excellent publications.

### A List of Current Clients

Keeping a list of your current or recently active clients in your datebook may be very helpful if you need to cancel or reschedule appointments, or reach clients in an emergency. Of course, such a roster could be an obvious breach of confidentiality and a significant risk. One way to reduce the risk is to write only a client's initials and phone numbers and employ a simple encryption that will baffle most people: Simply substitute the next (or second or third) letter in the alphabet or digit in sequence for the true initials and phone number. For example, for your client Jan Grimly whose phone number is (123) 456-7890, write "kh2345678901." Using an earlier letter or number is an alternative, and you could make a little graphic (perhaps on the first page of your datebook) to jog your memory of the encryption method you have chosen. If you use a personal digital assistant (PDA) or hand-held computer for your information, you can use a password or encryption method. By the way, PDAs change so rapidly that I cannot discuss their features or recommend them in this infrequently revised book.

## 1.4   Basics of Record Keeping

One of the attractions of private practice is the freedom from agency-imposed requirements, and one of those most eagerly dispensed with is elaborate record keeping. Although you cannot escape the need for records, you can adopt record-keeping methods that are simpler and more closely tailored to your needs. Kagle (1991, p. 148) has an excellent discussion of the benefits of record keeping for the clinician.

You will need to keep both business or financial records and case or clinical records. Keeping them separately is simpler. Business records consist of your income and expense records, checkbook, payrolls, tax forms, business and professional licenses, billing forms, and so forth. Your accountant can help you set these up efficiently. (Get an accountant; it's a good investment.) For a detailed discussion of financial record keeping, see Chapter 2.

Clinical records (whose confidentiality must be protected) include your datebook or schedule, case records (including intake forms, treatment plans, progress notes, referral notes, periodic summaries, discharge plans, etc.), correspondence with clients and with others about clients, and the like. It is also a good idea to keep telephone and office visit logs in the event that a lawsuit calls for a reconstruction of events.

For guidance in recording the intake and initial evaluation of a case, see the forms in Chapter 5. Chapter 6 covers treatment plans and how to record the progress of treatment. For a full discussion of confidentiality concerns, see Chapter 7.

The remainder of this chapter provides an overview of clinical records, including the reasons to keep them, the nature of their contents, and their physical structure and organization. It also includes a discussion of how to maintain the security of your records, and how long to retain them.

## Why Keep Records?

**First, records must be kept to comply with your profession's ethical expectations.** For example, Standard 6.01 of the APA ethics code (APA, 2002) states: "(a) Psychologists create . . . records and data relating to their professional and scientific work in order to (1) facilitate provision of services later by them or by other professionals, . . . (3) meet institutional requirements, (4) ensure accuracy of billing and payments, and (5) ensure compliance with law." On the basis of these guidelines, many states (e.g., Pennsylvania) are *requiring* licensed mental health practitioners to keep records. You cannot disregard these requirements on the basis of expediency, concern for confidentiality, or a feeling that "My notes are only about process and are illegible, so they would be of no use to anyone else." If challenged by an ethics committee or in court, you will be held to your profession's standards, simply because you present yourself as a practitioner. **Not keeping records is now grounds for a malpractice claim.** Having no records is illegal and unprofessional, thus demonstrating poor care. "An inadequate record will itself be seen as evidence of sub-standard care, no matter what care was actually provided" (Weiner & Wettstein, 1993, p. 179). Reid (1999, p. 12) phrases this as "Skimpy notes imply skimpy care."

**Adequate record keeping allows you to defend yourself.** Records will be your basic defense in the event of a malpractice or ethics complaint or other litigation. See Soisson et al. (1987) for the specific advantages of having good records in defending a malpractice claim.

**In addition, your records document your provision of services.** This is a legal obligation and is necessary to receive payment from anyone. "Courts and external review bodies view the absence of documentation in the record about an event as evidence that it never occurred, no matter what the subsequent claims of the clinicians" (Weiner & Wettstein, 1993, p. 179).

**Records document the thoroughness of your assessment if the untoward should happen.** They help you to organize your thoughts about a patient and case. Your records establish a baseline of current functioning for structuring treatment or for evaluating progress and the impact of providing services.

**Records have many additional uses.** Your records show whether a client meets an eligibility requirement (e.g., disability). They may be useful for some presently unknown hindsight evaluation (perhaps a psychological autopsy or the establishment of disability's onset) or for the patient's own use. They are needed for supervisory review, consultation, peer review, quality control, and statistical reporting. They may be needed to maintain the client's continuity of care in future therapy or with other therapists. They provide clues as to which treatments have been successful and which are to be avoided. They offer crucial information for interdisciplinary communication. They allow you to review past successes at a future time. They replace memory, which is often inaccurate. Records are useful for self-education and student education, or for research. Lastly, you need to keep records because you are being paid to.

To summarize, **keeping records is not optional.** If you currently do not take notes or take insufficient ones, you are not alone: 7.6% of the psychologists responding to one survey (Fulero & Wilbert, 1988) did not keep sufficient records or kept none. If you are among this group, you are playing with fire as well as doing your clients a disservice. Change now; set up your record-keeping practices before the sun goes down again.

## What Should Be in the Records?

The following information must be provided in sufficient detail to allow another therapist to take over the case and to allow regulatory and administrative review of service delivery:

- Client identifying data.

- Dates of service, types of service, fees.

- Assessment.

- Plan for intervention.

- Other materials (e.g., consultations, summary reports, testing reports, supporting data, releases).

This is a very minimal list and does not support all the reasons for record keeping as described above. *The Paper Office's* content and forms are designed to exceed these guidelines. Much more detail on what to include in notes can be found in Section 6.2.

I agree with Knapp (1992a) that records should be the following:

- **Comprehensive.** All the relevant data should be included: names and addresses, fee arrangements, dates and kinds of services rendered, results of consultations and testing, correspondence, releases, reports prepared, notes of phone calls and meetings, progress notes, and discharge summary.

- **Objective.** Facts need to be separated from opinion; observable behaviors need to be included.

- **Substantive.** The diagnosis, presenting problem, treatment plans, and your rationale for each of these should be contained in the records.

- **Consistent.** Your behavior should match your treatment plan and diagnosis, or you should document the reasons for any inconsistencies.

- **Retrievable.** Your notes need to be readable, your records findable, and your charts organized.

- **Current.** You should make your notes in a timely fashion.

- **Secure.** You must make certain that your records are inaccessible to unauthorized others. All of these characteristics are discussed below.

## The Physical Structure for Organizing Your Case Records

The Health Insurance Portability and Accountability Act (HIPAA) of 1996 states that, if you keep psychotherapy notes, they must be kept "separate" from the rest of the medical record, so be sure to adapt the records system you choose to meet this requirement. See Section 6.2 on keeping psychotherapy notes and Section 7.8 on HIPAA.

As indicated above, each client must have a range of specific information in his or her record. It is a challenge to keep all of this information logically separated and yet easily accessible. Here are some possibilities. The first two methods are variations on using the traditional manila folder, and the third uses a three-ring binder. I also briefly discuss computerized record keeping.

### The Basic Manila Folder Method

**FORM 1**

You can use an ordinary manila folder for each client. Although this format is simple and cheap, it has liabilities: Loose pages can get lost or misplaced; also, pages and entries are kept in the sequence in which they were created, and so information is not organized by topic or relevance. This traditional, even classic approach to record keeping can be improved by developing a checklist of the contents (see Form 1), which can be printed on the outside of each manila folder. There is no indication of the client's name on the outside, for privacy reasons. You should tailor Form 1 to your own office procedures and forms.

If your state's privacy regulations are, for any population, service, or provider, preempted by HIPAA's rules, you should modify the section "Informed Consent Materials" as appropriate. For example, if you only need to "notify" the client of his or her rights, you might add a box with "I certify that I have made the effort to explain or have had my client read the rules on disclosure of PHI (protected health information)." See Section 7.8 for more on the notification procedure.

### The Folder with Sections

The major medical publishers have systems specifically designed for recording of patient care efforts. For example, these may have dividers preprinted with various headings ("In-

# Checklist for Client Records

Client # _____   Intake date _____

## 1. Informed consent materials

| | Date | By whom? |
|---|---|---|

❏ Information brochure for clients given and signed*

❏ Risks, benefits, outcome, alternatives of treatment discussed and noted

❏ Handout on limits of confidentiality given and signed*

❏ Duty to warn, danger to self/others discussed and noted

❏ Requests for records from others signed and sent*

❏ Payment policy discussed, agreement to pay signed*

❏ Consent/contract to treatment given and signed*

❏ Consent for follow-up given and signed*

❏ Consent to evaluate without commitment to treat discussed and noted

❏ Other consents discussed and noted (research, recordings, )

## 2. Further evaluations or consultations needed—indicate questions to be addressed

❏ Medical: _____   ❏ Psychiatric: _____

❏ Vocational/educational: _____   ❏ Other: _____

## 3. Case management information

a. Referral received:  Date _____  By whom? _____

b. First contact:  Date _____  By whom? _____

c. Intake completed:  Date _____  By whom? _____

d. Initial treatment plan sent to MCO:  Date _____  By whom? _____

Consultation with MCO reviewer named: _____  Authorization number: _____

Number of sessions authorized: _____  Review scheduled for: _____

e. First reauthorization request:  Date _____  By whom? _____

Consultation with MCO reviewer named: _____  Authorization number: _____

Number of sessions authorized: _____  Review scheduled for: _____

Second reauthorization request:  Date _____  By whom? _____

Consultation with MCO reviewer named: _____  Authorization number: _____

Number of sessions authorized: _____  Review scheduled for: _____

Third reauthorization request:  Date _____  By whom? _____

Consultation with MCO reviewer named: _____  Authorization number: _____

Number of sessions authorized: _____  Review scheduled for: _____

f. Forms and records requested and released*

| Req. date | Form/record | Sent to | On date | By |
|---|---|---|---|---|
| | | | | |
| | | | | |
| | | | | |

---

**FORM 1. Checklist for client records.**  Asterisked (*) items are materials that can be found in this book.

From *The Paper Office*. Copyright 2003 by Edward L. Zuckerman. Permission to photocopy this form is granted to purchasers of this book for personal use only (see copyright page for details).

take," "Treatment Plan," "Legal Stuff," etc.) in a standard hospital or medical office chart. Different colors of paper can be used for each section, with the most frequently used pages in ordinary white. Look at all the options before you decide. Even if it costs more, a more usable record-making system will pay for itself very soon. How much do you charge other people for your time? How much of it do *you* waste each month searching in your folders?

### The Three-Ring Binder Method

Allow me to introduce Zuckerman's Unpretentious Clinical Keeping-of-Records System (ZUCKRS). It is a simple three-ring binder that holds all the materials about each active patient in a separate section and can be carried to the office each day. Although this system is almost embarrassingly low tech, it has been adopted by many of the therapists who have seen it.

*The Binder.* A plain vinyl-over-board binder without lettering or logo, in a dark color (like a dark blue suit), is always acceptable. Taste enters here: Neon pink will probably assure that you do not leave your book behind, but it may (or should?) clash with your office decor. You can express your taste, but inconspicuousness maybe prudent. If your ego decides the binder is a good idea, use your therapy talents to overcome your feeling that binders are not for adults, or to curb your grandiose inclination to buy the alligator leather version. Different colors for different settings or offices do make sense. If your accountant encourages you to make capital investments, there are heavy-duty designs with piano-hinged covers and other features for tech lovers. The "D-ring" design is not necessary but may be easier on the pages. Buy the best quality, because the rings will meet evenly and the pages will not get caught. Use a binder sized for your current practice, and replace it with larger ones as your practice grows, but keep it underfilled for convenience.

*Paper.* You need filler paper designed for three-ring binders. This is discounted in August during back-to-school sales. It tears less when there is at least ¼" of paper next to the holes. When marked "college-ruled," it has lines a little less than ¼" apart. Cheaper filler paper is 8" × 10½", slightly smaller than a regular 8½" × 11" page, such as you would use for a form. Forms will then show at the outside margin or edge of the page, and this may be useful. Whatever kind of paper you choose, make it your standard. Use it for writing all your professional work, and always keep a supply of it everywhere you write. You will save great effort and time. This method allows you to keep all your professional work (teaching notes, consultations, bestseller-in-progress, etc.) in separate three-ring binders cleanly and efficiently. Using colored paper for different parts of the client's record is trendy, but, except for yellow, it won't photocopy as well as white. You will also need a three-ring punch for your forms and paperwork received.

*Dividers.* The common Mylar-reinforced dividers, especially with colored tabs, are usable. But better are the very wide dividers (9" × 11") made of the heaviest paper material or solid plastic, which are available at real stationers. These will last much longer and be neater. It is probably best not to write patients' names on the tabs or the edges of your forms for security reasons. Many people can easily read upside down. If you use alphabetical tabs, you will be able to find a client's section quickly, but you will have to separate Smith and Smythe somehow. It may be easier simply to place clients in alphabetical order but to use unnamed dividers. The few seconds spent searching for the record can be a way for both the patient and therapist to focus mentally on what is going to be their work in the hour.

*Checklist for the Contents of Each Client's Section.* The following are listed in sequential order, not in order of importance. These contents are discussed and specific forms or sample documents are provided later in *The Paper Office* as indicated.

❏ A billing form (see Section 2.5).

❏ First-contact record (Form 20) and similar records (see Section 5.2).

❏ Progress or session notes, and homework done by the client (see Section 6.2).

❏ Some blank paper for recording the session notes.

❏ Documentation of informed consent—for example, a signed copy of the client information brochure (see Section 4.2), and other forms and materials regarding treatment and consent to evaluation that appear in Chapter 4.

❏ Psychological testing done by you.

❏ Previous records (medical, psychological, educational, etc;) that you obtain (see Section 7.4). These would include copies of release forms you have used.

❏ Correspondence from, to, and about the client.

❏ Newspaper or other clippings about the client, or clippings that the client brings in.

❏ Anything else you think is relevant at present or in the future.

## Computerized Client Records

The simplest way to keep clinical records on a computer is to create a folder or directory for each client, and to add a file or page for each visit. You can do this by creating a blank progress note (see Forms 41 and 42 for formats you can adopt) as a "template" or "stationery," and opening it each time you want to make a record. Fill in the current information, save it to the client's folder or directory, and entitle it with the client's initials and today's date. If you don't want to write so much, you can just open a file in each client's folder or directory called "Progress Notes" and add to what you have written before. Many of the computerized billing programs also now offer some way to incorporate progress notes. There are also separate computerized progress note programs such as ICANotes (http://www.icanotes.com), and larger record-keeping programs such as QuicDoc (http://www.quicdoc.com), which may suit your needs and style. Keep in mind, however, that there are security considerations with all computer records; these are discussed in the next section.

## When a Case Is Closed

After termination, or if the records become too bulky, a client's pages can be transferred from other formats to a manila folder and filed for "permanent" storage in a locked cabinet. If you indicate the dates of service provision on the outside, it will make it easier to prune your records after 15 years or whatever number of years you select as a disposal date (as suggested by Constance Fisher, PhD, of Pittsburgh, PA). See Section 1.6, below, on retention of records and their disposal.

# 1.5    Record Security

Keep all your case records, including the identifying data in your billing system, in a locked and secure place (APA, 1981). But remember Daniel Ellsberg's psychiatrist and the Nixon "plumbers"; no place is totally secure. A three-ring binder (see above) can be kept in your personal possession, which is sometimes better.

The final HIPAA Security Rule (Part 142), which had not been released as this book was going to press, will include regulations and technical procedures about maintaining the security of records. As soon as it is available, I will post an addenda to my recommendations at http://www.hipaahelp.info and http://www.thepaperoffice.com.

Computerized records, even billing information, must be secured as well. Many therapists quaintly insist on a paper "hard copy" backup of computerized records, without realizing that by printing out their records they have increased the risk of disclosure from almost zero to fairly high, because many more people can read paper than can use a computer: Some word processors include encryption, but if yours does not, buy and *use* an encryption program such as Norton Utilities or Zimmerman's Pretty Good Privacy, which is unbreakable and free. You can get information about it at http://www.pgp.com/products/freeware/default.asp. The site http://www.epic.org/privacy/tools.html offers tools for encrypting telephone calls, e-mail, your hard drive, and anonymous e-mailers. However, if these sites are no longer working, try a search of the Internet under PGP and Zimmerman.

An unresolved issue at present is the "probative value" of computerized records. How much trust can we place in a document that can be as easily altered as notes kept on a computer? Methods for authenticating documents such as digital signatures are just becoming available, and we should adopt them for our records as soon as practical. For a start, see the Digital Signature Guidelines from the American Bar Association at http://www.abanet.org/scitech/ec/isc/dsgfree.html.

Secure your computerized records from disasters as well as prying eyes. Design a simple-to-use and practical-to-implement regular backup program for your computer records. Many computer programs' manuals will teach you how to set up one. (Yes, I know we all say we do this, and most of us still don't. I do now, but only after a painful disaster.) The simplest backup method is to make a copy each week of your clinical files to a floppy disk or CD-RW and store it off-site in a secure place. More sophisticated programs allow this to be done automatically on a schedule and only for those files that have changed.

If your computer ever needs service or upgrading, anyone at the repair facility can read your clinical files if you have not password-protected them, so this is a must. Finally, when you sell or give away your old computer, you should erase the files on your hard drive. Deleting the files or putting them in the Trash/Recycle Bin is not enough; when you do this, only their addresses are removed. You need to use a program like Burn (Macintosh), or Eraser or DiskVac (for Windows), to make them truly unrecoverable.

Records can be lost, stolen, damaged, or destroyed. In an article in Practice Strategies ("Tips from an Attorney . . .," 1988) suggests the following: (1) Don't panic. (2) You may not need the records of clients you saw years ago. (3) Copies of your reports may exist in the files of others (such as insurance companies, attorneys, school systems, etc.), and you can request these. (4) Notify your professional insurance carrier and ask whether it will pay the costs of recovery. (5) Inform current clients of the problem. Review their treatment plans and status with them. (6) Write a synopsis for clients who are likely to need their records, such as those in litigation.

# 1.6    Retention of Records

When therapy ends and the case is closed, the records need to be preserved so that you can do the following:

- Comply with laws and ethics.

- Assure continuity of care (such as patient transfer).

- Defend yourself from some belated accusation. Despite statutes of limitations, the laws are in flux, and court decisions have extended the client's time to sue (e.g., "2 years after the discovery of damage").

- Qualify the client for some services in the future (e.g., Social Security disability, a special college program for a person with a learning disability).

- Restart a case because a patient returns for treatment.

- Cope with some other situation that is presently unforeseeable.

## How Long Should Records Be Kept?

When deciding what records to keep and for how long, you should consider your state's "statute of limitations" and the common rules of "5 years or more after a minor reaches majority" and "5 years after the end of treatment." The Internal Revenue Service requires you to keep business, not clinical, records of your income for 7 years. The APA's guidelines for clinical psychologists (APA, Committee on Professional Practice and Standards, 1993) mirror the federal policy: the full record for 3 years (after last contact or completion of services), and the full record or a summary for 12 more years for client welfare. For example, Social Security disability, Title II, can entitle a client to payments if he or she was disabled within 5 years of last working/paying FICA taxes. State laws vary. Different areas of law have different rules; malpractice may have a 3-year time limit, whereas the limit for breach of contract may be 6 years.

The practice brief entitled *Retention of Health Information (Updated)* is available at the American Health Information Management Association Web site (specifically, at http://www.ahima.org, where you can find it using the Search tool). It lists medical retention requirements (and makes recommendations where no official rules exist) by state as well as nationally, and also provides any special rules based on the specific type of medical record.

An additional consideration is that because of changes in the technology, old records may not be readable on newer word processors, or the media may no longer even be in use. For example, save your records as ASCII code ("plain text" or "text only"), which will never be unrecognizable. Similarly, floppy disk drives are disappearing from computers now, and so records maintained on them will soon be inaccessible. Devise a plan to remind yourself to transfer *all* old records when you update your computer.

Note that generally there is no statute of limitations on filing a complaint before a licensing board, and that records will be your best defense. On the other hand, records can become outdated and therefore invalid or of limited utility (see above). If you have to release such records, make sure to inform the recipient of these limitations. When you are asked for a record, see Section 7.3 on releasing records.

## Suggestions on Retaining Records

- If you have a secure space, keep the whole record forever for your own protection.

- Children's records should be retained until 5 years after they reach their majority, even though their findings may become out of date. Write that "discard date" on the outside of the folder when you close the case and store the record.

- Keep adults' records for 12 years, or keep a summary forever. Write the 12-year "discard date" on the outside of the folder when you store the record.

- At your established "discard date," destroy the records or offer to give them to another professional caring for the client. Design a mechanism to find a current address at some specified future time, and to send each patient a letter giving him or her the choice of having records transferred to a successor therapist whom they have seen or are seeing or another practitioner (or anyone who would understand the issues) chosen by the patient. Do not offer clients the choices of receiving the records directly or of destroying the records, because (1) they cannot anticipate the needs for the records; (2) they do not own the records; (3) they do not have the training to understand the records; and (4) the records may be needed by you.

- Whatever procedures you choose, be sure to document it in sufficient detail, and keep copies of your plan where your attorney, your family, or another therapist can find it. Also, be absolutely consistent in using your procedures, because any exceptions would suggest to a malpractice attorney that you have something to hide. Lastly, develop some standard form for recording which records you disposed of, when, and how, for both documentation and defense. I recommend that you keep only a list of the names of clients and the beginning and ending dates of your treatment.

## Disposal of Your Records

Even when destroying records, you have to maintain their confidentiality. You can't just throw them in the trash. A simple shredder isn't expensive but takes time. You might organize a group of your peers with old records to take them all to a professional disposal firm (look in the Yellow Pages under "Records Management") and get a "Certificate of Destruction."

## Preserving Your Records When You Close Your Practice, Retire, or Die

You are ethically and legally responsible for protecting the confidentiality of and access to your records if you should become unable to care for them, according to Standards 3.12 and 10.09 of the APA ethics code, (APA, 2002). Closing of your practice because of your moving, disability or incapacity,[1] temporarily or permanently retirement, loss of license to practice, or "untimely demise" requires assuring the well-being of your patients, and so there are significant ethical, legal, and practical matters to be addressed.

There do not appear to be any official guidelines for a "succession plan" or "professional will" for closing psychological practices, so the suggestions below have been gathered from many sources and the guidelines of other professions. I have organized them into two large sections. The first addresses closing your practice over a period of time, as would happen when you retire or move. The second section addresses what to do now to prepare for the possibility of unexpected death or sudden incapacity. Because you cannot foretell your demise, I recommend that you negotiate all these arrangements with your colleagues, THIS MONTH.

### Closing Your Practice

Despite what you may have heard, practices are rarely worth much, as they are so personal. Rather than selling my own practice when the time comes for me to retire, my preference would be to pay another professional to assume the duties of safeguarding my records and responding to calls and mail, and to explicitly allow a "bridge therapist" to refer or to accept as clients any who might call expecting to reach me.

*Your Obligations to Clients: Continuity of Care.*  If you retire or otherwise close your practice, you have obligations to current clients. With some, you will finish up therapy if you have the time. You may need to transfer other clients. All will need to be informed that you are leaving practice, when your office will close, and how they may obtain their records should they need them. They must be given sufficient time to make the best resolutions and least traumatic alternative arrangements (I would think not less than 60 days, depending on how often you are seeing them, but the earlier the better). You should make clear recommendations for those you believe require continued services. You simply cannot discontinue with clients in need, because this can be seen as "negligent abandonment"— which is both unethical and grounds for a malpractice suit against you or your estate. Of course, make sure those practitioners to whom you refer clients are both available and offer appropriate and high-quality services, in order to avoid problems with "negligent referrals." It is entirely appropriate for you to make the initial calls to these successor therapists.

If you are retiring, indicate when you will stop taking new patients and let your caseload wind down, which will be easier on you and others. But, because you may not have the time, prepare, **this week**, a letter to be sent to your current and recent clients (the last 18 months seems reasonable to me) notifying them of why you are closing up shop; exactly when the office will close; who will have your records, and how to reach them; whom clients can call in an emergency; what other therapists and community resources (agencies,

---

[1]This term is preferable to "incompetence" for its precision.

professional organizations) are available if they want more services; and so on. Make it clear that it is the clients' choice to pursue additional services and that the confidentiality of their records will be preserved. A copy of this letter (and any returned mail) should be placed in each client's file. Post a copy of this letter in your office and any other suitable places. Have your staff remind clients of the date of your closing your practice. Finally, place copies with your will, your life insurance policy, and other places your successor might look.

Legal consultants have recommended to physicians an even stricter policy. They suggest sending the above-described letter by registered mail (return receipt requested) for high-risk patients. They suggest that you enclose a medical record release authorization form (for requesting copies and transferring records to another physician), state the length of time (in years) that the records will be retained, and provide a permanent mailing address or post office box number for all future record requests. You must arrange for someone to maintain the address and respond to requests for records, for the time periods mentioned below.

*The Duties of the Custodian of Your Case Records.* You must protect your records' confidentiality and security (against theft, prying eyes, accidental discarding, etc.), preservation (against fire, rodents, water damage, etc.), and access (for a successor therapist, defense against a complaint or suit, response to a subpoena, etc.). These needs will be present even after your death or a client's. The following checklist will help you address them.

❑ Devise a letter of explanation for your successor therapist or custodian about your files. The letter should cover such items as how client records are filed and named (by last name, by date of last contact or discharge,[2] by a case number,[3] etc.) where they are kept,[4] the shorthand or abbreviations you have used in your notes, and destruction schedules and procedures. It may be appropriate to explain where to find the office keys and your appointment book (Spayd & Wiley, 2001).

❑ Close out case records with summaries, and bring all case notes up to date. Respond to any unfinished correspondence.

❑ Destroy some out-of-date records, following your usual procedures, so there will be less to transfer.

❑ Microfilming your records may make sense. Look under "Document Management" or "Records Management" for companies in the Yellow Pages.

❑ Actually transfer the records physically to your records' custodian, or contract to have this done.

---

[2]So that the files can be pruned regularly by destroying files older than the number of years they legally must be kept.

[3]And, if so, where to find the cross-index of names and numbers.

[4]With the keys for your locked files and the locations and passwords for your computerized records, both clinical and financial.

❑ Send copies of the letter described earlier about closing your practice and who will have custody of your records to the following:

> ❑ Your state licensing board. If you wish either to surrender your license or to become inactive, request this as well.

> ❑ Your state and national and other professional associations, and any other professional committees, groups, or organizations to which you belong or pay dues. Resign or choose an inactive status rather than letting your membership lapse for lack of dues.

> ❑ Your referral sources, and those who refer to you.

> ❑ Your professional friends.

> ❑ Your professional insurance carrier.

> ❑ Your billing service, if you use one.

> ❑ All managed care organizations (MCOs), health maintenance organizations (HMOs), insurance companies, hospitals, preferred provider organizations (PPOs), health plans, and similar clinical entities with which you have done business (prepare a list of these organizations). Note that the letter described earlier may not be sufficient for such organizations if you must also address the issues of unpaid bills.

*Your Financial and Contractual Obligations.* The following checklist will aid you in resolving any outstanding financial or contractual issues.

❑ Meet with your lawyer, banker, accountant, financial advisor, and others to review any unmet obligations you have. Draft any needed letters, notifications, forms, or agreements.

❑ Review the procedures for dissolution that are written into any partnership, professional corporation, or professional association agreements. Take the appropriate legal, financial, or other actions.

❑ Deal with all your rental agreements and leases—office space, cars, equipment, utilities, telephone, Internet access, advertising contracts (Yellow Pages), Web pages, cleaning contracts, and so on.

❑ Devise a plan for the formal dissolution of your business entity (i.e., distribution and liquidation of assets; notification of the appropriate state authorities, such as the Secretary of State; business account dealings). Your professional lawyer should handle this along with your accountant, so make sure they are notified of your circumstances.

❑ Arrange to dispose of your real assets. Used office equipment typically brings 10 to 50 cents on the dollar, depending on age and condition. Decide who is to receive it, or donate, sell, or otherwise dispose of your office equipment, supplies, and any other real property or real estate.

❑ Decide about your accounts payable and accounts receivable. Decide on an appropriate collection process and assign responsibility for it.

❑ Create a plan to make timely payments of federal, state, local, and other taxes; employee insurance; workers' compensation premiums; and the like.

❑ Make arrangements for ethical disposal, sale, or transfer of your psychological tests, biofeedback equipment, or other professional materials.

❑ Make arrangements for your professional liability insurance. Purchase a "tail" for your professional liability insurance if you have a "claims-made" policy (see Section 3.3). You (or your estate) can still be sued or complained against after you close up shop, and a tail protects against future complaints about your previous actions. Some insurance companies offer this at no cost if you have been a client for a while, but they must be notified. If you have the time and have had a number of high-risk cases, consider raising your coverage significantly for the last year of your practice, as your tail's limits will be based on the coverage limits in force during this time.

❑ Do not cancel premises insurance when you move out; wait until you are no longer the legal tenant.

❑ Consider cancelling your journal subscriptions. What professional roles do you intend to maintain in retirement?

Eric Marine (n.d.) suggests making a time line chart to organize your planning. His online article is on the topic of preparing to close a practice. Also see Ragusea (2002).

### If You Should Suddenly Become Incapacitated or Die

If you become incapacitated, there are at least three professional roles for which you should leave instructions so these can be filled by one or more persons. A **successor professional** will provide at least emergency or brief services (as a "bridge therapist") to your clients and may take on their cases. It would be best to have several named successors, in case one is unavailable when an emergency arises. Second, the **executor of your professional will** is the one responsible for carrying out its provisions. Last, the **custodian of your records** maintains their security and legal release. This may be the same person as either of the others but can be different for reasons of practical access and longevity. Do not simply ask a friend or friends to assume these obligations as a personal favor; too much is involved. Select and negotiate these functions with trusted colleagues. Arrange remuneration for each role out of your collectibles or estate. Pay the custodian for the costs of storage and the burdens of maintaining the security and potential access as a necessary expense of your retirement or estate.

Devise now a contingency plan for your practice. Then discuss it with your family, some colleagues, and your staff, and arrange for your lawyer to incorporate it into your personal will. Assure that your plan, which is called here a "Letter of Instructions," is very readily accessible to all those who must carry out your directions. It should address all the concerns and issues raised above, as well as some that arise because of sudden loss. The checklist that follows can guide you in devising a contingency plan.

❑ Arrange for a staff member, specific friend, or family member to notify others of your disability or death. Besides those described above, rapid notification should be given to your professional and family lawyers and your accountant. You should include all the ways of reaching each of these persons in your Letter of Instructions.

❑ Because a situation might arise suddenly in which you are unavailable, a list of all of the ways and places in which you could be contacted by those concerned about your well-being should be easily available to your staff and family. Your staff should have "all contact information for [your] spouse, life partner, adult children, or anyone else who would likely know of [your] whereabouts or sudden health problems" (Tracy, n.d). Tracy suggests that staff members should be formally permitted to make such calls and be told to wait no longer than an hour after your unexplained absence before making such calls. Train your staff in all these procedures.

❑ Since I have recommended that all records be maintained indefinitely, your custodian will have to make a similar "Professional Will" for the maintenance of your records in the event of his or her own retirement, disability, or death.

❑ If you have not prepared a letter (see above), your executor should be instructed to write a brief letter explaining your death or incapacity and the closing of your practice. This can be given to all current clients and mailed to all recent clients so that all are informed rapidly, explicitly, and simultaneously. It should address the relevant issues described here, such as access to records and referrals. In addition, the executor should place a notice in the newspaper of your demise.

❑ Arrange a method to remind yourself regularly to review and update your Letter of Instructions as necessary. Your practice or that of your executor may have changed.

❑ If you should die unexpectedly, a brief message should be placed on your answering machine or with your answering service for future potential clients who call your office when referred by friends, colleagues, or advertisements. Try to arrange for these messages to be available for the next 12–18 months.

❑ Prepare a letter for your successor professional to send to those who call and to any professional mail you receive, which explains the circumstances and suggests options.

❑ You must be explicit about your accounts receivable. Make sure your executor can legally accept monies due you and pay your bills.

❑ Create a plan for your professional successor to make timely payments of federal, state, local, and other taxes; employee insurance; workers' compensation premiums; and the like.

# CHAPTER 2

# Financial Tools
# and Procedures

## 2.1    Setting Financial Policies for Your Practice

> *Money matters will be treated by cultured people in the same manner as sexual matters, with the same inconsistency, prudishness, and hypocrisy. The therapist must be determined not to concur in this attitude, and in his [sic] dealings with patients to treat money matters with the same matter-of-course frankness that he wishes to induce in them in matters relating to sexual life.*
> —SIGMUND FREUD (1913/1958, p. 131)

The provision of therapy is both a business and a profession. As a business, it involves unavoidable dealings with money, and this is often problematic for therapists. They enter the field with a commitment to human service. Many have been trained at public expense or have worked in a public service setting; they may believe that making a profit from the misery in others' lives is unjust. However, the simple truth is that a therapist who does not succeed as a businessperson will not be able to work independently.

As a therapist, you *must* make decisions about many aspects of the business relationship with your clients. Choose options that seem fair, protective of both parties, and enforceable; then communicate them clearly, both orally and in writing. You will need policies to answer the following questions:

- When will you discuss money with the client?

- How much will you charge?

    Will you have different charges for different activities, or a per-hour charge for everything you do?

    Will you give discounts, do free therapy, or use a sliding scale of charges based on income?

    Will you charge for broken appointments, and if so, how much?

- How will you handle insurance coverage?

    Will you accept only what the client's insurance will pay, and not collect anything from the client? (The insurers view this as potential fraud; see below.)

    Will you require "assignment of benefits" (be paid directly by the insurance company), or trust the client to pay you?

    Will you prepare insurance claim forms for patients, or simply supply a bill they can submit?

    Will you join managed care organizations' (MCOs') "panels" of providers and "participate" (i.e., agree to provide services at the rates set by third-party payers)?

- How will you handle delinquent accounts and when?

    Will you only send reminders and rebill, or use collection letters?

    At what point will you use collection agencies? Lawyers? Small-claims court? At what point will you write off bad debts?

    When will you discontinue seeing a patient for not paying your fees?

When you have made these decisions, incorporate them into your means of gaining informed consent (see Section 4.2, the client information brochure).

## About Fees

Because few professional training programs teach about fees, some basics are covered here.

One of the "professional pleasures" offered by private practice is the freedom to take on a case that interests you without regard to the client's ability to pay. Do not let greed or fear take away this freedom. As you might guess, the belief that "paying for therapy is therapeutic" is endorsed most strongly by psychoanalysts and least strongly by social workers. It has repeatedly not been scientifically supported, and its popularity is generally declining (Pope, 1988c). A review of the literature found no clear relationship between fee paying and outcome (Herron & Sitkowski, 1986). Ethically, free therapy cannot be of a lesser quality than paid therapy, so do not try to cut corners; learn to live with this, or do not do *pro bono* (unpaid) work at all. The American Psychological Association (APA) strongly recommends that all psychologists do some unpaid work. The amount of such work is left to the conscience of the individual clinician. If a client has an unexpected and long-lasting loss of income, and neither termination nor transfer is desirable, you might consider your work *pro bono* and bite the bullet.

"Professional courtesy" (discounts to peers, health care providers, students, clergy, etc.) is rapidly disappearing because of social changes and the prevalence of health insurance. If a client who might be entitled to professional courtesy asks for it, you could probably offer a discount of 10% without too much pain.

Most therapists do not raise a private client's fee during the course of treatment, unless treatment lasts many years and inflation raises the client's income. Clients and third-party payers seem not to mind some raises over time. I suggest that you evaluate your fees yearly and indicate this in your client information brochure.

Finally, if you are terminating a client for lack of payment, be cautious and thorough, and try to get a payment plan agreed to. If it appears that it will be a sticky situation, consult with a colleague about issues of abandonment, client welfare, and the like, and note the consultation in your records. See also Section 6.3 on termination.

## Ethical Guidelines on Fees

Pope (1988c) has examined the laws and ethics pertaining to fee policies and procedures. The following discussion is based on his suggestions for avoiding common pitfalls.

**Ethically, you must make financial arrangements in advance of treatment,** so that consent to treatment is fully informed. Standard 6.04a of the APA ethics code (APA, 2002) requires that "As early as feasible in a professional or scientific relationship, [the psychologist] and the client/patient or other recipient of psychological services reach an agreement specifying the compensation and the billing arrangements." It is best to have clients know your charges before you even meet for the first time, so that they are not seduced by your interview into forming a relationship that then imposes financial hardship or is even exploitative.

You should know by the end of the first evaluation hour, from the social history information you have obtained, whether a client is able to pay you. **Therefore, give no "free initial consultations,"** because the client is by then committed to you, having revealed his or her personal issues. (This is called "undue influence" by lawyers.) Also, charging from the beginning of therapy sets a positive and equitable expectation that the client will indeed get and has a right to "what he or she paid for."

Tell the client your policies on raising fees during the course of treatment, charging for missed appointments, the maximum balance due you will tolerate, your use of a collection agency, and so forth. Make certain that the financial arrangements are fully understood by the client. For this a written fee policy is essential, and this policy should be stated in your client information brochure.

Fee splitting—that is, taking a fee or paying a percentage or dollar amount solely for making a referral—is still open to interpretation. The rules in psychology (APA, 2002, Standard 6.07) allow fee splitting when the dividing of payment is based on the services provided and not simply on making the referral. However, this is too vague to enforce, local rules differ, and arrangements are often complex. In an agreement with the Federal Trade Commission (APA, 1992), the APA agreed not to prohibit paying for referrals.

Accepting payment for your services in anything but money is "barter." Barter is an ancient, flexible, and honorable method, and gives more people access to your services. The APA code of ethics (APA, 2002, Standard 6.05) allows barter and offers some minimal standards and guidelines. Woody (1999) offers a thoughtful discussion of the risks and guidelines if you wish to use barter. However, barter presents great potential for abuse, exploitation, conflicts, and distortion of the professional relationship. I strongly recommend that you **do not barter** or exchange therapy for either goods (whose value can be questioned) or services (as this creates a dual relationship—i.e., that of employer–employee). Barter is a frequent source of ethics complaints. If a client has no money and you wish to help, offer your services *pro bono.*

## Setting Your Fee

Your "fee" is the amount you are willing to sell your services for. This should be the same as the amount you actually charge every client. Routinely accepting a lower fee by waiving insurance copayments is seen as fraud by third-party payers; when you do this, your actual, collected fee is not the stated fee you are charging the insurers. If you decide to accept a lower payment from a client in financial distress or for any other reason, do so only occasionally, with good reasons, and document your rationale in detail in your notes. Make sure you can justify the fee you set for each client; you may have to.

There is no standard method for setting fees; but here are some options:

- **Cost-plus pricing** is determining your fee by adding together your fixed and variable costs plus a profit. This is the traditional pricing method in many businesses, although not in private practice. If you take the time to compute your costs (your "nut"), it will allow you to know whether you are really making a go of your practice. However, do not try to add, say, 10% for "administrative expenses" when a patient requires billing or add on 20% for "extended contacts with MCOs and authorization." First, your contract with an MCO will clearly state that you may not bill any of its clients separately for any other charges and that the MCO will not pay such charges. Second, the MCO will see this as illegal because you will be charging insurance-covered patients an inflated fee, not your agreed-to fee.

- **Competitive pricing** is setting your prices to match, exceed, or underprice your competition, depending on whom you see as your competitors. Psychiatrists charge the most, with psychologists charging 80–90% of that, and social workers charging 70% or less. Counselors and psychiatric nurses charge about 50%. The newsletter *Psychotherapy Finances* publishes a fee survey each year, with enlightening information and comparisons. Setting your fee at 90% of the UCR (usual, customary, and reasonable) fee of your peers in the area will prevent difficulty with the insurance company, but 100% is quite reasonable.

  You can use what Medicare has computed as appropriate fees to set your own. The procedure for computing these fees is quite complicated, based on your geographic price cost indices, which have work, practice expense, and malpractice components; relative value units; phase-in dates; and so on. The Centers for Medicare and Medicaid Services (formerly the Health Care Financial Administration [HCFA] Web site has all the information at http://www.hcfa.gov/stats/cpt/rvudown.htm. Or you might simply ask your local Medicare intermediary to send you a fee schedule.

  A colleague, Gordon Herz, PhD, of Madison, WI, not only has provided the information above; on his Web site (http://www.mentalhealth-madison.com/Rate_the_Insurer.htm), he has very generously collected information provided by therapists from around the country on reimbursement fees. Clinicians also offer grades from A to F on their experiences with the companies, using Herz's "Therapists' Insurer Profiling Scale," on the dimensions of credentialing process, paperwork, intrusiveness of case management, consideration of patient needs, and speed of reimbursement. If you use the information there, please also contribute your own experiences.

One last point about comparative fee setting deserves mention. Because of antitrust laws, professionals cannot conspire with each other in order to fix rates. You cannot say to another practitioner, "I won't accept less than $75 an hour, and you shouldn't either." On the other hand, professionals are free to exchange information about rates (as above), just as "advertising one's rates in the Yellow Pages, in brochures, or as part of written practice policies is okay. In fact, it may be very helpful to the competitive process" (Sahid, 1998). Sahid offers these basic rules: "1. Practitioners should not discuss their fees with competitors. 2. Never suggest a fee as a line-in-the-sand that would prompt a boycott or refusal to contract with a managed care firm. 3. If you sign a contract with a managed care firm, the rate agreed to is your fee."

- **Pricing by negotiation** is accepting a price that is arranged in the marketplace of buyers and sellers. With private-pay patients, be mindful that they are needy and therefore not your equals in negotiating a fee. The negotiation process requires self-esteem and autonomy, which patients often lack. They also usually lack an appreciation of your (quite high) costs in providing your services. As you know, the actual buyers of mental health services for many clients are their employers or their employers' delegates—the whole panoply of MCO contractors. They do not appear to lack self-confidence and negotiation resources. Although there are alternatives to managed care (see especially Ackley, 1997) developing a knowledge base in this area will be essential for most therapists.

- **Pricing by time** is charging for time, not for the services provided. This means charging everyone the same rate for any kind of service (therapy, consulting, teaching, supervising, etc.). Because it is rarely possible to charge for preparation, teaching and lecturing tend to be underbilled. You can try to reduce these costs by specializing in only a few topics at a time and by selling these preparations to several audiences.

- **Pricing by setting an income goal** is setting a yearly income goal, dividing it by the number of hours you want to work, and calculating your hourly charge. This is worth considering for life or financial planning. Is this a self-esteem test? Is this a test of how role-socialized you are? Did you pass?

## Other Fee Arrangements

### Offering Discounts

Discounts can take several forms. First, MCOs demand a lower fee, with the rationale that it is a discount for a bulk order. They promise to send you many referrals, keep you busy, and fill your empty hours, and so they contend that they deserve a lower price than if you had to recruit and negotiate with one client at a time. See Section 3.12 for more on managed care.

You can offer discounts for various reasons, and most businesses do. However, you must make the rationale perfectly clear to the client and any insurance company, make it consistent with your state's insurance and business laws, and be entirely consistent in its application. It is altogether proper to offer clients who need less of your time a lower fee. A 20% discount for clients who pay by check, cash, or credit card at the time of service and do not need any paperwork or phone calls for insurance or any other reason is justified. Clients usually feel that they got a bargain and earned the discount. Sending a yearly statement indicating only dates of service and payments made without a diagnosis or procedure code and to be used for the client's income taxes or medical savings account is the only paperwork provided. This is the policy of the Boulder, CO, Psychotherapists' Guild and many others.

Charles H. Steinmeyer, PhD, of Warren PA, offers what he calls "no-nonsense fees" for therapy and consultations, which make the discounts more specific. From his established fee, he deducts dollar amounts for no phone calls to MCOs or insurance companies, for no filling of claims forms, for no reports or treatment plans sent, and finally for no bills sent. If any of these are needed later, he charges for them at the rates indicated originally. The results are complete confidentiality, no nasty surprises if an MCO refuses to pay, and a predictable cash flow for both parties.

### Sliding Fees

Sliding fee scales provide discounts, but often awkward ones. Unless their use is proceduralized, they are discriminatory, and any bureaucracy will be unfair to some clients because everyone's circumstances are different. Also, since you are no longer charging everyone the same fee, insurers may see this as at least a violation of your contract. See below.

### Treating an MCO Patient without Using MCO Benefits

Making arrangements for payment with an MCO patient is complicated by your contract with the MCO. If you are on the panel and the patient wants to use MCO coverage, you are obligated to accept the MCO fee you agreed to as full payment and not to bill the patient for the difference between that fee and your (usually much higher), regular fee (this is called "balance billing"; see Section 2.7). However, if the patient does not wish to use his or her MCO coverage, or if the service you will provide is not covered by your or the client's MCO contract, or if the benefits have been used up or have been denied, then you and the client can work out any mutually agreeable financial arrangement.

### Self-Pay Arrangements for Confidentiality

If you offer clients the option of not using their health insurance, the records you create (which you must keep both to be ethical and to protect yourself) need never leave your office. However, the clients are very likely to be asked in the future, "Have you ever been treated for a mental disorder?" or something similar. Should they say no, knowing that your records will not then be requested? What about some future legal proceeding that brings their current mental state into question and for which your records may help them (or not)? When I have raised this question with my peers, I have received several suggested courses of action.

If a client wants to consult you about a "problem in living" and you work on that, with no mention of a "psychological condition," then the client can answer honestly that no such condition was diagnosed or treated. Similarly, Miller (2001) has indicated:

> I consider a diagnostic evaluation to be a separate service that I only conduct if the patient requests it. Therefore, when I see a self-pay client, I do not record a diagnosis. . . . for the vast majority of my clients, I am providing psychological consultation for personal and interpersonal issues. In other words, my clients are merely exercising their right to talk with or consult with a psychologist, and there is no reason that they need to carry a DSM-IV diagnosis because they wanted to exercise that right. Therefore, if I have not diagnosed them, they can say that they have never been treated for a psychiatric condition. (Miller, 2001, p. 78)

Miller (2001) also reports on a survey of psychologists that supported this position in hearings by the Colorado licensing board, which was considering requiring a DSM-IV diagnosis and other clinical information on each case.

> Consumers only want a diagnosis when it will clearly lead to better treatment or some benefit greater than the potential discrimination or stigma. In psychotherapy, many times the DSM-IV diagnosis does little to guide treatment, and it is often not necessary. Moreover, there is no clear dividing line between psychotherapy and the processes of problem solving, consultation, or coaching—services that do not require a diagnosis. Considering the negative repercussions of a mental health diagnosis, it is not surprising that in many situations consumers wish to be able to talk with a professional or use the tool of psychotherapy without either a diagnostic evaluation being conducted or a diagnosis being recorded. The petition documents that a large portion of psychologists support the right to talk with a mental health professional without receiving a formal diagnosis. (Miller, 2001, p. 78)

### Pricing Forensic Services

Forensic testifying is commonly billed at double your clinical rate and includes all time out of the office (i.e., travel time), because your time to testify is so unpredictable that you should not schedule any clients afterward. Charging for half a day is a common minimum, as is requiring to be paid several days before testifying. Of course, never either accept or defer a fee contingent on the case's outcome, because this will be seen as compromising the independence of your opinions. (Expect to be asked about this by opposing counsel.) You are likely to be asked to meet with "your" attorney beforehand and should bill for this time, as for any other services to clients. Be careful with any notes you might take at this meeting, as they are "discoverable" (i.e., subject to a subpoena) by the other side.

Providing a deposition in your office is simpler than actually testifying, and so charging your usual clinical fee, plus the time needed to review your files or other related activities, is reasonable. For any deposition, negotiate with the attorney the number of hours, keeping in mind the number of clients you must cancel and reschedule. Again, make certain to be paid in advance and stop when the paid time is up. It is not uncommon for depositions to take longer than expected, and for attorneys to try to get you to bill opposing counsel for the additional time, so be assertive. Any case materials you bring to a deposition are likely to be copied for the other side, so be very selective and don't let an attorney have any originals.

*Pricing School Services*

If you plan to do school consultation or training, develop a letter explaining your services (in nontechnical terms, if possible) and fee schedules. Give it to any school personnel who inquire about your services, and provide an estimate of the amount of your time required. Their response should be a sentence and signature on the estimate, or a letter agreeing to accept responsibility to pay for the services.

If a parent wants to use some insurance or agency resources to pay your fees, make it clear that you will bill the parents; that they must talk to a case manager to arrange payment for your several hours of consulting; and that this service is not testing or therapy and will not be billed at a discounted rate under any MCO or health maintenance organization (HMO) plan. You may have success in getting the school to pay for your staff training services after you have done your work with the child (and thus make your fees a worthwhile cost to the parents), especially if the previously provided school services have been unproductive.

*Providing Service Pro Bono*

> Sometimes give your services for nothing, calling to mind a previous benefaction
> or present satisfaction. And if there be an opportunity of serving one who is a
> stranger in financial straits, give full assistance to such.
> —HIPPOCRATES (cited in Jones, 1923, p. 319)

Although it is not required, offering your services without charge has a long history among professionals. It is not required by the APA ethics code (APA, 2002), but it is highly recommended in Principle B. Many therapists dedicate a percentage (5–15%) of their practice to *pro bono* services as part of their responsibility to society.

## Discussing Fees

The resistance to setting up a fee arrangement in the first session comes almost completely from the therapist. If you say, "We can worry about the money later," you are increasing your uncollectable fees by 20%. It is also unethical because it prevents informed consent. One simple way of discussing fees is to raise the issue toward the end of the first session, after you have discussed the length of treatment. You can use phrasing like this:

"There is one more issue we must talk about, and that is fees. My regular fee is $_____ per session. Take a minute and consider what I have said about how long your treatment should take, and weigh your income and expenses, and tell me if you can afford that."

I find that most clients agree to pay this amount. If they say they cannot or appear very reluctant, I usually say, "Well, in light of your situation, tell me what you can afford and I will accept that."

I have used this policy for years with few abuses or regrets. If you adopt it, be aware that you are at risk even if you do not put anything like this in your client information brochure, because a patient may complain. It may be better to develop a credit policy for all patients. This is also a good time to introduce or reinforce paying for each session at its end. Note that these policies do not apply to those who have you bill their insurers or use MCOs.

If someone other than the client pays the fee, make that responsibility clear to the payer with a formal agreement (see Form 28). Also make it clear that this arrangement does not entitle the payer to confidential information. When the client is a child, however, parents do have the right to general information on progress. This should be spelled out in detail in your client information brochure (see Section 4.2).

### Tips on Collecting Fees

- **Simply do not allow clients to run up large unpaid bills.** You should allow no more than two sessions without payment to elapse before you raise the issue with a patient, because you cannot terminate a client in great psychological need just for financial problems. If you extend credit, you should set a dollar limit, such as $1,000, on a maximum balance.

- Big balances may tempt patients to devise malpractice suits or ethics complaints to escape them. This is a major source of such complaints.

- The longer the delay, the smaller the collection. The established wisdom of collection agents is that if a payment is over 90 days late, you will collect 50% or less.

- If you allow a patient not to pay, you will both feel rotten. It sets a poor example of your not handling disagreeable and important issues or delaying their handling. The patient may come to believe that you are not a good therapist.

- You may need a simple book of two-part receipts for the few patients who pay cash. Don't waste your money on custom-printed receipts unless you use the form for other purposes (see Form 3).

- If a client gives you a check that makes you suspicious, cash it *immediately* at the client's bank. If the account does not have sufficient funds, don't try again until you know the check will clear—you can call the bank every day or two and ask if the funds are there. When the account has the funds, cash the check immediately.

## <u>2.2</u>   The Income Record

A record of your income is essential and can be as simple as a single page of inexpensive, ruled 8½" × 11" accounting paper for each month with appropriate headings. Figure 2 shows the type of income record I use, shortened here for space reasons, but you should adapt it to your style and needs.

For each month I use a fresh sheet with eight columns, as shown in the figure. The date each check is received is recorded in the first column. I write the number of the check in the next column. This will assist in clarifications with a client should confusion arise, but this column is optional. The last name of the person who gave me the check is recorded in the third column. I add initials if the name is common and if I might take on another patient by that name.

The next three columns, "Office 1," "Office 2," and "Paychecks," correspond to categories I need to keep separate for tax purposes or for evaluating programs. I have two offices in different communities, so taxes are paid to two municipalities accordingly. Paychecks, from which taxes have already been deducted, are recorded in the third column. The "Other" column is reserved for special income that does not fit these labels.

I make deposits to my practice's checking account weekly. I cluster the checks in each deposit with a large bracket, and write the total amount and date of deposit in the last column. At the end of the month, the totals are recorded at the bottom of the page for each column, and a grand total is computed. I use the monthly totals for estimating quarterly taxes to be paid. As your practice grows, actually endorsing each check with your signature and account number becomes tiring. Instead, you can obtain a stamp that says "For Deposit Only" with your account number and name. The stamp also allows your staff to make up your deposits.

## Monthly Income Record

For:  July 2002

| Date | Check # | Source of income | Office 1 | Office 2 | Paychecks | Other | Deposits |
|------|---------|------------------|----------|----------|-----------|-------|----------|
| 4 | 207 | Lenin | 100 | | | | |
| | 456 | Nixon | 75 | | | | |
| 6 | 129 | Stalin | | 100 | | | 575.00 (7/10) |
| 8 | 567 | Hoover, J. E. | | 200(I)[1] | | | |
| | 130 | Stalin | | 100 | | | |
| 11 | — | Lenin | 100($)[2] | | | | |
| | 459 | Nixon | 75 | | | | |
| 12 | 938 | Bonaparte | | 68 | | | 1,064.33 (7/17) |
| 14 | 004 | Lecture to CIA | | | | 100 | |
| 15 | 888 | Lecture to NSA | | | | 100 | |
| 15 | 996 | NIMH | | | 621.33 | | |
| Subtotals | | | 350 | 468 | 621.33 | 200 | |
| Grand total | | | | | | | 1,639.33 |

[1] If it was an insurance payment, a letter "I" can be inserted to clarify the source.
[2] If a client pays you in cash, you can insert "$" to keep your records clear.

FIGURE 2.  Sample monthly income record.

# 2.3   The Expense Record I: Your Checkbook

There are two components to recording your professional expenses. The first is your business checkbook, and the second is an expense summary, completed on a monthly or quarterly basis. Remember that every legitimate and necessary business expense (because it is deductible against income) is really very valuable to you. The true cost of purchases for your business is about 50% of what you pay, because they are tax-deductible, and you are probably in the 50% tax bracket (federal income tax of 28%, state and perhaps local income taxes of about 5%, FICA of 15.7%, sales tax of about 6%, etc.). This is the way the U.S. Congress, in its wisdom, has set up the country. Enjoy it. Buy whatever will make your business easier and more efficient.

## Choosing a Checking Account

A checking account used exclusively for your practice is crucial in business record keeping. Accurate and full documentation of business expenses is a source of self-direction, as well as a safeguard against the anxieties of an audit. A checking account is also essential for paying your business-related obligations.

Try to avoid getting a business account, which has all kinds of fancy expenses associated with it. A personal account may also make it easier to get a card to use automatic teller machines for convenient deposits. Choose the least expensive account possible. Each bank has marginally different offerings, so investigate the various features. Basically, you want the highest interest and lowest bank fees for your lowest minimum balance. Consider the following (in order of cost importance): (1) the costs of services such as informing you of an incorrect deposit calculation, overdraft protection/loans, and especially the handling of "bounced" checks you deposit; (2) the lowest cost of monthly service charges for the size of your practice; (3) interest-bearing checking accounts and their minimum balance requirements for paying interest; and (4) the lowest minimum balance required to prevent a service charge. Several "checks by mail" companies are cheap, and checks are a major expense.

## Guidelines for a Business Checkbook

- The smallest size of checks is perfectly acceptable, cheaper, and easier to store both at home and in your wallet. Plain blue or yellow checks are fine. Never let your 3-year-old select the balloons-floating-in-the-sky design (as I did once).

- Buy the smallest number of checks at a time (200 or fewer), as larger quantities aren't usually cheaper and the check printer can get them to you in less than a week.

- Many prefer the three-checks-to-a-page format with a 6" × 8" check register, because both fit into a 7" × 9" loose-leaf binder that will stand up neatly in a bookcase or on the desk with other books.

- Many businesses use "one-write" checkbooks, in which the writing of a check automatically (with carbon on the back of the check) creates a ledger entry on the page behind it. The amounts are assigned to columns that correspond to tax or other financial purposes. For example, some column headings could be "Auto Expenses," "Rents," "Professional Library," and "Office Expenses." This simplifies bookkeeping by allowing the column totals to be used for tax accounting. This system, however, has several limitations for a small practice: The book is cumbersome; if you take a check with you and fill it out at the store, you will have to enter it into the checkbook the old-fashioned way; the checks are large, have to be specially ordered from a commercial printer, and cost more; finally, the time saved is minimal for the small number of checks most therapists write each year.

- If your practice is large, or if you only deposit checks monthly, get the deposit slips that allow you to list 16 or 19 checks on the back, and not the smaller deposit tickets (which sometimes will require you to use several).

- You may want to balance your account monthly, or you may prefer to let it go if it is in the ballpark, to save time. Some people round up the amounts of all checks and thus ensure that they will have a surplus cushion.

- Start a new check register each tax or calendar year, even if it is not used up, for simplicity of record keeping.

- If you are comfortable with keeping accounts on your computer, Quicken (http://www.quicken.com) is the standard program for bookkeeping, meets the needs of small practices, is not expensive or hard to learn, and easily imports and exports to other programs for tax time. If you need more resources for operating a more complex business, look at QuickBooks (http://www.quickbooks.com).

### Choosing a Credit Card

Although the issue of a business credit card is not directly connected with that of a business checking account, I'd like to mention it briefly in passing. It makes sense to get a separate credit card for your business and avoid using it for personal purchases. If you have more than one business, get a card for each. Write a note on an adhesive slip on each card to keep each card's use clear. Get bank cards (Visa or MasterCard) for all your accounts to save costs. The "Gold" versions are as good as the private cards in terms of offered services you really can use, such as rental car insurance coverage. If they are both or all from the same bank and all come due at the same time, you will save on postage when paying your bills. If you maintain a large balance each month, look for the lowest interest rates; if you pay off your balance, look for no yearly fees, and lowest costs for advances and other fees.

## 2.4   The Expense Record II: Monthly/Quarterly Expense Summary

FORM 2

The second step in systematic recording of expenses is having a running summary of your expenses. Form 2 offers a list of headings in standard accounting format that match the categories on business and personal income tax forms. You need enter only each expense's date and amount, and so you can place many checks, receipts, bills, and so forth on the same horizontal line. The line and section totals (e.g., auto expenses) can be entered into

# Business Expenses

Month: _____   or   Quarter:  1  2  3  4   of   Year: _____

| | 1 | 2 | 3 | 4 | Total |
|---|---|---|---|---|---|
| Prof. services: Accounting | | | | | |
| Legal expenses | | | | | |
| Secretarial | | | | | |
| Supervision/consultation | | | | | |
| Professional liability insurance | | | | | |
| Professional licenses | | | | | |
| Professional library | | | | | |
| Professional dues | | | | | |
| Advertising | | | | | |
| Auto expenses: Loan | | | | | |
| Fuel | | | | | |
| Insurance | | | | | |
| Repairs | | | | | |
| Supplies | | | | | |
| Registration fees | | | | | |
| Other | | | | | |
| Bank fees, checks | | | | | |
| Business entertainment | | | | | |
| Business gifts | | | | | |
| Office expenses: Supplies | | | | | |
| Supplies | | | | | |
| Equipment | | | | | |
| Subscriptions | | | | | |
| Rent(s) | | | | | |
| Telephone | | | | | |
| Answering service | | | | | |
| Utilities | | | | | |
| Repairs | | | | | |
| Postage | | | | | |
| Printing | | | | | |
| Refunds given | | | | | |
| Taxes paid (on business): | | | | | |
| Business privilege | | | | | |
| Property | | | | | |
| Sales | | | | | |
| Training/Prof. development | | | | | |
| Travel, meals | | | | | |
| Miscellaneous (small amounts): | | | | | |
| | | | | | |
| | | | | | |
| Other (specify reason & payee): | | | | | |
| | | | | | |
| | | | | | |
| Cash expenses (total and staple receipts on back ): | | | | | |
| | | | | | |

**FORM 2. Monthly/quarterly expense summary.**   From *The Paper Office*. Copyright 2003 by Edward L. Zuckerman. Permission to photocopy this form is granted to purchasers of this book for personal use only (see copyright page for details).

your federal and state quarterly estimated income tax forms, so that you do not overpay or underpay your taxes. When you have completed a year's worth of these, you will also have a good sense of where your money is going, feel more comfortable with the business side of your practice, and be able to plan better.

# 2.5  Methods of Billing

The simplest and cheapest method of billing is *not* having to bill: Have clients pay at the time of each session.

### Credit Cards

The second simplest method of billing is to accept credit card payments. This ensures full payment, avoids the delay of billing, and makes payment certain. Business supply stores and banks can help you become a "vendor" or open a "merchant account" to accept credit cards. As to costs, in April 2001 I saw a $50 setup fee and then 3% plus $0.50 per transaction with a $15/month minimum. Be warned, however, that credit card companies have sold their lists of transactions, so you should inquire about the card issuer's privacy policies to avoid embarrassing your clients in the future.

Most clients, however, still need records of the services received and of their payments to you, for tax purposes or for reimbursement from health insurance. To save yourself grief, find a billing method that works for you in terms of your resources (time, secretarial help, computer access, size of your practice), and use it until something *markedly* better comes along. The common options are covered below.

Whichever of the following options you choose, **you should bill often**. I know this is a burden, but you will collect more money in the long run.

### Statements

If your office help is cheap and reliable, sending out statements could work for you. However, putting together traditional, typed, letter-like statements is time-consuming, because so much writing is needed each month. Use a statement card, writing in each month's contacts, charges, and payments, and then compute a balance due. Then send out a photocopy of this 5¾" × 8½" card each month in a #9 window envelope. Medical printers offer the materials needed.

### SuperΨbills

Some therapists have adopted the SuperΨbill approach. It has a three-part "no-carbon-required" form with diagnostic codes, patient insurance submission instructions, service codes, and your practice's identification imprinted on it. You only have to make checkoffs and mail it out. CD-ROM versions are available from Medical Office Connection (http://medicaloffice.com). Also, some computerized billing programs will print a kind of "super-bill."

### Computerized Billing Programs

Mental health billing is the most complex area of medical billing. To meet the needs of practitioners, there are about 25 computerized billing programs publicly available. The simpler and cheaper ones serve those in solo practice, and the more complex and expensive ones serve large groups or health care organizations. Programs construct a bill to give to clients, track MCOs' session limits, bill multiple payers separately, keep progress notes, send out reminders, and help with treatment planning. The evaluation of these programs is beyond the scope of this chapter, but if you bill more than 25 clients a month and do not have an ace billing person working for you, you should investigate them. Most are advertised in your professional newsletters.

### Billing Services

There are companies that will do your billing for you. Look under "Billing Services" in the Yellow Pages or ask around. Billing services will provide a variety of valuable services, including allowing you to accept credit card payments, as well as electronic claim submission. They can bill all kind of insurers and third parties, using these parties' current forms, procedures, and policies, and with faster turnaround on your accounts receivable. They offer help with audits by payers, verification of benefits, and toll-free assistance, and they can save you postage (although your telephone bill for faxes may go up a little). They send nicely printed bills to the client, bills to third parties with all the needed information ("clean claims"), and monthly reports on the status of your accounts receivable. The cost to therapists is based on a percentage of the amount collected, usually between 6% and 8%. Before signing up, ask how they deal with billing mistakes—they should have at least a big "errors and omission" insurance policy. Evaluate the forms they want you to use, and how they deal with insurance company denials (do they simply pick the "low-hanging fruit" of easy cases, or are they persistent but not too aggressive?). Be sure to get and check some references, and to confirm how long they have been in business and how many clients they have. Remember, you will be held responsible for their actions—if not legally, then ethically (APA, 2002, Standard 6.06).

### A Weekly Summary for Billing

If you have someone else make up and send out your bills, you will need to specify whom to bill and for what services; the format below will do that. It is slightly modified from one designed by Mason B. Scott, EdD, of Pittsburgh, PA, and is especially useful if clients are seen several times a week. It is also suitable for billing consultation hours and other indirect or non-client-related services. This form is filled out by the therapist from (or instead of) an appointment book. Make all entries in pencil, and select appropriate service codes for your practice.

When a client comes in, the billing code (BC) box is marked with a slash ("/") to show that the client was seen and should be billed; when the client is actually billed, a backslash ("\") is used to form an "×." If the client cancels, // is used to indicate that the client is to be billed. If the therapist cancels or some other unusual circumstance arises and the client is not to be billed, /// is used. The form can also be used for keeping track of phone calls to clients: Each name and number is entered, and when the call is completed, the name is crossed out with a single horizontal line. Calls to be billed are marked with a slash in the BC box, as appointments are. Calls not completed are rewritten to the next week's form. The form is sent weekly to the person doing the billing, who has a list of names and usual charges, and so creates the bills that are sent out each month.

## Billing Summary

Name of service provider: _____          For the week of _____ to _____

| Client's name | Mon. | | | Tues. | | | Wed. | | | Thurs. | | | Fri. | | | Sat. | | |
|---|---|---|---|---|---|---|---|---|---|---|---|---|---|---|---|---|---|---|
| | BC | Hr | SC | BC | Hr | SC | BC | Hr | SC | BC | Hr | SC | BC | Hr | SC | BC | Hr | SC |
| | | | | | | | | | | | | | | | | | | |
| | | | | | | | | | | | | | | | | | | |
| [Add as many lines as you need] | | | | | | | | | | | | | | | | | | |
| Totals | | | | | | | | | | | | | | | | | | |
| Grand total | | | | | | | | | | | | | | | | | | |

**Billing codes (BC):** / = Seen; / = Cancelled but to be billed; / = Cancelled but not billed; \ = Billed. **Hr:** Number of hours.
**Service codes (SC):** C = Consultation; P = Psychological examination; NP = Neuropsychological examination; I = Interpretation; RP = Report preparation; RR = Records review; D = Deposition; T = Testimony; PC = Phone consultation. If no code is indicated, bill for 1 hour of psychotherapy. ExT = 1.5 hours of psychotherapy.

## A Record of Services Provided

Some therapists, in lieu of a bill, provide the patient with a form like Form 3 after every visit. Professional billers call it "a walk-out statement." It has the advantages of (1) replacing a monthly cumulative "statement"; (2) providing a reminder at the end of the session to pay and a receipt for payments made; (3) indicating and reminding the client of the next appointment; and (4) being a record of services provided for client-submitted insurance claims.

**FORM 3**

Form 3 also documents each visit with a signature and confirms the client's consent to receiving services. You can use this form when you think a client has some undefined or unarticulated reluctance about treatment; have the client sign the form as soon as he or she comes in. Clients will go along with almost any procedure if you make it seem matter-of-fact and customary. Lastly, the form reinforces the client's assumption of financial responsibility for your fees.

This form is based on one used by Irvin P. R. Guyett, PhD, of Pittsburgh, PA. If you want to print it up by the hundreds, it can be made into a no-carbon-required form, which will create a copy for the client and one for you or your bill-generating person. Under "SS/Fed. EIN #," add your Social Security or federal employer identification number. The latter you'll need if you employ anyone (i.e., give him or her a W-2 form). Insurance companies

## Record of Services Provided

SS/Fed. EIN #: _____ State license #: _____

Client: _____ Date of service: _____

Diagnoses (DSM/ICD codes): _____

Services performed (CPT or other codes): _____ Service location (if different from above):

_____ _____

_____ _____

This is session number _____ of a total of _____ visits authorized by your managed care organization on _____.

| Fee | Adjustment | Charges | Amount paid | Balance due |
|-----|-----------|---------|-------------|-------------|
|     |           |         |             |             |

Signature of client, which indicates consent to services and acceptance of final responsibility for payment, regardless of any third-party benefits: _____

Therapist's signature: _____

Date of our next appointment: _____, the _____ of _____, at time _____ A.M./P.M.

**FORM 3. Record of services provided.** Adapted from a form devised by Irvin P. R. Guyett, PhD, of Pittsburgh, PA, and used by permission of Dr. Guyett.—From *The Paper Office*. Permission to photocopy this form is granted to purchasers of this book for personal use only (see copyright page for details).

require one or the other of these numbers to pay you. You can replace "State license" with another indication that you are a credentialed and payable professional, if you so desire. It is often useful to print a number of diagnostic codes and their titles in the "Diagnosis" space, which you can simply circle, to save time. Under "Services performed," you can print appropriate codes and their titles as well, although none are offered here because they change fairly often (for a discussion of *Current Procedural Terminology* [CPT] codes, see Section 2.7).

Any client submitting an MCO insurance claim will need to have an HCFA-1500 form completed (see Section 2.7) or a similar form devised by his or her MCO. However, for "self-pay" clients or those who use indemnity insurance, Form 3 can be modified to meet the client's information needs for tax purposes or reimbursement by simply adding a column at the left side for the dates of service.

On the line for diagnoses, you can enter either the name or code number or both. Using only the code number may increase confidentiality. Use either ICD or DSM codes, and circle to indicate which. Each session gets its own line. It may seem distrustful, but when you complete the form, routinely initialing or signing under the last visit entry will discourage the client from adding sessions to increase a deductible medical expense or illegally recover additional reimbursement.[1] You can use the back of your original to record when you mailed the last copy of this form or any special financial arrangements you made. Keeping the original in the front of the client's case file can help you know the client's balance and address any payment problems early.

## 2.6   Collecting Overdue Fees from Clients

*Note.* Collecting from insurance companies is covered in Section 2.7.

Regular billing gives you a good grasp of your accounts, so that you will know when someone slips from 30 to 45 days behind. The later a client is in paying, the less likely it is that you will collect the full sum owed you; the curve is steep and negatively accelerated.

If you are squeamish about dunning your clients for money or think that it negatively affects the intimate therapeutic relationship, find another way to assure that you will be paid, or you will have to leave private practice. You can work it through with your own therapist (more work and more costly), hire someone to dun clients (cheaper and easier), use a paperwork solution such as that described below, or have your secretary (or spouse, calling as your office manager) call the slow payers.

However, keep in mind that collection efforts are a frequent cause of ethics complaints (see Section 3.1). Whichever method you choose, proceed with caution.

---

[1]If you are concerned with this kind of fraud, and if you complete bills on a computer, try to choose a font not widely available so that your bill cannot be added to without making the additions obvious. Thousands of fonts are available on the Internet at no cost.

## Calling the Client

A face-to-face discussion with you is the best, but a phone call is a good way to assure payment. A second choice is a personal call from a secretary or office manager. This has been shown to be many times more productive than using the mail. Be sure, though, that whoever makes the call understands the limitations on what he or she can do and say. Read up on the federal and state laws and practices in this area before starting. In general, the caller must always be polite, show concern for the client's best interests, listen to explanations, offer to work out a payment schedule, and follow up methodically. Calls may be made only between 8 A.M. and 9 P.M. The caller should carefully note his or her efforts and the client's response on a 3" × 5" "tickler card," which can go into your "tickler file."

The most common version of a tickler file is a set of index cards with spaces for the client's name and today's date. As of today, indicate the days the account is past due, the action taken, its results, and the follow-up date. Last, indicate the final action taken (amount paid, sent to collection, etc.). These cards are filed, and, after the action is performed, refiled behind 70 dividers: 3 sets of 31 for the days of the next 3 months, and 9 more for the rest of the year.

## Sending a Note on the Bill

When there is a larger-than-expected unpaid balance, or a payment is more than 30 days late, I attach a yellow Post-It Note (removable so the bill can still be submitted to the insurance company) to the bill. Since such a client's case is usually closed, the note usually says something like "Is there some problem with this account?" or "Are you having a money problem?" or "Is there some trouble with your insurance company?" It then requests or informs the client of action: "Please call/talk to me if there is some difficulty with this," or "Can you pay me something on this account?" or "I will call you next week about this."

## Sending Collection Letters

Collection letters seem to work better than notes on the bill. Meek (1987) provides an excellent discussion of such letters in just three pages. For those of you who have never received them, collection letters come in increasing intensity of wording (and often of paper color as well). The "first-level" notes are increasingly demanding in tone, but all indicate a willingness to talk and work out a payment plan. The "second-level" letter informs the client that you will no longer provide services until payment is made. The "third-level" letter threatens legal action.

## Other Methods

If a bill is several years old, and you don't want to sue now but might in the future, you can extend the debt's payment time. Try to get an acknowledgment of the debt (by a dated signature on a letter), a small payment, or even a promise to pay. Sometimes people's financial situations change and they will actually pay their debts off. Ask; it's cheap to try.

As the third-level collection letter suggests, you can use small-claims court in your district. It is simple and cheap, and no lawyer or other professional is required. It is almost always successful, but you need to decide the following: (1) Have you tried all other methods first? (2) Is there anything to collect? Does the client have the money? and (3) Do you want to make an enemy for this much money? The journal *Psychotherapy Finances* discusses small claims court in its binder *Guide to Private Practice*, and Hussey (1986) also provides a good discussion.

The APA allows the use of collection agencies, but you must inform the client first and provide him or her with the opportunity to pay before proceeding (APA, 2002, Standard 6.04e). Indeed, never turn over a debt to a collection agency without first having spoken with the client. Surprising the client with a call from a collection agency may provoke a retaliatory ethics or malpractice complaint. Hussey (1986) has good advice on collection agencies.

Investigate and carefully read your contract with a collection agency, to reduce problems. Some problems I have heard of include being locked into a single agency for collecting your money; being required to pay a fee if you discontinue having an agency collect for you; having collection activities dropped if you or the agency is sued or threatened with a suit by the client; receiving very limited (and often ineffective) investigation to find a client who has "skipped out"; and having to supply a lot of material to support your bill. Overall, some agencies are clearer and fairer than others, so be thorough and ask lots of questions.

As a final reminder, if patients are not allowed to get behind in their payments to you, sophisticated collection methods will not be needed. Have clients pay upon receipt of services, or bill early and often. **Don't let patients get behind in their payments to you!**

## 2.7   Billing Third Parties—and Getting Reimbursed

In the old days, you had a professional relationship only with the client (first party) and not with the insurance company (third party). The client paid you and then might recover payment from the indemnity insurer with whom he or she had a contract. These days you are more likely to have a contract with an MCO, a preferred provider organization (PPO), or an HMO, and so you *do* have a professional relationship with a third party.[2] Your contract will stipulate all the billing procedures and limitations.

### Advice on Procedures for Clients with Health Insurance

Before you provide any services, you should confirm that the client is indeed covered for your services. This is called "verification of coverage." Both indemnity policies and an MCO's procedures are invariably complex and time-consuming. See the behavioral health insurance benefits questionnaire (Form 7) in Section 3.12, for a list of questions to guide you through your calls to an indemnity insurer or MCO.

---

[2]The term "MCO" ("managed care organization") will be used from this point onward in this book to encompass all similar legal, financial, and organizational structures, which may be called preferred provider organizations (PPOs), health maintenance organizations (HMOs), or the like. For all practical purposes they are the same for the mental health clinician, because in each case a third party (the MCO) is making decisions that restrict treatment of the client (the first party) by the clinician (the second party).

There is a standard form for submitting almost all health insurance claims, called the HCFA-1500. It is revised occasionally and is available from printers, who will place your practice information in the appropriate block. It may also be available from the insurance companies who require you to submit it.

The HCFA-1500 can be completed in several ways, depending on the size of your practice and wallet:

- Computer-based billing/office management systems do a superb job. This is their biggest selling point. Most of these programs now can even submit your bill to an insurer over the phone lines with a kind of e-mail called "electronic claim submission."

- You may be able to set up your computer and printer with a template in a word-processing or data base program to print the essential information onto preprinted or photocopied HCFA-1500 forms. In a March 2001 Internet search, I found programs that just fill out HCFA-1500s, ranging in cost from $42 to about $200. The forms can be downloaded as well.

- You can fill out one master form (such as the HCFA-1500 or the form from the client's insurance company) for each patient, make several photocopies, and enter (by hand or typewriter) the current billing period's services-provided information. Repeat on another copy of the form each month. This is cheap, simple, and really quick if you have only 10 patients who need this kind of billing.

By October 2003, the HCFA-1500 is likely to be replaced by other forms with different service and billing codes; however, these transaction codes (Part 162 of HIPAA) had not been decided upon as this book was going to press. The developers of all electronic billing programs and the health insurers with whom you deal will provide you with all the materials you will need before this deadline.

If you must share more information than patients' names, dates/kinds of services, and diagnoses with the insurance company, another person, or any other third party, be sure to get a release-of-information form signed (see Section 7.5 for various types of these forms).

## What You Need to Know for Insurance Processing

If you do not have the following information and skills, learn them from private seminars, other billers, training programs provided by the larger insurers (e.g., Blue Cross/Blue Shield), or national training organizations.

- Know which of your services are reimbursable and for what amounts. *Physicians' Current Procedural Terminology* (CPT; for the most recent edition, see American Medical Association, 2002) is an enormous multivolume publication defining all recognized health treatment practices. You will need CPT code names and numbers to bill for your services. As a therapist you only need to know a few codes, but these must be current. CPT codes that cover psychotherapy and some assessment were supplemented in 2002 with codes for the application of typical psychological methods to assessing and treating medical disease-related problems and medical diagnoses. This is a tremendous advance, finally recognizing (and ultimately paying for) biopsychosocial interventions, and you should consider the implications for your practice. Two codes, 96150 and 96151, cover assessments and reassessments, respectively, to identify the biological, psychological, and social factors important to the prevention, treatment, or management of physical health problems. Four codes (96152, -3, -4, and -5) can be used to reflect services (to an individual, group, and family with and without the client present) to modify the psychological, behavioral, cognitive, and social factors affecting the client's psychological functioning, health, and well-being. They do not apply to patients with psychiatric diagnoses, and cannot be reported on the same day as the psychiatric codes. Medicare will reimburse immediately, although private insurers will be slower to pay for these services. Others such as social workers, nurses, and physical therapists can also utilize these codes.

- Using the ICD codes may have advantages over the DSM codes. If you are treating a psychological condition related to a medical one, or if you are doing neuropsychological evaluations or treatments, use the medical ICD codes. They are reimbursed more routinely, with less resistance, and often at higher rates by Medicare, Medigap policies, commercial carriers, and MCOs, and the parallel CPT codes may allow you more hours for assessment or services. If you are treating a psychological condition and using psychological methods, use both a psychological CPT code and a DSM diagnostic code. Do not use the psychological procedure codes with a medical diagnosis, and vice versa. Different procedures can be provided to the same patient for different diagnoses—that is why there is a space on the HCFA-1500 form for a diagnosis code next to each procedure code's space. There may be limits on similar procedures performed during the same visit. For more on these issues, at least for neuropsychology, see http://www.NANonline.org/ and search the section on "Professional Issues" and then "Billing and Reimbursement."

- Know what forms and terms to use. You will need the HCFA-1500 or the insurer's own billing form. Be familiar with the jargon of billing (e.g., "duration of session," "place of service," "coinsurer," "verification of benefits," etc.). Understand deductibles, copayments, coordination of benefits, and percentage coverages, as well as how they are computed. Small (1993) is an excellent resource and guide to all these aspects and details.

- Understand how to get around companies that deliberately delay payment and devise obstacles, or at least know how to pursue these organizations energetically. Payment of some of your perfectly legitimate claims is likely to be refused, and so to get paid, you must appeal those "denials." Although this topic is too detailed and changeable for discussion here, you can find three pages of advice and suggestions on this process at http://www.psych.org/pract_of_psych/reimb_denial.cfm.

- This may seem obvious, but given the behavior of MCOs, make certain to get (even if you have to make many calls) the "certification letter" that authorizes you to bill an MCO for the services you are going to perform. This is the only support you have for a claim that might be "lost in the mail," "never received in this office," or just has "no record of that contact or agreement."

- Obtain precise information concerning the lifetime and annual deductible or limitations.

- Be sophisticated about how to use time of billing to your advantage. For example: are yearly deductibles based on calendar years or on 365-day periods from diagnosis or initiation of service?

- Make arrangements for the "physician referral" issue.

## Billing for Medicare Patients

The various government programs are confusing, but do not reject the provision of services to Medicare-covered clients too quickly. Although there are some bureaucratic complexities, there are many benefits—reliable and fast payments; billing on additional codes for more complete and realistic reimbursement; and grateful patients and families. What each Medicare program means for psychotherapists is beautifully explained in Norris et al. (1998).

The APA Practice Directorate has a new, free, and very comprehensive *Medicare Handbook*, which can be ordered from 202-336-5889 and is also provided online at http://www.apa. org/practice/medtoc.html. This is the single best source of information for psychologists, and reading its approximately 35 pages will be well worth your time. The APA Practice Directorate's site at http://www.apa.org/practice/prof.html has other relevant resources, such as *The Basics of Medicare Audits, State Medicaid Reimbursement Standards for Psychologists,* and *Medicare Private Contracting: Plus or Minus?*

According to the 1989 Medicare law, you must notify the patient's primary physician after treatment has begun unless the patient specifically requests that no notice be given. You should discuss the desirability of this notification, carry it out by letter or phone if the patient agrees, and document these steps and this decision in your notes (see Section 4.2).

## Checklist for Avoiding Illegal and Unethical Billing Procedures

The APA code of ethics (APA, 2002) states simply that "Psychologists' fee practices are consistent with law" (Standard 6.04b) and that "Psychologists do not misrepresent their fees" (Standard 6.04c). This makes accurate billing an ethical responsibility and subject to ethical as well as legal risk. Kovacs (1987) examines billing practices that put you at legal risk. Here is a checklist of ways to avoid such risks:

- ❏ Bill only for services actually rendered, not for missed or shortened appointments. (You can collect for these from the patient under most conditions, but read your MCO contract. See Section 4.2.)

- ❏ Bill only in the name of the patient. If you see a couple, do not bill both members as individuals. Billing for only one person when you are doing relationship therapy is incorrect and illegal. Similarly, bill members of a therapy group for group therapy, not as if they were individual therapy patients.

- ❏ Miller (2000), in an online article, states:

    Insurance companies generally refuse to pay for couples therapy claiming that their policies do not cover marriage counseling. Although many clinicians and patients have assumed that there is nothing that can be done, in most cases, there is a way to obtain reimbursement for couples therapy. The key to overcoming the denials is understanding the issues and how the denials involve "downcoding to avoid payment." Armed with this information, assertive clinicians can do something to stop managed care's erosion of mental health services.

I strongly recommend this article (and other materials on the same site, http://www.psychotherapistsguild.com/refusal.html).

❏ Do not mislead the insurance company into believing that you provided a service when in fact a trainee or assistant did, even if the insurance company will not pay for services provided by others (as it should). This is an issue we should take up with lawmakers.

❏ Charge the insurer only the fees you and the client agree upon. If the patient really cannot afford your fee, (1) lower it or (2) refer him or her to another provider or clinic.

❏ Do not bill for double your usual fee, so that the insurance company will pay half and you will then receive your usual fee.

❏ Do not try to collect more than 100% of your fee by billing two insurers when a patient is covered by his or her own and a spouse's plan (Knapp, 1994). However, it may be acceptable to bill the second insurer for the part not paid by the first; read the contract under "coordination of benefits."

❏ Accepting the actual amount paid by a third party as full payment of your fee when it is not your agreed-on, posted fee is fraud. If you have told the third party your fee is $x$ dollars, and now you in effect accept less as full payment and do not collect the patient's part, this is submission of a false claim, or violation of the anti-kickback provisions of your contract with the payer. Do not advertise or state in your client information brochure that "Medicare is accepted as payment in full" or "Insurance is accepted as full payment." State in writing your financial policy concerning waiving the copayment only for the indigent, and define your criteria for "indigent." Do not offer the waiver; let the client ask for it. Do not routinely claim to the third party that a patient's financial hardship prevents his or her payment. Investigate and document the client's income and insurance coverage before waiving the copayment. Do not fail to make a good-faith effort to collect the client's part of the fee (the copayment) unless you have documented his or her indigence. Document your collection efforts. These are burdens, but the risks are high.

❏ It is common practice to collect part of your fee from the client's health insurance and copayment, and, if that does not cover your fee, to bill the client for the rest. In fact, this practice is incorporated into several of the forms in this book. With indemnity policies this is reasonable and legal, but with an MCO contract this "balance billing" may be forbidden. Such contracts require you to agree not to charge the client for the part of your regular fee that you have forfeited to become a managed care provider. They usually go further to indicate that if the MCO rejects your claim for payment for services you have rendered, you can only collect the copayment and not the rest of the fee (for which you had billed the MCO). Read your contracts very, very carefully.

❏ Do not change the diagnosis or the CPT code so that the insurance company will pay for your services or pay more (this is called "padding the bill" or, more currently, "upcoding"). For example, do not label what is truly a V-code diagnosis "adjustment disorder," or turn "adjustment disorder" into "dysthymia," or change "biofeedback" into "psychotherapy" if these are not accurate. "It's dishonest, and you're telling the patient that you think it is fine for both or you to become criminals for the price of a few sessions" (Reid, 1999, p. 63).

❑ Don't "cream and dump." That is, don't see those with insurance until their coverage is exhausted and then refer them away.

❑ Do not pretend that you were "too busy with clinical issues to worry about the paperwork," or say that you "trusted your assistant," or use other excuses for fraudulent billing.

**Failure to follow these rules can result in your being prosecuted.** You may then be convicted of insurance fraud, perjury to commit fraud, or collusion with the patient; you can subsequently be fined and jailed (I have heard that psychologists have served time for insurance fraud). Fraud, perjury, and collusion are all felonies and will usually cost you your license and livelihood. The federal government has recently enlarged its crackdown on fraudulent health care billing, and the Office of the Inspector General has issued elaborate new rules on compliance. (See http://org/hhs.gov/fraud.html for more information.) Furthermore, illegal practices are not good for the patient to see or to participate in.

## Late Payments from Insurers

Insurers must either pay or deny a claim within a limited time period (usually 30 days) after it is submitted. You can threaten to report insurers to the state insurance commissioner if they are too slow. If you can do so, and it is worthwhile to you, monitor the progress of all claims you submit, and keep after the insurers on old claims. Computerized billing programs can often do this automatically.

To assure that the insurance company has gotten the mail he sends, Irvin P. R. Guyett, PhD, of Pittsburgh, PA, includes a self-addressed postcard that the insurance clerk is to sign, date, and return to indicate receipt of the forms. If the postcard is not returned in 10 days, he sends the same materials again with a card and a note. The note clearly indicates that this is a second submission, because the first was apparently lost in the mail or in the insurance company's office, as he did not receive the return card. If appropriate, a call before the resending may speed things up, because the insurer doesn't want the extra paperwork.

A form letter to the insurance company reminding it of an unpaid claim may be productive. You may use a simple letter like this:

To:    [Insurance company]

Re:    Payment not received on insured [name]: _____
       Insured's identification no.: _____
       Patient (if other than insured): _____

Dear _____ :

In reviewing our files, we find no record of receipt of payment on this claim, and so have enclosed a duplicate copy of the claim we submitted originally on _____.

Please process this claim as soon as possible, as services were rendered in good faith some time ago. We thank you for your immediate attention to this matter.

Usually, insurers will respond to such a letter by indicating that some information is missing on the claim form you submitted. Insurance companies have been almost universally delaying payment by asserting that the forms submitted are incomplete—are not "clean claims." It has become so severe a problem that Pennsylvania finally passed a law (Act 68 of 1998) compelling timely (within 45 days) payment of "clean claims" or payment of interest on the balance due. Your state may have similar laws and procedures. If your state does not, pursue such legislation. If it does, enclose a copy with your claims. Do not assume that an insurance company or MCO is either competent or honest at this point in time. However, if company personnel tell you that information is missing, remedy the situation immediately (a fax machine is very handy here). If what they ask is confidential, write to them supplying alternative information (see Section 7.5).

If you find that a particular insurer repeatedly delays payments (some insurers have apparently chosen this method to increase their profits), include stronger language in your letters, and quote or cite your state's rules on timely payment. Also, send copies of all your communications with the insurer to your state's insurance commissioner, and note this policy at the bottom of all future letters to the insurer.

## Authorization of Benefits

Sometimes patients may receive payments from their health insurance for services you have provided and then fail to pay you. You can prevent this, as well as simplify the financial part of their lives, with the very standard procedure that the sample letter below supports. In addition, when you experience problems with receiving payment, having such a letter may allow you legitimate access to a client's benefit information and previous records to respond to denials based on "preexisting conditions"[3] if the client has left treatment, as is likely.

[Letterhead]


[Date]
[Name of insurer]                                                    [Name of patient or insured]
[Addresses]          [Patient's or insured's identification number or Social Security number]

Dear _____:

Your health insurance may cover part of the costs of your treatment here. I would prefer that the insurance company pay its obligations directly to me, rather than paying you and then having you pay me. In order to make that arrangement, I need your signature below. Please read the next two

---

[3]Like the term "preauthorization," which means "authorization," use of this term by insurance companies demonstrates the failure of their employees' education. They mean, of course, "existing conditions."

paragraphs and sign where indicated. If you have questions or would like to discuss this, please give me a call.

**This is a direct assignment of my rights and benefits under this policy.** I hereby request that payment of authorized Medicare, Medigap, and/or other health insurance plan benefits be made on my behalf to the therapist named above for services provided. I authorize this therapist to release to my third-party payer/insurer and/or to the Centers for Medicare and Medicaid Services and its agents, as necessary, any medical information needed to determine the benefits payable for related services. This authorization shall be considered valid for the duration of the claim. A photocopy of this authorization will be considered as effective and valid as the original.

I understand that I will be personally responsible for any amount denied, or any remaining amount owed for services partially covered by my third-party payer/insurer. This payment will not exceed my indebtedness to the above mentioned assignee, and I agree to pay, in a current manner. I agree to pay any costs incurred by this therapist in collecting such fees.

_____          _____

Signature of patient (or insured, parent, or guardian)                    Date

_____ Copy received by client          _____ Copy held by therapist

# 2.8    Marketing Your Practice Ethically

Marketing is required for the independent practice of psychotherapy. Clients will not just walk in off the street, and so you must either approach them directly (advertising, giving presentations, etc.) or have clients referred to you (by other professionals, insurers, ex-clients, agencies, etc.). There are many ways to get your practice known to others (see the list of books in Appendix A) but the best marketing for professional services is word of mouth, and so this section will focus on reaching ex-clients and the professionals ("gatekeepers") who might refer patients to you.

Ex-clients are the best sources for referrals, because they have already been persuaded that you can help them. Using testimonials from ex-clients is considered proper, but psychologists have generally frowned on such testimonials because they are so easily distorted. Only those who liked your services would be asked to testify, and few testifiers have had any experience with competing services. Bear in mind also that Standard 5.05 of the APA's code of ethics (APA, 2002) forbids asking or using current clients for testimonials, because it would be potentially exploitative. Also, traditionally one does not approach active clients of other therapists. Some view this injunction to be both paternalistic (after all, these are adult and experienced consumers who can make informed choices) and not in the best interest of the clients, who may receive better services from you than from their current therapists. The APA ethics code (APA, 2002) offers guidance that emphasizes consideration of the client's welfare, full discussion of these issues to minimize confusion and conflict, and proceeding with caution and sensitivity (Standards 10.04 and 5.06).

Physicians (not "doctors," please) are often good referral sources. Some specialties have enormous caseloads (10,000 patients in an internal medicine or gynecology group is common), have many patients with psychological problems, and often want to refer their troubled or troublesome cases. Their offices may even call and make the appointment if you are easily accessible. When you visit (as you should), ask whether you can leave educational brochures in a rack in their waiting rooms.

As noted in Section 2.1, beware of fee-splitting arrangements. Paying for referrals is common and ethical in many businesses, but psychologists' practices are not purely businesses. The APA ethics code (APA, 2002) specifically forbids this (in Standard 6.07), because being paid for making referrals to one service provider and not to another is likely to distort the referrer's views of what is best for patients. You may have to clarify this point with some potential referrers.

Your fellow clinicians can be an excellent source of referrals if they are simply (and repeatedly) informed of your availability and specialties on a regular basis. Below, you will find several means for making your services better known.

As required by Standards 5.01 to 5.04 of the APA ethics code (APA, 2002), you must be accurate in representations of your credentials, qualifications, and promises in mass media advertisements, in all forms of publicity, and when offering workshops for the public. Ads in the Yellow Pages generate many referrals, but they are sometimes of lower quality: People often call in the heat of an argument or crisis and may not show for the appointment. They do not cancel, as they think they will have to explain, feel guilty, apologize, or even get talked into coming. Or they may not understand the "rules of the game" of therapy and need socializing into the way this special relationship is conducted. As the "gatekeeping" function becomes more professionalized by MCOs, HMOs, EAPs fewer people will use the ads in the Yellow Pages. Referrals will be almost exclusively by networks.

If you want encouragement, information, and guidance on various marketing activities (e.g., surveying community needs and resources; writing and placing advertisements; creating newsletters; designing and presenting workshops to the community, peers, and businesses; etc.), see the books listed in Appendix A on practice development and marketing.

## Practice Announcement Letters

A letter is a simple and effective way to tell potential referrers that you are available. Below is a copy of a letter I sent to the medical staff when I joined a local hospital. It will need to be tailored to your orientation, professional situation, methods, audience, and comparative advantages, but it is a useful model of how to approach physicians. Keep the letter undated, as you should not send this announcement to every staff member at one time; if you do, you will be inundated with referrals to which you cannot respond. Try five per month for those you meet at the hospital. Indicate what you *don't* do (e.g., testing or child therapy) or treat, as well as what you do, or you will get inappropriate referrals and annoy your referral sources. I believe it is crucial to identify one or two specialties, so that the referrer has a "hook" to "hang your name on." Without these, you will blend into the undifferentiated mass of "service providers" and be ignored. With physicians, I have used "collaboration" or "consultation" to describe my practice model and found ready acceptance. Additions to this letter might address costs by indicating which MCO panels you are on; whether you offer a sliding fee scale and/or do *pro bono* work; and whether you have a waiting list, or will refer any who cannot afford to see you to appropriate community resources. For some settings, if you are a psychologist, you may have to explain the APA's ethics code's opposition to fee splitting.


[Letterhead]


[*No date*]

Dear Dr. _____:

May I take a moment of your time to briefly introduce myself? I've just joined you on the staff here at _____ Hospital and opened an office for the general practice of clinical psychology in the Medical Arts Building.

I treat adults (but not children) for depression, anxieties, phobias, and similar emotional disorders, using behavioral and cognitive methods that have clear scientific support of their effectiveness and efficiency. They do not involve extensive exploration of a patient's childhood or unconscious mind. Instead, my methods are active, directive, and educative; I aim at solving the problems the patient faces here and now.

I am keenly interested in treating conditions such as _____, _____, and _____ in close cooperation with physicians, who would of course retain the overall medical responsibility for their patients.

My background includes a PhD in clinical psychology from the University of Pittsburgh and a year-long full-time internship, both of which were approved by the American Psychological Association for training in specifically *clinical* psychology. I have worked for more than a dozen years in psychiatric hospitals, community mental health centers, and centers for the treatment of mental retardation, as well as in consultation/liaison and independent practice. Because I am a fully licensed psychologist, my fees are often partly covered by a patient's health insurance.

The research on the psychological needs of medical patients has uniformly indicated a high level of benefit from psychotherapeutic services, so if I can be of any assistance to you or your patients, please do not hesitate to call on me.

I have been warmly welcomed here and eagerly anticipate productive years of providing effective services to patients. Since my office is close by, I would be happy to come to meet with you, even briefly, at your convenience.


Sincerely,


_____

[Signature]


P.S. I have been very active in the psychotherapeutic community in Pittsburgh, and so if a patient of yours needs a specialized service, I may be able to refer him or her to someone who can meet this need. I would be happy to answer your questions or your patient' questions at any time and will respond to all phone calls very promptly.

## A Referral-for-Psychotherapy Questionnaire

FORM 4

It has been repeatedly established that physicians, even those with extensive training to do so, do not refer their medical patients for the therapy they recognize that the patients need. Form 4 aims to clarify the criteria for referral and treatment, and so to increase appropriate referrals.

Form 4 is based on one developed by Charles H. Steinmeyer, PhD, of Warren, PA. It may be used as an introduction to or a follow-up with potential referrers. It is designed to assess clients for the usual level of intensity and range of problems seen in office-based treatments, but you may find that those who score lower are suitable for some more specialized services you could provide. Substitute other questions based on your practice's patterns and services.

The "Total Score" interpretations have not been validated empirically. The general idea is that someone who gets 2's or less on all items is probably inappropriate for outpatient therapy, and someone who gets some combination of all 3's and 4's has a good chance of being appropriate for verbal psychotherapy.

A good strategy might be to deliver or mail a few copies, and when a referral is made, send more copies so the referrer has them easily available. If you send them in a manila folder with your cards, curriculum vitae (CV), appointment cards, and other materials, these are more likely to be filed and found when needed.

## A Referral Form for Group Therapy

FORM 5

We all know that group therapy can be very productive, can be time- and cost-efficient, and can address and resolve unique issues. Why don't mental health clinicians make better use of groups? The main reason is that they don't have a sufficient flow of clients to organize them into groups. How then can you increase the flow of suitable referrals? By "publicizing" your groups to all potential referrers. Form 5 is designed to explain concisely what a therapy group is about and for whom it is appropriate. It provides the essential information the referrer needs to make intelligent recommendations. Circulating it often and widely should generate a flow of new clients. The form is modified from one devised by Mickie Rosen, MS, ATR, of Huntington Valley, PA, for the Delaware Valley Group Psychotherapy Society's Referral Service.

## "Thanks for the Referral" Notes

Thank-you notes for referrals are sent as a professional courtesy, to document continuity and comprehensiveness of care, and to encourage more referrals.

During the first session with a referred patient, discuss and decide with the patient, how much he or she wants the referrer to know about the treatment. A "Yes" response to the appropriate question in Section B of Form 23 (the client demographic information form) is a sufficient release to inform the referrer that the patient showed up and is being evaluated. When it would be better to send a report of your findings, diagnosis, duration and nature

# Criteria for the Appropriateness of a Referral for Verbal Psychotherapy

Name of patient: _____  Date: _____

Name of evaluator/referrer: _____  Phone: _____

**Criteria**                                                                                            **Score**

A.  Insight (patient's understanding of the nonmedical problem as having psychological roots):        _____

   1 = Patient denies that there is a *psychological* problem.

   2 = Patient blames others for or rationalizes the problem.

   3 = Patient acknowledges a problem, although inaccurately understood.

   4 = Patient presents a treatable psychological or interpersonal problem.


B.  Reality testing (Patient's ability to perceive and respond to consensual reality):                _____

   1 = Disorientation, delirium, hallucinations, etc.

   2 = Marked delusions.

   3 = Isolated misinterpretations of common realities (interpersonal, social).

   4 = No recorded or observed misinterpretations of reality.


C.  Memory functioning (patient's ability to retain in-therapy learnings):                            _____

   1 = Patient has a clearly established new-learning memory disorder.

   2 = Possible memory disturbance (vagueness, gaps).

   3 = Memory function limited by patient's denial.

   4 = No demonstrated or suspected memory disorder.


D.  Communication ability (Using verbal skills):                                                      _____

   1 = Absent communication function (mute, aphasic).

   2 = Impaired communication function (mental retardation, disability).

   3 = Weak communication functions (withdrawal, reluctance, passivity).

   4 = No demonstrated impairments.

*(cont.)*

---

**FORM 4. Referral-for-psychotherapy questionnaire (p. 1 of 2).** Adapted from a form devised by Charles H. Steinmeyer, PhD, of Warren, PA, and used by permission of Dr. Steinmeyer.—From *The Paper Office*. Permission to photocopy this form is granted to purchasers of this book for personal use only (see copyright page for details).

E.  Abstraction or conceptual function (ability to generalize across situations):  ____

   1 = No demonstrated abstract ability—"concrete" thinking.

   2 = Weak or basic "functional" understanding.

   3 = Overly or inappropriately abstract thinking.

   4 = No demonstrated impairment.


F.  Thinking processes (patient's ability to participate in problem solving):  ____

   1 = Incoherent, confused, or grossly illogical thinking.

   2 = Flight of ideas, pressured speech, or tangential thinking.

   3 = Distractibility, lessened concentration or attention, preoccupation.

   4 = No notable impairment of thinking process.


Summary of appropriateness for verbal psychological intervention:  Total score: ____

   16–24 = Appropriate—Psychological methods are *very likely* effective for major
            problem(s). Please refer for treatment.

    8–15 = Questionable—Some psychological methods are *possibly* appropriate for some
            areas or aspects of the problems. Evaluate more fully or refer for evaluation.

    1–7  = Inappropriate—Psychological methods do not apply to the areas of this
            patient's problems. Consider other interventions to stabilize patient.


Your current diagnosis or diagnoses of this patient:




Comments or questions on other aspects or areas:




I appreciate your considering my services and promise to get right back to you on my evaluation of this patient.

## Group Therapy Referral Form

Dear _____:

We all know the benefits of group work for clients and professionals. This letter is to let you know of a group we host and ask you to consider referring your clients to participate in it.

Thank you.

_____

[Signature]

**Title of group:** _____

**In one sentence, this group is:** _____

_____

Purpose of the group:  ❑ Therapy    ❑ Support    ❑ Supervision    ❑ Training    ❑ Education

   ❑ Other: _____

General location of group: _____

Contact person: _____  Day phone _____  Eve. phone: _____

This group is:  ❑ In progress    ❑ Now forming    ❑ A potential new group

### Membership criteria

Target population:

   ❑ Children    ❑ Adolescent    ❑ Young adults    ❑ Adults    ❑ Senior citizens    ❑ Couples

   ❑ Families    ❑ Women    ❑ Men    ❑ Persons with disabilities    ❑ Persons with mental retardation

   ❑ Other: _____

Prior therapy experience:    ❑ Unnecessary    ❑ Helpful    ❑ Required

Marital status:  ❑ Irrelevant    ❑ Never married    ❑ Married    ❑ Separated    ❑ Divorced    ❑ Widowed

Educational status:  ❑ Irrelevant    ❑ Grade school    ❑ High school    ❑ College    ❑ Special education

Any exclusionary criteria for the group?: _____

### Meetings        ❑ Not yet set

   Day of the week/month:   S   M   Tu   W   Th   F   S        Time: From _____ to _____

   Duration of group: _____ weeks or months   or   ❑ Ongoing

   Each session lasts:  ❑ 1 hr.   ❑ 1.25 hrs.   ❑ 1.5 hrs.   ❑ 2 hrs.

   The group meets:  ❑ Weekly   ❑ Monthly   ❑ 2×/month   ❑ 3×/month   Other: _____

*(cont.)*

---

**FORM 5. Referral form for group therapy (p. 1 of 2).**    Adapted from a form devised by Mickie Rosen, MS, ATR, of Huntington Valley, PA, and used by permission of Ms. Rosen.—From *The Paper Office*. Copyright 2003 by Edward L. Zuckerman. Permission to photocopy this form is granted to purchasers of this book for personal use only (see copyright page for details).

## Foci of the group

Diagnoses

- ❏ Adjustment reactions
- ❏ Generalized anxiety disorder
- ❏ Obsessive–compulsive disorder
- ❏ Mood disorders
- ❏ Borderline personality disorder
- ❏ Substance abuse/dependence
- ❏ Psychotic disorders
- ❏ Eating disorders
- ❏ Fears and phobias
- ❏ Sexual dysfunctions
- ❏ Narcissistic personality disorder
- ❏ PTSD
- ❏ Psychosomatic disorders
- ❏ AIDS
- ❏ Other: _____

Problems

- ❏ Financial stress
- ❏ Coping with disabilities
- ❏ ACOA
- ❏ Alzheimer's support
- ❏ Cancer support
- ❏ Coping with chronic illness
- ❏ Coping with incapable parents
- ❏ Dysfunctional families
- ❏ Infertility
- ❏ Midlife crises
- ❏ Sexual abuse
- ❏ Physical abuse
- ❏ Unwanted pregnancy
- ❏ Weight control
- ❏ Chronic pain
- ❏ Other: _____

Issues

- ❏ Death and dying
- ❏ Marital issues
- ❏ Career/job search
- ❏ Minority issues
- ❏ Parenting issues
- ❏ Stress management
- ❏ Stepparenting
- ❏ Men's issues
- ❏ Women's issues
- ❏ Gay/lesbian issues
- ❏ Retirement
- ❏ Mourning/loss
- ❏ Nutrition/health
- ❏ Single parenting
- ❏ Widowhood
- ❏ Other: _____

## Orientation/leadership style

- ❏ Psychoanalytic
- ❏ Gestalt therapy
- ❏ Group-as-whole
- ❏ Psychodynamic
- ❏ Socialization
- ❏ Twelve-Step
- ❏ Interpersonal
- ❏ Cognitive therapy
- ❏ Other: _____
- ❏ Transactional
- ❏ Behavioral

## Group directors' information

Leader's name: _____

Address: _____

City: _____ State: _____ Zip: _____

Day phone: _____ Evening phone: _____

Highest degree: _____ License #: _____

Cotherapist's name: _____

Address: _____

City: _____ State: _____ Zip: _____

Day phone: _____ Evening phone: _____

Highest degree: _____ License #: _____

Supervisor's name: _____

Address: _____

City: _____ State: _____ Zip: _____

Day phone: _____ Evening phone: _____

Highest degree: _____ License #: _____

**Questions?** Please call: _____ at: _____

The best times to call are: _____

## Comments, suggestions, and other points

We thank you for your time and consideration.

of treatment, progress notes, and the like, then get a signed release-of-information form (Form 50) before calling or writing to the referrer. See the next section on progress notes.

If the client does not show up, you should inform the referring professional, because this is important information about the client's compliance with the referrer's treatment recommendations. Although you won't have the client's permission to release information about the client's status, I think that since the referrer knew of the referral (having made it), the client knew of it (having agreed to the appointment), and you knew of it (having set up the appointment), there is no breach of confidentiality.

You do not need to give any notification to former or current clients who refer others, because of general reasons of privacy. Also, a nonprofessional's recommendation to a friend or associate is only personal advice, and the recipient is free to ignore it.

Here are some tips on "thanks for the referral" note formats:

- Medical and other printers offer name-imprinted note cards for thanking referrers, but some of these, even though colorful and simple, may be rather impersonal for a psychotherapist.

- If your referrer is a physician or anyone likely to keep a "chart" on this person, you might consider typing or printing your note on a large label so that it can be easily incorporated into the referrer's chart.

- A common and professional format is to send a note like this:

[Letterhead]


[Date]

Dear Dr. _____:

Please accept my thanks for referring _____ to me for professional services.

If it is appropriate, and with a signed release from the client, I will provide you with a written or telephone summary of my clinical impressions and recommendations soon after our meeting. If for some reason the appointments are not completed, I will let you know.

If you have any questions or other concerns that you would like me to respond to in this client's case, please contact me immediately.

I sincerely appreciate your confidence in my services, and again thank you for this referral.

Very truly yours,


_____

[Signature]

Other suitable phrases for closing this note include the following:

. . . appreciate your vote/expression of confidence.

. . . promise to continue to provide the same high level of care to your referral that you have come to expect of us.

. . . proud that we have inspired your confidence.

Thank you for involving me in the ongoing care and treatment of your patient. I thank you for your kind referral, and I am looking forward to being of service.

Your confidence and trust are sincerely appreciated.

Again, thank you for your recommendation.

## Sending Progress Notes to the Referrer or Cotreater

Any referrer wants to know, at a minimum, whether a client contacted you and entered into treatment. That is why the client demographic information form (Form 23) has a question to get permission to tell the referrer that the referral was completed. Medicare requires that you inform the client's physician of your providing treatment (see Section 4.2), and, as a courtesy, you should keep all those who are continuing to provide care informed of progress and problems. The APA ethics code (APA, 2002) no longer specifically requires you to coordinate your treatment with the client's physician, but does strongly suggest it.

The contents of your letter should be tailored to the referrer's involvement in treating the client and the client's needs for privacy. If the referrer is no longer involved in the client's care, a simple thank-you note may be all that is needed. If you are actively collaborating with the referrer and sharing interventions (e.g., having a physician write the client's psychiatric medications), more details about changes in symptomatic behaviors, side effects of medications, failure to adhere to regimens, changes to treatment plans, advice on management, and the like would be appropriate, as would more frequent correspondence.

### Checklist for the Contents of a Progress Letter

Since you will be treating all kinds of patients, I have not offered a form here, but the contents should include at least these:

❏ Name and identifying numbers.

❏ Dates of service.

❏ Diagnosis or diagnoses, and especially any changes to these.

❏ Brief case formulation.

❏ Target symptoms, goals, etc.

❏ Kind(s) of treatment(s) you provided.

❏ What information you have given to the patient.

❏ Problems or information of relevance to the referrer or cotreater in managing the case.

❏ Response to treatment.

❏ Cooperation, motivation, adherence.

❏ Prognosis and expected duration of treatment.

❏ A closing expression of appreciation, hope that the information is of value, indication of your continued availability for consultation, and the like. (See Zuckerman, 2000, for many alternative phrasings for closing a note or report.)

### Suggestions

■ Most professionals avoid reading more than a page, and an outline or checkoff format for sending progress reports to a referrer will save time for both of you.

■ An outlined progress note can be created during a session with the client. This can become an opportunity to review progress and goals, as well as getting informal permission.

■ Since you are sending information to another professional, you need your patient's written permission. It is better to get a current release-of-information form (Form 50) signed near the time you send this information than to rely on an older one from the intake, when the client did not know what you might send or say.

■ For convenience, get permission to make telephone consultations with the referrer or collaborator by including this option on the release form.

## Where Do Your Referrals Come From?

The value of collecting information on the sources of your referrals can be expressed in terms of the old "80/20 rule": 80% of your patients come from 20% of your referrers.[4] The problem is that you may not know who those 20% are, and so may not be able to work better with them to increase those referrals. Creating a client log or form with the general headings provided below will help you to clarify the situation and understand which networks include you. It will give you a clearer and more objective picture of your practice's perceived orientation and visibility, so that you can decide whether you wish to change to meet your goals. When you create your own log, please adapt the headings below to the categories that suit your practice best.

If you keep this client log with your billing forms, you can fill it out monthly for all new pa-

---

[4]How do I know? It is a universal rule—just as 20% of your patients cause 80% of your billing problems, or 80% of your joy comes from 20% of your companions. The 80/20 rule is usually attributed to Vilfredo Pareto (1848–1923), an Italian economist. For more entertaining and thought-provoking examples, see http://www.csun.edu/~jmotil/Paretoisms.

tients. Alternately, you can complete it at intervals, perhaps when you file your quarterly estimated taxes.

### Characteristics of New Clients

| Client's initials | Date called | Referred by/ code† | Age* | Sex* | Zip code* | Diagnosis* | Other |
|---|---|---|---|---|---|---|---|
| | | | | | | | |

†These can be coded as follows Yellow Pages, Newspaper ad., MD, Attorney, MH professional (names or disciplines), Ex-patient, Agency, Ex-training setting, Peers, Public speaking engagement, etc.

*These categories should be modified to suit the goals of your practice. Zip codes can inform you of the geographic range of your client base, can indicate how far people will travel, and can guide your placement of advertisements or other marketing efforts.

### Record of Referrals Received

In addition, for collaborative or marketing purposes, you might reorganize these data by referral source.

Referral source:

Name:

Address:

Phone:

| Name of client | Date of first contact | Thank-you sent? |
|---|---|---|
| | | |

Comments (typical referral problems or diagnosis, preferences for feedback, needs, etc.):

### Analyzing and Using the Data on Referral Sources

At intervals, you should examine your log of client characteristics and collect some simple totals and percentages. Entering these numbers into a data base will allow you to pose interesting questions such as these:

- Does the referrer who sends me the most cases with $X$ diagnosis also have a lot of clients with $Y$ diagnosis whom he or she is not sending to *me*?

- Has referrer $R$ begun to send me lots more clients or ones with different diagnoses than he or she did a year ago because of my marketing efforts with him or her?

- Am I getting a lot of new clients who live or work in a particular area, and so might I consider opening an office for their convenience?

- Am I getting a lot of new clients with diagnosis $D$, and so might I get more training in, advertise, or teach this specialty?

- Which of my advertisements are most and least productive?

- How well do the actual number and percentage of clients from each referral source, in each age group, by diagnosis, and so on fit the projections for my practice that I made last year?

Examining the patterns will allow you to answer questions about your practice that will help you achieve your personal and professional long-term aims. For example:

- What is the number of new referrals I need to meet my practice/income goals?

- Compared with last month and with last year, am I meeting my goals?

- What are my new goals for next quarter?

- What are some new methods to meet these goals?

Clement (1999) is an excellent resource for more ideas on the practical value of such information.

## Collecting Feedback on Your Psychological Reports

The essential reason for doing evaluations—whether they involve testing, interviewing, or observations—is to collect information that shapes the decisions to be made about the treatment of individuals. And if you do any kinds of evaluative reports, the essential information you need to do your best evaluations is feedback on the value of your reports from their consumers.

The list of questions below can be used to structure a simple letter, which will demonstrate that you care about satisfying the needs of the recipients of your reports and will provide you with information to improve them. You should send it at least yearly to school personnel, therapists, the courts, or other colleagues/professionals who make referrals to you. Modify the words if you evaluate children or are sending this to parents or other consumers. If you do educational evaluations, you might review Ownby's (1991) form for some language.

1. Did the report give you information beyond what you already knew?

2. How helpful and realistic were . . . (here offer a list of sections and contents of your reports, such as recommendations for therapy or training, coping with symptomatic behaviors, etc.)?

3. Did the report fail to address areas of concern to you? If so, which?

4. Do you have any suggestions or comments?

Conclude the letter by expressing gratitude for the recipient's time and concern.

# CHAPTER 3

# Reducing Malpractice Risk by Operating Ethically

## 3.1 Ethics and Malpractice

*Study widely.*
*Question thoroughly.*
*Deliberate carefully.*
*Analyze clearly.*
*Act conscientiously.*
—The sage kings Yao and Shun,
as described by YAMAZAKI ANSAI

### Why Are Ethical and Legal Issues So Complicated

Abstract ideas of right and wrong can be simple. Unfortunately, the real world can be quite complicated:

- Principles must be stated abstractly to be comprehensive, and yet each case and situation is unique. "Should" and "must" are often too vague to direct specific actions; actions require precise answers (when, how, where, etc.).

- Ethics and laws can sometimes conflict, such as when the client's best interests require confidentiality but the law requires disclosure. Two ethical imperatives can also be in conflict in a particular situation.

- Therapy's goals may conflict with ethical guidelines. For example, full disclosure of a treatment's risks is necessary for informed consent, but may weaken a client's motivation for therapy. Offering success rates may make him or her disappointed with the therapist or hopeless about therapy's outcome.

- There are many ways to view a case and its issues; some views may be in conflict, and we cannot know all of them. Even experts will differ in their interpretations, recommendations, and judgments, as each can have different conceptual bases.

- The field of psychology keeps evolving. Laws and court decisions keep changing. Each state has different laws; departments within a state government can have different rules; and there are gaps and overlaps in the laws and rules.

In addition to the points made above, keep in mind that written standards for ethical behavior can be of two kinds: "minimal standards," which are mandatory, with punishment for violations; and "aspirational standards," which are not mandatory and do not involve punishment for violations, but toward which we are expected to strive. Furthermore, Haas et al. (1986) found that "When psychologists are faced with a variety of ethical dilemmas, they will often make decisions based on their personal value systems and not on the basis of defined ethical principles" (p. 321). Such decisions may "feel right," but how can we be sure that this is good enough to protect us legally and ethically? How can we do better? As professionals committed to empiricism, let's look at the data.

## The Major Malpractice Risks for Clinicians

Pope (1989a) reviewed the data on malpractice against psychologists from January 16, 1986, to July 1, 1988, and found 27 major causes for successful suits. His findings are summarized in Table 1. The major issues are indicated in boldface, and the causes are ranked by the percentage of claims each represents. Note how few "failure to warn" cases there were (ranked 23rd), although such cases generate a lot of therapist anxiety. Note also how relatively large problems related to fee collection were (ranked 5th), despite which many therapists vigorously pursue monies owed them.

Other data come from a report by the American Psychological Association (APA) Committee on Ethics (1988). This committee reviewed complaints over a 5-year period and found a pattern similar to that found by Pope. The majority of ethics complaints came from the following small number of issues:

- Dual relationships, including sexual intimacies (23%).

- Violations of various APA practice and research standards and guidelines, or of governmental laws and institutional regulations (16%).

- Therapist behavior that violated or diminished the legal or civil rights of others (8%).

- A professional's failure to preserve appropriate confidentiality of patients or students (4%).

More recent experience (Sam Knapp, personal communication, October 2, 1996) suggests two additional areas of concern. First, child custody evaluations, which by their nature leave someone unhappy, have produced a large number of complaints on the issues of breach of confidentiality, and violations of the ethics of assessment. Second, the treatment of adult survivors of childhood abuse using recovered memories has resulted in high awards in malpractice cases. The best advice may be simply to avoid this approach, and if

TABLE 1. Major Causes of Successful Malpractice Suits against Psychologists

| Cause | % of costs | % of claims |
|---|---|---|
| 1. **Sexual impropriety** | 53.2 | 20.4 |
| 2. **Incorrect treatment** (i.e., using treatments the therapist was not qualified to perform by lack of training or experience) | 8.4 | 13.2 |
| 3. Loss (to the patient) from evaluation (performed by the psychologist) | 2.6 | 8.5 |
| 4. **Breach of confidentiality or privacy** | 1.3 | 6.4 |
| 5. **Countersuit for fee collection** (improper fee setting, billing, or fee collection methods) | 1.3 | 6.2 |
| 6. **Suicide of patient** | 11.2 | 5.8 |
| 7. **Diagnosis: Failure to or incorrect** | 3.7 | 5.4 |
| 8. Defamation: Libel/slander | 0.7 | 4.4 |
| 9. **Improper death of patient or others** | 2.0 | 3.2 |
| 10. Miscellaneous (the meaning of this category was unclear to Pope) | 0.8 | 3.1 |
| 11. Premise liability (e.g., a client was hurt in the office by falling) | 0.1 | 2.4 |
| 12. Violation of legal regulations | 0.5 | 2.6 |
| 13. Bodily injury | 1.6 | 2.2 |
| 14. Loss of child custody or visitation | 0.2 | 2.2 |
| 15. Violation of civil rights | 1.1 | 2.1 |
| 16. Licensing or peer review | 0.2 | 2.1 |
| 17. Poor results | 0.1 | 1.7 |
| 18. Undetermined (i.e., the causes of action were undetermined) | 7.9 | 1.5 |
| 19. Breach of contract | 0.1 | 1.4 |
| 20. Assault and battery | 1.5 | 1.2 |
| 21. Failure to supervise properly | 0.3 | 0.9 |
| 22. **Undue influence (these are basically dual relationships)** | 0.4 | 0.6 |
| 23. **Failure to warn** | 0.6 | 0.4 |
| 24. Abandonment | 0.1 | 0.3 |
| 25. False imprisonment/arrest | 11 cases, average cost $935 | |
| 26. Failure to refer | 1 case, cost $2,141 | |
| 27. Failure to treat | 2 cases, average cost $38 | |

*Note.* The data are from Pope (1989a).

you do use it to be very clear about boundaries (see Section 3.4). Lastly, a recent survey by Montgomery et al. (1999) indicated that issues of supervision may be a largely unrecognized area of increased risk (see Section 3.13 for ways to reduce this risk).

This may seem like a long list. Do you have to worry about everything you do as a therapist? The answer is no. Nearly all malpractice complaints stem from just a few issues, and most are in areas over which you have excellent control. Over 60% of the claims in Table 1 and the majority of complaints noted by the APA Committee on Ethics originated in sexual improprieties, dual relationships, substandard diagnosis or treatment, lapses in the duty to protect, and poor office administration. You can reduce or eliminate the vast majority of risks in these areas if you are clinically competent and self-aware, if you consult fully with others, and if you create an adequate written record to document your actions and the reasons for them. Here is the good news in all this: **Almost all malpractice cases arise not from unforeseeable problems, but from ones that could have been avoided if only they were recognized and anticipated** (Bennett et al., 1990).

In some cases, the issues are so clear that lists of dos and don'ts can be created for them. I have included these in this book where appropriate. More importantly, some principles are so clearly formulated that they can be incorporated into your practice simply by using the forms, sample documents, guidelines, and checklists in this book. In fact, that is a major concept underlying this book: If you build the ethics into your paperwork, you greatly reduce your risk of malpractice.

## Four Steps toward Ethical Self-Protection

1. **Be realistic.** Ethical dilemmas can and may happen to you.

   One barrier to improved ethical practice is arrogance. "Pride goeth before a fall," but arrogance is hard to avoid when capable people are asking your advice every day, listening carefully, paying you, and being grateful. Do not let false pride, denial, panic, ignorance, or rumors cause you to avoid acting to protect yourself and your clients.

2. **Learn the rules.** The fact that you have the client's best interests at heart, are well intentioned, or like the client doesn't ensure that you are acting ethically. Don't assume that ethical niceties and picky little rules can be ignored because you are a "good guy/girl." These rules have usually been carefully worked out after painful experiences.

   First, get, read, and keep available copies of your state's licensing law and all the ethical codes or principles you operate under. You need to be mindful of the legal context in which you operate. There are many codes of ethical standards. Which ethical standards apply to you? It will be the code of the group you align with by education or by the title or description you offer of your services. You will also, perhaps surprisingly, be held to the standards of any group an ordinary citizen would see you as belonging to. Even if you are not certified by the American Association for Marriage and Family Therapy, a court is likely to hold your practice to this group's standards if you identify yourself as a "marriage counselor" or "family therapist."

   For a dozen perspectives on the old (1992) APA code of ethics, see a special section of the journal *Professional Psychology: Research and Practice* (Vol. 25, No.4, November 1994). For interpretations of each section of that code, see Canter et al. (1994). Read the current literature, and attend continuing education programs in the areas of ethical practice. For short overviews of the issues, see Hulteng and Goldman (1986) and Ewing (1983). A readable and brief survey of all the ethical issues from the perspective of the practicing clinician can be found in Haas and Malouf (1995).

   In addition, join your profession's associations. Their newsletters and listservs will keep you ahead of changes in laws, regulations, and court decisions. Their boards, ethics committees, and professional staffs are available to offer useful guidance.

3. **Develop an ethical consciousness.** Ethics education should result in a "learned disease." This is an awareness of vulnerability, complexity, and multiple perspectives. It is almost an operational definition of an ethical consciousness. It will give you a "gut feeling" to guide and warn you. This anxiety should motivate thoughtfulness, consultation, conservatism, foresight, contingency planning, and empathy. The development of an ethical sensitivity will help alert you to the ethical aspects and implications of all your professional activities. For practice, a book by Stromberg et al. (1988, pp. 235–271) contains a table of more than 100 situations in which the practice of psychology raises legal or ethical questions. For documentation concerned, a book by Moline et al. (1998) has similar vignettes.

To develop and maintain an ethical awareness, repeatedly evaluate the ethical implications of your decisions. Ask yourself "What if . . . ?" questions from a "worst-case scenario" perspective and from the perspective of a hostile complainant (patient, peer, or lawyer). Be especially careful about novel or uncommon practices. If what you are doing with a client, or are considering doing, is unusual among your peer professionals, get at least one consultation on its ethical correctness *before* proceeding. My own rule is this: If you don't personally know anyone else who is doing what you are considering doing, be extraordinarily cautious.

4. **Tighten up your procedures.** By using checklists and similar procedural devices, you can anticipate problems and head them off. Such procedures can remind you of legal obligations, shape the questions you ask, and offer easily incorporated risk management strategies. Read each section of this book that applies to your practice, evaluate the forms and sample documents, modify them as necessary, make photocopies, and *use them* with every one of your patients.

# 3.2    Legal Aspects of Malpractice

## When Do Patients Sue?

Lawsuits represent about the last stage of breakdown in human relationships. They tend to occur in therapeutic contexts under the following conditions:

- When patients are disappointed with the outcome of treatment.

- When patients think they have had a bad outcome and attribute it to the therapist's incompetence or negligence.

- When patients believe they have been exploited or "used" financially, emotionally, or sexually.

- When patients are presented with a bill larger or later than they expected.

## What Is Malpractice?

Negley (1985) offers this definition: "Malpractice is a deviation (by omission or commission) from the standards of professional care which then results in an injury" (p. 243). From the viewpoint of a plaintiff's attorney, a potentially successful case must have these three elements: a serious injury, regardless of the extent of the violation of the standards; a "deep pocket" belonging to an insurance company or an institution; and someone's behavior that caused the injury.

Soisson et al. (1987) summarize what a plaintiff must demonstrate to support a malpractice claim as follows:

"a. The practitioner owed a duty to the plaintiff that was based on an established therapeutic relationship" (p. 498). That the relationship was "therapy" is the simplest part to demonstrate and is not of much concern here.

"b. The quality of care provided by the practitioner fell below the standard of care expected of the average practitioner" (p. 498) This standard used to be determined on a local basis, but is now interpreted by the courts on a regional or national basis. The comparison may be based on the specialty advertised or offered to the patient, or the care offered by other practitioners of a particular school of thought (Knapp, VandeCreek, & Tepper, 1998, p. 88).

"c. The patient suffered or was caused harm or injury" (Soisson et al., 1987, p. 498).

"d. The practitioner's dereliction of duty was the direct cause of the harm or injury" (p. 498).

Many kinds of behaviors can result in liability: negligence, breach of contract, intentional misconduct, defamation, invasion of privacy, failure to prevent an injury, and so on (King, 1977). Wilkinson (1982) adds liability for self-inflicted injuries and suicide, harm by the client to third parties, errors in judgment concerning patient management, harmful treatment methods, and sexual misconduct. Perhaps it should be emphasized that neither a bad outcome nor a mistake is proof of malpractice (Knapp, 1994).

## The Good News (for Us): The Real Risks Are Small

Medical malpractice suits are rarely successful; the risk of a loss at trial is surprisingly small. Although 100% of those consulting malpractice attorneys are angry at their doctors, only 20% have sufficient facts to file complaints (and some of these are mistaken). Only 10% of lawsuits against physicians go to trial, and in them defendants are exonerated 70–90% of the time; 75% of suits filed are won by the physicians and 60% are resolved without payment to the patients (Barge & Fenalason, 1989). Charles (cited in Barge & Fenalason, 1989) has reported that four of five cases are settled without payment to the plaintiffs, and that in three-fourths of those that go to trial, the physicians are vindicated. Furthermore, "For those who do win . . . the median award is $36,500" (Charles, in Barge & Fenalason, 1989).

## The Bad News (for Us): Malpractice Accusations Hurt

As the saying goes, "You can't win a malpractice lawsuit, but you sure can lose one." And you can do so very badly. The actual costs, losses, and hassles pale before the self-doubt, public humiliation, and anxiety. You can be sued for more money than you have or will ever have. Your insurer will at best pay only part of the judgment (but generally most of your defense), and will try to settle the case early (if this is successful, you may be seen as guilty by your peers even if you are innocent). You will spend countless hours sitting in court (where you *are* on trial), giving depositions, having conferences with lawyers, getting support from friends, and engaging in endless self-reproaches and tears. If you are convicted of a felony, you will lose your license and have to find a new line of work. Yet another consequence of malpractice is being entered into the National Practitioner Data Bank/Healthcare Integrity and Protection Data Bank (P.O. Box 10832, Chantilly, VA 20153-0832; http://www.npdb-hipdb.com). Maintained by the U.S. Department of Health and Human Services, it lists those practitioners who have had medical malpractice payments made on their behalf; actions taken against their licenses or clinical privileges; actions taken by professional societies against them; and judgments or convictions for health care fraud, criminal convictions, and similar decisions. Although those entered can get information on their entries, the public cannot and may never be able to. However, health care organizations, licensing boards, and insurers can access this list, and so entry may greatly limit your future ability to practice.

There are very sensitive portraits of the effects of just being accused in Charles (1985), Charles et al. (1988), Rosenthal (1976), and Wilbert et al. (1987). Indeed, Charles et al. (1985, 1988) have described the "malpractice stress syndrome"—a pattern of behaviors, feelings, and thoughts that is much more likely to appear in those involved in a malpractice case than in those not so involved. The sued are more likely to feel depressed, ashamed, misunderstood, defeated, tense, angry, and frustrated. They experience headaches, insomnia, and similar symptoms; drink alcohol excessively; and have suicidal ideation. They stop seeing certain kinds of patients, consider retiring earlier, and discourage their children from entering their profession. More recently, Schoenfeld et al. (2001) have extended these findings.

## What to Do If You Are Complained Against: A Checklist

The following checklist concerns lawsuits, but also generally applies to having a complaint alleged against you with an ethics or licensing board. It is based on recommendations from Wright (1981a, 1981b), Woody (2000), the American Professional Agency (1992), and others.

- ❑ **If you are served a summons or a subpoena, accept it, but don't overreact to it.** Control your anxiety; don't panic. Keep these points in mind:

    If a large number of allegations are made, this "shotgun" approach is standard practice, and most of the time they are all settled at once.

    Exaggeration and "legalese" are to be expected.

    Lawsuits are not unusual in our society. The vast majority of complaints and lawsuits are frivolous and go nowhere.

    Resolution will take years (from 1 to 3 years, usually).

- ❑ **Call your professional liability insurance agency immediately and supply the information its staff members request.** They will open a file, assign a claims manager at their office, and call a local lawyer. Meet with this attorney as soon as possible. Remember that these contacts with a lawyer *are* privileged communications. If you need more effort or a different approach, hire your own personal defense attorney. Do not make any notes until you have established a relationship, as these documents are not privileged unless done for an attorney.

- ❑ **Assemble all relevant documents and records.** Do not alter, add to, or destroy any documents. Show them to no one except your lawyer. Do not release any documents unless your attorney instructs you to do so. Make and keep copies and originals of everything. Do not offer more than is relevant.

- ❑ **Read the relevant literature.**

❏ **Educate your lawyer about the strengths and weaknesses of your case.** If this is a complaint to the licensing board, consult with your lawyer and prepare a carefully considered reply to the board. The client is likely to read this reply, so be circumspect. Do not divulge confidential information unless you have the client's consent or a subpoena from the board.

❏ **Assume a defensive stance.** Admit nothing and make no self-incriminating statements to *anyone* not covered by confidentiality. If it is a current client, end the therapy immediately with a letter (created with the help of your attorney) advising the client to transfer and offering a few referral names. See Section 6.3 on termination.

❏ **Do not communicate with the client or the client's lawyer by mail or in person. Do not play therapist any more.** Do not attempt to "therapeutically resolve" the issues or to "negotiate" a resolution. These communications are not privileged and can be used against you. Have everything from or to the client or the client's attorney go to and through your attorney.

❏ **Do not play lawyer and attempt to settle the matter.** Don't meet or talk with the client or the opposing lawyer unless your attorney is present. If you do meet with the client's attorney, be sure the client has consented to that conversation. Follow this rule even if you are told that another therapist is the target of potential litigation. Inform the patient's attorney and "Bill the [patient's] attorney for your time, just as you would bill the patient. To not bill might imply that you owe the patient something because of improper care" (Barge & Fenalason, 1989).

❏ **Do not discuss your claim with *anyone* (except perhaps your legal spouse) without the agreement of your personal attorney.** Consultation with a trusted colleague or close friend may seem valuable, but such conversations are not privileged and can later be used against you. If you do talk to experts in ethics, any lawyers other than your own, or any institutional colleagues, do so only in hypothetical terms. Limit discussions with colleagues to the process of being sued or ways to cope with the stress, and do not discuss details of the case, the care you provided, or any other confidential information. Personal therapy for the stress and other personal issues related to a claim, however, may be valuable, and such conversations *are* considered privileged communications because you are then a client.

❏ **Continue to work at your profession to the same high standards.**

Do not feel ashamed because you are sued. Remember (as you have no doubt told clients), the fact that someone didn't like what you did does not prove you did anything wrong.

Don't let yourself get depressed or overly concerned. Control your anger as well. Learn to compartmentalize your life.

Remember that being complained against doesn't mean you are a jerk, stupid, or incompetent.

❏ At some point, attorneys will start to talk about **a settlement**. Discuss any proposals fully with your personal attorney, and weigh the many factors and implications carefully. Do not rush, and make sure you have the resources before you "do the right thing."

❏ When it is all over, **create a summary of the case and its outcome**. You will need this in later years, when you apply for panel membership and other opportunities. "When the ordeal is over and the dust settles, celebrate your survival and get on with your life. Acknowledge the lessons you've learned, make amends where you need to, and move on" (Boedecker, 1995, p. 3).

❏ If you are accused, read Wright (1981a, 1981b); if you are sued for malpractice, read Cohen (1979, pp. 274–283). It would even be wise to read both in advance.

# **3.3**   **Professional Liability ("Malpractice") Insurance**

*Disclaimer*: These issues are complex; needs are individual; and policies differ in many details. The following is intended as an overview, so do not base your insurance decisions solely on this summary, but examine the policies and ask questions.

## Introduction

You may ask, "Do I really need professional liability insurance?" It covers more than "malpractice," the name that is often used by clinicians. You could buy no insurance (called "going bare"), which *might* reduce your risk of some kinds of suits (because plaintiffs' lawyers look for those with "deep pockets" to make a case worth taking on), and it will save a few hundred deductible dollars a year. However, such a plan offers no protection for your personal assets or assistance with the expenses of defending yourself in either a suit or the much more likely licensing board complaint. Without insurance, you assume all the risks of practice by yourself. Buying insurance is a way of risk sharing. If you are considering "going bare," read more about the risks, assess your exposures, and consult your lawyer. If a court judgment goes against you, you can lose all your current assets and future resources (inheritance, future income, spouse's income, etc.). You could also lose your license and thus your profession.

## Occurrence-Based versus Claims-Made Policies

Professional liability insurance changed in many ways in the 1990s because of competition among insurance companies, patterns of suits and settlements, and the cyclic nature of the insurance business. The standard form of coverage, called "occurrence-based," was almost completely replaced by one called "claims-made." However, both are still available, and either one may be a better fit for your needs. Most of us had the occurrence-based plans, and most of us, to save money, have switched to the claims-made plans without much to worry about. Problems generally arise only if we wish at a later date to switch back to an occurrence-based plan or wish to switch carriers (insurance companies). As we go through this discussion, refer to Figure 3.

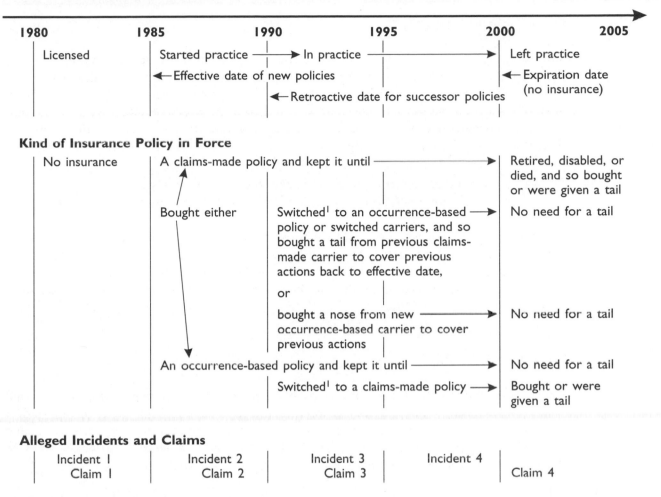

### Alleged Incidents and Claims

| Incident 1 | Incident 2 | Incident 3 | Incident 4 |
|---|---|---|---|
| Claim 1 | Claim 2 | Claim 3 | Claim 4 |

¹Or were canceled/dropped, or the claims-made policy's company stopped writing professional liability coverage or went bankrupt or was bought out and changed its business, or any other reasons.

Incident 1 would be covered only if you had bought prior-acts "nose" coverage in 1990. It would not be covered under the occurrence-based policy or even a claims-made policy bought in 1985, because it occurred before the effective dates of either kind of policy.

Incident 2 would be covered under either the claims-made policy (if the claim was made after the effective date, 1985, and before the expiration date, 2000, of the policy) or the occurrence-based policy (no matter when the claim was made).

Incident 3 would be covered under either claims-made policy (the 1985–2000 policy or the 1990–2000 policy) but only if the policy were in force when the claim was filed (after the retroactive date—1990). If it were reported after 2000, it would only be covered under the tail coverage bought in 2000. It would be covered under the occurrence-based policy bought in either 1985 or 1990.

Claim 4 would be covered by an occurrence-based policy, or only if you bought or received a tail (since you last had a claims-made policy).

---

FIGURE 3. An illustration of your coverage in claims-made and occurrence-based policies over time.

### Claims-Made Policies

Simply put, a claims-made policy covers claims (accusations of malpractice) made against you during the years you are paying for the policy. It does not matter when the incident on which a claim is based occurred, only when the claim is made. More technically, it covers most of your professional activities that occurred after the effective date of your initial policy (or the retroactive date of the successor policy), or after the termination date if you purchased a "tail."

A "tail" or "extended reporting period" covers the time period starting with the end of your claims-made coverage and moving forward in time. The language is confusing, because we usually think of a tail as being behind us in time, but here it is understood as the continuing tail of risks assumed by the insurer and it moves forward in time. You can buy a tail from your previous claims-made carrier. These are often free or not very expensive if you have been insured for a few years. The reason they cost so little is that you will no longer be adding risks by seeing clients, and the risk assumed by the insurer actually declines over time.

### Occurrence-Based Policies

Simply put, an occurrence-based policy covers incidents that occurred during the time the policy was in force (being paid for), without regard to when a claim is made or reported. If you are accused of an incident that is alleged to have occurred after your policy's effective date (first day of coverage) and before its termination date (when you canceled it or stopped paying for it), an occurrence-based policy will cover it.

If you choose or are forced to switch from a claims-made to an occurrence-based policy, you will need coverage for the previous years of practice no longer covered by a claims-made policy. You may be able to buy a tail from the claims-made carrier that you are leaving, or you can buy "nose" coverage from your new occurrence-based carrier. The "nose" (the opposite of a tail), called a "prior-acts rider," covers those actions you took before being covered by the new occurrence-based policy. When you buy prior-acts coverage, make sure its effective date is extended backward to the effective date of your previous claims-made policy.

### Changing from One to the Other

Generally, you are likely to switch to or maintain your claims-made policy, because all other features being equal, the cost of buying the tail is delayed (and so costs less). The cost of buying it is smaller because it is, in effect, "built into" an occurrence-based policy.

However, a change may be forced upon you by a policy's cancellation, a carrier's withdrawal from the professional liability business, or other changes in the world of insurance, so it is worth considering. If you choose or are forced to switch from a claims-made to an occurrence-based policy, you will need coverage for the previous years of practice no longer covered by a claims-made policy. You will need a nose from your new carrier or a tail from your old carrier.

## Points of Comparison and Advantage

### Costs

In the long run, the two types of policies will cost nearly the same; in the short run, however, a claims-made policy costs less over the first few years and may stay lower over time. The premiums will always be higher for occurrence-based coverage, because you are essentially paying for a built-in tail coverage (see below). On the other hand, after you end your occurrence-based coverage, there is no need to spend money to buy a tail whose price you cannot anticipate years in advance.

The first few years' premiums (your costs) for claims-made coverage are less than those for an occurrence-based policy. This is true simply because the current premium covers only this current year's risk exposure, which is less than that accumulated in the collective previous years of your practice because you will see fewer patients this year than the total you saw in all the previous years. In addition, the full cost of a claim is rarely paid during the year it is reported. Thus the policy "matures" (rises in cost) over 4 to 7 years' time to reflect the increased risk exposure and likelihood of claims accumulated over the years. Claims-made premiums may stay lower than those of occurrence-based policies, as the premiums are more tightly linked in time to the actual loss experience of the insurer.

To compare costs, compute the costs for at least 5 and preferably 10 years. Add the premiums of each year until a claims-made policy matures, average them, and add the costs of a tail when comparing the claims-made policy to an occurrence-based policy. These figures are available from each company, no matter what the person who answers the phone says, because all companies are registered with your state's insurance commissioner.

### Limits of Liability Coverage

An advantage of claims-made policies is that you can purchase higher liability coverage (more dollars) at any year's renewal to protect you against the rising size of awards. Of course, this additional coverage will cost you more, but the flexibility is valuable in the face of the inflation in settlement costs and the size of claims awards. With an occurrence-based policy, there is no way to make your coverage for past incidents retroactively larger; you specified the limits for each year each time you renewed the policy.

The two types of policies are not equivalent, so evaluate your needs and risk tolerance. Here is a large difference, as described by Bogie (2002):

> Say you have a $1 million occurrence[-based] policy which you renewed each year for ten years. You would have $1 million coverage for each and every one of those ten years. Compare it to a $1 million claims-made policy with the unlimited tail . . . which you renewed for ten years. You would have $1 million in total covering the entire ten-year period.

On the other hand she says:

> Remember, psychologists aren't sued very often, and when sued, the vast majority of claims cost well under $100,000. Few psychologists are sued more than once in their lifetime. Given these trends, stretching your liability limits over a number of years with a claims-made program is not particularly risky.

*The Effects of Time*

A major disadvantage of occurrence-based policies is that a claim may be made against you many years after an alleged act occurred, and therefore it would be covered under a policy written many years ago. This has several limitations: (1) The policy probably had lower liability limits, and so fewer dollars are available to pay all the claims made under your policy; (2) it may have had different features, no longer matching today's types of risks and claims; and (3) it may have been with a carrier no longer in this business and not eager to defend a claim from a nonpayer of premiums.

Claims-made policies have a parallel limitation: If many claims are made in a single year, even for acts over several years, they could exceed the limits of such a policy.

## Guidelines and Issues to Consider When Purchasing Liability Insurance

1. **Never lie or omit anything on an application,** as the insurer can easily deny coverage because of false statements or failure to stay within policy limitations (such as your not really being in "part-time" practice).

2. **Become well informed. Read your current policy or that of a friend.** Review the materials listed in Appendix C of this book.

   ■ Policies are only a few pages long but very educational.

   ■ Policies differ greatly, and if there is a problem, you will be held to the language of your policy. Some polices seem to be almost unchanged from a general business liability form or one for all professions, whereas others understand and speak to therapists.

   ■ **Examine the differences between the policies** to see which small differences, if any, are highly significant for your practice, history, and future professional plans. Later in this section, I offer checklists on which to compare plans' features, and Appendix C lists the sellers of such insurance for psychologists.

   ■ **Do ask each insurer you are considering for a specimen policy,** because their marketing materials and "summaries" may not give you enough information for your particular practice, may make misleading yes–no comparisons, and may incorrectly describe their competitor's products.

   ■ **If you call with more than routine questions, talk to a "licensed agent"** and not just the person answering the phone, because only licensed agents are legally required to provide complete information.

3. **Liability limits numbers are stated as two numbers of dollars**—for example, "$1 million/$3 million." The first is the maximum to be paid for a single claim (even if it includes more than one person), and the second is the maximum to be paid for all claims filed against the policy in any one policy year. Buy the coverage limits to protect your life's assets. Evaluate your personal assets, present and future, in need of protection as well as the risks of your practice activities.

- Higher coverage is not much more expensive than the lower coverage.

- The most commonly purchased coverage is the $1 million (per claim)/$3 million (aggregate—multiple claims in one policy year) form.

- Check to see whether the (substantial) costs of defense may be deducted from the limits the company will pay. If so, consider buying higher coverage

- If you need even higher limits (e.g., for a group practice), talk with the agency.

4. **Choose the program administrator or agency that provides the best service,** because you will almost never deal with the actual insurance company—the "carrier" or "insurer" that would pay a covered claim against you. The "program administrator" or "agency" is the office that sells the policy you buy, bills and collects your payments (premiums), evaluates claims made against you, etc. For psychologists, the two largest agencies are (a) the American Professional Agency and (b) Trust Risk Management Services for the APA Insurance Trust (APAIT), which is the insurance-selling arm of the APA. Call and ask a few simple questions.

   - Can you reach informed and experienced persons when you have questions? Are their answers accurate and complete? Are they educating you or just selling insurance? Are they forthcoming about any limitations?

   - When you have legal questions, can you speak to a licensed agent or only a sales person? Are there delays and barriers to access these persons?

   - Can you understand the answers? Can you use the answers in your decisions?

   - Do they answer promptly? Repeatedly?

   - What do they say about the other companies' policies? Do they know the differences?

   - Do they send you any materials they promised?

   - Are their bills and forms clear and not too burdensome (because you will be filling them out at each policy renewal year?

   Then call the other companies and see how they do.

5. **Consider the stability and size of the insurance company (the "carrier")** that actually provides the coverage.

   - Look for A. M. Best ratings of A+ or A, and similar high ratings by others.

   - Evaluate the years the carrier has been insuring your kind of professional, the number of states it operates in, and the number of professionals it insures; longer, larger and more will make the carrier more skilled in handling such claims and less likely to pull out of the business.

- Insurance companies new to malpractice can offer lower rates because they have fewer payouts. This must be balanced against such a company's ratings of size and financial security.

- You will need to buy tail or nose coverage if you change carriers (insurance companies).

- You may want to stay with the same carrier and program administrator out of loyalty to the professional association, or in order to avoid a reexamination of a closed complaint against you.

6. **Check into the availability or size of discounts** offered to the following:

   - Those who have taken continuing education courses, especially courses in ethics or risk management.

   - Part-time practitioners (usually working 20 hours per week or less). Find out how this status is determined by each insurance carrier, as it can differ.

   - Females.

   - Members of the National Register or other certifying boards.

   - Part-time professional employees of yours. (Generally, such professionals should have their own liability coverage as well.)

7. If the premium is substantial, **evaluate the availability of periodic payments** throughout the year (especially when there is no finance charge).

8. **Investigate the costs and availability of coverage for agencies, facilities, or other organizations for which you work** (called "additional insureds") and which require you to have insurance to protect them.

   - Generally, if you are the sole employee of a professional corporation, you do not need to buy additional coverage for the corporation; however, if there are other practitioners, discuss your situation with the agency. There may or may not be an additional charge for partnerships or corporations.

   - What is the size of the additional costs to add independent contractors or consultants to your coverage?

   - If you are in a partnership or joint practice that has a claims-made policy, and you then leave the practice, you should be covered by the policy. Check with the program administrator to see how this is actually arranged.

9. Even if you are not near retirement, you might have to quit practice due to disability or other reasons. Therefore, **investigate the cost of a tail** and the guarantee of its availability.

10. **Most policies will not pay fines, penalties, or damages (punitive, exemplary, or multiplied).** These are simply excluded and will be levied against your assets if

awarded (the bad news). These are very, very rarely imposed in our area, as malice and repetition are required (the good news).

11. **Weigh the absence or size of a deductible** for awards made against you. To evaluate the cost of a deductible, multiply its dollar amount by the probability of a suit in 1 year (on the order of 4–8% for psychiatrists, about half that for psychologists), and subtract this amount from the yearly cost of any policy that does not have a deductible.

12. **See how the policy pays the actual defense costs in a suit** (investigation, bonds, legal fees, court costs, costs of expert testimony), as well as defenses before licensing and other regulatory bodies.

   - The options are as follows: "without limit" (best); "above the liability limit," with some limit (typically $15,000 to $25,000—acceptable); "deducted from your liability limits" (not good); or pays none of them (worst). You should know that these payments only last up until admission of guilt or conviction.

   - Board hearings are already more frequent than suits and becoming much more so. The issue is too complex to go into here, but be aware that boards work on "administrative law," which is neither criminal or civil law. There is little consistency across states in complaint handling, because states locate their investigation and enforcement mechanisms in different governmental structures (e.g., a case may be handled as a civil, a criminal, or a consumer protection matter).

   - Low limits of payments (e.g., $5,000) are easily exceeded. (How many hours of attorney time would those dollars cover?) When costs exceed your limit because the case is or becomes complex or longer, you will have to pay the attorney yourself, and it is unlikely that you will want to switch to another attorney and start all over at your expense.

   - The coverage for defense in a hearing before a state licensing board may not be as advantageous as it seems. In my opinion, it will tend to involve lawyers from the beginning of the process; this may make the process, which might have been collegial, more adversarial and litigious. Remember, many complaints are dismissed or resolved at this early stage. On the other hand, having an attorney may support some due process and adequate investigation, which the board may not offer you otherwise.

   - It might be advantageous to you to hire an attorney (at your own expense) from the beginning as a consultant to monitor the case and advise you of your options, if not to represent you at the hearing, negotiations, or trial.

   - As soon as you notify your plan administrator of a complaint or suit, the administrator will select an attorney from their list of attorneys near you who have the appropriate experience. You should ask about how the attorney is being paid by the insurer (capitation, discounted fees to get the referral [managed legal care], bill against a retainer, salary, fee-for-service billable hours, etc.). Use this information to evaluate how much service you will get before you use up your coverage, and ask what will happen then. Also evaluate any financial pressures on the attorney to settle.

13. **Will the policy pay you for the income lost** when you are defending a claim against yourself by giving depositions, consulting with your lawyer, and attending hearings or a trial? What is the limit to these payments per day or in total? Some policies will only pay if you are a defendant in a criminal case, and some when you are before a board of inquiry.

14. **Does the policy offer coverage when you act as a supervisor** (to nonemployees), and if so, what is its cost? Claims for negligent supervision can be made against you even if you never saw a patient. Is the number of your supervisees larger than the policy allows? Do you have to see a patient to be covered?

15. **Examine statements about location of your services.** If you practice in several states, or outside the United States, make sure your activities are covered.

16. **The policy should cover "all your professional activities"** and exclude none.

    ■ If you serve as a peer reviewer or on an ethics panel, make certain you are covered against claims of negligence or maliciousness by either the sponsoring organization's policy or your own malpractice policy.

    ■ Check the coverage for special treatments (hypnotism, biofeedback, divorce mediation, group therapy, or whatever you do). Other complex risks are collaborating with physicians and forensic testimony.

    ■ Examine the coverage for "Good Samaritan" acts if you might provide this kind of service.

17. **Evaluate each policy's "consent to settle" aspects.**

    ■ The best policies require your agreement before settling, which is called "unlimited consent to settlement."

    ■ Generally, if you refuse to accept a settlement that the insurance company recommends (and that the plaintiff, suing you, accepts), the carrier will not cover any further defense costs and you will have to pay those. Furthermore, if you then lose the case, the company will not pay more than it could have settled for.

    ■ In the worst case, you may have no choice but to accept a settlement your carrier agrees to (a "hammer clause"). Try for some language that allows you some leeway and power.

18. **Does the insurer or agency offer high-quality, low-cost risk management seminars** and educational efforts? Do these offer continuing education credits? Is telephone "legal" or risk consultation available when you are worried? If so, how good is it?

19. If you are a psychologist, **the APAIT "endorsement" is a value that is difficult to weigh.**

    ■ As noted above, APAIT is the insurance-marketing arm of APA. It is a significant profit center for APA, and so its interests are not identical with those of clinicians in practice.

- By the way, you will not see booths from other professional insurance companies at the APA conventions because APA will not allow competition for any "member benefits" it offers. APAIT's costs of advertising in APA journals are also not the same as those charged to its competitors, and so you will have to make the effort to get information from other providers. See Appendix C.

- You won't have to pay APA dues if you select a policy other than from APAIT. Ask yourself if you would otherwise belong to APA, and if not, reduce the yearly cost of the policy by your APA dues when comparing policies.

20. If you intend to practice for only a few years, an occurrence-based policy will save you the costs of buying a tail (but do the math for yourself).

21. Having tail coverage is becoming more important, because the courts are now accepting suits beyond the old statutes of limitations, and if you work with children they may file claims when they become adults. Note that when you buy a tail, the size of the tail fixes the total amount of money available to pay all the claims that may be made against you in the future. Since the tail's size depends on the liability limits you chose in your last renewal, consider raising these limits substantially.

22. If there is any doubt that a company will still be solvent in 15 years, do not consider its occurrence-based policy.

## Checklists for Comparing Professional Liability Insurance Policies

Specific information on policies is not easy to acquire. The two largest "insurers"—the American Professional Agency (a true broker) and APAIT (the insurance-marketing arm of APA, with Trust Risk Management Services as the broker)—offer nonoverlapping information, and the other agencies (listed in Appendix C) vary in their enthusiasm for providing information before you sign up. Below are listed the main questions you should ask when examining the offerings of an insurer; there may be others, depending on your practice, local laws, history, and projected needs.

### What Kinds of Activities Are Covered?

There are dozens of possible exclusions for actions and situations not covered. Read the actual policy (not a summary) carefully, and evaluate which exclusions you can live with. Are the following included?

❑ "All professional activities" (best), or only those specified or those not excluded?

❑ Serving on an ethics board, state psychological association, hospital committees, or the like.

❑ Sexual misconduct liability (not just the costs of defense before a licensing board or in a civil suit, but payment of judgments against you; amount of coverage, if any, is usually small—a "sublimit"). Your employees should be covered, as well as yourself.

❑ "Vicarious liability" for students, supervisees, employees, and independent contractors. This is most important in group practices and in collaboration with other professionals. If you have any uncertainties, seek professional guidance.

❑ Personal injury (slander, violation of rights of privacy, malicious prosecution, etc.).

❑ Advertising injury (false advertising, libel, copyright infringement).

❑ Premises ("slips and falls") liability. Try to get this included.

❑ Contractual or fee disputes (e.g., breaking a contract, with a managed care organization [MCO]).

❑ And others: discriminatory acts; nonprofessional administrative activities; cases against another professional with the same insurance carrier; dishonest, criminal, fraudulent, or malicious acts; and any business relationship.

*Note.* Confirm the availability and cost of any of these risks that are of interest to you, and make sure that the coverages are in addition to the policy's usual limits.

### Payment for Costs of Defending a Claim

❑ Are there limits per incident, per year, or lifetime? (My advice: Act on your fears and buy the bigger coverage.)

❑ Are lost wages during defending a claim or board hearing covered? ($ _____ per day, to a limit of $ _____).

❑ Are your other costs included (hotels, transportation, etc.)? This is not really much money, so it is not an important coverage.

### Support

Look for the following:

❑ Free, anonymous, convenient, unlimited ability to talk to a lawyer, psychologist, or other appropriate professional for advice on prevention and risk management. (Perhaps make a test call?)

❑ The educational value, usefulness, and cost of risk management seminars or other materials.

❑ The educational value and usefulness of mailed or online materials.

### Agency

Ask yourself these questions:

❑ Does the person who answers the phone exhibit general knowledge of the field, quality of explanations, sensitivity to your concerns, responses that are valuable to your decision making, and knowledge of other companies' policies?

❑ Can you speak to a Licensed Insurance Agent, or just the unlicensed (though trained) clerical/administrative person who answers the phone?

❑ Did the agency send a "specimen" policy when specifically asked?

❑ What is the agency's experience (years, number of policy holders) in dealing with therapists?

### Application Form

Examine the application form for these characteristics:

❑ Complexity and burden (because you will be redoing it every year).

❑ Specific language of history questions, especially if you have had an ethical problem.

❑ Intrusiveness and history requested. (Some states allow questions to discover whether your "personal habits" constitute a "moral hazard.")

### Specimen Policy

You will be bound by the terms of the actual policy, not the simplified description of it that agencies all send. Ask yourself these questions about the specimen policy:

❑ Is it in "plain English"?

❑ Is it tailored for therapists versus generic professionals, or (worse) is it a generic liability policy?

❑ Is it written to exclude (by naming) or to include all your professional activities?

### Insurer, Carrier, or Insurance Company

Ask the following questions:

❑ What is the carrier's A. M. Best rating? (A+ to C–; A or A+ is fine.)

❑ Is it an "admitted carrier" in your state?

❑ What is its experience (years, number of policy holders) in dealing with therapists?

❑ In which states does it sell policies? (New York's laws are generally considered the most thorough)?

## Rates and Costs

*Warning*: Cost should not be a determining factor in your insurance purchase. I recommend the following:

❏ Get prices for $1 million/$3 million coverage.

❏ To compare costs, compute the costs for at least 5 and preferably 10 years.

❏ Consider also the costs of APA membership for APAIT coverage if you are a psychologist but do not have other reasons to be an APA member.

## Tail or Nose Coverage

Ask these questions:

❏ Is there guaranteed availability of a tail? Are there limitations on availability (e.g., if you had a sexual misconduct accusation, or perhaps were not insured for the last 5 years with the company)?

❏ What is the cost of a tail for a set number of years of coverage ("length")? (Advice: I cannot see where anything less than an unlimited tail makes sense in terms or risk management. If you raise your coverage in your last year of practice to get a larger tail, and have to pay for the tail, your costs will go up.)

❏ What is the cost (if any) of a tail upon death, retirement, or disability (i.e., how many years must you have been insured to get it free)?

❏ What is the cost of prior-acts coverage (a nose) if you are switching from a claims-made policy or switching insurance agencies or carriers (in which case you can buy either a nose or a tail, but noses are cheaper than tails)?

## Credits and Discounts

Look for credits and discounts (percentages) on your rates for the following:

❏ Being new to practice (first- and second-year discounts).

❏ Part-time practice.

❏ Continuing education courses and credits.

❏ Ethics or risk management continuing education courses.

❏ Being a female.

❏ Board certification (National Register, American Board of Professional Psychology, etc.).

*Other Issues*

❏ If you work in different states or areas, is coverage "worldwide" or at least "in the United States," or is it confined to your office or offices?

❏ How much control over a settlement do you have?

❏ Can premium payments be spread over a year with no finance charge?

*Issues for Group Practices*

For group practices (partnerships, general business corporations, professional corporations, or professional associations), consider the following issues:

❏ Is your (and your employees') work outside your main employment setting covered? This matters if you (or they) do some "moonlighting,"such as consulting or teaching outside your office.

❏ What is the cost of coverage for "additional insureds" (consultee organizations, part-time employers, etc.)? Do you have to cover MCOs on your policy?

❏ Are there different rates? You may be charged the "insured" rate; employees with a master's degree or higher may be charged a "professional" rate; and any others a "paraprofessional" rate. Clerical workers are not usually charged separately, but look at the application form. These are all for W-2 employees; your independent contractors ("1099s") are not covered and need their own policies.

❏ If you hire staff members before the next renewal date, are they automatically covered?

❏ Can you get different limits for each therapist ("severability of limits")? If one member of the group has a practice that requires high-limit coverage, he or she can get that without having everyone else pay the same (higher) premiums.

❏ Are there discounts for multiple MDs or PhDs?

❏ Can you keep your coverage if you leave the group?

❏ If you have 15 or more employees, you may need employment practices liability insurance (EPLI) coverage.

*Note.* If you do have more complex arrangements, consult a licensed agent or broker.

## Other Kinds of Insurance You Might Need

*Disability or Income Protection*

You are much more likely to become disabled than to die, and your disability will disrupt your finances almost as much as an adverse malpractice judgment, so prepare for it with disability insurance. Be aware that loss of income if your license is revoked due to malpractice is not covered by this insurance. Disability insurance is moderately expensive, but less so if you buy it at a younger age.

### Premises Liability

If anyone (not just a patient) is injured while in your office, premises liability insurance can protect you. The professional liability policies often offer this coverage as a component, and the better ones include it free of charge, but do ask.

- Some include premises liability coverage with a policy for office property (see "Office Property," below), for business interruption (due to damage to the office), or the like. Your office or renter's insurance policy probably already covers this.

- You will need a separate policy for a home office; see your home insurance's agent about a "rider," which is inexpensive.

### Office Overhead/Expense

If your office expenses (rent, loans, advertising, car, staff) are a large part of your income, and you *must* pay them because of contracts you signed, you can buy insurance to pay these expenses if you are ill or injured. Such insurance is moderately expensive.

### Office Property

Finally, consider insurance to cover your office equipment, such as computers and furniture. Select more than you think you'll need, because prices rise and the process of replacing is costly. "Replacement cost" is much better than "current value" when you have a loss. If you work at home, you will need a separate policy or a rider on your homeowner's policy to cover the cost of replacing your office equipment. Such insurance is inexpensive.

## 3.4   Ways to Reduce Your Risk of Malpractice

*Note.* For a discussion of reducing your risk of malpractice in billing, see Section 2.7.

### Twenty-Two Steps for Risk Reduction

As long as you are practicing, you can never totally eliminate your risk for malpractice, but here are 22 concrete steps that can very significantly reduce your risk.

1. **Assure the continuity of each patient's care.** You do not have to accept everyone as a patient, but once you have accepted a patient, don't neglect or abandon him or her. See Section 6.3 on termination.

2. **Practice competently.** The central protective rule of ethics is to stay within what you

know. It is hard to know exactly what we don't know, or to know beforehand what we don't know well enough. Clinical knowledge comes from direct training by experienced teachers (supervisors); from work at regionally and professionally accredited educational institutions (e.g., internships); from training workshops by leaders in the field; from relevant and prolonged consultations; from your own well-considered experience over substantial time; and from thoughtful reading, writing, and teaching. In general, always keep the following guidelines in mind:

- Never do what you are not legally entitled to do. Do not practice medicine, law, or pharmacy if you are not so credentialed.

- Do not try to do everything you *are* legally allowed to do. You are *not* competent to handle everything that walks in the door.

- Moreover, you are probably not really competent to do some things you were exposed to if you did not receive the necessary high quality of training.

- Make clear the real areas of your competence in your communications to patients, both orally and in writing. Inaccurate expectations can be the basis for a complaint.

- If you do assessments, use "a well-defined and systematic method of interpreting test findings and be able to support your findings in court" (Cohen, 1990, p. 660). See also Section 3.6 on malpractice in testing.

- Don't use shortcuts (sending tests home with clients, or depending excessively on computerized test interpretations).

- Do not do custody evaluations without considering the inherent conflicts and the potential for dissatisfied clients. Take many precautions. Glassman (1998) reviews the issues and makes many useful suggestions. The publication of APA's guidelines for custody evaluations (APA, Committee on Professional Practice and Standards, 1998) includes many resources and definitions as well as suggested behaviors. The APA code of ethics (APA, 2002) requires the psychologist to "clarify at the outset . . . the probable uses of the services provided or the information obtained" (Standard 10.02). The received wisdom is that doing custody evaluations will result in a high frequency of licensing board complaints. Kirkland and Kirkland (2001) examined a good data set and found that (a) yes, there were some such complaints, and dealing with and defending against these were very stressful, costly, and time-consuming; (b) the numbers of complaints were actually very small (2,413 in 34 states in 10 years up through 1998) outside of California, which had two-thirds of the complaints; (c) only about 1% of the complaints resulted in any findings of fault and punishment; and (d) even these resulted in generally mild punishments.

- If you operate in the area of "health psychology" or "behavioral medicine," be especially careful not to "practice medicine without a license." Maintain full, continual, and two-way communication with physicians, and define your roles and knowledge base carefully (Knapp & VandeCreek, 1981).

3. **Get fully informed consent.** Require competent, informed, and voluntary consent for everything you do. Inform clients fully about the limits of confidentiality, *before* they reveal something you cannot keep confidential. See Chapter 4 on obtaining consent.

4. **Maintain confidentiality.** Know the limits of the confidentiality you can offer, and do not promise more than you can deliver. See Chapter 7 on confidentiality.

5. **Communicate fully.**

   - Communicate completely. Keep your patients' expectations reality-based.

   - Communicate openly. Become curious about difficulties and failures of communication. Be willing to hear complaints nondefensively.

   - Communicate honestly. Don't pretend to clarity you don't have; the best direction is not always clear, and each case is a little different. Issues and decisions can remain clouded. We can only use our best judgment based on our knowledge, skill, and experience, but we can use all of it and share our concerns.

   - Communicate clearly, especially in regard to money, fees, and insurance.

   - Communicate regularly. Your patient handout forms, initial evaluation remarks, and regular feedback on progress are crucial here.

   - Don't be distant. Be kind and warm where appropriate. Show that you care about the client's welfare and are "doing everything in [your] power to help" (Pressman & Siegler, 1983, p. 109).

6. **Supervise fully.** When you supervise, be thorough and be available. Monitor your students, teammates, and employees closely. Supervision is always a difficult balance between paternalism and the encouragement of autonomy, between risk assumption and self-protective fears. Have your supervisees obtain their own professional liability insurance, if possible. If not, you must provide it under your policy; in either case, remember that you will be held responsible for their actions. Bear in mind that your employees can commit malpractice. Prevention should include training in confidentiality, collections, filing, scheduling, and any other areas that occur to you. See Section 3.13 for more guidance.

7. **Keep abreast of new developments on both the clinical and legal fronts.** You must know what is considered high-quality in the field, so you have to keep up with current developments. Put aside time and energy for professional development (more than the minimum required for continuing education credits). Continuing education on both your methods *and alternative ones* is essential; go to the presentations of those you disagree with. Keep aware of the development of the legal aspects of professional work as well. Remember that the half-life of the knowledge base gained in a PhD program is (at the very most) 10 years.

8. **Consult frequently and formally.** Get consultation when things aren't going well with a patient, whenever you have some unease about something, and definitely when you are considering breaking any rule. Do not delay! If you have doubts or are

uncomfortable about your conceptualization or treatment, consult with a colleague and/or your attorney. "Consult" with clients' former therapists by getting records and asking questions. Thomas Gutheil, the renowned clinical ethicist, has put this most succinctly and memorably: "Never worry alone" (quoted in Reid, 1999, p. 9). Nonmedical therapists (and many medical therapists) should consult clients' physicians about any medical questions.

9. **Take seriously and evaluate thoroughly any evidence of suicidal ideation or intent.** See Sections 3.10 and 3.11.

10. **Have a contingency plan.** It is much more difficult to plan after a client becomes dangerous to self or others. Your plan should include resources for family or support system contact, special consultations for both you and the client, medications, referrals, hospitalization, police contacts, contacts with your lawyer, and so on. Tell your client about your options and your duty to warn (see Section 4.2). It may be too late to do this when the client is dangerous, so write this need into your datebook this minute.

11. **Refer carefully.**

   - Refer clients when the problem they present is one with which you have little experience or training.

   - Refer only to others who have the necessary areas of competence. Get feedback from those clients you refer and respect, so that you know who is competent and who is not among your possible referral resources. There is a kind of malpractice called "negligent referral."

   - Ethically, a client who does not improve under your care should be referred elsewhere, even when a colleague with the necessary competence seems hard to find or the client is reluctant to start again. At the minimum, the client must be informed and allowed to choose. Document the options, the choices made, and their rationales.

12. **Be conservative in your treatments.** You are required by the ethics of your profession to act prudently and reasonably. If you do not, you are exposing yourself to risk, because you are exposing your patient to substandard treatment.

   Having a theoretical rationale for a treatment does not make it ethical; nonetheless, base all your psychotherapeutic interventions on a well-established theory (Woody, 1988, p. 211). This does not mean that you must *always* follow a recognized "school" with at least a minority of adherents, but courts are likely to move in that direction. Your treatment does not have to have an empirical justification, but it must be seen as acceptable by a significant number of your peers. In general, it will be hard for a court to find fault with the prudently reasoned use of a new and professionally or scientifically supported method by a therapist with strong credentials and no personal gain in sight.

   If your treatment lacks this prudence, call it "experimental," tell the patient of other treatment options, get more detailed informed consent, and discontinue it at the first sign of harm to the patient. It is a continuing and difficult professional struggle to balance the use of a scientifically tested method, which (in theory) protects the patient, against the need to tailor any method to the unique client and the need to innovate (for future clients' benefit). This balancing is an inescapable ethical dimension of high-quality practice.

13. **Don't promise a cure.** Be careful when discussing the effectiveness of your treatment approach, and do not allow a client to develop expectations that will not be fulfilled. Promote realistic expectations of treatment outcomes, not overly optimistic expectations of success, by utilizing standardized conceptualizations and classifications and by making probabilistic statements (Cross & Deardorff, 1987, p. 75).

14. **Document.** Get a relevant case history, especially of substance use, violence, homicide, suicide, all previous episodes and treatments, lawsuits, and the like (see the intake materials in Chapter 5). Keep clear, concise, and complete records. Use behavioral descriptions, not just diagnoses, labels, or shortcut jargon. Record the essentials. Pressman and Siegler (1983) suggest: "One way to think about what the medical record should contain might be to think about what you would want to see if you were called in as a new consultant on the case in order to understand the history and to start a course of treatment" (p. 109).

   Document your thinking, reasoning, and judgments as well. Record diagnoses, prognoses, progress, and evaluations of outcome. Record your instructions to clients, handouts given to clients, and after-hours calls. Document no-shows (and your responses), consultations, and your arrangements for another professional's covering for you, and for which patients. See Chapters 5 and 6 for a full discussion of clinical record keeping.

15. **Diagnose.** If a case should come to a courtroom, a therapist cannot "hide behind the notion that since his or her theory of therapy does not rely on psychodiagnostics, [no diagnostic evaluation was performed]" (Woody, 1988, p. 211). A good history may be all that is necessary and *reasonable* (the key word). The extent and nature of this evaluation process depend on your professional discipline as well. Malpractice claims for "misdiagnosis [negligent or improper diagnosis] generally require the use of egregiously inappropriate" methods (Stromberg et al., 1988, p. 453).

   A care provider has an obligation (a) to diagnose accurately and thus treat properly; (b) to ensure that a patient who presents with an emotional problem does not suffer from an undiagnosed and untreated coexisting or contributing medical illness; and (c) to provide adequate biological treatment. This burden is especially heavy on care providers who are biased against, lacking proficiency in, or reluctant to obtain consultation for such treatment. In a representative and most instructive case with a negative outcome, the court stated that "the question is not whether the physician made a mistake in diagnosis, but rather whether he failed to conform to the accepted standard of care" in his procedures and judgments (Stromberg & Dellinger, 1993, p. 7). In order to document your own clinical judgments, administer psychological tests as necessary.

16. **Avoid fee disputes and the accumulation of a large debt.** Never turn a debt over for collection without a personal conversation by you (not your secretary or office manager) with the client (not a spouse or other).

17. **Be alert to a patient's dissatisfaction with you.** This may be why the patient is not paying your bill, attending sessions regularly, or complying with treatments. Other early warning signs of dissatisfaction may include a patient's being overconcerned with your fees; being overly critical of a previous therapist or treatment (and therefore likely to be dissatisfied with yours); and having unrealistically high expectations of therapy's outcome (which are bound to be dashed). Of course, all of these should be dealt with as issues in therapy. In addition, factors such as lack of "psychological-mindedness" and entering therapy under external pressure may direct a patient to seek a way out of therapy, to gain revenge, and to make a profit all at the same time—by filing a complaint or suit. Of course, any patient's dissatisfaction should be responded to immediately, but this may also be the first warning of a complaint or suit.

Pay careful and immediate attention to any patient's disappointment or to failure of any expectations. If you are distant, arrogant, not readily available, or hard to talk to, then a patient may begin to question your competence. Remember that patients are usually not qualified to judge your clinical competence; they can only judge you as they see you, based on your actions as a human being. This is why testimonials from patients were forbidden until the 1992 revision of the APA code of ethics and even now testimonials from current patients are not allowed (APA, 2002, Standard 5.05).

18. **Respect the complexities of families and couples.** Be aware that family and marital therapies raise sticky complexities regarding the therapist's responsibility to each person, particularly regarding confidentiality and informed consent. The therapist's own values (about preserving a marriage, extramarital affairs, sex roles, etc.) add to the complexities. Margolin (1982) addresses these issues sensitively and clearly, and advises being open and straightforward with the clients. Her article is required reading for anyone who is designing consent procedures for couples or families.

19. **Don't work if you are burned out.** A significant risk factor for unethical practice is therapist burnout. If you identify with several of the items on this short list, read some of the books on therapist burnout, (e.g., Grosch & Olsen, 1994; Pearlman & Saakvitne, 1995), and seek consultation.

- Do you feel pessimistic or even cynical toward clients?

- Have you experienced persistent and interfering daydreams during sessions?

- Have you had hostile thoughts toward any client?

- Are you bored with your clients? Are they beginning to sound the same?

- Do you find yourself overly quick to diagnose?

- Are you overusing medication as treatment for the client or yourself?

- Are you blaming the client?

20. **Terminate properly.** See Section 6.3 for guidance in avoiding abandonment and other problems.

21. **Consider screening clients for litigiousness.** You might think about excluding from your practice clients you believe are likely to file lawsuits at some point.

22. **Consider limiting the scope of your practice.** You might limit or plan in the future to limit your practice to a single or a few specialized clinical domains.

## Other Risk Areas for Malpractice

The 22 steps above pertain to psychotherapy with *adults*. The assessment and treatment of children raise other issues. An excellent yet brief introduction to how the ethical principles play out for children and adolescent clients can be found in Barnett et al. (2001).

A second risk area of increasing frequency is the counseling of HIV-positive clients who engage in high-risk activities, such as needle sharing and unprotected sexual intercourse. See Section 3.10 for more on this issue.

In your writing and publishing, you should be alert to the ethical and legal consequences of scientific fraud, misinformation, plagiarism (uncredited taking of words), duplicate publication (publishing the same or essentially the same findings more than once in order to get more publication credits on your resume), piecemeal/serial publication (unnecessarily separating your findings so you can publish them in several articles to get more publications), and failure to credit authorship properly. An excellent guide to the last of these problems is provided by Fine and Kurdek (1993).

In no other profession do culture, socialization, roles, and world view matter more than in clinical work. We should be aware and respectful of clients' customs, parenting styles, acculturation, expectations of therapy and healing, and any other factors that play major roles in our work. We have both an ethical obligation (APA, 1993; APA, 2002, Principle E) and a clinical need to be sensitive and competent in dealing with those with different backgrounds. It goes without saying that we should be aware of the common cultural, ethnic, religious, racial, and sexual orientation differences. However, we also need to examine our beliefs about fat and body size, age, gender, income and social class, disabilities, illiteracy and language use, and other such areas of difference. We must work for insight into our own values, biases, and prejudices, and our expectations of roles and obligations, likely conflicts, and communication styles. (Goode, 2000, offers a fine checklist to raise awareness.) We must enlarge our sensitivities to cross-cultural issues of institutional oppression, racism, sexism, elitism, ageism, beautyism, and similar distortions, so as to avoid limiting our clients' potentials.

Lists of culture-specific characteristics that affect psychological functioning are available for many subcultures and ethnicities (Paniagua, 1998; Geissler, 1998). Although such information is often valuable, assuming that all members of a group will have all these characteristics is stereotyping; there is much variation within any group. It is probably best to use these characteristics as hypotheses to be modified or discarded during treatment.

General resources for developing cultural competence include a chapter by Barnett and Polakoff (2000), which is a brief overview, and books by Sue and Sue (1999) and Paniagua (1998). More specifically, a book by Orlandi et al. (1992) deals with substance abuse/dependence, and books by McGoldrick et al. (1996) and Okun (1996) deal with family therapy.

## Risks in Repressed-Memory Therapy

Exercise extreme caution if you are considering doing repressed-memory work. In 1992, there were hardly any claims on this issue; by 1994, fully 16% of all professional liability claims against mental health professionals were connected with repressed-memory (Marine, cited in "Repressed Memory Claims Expected to Soar," 1995). The most comprehensive resource is a book by Knapp and VandeCreek (1997b), which should be read before proceeding in this area. A careful reading of at least four articles by Kenneth S. Pope is highly recommended (Pope, 1995, 1996, 1997, and 1998) for understanding the scientific basis for this therapy. Gutheil and Simon (1997) offer wise guidance in managing the risks of recovered-memory therapy, and Brown (1998) provides guidance on treatment. If you want to persist in this type of work, Nagy (1994) and Marine and Caudill (1996) recommend that you do the following:

- Rule out, or at least investigate fully, any medical or physical causes for the client's symptoms.

- Consider all alternative methods that are appropriate to the goals. Document your weighing of these and your reasons for rejecting the alternatives and pursuing this method.

- Devise a complete and balanced statement of the risks and benefits of recovering memories, and have the client read, discuss, and sign it.

- There are significant doubts about the veracity of memories recovered under hypnosis or during drug-assisted interviews (using Amytal or Brevital, so-called "truth serums"), and so more detailed consents should be obtained before these kinds of explorations are conducted. I have been unable to find a consent form for hypnosis, but there is a great deal of patient education material available from which you could construct one.

- Do not use statistics extrapolated from small samples or other weak data correlating childhood abuse with symptoms or disorders (e.g., common clinical phenomena) as a basis for concluding that abuse occurred.

- Know your local laws (especially on the reporting of abuse) and local ethical codes about areas of competence, documentation, and so on. The HIPAA procedures will be used only where the state rules for privacy are less stringent, so you must consult your state's professional organizations and know your local rules before you adopt the HIPAA forms and procedures.

- This area is rapidly evolving, so know and keep up to date with the flood of litigation in this area (so you will know how to respond if your clinical case becomes a forensic case), your professional liability coverage and obligations, the mental health professions' statements on these issues, and current research and practice. (See Appelbaum, 2001.)

Although one cannot prevent a suit, the following precautions should greatly reduce one's risk of being accused of "implanting false memories." They were developed by George F. Rhoades, Jr., PhD, of Aiea, HI, and are presented here (with some slight modifications and reorganization) with his kind permission.

1. Obtain all records from previous therapists.

2. Obtain fully informed and repeated consent for the following:

   a. Hypnosis.

   b. Innovative (or uncommon) techniques.

   c. Working in the area of "recovered memories."

3. Don't "lead" your client in the recovery of his or her memories.

   a. Some clients may embellish memories to please you in your quest for more details.

   b. Don't suggest types of abuse or possible perpetrators.

   c. Don't jump to conclusions; allow the client to recover his or her own memories.

   d. Don't push a client to discover and process memories too quickly.

   e. Don't tell your client that he or she has the "characteristics of an abuse victim."

   f. Don't search for "dissociated" memories.

4. Don't overestimate the accuracy of "recovered" memories.

   a. Be aware of the processes that can affect memory.

   b. Be aware of possible contamination effects on memory, inside and outside of therapy.

   c. Be willing to educate your client regarding memory functioning and its limitations and vulnerabilities.

5. Don't tell your clients that you "know" that their memories are true.

   a. Unless you were physically present or had independent corroborating evidence at the time of the abuse, you cannot verify that abuse.

   b. You may, however, offer your opinion regarding diagnostic impressions of a client, the process of the patient's memory recovery, and the relation of his or her account to current research and/or knowledge of memory and abuse.

   c. Process with the client his or her possible "need" for the therapist to "believe" the details of the reported abuse.

6. Remember your role—that of a therapist, and not of a police officer, an investigator, or the like.

7. Don't accuse an individual of sexual abuse, but comply with the abuse reporting laws in your jurisdiction.

8. Don't encourage the confrontation of reported perpetrators.

9. Don't tell your clients to "cut off" contact with the reported perpetrators or other family members. The therapeutic environment may be used to discuss the possible implications of major life changes, before choosing and acting on said changes.

10. Don't encourage legal action/retribution of clients against reported perpetrators.

11. Don't breach confidentiality.

    a. Adult clients have the right of confidentiality (within the limits of local abuse-reporting laws). Don't speak to family members without written permission.

    b. After written permission is obtained, inform concerned parties regarding the therapeutic process and the therapist's limits in disclosure.

12. Don't recommend to your clients books or support groups that you are unfamiliar with.

13. Don't look at your clients as possible subjects for a "good [scholarly] article," a "good [popular] book," and/or an interview by the mass media.

14. Document the treatment process:

    a. Treatment goals and progress toward goals.

    b. Therapeutic interventions.

    c. Patient's statements regarding progress and interventions.

    d. The history (sequence, context) of the recall of the "recovered" memories.

15. Don't utilize hypnosis without adequate training and supervision.

16. Be a reality check for your client.

17. Seek supervision/consultation.

18. Be willing to refer a client who requires skills you don't possess or when therapeutic benefits have been maximized in your therapeutic relationship (i.e., no progress is being made).

## 3.5  Evaluating the Ethicality of Proposed Treatments

There are hundreds of types or schools of psychotherapy and thousands of interventions. How can you evaluate the ethicality of a technique with a particular client? Each psychotherapist should be able to answer the questions in Table 2, a questionnaire prepared by the Association for Advancement of Behavior Therapy (1977), about every treatment provided

**TABLE 2. Checklist for the Ethicality of Proposed Treatments**

A. Have the goals of treatment been adequately considered?
  1. To insure that the goals are explicit, are they written?
  2. Has the client's understanding of the goals been assured by having the client restate them orally or in writing?
  3. Have the therapist and client agreed on the goals of therapy?
  4. Will serving the client's interests be contrary to the interests of other persons?
  5. Will serving the client's immediate interests be contrary to the client's long-term interest?

B. Has the choice of treatment methods been adequately considered?
  1. Does the published literature show the procedure to be the best one available for that problem?
  2. If no literature exists regarding the treatment method, is the method consistent with generally accepted practice?
  3. Has the client been told of alternative procedures that might be preferred by the client on the basis of significant differences in discomfort, treatment time, cost, or degree of demonstrated effectiveness?
  4. If a treatment procedure is publicly, legally, or professionally controversial, has formal professional consultation been obtained, has the reaction of the affected segment of the public been adequately considered, and have the alternative treatment methods been more closely reexamined and reconsidered?

C. Is the client's participation voluntary?
  1. Have possible sources of coercion on the client's participation been considered?
  2. If treatment is legally mandated, has the available range of treatments and therapists been offered?
  3. Can the client withdraw from treatment without a penalty or financial loss that exceeds actual clinical costs?

D. When another person or an agency is empowered to arrange for therapy, have the interests of the subordinated client been sufficiently considered?
  1. Has the subordinated client been informed of the treatment objectives and participated in the choice of treatment procedures?
  2. Where the subordinated client's competence to decide is limited, have the client as well as the guardian participated in the treatment discussions to the extent that the client's abilities permit?
  3. If the interests of the subordinated person and the superordinate persons or agency conflict, have attempts been made to reduce the conflict by dealing with both interests?

E. Has the adequacy of treatment been evaluated?
  1. Have quantitative measures of the problem and its progress been obtained?
  2. Have the measures of the problem and its progress been made available to the client during treatment?

F. Has the confidentiality of the treatment relationship been protected?
  1. Has the client been told who has access to the records?
  2. Are records available only to authorized persons?

G. Does the therapist refer the client to other therapists when necessary?
  1. If treatment is unsuccessful, is the client referred to other therapists?
  2. Has the client been told that if [he or she is] dissatisfied with the treatment, referral will be made?

H. Is the therapist qualified to provide treatment?
  1. Has the therapist had training or experience in treating problems like the client's?
  2. If deficits exist in the therapist's qualifications, has the client been informed?
  3. If the therapist is not adequately qualified, is the client referred to other therapists, or has supervision by a qualified therapist been provided? Is the client informed of the supervisory relation?
  4. If the treatment is administered by mediators, have the mediators been adequately supervised by a qualified therapist?

*Note.* Reprinted from the Association for Advancement of Behavior Therapy (AABT, 1977). Copyright 1977 by the AABT. Reprinted by permission.

to every client. You may not usually consider these questions so formally, but if you are considering any treatment that is unusual, controversial, or experimental, it will be in your long-term best interest to consider answering these by "thinking out loud for the record" to show that you have arrived at your treatment plan thoughtfully.

For a review of the variables in ethics decision making, the models employed, and a comprehensive and integrative model suitable for clinical work, see Hansen and Goldberg (1999).

# 3.6  Avoiding Malpractice in Psychological Testing

Pope (1988d) offers 17 specific ways for avoiding malpractice in the areas of assessment, diagnosis, and testing. This section is loosely adapted from his recommendations.

## Require the Client to Give Consent

The APA code of ethics (APA, 2002) specifically requires informed consent for testing (Standard 9.03) and refers to a fuller discussion of the meaning of informed consent in Standard 3.10. For more on this issue, see Section 4.1. As to HIPAA, while the APA filed a request (Newman, 2002) that "test data" (psychological tests, protocols, and findings and test materials such as manuals and scoring keys) be treated with the same high privacy requirements as psychotherapy notes, this did not become a part of the final Privacy Rule of August 14, 2002. I presume, first, that test data, when included in a client's medical record, would be considered protected health information (PHI) and thus would be subject to the rules about PHI, including the "minimum necessary" requirement (per HIPAA Section 164.502[b]), which is designed to prevent "sending the whole chart," and, second, that where they exist, each state's rules about test data will apply. Where there are no state rules about test data, the HIPAA rules offer no meaningful protection.

Consent must be all of the following:

- **Competent.** The client must be both old enough and sufficiently intellectually competent to understand the consequences of giving consent, to understand the choices, to make a consistent decision, and to act in his or her best interests. Obviously, for children, persons with mental retardation, and others, the substitute consent of a competent and appropriate adult needs to be obtained. This issue is of greater ethical concern when the purpose of testing is to determine competence (e.g., to make a will or life-planning decisions).

- **Voluntary.** Clients must know that they have the option to refuse or discontinue testing without punishment. They must also know the situational consequences if they do not participate (such as loss of disability benefits, promotions, etc.; Sweet, 1990). You and an unbiased peer should be able to agree that a client is not feeling threatened or just being agreeable in consenting.

- **Informed.** Clients must know the purposes, nature, and consequences of the assessment. Specifically, clients must be told all the significant consequences of the testing that can be anticipated, and they must understand the issues, such as conflicts of inter-est or the ramifications of the results. These are especially important in forensic evalua-tions. The issues must be explained in terms familiar to the clients. Also, you must be sure to document that these explanations have been given. Clients must be informed that they have the "right to know the results, interpretations made, and the bases for [the psychologists'] conclusions and recommendations" (APA, 1981; p. 637). Any local variations on this theme must be included. Clients must be informed about the nature of tests and therapeutic techniques you will use (while keeping in mind the constraints of test security, expectancies, and practice effects). Make certain that you know, and fully inform the clients about, *all* those who will have access to the test report and the raw data. And, lastly, all of this should occur before the testing begins, so you will be in compliance with all laws and your conscience will be clear.

## Know the Rules

First, you must know the appropriate standards and guidelines of your discipline. Profes-sional organizations have published many guidelines (see Appendix D) with which you should be familiar. Generally, you will be held to the national standards, so learn them and provide services at a high level of quality and integrity.

In addition, you must know the current state and local laws. Conflicts between what you promise a client (such as confidentiality of some information divulged to you), and what the governing laws require can be avoided if you know all the applicable laws (such as those concerning clients with both substance abuse and developmental disabilities). For example, which takes precedence—workers' compensation law or mental health law? The book by Stromberg et al. (1988) is an excellent source for guidance. Lastly, if your state's rules are less stringent in protecting privacy, the HIPAA rules and procedures will apply, so you must be familiar with them as well.

## Stay within Your Areas of Competence

Weiner (1989) has argued that it is possible to be competent at psychological testing with-out being ethical, but that it is not possible to be ethical without being competent. Don't do everything you are licensed, trained, or even degreed to do. Make certain you are fully trained and practiced in administering, scoring, and interpreting each test you use. If you were last trained in test administration years ago, a consultation with a colleague who ob-serves you may be very enlightening and may improve the validity of your testing. Don't use a test if your administration will be invalid, or if your knowledge is insufficient to in-terpret *all* potential findings validly and fully.

In a remarkably simple and elegant analysis, Moreland et al. (1995) identified seven fac-tors and 86 areas of test user competence, and then, taking critical incidents of test mis-use as guides, developed empirically based test purchaser qualification forms. They have listed 12 minimal areas of competence and the seven factors. Ethical guidelines can be drawn from this list such as "Don't coach anyone" and "Refrain from labeling people with derogatory terms like 'dishonest' on the basis of a test score that lacks perfect valid-ity."

## Administer Tests the Way They Were Designed

- You must understand the technical aspects of measurement, validation, and evaluation design; the tests, procedures, and materials used; and their limitations and appropriateness for the subject.

- Follow the standardized procedures *exactly* when you are administering and scoring a test, to ensure validity.

- Use only tests whose manuals have the necessary and currently appropriate reliability and validity data. The manuals should also have detailed procedural descriptions of the methods of administering, scoring, and interpreting the tests' results.

- Use the most current, reliable, and valid version of a test. Although the APA code of ethics (APA, 2002) specifically forbids the use of obsolete or outdated tests (Standard 9.08), Sam Knapp (personal communication, October 2, 1996) reminds me, "It can be justified to use an earlier version of a test under some circumstances, for example, in doing a test–retest with a particular patient."

- Test security, always a good idea, is required by the APA code of ethics (APA, 2002) in Standard 9.11. For this reason, do not quote the questions asked (especially from copyrighted tests) in your reports. Instead, describe the stimuli in general terms. Similarly, keep the tests, materials, and manuals unavailable to potential clients and to unsophisticated users. Do not let clients take a test home (this ensures that no one will assist the clients in answering as well).

## Interpret and Report Your Findings Carefully

- It is probably a good idea to write your report as if persons besides the referrer will someday read it. If you are not fully comfortable justifying (perhaps in court and to a hostile opposition) any statement, either leave it out or modify it.

- Don't go beyond your findings: Do not, in your report through defensiveness or arrogance, go beyond your data. The APA ethics code reminds us that psychologists must recognize the "limitations of their interpretations" of assessment results (APA, 2002, Standard 9.06).

- Treat test results as hypotheses, not factual pronouncements. After all, they are only behavior samples from the universe of possible behaviors. When you use an automated scoring and interpretation service, you must understand the decision rules that transform the raw data into interpretative statements, as well as the psychometric properties of the program (especially its reliability and validity).

## Be Alert for Biasing Factors

- Know and keep in mind the assumptions behind your orientation, and struggle to understand how these can blind you to evidence, shape your expectations, and bias your results. Again, the APA code of ethics (APA, 2002) gives guidance for sensitivity and circumspection in test administration and interpretation in Standard 9, especially Standard 9.06.

- Seek out and attend to personal, social, and cultural factors that can bias your results. As noted earlier, these may include ageism; "beautyism" (the influence of weight, height, coloring, and prettiness); ethnic preferences and beliefs; racism; sex-role stereotypes; your social class; "personal allergies" to some people; your financial gain from some findings or diagnoses; sympathy with the "victim"; hostility to the "aggressor"; blaming the "victim"; supporting the "downtrodden"; your personal liberalism or conservatism; feelings about those who smoke, drink, abstain, and/or are "in recovery"; biases for or against various religions or degrees of religiousity; and other less well-defined feelings that can interfere with careful analysis.

- Understand and always give full weight to the "low base rate" phenomenon, which can severely limit the accuracy of any variable's identification. Similarly, appreciate the effects of a high base rate, and know the local base rates of the phenomena of interest.

- In your report, state clearly all possible limitations of and reservations about reliability and validity:

  Environmental factors: room lighting, a client's poor hearing or need for glasses, interruptions, noise.

  Communicational factors: the client's hearing, speech, and facility in English (written, read, heard, and spoken). For example, the Minneapolis Multiphasic Personality Inventory (MMPI) requires an eighth-grade reading level.

  The client's personal aspects: age, sex, education, and ethnic/cultural background.

  Any differences between the client and the norming population, which might invalidate the use of a test for this client. When such differences exist, weight them.

## Be Aware of Forensic Issues

As noted in Chapter 2, never either accept or defer a fee for forensic evaluations contingent upon the outcome of the trial (because doing so appears to compromise your professional independence), and do not base custody evaluations on less than full evaluations of all parties. Anderten et al. (1980) add several other considerations for forensic evaluations:

- Be especially careful to be objective and impartial, resisting pressure to support the position of the side that hires you.

- Work with your attorney to assure that *all* of your relevant findings will be heard in court.

- Make your first priority the client's well-being, not your loyalty to the attorney or agency.

### Be Thorough

- Consider possible physical causes of any and all findings, and pursue their investigation.

- Always obtain and review previous testing and treatment records.

The APA code of ethics (APA, 2002) requires providing feedback to clients in Standard 9.10. The best brief overview of the ethical obligations one assumes when providing clients with feedback on tests results is provided by Pope (1992). For a release form, see Section 7.5 and Form 50. Finally, as always, you should stay current on the literature, the issues, and the evolving state of the assessment arts.

## 3.7  Boundary Issues

Several of the ethical problems described earlier can be understood as "boundary issues": failure to clarify or maintain differences between client and therapist; crossing the boundary between friend and therapist; not keeping your private life out of your work; forming sexually intimate relationships in therapy; and so on. Excellent reviews of these issues can be found in Smith and Fitzpatrick (1995) and Gutheil and Gabbard (1993). A very good self-educational questionnaire exploring the consequences of boundary confusion is the Exploitation Index (Epstein & Simon, 1990). Boundary issues stemming from "dual relationships" in general, and from client–therapist sexual intimacy in particular, are discussed in detail in the next two sections.

Take the time to answer the questionnaire presented in Figure 4. To gain most from it, consider all your clients when answering it; not just the one it asks about. The questions are likely to raise your consciousness of how these issues can distort your work. I am indebted to Estelle Disch, PhD, of Cambridge, MA, for her permission to reprint it, and to Sam Knapp, EdD, of Harrisburg, PA, for suggesting the addition of the last four items.

## 3.8  Dual (or Multiple) Relationships

### What Are Dual Relationships?

"Dual relationships" exist whenever a therapist interacts with a client in more than one role or capacity as therapist, such as also being a business partner, teacher, consultant, or sexual partner. The relevant portion of the APA code of ethics (APA, 2002) is Standard 3.05. In psychiatry, most of these are called "double agentry."

### Why Avoid Dual Relationships?

Performing any role besides that of therapist can create goals, needs, and desires that are yours and not the client's. Dual relationships may lead to conflicts between your interests and the client's, and so you may not put the client's interest first. **Thus dual relationships**

# Are You in Trouble with a Client?

The purpose of this checklist is to alert you to boundary issues that might be interfering with your ability to work effectively with a particular client. Be particularly attentive if the situation persists even after you have attempted to change it. Answer either true or false to each question and add any explanations or details.

Client's initials or pseudonym: _____ Date: _____

1. This client feels more like a friend than a client. ❑ True ❑ False

2. I often tell my personal problems to this client. ❑ True ❑ False

3. I feel sexually aroused in response to this client. ❑ True ❑ False

4. I want to be friends with this client when therapy ends. ❑ True ❑ False

5. I'm waiting for therapy to end in order to be lovers with this client. ❑ True ❑ False

6. To be honest, I think the good-bye hugs last too long with this client. ❑ True ❑ False

7. My sessions often run overtime with this client. ❑ True ❑ False

8. I tend to accept gifts or favors from this client without examining why the gift was given and why at that particular time. ❑ True ❑ False

9. I have a barter arrangement with this client. ❑ True ❑ False

10. I have had sexual contact with this client. ❑ True ❑ False

11. I sometimes choose my clothing with this particular client in mind. ❑ True ❑ False

12. I have attended small professional or social events at which I knew this client would be present, without discussing it ahead of time. ❑ True ❑ False

13. This client often invites me to social events and I don't feel comfortable saying either yes or no. ❑ True ❑ False

14. This client sometimes sits on my lap. ❑ True ❑ False

15. Sometimes when I'm holding or hugging this client during our regular therapy work, I feel like the contact is sexualized for one or the other or both of us. ❑ True ❑ False

16. There's something I like about being alone in the office with this client when no one else is around. ❑ True ❑ False

17. I lock the door when working with this client. ❑ True ❑ False

18. This client is very seductive and I often don't know how to handle it. ❑ True ❑ False

19. This client owes me/the agency a lot of money and I don't know what to do about it. ❑ True ❑ False

20. I have invited this client to public or social events. ❑ True ❑ False

21. I am often late for sessions with this particular client. ❑ True ❑ False

22. I find myself cajoling, teasing, or joking a lot with this client. ❑ True ❑ False

23. I am in a heavy emotional crisis myself and I identify so much with this client's pain that I can hardly attend to the client. ❑ True ❑ False

*(cont.)*

**FIGURE 4. Are you in trouble with a client?** Questionnaire for assessing boundary issues, devised by Estelle Disch, PhD, of Cambridge, MA, and reprinted here by permission of Dr. Disch. (Items 48–51 were suggested by Sam Knapp, EdD, of Harrisburg, PA.)

Figure 4 (*cont.*)

24. I allow this client to comfort me. ❑ True ❑ False

25. I feel like this client and I are very much alike. ❑ True ❑ False

26. This client scares me. ❑ True ❑ False

27. This client's pain is so deep I can hardly stand it. ❑ True ❑ False

28. I enjoy feeling more powerful than this client. ❑ True ❑ False

29. Sometimes I feel like I'm in over my head with this client. ❑ True ❑ False

30. I often feel hooked or lost with this client and supervision on the case hasn't helped. ❑ True ❑ False

31. I often feel invaded or pushed by this client and have a difficult time standing my ground. ❑ True ❑ False

32. Sometimes I hate this client. ❑ True ❑ False

33. I sometimes feel like punishing or controlling this client. ❑ True ❑ False

34. I feel overly protective toward this client. ❑ True ❑ False

35. I sometimes drink or take drugs with this client. ❑ True ❑ False

36. I don't regularly check out what the physical contact I have with this client means for the client. ❑ True ❑ False

37. I accommodate to this client's schedule and then feel angry/manipulated. ❑ True ❑ False

38. This client's fee feels too high or too low. ❑ True ❑ False

39. This client has invested money in an enterprise of mine or vice versa. ❑ True ❑ False

40. I have hired this client to work for me. ❑ True ❑ False

41. This client has hired me to work for her/him. ❑ True ❑ False

42. I find it very difficult not to talk about this client with people close to me. ❑ True ❑ False

43. I find myself saying a lot about myself with this client—telling stories, engaging in peer-like conversation. ❑ True ❑ False

44. If I were to list people in my caseload with whom I could envision myself in a sexual relationship, this client would be on the list. ❑ True ❑ False

45. I call this client a lot and go out of my way to meet with her/him in locations convenient to her/him. ❑ True ❑ False

46. This client has spent time at my home (apart from the office). ❑ True ❑ False

47. I'm doing so much on this client's behalf I feel exhausted. ❑ True ❑ False

48. I have given this client a ride home. ❑ True ❑ False

49. We have had lunch/dinner during sessions. ❑ True ❑ False

50. This client has performed minor favors for me, such as returning library books or picking up dry cleaning. ❑ True ❑ False

51. I have accepted valuable gifts from this client. ❑ True ❑ False

**impair your unselfish judgment, which is the essence of being a professional.** In addition, such relationships can have these negative effects:

- They limit the effective handling of the transference and other relationship variables.

- They usually close the door to future therapy if it is needed.

- The power differential inherent in the therapy relationship may be exploited through seducing or intimidating the client into the other relationship.

- In addition, when clients are exploited in dual relationships, complaining about it is much more difficult for them than complaining about most other issues, like fees. The clients must overcome the power differential and transference in order to assert their own needs. The risks to a client are usually much greater than the risks to a therapist. For example, in a complaint, confidentiality may be broken and the therapist can say, allege, or deny almost anything about the client's life, thus putting the client on trial.

Harmful dual relationships usually stem from "subtle, gradual, and innocuous beginnings" (Pope, 1988a, p. 17). They may arise from inattention to the dynamics of the therapeutic relationship, or from a desire to be of even more help to a patient. They can also arise from the patient's own manipulation (because of pathology, transference, or other sources); in these cases, "dual" relationships often become "duel" relationships.

## Types of Dual Relationships

There are many types of dual or multiple relationships, and therapists must be alert to all the possibilities. Pope (1988a) lists 18 real-life scenarios (and I have added some others), which can be simplified into the following general kinds of relationships.

### Double Roles

Double roles include being a therapist as well as a supervisor, teacher (see below), dissertation committee member, evaluator, or research supervisor to the same person. Another example of double roles is providing therapy to current social acquaintances or business contacts, or to former ones when the old relationship was intense. Any such double roles are likely to distort the therapy relationship.

Being both a therapist and a friend is a third example of double roles. A "friend" is defined as someone with whom one socializes outside the therapy office (or the friend or close relative of such a person). There are many distinctions between friendship and therapy, and the patient handout provided a little later (Handout 1) describes some of them. A policy is also included in the sample client information brochure (Section 4.2), and you may wish to make additions to this list from your own experience. You may even wish to expand upon the list in Section 4.2 for a separate handout; if you do so, please share the results with me.

Other examples of double roles include the following:

- Having any kind of sexual relationship with a former or current client (see Section 3.9).

- Having any kind of business relationship with a former or current client (that of employer, coauthor, consultant, advisor, mentor, partner, lender, debtor, etc.).

- Providing any kind of psychological services to the children of your employees; to children of colleagues, friends, or frequent social, political, or business contacts; or to children you coach in an athletic activity.

- In regard to students (see above), always refer your current students seeking therapy, and be careful about relationships with those who might become your students. It may even be better to remain somewhat distant, have only casual contacts, or meet only at social events associated with the university until a student graduates and one of your roles terminates, before entering a closer friendship with this person (Koocher & Keith-Spiegel, 1998).

## Double Professions

The term "double professions" means serving in a second professional capacity with your patients, such as practicing law/medicine/financial advising (or any other profession) without a license (Pope, 1988a).

## Double Financial Relationships

Double financial relationships are a third type of dual relationships. Trading or bartering therapy for legal or professional services (e.g., tutoring), goods, or discounts—either on a dollar-for-dollar value or on a task-for-task basis—puts you into an additional commercial role. In this role your goals are, or appear to be, in conflict with those of your clients. That is, you seem to be providing services at the lowest cost to you but the highest cost to them.

## When Dual Relationships Are Not Avoidable: Weighing Their Effect

Multiple relationships are unavoidable in rural areas, in the military, and in most small communities. The central issue is the avoidance of *conflicting* roles. The APA ethics code (APA, 2002) notes that "Multiple relationships *that would not reasonably be expected to cause impairment or risk exploitation or harm* are not unethical" (Standard 3.05; emphasis added). Thus the code does not forbid dual or multiple relationships, but puts the burden of keeping them harmless on the psychologist. Eleven guidelines for doing so are offered by Barnett and Yutrzenka (1994).

In an intelligent and thoughtful article, Gottlieb (1993) proposes that since dual relationships are often unavoidable and are not prohibited outright, their variable effects ought to be weighed on three dimensions: "power," "duration," and the clarity of the time limits of the relationship, which he calls "termination." Essentially, relationships with low power differentials, briefer contacts, and clear time boundaries are less risky for exploitation, require less consultation, require less extensive and detailed informed consent, and so on. For example, vocational testing is lower on all three dimensions than intensive psychotherapy. For carefully reasoned arguments and suggestions about defining which multiple relationships are harmful and which are not, see Sonne (1994) and Gonsiorek and Brown (1989). Staal and King (2000) have adapted Gottlieb's model for military psychologists, and Younggren's (2002) article is helpful in evaluating the ethics of a dual relationship.

If you recognize that you are deep in conflicting and risky dual relationships with a patient, Kaplan (1990) recommends that you do the following:[1]

- Don't wait until the patient makes it clear that a problem has developed. Act.

- Get consultation about (1) the dynamics of the dual relationships, (2) how best to end the dual relationships, and (3) how to create the least harm to the patient.

- Review your malpractice insurance policy and inform your carrier. Talk to an attorney to learn how to limit your liability.

- With the patient's agreement, try to get a mediator to devise a "mutually agreeable, constructive solution which works toward restoration of a healthy therapeutic relationship or, in the alternative, develop a means to terminate both . . . relationship[s] without harming the patient through abandonment" (Kaplan, 1990, p. 30).

- Arrange for an independent evaluation of the patient to determine whether the patient has been harmed and to develop future treatment recommendations" (Kaplan, 1990, p. 30).

- Document all interactions with the patient and your memories of how the dual relationship arose.

- Document any agreements with the patient, and have them reviewed by both your own counsel and the patient's.

### Preventing Trouble

**HANDOUT 1**  A handout on dual relationships is presented as Handout 1. It is intended to be used for patient education, and thus to lessen troubles in this area. It can be left in your waiting room or handed to a patient when questions or a potentially risky situation occurs.

## 3.9  Sexual Intimacies in Therapy

Sexual relationships with patients are a particularly toxic type of dual relationship, and they constitute a plague in the health professions. We must greatly extend our efforts to prevent them through consciousness raising, training, supervision, investigation, and punishment. The APA code of ethics (APA, 2002) says flatly in Standard 10.05 that "Psychologists do not engage in sexual intimacies with current therapy clients/patients," and in Standard 10.08 that they do not do so "with a former client/patient for at least two years

[1]This list is adapted from Kaplan (1990). Copyright 1990 by the Illinois Psychological Association. Adapted by permission.

## Limits of the Therapy Relationship: What Clients Should Know

Psychotherapy is a professional service I can provide to you. Because of the nature of therapy, our relationship has to be different from most relationships. It may differ in how long it lasts, in the topics we discuss, or in the goals of our relationship. It must also be limited to the relationship of therapist and client *only*. If we were to interact in any other ways, we would then have a "dual relationship," which would not be right and may not be legal. The different therapy professions have rules against such relationships to protect us both.

I want to explain why having a dual relationship is not a good idea. Dual relationships can set up conflicts between my own (the therapist's) interests and your (the client's) best interests, and then your interests might not be put first. In order to offer all my clients the best care, my judgment needs to be unselfish and professional.

Because I am your therapist, dual relationships like these are improper:

- I cannot be your supervisor, teacher, or evaluator.
- I cannot be a therapist to my own relatives, friends (or the relatives of friends), people I know socially, or business contacts.
- I cannot provide therapy to people I used to know socially, or to former business contacts.
- I cannot have any other kind of business relationship with you besides the therapy itself. For example, I cannot employ you, lend to or borrow from you, or trade or barter your services (things like tutoring, repairing, child care, etc.) or goods for therapy.
- I cannot give legal, medical, financial, or any other type of professional advice.
- I cannot have any kind of romantic or sexual relationship with a former or current client, or any other people close to a client.

There are important differences between therapy and friendship. As your therapist, I cannot be your friend. Friends may see you only from their personal viewpoints and experiences. Friends may want to find quick and easy solutions to your problems so that they can feel helpful. These short-term solutions may not be in your long-term best interest. Friends do not usually follow up on their advice to see whether it was useful. They may *need* to have you do what they advise. A therapist offers you choices and helps you choose what is best for you. A therapist helps you learn how to solve problems better and make better decisions. A therapist's responses to your situation are based on tested theories and methods of change. You should also know that therapists are required to keep the identity of their clients secret. Therefore, I may ignore you when we meet in a public place, and I must decline to attend your family's gatherings if you invite me. Lastly, when our therapy is completed, I will not be able to be a friend to you like your other friends.

In sum, my duty as therapist is to care for you and my other clients, but *only* in the professional role of therapist. Please note any questions or concerns on the back of this page so we can discuss them.

**HANDOUT 1. Patient handout on limits of the therapy relationship.**    From *The Paper Office.* Copyright 2003 by Edward L. Zuckerman. Permission to photocopy this handout is granted to purchasers of this book for personal use only (see copyright page for details).

after cessation or termination of therapy." (See later in this section for clarification of this latter prohibition.)

## What Is Meant by "Sexual Intimacies"?

Although there is no precise agreement on the definition of "sexual intimacy," the following statements are made in the professional liability insurance policies of several professional organizations.

The American Professional Agency's (1992) policy (from the Executive Risk Indemnity, Inc.) defines "sexual misconduct" this way:

> any type of actual, alleged, attempted, or proposed physical touching or caressing or suggestions thereof by *You* or by any person for whom *You* may be legally responsible, with or to any of *Your* past or present patients or clients, or with or to any relative or member of the same household of any such patient or client, or with or to any person with whom such patient or client or relative has an affectionate personal relationship, which could be considered sexual in nature and/or inappropriate to any psychological services being provided. (American Professional Agency, 1992, p. 6; emphasis in original)

The policy sponsored by the American Psychiatric Association (Psychiatrists' Risk Retention Group, 1996) for its "Members" excludes coverage for "undue familiarity with the claimant" and for "mishandling of the transference or counter-transference phenomenon":

> Undue familiarity means, with respect to a patient, a former patient, or a member of the patient's immediate family or household (hereinafter the "claimant"), any actual or alleged sexual or social relationship between a Member and the Claimant or any actual or alleged physical contact by a Member of such Claimant, or any other demonstrated intention or act for the purpose of sexual gratification or stimulation, including but not limited to, with respect to such Claimant, any actual or alleged mishandling of the transference or counter-transference phenomena, harassment, or abandonment. (Psychiatrists' Risk Retention Group, 1996, p. 12)

The policy for psychologists from the APAIT (Chicago Insurance Company) states that it

> does not apply to any *Claims* made or Suits brought against any *Insured* alleging, in whole or in part, sexual assault, abuse, molestation, or licentious, immoral, amoral, or any other behavior which threatened, led to or culminated in any sexual act whether committed intentionally, negligently, inadvertently or with the belief, erroneous or otherwise, that the other party is consenting and has the legal and mental capacity to consent thereto, that was committed, or alleged to have been committed by the *Insured* or by any person for whom the *Insured* is legally responsible. (Interstate Insurance Group, 1994, p. 4, emphasis in original)

As you can see, current policies are very broadly written. In addition, state laws differ in defining sexual behaviors; some indicate only heterosexual genital intercourse, while others include kissing and sexual touching but may be silent on other kinds of sexual expression.

## With Whom Are Sexual Intimacies Prohibited?

Sexual intimacies are not allowed with "clients" of any kind, including supervisees, trainees, students of yours, or any persons in a professional relationship with you (e.g., business partners or employees). In parallel, the APA ethics code (APA, 2002) says that you should not do therapy with former sexual partners (Standard 10.07).

Standard 10.06 of the APA code (APA, 2002) also forbids sexualized relationships with "individuals [who psychologists] know to be the close relatives or significant others of current clients/patients." This definition includes all members of a client's household, and it may even include anyone (such as an ex-spouse or a boyfriend or girlfriend) with whom any of these persons has or had a close emotional relationship. Although this is the most stringent exclusionary approach, it may be better to be safe than sorry, in light of the direction the field is going.

Stromberg and Dellinger (1993) raise the question of how state regulations define "patient" or "client." This may be of considerable importance to psychologists, who often have a wider spectrum of possible professional relationships than do psychiatrists or social workers. For example, psychologists see assessment subjects, organizational clients, research participants, employment counseling clients, and the like. Obviously, psychologists have to know the answer to this question and be circumspect; regulators tend to think in polarities, whereas psychologists may evaluate patienthood in terms of the intensity, duration, and intimacy of the relationship. Haspel et al. (1997) provide both excellent discussions of the definitional issues and quoted definitions from many states' laws.

## Who Is Prohibited from Engaging in Intimacies?

You as the therapist are prohibited from engaging in sexual intimacies, of course, but those you employ or supervise are also prohibited.

## The Damage to the Client and to Therapy

Therapist–client sexual intimacies are universally prohibited because they betray the trust the client has in the therapist's putting the client's needs first. The harm to the client can be extensive (Pope, 1988b). There have been problems with the collection of empirical data in this area; as a result, we have only the upper and lower limits of occurrence rates, and descriptions of some of the damage from these relationships (Williams, 1992).

Frequently reported consequences to clients (Bouhoutsos et al., 1983) include ambivalence, distrust of men or women, and distrust of therapy. The victims become "therapeutic orphans." They may have flashbacks, nightmares, and other recollections, and/or depression, hospitalizations, and suicides. They may exhibit relationship problems, with confusion about identity, boundaries, and roles. They may experience feelings of anger, abandonment, exploitation, devastation, guilt, emptiness, and isolation; they may also show suppressed rage, emotional dyscontrol, and mood swings.

Pope (1988b) has described the "therapist–patient sex syndrome" as similar both to posttraumatic stress disorder and to the sequelae of child or spouse abuse, rape, and incest. According to Pope, this syndrome involves "(a) ambivalence, (b) a sense of guilt, (c) feelings of emptiness and isolation, (d) sexual confusion, (e) impaired ability to trust, (f) identity, boundary, and role confusion, (g) emotional lability . . . , (h) suppressed rage, (i) increased suicidal risk, and (j) cognitive dysfunction . . . " (1988, p. 222). Folman (1990) has suggested that 11 psychotherapy processes are all affected negatively by sexual contacts: transference, countertransference, trust, confidentiality, resistance, privacy, intimacy, boundaries, self-disclosure, use of touch, and termination. Theory suggests that the effects may differ for men and women, may be worse if the therapist initiates the intimacies and is married, and may also be worse if the client has been victimized before. In summary, if any of the negative consequences described here is likely to occur, they are so serious that taking the chance that a patient *won't* be harmed is unethical. As clinicians, we do have a minimal ethical duty: "At least do no harm."

## Negative Consequences to the Clinician

The helping professions no longer ignore sexual relations with clients. It appears that, in fact, the trend is toward greater enforcement, condemnation, and punishment. If you need reinforcements for abstaining from sexual intimacies, here are some from Keith-Spiegel (1977) and others:

- Subsequent therapists will support and encourage your ex-client to complain.

- Your client/lover will expect commitment, or at least a continuation of the relationship, from you; you will then have to deal with a spurned lover, not a helped client.

- The mass media love these cases. You will be publicly pilloried.

- Some states make ethical violations illegal, so you can lose your license.

- As of 2001, 18 states have criminalized sexual contact between therapists and clients. It is a felony, and the maximum sentence is often 20 years in prison and a fine of $150,000.

- Intimacy with a client is likely to result in multiple legal problems. Gary Schoener, an expert in this area, says, "I call it a triple whammy. First, a criminal case can result in a prison term or probation and a large fine. Second, a criminal conviction makes it more likely that a therapist will lose a civil case and have to cough up monetary damages. Third; criminal conviction usually makes it an easy and fast job for a state board to revoke professional licenses" (Schoener, quoted in Foster, 1996, p. 25).

- R. Folman (personal communication, August 29, 1996) reports that several therapists have made suicide attempts when confronted with accusations of sexual improprieties.

- You cannot really win if you are sued; you will experience excruciating stress, lost money, and conflict with your significant others. Your professional liability insurance probably won't cover the damages awarded: Insurers generally cover only up to $25,000 for sexual cases, and many will not cover these at all. Current practice is for the insurance company to offer the $25,000 only for the defense of the claim, and nothing to settle the claim or pay any damages awarded. Therefore, you alone will be fully responsible for any damage awards. Insurance companies use the rationale that their policies don't cover intentional or knowing misconduct, and that your ethics code and the literature have put you "on notice" that these are wrong (Stromberg & Dellinger,

1993). Moreover, you can even be sued by the patient (and his or her significant other, if any) for such things as intentional infliction of harm (Stromberg & Dellinger, 1993, p. 9).

## Not Me! I Would Never!

Misconceptions and distortions abound about sexually intimate and abusing therapists. Pope (1989b) has identified categories and scenarios for therapists who became sexually intimate with patients. On the basis of his work and that of others, we can debunk a number of erroneous ideas as follows:

- It is not true that only poorly trained therapists get sexually involved with patients.

- It is not true that only jerks get sexually involved; respected, influential, successful, or prominent therapists also do the same.

- It is not true that the sexually active therapist is seen as a hero. Such a therapist's sexual behaviors will be seen as exploitative and motivated by feelings of inadequacy (Keith-Spiegel, 1977).

- It is not true that sexual intimacies can be simply an extension of sex education or sex therapy

- It is not true that sexual intimacies can be a component of trailblazing or innovative therapy.

- It is not true that sexual intimacies may be justified if the consequence of refusal would be the client's suicide or something else as serious. (If this idea even flickers though your mind, consult a peer to examine this rationalization and find ethical alternatives.)

- It is not true that abusing therapists will only abuse one sex, so confining their practice to the other sex will safeguard their clients.

- It is not true that the termination of therapy legitimizes the intimacy. You cannot simply discharge or refer a patient and then pursue a relationship.

- It is not true that waiting a year after discharge means "it can't be transference" and thus it is all right.

- It is not true that "anyone can get carried away with passion." You will be held responsible for your behavior.

- It is not true that sincerely believing that sexual attraction is totally inappropriate and harmful protects a therapist from being sexually attracted (Bennett et al., 1990).

- The Group for the Advancement of Psychiatry (GAP, 1990) offers some common rationalizations that have led therapists into trouble:

"If we had met socially I'm sure we would have had a great relationship right from the start. Why should we be penalized by our bad luck in meeting this way?"

"We are both mature people, and basically healthy, so we can handle the relationship despite any transference distortions."

■ It is possible that real true love—not just transference—can happen in therapy, but it is not at all certain that a client and a therapist can accurately distinguish it. Therapists and clients have married after the therapeutic issues are resolved, but the burden of demonstrating that such a relationship is not exploitative rests completely on the therapist. See below.

## Is Sexual Intimacy with a Client *Ever* Acceptable?

### The Safest Course: "Never"

Sexual intimacy with a client is *never* acceptable, even if the therapy is over. **It is always your responsibility to say "No." "Never—without time limits"** is the safest course. As of December 1988, the American Psychiatric Association felt that "Sexual involvement with one's former patients generally exploits emotions deriving from treatment and therefore almost always is unethical" (quoted in GAP, 1990, p. 59).

For psychologists, the code of ethics (APA, 2002, Standard 10.08) sets a 2-year posttherapy time limit, but after that the psychologist is responsible for demonstrating that the relationship is not exploitative (Standard 10.08b). This is slippery; a therapist in love/lust/loneliness is likely to be a poor judge of these issues. It is educational to read the APA code's list of criteria for evaluating potential exploitativeness: the length of time since termination; the nature, duration, and intensity of the treatment; the circumstances of termination; the client's personal history and present mental status; the chances of adverse impact on the client; and any statements or actions by the therapist during the course of therapy *suggesting or inviting* the possibility of a posttermination sexual *or romantic* relationship with the patient (APA, 2002; modified and emphasis added).

Individual states, however, are enacting laws concerning the time limits. Florida (Fla. Stat. Chapter 21U-15004) considers the therapy relationship "to continue in perpetuity," whereas California believes in a 2-year limit (Cal. Civil Code Section 43.93), as do Ohio and Minnesota. There is also much uncertainty about the statute of limitations for suing. Generally it has run from the time of the incident, but courts are now accepting the idea that the statute may not start until the harm is discovered or recognized, and this may be years later. "Thus, in essence, most courts are bending over backwards to permit patients to proceed with suits against abusive therapists—even if their mental state caused considerable delay in doing so" (Stromberg & Dellinger, 1993, p. 10).

Because of the many options and factors involved, therapists who are sexually involved with clients or ex-clients can never be sure that they will not be sued for sexual intimacies, no matter how long it has been since the termination of therapy. For all these reasons, "never" is safest for both you and your clients.

*Other "What If . . . ?" Situations*

- Sex with a client is not allowed even if you believe it is in the client's best interest (as sex therapy, as a means of raising his or her self-esteem or sexual confidence, as a restitutive emotional experience, etc.) If you are afraid that discontinuing a sexual relationship will have negative consequences, these consequences may happen anyway. Consult.

- Sex is not allowed even if the client is a consenting adult who wants to have sex, initiates it, authorizes it, says it's OK, promises it will be no problem for you, pleads, or the like. In the laws making therapist–client sex a felony, consent (by the client) is specifically ruled out as a defense to be used by the therapist. So if you and a client have sexual intimacies, you are guilty *de jure.*

- Even if what you feel for a client is "true love," sex is not allowed. Sorry, but your feelings do not count here. It is probably unethical even when you fully intend to marry a client or ex-client. Plans change; promises don't.

- Sex, of course, is not allowed with force, seduction, drugs, threats, or intimidation.

- If you think, "Sex outside the office is OK because it is not therapy," think again. Sex is not allowed even if you never discuss therapy, because it is the role conflict—not the actions or location—that is harmful.

- Sorry, but even *flirting* is out. This is not a legitimate or reliable way to raise the self-esteem of a patient.

- *No* kind of sex is allowed. Remind yourself that sexual activities are not just limited to intercourse, not just genital, not just heterosexual.

- Regarding touching: The safest rule, "never touch," may seem too conservative and crippling to both parties. Durana (1998) and Downey (2001) review the literature and offer legal and clinical guidelines. Smith et al.'s (1998) book is comprehensive and authoritative. Some guidelines from Meiselman (1990, p. 138) were originally devised for treating adult women who were sexually abused as children, but seem sensible and well reasoned:

  "Wait for the client to spontaneously initiate touch or indicate a willingness to be touched." This allows the client to retain control and security.

  "Specifically ask for the client's permission before touching her in any way." This allows cognitive reinforcement of affects and supports the client's control of her (or his) body.

  "Avoid falling into a routinized pattern of touching," because "establishing a custom of touching can cause the client to feel coerced into allowing touching . . . when she would prefer to avoid it."

  "Decline any form of touch that seems likely to be sexually stimulating to either party." Be aware that *any* touch can be sexualized, and the contact may be erotic only to the patient. This rule reinforces boundaries and the rule that both parties have the right to say "No."

## A Checklist of Preventive Measures

❏ Inform clients early in therapy about ethical limits. (See, Handout 1 and Section 4.2.)

❏ Reduce your vulnerability by doing nothing but therapy in the office, keeping the office businesslike, and perhaps never being alone in the office suite with some clients.

❏ Be sensitive to how each client may interpret your nonsexual or affectionate behaviors, conversation about sexual topics, jokes, efforts to be helpful, and so forth. Even simple touches and expressions of concern can be misinterpreted. Think how the patient will interpret your touching him or her. Explain what you are doing and why before you do it, so that it will not be seen as a sexual overture (Bennett et al., 1990).

❏ Monitor your feelings throughout the therapy. If your attraction or fantasies become strong or distracting, consult immediately.

❏ Ask yourself: What effects will a sexual relationship with this client have on my other important relationships?

❏ Remind yourself: You really need this career. You have worked hard and long for it, and you are, or will be, very good at it. Don't throw it away for a little "fun." There is an old saying (and not only for men): "Don't let the little head do the thinking for the big head."

## What to Do If a Client Asks You for Sex

If a client asks you for sex, plan your reaction carefully, because this is a high-risk situation for you and a high-vulnerability time for the client. Maintain the client's self-esteem (perhaps say that you are flattered), and clarify the request. In particular, explore the issues therapeutically:

■ Is the client attracted to your role or power, or to you as a person?

■ Are there transference, avoidance, authority, or parental issues?

■ Is the client subverting the therapy to avoid confrontation and change?

■ Is the client setting up another defeat of a therapist, failure of treatment, or failure of his or her own efforts? (Any of these could be a reflection of infantile, narcissistic, or helplessness needs.)

Rutter (quoted in Foster, 1996, p. 27) offers this observation:

A client trying to seduce a therapist may be repeating past injuries, but is also most likely searching for a response that will discourage this repetition. The client is doing exactly what patients are supposed to do when they see their doctors: bringing her [sic] illness to her therapist, her self-destructive pattern, in the only way she knows how, by repeating it with her therapist, right there in the room. Along with her hunger for warmth and affection, she is showing her therapist that she has always been out of control of her own sexual boundaries. The therapist can either victimize her as others have, or he can offer her a way to begin recovering from her past injuries.

When you say "No" to the client (as you must), make the "No" solid. Do not be ambiguous. Don't say "Only if . . . ," or "When . . . ," or even "No, but . . . ". Say, "It is unethical and would be harmful to you. Not after therapy is over. Never, under any conditions." Set and keep rigid boundaries, but also use this incident as grist for the therapeutic mill.

## Consciousness Raising

In an appendix to their book, Pope and Bouhoutsos (1986) offer a list of situations in which the risk of sexual intimacy with a client is high. Their list is rephrased below, with some additions, for consciousness-raising purposes.[2]

You are at increased risk when you are:

- Preoccupied with your personal problems when in therapy.

- Playing the authority on everything and becoming angry when challenged.

- Dressing, talking, or acting in a flirtatious or seductive manner with a patient.

- Prescribing that a client dress, talk, or act in a flirtatious or seductive manner. You are at some increased risk of the patient's misunderstanding when you prescribe seductive behavior (as in dating skills training or sexual therapy), or especially when you have him or her rehearse with you. Therefore, be extra careful to get fully informed consent. Also, you might want to involve a consultant or a witness to your therapy plan and methods.

- Prescribing sexual behaviors for your vicarious pleasure, curiosity, voyeurism, or sense of power.

- Prescribing abstinence or proscribing some relationship because you are jealous.

- Discussing sexual material because of your own interests rather than the patient's clinical needs.

- "Dating" your patient—taking him or her out for lunch, a drink, a film, or an art gallery. Treating agoraphobia *in vivo* might lead to these situations.

- Scheduling a patient so that you have lots of time with him or her (last patient of the day), or can be alone together, or can have extra sessions with him or her.

- Wallowing in a "mutual admiration society": giving or receiving excessive compli-

---

[2]Most of this is adapted from Pope and Bouhoutsos (1986). Copyright 1986 by the Greenwood Publishing Group, Inc. Adapted by permission.

ments, basking in the glow of the client's appreciation while ignoring or minimizing the distortion, and rationalizing away either party's limitations.

■ Not examining your attraction or arousal in light of the therapy's dynamics and your own psychological state and needs, and not offering an appropriate and therapeutic response.

■ Isolating the patient from other sources of assistance so that you become his or her "life-line," and he or she is less likely to tell another professional of your sexual relations.

■ Isolating yourself from consultation, peers, supervision, and education.

■ Believing that in the case of this patient, there are special mitigating factors that make sex OK (GAP, 1990, p. 58).

By far the most common scenario in which sexual improprieties arise is one in which a male therapist (or, rarely—5–10% of the time—a female therapist) has personal problems that temporarily distort his (or her) judgment. Therefore, if you are compromised by such problems, do not work. Rest and recuperate; get consultation and education. Everything is more difficult to get out of than into. If you discover or even suspect that you are at risk, **get help immediately!** Seek consultation, personal therapy, time off, or whatever you need.

## What to Do If You Are Attracted to a Client

"Attraction" means finding a client strikingly physically attractive, amazingly witty or sensitive, alluringly comfortable for you, or the like. Here are some guidelines for what to do if you find yourself feeling attracted:

■ Step back mentally and ask yourself whether this presentation has previously been a strategy of the client's for getting his or her needs met. Ask how such a strategy plays into your own needs and situation. Consider your own issues, such as rescue fantasies and needs to be admired, found attractive, be in control, or be depended upon. In addition, how are your intimate relationships going now?

■ How have you previously resolved such attractions? Remember, therapists should meet clients' needs, not vice versa.

■ Irvin P. R. Guyett, PhD, of Pittsburgh, PA, advises: If you find yourself fantasizing about the client outside the session or your fantasies are amplified in the next session, consult a peer.

■ If you are attracted, do *not* discuss this attraction with the client until you have consulted a peer first. You must fully understand your side before putting anything more on the client.

■ It is still your responsibility to deal with both your own and the client's urges, fantasies, and attractions in a therapeutically productive way, or you may be at risk of malpractice even without the sexual contact. That is, you may be ignoring or not meeting the client's needs but meeting your own, and so you are providing inadequate or even incompetent services.

■ Some advise immediately referring a client to whom you develop romantic feelings; however, besides resembling abandonment and punishing the client, this is avoidance of your or the client's feelings. It is likely to be better in the long run to process these feelings with your supervisor or consultant and to resolve them.

■ Ask yourself: Can I control my impulses? Can I be open about this problem and my feelings with a colleague? If you cannot resolve the feelings, terminate the therapy and refer the client, before you get into deeper trouble.

■ Pope (1987) outlines a successful case treatment of a therapist who was highly attracted to a client. This may be useful reading. The best condensed and up-to-date overview of the facts, consequences, and issues is also by Pope (2000).

## Reporting Another Therapist

What if you recognize the damage done to a patient by a previous sexual relationship with a therapist, but the patient does not? Of course you will work with the patient on this issue, but do you have to report it? Generally, the answer is yes (APA, 2002, Standard 1.04 and 1.05), because you have a duty to care for the patient. Unfortunately, fewer than 3% of such cases are reported to licensing boards (Parsons & Wincze, 1995).

What if a client *falsely* accuses a previous therapist of sexual misconduct? Good starting sources for some information about false accusations of sexual improprieties are Gutheil (1992) and Sederer and Libby (1995).

## Client–Therapist Intimacy: Appropriate and Inappropriate Conduct

HANDOUT 2    The purposes and functions of Handout 2, presented below, are as follows: (1) to reduce the rate of inappropriate sexual behaviors on the part of clients; (2) to increase the rate of clients' reporting of sexual exploitation by all kinds of professionals; and (3) to protect you if you are misunderstood or even accused of sexual improprieties, because this form states your rules of practice. The handout is valuable because it is written for consumers, in a narrative and casual style. Its message and tone are empowering; it addresses questions of ethics, harm, love, and discomfort with sexual behavior in therapy; and it offers options for reacting, taking action, and handling the emotions stirred up by sexual behaviors in therapy.

This handout is not suitable for routine distribution to every client, because the reading may be burdensome for those who have not had ideas or experiences along these lines. Also, it may stimulate inappropriate thoughts in clients who are borderline, psychotic, or dependent.

You should be the one to ask or bring up the subject of this handout, because the client may be feeling too ashamed, confused, or guilty to do so. It can be given to a patient when it is topically appropriate, or it can be made available in a three-ring binder, along with other patient education materials and some of your forms, in your waiting room. You might sug-

## Client–Therapist Contact: Proper and Improper Conduct

This brochure has been written to help you understand what is proper and improper conduct for a therapist, and what responses are available to you as a consumer. It may raise issues that you have not considered before. However, if you are well informed, you will be better able to make sure your needs get met in therapy.

Although most therapists are ethical people (that is, good and law-abiding people) who care about their clients and follow professional rules and standards in their practice, there are a very few who do not consider what is best for their clients and who behave unethically. These issues apply to any mental health worker: psychologists, psychiatrists, social workers, counselors, clergy, nurses, or marriage and family therapists.

### Therapist Behaviors That May Not Be OK

There will be times in your therapy when it might be important, even if it is very uncomfortable for you and your therapist, to discuss your feelings and concerns about sex. In fact, such discussions may be needed if you are to benefit from your therapy. **However, sexual contact is never a proper part of any sex education or sex therapy.**

Many caring therapists sometimes show their feelings through touch. These forms of physical contact in therapy, such as a handshake, a pat on the back, or a comforting hug, may not concern you. But you are the best judge of the effects that any touching may have on you. If your therapist engages in any type of physical contact that you do not want, tell him or her to stop, and explain how you feel about that contact. A responsible therapist will want to know about your feelings and will respect your feelings without challenging you.

If your therapist makes sexual comments or touches you in a way that seems sexual to you, you are likely to feel discomfort. Trust your feelings. Do not assume that your therapist must be right if it feels wrong to you.

There are warning signs that a therapist may be moving toward sexual contact with you. The therapist may start talking a lot about his or her own personal problems, giving you gifts, writing letters to you that are not about your therapy, or dwelling on the personal nature of your relationship. Or the therapist may create the idea that he or she is your only source of help by criticizing you for standing up for yourself, or by telling you how to behave with a sexual partner. A red flag should definitely go up if your therapist discusses his or her own sexual activities or sexual attraction to you. Other signs include making remarks intended to arouse sexual feelings, or forms of physical seduction, such as sexual touching.

*(cont.)*

**HANDOUT 2. Patient handout on client–therapist contact (p. 1 of 3).**     Adapted from the Alabama Psychological Association (n.d.). Copyright by the Alabama Psychological Association. Adapted by permission. (This was adapted in turn from a longer brochure by the American Psychological Association [APA], Committee on Women in Psychology [1989]. Copyright 1989 by the APA. Adapted by permission. The APA grants purchasers of *The Paper Office* the right to make photocopies for personal use only. Further use of this material without the express written permission of the APA is strictly prohibited.)—From *The Paper Office.*

## Attraction to Your Therapist

It is normal for people in therapy to develop positive feelings, such as love or affection, toward a therapist who gives them support and caring. These feelings can be strong and may sometimes take the form of sexual attraction. It can be helpful to discuss these feelings with your therapist in order to understand them. A caring, ethical therapist would never take advantage of your feelings by suggesting sexual contact in therapy or by ending therapy to have a romantic relationship with you.

Though sexual feelings sometimes occur, and discussion about them is often useful, sexual contact with your therapist cannot be helpful. Sexual contact in therapy has been found to be harmful to the client in many ways, including damaging the client's ability to trust. The harmful effects may be immediate, or they may not be felt until later. For this reason, sexual contact with clients is clearly against the rules of all professional groups of mental health workers (psychologists, psychiatrists, social workers, and so on).

## Actions You Can Take If You Believe That Your Therapist's Actions Are Not OK

Any time you feel uncomfortable about a part of your therapy, including therapist behavior that you think is improper, consider discussing this with your therapist. Your therapist should not try to make you feel guilty or stupid for asking questions, and your therapist should not try to frighten, pressure, or threaten you. If your therapist will not discuss your concerns openly or continues to behave in ways that are not OK with you, you probably have reason to be concerned.

When a discussion with your therapist about these behaviors does not help, you have the right to take some further action. You may wish to find another therapist and/or file any of several types of complaints. It is important for *you* to make the final decision about what course of action is best for your concerns and needs.

It may be very hard for you to think about making any kind of complaint against your therapist. You may worry that he or she will eventually find out about your complaint and be angry or hurt about it. You may also be concerned about possible harm to your therapist. There are several points to consider when you are trying to decide what is the best thing to do:

- Sexual contact between a therapist and a client is never a proper form of treatment for any problem. A therapist who suggests or engages in sexual contact in therapy is showing a lack of concern for you.
- Sexual contact in therapy is never your fault. Regardless of the particular things that have happened, you have placed your trust in the therapist, and it is his or her duty not to take advantage of that trust. If the therapist does this, you have been betrayed.
- A therapist who engages in sexual contact with a client is likely to do so more than once and with more than one client. If no one reports this behavior, other people may be harmed by the same therapist.

## Specific Courses of Action

Remember that you have the right to stop therapy whenever you choose. At the same time, you may also wish to make some type of complaint against the therapist who has acted improperly.

If you choose to make a complaint against your therapist, the process may become long and difficult. Other clients taking such action have felt overwhelmed, angry, and discouraged. It is very impor-

*(cont.)*

tant that you have support from people you can depend upon. Good sources of support might be family members, friends, support groups, a new therapist, or some type of advocate. Identifying and using good sources of support will help you feel more secure about the plan of action you have chosen.

You may wish to see another therapist to help you continue with your therapy, including dealing with problems resulting from the experience with the unethical therapist. It would not be unusual for you to have confusing thoughts and feelings about your experience and your previous therapist. It would also be understandable if you felt frightened about seeking, or had difficulty trusting, a new therapist.

You may also want an advocate to actively help you in making and pursuing plans. Try to locate a mental health worker who has had experience with other clients who have been victims of therapist sexual misconduct. He or she will be able to understand your situation, provide you with important information, and support you in your choice of action.

Many therapists work in agencies or other offices with supervisors. Consider talking to your therapist's supervisor or agency director to see what can be done.

You may want to contact the state and/or national professional group to which your therapist belongs. For example, many practicing psychologists are members of this state's Psychological Association and the American Psychological Association. These organizations have specific rules against sexual contact with clients, and each has an ethics committee that hears complaints. State and national professional associations do not license their members to practice psychotherapy; however, they can punish an unethical therapist, sometimes by expelling that person from membership in the organization. Such an action may make it more difficult for the therapist to get or keep a license to practice.

If your therapist is a licensed professional, you may want to contact this state's licensing board of the profession to which your therapist belongs. It has the power to take away or suspend the license of a professional found guilty of sexual misconduct.

Another option is to file a civil suit for malpractice, which would be done through a lawyer. To get a referral to an advocate or therapist experienced in working with victims of sexual misconduct, or to obtain information on filing a complaint, call or write to this state's professional organization.

Here are the addresses of some of the organizations mentioned above:

American Counseling Association
5999 Stevenson Avenue
Alexandria, VA 22304
703-823-9800

American Psychiatric Association
1400 K Street, N.W.
Washington, DC 20005
888-357-7924

American Psychological Association
750 First Street, N.E.
Washington, DC 20002-4242
202-336-5510

National Association of Social Workers
750 First Street, N.E., Suite 700
Washington, DC 20002-4241
202-408-8600

There are groups in many communities to help victims of sexual abuse, and you can usually find them through the telephone book's "Human Services" section.

Please write your questions on the back of this handout so we can discuss them. Thank you.

gest that a client "look through the book when you have a chance, because I want you to have this information." Perhaps 3–5% of new female clients will have had a sexual relationship with a previous therapist or other trusted professional. Although you should ask about this possibility in the first interview's history taking (this is why questions about it are included in the intake interview questions and guide—see Form 32), the client may not be ready to reveal this. You generally cannot ask this question repeatedly, but by leaving Handout 2 on your waiting room table, you have "normalized" the question, done some education, and told the client you are ready to hear about this relationship whenever the client is ready to reveal it. The same applies to domestic violence and battering.

Thorn et al. (1993) found that the use of a brochure or handout such as Handout 2 raised clients' consciousness about specific kinds of sexual abuse, and was very likely to prevent such abuse by therapists. Some patients who read this or similar materials may come to recognize that a previous therapist was sexually exploitative. You should be prepared to deal with this contingency legally, emotionally, and professionally through education or through referral.

This handout is based on one authored by the Alabama Psychological Association's (P.O. Box 97, Montgomery, AL 36101-0097; phone 334-262-8245) Committee to Prevent Sexual Misconduct. This was in turn adapted from a longer brochure published by the APA's Committee on Women in Psychology (1989), entitled "If Sex Enters the Psychotherapy Relationship," which is available online at http://www.apa.org/pi/therapy.html.

Insert the names, addresses, and phone numbers of your state's associations on page 3 of the handout, above the associations listed there, before you copy the handout for distribution.

For your education in client–therapist sexual contacts, there are several excellent books available. The one by Bates and Brodsky (1993) is half a detailed case study and half devoted to the legal struggles of this client–therapist team against a psychopathic abuser. Peterson (1992) addresses all kinds of boundary violations and their causes; this book is more wide-ranging and educational than those focusing only on specific ethical violations. The Pope and Bouhoutsos (1986) volume is older but not out of date, because of its detailed examination of violations and their consequences. Finally, a book by Pope et al. (1993) addresses the universal experience of feelings and not just the less common actions.

# 3.10 The Duty to Protect (and Warn)

In addition to the ethical duties discussed previously, therapists also have ethical and legal obligations to prevent their clients from physically harming themselves or other persons. If you believe a client is dangerous, you have to use all reasonable care to protect the potential victim of your client's violence. You must use your professional judgment and position to *protect*, not just the more narrow duty simply to *warn*. Actually, your duty is to take appropriate action, which is not confined to warning. You have a less clear but more general obligation as a citizen to protect your fellow citizens.

## The Legal Basis

The court's two decisions in the famous *Tarasoff* case (*Tarasoff v. Regents of the University of California*, 1976) established therapists' duty to protect. Since then, court cases have sent mixed messages about the limits of therapists' liability and required behaviors. But they have rarely held a therapist liable, and never when a professionally proper response was made. (This is good news for therapists.) **You will not be held responsible for a negative outcome if you have done what a good clinician should have—proper evaluation, planning, and implementation.** A review (Appelbaum, 1996) of suits against clinicians for warning others suggests that therapists should warn potential victims in order to avoid liability for subsequent violence, even though doing so opens the therapist to allegations of breach of confidentiality.

When adopting *Tarasoff*, the courts have usually followed three basic principles in assessing liability. These principles are (1) "foreseeability" of harm (a verbal threat or action taken), (2) identifiability of a victim, and (3) feasibility of therapist intervention. On the other hand, about 15 states have adopted "anti-*Tarasoff*" (or proconfidentiality) legislation or immunity statutes, which hold a therapist not liable if he or she fails to warn a victim. Furthermore, if therapists do break privilege in order to protect life, they generally will not be held liable for this breach under a doctrine of "qualified privilege" (i.e., if they can prove that there was a necessity to breach confidentiality). Some states have passed laws to limit a mental health practitioner's liability to situations where the therapist has actual knowledge of a danger to a specific person; even then, the liability is avoided if the therapist warns the target person and notifies the police. About half the states have some law about warning an identifiable victim of a serious threat. In Arizona, California, Kentucky, Illinois, Louisiana, Maryland, Maine, Montana, and Utah, you must notify the identifiable victim; in Minnesota, you must notify police only when you can't reach the victim; in Colorado, you must notify if the client is just "considering" (the client need not say he or she "intends" to kill). The states of Indiana, Massachusetts, Michigan, New Hampshire, and Tennessee offer you a choice among responses for protecting a victim, and Alaska and Washington have other requirements and arrangements. This list is not a substitute for knowing your state's rules in detail. Every state with a requirement to warn also protects you from any liability for warning.

## When Do You Have a "Duty to Warn"?

You have a duty to warn, and should reveal the threat of violence, when you have reasonable cause to believe that the patient is dangerous to a specific person. But what are the characteristics of "reasonable cause"?

First, the threat must be toward *a specific and identifiable target*. This must be a particular person, identifiable persons, or sometimes property, rather than a general group or category. The threat may arise through the patient's contemplation of a criminal act; so be attentive to all the consequences of such statements. The threat may also be toward the client's self, as in self-mutilation, suicide, or even self-neglect (such as failing to eat or drinking alcohol to the point of unconsciousness). Second, the threat has to be *believable*. It should be explicit, not vague; motives count, as does history.

In determining whether reasonable cause exists, you must use good judgment, professional skill, and knowledge at levels usually provided by your peers. However, you are "not liable for simple errors made in good faith and with reasonable professional judgment" (Brodsky & Schumacher, 1990, p. 668). You do not need to be a perfect predictor of dangerousness—only to exercise a standard of care that a reasonable member of your discipline, in your local community and in these particular circumstances, would use. Such a professional should have current knowledge in the areas of evaluating dangerousness and violence (the texts by Roth, 1987, and more recently by Eichelman & Hartwig, 1995, provide guidance in these areas). You must "take whatever other steps are reasonably necessary under the circumstances" (*Tarasoff v. Regents*).

## What to Do When You Decide to "Warn"

"Discharging your *Tarasoff* duties" (as the lawyers call it) depends on many factors. You must take "reasonable" and "necessary" steps to protect the potential victim or victims. These will, of course, vary with the circumstances and the local laws, but *may* include the following options. Good sense suggests that you should implement as many of these options as possible, based on local rules and consultation:

- Warning the intended victim.

- Notifying local law enforcement authorities.

- Contacting relatives or others who can apprise the potential victim of the danger.

- Initiating voluntary or involuntary commitment. (This will shift the burden of decision making to the courts.)

- Taking whatever other steps seem appropriate and necessary under the unique circumstances.

- Documenting all your thoughts and efforts.

State laws vary from offering specific steps (reasonable efforts to communicate the threat to victim and police—California, Kentucky, Louisiana), to simply warning the victim (Indiana, Massachusetts, Minnesota). In New Jersey, the therapist must do "any of the following: (1) arranging for the patient to be admitted to a psychiatric facility; (2) initiating procedures for involuntary commitment of the patient; (3) notifying local law enforcement authorities; (4) warning the intended victim; or (5) in the case of a minor who threatens to commit suicide or injury to herself, warning the patient's parents or guardian" (Stromberg, Schneider, & Joondeph, 1993).

We can expect to see more variations on this issue of protecting clients, and at least one deserves mention here: Does the therapist of a patient who is HIV-positive have a duty to warn the patient's partner of the medical risks of sexual activity if the patient refuses to cease the risky behaviors or tell the partner? See Lamb et al. (1989) and the APA's position as stated in Fox (1992). If you find yourself in this situation, do not face it alone; I urge you to obtain local, up-to-date legal and ethical consultation immediately. (See also the end of Section 7.1.) In general, public policy and court decision have indicated that physicians, who are more often in this situation, *may* (but are not required to) inform partners. Kalichman's (1995, 1998) books address many HIV-related issues, and Melchert and Patterson's (1999) and Chenneville's (2000) decision-making models offer much valuable guidance for therapists. Other excellent resources are the four appendices of references in Werth and Carney (1994) concerning ethical, legal, and professional issues; assessment and diagnosis; research design; and counseling diverse populations.

## Suicide

The duty to protect often extends to protecting patients from themselves. Although courts have rarely held therapists responsible for outpatient suicides, this situation is now changing, especially where the situational facts are clear. In general, the therapist is protected by performing the proper professional activities—thorough evaluation, careful consideration, and appropriate interventions. The treatment of a suicidal crisis is beyond the scope of this book. The major references are Bongar et al. (1998) and Blumenthal and Kupfer (1990). Kleespies et al. (1999) provide a superb analysis and set of recommendations for managing suicidal emergencies. The major journal is *Suicide and Life-Threatening Behavior.*

## Family Violence and Abuse

Cervantes (1992) indicates specific steps therapists can take to respond to their ethical and legal responsibilities to protect spouses and children from abuse:

- Developing a safety plan with clients.

- Knowing the legal protections available.

- Assessing for and reporting child abuse.

- Assessing for and reporting cruelty to animals.

The ethics of family therapy in cases of violence are considered by Willbach (1989). The APA's Committee on Professional Practice and Standards (1996) has offered guidance for those who treat abused children.

If you even suspect that a client has either endured or perpetrated abuse, you may have a legal duty to report the situation and an ethical duty to protect the abused person(s) (see Section 7.1). Precautionary measures should include the following:

- Examine all situations coming to your attention that might involve abuse.

- Just as people with hypochondria can get sick, even people with paranoia and people who lie can be victims. Be thorough.

- Keep your assumptions about perpetrators open (people of all classes, races, ages, etc., assault other people). In particular, be alert to your negative reactions to a possible perpetrator. If these continue to interfere with your objectivity, refer the case. Similarly, attend to your rescue fantasies.

- Know in detail, and obey, local laws' requirements about reporting abuse, and prepare your response thoughtfully.

- Get consultation if you are not familiar with the perpetrator's or other family members' personality patterns and choose not to refer.

- Document fully and sensitively the claims, your evaluation, and your actions. Because perpetrators or other family members may pressure abused persons to recant or modify their statements, be certain to record verbatim the information offered to you (about occurrences, circumstances, sequences, etc.).

# 3.11   Assessing a Client's Dangerousness to Self and Others

The preceding section has described, in general, your ethical duty to protect your client and potential victims of his or her violence. This section covers how and when to carry out that obligation. If you have *any* reason to suspect any risk, a comprehensive evaluation of the risks of violence is necessary. Be sensitive to your feelings, which may lead you toward or away from full and accurate assessment. Truscott et al. (1995) offer a summary of the literature and a model for clinical decision making in the outpatient treatment of violent clients; their model is simple and yet comprehensive. The most recent comprehensive reference in violence prediction is Monahan and Stedman's (1994) book. Polythress (1992) addresses testimony.

Here are the steps you should ideally take in dealing with the risk of violence.

## Prepare Ahead of Time

Monahan (1993) urges therapists to become educated in risk assessment, stay current with developments in the field, and be conversant with the laws of their jurisdictions. For example, you should obtain continuing education and otherwise keep up to date on working with spousal abuse.

In addition, indicate the limits of confidentiality in your educational procedures at the beginning of therapy (see Sections 4.2 and 7.1).

## Gather Information to Assess Risk

"Obtain reasonably available records of recent prior treatment and carefully review current treatment records" (Monahan, 1993, p. 243). Note the use of "reasonably"; this is meant to exclude "all possible" records. If a record is very old, if it concerns problems irrelevant to the risks at hand, or if it is likely to be unobtainable, you do not need to obtain it to be seen as acting like a responsible professional. However, it is advisable to obtain any record known to be relevant to violence, and to obtain usual records and read them for violence-related information. In addition, it may be advisable to ask the client for a release to question others who may know of the client's behavior, history, or motives (you can amend Form 47). If the client refuses, document this refusal.

In your deliberations, attend to the client's motivation. Beck (1990, pp. 702–703) suggests asking, "Are you angry at anyone? Are you thinking of hurting anyone?" If the answer is yes, it is important to follow this up with questions about specific thoughts the patient is having; about whom these thoughts are occurring; when, where, and how long these thoughts are occurring; whether the patient is worried about the control of these impulses; and whether the patient has acted on them or come close to acting on them. Bennett et al. (1990) suggest also assessing for beliefs in justified revenge or in the appropriateness or efficacy of violence.

## Evaluate the Risk Factors Present

### The Issue of Suicide

If people are responsible for their own behavior, why are mental health workers held responsible when their patients commit suicide? "Courts often conclude that suicide occurs within the context of 'diminished capacity' or diminished functioning; therefore customary views that patients are responsible for their own behavior do not always apply" (Knapp & VandeCreek, 1983, p. 18). However, courts usually recognize that suicide cannot be well predicted, but "professionals have been held liable when they ignored or failed to assess indicators of suicide" (Knapp & VandeCreek, 1983, p. 18). "Courts usually consider two fundamental issues: (a) did the professional adequately assess the likelihood that a patient was suicidal? and, (b) If an identifiable risk of harm was determined, did the professional take sufficient precautions to prevent suicide?" (Knapp & VandeCreek, 1983, p. 18).

The book by Bongar et al. (1998) is the standard reference on management of suicidality; see also Maltsberger (1986) on assessment. Jobes and Berman (1993) provide a thorough treatment of this area and offer incisive suggestions for managing risk. Their book also provides formats for recording the important issues for both therapists and clients, and some of their ideas have been incorporated into the materials offered here. Barnett and Porter (1998) give another good overview.

The assessment of a client's suicidality must be an ongoing process throughout treatment, because many factors can rapidly raise or lower the chances of a suicide attempt. To perform ethically, you must collect all the relevant information, weigh this information to the best of your ability, and document your conclusions and decisions. You are not expected to predict the future perfectly, only to do your job well. Your assessment can be based most securely on different sources of information and different ways of acquiring it. For example, you can assess known risk factors, which produce a general probability or likelihood of suicide but can't predict the specific likelihood for an individual. The checklist of suicide risk factors (Form 6; see below) facilitates the recording of the most widely recognized risk factors. A second source of information, and obviously most crucial, is your interviewing of the client. Finally, you can integrate all the information you have obtained on the suicide risk assessment summary and recommendations (Form 36). It is designed not only to summarize the risk factors and interview information, but to document your professional judgments about suicide. You may not need to use both of the forms, especially when early indications are that the suicide risk is not great, but they are desirable when the risk appears to be high.

*The Assessment of Suicide Potential: Risk Factor Analysis versus Predictions of Suicide.* Summarizing much research, Hillard (1995) stated that "none of these studies has identified factors that successfully predict suicide by an individual." Why not? The main obstacle is well recognized: Suicide is quite uncommon. Only about 12 in 100,000 persons per year commit suicide in the United States (National Center for Health Statistics, 1988). It is so rare that even a highly accurate test for suicide potential results in unacceptably high levels of false positives (which mean that time and money are wasted in investigating these cases) or false negatives (which mean, tragically, that interventions are not offered when they might help).

Although we can't predict suicide, we can assess risk. Risk factors are those variables that are significantly correlated with suicide, according to grouped data, though they cannot predict individual cases. Using them, we can design levels of intervention appropriate to the level of risk. For example, risk factors of race and sex are significant: 72% of suicides are white males; there are about 20 per 100,000 age-adjusted deaths for males, as opposed to 4.84 for females; nonwhite males make up 7% of all suicides, and nonwhite females 2% (Allen et al., 1994).

*Risk Factors for Suicide among Psychiatric Patients.* Among psychiatric patients, however, the suicide rates are much higher—about 6% on average, and as high as 20% among those with panic disorder (Rudd et al., 1993). These figures indicate that having a psychiatric disorder is a significant risk factor. Bongar (1992) and Hirshfeld and Davidson (1988), summarizing several studies, found the following points relevant:

- A psychiatric history (diagnosis, treatment, hospitalization) increases the risk of completed suicide. Having a psychiatric disorder/diagnosis raises the rate for males 8–10 times; having depression raises the male rate 80–100 times (and severe depression raises it 500 times). Risk is also increased with a diagnosis of schizophrenia or substance abuse. Caldwell and Gottesman (1990) report a lifetime suicide rate of approximately 15% for those with mood disorders (which is over 30 times the rate of the general population), and a rate of 10–13% for those with schizophrenia.

- Having been an inpatient increases risk from 5 to 40 times the risk in the general population.

- In the general population, males have a greater risk for attempts than females by a ratio of about 2.5:1; however, this ratio falls to about 1.5:1 for psychiatric inpatients because of the increase in female suicide completers.

- Older white males are the greatest risk group outside institutions, but the riskiest inpatient age groups are 25–40 for males and 30–50 for females.

- Alcohol use is implicated in increased risk in several ways:

  One in five victims of completed suicide is intoxicated, and many more attempters have used alcohol immediately prior to their attempts.

  Persons with alcohol use disorders are more likely than individuals with other diagnoses to communicate suicidal intent.

  The rate of completed suicide is increased for those with alcohol use disorders if there is a concurrent depressive disorder.

- A history of previous suicide attempts greatly increases the risk for completion, except among those with psychotic disorders, who may offer little or no warning.

- Refusal or inability to cooperate with treatment increases risk.

**FORM 6**

There are a number of other clusters of risk factors for suicide (see Zuckerman, 2000), and many of these have been incorporated into Form 6. Bear in mind that the factors have to be weighted; they change over time; and, of course, they have different meanings for different individuals. Also, remember (1) that low risk never means *no* risk; and (2) that risk factors are not simple predictors, have no established weights in a predictor equation, and must be integrated with other data. Form 6 is only a guide.

The purposes of this form are (1) to evaluate the risk of suicide, (2) to ensure and document the thoroughness of this evaluation for ethical and protective purposes, (3) to reduce the risk of suicide based on this evaluation, and (4) to initiate appropriate treatment of the suicidal client.

More formal assessment measures include scales of suicidal ideation (Beck et al., 1979; Reynolds, 1991), suicidal intent (Beck et al., 1974), and hopelessness (Beck, 1986). There are many other suicide evaluation scales, most with good empirical support. For example, Western Psychological Services (www.wpspublish.com) sells the Suicide Probability Scale (Cull & Gill, 1988), which has 36 questions that map onto four scales—Hopelessness, Suicide Ideation, Negative Self-Evaluation, and Hostility. There are norms for normals, psychiatric patients, and attempters, and it can be hand- or computer-scored. A version of the Reynolds (1991) Suicidal Ideation Questionnaire for adolescents is available from Sigma (www.sigma-assessmentsystems.com). To learn more about interviewing clients who may be at risk for suicide, you might want to read Wollersheim (1974), which offers specific phrasings and guidance for conducting a risk interview. Sommers-Flanagan and Sommers-Flanagan (1995) provide a structured way of asking and recording the relevant information on risk.

*Responding to a Suicidal Crisis.* There is no one foolproof treatment plan to follow in dealing with a suicidal patient, but make certain to act aggressively by implementing the plan you choose. I suggest that you determine *right now* what your referral and support resources are in your community; trying to find them with a crisis on your hands may be too late and is certainly more stressful. Make it a goal for this week to ask all your peers and anyone else who would know about who can help in a suicidal crisis (or any other crisis—violence, abuse, homicide, etc.), and get their exact names and phone numbers.

When you realize that a patient is suicidal, take precautionary measures such as the following:

- Hospitalization.

- Close, repeated, and continuing observation.

- Referral for appropriate services.

- Preventing access to means of self-harm (e.g., letting the patient have only small doses of risky medications, removing guns from the patient's home).

# Checklist of Suicide Risk Factors

Client: _____ Date: _____

The following ratings are based on my:

❑ Review of records (specify): _____

❑ Interview with staff, friends, relatives (circle and name): _____

❑ Observations of this individual over the last ❑ interview ❑ day ❑ week ❑ month

❑ Other (specify): _____

## Demographic risk factors

❑ European American or Native American ❑ Male

❑ Lowest socioeconomic class ❑ Protestant

❑ Suicidal partner ❑ Never-married or widowed status

❑ Divorced status (especially repeated divorce or divorce in last 6 months)

❑ Age: Young adult (15–24) or very elderly (75–85 or older)

❑ Medical, dental, or mental health professional, lawyer, etc.

## Historical risk factors

❑ A relative or close friend who died by suicide ❑ Criminal behaviors

❑ Checking off "suicide" on intake form or other assessments ❑ Self-mutilating behaviors

❑ Substance abuse or dependence ❑ History of abuse (physical, sexual, of long duration, etc.)

❑ Suicidal behaviors: ❑ Multiple threats/attempts of ❑ high lethality ❑ high violence ❑ high pain
❑ Clearly intended death ❑ Secretive attempts ❑ Anniversary attempts

❑ Other risk factors: ❑ Chronic psychiatric problems ❑ Frequent accidents

❑ _____

## Recent specific risk factors

Check applicable boxes and enter a code for time period at the "T: _____" as follows: 24 = within last 24 hours, ds = last few days, w = last 7 days or week, m = last 30 days or month, ms = last few or 2–4 months, y = last 12 months or year.

❑ Had passive death wishes   T: _____ ❑ Experienced fleeting ideation   T: _____

❑ Experienced persistent ideation   T: _____ ❑ Made threats   T: _____

❑ Made gestures   T: _____ ❑ Engaged in actions, rehearsals   T: _____

❑ Made suicide plans that involve a highly lethal method and a time without interruption   T: _____

❑ Made an attempt of ❑ high ❑ medium ❑ low lethality with ❑ high ❑ medium ❑ low potential for rescue   T: _____

❑ Seen recent/relevant media reports   T: _____

*(cont.)*

---

**FORM 6. Checklist of suicide risk factors (p. 1 of 2).**   From *The Paper Office*. Copyright 2003 by Edward L. Zuckerman. Permission to photocopy this form is granted to purchasers of this book for personal use only (see copyright page for details).

❏ Talked with therapist or other staff about suicide intentions/plans   T: ____

❏ Made a clear statement of intent to others   T: ____

❏ Written a suicide note   T: ____

❏ Described a practical/available method or plan   T: ____

❏ Given away an important personal possession   T: ____

❏ Made a will   T: ____

❏ Made funeral arrangements   T: ____

❏ Established access to means/methods   T: ____

❏ Other (specify): _____

## Current psychological risk factors (circle a number)

| | | | | | | | |
|---|---|---|---|---|---|---|---|
| ❏ Hopelessness | Absolutely hopeful | 1 | 2 | 3 | 4 | 5 | Absolutely hopeless |
| ❏ Psychological pain | Little | 1 | 2 | 3 | 4 | 5 | Intolerable |
| ❏ Vegetative symptoms (sleep disturbances, restlessness) | Low | 1 | 2 | 3 | 4 | 5 | High |
| ❏ Agitation, irritability, rages, violence | Low | 1 | 2 | 3 | 4 | 5 | High |
| ❏ Significant stressors (major or irrevocable losses, failures) | Low | 1 | 2 | 3 | 4 | 5 | High |
| ❏ Social support system (nearby friends, therapist, spouse/ partner) | Strong | 1 | 2 | 3 | 4 | 5 | Weak |
| ❏ Cognitive rigidity, poor problem-solving ability | Low | 1 | 2 | 3 | 4 | 5 | High |
| ❏ Actively involved in treatment, progressing | Yes | 1 | 2 | 3 | 4 | 5 | No |
| ❏ Physical illness | Well | 1 | 2 | 3 | 4 | 5 | Sick |
| ❏ Self-regard | Extremely positive | 1 | 2 | 3 | 4 | 5 | Extremely negative |
| ❏ Impulsivity (low self-control, distractibility) | Low | 1 | 2 | 3 | 4 | 5 | High |
| ❏ Depression (blunted emotions, anhedonia, isolation) | Low | 1 | 2 | 3 | 4 | 5 | High |
| ❏ Cognitive disorganization (organic brain syndrome, psychosis, intoxication) | Low | 1 | 2 | 3 | 4 | 5 | High |
| ❏ Other factors (homicidal intent, few/weak deterrents, motivated by revenge): _____ | Low | 1 | 2 | 3 | 4 | 5 | High |
| ❏ _____ | Low | 1 | 2 | 3 | 4 | 5 | High |
| ❏ _____ | Low | 1 | 2 | 3 | 4 | 5 | High |

Additional information on the items checked can be found in/at: _____

## Additional factors for a child or adolescent

❏ Gender:   ❏ Female (more likely to attempt)   ❏ Male (more likely to succeed)

❏ Age above 15   ❏ Rural resident   ❏ Strained family relationships

❏ Other stressors (legal difficulties, unwanted pregnancy, change of school, birth of a sibling, etc.)

Therapist: _____   Supervisor: _____

*This is a strictly confidential patient medical record. Redisclosure or transfer is expressly prohibited by law.*

- Providing backup services when you are unavailable.

- Consultation.

- Reviewing and keeping complete records.

Having collected the information on Form 6, you can use Form 36 to summarize your recommendations and plans for coping with this risk situation.

"No-suicide contracts" have become widely popular, despite the lack of evidence for their reducing suicides (Miller et al., 1998), because they are simple. They have no legal validity and have not protected professionals (Simon, 1999) in suits. In the context of a strong therapeutic relationship, however, proposing open communication about suicidality and restating shared goals and commitments can strengthen the "alliance for safety."

For a suicidal patient who (you believe) understands the issues and is competent to sign, you might consider a written "no-suicide contract" with wording like the following:

> I accept and acknowledge that I am responsible for my own actions. I do want to continue to live and improve my life. If I come to feel and believe that my life situation has become too difficult or painful, I will contact you, _____, my therapist, by phone at _____ or at _____. If I cannot reach you, I will call _____ at _____, or I will go to the emergency department of _____ Hospital.

This should be signed and dated by both of you. The wording should be expanded and tailored to the individual client, and should be subject to ongoing discussion and revision.

### The Risk Factors for Interpersonal Violence

The following variables, according to Monahan (1981) and Beck (1990, p. 702), are associated with increased interpersonal violence:

- Being male.

- Being 16–25 years of age.

- Moving frequently.

- Being unemployed.

- Living or growing up in a violent subculture or family.

- Abusing substances.

- Having lower intelligence.

- Having a history of violence (this is the best indicator)—fighting, hurting others, and violence against animals. Violence against property has to be separately evaluated for motivation and degree of control.

- Having appeared in court for violence, or having had inpatient psychiatric treatment for violence.

- Reporting own acts of violence.

- Committing more severe, recent, and frequent violent acts.

- Having weapons (or other means) available.

- Having identified potential or previous target persons available or accessible.

- Having multiple stressors (which may lessen frustration tolerance).

Obviously, there are no normative weights available for these factors, and they are based on grouped data rather than data on individuals, so use them with circumspection.

## Analyze the Information Gathered

Consider what additional information is needed and obtain the assessments. Examples may include assessments of paranoia or sociopathy, or of membership in a social grouping that condones or promotes violence. Richard E. Jensen, PhD, of St. Charles, IL, helpfully suggests considering all potential problematic behaviors: aggression, arson, elopement, suicide, robbery, property destruction, terroristic threats, and any other situation-specific behaviors. Jensen also suggests attempting, from records or other data, to assess these intervention-relevant factors: the "triggers" of the negative behaviors; the client's compliance with previous treatment and likely compliance with future treatment; and the client's attitude toward therapists, programs, staff, members, and so on.

In addition, assess the client for lessened internal controls. For example, psychosis, paranoid suspiciousness, organic brain syndrome, and substance use can all cause lessened control (Beck, 1990, pp. 702–703). Bennett et al. (1990, p. 66) note that the following may also lower internal controls: a history of impulsiveness or volatile temper; affective illness; beliefs in justified revenge or the appropriateness or efficacy of violence; and medication interactions.

Be alert to threats. If the client makes any threats, Bennett et al. (1990) advise evaluating their purpose. Is a threat real or manipulative? Is it self-justifying or self-protecting, or is it made in order to avoid some other consequence? Be especially alert to threats with specific details. Beck (1990) cautions that mention of time, method, contingency, location, victim, and use of the active voice are all indicators of greater likelihood in a threat.

Get consultation as well. The demonstration of a consensus, especially among professionals of several disciplines, proves that your care did not fall below a reasonable standard. You may need someone's assistance if pharmacotherapy or hospitalization is necessary.

Finally, it may be valuable, but is not generally necessary, to consider other foreseeable victims (such as coworkers) beside those identified by the patient.

## Document the Situation and Your Actions

"Record the source, content, and date of significant information on risk and the content, rationale, and date of all actions to prevent violence" (Monahan, 1993, p. 246). Your notes should show that you "understood the nature of the situation and that reasonable steps were taken in light of the facts" (Fulero, 1988, p. 186). Take full and thoughtful notes about any threat. Quote the patient's statements and answers to your questions; note your conclusions, your course of action, your rationale for choosing this course, and reasons you believe it is better than any other available choice. Your records should show how you thought out the issues in an ongoing way what happened, your evaluation, the options you considered, risk–benefit analyses, your judgments, the patient's involvement, the treatment plan to reduce risk factors, and so on.

## Manage the Risk

Make any environmental manipulations (e.g., removing guns) that may reduce the danger of impulsive actions.

**Before you break confidentiality, weigh the costs against the benefits,** such as protecting a possible target. The costs can include losing the trust of the client or even the opportunity to continue to work with the client and help him or her. Discuss the issues with the client before disclosure. This is rarely unproductive when it is handled as a part of therapy, and harm seems more likely when it is not discussed. Beck (1982) suggests involving the client in warning the potential target. It may even be possible to involve the potential target in the therapy (Knapp, 1994). But be cautious and modest in considering your resources.

This may sound strange, but you should attempt to get a release (see Form 47) to break confidentiality if a serious threat is made. Most violent people are desperate and ambivalent about their aggression, and are still competent to consent. Violent behavior does not, in and of itself, justify breaking confidentiality. In addition, do not break confidentiality when you have only suspicions but no client words or deeds. If you are uncertain, use judgment, consultation, and thorough, honest documentation. Do not act to warn just out of fear of a *Tarasoff* suit.

As an alternative to breaking confidentiality, **consider intensifying the therapy** and documenting the alteration and its rationale. The following are good ideas:

- Increase the frequency of sessions.

- Focus on anger, aggression, controls, consequences, alternatives to violence, and topics that stimulate violent thoughts.

- Pay more attention to minor threats.

- Work with the client to attend to the "triggers" and to change the violent behaviors and risks, but be aware that the client may lie to you about his or her changes.

- Follow up on any lack of compliance with treatment (Monahan, 1993).

- Do anything that will increase the "therapeutic alliance."

In addition, it is wise to **develop various protective interventions**:

- Develop a safety plan for both the potential target and the perpetrator.

- If the spouse is a target, consider couple therapy, but only if safety issues can be addressed and documented.

- Know your community's resources for targets of abuse and violence (shelters, support groups, police, etc.).

- Work with family members who can more closely observe the client.

- Consider hospitalization or police, actions that would serve to incapacitate the client (Monahan, 1993).

- Monahan (1993) also suggests "target hardening," or making the target less vulnerable (by decreasing salience or accessibility, hiring bodyguards, etc.). This is not a therapy area, so get consultation.

- "Communicate information and concerns about violence to the person responsible for making decisions about the patient, and make important items salient" (Monahan, 1993, p. 245).

**Gather your resources now; do not wait for an emergency situation.** In the next few days, collect names, phone numbers, addresses, and any procedural details for contacting the following: police in your and the client's area; psychiatric or other appropriate inpatient facilities; consulting psychiatrists; the local mental health authorities who can authorize hospitalization; lawyers and legal organizations you can consult with; colleagues familiar with the local scene and with the treatment of potentially violent individuals; and any other persons who, or agencies that, may be helpful.

For a specific client, routinely gather information on who is medicating or can medicate him or her; on friends and family members who can intervene, house the client, or separate him or her from potential targets; and on insurance coverage for emergency hospital care and/or other intensive treatment.

It is always possible that the client will not agree to your efforts to reduce the likelihood of violence. In these cases you might consider getting a more specific **waiver of your responsibility** any time a patient refuses to cooperate with an important treatment recommendation (Liberman, 1990). You could create a letter to be signed by the client to the effect that (1) he or she has been fully informed about your treatment recommendations; (2) refusing your specific treatment recommendation(s) may seriously compromise his or her health or have other adverse personal, social, vocational, medical, or other consequences, some of which have been discussed fully with the client and others may be as yet unforeseeable; and (3) the client voluntarily and with full understanding is choosing to refuse or not to cooperate with your recommendation(s). Examples offered by Liberman (1990) include a patient with severe bipolar disorder who refuses or discontinues mood-stabilizing medications; a patient with severe anorexia nervosa who refuses inpatient treatment; and those with signs of serious medical conditions who refuse evaluation, consultation, or treatments.

## Do Damage Control

If violence has occurred, do not make public statements of responsibility, and do not tamper with the record (Monahan, 1993). See Section 3.2.

## Limit Your Personal Vulnerability to Violence

Therapists are as vulnerable to violence as others are. Guy et al. (1992) found that about half of all the psychotherapists they studied had been threatened, harassed, or physically attacked by patients during their careers. These unwanted behaviors and fears included unwanted calls to their offices or homes; threats of malpractice suits; verbal threats against therapists; destruction of the contents of their offices; physical attacks on therapists or on their loved ones; threats against their loved ones; destruction of their homes; and even murder of therapists or their loved ones (Guy et al., 1992).

As a result of such experiences, many therapists have taken protective measures. These include refusing to treat certain clients or to disclose personal data to patients; prohibiting clients from appearing at one's home; relocating one's office to a "safe" building; specifying intolerable patient behaviors; discussing safety issues with loved ones; having no home address listing in the telephone directory; developing contingency plans for summoning help at the office; avoiding working alone in the office; hiring a secretary; terminating a threatening client; obtaining training in management of assaultive behaviors and self-defense for oneself and one's loved ones, installing a home security alarm system, developing a contingency plan for family members if a client appears at the home; avoiding solo practice; installing an office alarm system (you can add a hand-held remote control "panic button" to such a system at small cost—keeping this in public display as well as reach makes good sense); keeping a weapon at home and/or at the office; hiring a security guard; and other measures (Guy et al., 1992). It may be in your best interest to consider each of these for yourself and implement some of them today, before trouble strikes.

# 3.12 Ethical and Legal Issues in Working with Managed Care Organizations

Managed health care is pervasive, multifaceted, and evolving. Originally designed primarily to increase access and quality, and secondarily to control costs, it has done neither while deconstructing a world-class American enterprise—health care. Mental health has suffered disproportionately, in that no distinctions have been made between inpatient services (high cost and lesser effectiveness) and outpatient services (lower immediate and long-term costs with more effectiveness for almost all conditions).

The impacts of managed care on mental health services are complex, and they are addressed in detail in this section. The issues include ethical conflicts, the complexities of contracting with MCOs,[3] threats to confidentiality, dealing with MCO reviewers and restrictions on treat-

---

[3]As noted in Chapter 2 (see footnote 2 there), "MCOs" is used here as a blanket term for all similar organizations, such as preferred provider organizations (PPOs) and health maintenance organizations (HMOs).

ment, maintaining continuity of care, and the administrative burdens of treating MCO patients.

## Conflicts and Concerns

Working in an MCO environment raises ethical conflicts, some of which are no doubt familiar to you:

- Your loyalties can often be divided between your patient's needs and those of the controller of funding that employs you (the MCO). Neither you nor your patient chose the MCO (the patient's employer did), and yet you are under contract to the MCO.

- Decisions about care are often based on cost control (and reduction), and not on quality of services, long-term client benefits, the research on treatment's effectiveness, or your or your client's informed preferences. Thus you may be pressured to provide care you know (or should know) to be inadequate.

- You may be induced to treat problems and diagnoses beyond your expertise in order to prevent the costs of referral to more expensive specialists, inside or outside the "network of providers."

- Your client has essentially no confidentiality. You must either omit information from your records (which you may later need to demonstrate your thoughtful decision making if you are complained against or sued), or force the client to trust the MCO (which does not operate by your ethical standards or any other recognized, legal, or enforceable code of ethics). See below for more specifics.

- If you are not a psychiatrist, you should explain to clients that their MCO will very often require them to see a psychiatrist for medication evaluations (and almost always prescriptions), no matter what the clients or you believe is best. Noncooperation with this will lead to non-authorization for your payment and their care.

Miller (1998), in just a few downloadable pages (at http://www.nomanagedcare.org/eleven.html), offers more information on these and other ethical lapses from a client's point of view; I consider it essential reading. Because these concerns must be described to potential clients before treatment begins (in order to obtain their informed consent to treatment), Handout 3 is provided at the end of this section for the purposes of patient education. The following discussion covers these and other practical ethical issues that arise in working with an MCO.

A set of links to resources for dealing with HMOs and other forms of managed care can be found at http://www.americanmentalhealth.com/indexp.tpl.

## Joining an MCO Panel

If you wish to be paid by an MCO for providing clinical services to the employees (and their families) of companies that have hired the MCO, look in the Yellow Pages under "Health Maintenance Organizations" or contact the national offices of the handful of major

MCOs. Call their provider relations numbers and ask for the application materials you will need to join their "panels" of approved "providers."[4] You will find that almost all MCOs have full panels of providers and are not interested in your applying, unless you have a specialty they want or are located in an underserved area (yet with many "covered lives" living there). Before you apply, consider that MCOs generally will not accept onto their panels, or will simply not make referrals to, those who practice styles of therapy they disapprove of. MCOs that seek you out and ask you to join their panels are likely to be setting up a "network of providers" before bidding on employers' MCO contracts. The panel application paperwork is very detailed and time-consuming, as is the often yearly "recredentialing" process. Try to use a name with a first letter that is early in the alphabet, as MCO staff members usually go down an alphabetical list when making referring phone calls. Never pay a fee to join a panel or to be recertified—a sure sign of a weak company. You may find some MCO criteria burdensome such as completing clinical evaluations and the paperwork for "initial certification for treatment" within a day or two, or being able to see referred clients "immediately." MCO staffers have been known to make calls to clinicians presenting themselves as patients and asking to be seen as soon as possible, to check on your compliance with the latter point.

## Complexities in Your Contract with the MCO

*You must understand every part of the contract you sign.* This may seem obvious, but you will need to do repeated readings, as well as obtain the assistance of peer consultation and your lawyer to grasp the implications of the contract's language (see Stout et al., 2001, for an introduction to the language of MCOs). Here are some examples:

- Do not assume that you are offered the identical contract other psychologists have been offered in your area, or that this year's is identical with the one you signed last year. Note that "evergreen renewals" allow an MCO to renew your contract without any negotiation on your part.

- Read not only the contract but all of its "attachments," such as the provider manuals in which more obligations and responsibilities are spelled out. These are in "incorporation by reference" statements.

- Understand the ways you are assuming risks by agreeing to "withholds" (payments for your services that are not paid to you unless you provide services the way the MCO wishes); "case rates" (in which you are paid a flat rate for a specific diagnosis regardless of a client's needs, and if these needs exceed the number of sessions agreed to, you will have to provide unpaid extra sessions); or "capitation" (in which you receive a flat payment, the "per member per month" [PMPM] payment, to provide all the services a client needs). A full discussion of capitation is beyond this book and beyond solo practitioners, but variations of all three of these types of payment will be offered to therapists.

---

[4]You did go to "provider" school, didn't you? The entire language of managed care is that of a business model like manufacturing (with completely interchangeable parts). Although this model has been successful in many areas of American life, it seems completely inappropriate for providing health care, especially for chronic or relapsing conditions.

- An indemnification or "hold harmless" agreement states that if the MCO is sued by a patient for the actions of the provider, then the provider cannot hold the MCO responsible in any way for the outcome. Generally, your insurance will cover your actions and those of any employees you have included in your insurance application, but not the actions of your nonemployees. Common sense would indicate that you should avoid signing an indemnification agreement that holds you responsible for the acts of nonemployees.

- Beware of "noncompete" or "exclusivity" clauses, which prevent you from having business relationships with competing programs, even after you have left the first MCO.

- "No-disparagement"and "gag" clauses prevent you from criticizing the MCO, discussing treatment options that the MCO won't pay for, mentioning financial incentives given to you or other providers, criticizing adverse decisions made by the MCO, or the like. These limit your ability to practice as you believe best, advocate for your client, and appeal a denial of payment. These"gag" rules may be disappearing because of new laws, but do read your MCO contracts carefully. The risk to you is that you may be sued or complained against for failure to treat properly when you knew or should have known that a different kind of service was needed, and yet you could not recommend or refer for it because of your MCO contract. You are still responsible for your client's care.

- "Termination without cause" provisions allow an MCO to remove you from its panels with 60 or 90 days' notice for any reason. Of course, this could be a financial disaster to you, would limit the continuity of your care, and might not be in the client's best interest. Best would be allowing only termination with a list of specified causes, but also ask about the MCO's appeals process for these types of termination, and try to make them work both ways.

- "Severability" clauses keep the rest of the contract binding, even if one part is declared illegal or unenforceable.

- Examine the billing parts to evaluate your ability to do "balance billing" (see Section 2.7). Also evaluate the time and effort costs to you of utilization review, authorization-concurrent and retrospective reviews, and the appeal mechanisms. For example, in a retrospective review, if the MCO, after examining closed and paid-for cases, decides that you should not have treated the clients, it will expect you to return the money it paid to you.

## Beginning to See MCO Clients

Clients will call their MCO and the MCO staff will refer them to you (and probably several other providers), or clients will call you because they see your name in the MCO's pamphlet of providers' names. Those referred by the MCO have had a session or two "preauthorized," but before you see self-referred clients, you must obtain preauthorization for being paid for the MCO. This will involve at least one phone call to "certify or verify their benefits"—that is, to determine whether the mental health services they are seeking are currently covered by a particular MCO contract. After meeting a self-referred client you will have to complete and submit an assessment and treatment plan, often called an "initial treatment plan" or "individualized treatment plan" (see Form 38), with a great deal of information on the client's history and functioning. An MCO typically requires a clinician to provide a diagnosis, treatment plan, evaluation of the patient's level of performing activities of daily living, assessment of substance use/abuse, and evaluation of the lethality of any suicidal plans, so that the "medical necessity" (see below) of treatment may be determined. It is not uncommon for MCOs to take weeks to decide to accept (or even refuse) your proposed treatment plan, during which time you may suffer financial hardship and your client emotional hardship. If your proposed treatment is acceptable to the MCO, you will have a small number of visits "authorized." Before these are used up, you must decide whether your client will need more treatment; if so, you must submit an "outpatient treatment report" (OTR), which is a kind of progress note on how the client is functioning and a revised treatment plan. Generally, you must indicate progress toward treatment goals for the authorization of further services. Because you ethically may not lie about levels of function, treatment may be denied to those who could benefit from it but who are not severely incapacitated.

After you begin seeing clients (which may not be soon—most clinicians receive only a few referrals per year), the MCO will start a "profile" on how many sessions you typically use per case (and perhaps how frequently you see clients); how much difficulty you cause the MCO when seeking authorization for services; and how you meet many other undisclosed criteria. This profile will be used to decide whether or not to offer you referrals and "recredentialing."

Lastly, despite your timely submission of forms and information to the MCO, there may be extensive delays (1) before decisions are made and (2) before payment is received by you, even after authorization. The first type of delay places you and your client in anxious limbo, and the second is solely your burden.

## Initial Discussions with the Client about MCO-Related Ethical Issues

Securing informed consent involves discussion with any potential client prior to treatment about its risks and benefits (see Chapter 4). Managed care brings additional risks beyond the clinical ones, such as those concerning confidentiality and continuity of care. Having a client read and review an OTR form will make more concrete and believable the information sought by MCOs and the concerns you raise in your discussion. The form will also be a stimulus for the client to weigh the use of MCO benefits. Examples can be found at www.valueoptions.com/provider/forms/outpatienttreatment(11).pdf and at www.magellanprovider.com/HnbkAppxA/appa_trrtool.pdf.

### Confidentiality

The lack of confidentiality in managed care treatment has received wide publicity, but the potential client must be informed in advance of the specific implications for mental health treatment, to give him or her the ability to refuse such treatment.

When MCO staff members refer a patient, they expect the therapist to provide them with a diagnosis, treatment plan, and a great deal of information on the patient's life functioning.

The MCO's reviewers then assess the "medical necessity" (see below) for treatment before its authorization. Because this process requires the gathering of much detailed information in many areas of life, it can be intrusive. Appelbaum (1993) notes that you must disclose to the patient the "nature and extent of information that may have to be released to managed care reviewers" (p. 254), as well as the lack of ethical and legal limitations on the disclosure of this information within the MCO and possibly the client's employer. Similar sensitive information will be regularly required for treatment reauthorizations, internal reviews, and in-your-office reviews. The fate of this information and its consequences for the client are almost always uncertain.

This information is often transferred to the MCO by fax or electronic methods, which do not necessarily have the same legal and technical privacy protections as paper reports. When the information has left the therapist's office, there are few legal constraints and no effective ethical constraints on what happens to it. In addition, the training and skills of the MCO personnel receiving and evaluating this information are uncertain. These people are not controlled by the laws and ethics that apply to licensed psychotherapists. Reviewers are not (at least at the initial levels) mental health professionals; even at higher levels, they may not be clinicians or therapists. Only a few MCOs require even a professional of your discipline to review your treatment. Given these factors, I advise the following:

- You should have a more detailed discussion with the client of the issues described here, have the client read Handout 3, and get a more specific release-of-information form signed (you can use Form 47) before talking to an MCO reviewer.

- You should discuss with the client the probable consequences of releasing this information to the MCO, where it will become part of a permanent medical record.[5] It is likely that this record will be accessible to many other organizations over time, such as when the client applies for health or life insurance, security clearances, mortgage loans, or jobs. Of course, this information will not be shared for these purposes without the client's permission. The issue here is that once recorded, it *must* be disclosed, or the client will have to forgo ordinary opportunities like getting a job or a mortgage. Such honest discussion may or may not lessen the tendency of clients to be forthcoming and self-disclosing when advised of an MCO's confidentiality rules (Kremer & Gesten, 1998).

- Releasing detailed information may be countertherapeutic with some borderline or paranoid patients. You should decide what to do and may have to forgo MCO payments with these patients.

### Informing the Client about MCO Coverage, Benefits, and Limitations on Treatment

Clients must be informed of the limits of the benefits available to them under their MCO coverage. This should include both the written limits and your own experience of the services frequently authorized (which are nearly always less than optimal). They should be

---

[5]Consider the following. The Medical Information Bureau is the most likely repository, but the information is not in your words or in a narrative format. It is coded and simplified for the use of insurers, and thus open to distortion. When MCOs and similar organizations merge, their data systems must merge too, and so data may be distorted. When mental health data are recorded in medical data bases, the level of confidentiality may be lowered to that of the medical data.

fully informed about the limitations on from whom they can receive treatment without having to pay more out of pocket.

- The client must accept the MCO's intention to pay only for treatment to return the client to baseline levels of functioning. When this has happened, you and the client must renegotiate your contract, including goals, methods, and payment for further services.

- MCOs tend to approve only very brief treatment, which may not be clinically appropriate for all patients. Their present and apparently universal philosophy of treatment is that briefer is better. In the experience of many clinicians, this seems to prevail no matter what the diagnosis, history, or need, but I have seen no good data on this point. MCOs' definition of "brief" is often too short (6–10 sessions) to be effective for many diagnoses, according to the literature (which suggests 20–30 sessions for effectiveness with anxiety disorders and depression). Yet MCO personnel themselves have little or no valid research support for requiring brief therapy (see Miller, 1998). Because they are usually not clinicians, they are not your consultants or your supervisors, and therefor legally unable to offer direction for treatment. (However, as you will see in Form 38, it is often useful for later discussion to record their comments and suggestions.)

- MCOs restrict the range of clinicians a client may see to those on their approved "panel" of providers. MCOs represent to employers and their "covered lives" that these providers are highly qualified and so raise the quality of care provided. They are certainly clinicians who accept MCOs' lower-than-customary fees and possess some minimal credentials, but this says nothing about the appropriateness or quality of care delivered.

- A few MCOs will pay a great deal less for treatment by providers not on one of their panels, but most MCOs will pay nothing for such "out-of-network"services.

- A client's insurance coverage and MCO may change during your treatment; reviewers and other staff members at the MCO may give you inaccurate information; or they may later deny payment for previously authorized service ("retroactive denials")—all of which change the true costs of treatment for the client. The client should be informed of these possibilities and, in your experience, their likelihood.

## Verification of Coverage

An MCO will not authorize an "episode of treatment" (your services) unless a client's policy specifically covers the particular services (defined by *Current Procedural Terminology* [CPT] codes) and, of course, the MCO believes the services to be "medically necessary" (discussed later in this section). Most clients are woefully uninformed or misinformed about their actual coverage, and so you must decide first whether you or they will make the arduous calls to the MCO. Clients are also not in the best position to learn the intricacies of behavioral health insurance when they come for help, and many simply give up (which MCOs apparently count on). You or your staff are usually better motivated, informed, and persistent, and your clients will be grateful for your relieving them of this burden. The questions in Form 7 address all the variables in MCO policies (as well as of indemnity insurance policies) of which I am currently aware. When you are calling to ask about excluded diagnoses or other issues, try to ask about several, even if not all of them

**FORM 7**

## Questionnaire for Determining Behavioral Health Insurance Benefits

Try to get an answer to each question, and make longer notes if you need to, so you can be clear about the coverage. You will need to have this information before you call:

Patient's name: _____

Patient's date of birth: _____ Patient's ID/SS #: _____

Policy holder's name (if different from patient): _____

Policy holder's date of birth: _____ Policy holder's ID/SS #:_____

Policy holder's employer: _____

Address of policy holder's employer: _____

Name of MCO or other insurer: _____

Policy #: _____ Group #: _____ Renewal date: _____

Name of any behavioral health subcontractor: _____

| Phone # | Buttons or prompts | Date(s) called | Name(s) of representative(s) spoken with |
|---|---|---|---|
|  |  |  |  |
|  |  |  |  |

1. Is this specific patient covered under this policy? ❑ Yes ❑ No

2. Are services for treating "mental and nervous disorders" covered? ❑ Yes ❑ No

   Are services for treating "drug and alcohol disorders" covered? ❑ Yes ❑ No

3. Is "outpatient psychotherapy"or "outpatient mental health/behavioral health treatment" for these disorders covered? ❑ Yes ❑ No

4. Will the insurance pay for these kinds of treatment?

   Individual psychotherapy ❑ Yes ❑ No

   Family therapy ❑ Yes ❑ No

   Psychological testing ❑ Yes ❑ No

*(cont.)*

**FORM 7. Behavioral health insurance benefits questionnaire.** From *The Paper Office*. Copyright 2003 by Edward L. Zuckerman. Permission to photocopy this handout is granted to purchasers of this book for personal use only (see copyright page for details).

Drug and alcohol treatment     ❏ Yes    ❏ No

Medication prescription and monitoring     ❏ Yes    ❏ No

❏ Other: _____

5. Does the insurance company require either DSM or ICD diagnoses, or both, or neither? (Circle)

6. Are services provided by a licensed psychologist, social worker, or other mental health professional covered?

    a. Are additional credentials required?     ❏ No    ❏ Yes
      (If yes, which? _____)

    b. Is referral by a physician required?     ❏ No    ❏ Yes

    c. Is supervision by a physician required?     ❏ No    ❏ Yes

    d. Is consultation with a physician required?     ❏ No    ❏ Yes

7. Is this therapist a "participating" or an "eligible" provider under this particular insurance plan?     ❏ Yes    ❏ No

8. Is there an exclusion for "preexisting" conditions? Are these present in this case?

9. Are there excluded diagnoses? (Ask about ADHD and learning disorders, ODD, borderline personality disorder, conduct disorder, chronic pain, or others as relevant.)

10. Is there a "copayment" that the client must pay for each treatment session?     ❏ No    ❏ Yes
     (If yes, how is it calculated? _____)

11. Is there a deductible that must be paid by the patient before the insurance company    ❏ No    ❏ Yes
     will pay anything?       (If yes, how much is it? $ _____)

     Is this deductible per year, per calendar year, per person/client, per family, per diagnosis (underline which) or some combination of these? _____

12. Will the insurer pay the entire amount of allowable charges (after the deductible) for    ❏ No reduction
     mental health services, or does it reduce the coverage for mental health services?    ❏ Yes
                               (If yes, how much? $____ or ____%)

13. Is there a limit on the amount the insurance will pay for mental health services in a year    ❏ No    ❏ Yes
     or a lifetime? (If yes, $____ per year and/or $____ in lifetime. How much of this remains available? $____)

*(cont.)*

14. Is there a limit on the number of visits/sessions per year or by diagnosis?　　❑ No

　　❑ Yes, _____ per year.　　❑ Yes, by diagnosis: _____

15. If the spouse, the parents of a child patient, or the whole family is seen are these visits　❑ No　❑ Yes
covered differently than visits of the patient alone?　(If yes, how? _____)

16. Will the policy pay for sessions longer than 1 hour?　　❑ Yes　❑ No

17. If we must meet for two sessions on a single date, will insurance pay for it or for　　❑ Double
only a single session per day?　　❑ Only one session

18. Will insurance pay for more than one session per week?　　❑ No

　　❑ Yes, but only _____ sessions per week　❑ Yes, as decided by the professional

19. Coordination of benefits: What rules apply if more than one insurance company is providing coverage for this patient and claims are submitted to both companies? (Which has priority?)

20. Are there any other rules, requirements, forms, or procedures that we should be aware of?

21. Authorized treatment: _____

Starting date: _____　Number of sessions: _____　Dollar limit: _____

Authorization renewal date: _____

22. Where are claims forms to be sent?

are appropriate for the client you are calling about. This is both for your information and for confidentiality purposes, so that an MCO staffer cannot associate a particular client with a particular condition. If you wish to have clients gather this information, you can give them Form 27 (the financial information form) instead of Form 7.

## Dealing with MCO Reviewers

MCOs "micromanage" therapy by requiring frequent, detailed telephone consultations with their "care coordinators" or reviewers and submission of OTR forms in order for you to receive reauthorization for a small number of continuing treatment sessions. There are exceptions to this, but it is still the most common procedure. To protect yourself against MCO disorganization, mistakes, and deceit, the late John Roraback, PhD, of Moline, IL, suggested that clinicians tape-record their calls to MCO reviewers. If you decide to do so, perhaps notify the MCO in a tactfully worded letter. Obviously, these approaches would be seen as hostile by the MCO, but they would serve to protect you in cases of legal actions over adverse consequences to a patient, so you might be selective. Make certain you receive and keep the written authorization from the MCO for every client and "episode of treatment."

From the other side, the guidelines below are from Bruce Barrett, MA, CPT, of Duxbury, MA, who was a medical reviewer. They are reproduced with his kind permission.

1. Always assume that reviewers really do have patients' interests in mind. They really believe that short-term treatment in the least restrictive setting works best, and that they have the research studies to support their position. They also see the money being spent as the patients' money (which it is—it's part of the compensation package at their employment).

2. Don't confuse a life threatening diagnosis with a life threatening patient status. For example, bulimia nervosa is a life-threatening disorder, but a patient with bulimia nervosa may not be currently in a life-threatening status. You'll need to document the current facts to show that the patient's present condition warrants the treatment you're planning now.

3. Failure in outpatient treatment is often necessary before inpatient treatment will be approved. Documenting patient behavior that shows this failure (rather than therapists' impression, feelings, or anticipations, accurate as they may be) is what reviewers look for.

4. Make sure you really do what you tell a reviewer a patient really needs. You remember your reviewers—they remember you, too, and they keep notes.

5. Be ready to appeal decisions of payment denial. It may be that your patient has to do this, but you can help by knowing the procedure. Insurance companies have higher-skilled professionals to review denials and appealed claims, although in my experience the first-line reviewers are pretty sharp, too. Overturned denials are typically the result of clearer documentation of the need for treatment.

6. Don't bother trying to get or keep the patient in the hospital because you or some other key treater is away, busy, on vacation, or sick. Hospitals don't charge your pa-

tient's health care treasury less for the slow weekends, so discharge on Friday, not Monday.

7. Learn the criteria for admission, continued stay, and the various other levels of treatment (partial hospitalization, outpatient care, etc.) for the various conditions you treat. Learn them as well as you would if you were a reviewer, or a consultant to an insurance company. Then learn (from the reviewers, if possible) what manner of documentation—what type and quality of case facts—they use to make their decisions.

8. Rely on objective and behavioral data in your case notes. "Spouse reports patient binged and purged three times in last 24 hours" is much more useful than "This patient is getting worse and needs an inpatient stay." Patient self-report helps, too, even when there is clear evidence of denial (e.g., "Patient reports feeling better than ever, despite relapse of purging").

9. Denial and other forms of patient-based unreadiness for treatment can be tricky, but reviewers know that, too. Showing evidence that a patient's degree of denial is colossal, and might be broken through with intensive (inpatient or partial hospitalization) treatment, can be impressive to a reviewer.

10. Make sure it all fits together—diagnosis, need for treatment (patient condition), intensity of treatment planned, and intensity of treatment delivered. Hyperbole in the need for treatment, when coupled with routine scheduling of appointments (or even scheduled gaps in treatment), stands out like a sore thumb. A life-or-death patient condition calls for urgent action and timing from the therapist.

## Continuity of Care Concerns

As soon as you accept patients, you have a duty to provide high-quality care until you discharge them. But, because of MCOs' limitations on treatment you are likely to have patients for whom MCOs refuse to authorize more treatment but who are not ready for discharge. Therapists have the ethical obligation—and may, under managed care, have a contractual obligation—to continue to treat patients whose benefits become unavailable or exhausted. There are three other aspects of maintaining continuity of care.

First, "If managed care refuses payment, you are legally required *at least* [to] (1) provide clinically necessary *emergency* services regardless of payment" (Stromberg & Dellinger, 1993, p. 13; emphasis added). You cannot abandon a patient in crisis, regardless of the financial situation.

Second, a therapist has the additional obligation to appeal an MCO's decisions to deny services that the clinician has recommended. If your client could benefit from more treatment but is not severely incapacitated, authorization may be denied, and ethically you may not falsify levels of functioning. Appelbaum (1993, p. 254) notes the "possibility that payment for therapy might be terminated before either the patient or the clinician believes that the goals of treatment have been achieved." If the client continues to need care, in the clinician's opinion, the clinician must appeal the MCO's decision. Note, however, that this process is entirely under the auspices of the MCO, which makes all the rules. Appelbaum (1993) says, "At a minimum, a clinician whose patient has been denied payment for care that he or she believe is indicated, may have an ethical obligation to contest, on the patient's behalf, the decision of the managed care entity" (p. 253). Stromberg and Dellinger (1993) make this point even more strongly: "If managed care refuses payment, you are legally required [to] (2) energetically seek approval for additional services the patient genuinely needs" (p. 13). The clinician should make some effort at the initial appeal level. A decision on whether to continue to secondary levels of appeal needs to be made after "consultation with the patient, taking into consideration the likelihood of success, whether the patient still desires to proceed with treatment, and the availability of alternative means of paying for care" (Appelbaum, 1993, p. 253).

Third, since an appeal is rarely successful, alternative treatment resources must be considered:. You should ask yourself and the client:

- Can the client afford to obtain care from an out-of-network provider at higher cost?

- Can the client pay out of pocket for your therapy?

- Is the client willing to proceed with your therapy during the appeals process, risking being held responsible for the charges accrued in the interim?

- Are there free or less expensive alternative sources of care to which the client can be referred, if you find them competent to treat, and the client finds this referral acceptable?

- Are you willing to continue your care at a reduced rate or without payment?

- Are you willing to terminate the client?

However, read your MCO contract carefully. It may in fact require you to discharge the patient. Or it may require you to continue to treat the patient after benefits are exhausted, if he or she still needs treatment; it may even prevent you from charging the patient for this treatment.

## Educating Clients about Managed Care

HANDOUT 3

Handout 3 is designed to inform clients of the practical, financial, legal, and ethical implications of managed care. Before using it, read and decide whether it is accurate for your location, contracts, profession and experience. For example, if a patients' bill of rights is passed in your state or nationally, or the Health Insurance Portability and Accountability Act (HIPAA) rules (see http://www.ahrq.gov/data/hipaa1.htm) are being applied, or your state has legal precedents like the *Jaffee v. Redmond* (518 U.S. 1, 1996) case (see http://www.psa-uny.org/jr/and DeBell & Jones, 1997), you should modify the statements about confidentiality in this form. Some sentences that are highly critical of managed care are offered in italics, and you might choose to delete them if your practice is dependent on MCO. The next-to-last paragraph offers clients the possibility of paying you directly and thus not creating any records outside your office; this may not be allowed under your MCO contracts when the MCO has made the referral and "covers" a client's life. A few sentences are adapted from Higuchi (1994), who provides a good review of the legal issues. I must thank Jackson Rainer, PhD, of Norcross, GA, and Charles H. Steinmeyer, PhD, of Warren, PA, for improving this section and handout through their reviews.

## What You Should Know about Managed Care and Your Treatment

Your health insurance may pay part of the costs of your treatment, but the benefits cannot be paid until a managed care organization (MCO) authorizes this (says they can be paid). The MCO has been selected by your employer, not by you or me. The MCO sets some limits on us, and you need to know what these are before we go further.

### Confidentiality

If you use your health insurance to help pay for psychotherapy, you must allow me to tell the MCO about your problem (give it a psychiatric diagnosis). You must also permit me to tell the MCO about the treatment I am recommending, about your progress during treatment, and about how you are doing in many areas of your life (functions at work, in your family, and in activities of daily living). I am not paid separately for collecting, organizing, or submitting this information, and I cannot bill you for these services. All of this information will become part of the MCO's records, and it will be included in your permanent medical record at the Medical Information Bureau, a national data bank. The information will be examined when you apply for life or health insurance, and it may be considered when you apply for employment, credit or loans, a security clearance, or other things in the future. You will have to indicate that you were treated for a psychological condition and release this information, or you may not get the insurance, job, loan, or clearance.

All insurance carriers claim to keep the information they receive confidential, and there are federal laws about its release. The laws and ethics that apply to me are much stricter than the rules that apply at present to MCOs. *There have been reports in the media about many significant and damaging breaches of confidentiality by MCOs.* If you are concerned about who might see your records now or in the future, we should discuss this issue more fully before we start treatment and before I send the MCO any information. You should evaluate your situation carefully in regard to confidentiality. For some people and some problems, the privacy of their communications to their therapist is absolutely essential to their work on their difficulties. For others, their problems are not ones that raise much concern over confidentiality.

### Treatment

The MCO will review the information I send it and then decide how much treatment I can provide to you. *The MCO can refuse to pay for any of your treatment, or for any treatment by me. Or it may pay only a very small part of the treatment's cost, and it can prevent me from charging you directly for treatment we agree to.* Finally, it can set limits on the kinds of treatments I can provide to you. These limited treatments may not be the most appropriate for you or in your best interest. The MCO will approve treatment aimed at improving the specific symptoms (behaviors, feelings) that brought you into therapy, but it may not approve any further treatment. The MCO will almost always require you to see a psychiatrist for medication evaluations (and prescriptions), *whether you or I think this is appropriate.*

*(cont.)*

**HANDOUT 3. Patient handout for education about/informed consent to managed care (p. 1 of 2).** From *The Paper Office.* Copyright 2003 by Edward L. Zuckerman. Permission to photocopy this handout is granted to purchasers of this book for personal use only (see copyright page for details).

When it does authorize our treatment, the MCO is likely to limit the number of times we can meet. Your insurance policy probably has a maximum number of appointments allowed for outpatient psychotherapy (usually per year, though there may be a lifetime limit as well), but the MCO does not have to let you use all of those. It may not agree to more sessions, even if I believe those are needed to fully relieve your problems, or if I believe that undertreating your problems may prolong your distress or lead to relapses (worsening or backsliding).

If the MCO denies payment before either of us is satisfied about our progress, we may also need to consider other treatment choices, and they may not be the ones we would prefer. We can appeal the MCO's decisions on payment and number of sessions, but we can only do so within the MCO itself. We cannot appeal to other professionals, to your employer, or through the courts. This state does not have laws regulating MCOs —that is, laws about the skills or qualifications of their staff members, about access to medical and psychological records by employers and others, or about the appeals process.

You should know that my contract or your employer's contract with a particular MCO prevent us from taking legal actions against the MCO if things go badly because of its decision. *My contract may prevent me from discussing with you treatment options for which the MCO will not pay.* I will discuss with you any efforts the MCO makes to get me to limit your care in any way.

The particular MCO in charge of your mental health benefits can change during the course of your treatment. If this happens, we may have to go through the whole treatment authorization process again. It is also possible that the benefits or coverage for your treatment may change during the course of our therapy, and so your part of costs for treatment may change.

Lastly, even if we send all the forms and information to the MCO on time, there may be long delays before any decisions are made. This creates stressful uncertainty and may alter our earlier assumptions about the costs and nature of your treatment.

## Our Agreement

If, after reading this and discussing it with me, you are concerned with these issues, you may have the choice of paying me directly and not using your health insurance. This will create no record outside of my files. This possibility depends on my contract with the MCO.

I have read and understood the issues described above and willingly enter treatment accepting these limits. I give my therapist permission to submit information in order to secure payment for the mental health services to be provided to me.

❏ Yes, I want to review and/or receive copies of any written materials you send to my MCO.

❏ No, that is not necessary.

| | | |
|---|---|---|
| Signature of client | Printed name of client | Date |

If you have a managed care arrangement that involves capitation[6] (payments to you by the MCO of a fixed amount—the PMPM rate—to provide for all the mental health needs of the "covered lives") or a case rate system (in which you are paid a lump sum per case, usually regardless of diagnosis, and no matter what kinds of care the client needs), you should disclose this to all new clients. Why? Because these arrangements, just like MCOs' excessive paperwork, use of "medical necessity" criteria, limited or even "phantom" panels of providers, and other cost controls, serve to constrain and ration the care available (Miller, 1998), and clients should be informed of these limitations to be able to consent to enter treatment. For example, Rosenthal (2000) found that case rate payments resulted in reduction of numbers of sessions by 20–25%, compared to sessions for clients seen on a fee-for-service basis (payments for each session).

## The Concept of "Medically Necessary" Care

"Medical necessity" is a concept created by MCOs and has no history or basis in economics, insurance, medicine, psychiatry, or psychology. It was based on the belief that services were being overused (i.e., treatment was being provided when it was not necessary), and that this was the cause of the great increases in health care costs in the 1970s. (More recent research has called this into question.) MCOs sold employers the idea that they could substantially reduce health care costs by limiting care to "medically necessary" services. The concept is used to control access to different kinds of services by the MCOs. For about a decade, health care costs to employers did indeed grow more slowly or level off. Providers, especially hospitals, were paid a lot less, and MCOs made huge profits. Cost cutting peaked in the early 1990s, and so did the profits of MCOs and similar arrangements.

However, "medical necessity" is still universally used to control payments to providers. The criteria for "medical necessity" vary among disorders and also across MCOs; are considered business secrets and so are not publicly available; and have never been subjected to empirical evaluation. The MCO reviewers' opinions of what is "medically necessary" care will be based on their training in the MCO and is unlikely to match your professional views or your clients' expectations of kind or duration of treatment.

**FORM 8**    Form 8, a medical-necessity-for-psychotherapy checklist, is modified from one by Allan J. Comeau, PhD, of West Los Angeles, CA, and is used with his kind permission. It was designed to improve documentation to third-party payers and to assist with thinking through decisions about continuing or reducing/ending treatment. Because MCOs use the criterion of "medical necessity," in dealing with their reviewers it may be advantageous to discuss a case from this perspective. Presumably a reviewer will have a good deal of clinical information at hand, and this form summarizes your conclusions and (ideally) will lead the reviewer to see the case in the way you indicate.

## Coping with Administrative Burden, Fees, and Payments

MCOs have been able to shift the administrative burdens of insuring clients to clinicians. A provider now has to determine whether a potential client has current coverage for the proposed services; determine whether a required referral from the client's primary care physi-

---

[6]From, perhaps, either the German *Kaput* for "finished and done," or the Latin, as in "to capitulate" or "decapitation."

## Checklist for Determining Medical Necessity for Psychotherapy

Patient:_____ Identification number: _____

Based upon my ongoing assessment, the above-named patient requires continued psychotherapy and or psychotherapeutic case management for the following reasons:

❏ This patient has a history of regression to a lower level of functioning without ongoing psychotherapy services.

❏ This patient has improved considerably in the past, but his or her functioning and condition deteriorated following a reduction of frequency in therapy visits.

❏ This patient has a history of noncompliance with other essential components of his or her care (medications, day treatment, attendance, sobriety, etc.), and psychotherapy helps this patient to improve his or her level of adherence to planned treatment.

❏ This patient's current level of functioning is such that psychotherapy and/or case management services are needed to support maintenance at this (lower) level of functioning.

❏ This patient's current Global Assessment of Functioning (GAF) score is below 70 (with difficulties in social, occupational, or school functioning, etc.). Psychotherapeutic treatment is essential to support stabilization.

❏ This patient's GAF score is below 60 (with moderate or greater difficulty in social, occupational, or school functioning, etc.). Psychotherapeutic treatment is essential to promote stabilization.

❏ This patient's GAF score is below 50 (with severe difficulty in social, occupational, or school functioning, etc.). Psychotherapeutic treatment is essential to assist with stabilization.

Additional information:

_____

_____

I therefore recommend these methods and frequency of treatment:

❏ Individual psychotherapy at the rate of _____ sessions per week/month.

❏ Group psychotherapy at the rate of _____ meetings per week/month.

❏ Collateral therapy at the rate of _____ meetings per week/month.

❏ Clinical case management at the intensity of _____.

❏ Other: _____

Thank you for your attention to this matter.

Sincerely,

_____          _____
        (Signature of clinician)                                Date

**FORM 8. Medical-necessity-for-psychotherapy checklist.** Adapted from a form devised by Allan J. Comeau, PhD, of West Los Angeles, CA, and used by permission of Dr. Comeau.—From *The Paper Office*. Permission to photocopy this form is granted to purchasers of this book for personal use only (see copyright page for details).

cian has been formally made; keep track of the number of sessions authorized and received; renew the authorization before that number has been used; provide a claim form that perfectly matches the MCO's needs (a "clean claim"); send it to the MCO's preferred and current staff and addresses; and so on. Clinicians routinely report that they (or their office staff) spend about 30% of their work time on such paperwork issues. Some offices have found calling in the early mornings to be more time-effective. Also, because you will usually be put on hold, the use of a speakerphone will allow you to do other work while you wait.

It is clear that MCOs have not developed equivalently efficient administrative practices. They routinely "lose" the papers mailed and faxed to them; give incorrect information on coverage, clients, and fees to clinicians; or delay or simply do not respond by mail, phone, fax, or e-mail. They routinely fail to notify providers of changes in their procedures, and then refuse payment when these new rules are not complied with. On occasion they pay less than what was accurately billed (and rarely even apologize for these "errors"). They have been stretching out the time they take to pay their bills. Their staff turnover, mergers, and inadequate training interact to make them extremely inaccurate. They obviously have no incentive to improve their functioning, and have changed only when compelled to by laws such as those requiring timely payment for claims (with interest being charged—of course, the interest rates are less than the costs of improving their services). Many clients and clinicians simply give up on pursuing claims, and there are no criminal or civil penalties for this sort of inefficiency by an MCO.

## What Can a Clinician Do?

1. Get paid more?

   ▪ The fees MCOs have been paying have generally been going down, so you will not be able to raise your fees to cover these additional costs, or to keep pace with inflation and your costs of doing business.

   ▪ Join only panels that pay a fee that allows you to make a reasonable profit. For some clinicians, this may not be possible or may become impossible.

   ▪ Locate your practice where there are few providers but many "covered lives," so you will get many referrals from MCOs and can make a profit because of your efficiency.

   ▪ Provide services that MCOs value highly but cannot find providers to perform. If you specialize in newer or rarer services, explore with the MCOs whether they are in need of such services before applying for their panels. Try to negotiate a higher fee for these unusual services. Reviewers may, and their supervisors usually are, authorized to negotiate fees.

   ▪ See MCO patients, but only as an out-of-network-provider (not on the patients' MCO's panel, although you may be on other MCOs' panels). Again, the MCO must want your services and be willing to pay a higher fee than it pays to its panelists.

   ▪ Discuss the true costs and risks of using "extremely basic/minimal MCO coverage" before accepting a person as your client. If it is legal to do so, offer the client a discount of, say, 25% for services without MCO paperwork, no diagnosis, and payment at the time of service.

2. Recover your administrative costs?

■ Your MCO contract generally will not permit you to bill the MCO or the client for the additional time needed to complete paperwork, call the reviewers, and similar administrative burdens, or for using client time to fill out OTRs and other MCO forms, but check. If you routinely have clients sign a form agreeing to accept financial responsibility for all nonreimbursed costs (such as Form 27), you might consider billing the client for your administrative costs, where this is legal.

3. Complain to your state's insurance commissioner and to your legal representatives?

■ An MCO is only vulnerable to laws with teeth. Your state is unlikely to have laws like these (the insurance lobby has been very strong in recent years), so join with your state professional organizations, clients, and consumers to lobby. Call and write to your representatives.

■ When you have to resubmit a bunch of OTRs (outpatient treatment reports) or similar documents, consider sending an explanatory cover letter with the date you sent the first (now "lost") OTRs, and a copy of this letter to the insurance commissioner of your state.

■ Go to Gordon Herz's Therapists' Insurer Profiling Scale Web site (http://www.mentalhealth-madison.com/Rate_the_Insurer.htm). Read others' experiences with each MCO, and submit your own.

4. Complain better to the MCOs?

■ Document all calls and paperwork sent (to whom, when, where, for what, length of call, etc.). After the first call, ask to speak to a supervisor,

■ After a few discussions with supervisors, try to arrange a face-to-face meeting to discuss problems and solutions with someone at the MCO.

■ If it is harder for the MCO to drop you (by simply not sending your referrals) than it is to deal with the additional paperwork your complaints to the insurance commissioner will generate, the MCO's personnel may deal more efficiently with you.

■ Have one of your staff members call each MCO on each claim submitted more than 2 weeks ago and not yet paid. This is burdensome and costly, but it will be so to the MCO as well.

■ When you are told that client paperwork was "not received," you could become very concerned or even frightened that a document with "confidential medical information" has gone astray. Confirm that you have mailed it correctly, and conclude that it must have been lost in their office. Because the "not received" gambit is so widespread, MCO staffers will not admit to finding the paperwork if you propose calling back later to check on their search efforts. Instead, point out that if

# 3.13  Legal and Ethical Aspects of Supervising and Being Supervised

As clinicians, we all participate in clinical supervision during our careers, often both as supervisees and as supervisors. We do this because of our faith in the necessity of face-to-face assessing, teaching, monitoring, and mentoring to raise skill levels, model sophisticated skills and attitudes, socialize the novice into a profession's world view, and so on.

Being supervised is like an apprenticeship with a master to integrate the theory learned in training (in school as well as self-education) with the development and application of skills to the needs of real-world patients. In contrast to "consultation" with an independent peer or organization, "supervision" suggests the monitoring and control of the supervisee's practice by the supervisor. In the professions, there is an expectation that the supervision is educational and the relationship will terminate when the skills have been passed on. Formalizing the supervision relationship by contract with peers, associates, or others from whom you can learn or to whom you teach is a small step but a legally protective one, and it is implied by Standard 7.06 of the APA ethics code (APA, 2002). See Form 9 below for an example of such an agreement.

Most supervision takes place either on a one-to-one basis or in a seminar format. However, it also includes the use of cotherapy and team therapy, formal assignments and teaching, modeling by the supervisor, and formalized mentoring outside the classroom. The Internet is bringing other possibilities.

## Risks and Responses

1. **Supervising is a special skill.** Some circumspection is needed by clinicians who are considering becoming supervisors. A high level of clinical skill is a necessary but not sufficient qualification for a supervisor, because students need more than demonstrations to learn sophisticated procedures. Some clinicians may be well able to do, but not to explain or teach. Furthermore, knowledge alone is insufficient to assure its being passed on, because "telling is not teaching," and showing does not address the situation of the learner. Also, clinicians may approach supervising from the perspective of their favorite school of therapy, which may not be appropriate or sufficiently flexible for the demands their supervisees face. Lastly, supervision based on a supervisor's own training experiences may simply pass on poor-quality or out-of-date skills. It is clear that being an effective supervisor requires more than a high level of professional skills as an experienced clinician.

    *Advice*: Training in supervision can be very enlightening and beneficial, and is probably necessary to reduce risk as well.

2. **Be aware of vicarious liability.** There is an old legal concept, *respondeat superior*, in which the master is held responsible for the actions of the servant; thus some clinicians may shy away from supervising, fearing its uncontrolled consequences. The law has held that the clients treated by your supervisee under your supervision are *your* clients. Although it is true that a supervisor can be held responsible for some actions of the supervisee ("vicarious liability") even when the supervisee is a licensed profes-

sional, incidents of this type have not been a significant professional liability risk factor, which should be reassuring.

*Advice*: A careful selection process, comprehensive discussions and training, continual monitoring, a clear contract, and inclusive liability insurance can reduce your risk to an insignificant level. Supervision should be timely, frequent, and of sufficient duration to allow competent monitoring of the supervisee, sufficient mutual understanding of the case, and evaluation of treatment.

3. **Do not exceed your areas of competent practice.** Just as you would not employ a method you didn't know well or treat a diagnosis you were unfamiliar with, you should not attempt to supervise in a clinical area in which you do not have demonstrated competence to perform supervision for which you lack sufficient skills. Supervisees must have been adequately trained to execute each treatment prescribed by the supervisor, even though the supervisor will be held responsible.

*Advice*: This may require you to refuse some supervisees or some clients for a supervisee, so plan ahead.

4. **Be aware of informed consent issues.** There are two issues here: the client's consent to be treated by a clinician who is being supervised, and the supervisee's consent to be supervised. First, according to Standard 10.01c of the APA ethics code (APA, 2002), clients must be informed about, understand the consequences (risks and benefits) of, and voluntarily agree to treatment by your supervisee. Specifically, they must be told that you are supervising, what your credentials are, that you will be reviewing the supervisee's records (and probably recordings of the sessions), and so on. This is part of their consent to treatment. HIPAA regulations allow the supervisees full access to the client's record because they are providing health care services ("treatment") to a client who had consented to share protected health information during the intake process. Second, your supervisee must be fully informed and consent to the supervision process you will pursue. According to Standard 7.06 of the APA ethics code (APA, 2002), processes for evaluating performance and providing feedback to students and interns are required to be specified.

*Advice*: The best ways to reduce these risks is simply to have a very clear contract. Form 9 addresses these issues. In addition, use the best evaluation methods available. Share them with the supervisee and negotiate their use, frequency, interpretation, and so forth.

5. **Consider confidentiality issues.** Understand that neither consultations nor supervision are privileged communications, so you and your notes could be dragged into court.

*Advice*: If a supervisee needs assistance on a case with significant legal implications, refer him or her to a lawyer. If he or she needs therapy for anxiety or depression, perhaps due to a stressful legal case, arrange for a therapist with the usual privacy protections. Do not become your consultee's "therapist," as this is a dual relationship and conflicts are easy to anticipate.

6. **Avoid exploitation.** Avoid dual relationships with a supervisee. The supervisor must be careful in relations with the supervisee that there is no possibility of exploitation.

Obviously, sexual relationships are forbidden (by Standard 7.07 of the APA ethics code; APA, 2002), but others are possible (such as supervising with business partners, relatives, spouses, friends, or prior clients).

*Advice*: Stick to doing only supervision with supervisees. Moreover, a supervisee should pay a fee for each hour and not use a percentage of the fees received from the clients, as this is fee splitting and still (usually) unethical.

*Advice to supervisees*: Your sessions should be constructive, so if you are not sure you are getting your money's worth, seek out another consultant. You can outgrow your teacher, you know.

## A Formal Agreement

**FORM 9**  Because of the pressures to formalize the context of supervisory relationships, Form 9, the agreement for professional supervision, addresses a variety of issues of relevance to the supervision relationship. This form incorporates some ideas from one developed by Kathleen Quinn, EdD, of Cheyenne, WY, for which I am most grateful.

Since supervision can be at many levels, some of the terms in the form have been placed in parentheses where they would apply only to those being supervised for pre- or postdoctoral internships or for licensure. It is written for psychotherapy supervision, so other clinical functions (such as diagnostic testing, case management, school consultation, mentoring and group supervision) will probably require additional or substitute paragraphs. If the supervision is for licensure or to meet some other formal goal, make sure the frequency, duration, and intensity are sufficient to meet the requirements. The means of emergency contact could include home phone numbers, cell phone, pager, answering service, or institutional switchboard. The form deliberately does not address the model of therapy, school, discipline, or approach, as these are likely to differ widely across supervision situations. This form would be inappropriate for online or peer-to-peer supervision. Lastly, it is not designed for specialized supervision, such as that of "burned-out," traumatized, or otherwise impaired professionals, or of professionals who are being rehabilitated or under supervision required by their licensing boards.

## A Record of Supervision Meetings

A format for supervision notes is offered below, but you should create a customized form for your goals, methods of practice, and types of contacts. This form should be agreed to by both the supervisor and supervisee. If the supervisee completes it, a copy should be furnished to the supervisor, so that everything is on the table and changes can be negotiated.

Notes can be written into the spaces provided, or the numbers can be used to organize narrative notes recorded on plain paper. This format provides a space for the supervisor's name and location, but it is best if more detailed information is also recorded. For example, you could indicate the following for each supervisor in full on the back of the first of these forms you use: the supervisor's agency, type of agency, or setting (e.g., private practice); full business address; telephone numbers (regular, home, emergency, fax, pager, e-mail,

## Agreement for Professional Supervision Services

### Introduction

This agreement has been created to address the legal, ethical, practical, and clinical issues of the supervision relationship. It can be added to or modified as the supervision process unfolds over time and across cases, and these addenda are indicated on the last page. This agreement is intended to articulate and clarify the complex mutual responsibilities of the parties involved, the procedures of the supervision, and the personal development needed to become a capable and responsible professional (deserving of independent professional practice).

### Parties

We, _____, (hereinafter called the "supervisee") and _____ (hereinafter called the "supervisor"), agree that the supervisor will provide professional supervision services as outlined below.

### Meetings and communication

The supervisee agrees to meet with the supervisor in person as mutually arranged or at these locations and times:

_____     _____
Location                                      Days, hours

_____     _____
Location                                      Days, hours

It is the supervisee's responsibility to initiate meetings as often as necessary to meet the goals of supervision, to meet his or her training needs, provide high levels of care to the clients involved, and to address other needs that may arise.

Besides our face-to-face meetings, we may use postal mail, telephone, video, e-mail, or other means to communicate. If we use e-mail messages or wireless phones to discuss cases or other confidential information, they must be encrypted. Electronic recordings will require the written consent of the clients involved.

Because we need to be able to reach each other easily and because emergencies may arise, the following arrangements for contact are made.

*Supervisee*

_____     _____
Days and hours of availability                Means of emergency contact

_____     _____
Days and hours of availability                Means of emergency contact

_____     _____
Days and hours of availability                Means of emergency contact

*(cont.)*

**FORM 9. Agreement for professional supervision (p. 1 of 4).**   Incorporates some ideas from a form devised by Kathleen Quinn, EdD, of Cheyenne, WY, and used by permission of Dr. Quinn.—From *The Paper Office*. Permission to photocopy this form is granted to purchasers of this book for personal use only (see copyright page for details).

*Supervisor*

_____       _____

Days and hours of availability                                        Means of emergency contact

_____       _____

Days and hours of availability                                        Means of emergency contact

_____       _____

Days and hours of availability                                        Means of emergency contact

When the supervisor is unavailable due to vacation or other events, the supervisor will assure adequate availability of a substitute supervisor and will inform this person of the supervisee's needs and situation.

## Frequency and Financial Concerns

The supervisee agrees to pay for services provided, up until the time either of us informs the other (in person or by written means) of his or her plans to end the relationship. The supervisee agrees to pay the fee of $_____$ per session for these services, starting on or about _____ and continuing at about the rate of about _____ meetings per _____. Vacations and other planned absences from supervision will be negotiated at least 30 days in advance.

## Records and Confidentiality

1. We both agree to keep records of our meetings, which will document the following:

   - The dates and times we met face to face or otherwise communicated.
   - The cases involved by name or case number.
   - The results of previous clinical efforts and interventions, the progress each case, the client's needs, and similar concerns.
   - Other relevant issues, such as ethical, legal, procedural, interpersonal, or organizational ones.
   - The supervisee's areas or skills in need of enhancement and progress toward mastery.
   - The recommendations and assignments given by the supervisor and assumed by the supervisee.
   - Discussion of the supervision process, procedures, and progress.

2. We will maintain these records in the same ways as we maintain clinical case records (as to confidentiality, availability, security, etc.).

3. We are both aware that these records are not privileged.

## Supervisee's responsibilities

1. Presentations to clients and informed consent.

   - The supervisee agrees to not misrepresent or advertise himself or herself in any way that might imply a competence or credential he or she does not have.
   - The supervisee agrees to explain to clients his or her professional achievements, status, or title, and to make it clear that he or she is being supervised. The supervisee will explain the supervision process and the supervisor's activities, profession, and credentials. The supervisee will explain that clients in therapy with the supervisee are legally considered to be clients of the supervisor. Clients will read and agree to the supervisor's client information brochure and other educational materials as needed.
   - The supervisee will obtain informed consent of clients to the information and record sharing involved in this supervision. Where direct observation and/or audio or video recordings will be made, the supervisee will obtain fully informed consent. Consent forms will be completed as appropriate.

2. Risk management.

   - The supervisee will inform the supervisor of any problems with any clients or cases as soon as possible. Any interactions with a client that raise any level of concern about risk to the client, family, peers, or others must be discussed with the supervisor immediately.

*(cont.)*

- The supervisee will abide by the appropriate national code of ethics for his or her profession and its guidelines and other similar materials, as appropriate to the kinds of services being rendered to clients and the characteristics of those clients.

- The supervisee will abide by the current rules and regulations of this state's professional licensing board.

- The supervisee will adhere to the policies and procedures of the employers of the supervisor and supervisee.

- The supervisee will obtain and maintain his or her own professional liability insurance coverage.

3. Supervisee's education.

- The supervisee recognizes that a major value of supervision is the learning of professional roles and associated behaviors.

- The supervisee agrees to use his or her best abilities to remain responsive to suggestions and recommendations.

- The supervisee agrees to bring to the attention of the supervisor any deficits the supervisee recognizes in his or her ability to perform the clinical functions involved in therapy or other clinical activities with clients.

- The supervisee agrees to complete readings and other educational assignments made by the supervisor. The supervisee may be asked to summarize or in other ways demonstrate the learning of the contents of these materials.

4. Clinical procedures.

- The supervisee agrees to meet with clients and perform psychotherapeutic or other clinical functions in a professional, reliable, and responsible manner.

- The supervisee agrees to implement to the best of his or her ability the recommendations made by the supervisor for the handling of each case.

- The supervisee agrees to develop adequate, appropriate, and current written treatment plans and will remain responsible for such. These will be reviewed at scheduled times with the client(s) and supervisor, and changes will be incorporated as needed.

**Supervisor's responsibilities**

1. Sensitivity, responsiveness, and flexibility.

- The supervisor agrees to try always to bear in mind issues of diversity, their many dimensions and influences, and to be sensitive and respectful of all differences among the client(s), the supervisee, and himself or herself.

- The supervisor agrees to attend to the boundaries, balances, and potential multiple relationships between the supervisor and supervisee. In all cases, the interests of the supervisee will be held primary.

- The supervisor agrees to maintain awareness of the sometimes fine line between doing supervision and providing psychotherapy. If the supervisor should decide that the supervisee can benefit from psychotherapy, he or she will make referrals.

2. Evaluation.

- The supervisor agrees to conduct an initial evaluation of the supervisee's knowledge, attitudes, and skills concerning the clinical activities that the supervisee intends to undertake and the supervisor to supervise. Other areas, as proposed by either party, may be assessed as well. Based on this comprehensive evaluation, both parties will formulate specific goals and methods for the content and nature of the supervision.

- The supervisor agrees to explain and obtain fully informed consent of the supervisee to any and all methods and procedures for the evaluation of the supervisee, their nature and timing, and any other persons who will also review the evaluations and results, before implementing any of them.

- If disagreements should arise that the supervisor and supervisee cannot resolve, they will take these difficulties to the supervisee's educational supervisor if the supervisee is in supervision as part of an educational program and if not they will consult with staff members of the local or state professional association.

*(cont.)*

3. Monitoring and risk management.

- The supervisor will review the supervisee's treatment plans, written notes, and audiotapes and/or video-tapes of selected treatment sessions on a periodic basis as decided by the supervisor. Direct observation of the services provided by the supervisee will be arranged if at all possible.

- The supervisor has legal responsibility for the supervisee's clients and will take all appropriate actions in their best interests.

- Supervision will include examination of and education in legal and ethical issues, as well as patient treatment issues.

- The supervisor agrees to abide by the appropriate national code of ethics for his or her profession and its guidelines and other similar materials as appropriate to the kinds of services being rendered to clients and the characteristics of those clients.

- The supervisor agrees to abide by the current rules and regulations of this state's professional licensing board.

- The supervisor agrees to adhere to the policies and procedures of employers of the supervisor and/or supervisee.

- The supervisor will maintain current professional insurance coverage and include the supervisee as required by law, regulation, or the insurer.

4. Supervisor's education.

- The supervisor agrees to continue to learn about supervision.

- The supervisor agrees to remain current in the model(s) and methods of assessment, therapy, legal and ethical issues, and similar clinical concerns.

5. Administrative responsibilities.

- The supervisor will maintain appropriate and necessary records of the experiences and services provided to and by the supervisee for licensure or certification, and will ensure that the criteria are met.

- The supervisor will provide evaluations, letters of recommendation, and similar document about the supervision and supervisee as requested by the supervisee.

I, the supervisee, have read the supervisor's office policy statements as well as the supervision statement above. I agree to act accordingly to everything stated there as shown by my signature below. I understand that this agreement can be terminated if either party does not live up to his or her responsibilities as outlined above. I agree to adhere to the contents of this agreement, until otherwise negotiated and formalized as addenda to this agreement.

_____     _____

Signature of the supervisee indicating agreement          Date

I, the supervisor, have discussed the issues above with the supervisee. I hereby agree to adhere to the contents of this agreement, until otherwise negotiated and formalized as addenda to this agreement.

_____     _____

Signature of the supervisor indicating agreement          Date

_____ Copy accepted by supervisee     _____ Copy kept by supervisor

Addenda or modifications to this agreement          Date

  1.

  2.

  3.

etc.); Social Security number; and any other information that might be needed in the future to substantiate that the supervision occurred.

### Supervision Record

1. Supervisor: _____   Agency/location: _____

2. Session's date: _____   Meeting number: _____   Duration: _____

   Individual or group? _____   Live or case consultation? _____

3. Preparation: (a) Supervisee's progress on tasks or homework from last session with client; (b) client case materials collected (paper and electronic records, genogram, consultations); (c) other materials collected (literature); (d) supervisee's concerns/issues to be raised (personal, family, case, theoretical, practical, organizational, ethical, conflicts); and (e) goals for the session.

4. Patients discussed (use initials): For each, discuss (a) problematic behaviors or concerns/main issues/progress/questions; (b) themes; (c) hypotheses; (d) treatment decisions made/tasks assumed.

5. Supervisor's comments/evaluations about: Supervisee's conceptualization of case/treatment/problems; interventions/implementation of treatments; handling of issues; self-awareness; process, clinical, or theoretical areas; evaluation of treatment; etc.

6. Skill development/training recommendations or suggestions made. If supervisee's performance is deficient, this must be made clear, and a remediation plan must be developed and implemented.

7. Signature of supervisor: _____

   Signature of supervisee: _____

## Consulting

Continuing professional consultations are essential for good clinical care; no one knows everything. Without consultations, you are less likely to ask advice when a question (clinical or ethical) comes up. Going it alone in murky waters is risky, if not self-destructive. Indeed, as noted earlier in this chapter, frequent and formal consultation with a respected peer is powerful protection against a malpractice verdict.

Consultation differs greatly from supervision. A consultant offers his or her expertise to an independent fellow professional who is not obliged to comply with any advice and retains full responsibility for his or her patients. Because there may be misunderstandings, get a letter of agreement about roles and responsibilities.

It is in your best interest to keep notes on your consultation sessions. These are separate from any case notes that would go into a patient's chart. I recommend keeping a separate three-ring binder in which you keep notes, photocopies, notes on readings, diaries, handouts, and anything else to support your consultation relationship and learning. These document the sessions (perhaps for a credential) and their content for defense if you are accused of an ethics or malpractice violation.

## Resources for Supervision and Consultation

There are many fine books on supervision and consultation, but only a few currently in print. Please see Appendix F for a list of books and journals.

# CHAPTER 4

# Getting Informed Consent

## 4.1 The What and Why of Getting Informed Consent

> *Informed consent is actually a statement about the moral atmosphere of the relationship between clinician and patient. In more practical terms, informed consent is a dyadic process, or dialogue that begins at the moment of eye contact and continues throughout the relationship."*
>
> —GUTHEIL (1993, p. 1005)

The relationship of therapist and client is complex and multidimensional. It evolves therapeutically, economically, and interpersonally. If this relationship is not spelled out, the client, therapist, ethics committees, insurance companies, and courts are all quite likely to interpret it differently. The relationship should thus be clarified as soon as clinically feasible; this process of clarification and of obtaining informed consent is not optional, but essential. The relevant parts of the American Psychological Association ethics code (APA, 2002) are primarily Standards 3.10 and 3.11 as well as 9.03 for assessment and 10.01 for therapy. But how can you be sure you have obtained such consent? What specific methods can you use to obtain it? This chapter answers these questions and offers five fully developed paths, or methods, you can use with clients to pursue their informed consent. Any of these methods, however, requires that four basic conditions be met.

### What Informed Consent Requires

Informed consent requires a **mentally competent** person who has a good **knowledge** of what will occur in treatment, freely **chooses** to be treated, and is **documented** in the record as such. If any of these is lacking, its absence must be documented, explained, and responded to. Let's look more carefully at each of these elements.

#### Mental Competence

Mental competence is presumed for all adults unless a court has decided that an adult is incompetent, or the adult has manifested clear signs of incompetence to you. Receiving a severe diagnosis or even being involuntarily hospitalized does not automatically presume incompetence. Some indicators of possible incompetence are psychosis, dementia, severe depression, suicidal behavior, and the like. In such cases, consult and/or refer if you lack the professional skills to evaluate the impact of these symptoms on the client's competence. Also note that the rationality of a decision is unrelated to the competence to make it (Group for the Advancement of Psychiatry [GAP], 1990, pp. 87 ff.) An irrational decision is defined as one that results in the person's suffering foreseeable harms without adequate reason (GAP, 1990, p. 87). If you need formal assessments of competence to make decisions about psychiatric treatment, the three scales developed by the MacArthur Treatment Competence Study are sophisticated and specific. They address denial of symptoms, assessment of cognitive functioning, and understanding of the explanations offered of treatments. The scales and manuals are free at the MacArthur Archive at http://macarthur.virginia.edu/treatment.html, and their use is also described by Grisso and Appelbaum (1998).

Competence is not "all or nothing." The extent of someone's competence depends on the issues of concern at the moment. A client may be competent to consent to some treatments and not to others; the latter may require resources he or she does not possess, now or at any time, such as the ability to foresee specific consequences in detail.

Competence is generally denied to minors, but local laws differ. A minor is usually anyone under 18 years of age. By law and presumption, minors cannot give consent or waive privilege because they are considered incompetent due to age. Consent must therefore be obtained from their parents or guardians. Residing with a child does not make an adult that child's legal guardian, and being a parent does not assure the parent's having legal custody to consent. If you need consent for a minor, find out who can give it.

In order to reduce barriers to treatment of minors, there are some legal exceptions concerning their competence to consent to treatment. For example, minors can generally seek treatment for sexually transmitted diseases or pregnancy without parental consent. Some states have extended this to drug and alcohol treatment and other diagnoses, or have allowed treatment in some settings. Consent to treatment by adolescents is complicated by their not-quite-adult legal and psychological status. The tendency is to give more weight to the thinking abilities of later adolescents and less to those of early adolescents. **You must know your local laws.** To illustrate, in Pennsylvania, the following questions need to be considered in deciding whether you need parental consent to treat an adolescent (Elwork, 1993): Is the treatment to be inpatient or outpatient? Is this a form of treatment an adolescent can consent to (e.g., drug/alcohol treatment), or not (e.g., treatment for mental illness)? Do you need parental consent to obtain records? Do you need parental consent for treatment, or do you only need to notify the parents of this treatment? Is parental notification a duty of yours or a right of theirs?

## Knowledge

Consent is "informed if all the risks and possible consequences of the procedure . . . along with alternatives have been explained . . . and . . . [the client] understands" (Cohen, 1979, p. 248). Note that this has two aspects: (1) giving adequate information and (2) ensuring that the client understands it. We need to examine each aspect in turn. First, how much information needs to be disclosed? Must every *possible* side effect be described?

"If a doctor knows (or should know) of possible complication[s] of the treatment, he [*sic*] is under a legal duty to disclose that information to his patient" (Cohen, 1979, p. 248). Not every possibility must be covered, but "only those risks which a reasonable man would consider material to his decision whether or not to undergo treatment" (Cohen, 1979, pp. 248–249). Reid (1999, pp. 27 and 77) suggests balancing significance and likelihood. Although the rare or benign effects of treatment may not require discussion, the more dangerous or more common an effect is, the more weight and time its discussion will deserve. Haas and Malouf (1995) recommend that if in doubt, it is probably better to give information and thus support the autonomy of the patient, than to withhold it and be accused later of paternalism. This is clearly subtle and complex in real-life practice, but some effort must be made in this direction with every patient.

Full knowledge involves giving the information that a rational person would want to have before making a decision. This usually requires you as the therapist to explain the following:

- Your approach and your qualifications.

- All procedures to be used, and any changes during treatment.

- The purposes of treatment—both the long-term and the short-term or immediate goals.

- Discomforts to be expected (e.g., conflicts with family members when a patient becomes more assertive).

- Foreseeable negative consequences, or "harms." "The harms which concern rational persons are death; pain (physical and mental); various disabilities; and loss of freedom, opportunity, or pleasure" (GAP, 1990, p. 80). They may also include some side effects of treatment.

- The anticipated benefits of this treatment.

- The option of no treatment and its consequences.

- Alternative treatments. A useful guideline for alternatives is to ask yourself whether some very differently trained but fully competent therapist might suggest some other treatment in this situation (GAP, 1990, p. 81).

Clients, even those without previous therapy experience, generally understand the ethical principles of therapy but are uncertain about more specific points (Claiborne et al., 1994). Furthermore, Jensen et al. (1991) found that clinicians and parents tended to agree on the content of informed consent discussions. Parents understood these purposes of therapy: to "talk things out"; to help problems get better; to get help for complex or very difficult problems; to improve parenting skills; and to improve relationships. They also understood the limits and risks of confidentiality (e.g., the mandatory reporting of child abuse, the possibility of having family secrets revealed). However, parents were more concerned than were clinicians with iatrogenic risks: the chance that problems might fail to improve or might get worse, as well as the effects of labeling (e.g., the children's being called "mentally disturbed" by others, the parents' being seen as inadequate) and other stigma-related issues (e.g., the possibility that the children's having been in therapy might cause problems in employability, school admission, etc.). It is important to note that in this study, demographics did not affect these issues' rankings of importance. Therefore, a uniform approach, such as a handout plus a discussion that is relatively standard but that can be tailored to the particular needs of clients, is empirically justified.

Clients' needs and therapists' approaches differ, and so different information needs to be provided accordingly. For example, the scheduling of therapy is often more problematic for clients at lower socioeconomic levels, so it should be discussed more fully (Graziano & Fink, 1973). Similarly, a study found that when those with more pathology were given more information on the limits of confidentiality, they revealed less than those given less information; those with lower pathology revealed most (Taube & Elwork, 1990). Labeling and other stigma-related issues are more important for some patients or families with a history of being stigmatized or a high risk of being stigmatized (Lidz et al., 1984). Inpatients and outpatients need discussion of different issues (Lidz et al., 1984). Families have different concerns from those of single adults or minors (Gustafson & McNamara, 1987).

Discussions of different therapeutic approaches may also require different content. For example, Widiger and Rorer (1984) argue that disclosure of therapeutic methods may cripple free association. If specialized techniques (such as biofeedback or hypnotherapy) are later introduced, additional informed consent is appropriate, even though a more general informed consent to treatment was obtained early in treatment. Those who use paradoxical methods should proceed with caution; these methods raise some serious questions about consent and require a more extensive consent-getting process.

As mentioned above, the offering of adequate information is not sufficient to ensure that a patient has knowledge sufficient for consent. The second requirement now comes into play; that is, the client must understand how the information applies to him or her. Such competence has two aspects: the comprehension of the meaning of what has been told, and its appreciation—that is, the realization that what has been said applies to him or her at the present time (GAP, 1990, p. 13).

To assure the client's understanding, it is important to remember these guidelines:

- Use simple, declarative sentences.

- Give explanations in language that is free of jargon (clinical, legal, or bureaucratic) and adjusted for the client's education or reading skills. Handelsman et al. (1986) suggest sixth- to eighth-grade language skill for consent forms. The forms in the field have not improved, and the research done on forms to consent to participate in research (LoVerde et al., 1989) indicates that things are getting worse, not better: In the 7 years studied, the forms got 58% longer, and they still required too high a level of education to be understood (22% required graduate school!).

- Communicate that any questions that occur to the client will be answered at any time.

- Respect the client's levels of cognitive functioning (especially memory abilities). One pitfall is "that information overload can prevent the obtaining of informed consent, perhaps as much as underdisclosure" (Haas & Malouf, 1995).

- Ask questions that probe the client's understanding, in addition to inviting and answering his or her questions.

- Make special efforts if English is the client's second language, or if there are hearing or cultural barriers.

- Understanding may be enhanced by the use of analogies and metaphors or even case vignettes, but beware of the client's drawing unrealistic conclusions from the parallels between the client in the story and himself or herself. Visual aids and graphics such as Venn diagrams and flow charts may help explain how things have worked and will work in causal terms.

- Couch your risk–benefit statements to the patient in terms like these (GAP, 1990, p. 10):

    ". . . while no completely satisfactory statistics are available, [I] believe that this combination of treatments offers the best chance of success."

    "The success rate of this treatment is about ____%. That is, about ____% of all patients receiving this treatment experience complete or substantial relief of their symptoms."

The best overview I have read of the issues involved in informed consent for psychotherapy with guiding wisdom on how to address them is a recent article by Beahrs and Gutheil (2001). Among other points, they note that addressing this process deliberately is likely to have at least these benefits: enhancing the patient's autonomy, responsibility, and self-therapeutic activity, and thus improving the likelihood of treatment success; lessening the patient's dependence, passivity, and tendency to put the therapist on a pedestal; reducing the therapist's liability because of clarification of responsibilities; and reducing the likelihood that the therapy will fall victim to therapeutic fads and cultishness.

### Choosing Freely

Treating patients without their consent is one type of "paternalistic behavior" (see GAP, 1990, pp. 27–44). Freely choosing to be treated, or "voluntariness," requires that the consent must be free from coercion, that is, free from powerful negative incentives such as "threats of severe pain or significant deprivation of freedom" (GAP, 1990, p. 12), that a rational person would find hard or unreasonable to resist. There should be a clear absence of coercion on your part. Bear in mind that others, as well as social reality, may exert coercion; this is not your responsibility unless you have control over the coercer (see GAP, 1990, p. 16, which is based on Mallory et al., 1986). Pressure is not the same as coercion; arguing forcefully for a course of action and voicing a degree of challenge may be quite appropriate at times (GAP, 1990, p. 82), especially when you feel the client's best interests are not being attended to.

The other side of the coin is that the client must know that he or she can withdraw from treatment at any time without being punished or suffering any consequences other than the loss of any benefits derived from the treatment. If there are other consequences, they must be described fully.

Patients can, of course, refuse treatments. Liberman (1990) wisely suggests obtaining a "written waiver" for situations where a patient's refusal to follow a treatment recommendation would threaten his or her health (see Section 3.11).

### Documentation

All of this therapist–client communication and rapport are consummated in the signing of a form, but the form cannot substitute for the interpersonal process of gaining informed consent. The form is not itself the consent; it is only the written evidence of the discussion and agreement. The APA code of ethics (APA, 2002) now requires that "Psychologists appropriately document written or oral consent, permission, and assent"(Standard 3.10d). If you do not get a signed form, you must carefully document in your notes what you have told the client about treatment, to demonstrate that you have indeed obtained informed consent.

If you cannot obtain consent before beginning treatment, document the reason why not (e.g., emergency, incompetence/proxy consent, court-ordered treatment, etc.) Then, if possible, get consent as soon as the crisis has passed. Everstine et al. (1980) recommend obtaining consent even in cases where treatment is compelled. The reason is that, though "legally empty, [consent] in many cases will very likely have clinical usefulness" (p. 832). The APA ethics code (APA, 2002) recognizes this issue and details responses in Standard 3.10b.

Remember also that a signed form, by itself, is not a guarantee that informed consent has been obtained. Vaccarino (1978) has reported that "legal actions for lack of informed consent have been brought despite the existence of a signed consent form" (p. 455). He emphasizes that consenting is an interpersonal, face-to-face, rapport-based, continual discussion process, and not a mechanical, paper-based one. Furthermore, studies of medical patients given written consent forms suggest that at best 60% of the information is retained, and so the discussion process is essential (Grunder, 1980; Ley, 1982).

## The Three Steps to Obtaining Informed Consent

The discussion above emphasizes that informed consent is an ongoing process, not a single act. How can you be sure you have obtained it? The following three-step process offers the best procedures.

**The first step is to have discussions covering the issues,** because discussion is the essence of informedness. Use either your memory, or, better, one of the following as a basis for the topics to cover in your discussion:

- The topics covered in the client information brochure (see Section 4.2).

- The questions in "Information You Have a Right to Know" (see Section 4.3).

- The contents of clients' rights statements (see Section 4.4).

- The contents of treatment contracts (see Section 4.5).

- A checklist made up from the materials above and your own understanding and ideas about the nature of your treatment.

**The second step is to document the client's agreement** with one (or, in complex situations, both) of the following:

1.  A signed consent form. Use one of these:

    - The client information brochure (see Section 4.2).

    - A treatment contract (see Section 4.5).

    - A consent-to-treatment form (see Section 4.6).

2.  Your notes concerning each of the relevant issues. The notes must document the following about both the discussions and the client's consent:

    - That you and the patient discussed all the relevant issues (for informedness).

    - That you answered all the patient's questions (again for informedness).

    - That the patient signed the form voluntarily.

    - That the patient was competent to consent. Use a statement such as the following: "After interacting with the patient for ____ minutes, observing his or her behavior and discussing many topics, I found no reason to suspect that the patient was not competent to consent to treatment."

**The third step is to keep the discussions about your treatment and their documentation ongoing.** This is especially important when there are difficulties or when you change the treatments you offer.

## Do Written Consent Forms Have a Negative Effect on Clients or Treatment?

Many clinicians are reluctant to use specifically worded consent materials such as those offered in this book, for fear they might turn away clients. They fear that the materials will create obstacles to (or distract clients from) treatment, or that their use will make a humane activity too formal and legalistic. Fortunately, empirical data are available to address these issues.

Handelsman (1990) has researched the effects of materials like these, in various combinations, for many years. He found that their use increased readers' positive judgments of the therapist's experience, likability, and trustworthiness; increased the readers' likelihood of recommending the therapist; and even increased self-referral by the (nonclient) subjects. More recently, Handelsman's team found that offering more readable forms with more specific information about the therapist "increased ratings of the attractiveness of the therapist, and of the relevance of and satisfaction with the forms. Personalized forms also tended to increase recall" (Wagner et al., 1998, p. 115). In an analogue but prospective study, Gustafson et al. (1994) found that providing information about risks and benefits did not affect parents' decision to seek psychological treatment for their children. Sullivan et al. (1993), in an analogue study, reported that subjects "gave higher ratings to a therapist who used an informed-consent procedure and reported more willingness to recommend him to a friend and go to him themselves" (p. 160).

In a study with university students in counseling, Dauser et al. (1995) found that providing a great deal of information on ethical issues (such as the limits of confidentiality, right to terminate, etc.), on the therapist's professional experience, and on what to expect in therapy (anticipated results, risks, alternatives, etc.) had no negative effects. There were no differences in no-shows or client-initiated terminations between those receiving more and those receiving less information. Those receiving more information felt they had a better understanding of what counseling would be like than did those receiving less information.

The limits of confidentiality constitute the topic of most concern to patients (Bratten & Handelsman, 1997). Beeman and Scott (1991) found that therapists believed that pursuing informed consent enhances autonomy and control, enhances the therapeutic relationship, satisfies ethical requirements, increases motivation for therapy, ensures appropriate expectations, views older adolescents as adults, satisfies legal requirements, results in fewer divorced-parent complaints, and selects only those wanting therapy. It appears that a majority of therapists do seek informed consent, although almost exclusively through discussions, which are of course very vulnerable to the pressures of current interests and the vagaries of memory.

To summarize, **the research does not support any negative effects of using consent forms, and suggests many benefits.** Yet, despite these findings, many therapists do not use a form for obtaining informed consent to treatment (Handelsman et al., 1986). It can be argued that a form has the advantages of being (1) a defense against malpractice; (2) a patient education tool; (3) an aid in socializing the patient into therapy; and (4) a means of therapist self-development. In my experience, about 60% of psychologists now use some paper form (usually a single page) for informed consent purposes. The main reason offered by the others for not doing so is the effort it takes to research its contents. This chapter offers the fruits of just such a research effort.

## The Five Paths to Informed Consent

We have now examined the basic requirements for obtaining informed consent: that your client be mentally competent to consent to treatment; that you communicate information about your qualifications and the treatment; that you make certain the client understands these; that the client choose freely to be treated; and that you document the entire ongoing process.

The remainder of this chapter offers five methods for conducting this process. In essence, they are five differing *paths* to consent. These are (1) giving and discussing a client information brochure; (2) offering clients a list of questions to guide discussion (here called "Information You Have a Right to Know"); (3) offering a list of clients' rights as a basis for discussion; (4) using a psychotherapy treatment contract; and (5) using a consent-to-treatment form.

# 4.2   The First Path to Informed Consent: The Client Information Brochure

## Kinds of Brochures

There are at least three kinds of brochures in wide use. Each is tailored to a specific purpose—namely, to advertise or market your service; to give patients specific information on specific conditions, procedures, and topics; or to initiate patients into, and assure informed consent for, therapy. Table 3 offers a more detailed description of each type.

In the table, I have named each of the brochure types according to its purposes. Other writers have called the advertising brochure, aimed at potential clients and possible referrers, a "practice" brochure; I find this ambiguous because it describes only some aspects of the practice. The advertising brochure could be the core of a package sent to potential referrers. You might add a cover letter explaining how you work with other professionals, your background and training, a letter-sized poster for their offices' bulletin boards, some business cards, a faxable referral form, and the like. Similarly, note that though the topical and client information brochures both provide factual information (which sometimes even overlaps), their goals and approaches are quite different. Although the fourth kind, the combination brochure, is quite common, I cannot recommend it. Designing separate brochures for each purpose will avoid confusing the readers with extraneous details and assure that all issues have been addressed.

I concentrate here on the third type, the client information brochure. This needs to be as comprehensive and protective as possible in order to achieve the goals listed in Table 3. A

**TABLE 3. Types and Purposes of Brochures Used in Psychotherapy**

| Type | Purpose | Possible contents |
|---|---|---|
| Advertising/marketing brochure | Describing your services in a very positive light so as to attract new clients. | Your resources, addresses, staff, credentials, ways to reach you, and so on. May also include testimonials (from ex-clients), invitations to visit, maps, photographs. |
| Topical brochure | Educating clients about specific topics. This is sometimes called "patient education." | Treatable conditions and the methods and benefits of therapy; health insurance, costs, and procedures; medications; child development and conditions; and many other common concerns. |
| Client information brochure | Assuring informed consent; conforming to ethical and legal concerns; creating a therapeutic alliance or contract; reducing malpractice risks; socializing clients into therapy; modeling openness; and so on. | Office procedures, such as intake, financial arrangements, appointments, clinical records, and the release of records. Also, the nature of therapy, appropriate goals, treatment planning, and assessment of progress. |
| Combination | Simplifying your paperwork or reducing its costs. | Various combinations of the contents described above. |

comprehensive client information brochure is the *core document of the treatment relationship.* It establishes the boundaries of your way of practicing, and is a therapeutic contract between you and your client. It should be thoughtfully constructed because it initiates and structures your relationship, which is the heart of therapy. You will generally be seen as having obtained initial informed consent if your client has read your client information brochure and has acknowledged in writing that he or she has done so.

Besides being a legal/ethical contract, the client information brochure can also enhance the process of therapy. Based on open exchange, it models an ongoing negotiation process. Collaboration with an informed client not only satisfies legal requirements, but facilitates trust therapeutically. In addition, the process of informing clients through an advertising brochure alone can elicit their fears, fantasies, and erroneous beliefs; if these are not addressed, they could hinder therapy (Cross & Deardorff, 1987, p. 64). The client information brochure permits handling of these issues earlier. Finally, this document serves to "socialize" or introduce clients into the procedures and expectations of therapists, and can be tailored to this aim. If you develop particularly fine efforts at socialization, please share them with me.

## How to Use the Model Client Information Brochure

At the end of this section, I offer an exhaustive model client information brochure. I have tried to include the full range of topics, not all of which may be relevant to your practice. It is designed to allow you to create a comprehensive and detailed brochure tailored for your own practice in just an hour or two. Spending the time to tailor a brochure to your needs will be a good investment, both ethically and professionally. Even weighing the parts you finally conclude are irrelevant can raise your awareness. To help with this task, I offer suggestions and commentary at appropriate points throughout the model brochure's text.

This brochure is very highly detailed, so as to be legally and ethically correct. It is written in standard U.S. grammar and word choice to make it widely applicable. Terms unfamiliar to the average client are explained in language the client can understand (APA, 2002). Note also that I have chosen a personal "I" style over an institutional, passive voice or a formal "we" version. You may prefer one of the other two; choose what feels most comfortable for you, but be consistent across all your documents.

If you are using the CD-ROM of forms and figures from this book, you can import this text and make the changes to it. You should pick and choose sections from this long version to match your specific practice needs. You can also change the format or margins, and add suitable wording to tailor it to your working methods, your locality, your clients, and your understanding of your practice. I generally call the model brochure "Information for Clients," but alternative titles might include "Welcome to the Psychological Practice of [Name]," "Introduction to the [Name] Clinic," or "New Client Introductory Information." Meek et al. (1985) use "Office Policy Statement." The brochure could also be titled by goal, such as "Ensuring Fully Informed Consent for Counseling." Others might prefer "Starting Our Work Together" or "How I Do Therapy."

Having the brochure conveniently available on your word processor is advantageous, because you can then print copies when needed and update it as your practice evolves. As a rule, when you find yourself telling three clients the same information, you should probably add it to your version of the brochure.

Other model brochures are widely available. Kachorek's (1990) is short and somewhat dated but well worded, and Schlosser and Tower's (1991) is extraordinarily extensive for doing assessments. At the APA Insurance Trust (APAIT) Web site (http://www.apait.org) is a model brochure written by Eric Harris, JD, EdD, and Bruce E. Bennett, PhD and at the Sidran site (http://www.sidran.org/consent.html) is one by Laura Brown, PhD, ABPP, each about five pages long. Doverspike (1997) offers several forms.

I recommend the use of the client information brochure as the most comprehensive method for getting informed consent. However, the use of even a very complete brochure for informing clients of the nature of therapy and of your practice's procedures has some drawbacks:

- There is no way to be certain that a client has understood what he or she has read, or even that he or she has read the brochure, unless you open a discussion.

- Risks and alternative treatments for an individual's particular difficulties are very difficult to convey in a generic, preprepared document.

- Most of these brochures require too high a level of psychological sophistication and reading skill (see Wagner et al., 1998, for a review and current findings). I know of no resources to help you choose wording for your brochure, so consider your least literate and least acculturated clients as you write it. Although I have made some efforts to simplify the one below, it is still at the college reading level, but this suits my clientele.

- The client has effectively lost the right to refuse information.

Therefore, it is worth considering the alternative methods presented later.

## The Model Client Information Brochure

The model brochure now begins, indented between vertical lines. The headings are headings that you can use in your own brochure. As you will see, my comments and suggestions are interwoven throughout.

### INFORMATION FOR CLIENTS

Welcome to my practice. I appreciate your giving me the opportunity to be of help to you.

This brochure answers some questions clients often ask about any therapy practice. It is important to me that you know how we will work together. I believe our work will be most helpful to you when you have a clear idea of what we are trying to do.

This brochure talks about the following in a general way:

- What the risks and benefits of therapy are.

- What the goals of therapy are, and what my methods of treatment are like.

- How long therapy might take.

- How much my services cost, and how I handle money matters.

- Other important areas of our relationship.

After you read this brochure we can discuss, in person, how these issues apply to your own situation. This brochure is yours to keep and refer to later. Please read all of it and mark any parts that are not clear to you. Write down any questions you think of, and we will discuss them at our next meeting. When you have read and fully understood this brochure, I will ask you to sign it at the end. I will sign it as well and make a copy, so we each have one.

### About Psychotherapy

Because you will be putting a good deal of time, money, and energy into therapy, you should choose a therapist carefully. I strongly believe you should feel comfortable with the therapist you choose, and hopeful about the therapy. When you feel this way, therapy is more likely to be very helpful to you. Let me describe how I see therapy.

My theoretical approach is based on . . .

The most central ideas in my work are. . . .

The goals of my treatment are . . .

Here you should create a general statement about therapy as you see it. Woody (1988, p. 207) calls this communicating your "standard of care." "The Therapy Process" by Meek et al. (1985) is an outstanding example of such a statement; it raises questions while asserting an approach. Eimer (1988) uses a three-stage model of therapy, the description of which is designed as a patient handout. Tailor your statement to your conception of the impact and value of your psychological services. It can include the general aims appropriate to therapy as you understand it. Include your model of working with patients (e.g., collaboration, education, problem solving, insight into dysfunctional patterns, redeciding, primal release, relearning through transference, working with outside groups, etc.). It is also appropriate to describe, under a separate heading, other services you offer (such as court testimony, relationship counseling, or psychological assessment). If these service descriptions become quite detailed, you should make them into separate handouts. Services you do *not* offer can also be specified, such as custody evaluations for relationship therapy patients.

It may be useful to indicate, if applicable, that you are not a physician (or "medical doctor," not just the ambiguous "doctor"), and so you do not use physical interventions such as medications. When discussing the kinds of treatment you offer, you can indicate that when medications are appropriate, you will work closely with the client's physician.

Hawkins and Bullock (1995) suggest that it would be proper to **indicate here any moral values you hold** that might conflict with clients' religious beliefs, or that might be adopted by clients through a process of convergence in which clients adopt their therapists' ideas on many topics. Hare-Mustin et al. (1979) suggest specifying and elaborating on any technique that might be at odds with the clients' values. For example, if you do relationship counseling, you might indicate that your obligation is to the mental and emotional health of the individuals, not to the relationship. A relationship cannot be a client, according to Koocher and Keith-Spiegel (1998), but Margolin (1982) differs on this point. If your treatment methods are experimental or even controversial, you should make this section even more detailed or prepare a special consent form. This applies, at present, to any therapy that aims to recover repressed memories of sexual abuse (see Section 3.4).

Another aspect of fully informed consent arises when you are asked whether you do "Christian counseling" (or have "Christian values" or something similar). It is both ethically appropriate and may be therapeutic to clarify what is meant before you reply. The "clinical integration" of religious and spiritual values into psychotherapy has grown rapidly. This is a complex area, so see Pargament (1997) and Shafranske (1996) for guidance. The caller may be seeking a Bible-based therapy (involving prayer, references to Bible stories, the teachings of Jesus, etc.). This potential client may be uninterested in therapy involving any secular theories, principles, or research. This is pastoral counseling, and you should either be so qualified or refer the client.

For those of us who are psychologists, there are several concerns in discussing "Christian values." First, we have an ethical requirement to respect the values of others (Principle E of the APA ethics code; APA, 2002). Second, we must make our own values and beliefs very clear to clients from the beginning so that clients can give informed consent to treatment. Third, we have an ethical requirement for cultural competence (Principle E). It seems very clear that evangelical Christians constitute a true subculture, so we must have the same level of cultural competence we require for working with other special populations. Lastly, the research shows that therapy is more successful when the client and therapist share more expectations. This suggests the benefits of exploring values early in the therapy process.

You should try to clarify a client's motivations for seeking a Christian counselor, to decide whether you can be responsive and effective. Potential clients seeking a therapist with "Christian values" usually want someone who is able to work within their world view. They may fear criticism or even condemnation of their behavior, and want to know that you share a common or at least compatible set of values. They may believe that a therapist with different values may wreak havoc with their current values. They may be seeking a "Christian counselor" because of pressures from their family members or their pastor.

Note that being "a psychologist who is also a Christian" is not a sufficient response, because there are so many kinds of Christians with so many value systems and so many issues on which they differ. Is a client concerned with going to hell for an unforgivable sin, struggling with Biblical condemnations of homosexual behaviors, seeking a morally acceptable resolution of an affair, unwilling to consider a divorce or an abortion, or suffering through a spiritual crisis because of a loss of faith? In light of the discussion above, you should, as part of your intake procedures, take a religious history (see Zuckerman, 2000, pp. 264–266) and then discuss the issues bringing clients for therapy and the religious context of their lives. Clarifying areas of difference between your own and your potential clients' beliefs that are likely to affect treatment seems essential for informed consent.

The following is the way my own brochure describes my approach, its central ideas, and its goals to clients:

> The type of therapy I do is called "rational–emotive behavior therapy," or REBT. It was developed by Albert Ellis, PhD, and is described in his dozens of books.
>
> We often believe that our behaviors and feelings are caused by what happens in the real world. However, this is not quite true. When we have any kind of experience, it does not affect us directly. Rather, we first give it a meaning through our beliefs about it. For example, if I hear a sound in the kitchen and believe it is made by my wife, I am not bothered

at all. But if I believe I am alone in the house, the same sound can bother me a great deal. Here we see that feelings and behaviors (my actions about the sound) flow from the active process of thinking about or adding meaning to the actual event (the sound).

Dr. Ellis separates beliefs into two kinds: "rational" beliefs, or ones based on reality and logic, and "irrational" beliefs, or ones based on false or unrealistic ideas. When we have irrational beliefs, we suffer from strong negative emotions (like rage, depression, and anxiety). When we act on the basis of irrational beliefs, our actions are often not effective and can even be harmful. If we have rational beliefs, we will experience more of the positive emotions (like pleasure, hope, and joy). We can still feel the mildly negative emotions, like irritation, sadness, and concern, but our behaviors will be more effective.

I think of my approach to helping people with their problems as an educational one. Anyone can learn to recognize irrational beliefs, dispute them, and replace them with more rational beliefs. We can, with practice, unlearn these beliefs and become happier persons who function better in the world. This is what I mean by an educational approach.

I want you to be able to use REBT without me. I encourage you to learn more about what methods are used in REBT; how well it works, and what possible problems or side effects it may have. I can lend you books and articles that explain how it works. Please return them when you no longer need them so I can lend them to other clients. I may also give you copies of articles or handouts that are yours to keep.

I usually take notes during our meetings. You may find it useful to take your own notes, and also to take notes outside the office. You could also tape-record our meetings to review at your leisure at home.

As to a client's note taking, I have found this useful for the same reasons I take notes myself: It is an opportunity to mull over what has been said; it aids my (or the client's) focusing as I decide (or the client decides) what to note; and it provides a record of what has happened and been said that I (or the client) can review. Occasionally, I have encouraged clients to keep a three-ring binder called "My Therapy" for notes, diaries, questions, clippings, photos, or any other relevant materials. It may be necessary to mention that these notes should be kept in such a way as to maintain their privacy, and even that clients might wish to destroy these at some future date.

Consider carefully before including the suggestion, as I do, that the client tape-record sessions. We all say things that we might later modify or withdraw, but a recording is fixed. You cannot ask a client to destroy recordings he or she has made, because they belong to the client. Also, such recordings would have to be maintained by the client in a secure manner and perhaps over a long time period. On the other hand, I have encouraged audiotaping by some patients when the educational content bears repeating, with the rationale that they have "had two sessions for the price of one." Be sensitive to the magical qualities of your taped voice for some clients. In most cases, when a client does not find making recordings beneficial, he or she usually simply stops bringing the equipment to sessions. See Section 4.6 and Form 17 if you are considering making tape recordings. Remember, recordings you make become part of your records and so can be "discovered" by an unhappy client's lawyer, and you must make arrangements for their continued confidential maintenance. In any case, do not tape-record without the client's informed consent.

By the end of our first or second session, I will tell you how I see your case at this point and how I think we should proceed. I view therapy as a partnership between us. You define the problem areas to be worked on; I use some special knowledge to help you make the changes you want to make. Psychotherapy is not like visiting a medical doctor. It requires your very active involvement. It requires your best efforts to change thoughts, feelings, and behaviors. For example, I want you to tell me about important experiences, what they mean to you, and what strong feelings are involved. This is one of the ways you are an active partner in therapy.

I expect us to plan our work together. In our treatment plan we will list the areas to work on, our goals, the methods we will use, the time and money commitments we will make, and some other things. I expect us to agree on a plan that we will both work hard to follow. From time to time, we will look together at our progress and goals. If we think we need to, we can then change our treatment plan, its goals, and its methods.

You might want to indicate that minor, major, and multiple problems take different amounts of therapy time (both frequency of sessions and duration of the therapy).

An important part of your therapy will be practicing new skills that you will learn in our sessions. I will ask you to practice outside our meetings, and we will work together to set up homework assignments for you. I might ask you to do exercises, to keep records, and perhaps to do other tasks to deepen your learning. You will probably have to work on relationships in your life and make long-term efforts to get the best results. These are important parts of personal change. Change will sometimes be easy and quick, but more often it will be slow and frustrating, and you will need to keep trying. There are no instant, painless cures and no "magic pills." However, you *can* learn new ways of looking at your problems that will be very helpful for changing your feelings and reactions.

In my brochure, **I do not address goals** except to suggest that they involve the reduction of symptomatic or distressing behaviors. I address the client's other specific goals during our interviews and in the treatment plan.

Most of my clients see me once a week for 3 to 4 months. After that, we meet less often for several more months. Therapy then usually comes to an end. The process of ending therapy, called "termination," can be a very valuable part of our work. Stopping therapy should not be done casually, although either of us may decide to end it if we believe it is in your best interest. If you wish to stop therapy at any time, I ask that you agree now to meet then for at least one session to review our work together. We will review our goals, the work we have done, any future work that needs to be done, and our choices. If you would like to take a "time out" from therapy to try it on your own, we should discuss this. We can often make such a "time out" be more helpful.

I will send you a brief set of questions about 6 months after our last session. These questions will ask you to look back at our work together, and sending them to you is part of my duty as a therapist. I ask that you agree, as part of entering therapy with me, to return this follow-up form and to be very honest about what you tell me then.

### The Benefits and Risks of Therapy

As with any powerful treatment, there are some risks as well as many benefits with therapy. You should think about both the benefits and risks when making any treatment decisions. For example, in therapy, there is a risk that clients will, for a time, have uncomfortable levels of sadness, guilt, anxiety, anger, frustration, loneliness, helplessness, or other negative feelings. Clients may recall unpleasant memories. These feelings or memories may bother a client at work or in school. In addition, some people in your community may mistakenly view anyone in therapy as weak, or perhaps as seriously disturbed or even dangerous. Also, clients in therapy may have problems with people important to

> them. Family secrets may be told. Therapy may disrupt a marital relationship and some-
> times may even lead to a divorce. Sometimes, too, a client's problems may temporarily
> worsen after the beginning of treatment. Most of these risks are to be expected when peo-
> ple are making important changes in their lives. Finally, even with our best efforts, there is
> a risk that therapy may not work out well for you.

The statement above presents a list of some risks in accordance with the requirements of informed consent. For example, Hurvitz (1976) found that progress in individual therapy may often disrupt a marital relationship. If you do this kind of work, you should include this point.

John Kachorek (1990, pp. 106–109) offers a very complete and well-reasoned handout of this type. It includes this statement:

> In therapy, major life decisions are sometimes made, including decisions involving separation
> within families, development of other types of relationships, changing employment settings
> and changing life-styles. These decisions are a legitimate outcome of the therapy experience as a
> result of an individual's calling into question many of their [sic] beliefs and values. As your
> therapist, I will be available to discuss any of your assumptions, problems, or possible negative
> side effects in our work together. (p. 107)

Some other possibilities for risks, according to Soreff and McDuffee (1993), are that

> symptom[s may be intensified;] the conflict may not be resolved; the emotional experience may
> be overwhelming or too intense to deal with at this time; the targeted behavior may not change;
> the patient may not be any more aware of himself [sic] than when therapy commenced; in spite
> of therapy, the patient still may not accept or forgive himself; the interpersonal experience may
> not be successful or corrective; the therapeutic experience may activate or reactivate conflicts,
> thoughts, or emotions that may in turn lead to disruptive behavior; new and different symp-
> toms may develop during therapy; the patient may have difficulty in terminating therapy. (p.
> 491)

The next paragraph of the model brochure describes therapy's benefits.

> While you consider these risks, you should know also that the benefits of therapy have
> been shown by scientists in hundreds of well-designed research studies. People who are
> depressed may find their mood lifting. Others may no longer feel afraid, angry, or anxious.
> In therapy, people have a chance to talk things out fully until their feelings are relieved or
> the problems are solved. Clients' relationships and coping skills may improve greatly.
> They may get more satisfaction out of social and family relationships. Their personal goals
> and values may become clearer. They may grow in many directions—as persons, in their
> close relationships, in their work or schooling, and in the ability to enjoy their lives.
>
> I do not take on clients I do not think I can help. Therefore, I will enter our relationship
> with optimism about our progress.

In your description of the benefits of psychotherapy (either orally or in writing), be careful not to promise a cure, or benefits so substantial that they approach a complete cure. Again, you are not in control of all or even most of the factors determining the outcome, and you especially do not wish to cause disappointment. You might also want to cite the meta-analysis of Smith and Glass (1977). However, recommending (even energetically) is not insisting and is not coercion, so don't be shy about the therapy you offer. Everstine et al. (1980) also discuss the benefits of personal growth and maturity.

## Consultations

This section of the brochure explains consultations. Depending on your practice, you might indicate here that you sometimes will suggest the need for psychological or educational testing, or for medication evaluation and prescription. If so, note the approximate cost of such referrals, and your usual arrangements for these referrals. If you are likely to refer clients to other professionals for services such as nutrition evaluation and counseling, exercise or martial arts training, vocational guidance, cosmetic surgery, credit counseling, shelters and protection agencies, or the like, this would be a good place to describe those options briefly as well. If you will be transferring protected health information (PHI) to a peer professional, those of a different profession, or any organization or group of professionals outside your own office or agency, HIPAA's privacy regulations *may* apply. In order to maintain the privacy of this information when sent to, say, a printer of monthly bills or a lawyer, HIPAA (which does not apply to nonhealthcare organizations) makes them your "Business Associates" and imposes duties on you to "satisfactorily safeguard" the privacy of the PHI you transfer by adding specifics to your contracts with them. Some of these "entities" could be related to you in "organized health care arrangements" and sharing PHI will be covered by the patient's initial "Notice of Privacy Practices" (see Section 7.8), while others will require you to obtain an "authorization" to release PHI, and still others will need to be considered under the regulations concerning "marketing." Face-to-face discussions with a patient about another's services or products are "marketing" but are exempted from the need for an authorization. The regulations are in Section 164.5 of the HIPAA Privacy Rule but are too detailed to be covered here.

> If you could benefit from a treatment I cannot provide, I will help you to get it. You have a right to ask me about such other treatments, their risks, and their benefits. Based on what I learn about your problems, I may recommend a medical exam or use of medication. If I do this, I will fully discuss my reasons with you, so that you can decide what is best. If you are treated by another professional, I will coordinate my services with them and with your own medical doctor.
>
> If for some reason treatment is not going well, I might suggest you see another therapist or another professional in addition to me. As a responsible person and ethical therapist, I cannot continue to treat you if my treatment is not working for you. If you wish for another professional's opinion at any time, or wish to talk with another therapist, I will help you find a qualified person and will provide him or her with the information needed.

Try to present alternative treatments evenhandedly for two reasons: (1) to present yourself as truly having the client's best interests at heart, and (2) to keep the client from thinking that, because you are discussing other helping programs so enthusiastically, you do not really want to work with the client (Hare-Mustin et al., 1979).

## What to Expect from Our Relationship

Sam Knapp, EdD, of Harrisburg, PA, offers the following wording as an introduction to this topic: "Psychological services are best provided in an atmosphere of trust. You expect me to be honest with you about your problems and progress. I expect you to be honest with me about your expectations for services, your compliance with medication, and any other barriers to treatment."

As a professional, I will use my best knowledge and skills to help you. This includes following the standards of the American Psychological Association, or APA. In your best interests, the APA puts limits on the relationship between a therapist and a client, and I will abide by these. Let me explain these limits, so you will not think they are personal responses to you.

First, I am licensed and trained to practice psychology—not law, medicine, finance, or any other profession. I am not able to give you good advice from these other professional viewpoints.

Second, state laws and the rules of the APA require me to keep what you tell me confidential (that is, private). You can trust me not to tell anyone else what you tell me, except in certain limited situations. I explain what those are in the "About Confidentiality" section of this brochure. Here I want to explain that I try not to reveal who my clients are. This is part of my effort to maintain your privacy. If we meet on the street or socially, I may not say hello or talk to you very much. My behavior will not be a personal reaction to you, but a way to maintain the confidentiality of our relationship.

Third, in your best interest, and following the APA's standards, I can only be your therapist. I cannot have any other role in your life. I cannot, now or ever, be a close friend or socialize with any of my clients. I cannot be a therapist to someone who is already a friend. I can never have a sexual or romantic relationship with any client during, or after, the course of therapy. I cannot have a business relationship with any of my clients, other than the therapy relationship.

In the paragraph above, it would be appropriate to add any rules you have that the client might inadvertently break or misinterpret. For example, some therapists have a rule never to touch a patient, mainly to avoid miscommunication (see Section 3.9). See Kertay and Reviere (1993) for a full discussion of and guidelines about touch. Or you may have a rule that the client establishes (perhaps with some assistance) the goals of therapy, and that you serve as his or her consultant in providing the means for those ends. Such clarifications are especially useful with borderline patients and those with a history of manipulation.

You might also want to add more specific information on these points:

Even though you might invite me, I will not attend your family gatherings, such as parties or weddings.

As your therapist, I will not celebrate holidays or give you gifts; I may not notice or recall your birthday; and may not receive any of your gifts eagerly.

Haas and Malouf (1995) offer excellent guidelines on the subject of gift receiving: express positive and caring feelings; do not immediately clinically process the giving; suggest an alternative (such as a gift to charity); and relax about most of these situations.

If you treat clients for addiction, they are likely to show up intoxicated at some point. Handling this is best done with paragraphs in your brochure (1) having them agree to attend treatment uninebriated and to give consent to random drug or alcohol tests, and (2) emphasizing the value of and need for honesty. On that basis, you can immediately confront them when you suspect substance use and then explore it therapeutically, rather than dismissing them from therapy (temporarily or permanently)—or, worse, ignoring slips.

## About Confidentiality

The section of the brochure on confidentiality is one of crucial legal concern. The APA ethics code (APA, 2002, Section 4.02) requires that the limits of confidentiality be communicated explicitly and in advance to all clients (clinical and organizational). It requires that you discuss the limits of confidentiality at the beginning of treatment and as any new circumstances warrant. The HIPAA Privacy Rule requires that you furnish clients with a "Notice of Privacy Practices," but if your state regulations are more stringent, you may not need to take this route to maintaining privacy. See Section 7.8 for more information on this form. As of 1990, Massachusetts law requires the therapist to furnish a handout to each client explaining the limits of confidentiality. Other states also require this kind of disclosure for informed consent, so this section of the brochure addresses this issue in detail. You might want to provide your clients (or selected clients) with a separate handout concerning only this issue; see Section 7.1 for such a handout and for more information.

> I will treat with great care all the information you share with me. It is your legal right that our sessions and my records about you be kept private. That is why I ask you to sign a "release-of-records" form before I can talk about you or send my records about you to anyone else. In general, I will tell no one what you tell me. I will not even reveal that you are receiving treatment from me.
>
> In all but a few rare situations, your confidentiality (that is, your privacy) is protected by state law and by the rules of my profession. Here are the most common cases in which confidentiality is *not* protected:
>
> 1. If you were sent to me by a court or an employer for evaluation or treatment, the court or employer expects a report from me. If this is your situation, please talk with me before you tell me anything you do not want the court or your employer to know. You have a right to tell me only what you are comfortable with telling.
>
> 2. Are you suing someone or being sued? Are you being charged with a crime? If so, and you tell the court that you are seeing me, I may then be ordered to show the court my records. Please consult your lawyer about these issues.
>
> 3. If you make a serious threat to harm yourself or another person, the law requires me to try to protect you or that other person. This usually means telling others about the threat. I cannot promise never to tell others about threats you make.
>
> 4. If I believe a child has been or will be abused or neglected, I am legally required to report this to the authorities.

Under the second exception above, you might consider noting that your records may be brought into custody or adoption proceedings (this is important if you see couples or families), or any other legal case in which a judge decides that a client's mental or emotional condition is an important element. Disability cases, worker's compensation hearings, psychiatric hospitalization, and criminal cases are some possibilities.

In the fourth exception above, I use the phrase, "If I believe a child . . . ". I have used "believe," but this word may not be accurate in your state. State laws differ in their language. For example, if the legal criterion is "what a reasonable person would suspect," this means that the level of evidence for reporting is lower than if the law were to say "believe." You must know your local rules. You might post a copy of the law in your waiting room, as suggested by David Clovard, MD, of Raleigh, NC.

An alternative phrasing for the third and fourth exceptions above is this: "As a therapist, my legal and moral duty is to protect your confidentiality, but I also have a duty under the law to the wider community and to myself, if there is harm, threat of harm, or neglect."

Obviously, you need to tailor the confidentiality section of your brochure to your specific situation, locality, and practice. For example, does your state have other exceptions to confidentiality besides those listed above, such as elder abuse? Be sure to modify this statement in light of your title, your profession's legal status, the state in which you practice, and the type of therapy you are doing. For example, if you see neuropsychology or rehabilitation clients and your state requires you to notify it of impaired drivers, you should indicate this rule. There is no substitute for exact knowledge and caution.

The statements above are not suitable for the treatment of minors. Set the ground rules with minors and their parents before therapy. See also Forms 11 and 12 for treatment contracts for minors, and Form 15 for a consent-to-treatment form for a child.

A different or fuller statement of the law in your locality, or for your profession, may be appropriate concerning consultations. You may use the patient handout on the limits of confidentiality (Handout 8) as a basis for your version.

> There are two situations in which I might talk about part of your case with another therapist. I ask now for your understanding and agreement to let me do so in these two situations.
>
> First, when I am away from the office for a few days, I have a trusted fellow therapist "cover" for me. This therapist will be available to you in emergencies. Therefore, he or she needs to know about you. Of course, this therapist is bound by the same laws and rules as I am to protect your confidentiality.
>
> Second, I sometimes consult other therapists or other professionals about my clients. This helps me in giving high-quality treatment. These persons are also required to keep your information private. Your name will never be given to them, and they will be told only as much as they need to know to understand your situation.

Knapp (1992b) has made a number of suggestions about communicating with a client's primary care physician (PCP), both in general and when the client is a Medicare patient. He suggests discussing the desirability of notifying the PCP, doing so in the most efficient way, and documenting this in the chart. If the client has refused, note this and the reasons offered. Knapp suggests this wording for your brochure:

> It may be beneficial for me to confer with your primary care physician with regard to your psychological treatment or to discuss any medical problems for which you are receiving treatment. In addition, Medicare requires that I notify your physician by telephone or in writing, concerning services that are being provided by me unless you request that notification not be made.
>
> Please check ONE of the following:
>
> ❑ You are authorized to contact my primary care physician whose name and address are shown below to discuss the treatment that I am receiving while under your care and to obtain information concerning my medical diagnosis and treatment.
>
> ❑ I do not authorize you to contact my primary care physician with regard to the treatment that I am receiving while under your care or to obtain information concerning my medical diagnosis

and treatment. I am providing you with the name and address of my primary care physician only for your records. (1992b, p. 7)

He then asks for the name, address, and phone number of the PCP.

I believe the HIPAA regulations allow the sharing of PHI with peer mental health clinicians or physicians without any other consent beyond the initial Notice of Privacy Practices. Note, however, that patients have some ability, under HIPAA, to restrict the sharing of their information (see Section 7.8).

An alternative phrasing for consultation is offered by Constance Fisher, PhD, of Pittsburgh, PA: "We consult with colleagues and specialists about our ongoing work. This pursuit of quality assurance never involves your name or any specifics through which you might be identified."

> For the purpose of these consultations, I may want to make audio or video recordings of our sessions. I will review the recordings with my consultant to assist with your treatment. I will ask your permission to make any recording. I promise to destroy each recording as soon as I no longer need it, or, at the latest, when I destroy your case records. You can refuse to allow this recording, or can insist that the recording be edited.

You should have the client sign a formal release (such as Form 17) if you are going to videotape sessions for consultations.

> Except for the situations I have described above, my office staff and I will always maintain your privacy. I also ask you not to disclose the name or identity of any other client being seen in this office.

> My office staff makes every effort to keep the names and records of clients private. My staff and I will try never to use your name on the telephone, if clients in the office can overhear it. All staff members who see your records have been trained in how to keep records confidential.

Make sure you fulfill this promise by designing a training program for all current and new staff members. See Section 7.2 for some guidance on this.

> If your records need to be seen by another professional, or anyone else, I will discuss it with you. If you agree to share these records, you will need to sign a release form. This form states exactly what information is to be shared, with whom, and why, and it also sets time limits. You may read this form at any time. If you have questions, please ask me.

You might want to add the following, again suggested by Constance Fisher, PhD, of Pittsburgh, PA: "We do not divulge the fact that you are a client or anything about you or your sessions to anyone, unless you request us (in writing) to do so."

Because you cannot foretell the needs for your records, I suggest retaining them for many years, or forever (see Section 1.6 on retention of records), and your clients should be advised of your policy. Here is my own statement:

> It is my office policy to destroy clients' records 15 years after the end of our therapy. Until then, I will keep your case records in a safe place.

There are two sides to this coin. Keeping records forever may protect you, but they are discoverable by opposing lawyers. The information in records can become very outdated and invalid, and so useless or even misleading. I think that therapists cannot automatically refuse to furnish records just because they might be invalid, so I suggest adding a statement to your cover letter warning of this issue (see Form 49).

Because your records must be available even when you cannot provide them (see Section 1.6), include a statement like this in your brochure:

> If I must discontinue our relationship because of illness, disability, or other presently un-foreseen circumstances, I ask you to agree to my transferring your records to another therapist who will assure their confidentiality, preservation, and appropriate access.

If you treat couples or families, the APA ethics code (APA, 2002, Standard 10.02) addresses some issues like confidentiality. Therefore, you might want to insert a notice like the following, before going on to address the topic of the information you give to insurance companies:

> If we do family or couple therapy (where there is more than one client), and you want to have my records of this therapy sent to anyone, all of the adults present will have to sign a release.

In 15 years of practice, I was contacted twice by the FBI when patients sought security clearances. However, this is not the only risk of receiving mental health treatment; other situations should be fully explored before a record is created and it is too late. For example, when all patient records are computerized, there is likely to be no way of segregating old records created under assumptions of confidentiality from new ones, or even from old medical records with different protections of confidentiality (as, for example, those created in different states). In addition, most medical diagnoses and treatments received have been recorded in the Medical Information Bureau's (www.mib.com) files and are accessed whenever one applies for life, health, disability, or long-term care insurance, as well as for other purposes. Routinely, diagnoses of depression affect one's eligibility for life insurance and the cost of such insurance, hiring for security-sensitive jobs and political ambitions (remember Senator Thomas Eagleton, George McGovern's ex-runningmate in 1972?). You should decide if you need to educate your clients about this issue before creating a record which would become eligible for inclusion in the files at the MIB.

> As part of cost control efforts, an insurance company will sometimes ask for more information on symptoms, diagnoses, and my treatment methods. It will become part of your permanent medical record. I will let you know if this should occur and what the company has asked for. Please understand that I have no control over how these records are handled at the insurance company. My policy is to provide only as much information as the insurance company will need to pay your benefits.

These are lively issues and of great concern. Federal laws like the proposed Patient's Bill of Rights, the HIPAA regulations, and the Employee Retirement Income Security Act (ERISA, 1974) "shield" interact with state laws, regulations, and our codes of ethics concerning privacy issues. The computerization of medical records, storage in multiple data bases with very different access rules, the use of encryption, and other pressures and events not foreseeable at present will shape your way of practicing. You will have to craft (and update) guidelines for your practice that you believe are in your and your client's best interest.

Many states have laws concerning clients' review of their own records, but few of those apply to private practice. For example, federal law is silent on drug and alcohol clients' inspection of their records (Drug Abuse Office and Treatment Act of 1972, Public Law 92-255), even when such clients are seen in private practice. But it defers to stricter state laws. These laws usually concern the following points: A client has a right to inspect records; to request corrections of inaccurate, irrelevant, outdated, or incomplete information; and to submit rebuttal information or memoranda. If your state laws do not offer clients the opportunity to review and modify your records, the HIPAA regulations on accessing and amending records (164.524 and 164.526, respectively) are very likely to apply (see Section 7.8).

> You can review your own records in my files at any time. You may add to them or correct them, and you can have copies of them. I ask you to understand and agree that you may not examine records created by anyone else and sent to me.

The laws may allow a professional or an agency manager to remove part of the record temporarily, if he or she determines that it might be detrimental to the client. This person must document the removal and its rationale (see Section 7.3). The client may appeal any limitation of access. If you design your procedures to work within these guidelines, and indicate your rules in your brochure, you will reduce your risk exposure greatly.

> In some very rare situations, I may temporarily remove parts of your records before you see them. This would happen if I believe that the information will be harmful to you, but I will discuss this with you.

## My Background

This section of the brochure gives your clients information about your professional background and training. Mention only your clinically relevant background; do not list social or political accomplishments, if these are irrelevant to being a therapist. You can include your areas of special professional interest, your publications, your supervisor status, and/or positions you hold in your professional organizations. If you present yourself as having any specialty, you will have to perform at, and conform to, the standards of others with full certification in that specialty. See Section 1.2 on the ethics of credentials. Few people are knowledgeable about therapists' credentials, so it may be helpful to offer explanations of such matters as licensure or levels of certification. You can also mention training, such as internships, qualifications, supervision, education, and positions held.

**If you are being supervised,** the APA code of ethics (APA, 2002, Standard 10.01c) requires that you inform clients of this fact and the supervisor's name where the supervisor has legal responsibility. I would suggest also including the supervisor's address and phone number as well, with the intention of heading off problems.

It is not unethical to include a statement of experience such as this: "I have over 20 years of experience in the delivery of psychotherapy, psychological assessment, and consultation to children, adults, and families." You can also list the full range of services you offer such as group, individual, relationship, and/or family therapy; evaluations of various kinds; consultations with schools, other clinicians, or lawyers; hospital and home visits; and so on.

> I am a psychologist with 25 years of experience. For the past 12 years, I have had my own office for the general practice of clinical psychology. I am trained and experienced in doing one-on-one and couple therapy with adults (18 years and over). Earlier in my career, I worked in clinics and similar settings. I hold these qualifications:
>
> - ■ I have a doctoral degree in clinical psychology from the University of Pittsburgh, whose program is approved by the American Psychological Association (APA).
>
> - ■ I completed an internship in clinical psychology, approved by the APA.
>
> - ■ I am licensed as a psychologist in Pennsylvania.
>
> - ■ I am a member of the APA.
>
> - ■ I am a fellow of the Pennsylvania Psychological Association.

I am a psychologist and I like the phrase "general practice of clinical psychology." But you might prefer to call yourself a "health psychologist," a "counselor," or another explanatory title. I have avoided the term "private practice," but an acceptable alternative phrase is "independent practice."

Although memberships do not certify competence, listing them informs the client of your adherence to that organization's codified ethical standards. Thus the client has recourse to the professional organization's ethics committee. You might consider stating in the brochure here that you accept and practice in conformity with the code of ethics of your license or certification in your state. This model brochure makes such a statement in a later section (see "Statement of Principles and Complaint Procedures").

### About Our Appointments

> The very first time I meet with you, we will need to give each other much basic information. For this reason, I usually schedule 1–2 hours for this first meeting. Following this, we will usually meet for a 50-minute session once or twice a week, then less often. We can schedule meetings for both your and my convenience. I will tell you at least a month in advance of my vacations or any other times we cannot meet. Please ask about my schedule in making your own plans.

The paragraph above describes the general time frame for brief therapy. You might want to be more detailed about the first session. It could be called an "initial evaluation session," for example, and you could specify that it includes open discussion of problems and concerns, history gathering, testing or questionnaires, and completion of forms (e.g., Form 27, the financial information form).

The scheduling of weekly appointments is traditional but not empirical. In a fascinating article, Zhu and Pierce (1995) suggest that, to the degree that the learning in therapy resembles the learning–forgetting curves seen in laboratory studies, the schedule of meetings ought to be negatively accelerated. As an example, they suggest meetings at 1, 3, 7, 14, and 30 days for optimal prevention of relapse. I would very strongly encourage you to consider such a schedule.

I suggest above that appointments can be scheduled for "both your and my convenience." An alternative wording might be "Changes in appointments should be made with as much advance notice as possible, as a sign of our mutual respect." Or "While I am willing to be flexible, I have found that therapy is more effective when it occurs at a regular time each week. I hope we can work toward this regularity of schedules." Or "Appointments can be scheduled during my office hours, Monday through Friday, 11:00 A.M. to 9:00 P.M." If you use this last format, you could indicate that appointments or calls outside these times will be charged at twice your usual rate.

Be careful not to use "session" and "hour" interchangeably (unless your session length truly is 60 minutes). Doing so may mislead some clients. Do not choose the length of your session on the basis of what your peers are doing; choose it on the basis of your particular style of doing therapy. Keep in mind your need for breaks, for time to write notes, and for moving around, as well as your office location. Therapists often schedule 1-hour sessions for individuals and 1½-hour sessions for couples. If you treat both individuals and couples, you can include both lengths at this point in your brochure.

> An appointment is a commitment to our work. We agree to meet here and to be on time. If I am ever unable to start on time, I ask your understanding. I also assure you that you will receive the full time agreed to. If you are late, we will probably be unable to meet for the full time, because it is likely that I will have another appointment after yours.
>
> A cancelled appointment delays our work. I will consider our meetings very important and ask you to do the same. Please try not to miss sessions if you can possibly help it. When you must cancel, please give me at least a week's notice. Your session time is reserved for you. I am rarely able to fill a cancelled session unless I know a week in advance. If you start to miss a lot of sessions, I will have to charge you for the lost time unless I am able to fill it. Your insurance will not cover this charge.

For the paragraph above, you can substitute the following:

> I will reserve a regular appointment time for you into the foreseeable future. I also do this for my other patients. Therefore, I am rarely able to fill a cancelled session unless I have several weeks' notice. You will be charged the full fee for sessions cancelled with less than 72 hours' notice, for other than the most serious reasons.

Repetition of this point on your appointment cards, on your bills, and on a sign in the office is recommended.

The quite reasonable charging for missed sessions can be complicated by your agreements with managed care organizations (MCOs) or Medicare, which generally forbid your charging a client for anything but the copayment. Read your contracts before including such a statement.

If you are able, should you charge no-shows, late cancellers, or late arrivers the full amount? Licensed psychologist Sheila Carluccio, MA, of Dickson City, PA, has made some excellent suggestions about this issue:

> Although it specifically states in my guidelines for treatment that I reserve the right to charge for cancellations, I reduce the charge for a missed session to $40.00 and am very specific that the charge is (1) not reimbursable through insurance and (2) charged in the event of frequent cancelling/no-shows, etc. We talk about the circumstances for missing the session. [For instance,] you'd rather go to the mall/keep forgetting to show up/don't "feel like" coming to a session? Then I'd have to charge. You have a sick child/got called to work mandatory overtime/you're

snowed in and can't make it? No charge. The guidelines are then signed as a treatment contract. In the event that difficulties arise, I refer back to this contract and we discuss it. Clients know from the beginning that being charged is something that they are choosing; at the same time I am giving clients the clear message that they need to be responsible for their own benefit (consistent treatment), that I have a respectable boundary, and that my time and their treatment is valuable. For most families living in my area $40.00 is nothing to sneeze at.

Another option is to charge but offer the client a timely replacement session—at your convenience, of course. What if you yourself are unable to make it to the session? A free makeup session would seem fair.

Constance Fisher, PhD, of Pittsburgh, PA, suggests having a clear, specific policy, such as the following: "Except for unpredictable emergencies (or because of a situation that would be seen by both of us as an unpredictable emergency), I will charge you 50% of the regular fee for any missed sessions." She chooses to implement this only with the second missed session.

Another possible statement is "If the appointment is not kept or is cancelled with less than 24 hours' advance notice, you can expect me to charge you for it." Some therapists add, "A retainer against such sessions, or for the closing session, will be requested at the initial meeting." For some therapists, the minimum advance notice for cancellation is 24 hours; this might then make a provision for weekends necessary, such as "Cancellations for a Monday appointment should be made no later than Thursday morning."

Note that the cancellation policy above is addressed to an individual client. If you treat families or couples, you need to make clear what you will do when everyone does not attend. (See Section 4.5 for some points concerning family therapy contracting.)

If you see children or adolescents, you should modify the following statement to suit your practice:

> I request that you do not bring children with you if they are young and need babysitting or supervision, which I cannot provide. I do not have toys, but I can provide reading materials suitable for older children.

You might also want to include a statement such as this: "You will be charged for any damage to, or theft of, property in this office by you or anyone for whom you are legally responsible." To this you might add, "I cannot be responsible for any personal property or valuables you bring into this office."

Depending on your methods, you might end this section with other information for clients, such as suggesting comfortable dress, requesting no smoking, asking that they avoid bringing food or drinks, or offering a note about your dog's or cat's presence (if you have an "office pet").

### Fees, Payments, and Billing

> Payment for services is an important part of any professional relationship. This is even more true in therapy; one treatment goal is to make relationships and the duties and obligations they involve clear. You are responsible for seeing that my services are paid for. Meeting this responsibility shows your commitment and maturity.

My current regular fees are as follows. You will be given advance notice if my fees should change.

*Regular therapy services:* For a session of _____ minutes, the fee is $_____ Please pay for each session at its end. I have found that this arrangement helps us stay focused on our goals, and so it works best. It also allows me to keep my fees as low as possible, because it cuts down on my bookkeeping costs. I suggest you make out your check before each session begins, so that our time will be used best. Other payment or fee arrangements must be worked out before the end of our first meeting.

*Telephone consultations:* I believe that telephone consultations may be suitable or even needed at times in our therapy. If so, I will charge you our regular fee, prorated over the time needed. If I need to have long telephone conferences with other professionals as part of your treatment, you will be billed for these at the same rate as for regular therapy services. If you are concerned about all this, please be sure to discuss it with me in advance so we can set a policy that is comfortable for both of us. Of course, there is no charge for calls about appointments or similar business.

*Extended sessions:* Occasionally it may be better to go on with a session, rather than stop or postpone work on a particular issue. When this extension is more than 10 minutes, I will tell you, because sessions that are extended beyond 10 minutes will be charged on a prorated basis.

*Psychological testing services:* $_____ per hour. Psychological testing fees include the time spent with you, the time needed for scoring and studying the test results, and the time needed to write a report on the findings. The amount of time involved depends on the tests used and the questions the testing is intended to answer.

*Reports:* I will not charge you for my time spent making routine reports to your insurance company. However, I will have to bill you for any extra-long or complex reports the company might require. The company will not cover this fee.

*Other services:* Charges for other services, such as hospital visits, consultations with other therapists, home visits, or any court-related services (such as consultations with lawyers, depositions, or attendance at courtroom proceedings) will be based on the time involved in providing the service at my regular fee schedule. Some services may require payment in advance.

I realize that my fees involve a substantial amount of money, although they are well in line with similar professionals' charges. For you to get the best value for your money, we must work hard and well.

You may want to specify different fees for activities with different time needs or costs. For example, fees for supervision may be lower. Fees for conducting in-service or other training sessions may be higher because of the preparation time involved. Court testimony may be priced by the half-day, since schedules may be uncertain. If you write reports for lawyers or others, you may want to state that these "must be fully paid for before they are provided in legally signed form or released to any third party." See also Form 51 for a release and contract with a lawyer.

You may wish to offer variations in your fee structure, but be careful to avoid seeming to have two fees—one for those who have health insurance and a lower one for those who do not—because the insurance company will see this as fraud. Instead, you can offer a discount on your regular fee, just as you do when you sign onto a panel of an MCO. You must however make this explicit on your bills by showing your regular fee, the adjustment, and the resulting charge. You could offer a discount to self-paying clients for payment in full at the time of billing or for payment in advance, but not for those who pay slowly. All of this must be explicitly stated in your information brochure for clients.

Other points that may need clarification can be included here:

- Will you accept a portion of the fee at the time of services, with the rest to be paid by the insurance company at a future date? If so, make this clear.

- Will you raise a client's fee during the course of therapy? The brochure has mentioned above that clients will be given advance notice of fee increases; this alerts them to the possibility. But if you anticipate a long treatment period and significant inflation, you should state your policy—for example, "I examine my costs yearly, and so may change my fees each new year." It may be too cautious, but consider never raising your charges to an individual client over the course of therapy, because it may appear that you are inflating your changes to gain more insurance reimbursement or in some other way exploiting the relationship (and this may trigger a complaint).

- Will you lower your fee if a client's insurance coverage is exhausted or if a client's financial circumstances change? (See Section 2.1 on financial policies.) You should decide and include a statement here.

- It's a good idea to repeat that payment is due at each session by hanging a sign about this in your waiting room. You can also have it printed on your appointment cards. Susan Hutchinson, DSW, LCSW, of Irvine, CA, advises clients in her office policy statement that she does not bill for the copayment; she thus reinforces payment for each session.

- If you offer payment by credit card, say so in this section. If you don't offer it, you may want to consider doing it (see Section 2.5).

- If your fee varies with the patient's MCO contract, you must indicate that this is so, or you may be misrepresenting your fee.

- If you make any other extra charges, such as a double rate outside your usual hours, it is helpful to put it here. This is the section clients will refer to when they check on charges.

> I will assume that our agreed-upon fee-paying relationship will continue as long as I provide services to you. I will assume this until you tell me in person, by telephone, or by certified mail that you wish to end it. You have a responsibility to pay for any services you receive before you end the relationship.

If you decide to bill some clients, you probably should put something like the following paragraphs into your brochure:

> Because I expect all payment at the time of our meetings, I usually do not send bills. However, if we have agreed that I will bill you, I ask that the bill be paid within 5 days of when you get it.

> At the end of each month, I will send you a statement. The statement can be used for health insurance claims, as described in the next section. It will show all of our meetings, the charges for each, how much has been paid, and how much (if any) is still owed. At the end of treatment, and when you have paid for all sessions, I will send you a final statement for your tax records.

The paragraphs above obviously should fit your office procedures. If you provide a "walk-out" receipt (see Section 2.5) at the end of each session, this is what a client should submit to the insurance company, and you won't need to send a statement. As regards tax deductibility, you could add, "Depending on your financial circumstances and total medical costs for any year, psychotherapy may be a deductible expense," and "Consult your tax advisor." Cost of transportation to and from appointments and fees paid may be deductible from the client's personal income taxes as medical expenses.

You may want to advise some clients to look into medical savings accounts (MSAs), because they can cover psychotherapy costs. The clients will need to pay for their own high-deductible health insurance (like the old Major Medical policies), and then establish MSAs, usually with a bank. The costs are low and the tax advantages are high for any client who can afford to pay several thousand dollars a year into such an account. A good starting place is http://www.hmopage.org/msaguide.html.

> If you think you may have trouble paying your bills on time, please discuss this with me. I will also raise the matter with you so we can arrive at a solution. If your unpaid balance reaches $_____, I will notify you by mail. If it then remains unpaid, I must stop therapy with you. Fees that continue unpaid after this will be turned over to small-claims court or a collection service.

A simpler alternative to the last sentence above is offered by Sam Knapp, EdD, of Harrisburg, PA: "Patients who owe money and fail to make arrangements to pay may be referred to a collection agency." Another alternative is to set a session limit on the amount owed.

For informed consent about confidentiality, it is also a good idea to indicate the kinds of information you will provide to those you hire to collect your old bills. A collection agency may get only the client's name, address, phone number, the amount owed, and the name of the therapist. (Collection agencies usually want more information if they need to locate an ex-client.) Small-claims court will get only the client's name, address, proof of services, and the amount owed to you.

Charging of interest or offering of credit requires you to comply with federal and state laws and forms. Therefore, use late fees or charge no interest. You can use "A late fee of 1½% of the unpaid balance will be charged each month" or "A late payment fee of $_____ will be charged each month that a balance remains unpaid."

You may want to indicate that you do not give refunds to unsatisfied customers (or to explain when you do give refunds).

> If there is any problem with my charges, my billing, your insurance, or any other money-related point, please bring it to my attention. I will do the same with you. Such problems can interfere greatly with our work. They must be worked out openly and quickly.

### If You Have Traditional (or "Indemnity") Health Insurance Coverage

Because I am a licensed psychologist, many health insurance plans will help you pay for therapy and other services I offer. These plans include Blue Shield and most Major Medical plans. Because health insurance is written by many different companies, I cannot tell you what your plan covers. Please read your plan's booklet under coverage for "Outpatient Psychotherapy" or under "Treatment of Mental and Nervous Conditions." Or call your employer's benefits office to find out what you need to know.

If your health insurance will pay part of my fee, I will help you with your insurance claim forms. However, please keep two things in mind:

1. I had no role in deciding what your insurance covers. Your employer decided which, if any, services will be covered and how much you (and I) will be paid. You are responsible for checking your insurance coverage, deductibles, payment rates, copayments, and so forth. Your insurance contract is between you and your company; it is not between me and the insurance company.

2. You—not your insurance company or any other person or company—are responsible for paying the fees we agree upon. If you ask me to bill a separated spouse, a relative, or an insurance company, and I do not receive payment on time, I will then expect this payment from you.

To seek payment from your insurance company, you must first obtain a claim form from your employer's benefits office or call your insurance company. Complete the claim form. Then attach my statement to the claim form and mail it to your insurance company. My statement already provides the information asked for on the claim form.

You should insert here whatever procedures you will perform (such as doing all the verification of coverage, billing insurers, billing for copayments, etc.) and what procedures are expected of the patient.

### If You Have a Managed Care Contract

If you belong to a health maintenance organization (HMO) or have another kind of health insurance with managed care, decisions about what kind of care you need and how much of it you can receive will be reviewed by the plan. The plan has rules, limits, and procedures that we should discuss. Please bring your health insurance plan's description of services to one of our early meetings, so that we can talk about it and decide what to do.

It may be helpful to list here the panels of MCOs and similar organizations to which you belong, and then describe the procedures they require you to follow. Managed care issues are complicated, and to get informed consent you might want to use Handout 3.

I will provide information about you to your insurance company only with your informed and written consent. I may send this information by mail or by fax. My office will try its best to maintain the privacy of your records, but I ask you not to hold me responsible for accidents or for anything that happens as a result.

If you think that the loss of confidentiality, lessened professional control of treatment, and the impact of a psychiatric diagnosis are significant concerns for clients, consider giving them Handout 3. Ackley (1997) also has excellent educational handouts about fees and insurance and about payment plans.

### If You Need to Contact Me

I cannot promise that I will be available at all times. Although I am in the office _____ through _____, from ____ to ____, I usually do not take phone calls when I am with a client. You can always leave a message with my secretary or on my answering machine, and I will return your call as soon as I can. Generally, I will return messages daily except on Sundays and holidays.

If you have an emergency or crisis, tell this to my secretary, who will try to contact me. If you have a behavioral or emotional crisis and cannot reach me or my secretary immediately by telephone, you or your family members should call one of the following community emergency agencies: the county mental health office at _____, or the crisis center at _____, or the _____ Hospital emergency room.

Reid (1999, p. 65) intelligently reminds us that we should not "equate constant personal availability with good care." Setting boundaries appropriate to the client, the circumstances, and your own needs is fully reasonable and therapeutic. You might include a statement that there may be times that you will be unavailable because of circumstances and that your staff knows what to do in case of problems or emergencies. The professional providing your coverage at these time will need access to records, phone numbers, and other resources of the practice. See Section 1.6 for more on making records available to successors.

You might indicate (only if it is true, of course) that you return all calls within 24 hours. The rule of immediate return is a good one to make, even if you have to work hard to keep it. You might also indicate hours for regular phone calls, such as 10 A.M. to 8 P.M., and say that calls outside these hours are treated as emergencies and charged accordingly. If it fits your style of practice, you could offer a regular hour each day during which you will be available to receive calls such as questions about homework. To reduce "telephone tag," you could specify a particular time each day during which you will return calls. Callers can then leave a number where they can be reached during that time.

For emergencies, you should add specific information for your situation. You might say, "In case of an emergency, call my answering service at _____. Tell the person who answers that you urgently need to speak with me, and ask him or her to locate me." Or, "In emergencies outside of my regular office hours, call me at home at _____. If you cannot reach me in a dire emergency, call your own medical doctor or go to the nearest emergency room." If you use a wireless phone or paging device, explain that here.

The following are some alternate phone policies: "I find that telephone therapy does not work as well as face-to-face therapy, and so I discourage it. I will generally suggest our meeting if you call with a problem that is not critical." Or "I have found that brief telephone calls work quite well for some purposes, and I am willing to arrange this." Or "If I feel that our work together calls for it, I will make special arrangements for telephone contact, and this service will be charged at my usual rate."

### If I Need to Contact Someone about You

If there is an emergency during our work together, or I become concerned about your personal safety, I am required by law and by the rules of my profession to contact someone close to you—perhaps a relative, spouse, or close friend. I am also required to contact this person, or the authorities, if I become concerned about your harming someone else. Please write down the name and information of your chosen contact person in the blanks provided:

Name: _____

Address: _____

Phone: _____ Relationship to you: _____

## Other Points

If you share office space with other therapists under any kind of financial arrangements, and especially if you operate together under an assumed business name (d/b/a) such as Therapy Associates, you will need to make clear to every client that you operate separately as a professional. This is mainly to avoid becoming involved in a complaint or suit against one of your "partners" but also to assure your clients of confidentiality. The APAIT offers sample phrasing for your brochure on its Web site (http://www.apait.org).

The APA code of ethics (APA, 2002, Standard 10.02b) suggests that you address the next point:

> If you ever become involved in a divorce or custody dispute, I want you to understand and agree that I will not provide evaluations or expert testimony in court. You should hire a different mental health professional for any evaluations or testimony you require. This position is based on two reasons: (1) My statements will be seen as biased in your favor because we have a therapy relationship; and (2) the testimony might affect our therapy relationship, and I must put this relationship first.

Before treating minor children you should have the consent of both parents, but in many cases this can become problematic. What if one parent refuses consent or withdraws it after treatment has been initiated? What if a parent plans to use your assessments and notes for a custody fight? Does your state's board have rules about this issue, or does your setting have relevant laws defining minors or about minors seeking treatment on their own? What effect would a custody decree or an accusation or finding of abuse have on treatment? See Section 4.5 for some guidance on consent to treating minors.

> Doing follow-up and outcome research is always educational. As a professional therapist, I naturally want to know more about how therapy helps people. To understand therapy better, I must collect information about clients before, during, and after therapy. Therefore, I am asking you to help me by filling out some questionnaires about different parts of your life-relationships, changes, concerns, attitudes, and other areas. I ask your permission to take what you wrote on these questionnaires and what I have in my records and use it in research or teaching that I may do in the future. If I ever use the information from your questionnaire, it will always be included with information from many others. Also, your identity will be made completely anonymous. Your name will never be mentioned, and all personal information will be disguised and changed. After the research, teaching, or publishing project is completed all the data used will be destroyed.

The next paragraph is protective of both you and the client (Berkowitz, 1995). A rare patient may ask you to remove or destroy some materials with the intention of removing your means of defense, and then complain against you or institute a lawsuit.

> If, as part of our therapy, you create and provide to me records, notes, artworks, or any other documents or materials, I will return the originals to you at your written request but will retain copies.

You can also indicate in this section any special rules you have—for example, about treating patients with active substance abuse/dependence, criminal or court-referred patients, spouse/child abusers, suicidal patients, patients with paranoid disorders, and so on. If you work with adults who have a history of childhood abuse, it may be a good idea to consider informing them about the possibility of suing their abusers for monetary damages. States are now enacting laws extending the "statute of limitations" in such cases; thus it may be useful, in order to protect yourself from charges of negligence, to inform such clients of the legal situation in your area of practice.

Finally, you can leave a space here to write in any additional issues that bear on each individual case.

### Statement of Principles and Complaint Procedures

> It is my intention to fully abide by all the rules of the American Psychological Association (APA) and by those of my state license.

The APA's rules include its ethical principles and code of conduct, its standards for providers of psychological services, its guidelines for delivery of specialty services by clinical psychologists, and others you care to mention. If you are not a psychologist, give the applicable rules and codes of your profession here.

> Problems can arise in our relationship, just as in any other relationship. If you are not satisfied with any area of our work, please raise your concerns with me at once. Our work together will be slower and harder if your concerns with me are not worked out. I will make every effort to hear any complaints you have and to seek solutions to them. If you feel that I, or any other therapist, has treated you unfairly or has even broken a professional rule, please tell me. You can also contact the state or local psychological association and speak to the chairperson of the ethics committee. He or she can help clarify your concerns or tell you how to file a complaint. You may also contact the state board of psychologist examiners [note that this name differs across states], the organization that licenses those of us in the independent practice of psychology.

Some would consider it unnecessary; pessimistic, or even masochistic to tell clients how to lodge a formal ethics complaint. But this information is essential for fully informing the consumer. Vinson (1987) found that the low level of reporting of sexual and other abuses by therapists was not attributable to lack of motivation, but to lack of information on how to file a complaint. Hare-Mustin et al. (1979) say that clients need to know what the legitimate grounds for complaints are, as well as what options are available for resolving them. Brown (personal communication in Branscomb, 1996) reported that in the state of Washington, where providing such information has been required since 1987, there has been no increase of complaints (frivolous or otherwise). This is, however, a complex clinical as well as ethical issue, with complicated options that are not well addressed in a small brochure. If a concern or complaint of any sort arises, document it. Do this even if you think it trivial or baseless.

> In my practice as a therapist, I do not discriminate against clients because of any of these factors: age, sex, marital/family status, race, color, religious beliefs, ethnic origin, place of

residence, veteran status, physical disability, health status, sexual orientation, or criminal record unrelated to present dangerousness. This is a personal commitment, as well as being required by federal, state, and local laws and regulations. I will always take steps to advance and support the values of equal opportunity, human dignity, and racial/ethnic/cultural diversity. If you believe you have been discriminated against, please bring this matter to my attention immediately.

In the list above of groups that can be discriminated against I have tried to be comprehensive—including, for example, "health status" as an indicator of HIV-positive individuals; "place of residence" in regard to low-socioeconomic-status areas or community mental health center catchment areas; and some other less usual factors. You should add to, or delete from, this list anything not applicable to your practice.

### Our Agreement

I, the client (or his or her parent or guardian), understand I have the right not to sign this form. My signature below indicates that I have read and discussed this agreement; it does not indicate that I am waiving any of my rights. I understand I can choose to discuss my concerns with you, the therapist, before I start (or the client starts) formal therapy. I also understand that any of the points mentioned above can be discussed and may be open to change. If at any time during the treatment I have questions about any of the subjects discussed in this brochure, I can talk with you about them, and you will do your best to answer them.

I understand that after therapy begins I have the right to withdraw my consent to therapy at any time, for any reason. However, I will make every effort to discuss my concerns about my progress with you before ending therapy with you.

To be sure you haven't promised a cure, you might want to insert language like this at the end of the brochure:

I understand that no specific promises have been made to me by this therapist about the results of treatment, the effectiveness of the procedures used by this therapist, or the number of sessions necessary for therapy to be effective.

I have read, or have had read to me, the issues and points in this brochure. I have discussed those points I did not understand, and have had my questions, if any, fully answered. I agree to act according to the points covered in this brochure. I hereby agree to enter into therapy with this therapist (or to have the client enter therapy), and to cooperate fully and to the best of my ability, as shown by my signature here.

_____          _____

Signature of client (or person acting for client)                     Date

_____

Printed name

Relationship to client:
  ❏ Self    ❏ Parent    ❏ Legal guardian
  ❏ Health care custodial parent of a minor (less than 14 years of age)
  ❏ Other person authorized to act on behalf of the client

Besides the signature, for your additional protection and assurance that the client has read every page, you could ask the client to initial each page at the bottom by including a statement like "Initial here to show that you have read this page."

---

I, the therapist, have met with this client (and/or his or her parent or guardian) for a suitable period of time, and have informed him or her of the issues and points raised in this brochure. I have responded to all of his or her questions. I believe this person fully understands the issues, and I find no reason to believe this person is not fully competent to give informed consent to treatment. I agree to enter into therapy with the client, as shown by my signature here.

_____          _____

Signature of therapist                                              Date

I truly appreciate the chance you have given me to be of professional service to you, and look forward to a successful relationship with you. If you are satisfied with my services as we proceed, I (like any professional) would appreciate your referring other people to me who might also be able to make use of my services.

❏ Copy accepted by client              ❏ Copy kept by therapist

---

# 4.3    The Second Path to Informed Consent: The Question List as a Guide to Discussion

The second method for obtaining informed consent comes from Handelsman and Calvin's (1988) proposal to provide the client with a list of questions and then conduct a discussion of the points the client raises. They describe the advantages of their approach as follows:

> First, it informs clients what information they have a right to [ask about] but preserves their right to request it or not. Second, it may be less overwhelming for clients. . . . Third, because the answers are not spelled out, the form requires a conversation between therapist and client to take place. . . . Fourth, the form has a fourth-grade readability level. (Handelsman & Calvin, 1988, p. 224)

In short, this approach is an admirably creative, flexible, and sensitive solution to a thorny problem.

The give-and-take of discussion incorporated into this approach is the essence of the process of getting informed consent. In practice, you can give the questions to the client at the end of the first session to take home and read. The client can then be asked for questions during the second session, and the form can be signed. (If, as is fairly often the case, the client has forgotten it, a new copy can be offered, discussed, and signed.) This, then, is **a structured interview the client conducts with you.** After answering the client's questions, you can write a note such as this: "I believe I have obtained fully informed, voluntary, and competent consent to proceed with treatment because we have covered everything on my [question list]." This procedure simultaneously (1) meets your legal responsibility to get an informed consent form signed; (2) meets your ethical responsibility to have the dialogue (questions and answers) that must logically and technically underlie informed consent; and, most importantly, (3) is clinically elegant, as it starts therapy off with openness—putting everything on the table not only by answering the client's questions, but by even giving the client the questions to ask.

Because the questions are in simple English and the client signs the list to affirm that he or she has had a discussion of the points and understands them, I believe that this procedure makes a legal challenge to the effect that the patient simply signed a form, and that therefore the consent was not really informed, far less likely to succeed.

**HANDOUT 4**

The questions to be offered in this section are adapted from the article by Handelsman and Calvin (1988). Several items have been added on the basis of Handelsman's later research (Bratten et al., 1993). Handout 4 (on pp. 212–213) provides the question list in a two-page format, which you can just photocopy and hand out.

You may want to discuss some questions with your clients other than the ones based in Handelsman and colleagues' work. For example, here are some questions to which you might prepare answers—either on paper for an educational brochure, or as an oral presentation in the question-and-answer format for proceeding toward fully informed consent.

What is a psychologist (or a psychiatrist, social worker, etc.)?
What is the educational background of a psychologist (etc.)?
What is a licensed psychologist (etc.)?
What types of problems are appropriate for consulting a psychologist (etc.)?
How do psychologists (etc.) differ from other types of mental health professionals?

What is psychotherapy?
Who does psychotherapy?
What kind of therapy will I receive?
What can I expect in my initial session?
How do I assess the usefulness of my therapy?
What if I feel I am not receiving proper treatment from my therapist?
What if I need medication?

You may want to add other questions or points suited to your practice. You can also review the client information brochure (in Section 4.2) for ideas to include and for options in answering the questions about how you practice, such as your financial policies. It will be essential for you to review your procedures and rehearse your responses to each of these questions. The answers you offer can be based on straightforward facts about diagnoses and treatment, or they can be designed to serve clinical goals, such as restraining of change or predicting changes to gain control of a symptom.

The questions based on Handelsman and colleagues' work, and presented later as a complete list in Handout 4, are now discussed. For clarity, the questions are set off from the text below in the same way as segments of the model client information brochure have been in Section 4.2.

### Information You Have a Right to Know

When you come for therapy, you are buying a service to meet your individual needs. You need good information about therapy to make the best choice for yourself and your family. I have written down some questions you might want to ask me about how I do therapy. We may have talked about some of them already. You are free to ask me any of these questions, and I will try my best to answer them for you. If my answers are not clear, or if I have left something out, or if you have more questions, just ask me again. You have the right to full information about therapy.

A. About Therapy

1. What will we do in therapy?

Obviously your answer to this should be tailored to your approach, but you might say something along these lines: "We will discuss fully what brought you to see me; explore your history and background; talk about all areas of your life, especially when, with whom, and in what settings you have problems; and discuss anything else that is important, so I can fully understand your situation." You could then discuss and describe treatments.

2. What will I have to do in therapy?

Perhaps you could say: "I will expect you to be open and honest about your thoughts and feelings; to help design homework; to do the homework assignments; to try out new ways of dealing with your feelings, thoughts, or other people; to keep track of your feelings and behaviors . . . " (add anything else you think appropriate).

3. Could anything bad happen because of therapy?

This question is designed to elicit a discussion of the possible risks involved in therapy, which might include the following: not improving, feeling worse temporarily, or a true worsening of the client's condition; conflicts with spouse/partner, relatives, or peers; divorce or breakup of a relationship; or some depression, fears, and doubts. Almost every therapy client is concerned about these things, but most clients do get better.

4. What will I notice when I am getting better?

Here you can focus the client's attention on specific areas chosen for their clinical utility. You might suggest that symptoms change in frequency, duration, intensity, or latency. You can predict reduced anxiety or increased optimism, self-confidence, energy, and courage.

5. About how long will it take for me to see that I am getting better?

The response to this question will depend on the client's presenting problems and prognosis. I often tell my clients that they should feel increased optimism in a few sessions, with lessened anxiety or depression in 10–15 sessions. I also tell them that others may notice changes before they do.

6. Will I have to take any tests? What for? What kind?

Obviously this depends on your approach and discipline, but symptom measures may be useful for assessing and documenting progress and outcome for both insurers and clients.

7. How many (that is, what fraction) of your clients with my kind of problem get better?

Most of us don't have this information, but we should. This may stimulate you to do some follow-up data collection calls.

8. How many (that is, what fraction) of your clients get worse?

This is a tough but critical question. Again, data collection may be needed.

9. How many (that is, what fraction) of people with the same kinds of problems I have get better without therapy? How many get worse?

DSM-IV (American Psychiatric Association, 1994) has information on the life course of some diagnoses.

10. About how long will therapy take?

Be realistic. Don't try to offer a low number of sessions because this is all the client's insurance will pay for, in cases where you know a low number will be insufficient. You can also discuss this in terms of short- and long-term goals.

11. What should I do if I feel therapy isn't working?

You might say this: "You should discuss this with me. We may be able to modify our treatment or your expectations might be inappropriate. We may need to add additional treatment methods. If we are not making progress I will seek consultation and may ask you to go to another therapist for a consultation. If we are really not making progress, I have an ethical obligation to discontinue treatment."

B. About Other Therapy and Help

1. What other types of therapy or help are there for my problems?

You can select from counseling, medications, group therapies, support groups, self-help groups, readings, and so forth, and from social agencies, clinics, schools, other practitioners, other orientations, and other disciplines.

2. How often do these other methods help people with problems like mine?

This is often a hard question for therapists to answer, because of interdisciplinary rivalry, ignorance of others' approaches, and fears of others' inadequacy in regard to training or skill. However, just as you would want complete and accurate information on alternatives before making a major decision, your clients deserve this discussion. Don't let your selfish interest in comfort outweigh a client's needs.

3. What are the risks or limits of these other methods?

You can indicate the costs, availability, location, and entry criteria of each alternative.

C. About Our Appointments

1. How will we set up our appointments?

2. How long will our sessions last? Do I have to pay more for longer ones?

3. How can I reach you in an emergency?

4. If I can't reach you, to whom can I talk?

5. What happens if the weather is bad or I'm sick and can't come to an appointment?

Options for all of these are offered in the client information brochure (see Section 4.2).

D. About Confidentiality

1. What kinds of records do you keep about my therapy?

Describe your records to the client, or, better yet, show the client the record forms you use.

2. Who is allowed to read these records?

Some possibilities are the client, members of the client's family, other clinicians, the referrer, the courts, insurance companies and managed care organizations, government departments, supervisors, lawyers, and collection agencies. You can explain release forms and their required contents (see Section 7.3).

3. Are there times you *have* to tell others about the personal things we might talk about?

Yes, and the usual situations are suicidal or homicidal threats, child or elder abuse/neglect, and court referral of cases. See also Section 7.1 on confidentiality and its limits.

E. About Money

Here is the time to discuss your financial policies. Make sure to rehearse answers to these questions, as this is hard for almost all therapists. See Section 2.1 on financial policies, as well as Section 4.2.

1. What will you charge me for each appointment?

2. When do you want to be paid?

3. Do I need to pay for an appointment if I don't come to it or call you and cancel it?

4. Do I need to pay for telephone calls to you?

5. Will you ever raise the fee that you charge me? When?

6. If I lose some of my income, can my fee be lowered?

7. If I do not pay my bill, what will you do?

F. Other Matters

1. How much training and experience do you have? Do you have a license? What are your other qualifications?

2. What kind of morals and values do you have?

Some clients seek out religious therapists, believing that such therapists will share their values (see, e.g., the discussion of requests for "Christian counseling" in Section 4.2). All therapists have a moral philosophy, as do all therapies. Besides general values such as trustworthiness and flexibility, it may be useful to discuss value issues that are most relevant to the presenting problem (e.g., loyalty, openness despite fear of consequences, gender role preferences, respect for authority or age, etc.).

> 3. To whom can I talk if I have a complaint about therapy that you and I can't work out?

You could say something like this: "If you have a complaint that we try to work out but can't, I may ask you to see another therapist for a consultation. The consultant can give both of us another perspective. If this doesn't help and you believe the issue is crucial, you can call the local psychological association and talk to the professional affairs officer to get direction and help."

> The list above deals with the most commonly asked questions, but many people want to know more. Feel free to ask me any questions you have at any time. The more you know, the better our work will go. You can keep the "Information for Clients" brochure (if given) and this list. Please read them carefully at home, and if any questions come up, write them on this page so we can talk about them when we meet next time.

Be sure to ask at the next session—and, indeed, periodically throughout treatment—whether the client has any further questions.

Handout 4 now presents the questions discussed above as a complete, two-page list.

# 4.4 The Third Path to Informed Consent: Lists of Clients' Rights

The third path to informed consent is less formal and more fluid, and therefore better suited to some therapists and clients than the question list. It is the offering of a listing of clients' basic rights in psychotherapy.

If you are going to use this approach, you should review the three lists presented below, add your own ideas, and then devise a list tailored to the style and needs of your practice. You must also modify these rights statements to fit your local and current circumstances before you distribute the list, and you should keep it current by consulting with your local ethics committee.

As of this writing, a national Patient's Bill of Rights has not been made law. However, if some version does pass, you should examine it for parts that apply to your way of practicing and incorporate or at least address those issues. The Mental Health Consumers' Bill of Rights as endorsed by all the mental health professions is available at http://www.mentalhealth.org/publications/allpubs/oel99-0003/default.asp and in the original publication, "President's Advisory Commission on Consumer Protection and Quality in the Health Care Industry," at http://www.healthqualitycommission.gov.cborr. It has also been published by Cantor (1999).

## Information You Have a Right to Know

When you come for therapy, you are buying a service to meet your individual needs. You need good information about therapy to make the best choice for yourself and your family. I have written down some questions you might want to ask me about how I do therapy. We may have talked about some of them already. You are free to ask me any of these questions, and I will try my best to answer them for you. If my answers are not clear, or if I have left something out, or if you have more questions, just ask me again. You have the right to full information about therapy.

A. About Therapy

   1. What will we do in therapy?
   2. What will I have to do in therapy?
   3. Could anything bad happen because of therapy?
   4. What will I notice when I am getting better?
   5. About how long will it take for me to see that I am getting better?
   6. Will I have to take any tests? What for? What kind?
   7. How many (that is, what fraction) of your clients with my kind of problem get better?
   8. How many (that is, what fraction) of your clients get worse?
   9. How many (that is, what fraction) of people with the same kinds of problems I have get better without therapy? How many get worse?
  10. About how long will therapy take?
  11. What should I do if I feel therapy isn't working?

B. About Other Therapy and Help

   1. What other types of therapy or help are there for my problems?
   2. How often do these other methods help people with problems like mine?
   3. What are the risks or limits of these other methods?

C. About Our Appointments

   1. How will we set up our appointments?
   2. How long will our sessions last? Do I have to pay more for longer ones?
   3. How can I reach you in an emergency?
   4. If I can't reach you, to whom can I talk?
   5. What happens if the weather is bad or I'm sick and can't come to an appointment?

D. About Confidentiality

   1. What kinds of records do you keep about my therapy?
   2. Who is allowed to read these records?
   3. Are there times you *have* to tell others about the personal things we might talk about?

*(cont.)*

**HANDOUT 4. Question list for therapist–client discussion (client's version) (p. 1 of 2).** Adapted from Handelsman and Galvin (1988). Copyright 1988 by the American Psychological Association (APA). Adapted by permission. The APA grants purchasers the right to make photocopies for personal use only. Further use of this material without the express written permission of the APA is strictly prohibited.—From *The Paper Office*.

### E. About Money

1. What will you charge me for each appointment?
2. When do you want to be paid?
3. Do I need to pay for an appointment if I don't come to it, or if I call you and cancel it?
4. Do I need to pay for telephone calls to you?
5. Will you ever raise the fee that you charge me? When?
6. If I lose some of my income, can my fee be lowered?
7. If I do not pay my bill, what will you do?

### F. Other Matters

1. How much training and experience do you have? Do you have a license? What are your other qualifications?
2. What kind of morals and values do you have?
3. To whom can I talk if I have a complaint about therapy that you and I can't work out?

The list above deals with the most commonly asked questions, but many people want to know more. Feel free to ask me any questions you have at any time. The more you know, the better our work will go. You can keep the "Information for Clients" brochure (if given) and this list. Please read them carefully at home, and if any questions come up, write them on this page so we can talk about them when we meet next time.

I, the client (or his or her parent or guardian), have gone over this list with the therapist, and I understand these questions and the therapist's answers.

_____          _____
Signature of client (or parent/guardian)                                      Date

_____
Printed name

I, the therapist, have discussed these issues with the client (and/or his or her parent or guardian). I believe this person fully understands the issues, and I find no reason to believe that this person is not fully competent to give informed consent to treatment.

_____          _____
Signature of therapist                                                         Date

❑ Copy accepted by client      ❑ Copy kept by therapist

## About Handouts 5, 6, and 7

**HANDOUT 5**  The first list (Handout 5) is based on one first published by Everstine et al. (1980), which has been widely reprinted. In regard to point 6, see Form 17 for a consent-to-record form.

**HANDOUT 6**  The second list (Handout 6) is adapted and simplified from one provided by Bennett et al. (1990), who describe it as a list of "rights generally agreed upon" (p. 119).

**HANDOUT 7**  The third list (Handout 7) is modified from a publication of the California Department of Consumer Affairs entitled *Professional Therapy Never Includes Sex* (Quinn, n.d.). This free, 20-page booklet describes the California laws and details how to report abuse, take legal and administrative actions, and find help for the victim.

Please examine each rights statement and modify it to suit your locale and style of practice. For example, telling a client that he or she cannot refuse court-ordered testing or therapy may insert you into a conflict between the client and the court, which would be better handled by them (Sam Knapp, personal communication, October 2, 1996).

## 4.5  The Fourth Path to Informed Consent: Psychotherapy Contracts

> *All treatment proceeds with a contract or a series of contractual agreements between therapist and patient that are either explicit or implicit in therapeutic discourse. The danger of an unarticulated contract is that it can be misunderstood, tacitly reconceptualized, or inconsistently applied, and thus misused. Such misunderstandings can increase exponentially in their impact, meaning and consequence over the course of treatment, resulting in an unexamined diffusion of and diversion from the therapeutic work.*
> —LIPMAN (1995, p. 996)

Contracts are not substitutes for a client information brochure. But they can establish a different therapeutic relationship from that established by the brochure. Contracts focus on more specific aspects of therapy activities. Some of the contract forms offered here expand information on the techniques or methods of therapy, and some focus more on the goals of treatment, the "rules" for therapy, or the risks of treatment versus the probability of success.

The treatment contract can be one component of the process of getting informed consent. The form is evidence of consent, but it is not a substitute for it; as mentioned earlier, courts have held in some cases that consent was not obtained despite the signing of a form. The client must be fully informed through discussions if consent is to be effectively and legally given. Only then should a contract form be completed and signed. As treatment evolves, the contract should also be renegotiated and redrafted. If you prefer less legalistic-sounding terminology than "contract," you can call such a form an "understanding" of an "agreement."

### The Nature of Contracts

Contracts have many advantages, as pointed out by Hare-Mustin et al. (1979):

- They reinforce equality, mutuality, and cooperation because they require negotiation.

- They clarify the relationship's goals, boundaries, and expectations.

## The Rights of Clients

1. You have the right to decide not to enter therapy with me. If you wish, I will provide you with the names of other good therapists.

2. You have the right to end therapy at any time. The only thing you will have to do is to pay for any treatments you have already had. You may, of course, have problems with other people or agencies if you end therapy—for example, if you have been sent for therapy by a court.

3. You have the right to ask any questions, at any time, about what we do during therapy, and to receive answers that satisfy you. If you wish, I will explain my usual methods to you.

4. You have the right not to allow the use of any therapy technique. If I plan to use any unusual technique, I will tell you and discuss its benefits and risks.

5. You have the right to keep what you tell me private. Generally, no one will learn of our work without your written permission. There are some situations in which I am required by law to reveal some of the things you tell me, even without your permission, and if I do reveal these things I am not required by the law to tell you that I have done so. Here are some of these situations:

   a. If you seriously threaten to harm another person, I must warn that person and the authorities.

   b. If a court orders me to testify about you, I must do so.

   c. If I am testing or treating you under a court order, I must report my findings to the court.

6. If I wish to record a session, I will get your informed consent in writing. You have the right to prevent any such recording.

7. You have the right to review your records in my files at any time, to add to or correct them, and to get copies for other professionals to use.

**HANDOUT 5. First clients' rights form.**   Adapted from Everstine et al. (1980). Copyright 1980 by the American Psychological Association (APA). Adapted by permission. The APA grants purchasers of *The Paper Office* the right to make photocopies for personal use only. Further use of this material without the express written permission of the APA is strictly prohibited.—From *The Paper Office*.

## Clients' Rights in Therapy

Clients generally have the right to:

- Know all about the therapist's experience and training.

- Discuss their therapy with anyone they choose, including another therapist.

- Know all about the terms of therapy, such as its cost, appointment times, privacy issues, and so on.

- Have any therapy procedure or method explained to them before it is used.

- See all the information about them in the therapist's files, or have it shared with another professional or group at their request.

- Ask the therapist about anything about therapy—and, if not satisfied, complain to the therapist's superior, or even file a complaint with the government or the therapist's professional group.

- Read a copy of the therapist's guidelines or rules about practicing therapy, such as the therapist's code of ethics.

- Refuse any test, evaluation, or therapy of any kind.

- If a client is ordered to be evaluated or to come to therapy by a court, however, there may be legal problems when he or she stops treatment.

In this list your rights are described in very brief terms, and this state's laws or rules may give them somewhat differently. If you want more information, please ask me, and we can discuss your actual rights in this state under its current laws and rules.

**HANDOUT 6. Second clients' rights form.** Adapted from Bennett, Bryant, VandenBos, and Greenwood (1990). Copyright 1990 by the American Psychological Association (APA). Adapted by permission. The APA grants purchasers of *The Paper Office* the right to make photocopies for personal use only. Further use of this material without the express written permission of the APA is strictly prohibited.—From *The Paper Office*.

## Client Bill of Rights

You have the right to:

- Get respectful treatment that will be helpful to you.

- Have a safe treatment setting, free from sexual, physical, and emotional abuse.

- Report immoral and illegal behavior by a therapist.

- Ask for and get information about the therapist's qualifications, including his or her license, education, training, experience, membership in professional groups, special areas of practice, and limits on practice.

- Have written information, before entering therapy, about fees, method of payment, insurance coverage, number of sessions the therapist thinks will be needed, substitute therapists (in cases of vacation and emergencies), and cancellation policies.

- Refuse audio or video recording of sessions (but you may ask for it if you wish).

- Refuse to answer any question or give any information you choose not to answer or give.

- Know if your therapist will discuss your case with others (for instance, supervisors, consultants, or students).

- Ask that the therapist inform you of your progress.

**HANDOUT 7. Third clients' rights form.**     Adapted from Quinn (n.d.). This document is in the public domain.—From *The Paper Office.*

- They "prevent misunderstandings about the responsibilities, methods, and practical arrangements of therapy" (p. 8).

- They clarify the roles of each person in the relationship: the therapist as possessing special skills, the client as offering personal knowledge.

- They increase both parties' accountability.

Contracts can also be made therapeutic for some clients by the planful placement of ideas under headings such as "Responsibilities" (e.g., completing all homework assignments) or "Possible Negative Effects of Treatment" (e.g., disappointment with therapy for not making the client's life better without the client's making any efforts). In phrasing a contract, as in phrasing a client brochure, do not underestimate the difficulties of therapy or promise change over which you have little control. Continually reevaluate progress and modify the goals as issues become better understood.

I want here to make a distinction between a "treatment contract" and a "consent-to-treatment form." An agreement can be negotiated that leaves out many of the goals, problem definitions, methods, and tactics; only the most critical items are stated. However, this form should be considered a consent-to-treatment form rather than a psychotherapy contract. These pared-down consent forms constitute the fifth path to consent and are covered in the next section. Here I offer the more detailed and specific contract approach.

Contracts should be tailored to your practice and to the client's individual situation. Sample contract forms are offered in the following pages: a contract for individual psychotherapy, two for treating children and adolescents, and one for group therapy. I also discuss important issues for contracts with families and couples.

## Checklists for a Psychotherapy Contract: Elements and Options

The contracts offered here do not cover all possible variations, and as written they may not suit your way of practicing. Below, I provide lists of the basic elements that a contract should include, together with a few additional options. These checklists are designed to help you create your own contracts. You can use one of the forms that follow as a general model, then pick and choose items from the lists below. Any items included in the client information brochure (see Section 4.2) could also be incorporated into a contract; I have not, however, duplicated all these possible inclusions here. These checklists are partially based on ideas developed by the Health Research Group (Adams & Orgel, 1975), as modified in Kachorek (1990, p. 105). They also incorporate ideas from Stromberg et al. (1988, pp. 164–165), Hare-Mustin et al. (1979), Bennett et al. (1990, p. 54), and Stuart 11975). The checklists' items are worded as questions about the content of the contract form.

### Agreement and Consent

❏ Does the form indicate clearly that this is an informal "agreement"? Its purpose is to indicate an understanding, or set of mutual expectations, between the client and therapist; its ultimate goals are clarification and communication. It is not an exhaustive, complete specification of all treatment variables and issues.

❏ Does the form fully inform the client of all relevant aspects and decisions, so that the client can consent to treatment as an autonomous adult?

❏ Does the form state that the client's consent to treatment is voluntary, and that he or she is free to withdraw from or discontinue treatment without penalty?

❏ Does the form tell the client that the contract will become part of the treatment record?

❏ Does the contract provide space for the signatures of both client and therapist indicating agreement, and the dates signed?

### Goals

❏ Are the goals of the psychotherapy with this client stated?

❏ Are they based on assessment of, and consultation with, the client?

❏ Have both long-term goals and short-term objectives been developed?

### Description/Listing of Techniques

❏ Does the form describe treatment techniques, or confirm that the client has been informed of them through discussion with the therapist or reading materials?

❏ Has the client been informed of any techniques that might be at odds with his or her values?

### Risks and Benefits

❏ Are the benefits to the client described fully, accurately, and without any promise of specific outcomes, results, cures, or guarantees?

❏ Are the risks to the client described, including contraindications, side effects, and undesirable or negative effects?

### Client Responsibilities

❏ Does the form state that the client will "cooperate fully" and "to the best of my ability"?

❏ Are specific client responsibilities indicated? These could include being on time for appointments, paying on a timely basis, doing homework, reading patient education materials, cooperating with educational efforts, and the like. On a more therapeutic level, responsibilities could include acting "as if" when initiating new behaviors, not canceling appointments when afraid, examining resistances to doing homework, and working courageously to overcome shame or humiliation.

*Therapist Responsibilities: Treatment*

Does the form state that the therapist will:

❏ Use his or her best efforts, skills, resources, training, experience, in good faith?

❏ Make use of the specific techniques in which he or she has been trained in the best interests of the client?

❏ Continually monitor the progress of the therapy?

❏ Operate responsibly, such as being on time, responding promptly to calls, being prepared, and the like?

❏ Fulfill other therapeutic responsibilities, such as encouraging the client's independence or rights to self-determination, not siding with one partner in couple therapy, and so forth?

*Therapist Responsibilities: Confidentiality*

Does the form indicate that:

❏ Professional standards and ethics will be respected?

❏ There are exceptions to confidentiality (see Chapter 7)?

❏ Permission is granted to the therapist to take notes and to record the sessions (see Form 17)?

❏ Permission is granted to the therapist to collect and publish anonymous and grouped treatment data?

❏ Written permission will be needed to disclose information about any specific clients?

*Meetings and Fees*

❏ Are the location, frequency, and length of meetings indicated together with how they are arranged?

❏ Is the client's assumption of financial responsibility stated?

❏ Are fees and charges explicitly stated, including fees for missed sessions?

❏ Is the form clear about when payment is expected?

❏ Are future adjustments to the fee, if they will be made, specified?

### Changing the Contract and Terminating Treatment

❏ Does the form state that any of the contract's contents may be renegotiated? Specifics may be mentioned, such as changing the nature, priority, or definition of the goals.

❏ Are the conditions of termination of therapy made clear? Specifically, the contract may be terminated by either party, but with some explicit advance notice.

### Provisions When Treating Families or Couples

❏ Does the form state your policy on nonattendance by a family member or one member of a couple?

❏ Does the form state your policy on how you will handle family secrets?

### Provisions When Treating Children or Adolescents

❏ Have you included a statement on parents' or guardians' legal rights to certain information?

❏ Does the form address a minor's right to a private life and your use of discretion in communicating with parents?

❏ Does the form state your policy on disclosing a minor's drug use, sexual behavior, or illegal actions, as well as confessions and similar privacies?

### Provisions for Group Therapy

❏ Does each group member agree to keep other group members' identities and information confidential? (*Note:* Client information revealed in group therapy is generally not considered to be legally privileged. Do not assert that it is unless you know that it is in your state.)

### Other Issues

❏ Are remedies for client dissatisfaction stated?

❏ Is a statement that the professional believes the client is fully competent to consent to treatment included?

## A Contract for Individual Therapy with an Adult

**FORM 10**    Form 10 is a generalized agreement for adult clients. Modify it to suit your way of working.

## Agreement for Individual Therapy

I, _____, the client, agree to meet with the therapist named below at the appointment times and places we agree on, starting on _____, _____, for about _____ sessions of _____ minutes each.

I have read the following materials on therapy, which have been provided to me by this therapist:

1. _____   3. _____

2. _____   4. _____

I believe I understand the basic ideas, goals, and methods of this therapy. I have no important questions or concerns that the therapist has not discussed. In my own words, I understand the following:

1. According to this therapy, the causes of my problems lie in: _____

_____

2. The main methods to be used in this therapy are: _____

_____

3. During these sessions, we will focus on working toward these goals: _____

    a. _____   b. _____

I understand that reaching these goals is not guaranteed.

4. I understand that I will have to do the following things/take the following actions:

    a. _____   b. _____

With enough knowledge, and without being forced, I enter into treatment with this therapist. I will keep my therapist fully up to date about any changes in my feelings, thoughts, and behaviors. I expect us to work together on any difficulties that occur, and to work them out in my long-term best interest.

At the end of _____ meetings, we will evaluate progress and may change parts of this agreement as needed. Our goals may have changed in nature, order of importance, or definition. If I am not satisfied by our progress toward goals, I will attempt to make change in this agreement, and I may stop treatment after giving this therapist at least 7 days' notice of my intentions and meeting with the therapist for one last time.

This agreement shows my commitment to pay for this therapist's services. It also shows this therapist's willingness to use and share his or her knowledge and skills in good faith. I agree to pay $_____ per session, and to pay at the end of each session. I agree to pay for uncancelled appointments or those where I fail to give enough notice that I will not attend. The only exceptions are unforeseen or unavoidable situations arising suddenly. I understand and accept that I am fully responsible for this fee, but that my therapist will help me in getting payments from any insurance coverage I have. I understand that this agreement will become part of my record of treatment.

I also give my permission for the therapist to audiotape/videotape our sessions for personal review and use with a consultant, who is also bound by the legal framework of privacy and confidentiality. I understand that any information in this recording that could identify me in any way will not be published or given out without my written consent.

My signature below means that I understand and agree with all of the points above.

_____   _____
Signature of client                                                                  Date

I, the therapist, have discussed the issues above with the client. My observations of this client's behavior and responses give me no reason, in my professional judgment, to believe that this person is not fully competent to give informed and willing consent.

_____   _____
Signature of therapist                                                               Date

❑ Copy accepted by client     ❑ Copy kept by therapist

*This is a strictly confidential patient medical record. Redisclosure or transfer is expressly prohibited by law.*

**FORM 10. Contract for individual adult therapy.**     From *The Paper Office.* Copyright 2003 by Edward L. Zuckerman. Permission to photocopy this form is granted to purchasers of this book for personal use only (see copyright page for details).

## About Contracts for Couples and Families

When you go from individual to couple and family therapies, the number of ways of interacting, and thus the number of ethical complexities, increases enormously. Although these complexities cannot be detailed here, there are two excellent reviews available: those by Patten et al. (1991) and by Hansen et al. (1989). The two most common ethical problems are the situations when only one partner comes for therapy and when there are secrets in the family. The provisions below can be incorporated into any of the paths to informed consent you select.

### Nonattenders

What can you do when one partner comes in without the other(s)? Here are some options:

- Do an individual therapy session in which you explore family-of-origin issues.

- Refuse to meet.

- Make a tape recording for the missing individual(s).

- Do a session and review it when you all meet next. You must decide what is to be shared, so as to prevent revelation of secrets and the development of an unfair alliance with the person who was present.

Deciding which option is best depends on the specific circumstances: If the session is early in therapy, before a full commitment and therapeutic alliance have been established, it may be best not to meet. You can explain how it would not be fair, describe how it could be counterproductive for the relationship with all parties, and ask the person present to trust you that this is better in the long run.

Although the treatment of choice in family therapy is to have all the family members attend, this may not be realistic for many families. Teisman (1980) has several suggestions: offering a single individual session to the nonattender(s), in exchange for attending a single family session; having short family sessions whose only goal is developing plans for engaging the nonattender(s); taping parts of sessions for review by the nonattender(s); having only one to three sessions for the attender(s); using leverage from the referral source; and cancelling sessions at which all are not present.

In couple therapy where one partner refuses to attend, Wilcoxon and Fenell (1983) suggest the clever use of a letter to the nonattender summarizing the research on one-partner therapy (which has a negative prognosis for the relationship), proffering an invitation to attend, and requesting a signed statement by both parties accepting the risks of one-partner therapy.

### Secrets

A couple's secrets typically concern an affair, wanting a divorce, or sexual attraction to another. There are several schools of thought on secrets:

- Wendorf and Wendorf (1985) argue that the therapist's position should be similar to the following: "I will decide when and how any information I become aware of is to be shared amongst all of us. I will do so in the best interests of the family."

- Hines and Hare-Mustin (1978) advise the therapist not to keep secrets, and to refuse calls between sessions which might reveal secrets. They do offer another policy: The therapist will keep the secret only with the intent of helping the individual divulge the secret.

- Margolin (1982), respecting the needs of the individuals present, argues for keeping secret only what one is asked to keep secret.

You will need to decide on a policy and communicate it to your patients *before* they reveal secrets.

Don-David Lusterman, PhD, of Baldwin, NY, includes this phrasing in his client information brochure:

> I will sometimes see you as a member of a family; if so my task may be to facilitate or improve your communication. At other times I may meet with one or another of you alone. If we do meet this way, the normal rules of confidentiality will apply. If issues come up in these sessions which you believe importantly concern your whole family, I generally will not communicate this information for you but will help you to speak to your family about any of these issues.

## Contracts for Therapy with Minors

### A Contract for Parental Consent to Therapy with a Minor

When one parent brings a child to your office, always ask about the other parent's involvement. You need to consider whether the other parent might have any objections; this can help you prevent later disagreements and perhaps legal/ethical complaints by feuding parents. My advice about the various possibilities in this situation (keep in mind that I am not a lawyer) is as follows.

Always ask about separation, divorce, and custody on intake. If there has been a custody decision, require the parent to bring the paperwork to the first meeting. It may be sufficient to get an oral agreement to treatment from the other parent (and document this in your notes), but if the parents seem litigious or conflicted about this issue, get both parents' formal written consent to their child's treatment.

Laws and regulations differ, but in general, you can evaluate or treat children from intact families with the permission of either parent and can do so until there is a custody decree. If only one parent asks for treatment, you might consider seeing the parent and child for just a single evaluation session to help clarify the issues, with the understanding that you will be allowed to contact the other parent and discuss his or her perceptions and the request for your services. Do not offer any findings or recommendations, but perhaps discuss how you might help both parents to work with their child around adapting to custodial changes and visitation. Be sensitive to the likelihood that you may be being contacted with the agenda of supporting a custody battle. Make an effort to clarify and resolve the issues with all involved parties. Weigh the impact of treatment on the family versus its possible benefits to the child (e.g., providing a safe haven) and your own legal and ethical risks before proceeding. What are the likely consequences of proceeding and the risks of not treating the child? Which options are going to be more distressing to the child and which less? It may be best to refuse to treat the child during a custody struggle or divorce proceeding unless you get a court order to do so.

After a divorce or custody decree, you must get the permission of the child's legal custodian, who may or may not be the physical custodian (if there is a difference in your state). Shared legal custody, which is by far the most frequent arrangement will require permission from both parents. If both originally agree to treatment and one later objects, the picture is cloudy. Generally, you can proceed with treatment, but be very careful. Do not initiate treatment of a child over the objections of a parent unless there is an emergency or other clear extenuating circumstances, such as the inability to locate the parent despite reasonable diligence (see below), or well-founded evidence of abuse.

As long as the other parent's rights have not been terminated, you should get the agreement of both parents that you will provide the noncustodial parent with general information (such as that and when you are seeing the child, his or her overall functioning and progress, treatment goals and plans, etc.). What if the other parent cannot be located due to homelessness or abandonment? You or the custodial parent must make reasonable efforts, such as sending certified mail to the other parent's last known address, or making some calls to find out whether anyone has a more recent address. Social Security can assist in cases where the parent is using its services. What if the other parent refuses to consent, refuses to pay, or sets up other barriers to treatment? This is a time for consultation and judgment. Always document the facts, your observations, and your thought processes leading to your decisions. After a custody decree, it will be best to have the court write your treatment into the custody decree.

**FORM 11**    Form 11 includes the minimum for written parental consent to assessment and/or treatment of a child, as suggested by Morris (1993). He indicates the need for a written consent unless the evaluation is court-ordered, the situation is a true emergency, or the child is committed to an institution employing you.

### A Contract for Therapy with an Older Minor

When you are dealing with a minor, especially an older child or adolescent, the minor as well as the parent/guardian needs to be properly informed and to consent. The APA code of ethics (APA, 2002) encourages seeking minors' assent and considering their preferences (Standard 3.10b). See Section 7.1 for more guidance. Form 11, above, is a contract for par-
**FORM 12**    ents' signature; Form 12 is a contract for older minors themselves and their parents to sign.

A major concern in treating minors, especially older children and adolescents, is balancing the degree of legal confidentiality available (little or none) with a minor's needs for privacy and trust in the professional. No perfect solution exists, but clarity about your rules, stated at the initiation of therapy, is essential. Taylor and Adelman (1989) encourage reframing the problem as finding ways to establish a working relationship in which information can be best shared. A discussion with parents and the child about the confidentiality issue should be a minimum. The parents can consent and the child can assent to the treatment and some ground rules about confidentiality. A signed and negotiated "letter of agreement" concerning specifics of confidentiality is advantageous at the onset of treatment, but is difficult to construct before the issues are explored. If you later discover explosive or high-risk behaviors, you can discuss and modify this agreement.

Young people may become "emancipated" and have adult rights when they marry, graduate from high school, or live on their own. It is important to clarify the legal status of young

# Agreement for Psychotherapy with a Minor

I, _____, the parent/legal guardian of the minor, _____, give my permission for this minor to receive the following services/procedures/treatments/assessments:

1. _____

2. _____

3. _____

These are for the purpose(s) of:

1. _____

2. _____

3. _____

These services are to be provided by the therapist named above, or by another professional as the therapist sees fit. The fees for these services will be $_____ per session of service, or $_____ for the full services.

This therapist's office policies concerning missed appointments have been explained to me. I have been told about the risks and benefits of receiving these services and the risks and benefits of *not* receiving these services, for both this minor and his or her family.

I agree that this professional may also interview, assess, or treat these other persons:

1. _____

2. _____

3. _____

Because of the laws of this state and the guidelines of the therapist's profession, these rules concerning privacy will be used:

1. _____

2. _____

3. _____

A report or reports concerning the therapist's findings will be available after this date: _____. Progress in this minor's treatment will be reviewed on or about this date: _____ and on a regular basis after that.

My signature below means that I understand and agree with all of the points above.

_____          _____
Signature of parent/guardian                                                    Date

I, the therapist, have discussed the issues above with the minor client's parent or guardian. My observations of this person's behavior and responses give me no reason, in my professional judgment, to believe that this person is not fully competent to give informed and willing consent to the minor client's treatment.

_____          _____
Signature of therapist                                                          Date

❏ Copy accepted by parent/guardian     ❏ Copy kept by therapist

*This is a strictly confidential patient medical record. Redisclosure or transfer is expressly prohibited by law.*

---

**FORM 11. Contract with parent/guardian for psychotherapy with a minor.** From *The Paper Office*. Copyright 2003 by Edward L. Zuckerman. Permission to photocopy this form is granted to purchasers of this book for personal use only (see copyright page for details).

## Agreement for Meetings with My Therapist

I, _____, agree to meet with the therapist named below, _____ time(s) per week starting on _____. Our meetings will last about _____ minutes. When we meet, we may talk, draw pictures, play games, or do other things to help this therapist get to know me better and understand my problems, strengths, and goals.

I understand that my parent (or parents) or my guardian has a right to know about how I am doing in therapy. I agree that this therapist may talk with my parent/guardian to discuss how I am doing. They may also talk about concerns and worries they may have about me. Or they may talk about things the therapist and I decide my parent/guardian needs to know about. Sometimes this therapist may meet with my parent/guardian without me. At other times we may all meet together.

The things I talk about in my meetings with the therapist are private. I understand this therapist will not tell others about the *specific* things I tell him or her. He or she will not repeat these things to my parent/guardian, my teachers, the police, probation officers, or agency employees. But there are two exceptions. First, because of the law, the therapist *will* tell others what I have said if I talk about seriously hurting myself or someone else. This therapist will have to tell someone who can help protect me or the person I have talked about hurting. Second, if I am being seriously hurt by anyone, this therapist has to tell someone for my protection.

I understand that sometimes I may not feel good about some things we may talk about in our meetings. I may feel uncomfortable talking to this therapist because I don't yet know him or her very well. I may feel embarrassed talking about myself. Some of the things we talk about may make me feel angry or sad. Sometimes coming to meetings may interfere with doing other things I enjoy more. But I also understand that coming to therapy should help me feel better in the long run. I may find that I will trust this therapist and can talk about things that I can't talk to anyone else about. I may learn some new, important, and helpful things about myself and others. I may learn some new and better ways of handling my feelings or problems. I may feel less worried or afraid and come to feel better about myself.

Any time I have questions or am worried about the things that are happening in therapy, I know I can ask this therapist. He or she will try to explain things to me in ways that I can understand. I also know that if my parent/guardian has any questions, the therapist will try to answer them.

I understand that my parent/guardian can stop my coming to therapy if he or she thinks that is best. If I decide therapy is not helping me and I want to stop, this therapist will discuss my feelings with me and with my parent/guardian. I understand that the final decision about stopping is up to my parent/guardian.

Our signatures below mean that we have read this agreement, or have had it read to us, and agree to act according to it.

_____     _____
Signature of child                                                         Date

_____     _____
Signature of parent/guardian                                           Date

I, the therapist, have discussed the issues above with the minor client and his or her parent/guardian. My observations of their behavior and responses give me no reason, in my professional judgment, to believe that these persons are not fully competent to give informed and willing consent.

_____     _____
Signature of therapist                                                    Date

❑ Copy accepted by client and parent/guardian        ❑ Copy kept by therapist

*This is a strictly confidential patient medical record. Redisclosure or transfer is expressly prohibited by law.*

**FORM 12.  Contract for psychotherapy with an older child or adolescent.**     Adapted from a form devised by Glenn W. Humphrey, OFM, PhD, of New York, NY, and used by permission of Dr. Humphrey.—From *The Paper Office*. Permission to photocopy this form is granted to purchasers of this book for personal use only (see copyright page for details).

people in your community and your caseload. Likely exceptions to the need for parental consent are emergencies, treatment for drug/alcohol abuse, and some sensitive medical conditions.

Form 12 is designed to be understood and signed by an older child or adolescent. It was originally written by Glenn W. Humphrey, OFM, PhD, of New York, NY, and is adapted here with his kind permission. To make it fit the client, replace or select the gender pronouns, and perhaps replace "the therapist" with your name and title.

## A Contract for Group Therapy

Orienting a client to a group experience is complex, and only the legal and ethical issues are addressed here, not the clinical ones. You may want to construct one or more additional handouts (about the "ground rules," ways members "work" to promote growth, the roles of leaders, contacts with member's partners, use of drugs/alcohol, violence, permission to make recordings, etc.) to support your initial evaluation and orienting efforts.

**FORM 13**  There are some unique risks and benefits you might discuss with the group or add to the contract in Form 13. Some possible risks, according to Soreff and McDuffee (1993, p. 492), include "disclosure of one's name or other information by a group member; emergence of extreme reactions, including disruptive behavior, in response to the intensity of the group experience; acquisition of others' symptoms and behavior from exposure to their psychopathology." Some possible benefits, also according to Soreff and McDuffee (1993, p. 492), include "insight into one's relationships; opportunity to practice interpersonal communication skills; recognition of how [one affects] others (group feedback); diminished isolation; increase in sensitivity to the reactions and feelings of others."

Many of the issues are the same in group therapy as in other therapy formats, but there are some important differences. **The legal and ethical rules of confidentiality** do not apply to group therapy, because the members are not professionals (or even cotherapists in the professional/ethical sense). The legal model in most states (except where there are laws specifically addressing confidentiality in groups) is that information shared with anyone besides a therapist, or a therapist's employee, is no longer privileged. Therefore, the central issue of ethical concern in groups appears to be the maintenance of confidentiality. For a wide-ranging discussion of ethical issues in group therapy (such as screening risks, informed consent, termination, etc.), see Corey (1984).

To increase the likelihood of confidentiality's being maintained, you can stress the rationale and importance of maintaining it from the first meeting onward, and model it in the discussions of earlier group interactions. Repeat the rationale when any new member joins or the topic comes up in a session, even in an indirect way. Offering many examples of breaking confidentiality seems to help people control their natural desire to gossip. If you see a member of the group in individual therapy as well, be especially cautious when raising issues with this person in the group to make certain the information was not given to you in the confidence of the individual session. If it was, do not share it or act on it in group sessions. Keep separate records for each kind of therapy.

Form 13 is a contract designed for groups. For various reasons, it may need to be modified or amended to be appropriate for a particular group:

## Agreement for Group Therapy

As a group member, I have rights and benefits as well as duties, and I understand that some of them are described in this agreement.

This group will be called _____ and will meet from _____ to _____ on _____ at _____. The total cost of this group is $_____, or $_____ per session. I agree to pay this fee even for group meetings I do not attend, unless I make other arrangements in advance.

The purpose of this group is to provide me with the opportunity to achieve the following goals:

1. _____

2. _____

3. _____

I agree to work in this group. This means openly talking about my thoughts and feelings, honestly reporting my behaviors, keeping my promises, and exchanging helpful feedback with other members of the group.

I will attend all meetings of this group from start to finish, even if I do not always feel like it. If I cannot attend, I will tell the group a week in advance (at the beginning of that meeting), or, if it is an emergency, call one of the leaders as soon as I know I cannot attend. If I decide not to go on or am unable to go on with the group, I will discuss my reasons with the group and its leaders, and I will give 2 weeks' notice to the group.

I will not socialize outside the group with any of its members or leaders. This is needed so that everyone will be equals in the group. If I happen to meet a member outside, I will tell the group at our next meeting.

I understand that this group experience is not a replacement for individual therapy. If issues arise that are not suitable for the group's process, I may benefit from individual therapy sessions, for which I will have to pay separately from the cost of the group therapy. I will discuss this with the group's leader(s).

I understand that the leaders are required by law to report any suspected child or elder abuse, or serious threats of harm to myself or another person, to the proper authorities.

With full understanding of the need for confidentiality (that is, privacy) for all group members, I accept these rules:

1. We will use only first names. I promise to tell no one the names of the group members, or in any other way allow someone not in the group to learn their names.

2. We will permit no children, spouses, journalists, or other visitors in our sessions.

3. We will not permit any kind of recordings of our sessions, even by our members or leaders.

4. I promise not to tell anyone outside the group about any of the problems, history, issues, or other facts presented by any group member, even if I conceal the name of the member.

*(cont.)*

---

**FORM 13. Contract for group therapy (p. 1 of 2).** From *The Paper Office*. Copyright 2003 by Edward L. Zuckerman. Permission to photocopy this form is granted to purchasers of this book for personal use only (see copyright page for details).

5. I understand and agree that if I break rules 1–4 often without meaning to, or if I ever break one of these rules on purpose, I will be asked to leave the group. I will also face a possible lawsuit in which I may have to pay damages. If I reveal private information, I give the offended person or persons the right to recover for damages to his, her, or their reputation for at least $_____. Also, this person or persons may recover for any other damages that can be proven.

6. I understand and agree that the leaders will keep a clinical case record on each individual member, and that this record will not contain information by which any other members can be identified. This record, kept in each member's name, can be shown to other professionals only with the member's written consent.

7. I understand that the leaders will keep another record about the group's meetings and the interactions of the members, and that this record will not be included in any member's records. This record may not be shown to anyone without the written agreement of all the members and the leaders.

8. Other points:

_____

_____

_____

_____

_____

I have read the points stated above, have discussed them when I was not clear about them, and have had my questions answered fully. I understand and agree to them, as shown by my signature below.

_____          _____
Signature of member (or parent/guardian)                                        Date

_____
Printed name

Please return a completed and signed copy of this agreement to one of the group's leaders, and you will receive a copy for you to keep.

I, a leader of this group, have discussed the issues above with the client (and/or his or her parent or guardian). My observations of this person's behavior and responses give me no reason to believe that this person is not fully competent to give informed and willing consent.

_____          _____
Signature of leader                                                              Date

_____
Printed name

_____          _____
Signature of leader                                                              Date

_____
Printed name

❑ Copy accepted by group member   ❑ Copy kept by leader

*This is a strictly confidential patient medical record. Redisclosure or transfer is expressly prohibited by law.*

- This version is designed to be given to *individual* group members. When anonymity is unnecessary, a single contract signed by all group members might do instead of separate contracts if it is to be a closed group.

- There is a provision prohibiting socialization outside the group meetings, but this may not be appropriate for some support groups. Or you might alter it to require full disclosure of all members' relationships to the group.

- If the group concerns domestic violence, you might want to add a paragraph giving permission for your full and continuing contact with the group member's partner.

- If you charge a down payment to reserve a place in the group, you may want to include that in your discussion of costs. You may also want to indicate that some fees are not refundable.

- You may want to require each individual to meet separately with the leaders on a regular basis.

- The provision for a monetary payment for damages in rule 5 is to support a breach-of-contract suit in the future if a member should reveal the contents of group discussions, identity of group members, or other confidential matters. This paragraph is loosely based on one from Morrison et al. (1975) as quoted in Bindrim (1980).

- You might consider adding to rule 5 a clause that if a group member sues another member for breaching confidentiality, the one being sued will "hold harmless" the therapist for any consequences of the breach. I cannot provide the language for this agreement, because state laws vary; consult your lawyer for the proper terms.

- For patient education, you might wish to flesh out this form with some of the rationales for group therapy. You could emphasize the processes of member-to-member interactions; feedback from multiple perspectives, and from peers as well as therapists; the potential for exploring socially uncomfortable topics; discovering that you are not alone; trying out interactions that are possible only in a group; and the like. You might indicate what the leader will do (e.g., serve as "referee" and coordinator, interrupt some kinds of criticism and attacks) and will not do (e.g., take sides, play "the authority").

- As to attendance, you might add more on the effects on the group of missing members, tardiness, leaving early, vacation arrangements, and so forth. Discussing expected attendance as a personal commitment one makes to others, each member's irreplaceability, and so on, may be useful at this early point.

- Similarly, the impact on the group's process of adding a new member or having one leave is usually an important clinical topic and may be noted here as such.

- Some may benefit from explanations of the normality of feelings of reluctance and concerns with exposure, and the roles of members as audience or "witness bearers" even when they have little to contribute.

- Rule 6, about access to the group notes, might be modified so that this record could be reviewed by any member without needing specific permission of the other members. If so, you would need to write the record in such a manner that it did not identify members or their issues, but recorded the topics and conclusions, interaction patterns, and other aspects you deemed important to record. However, you might choose to record the group's process so that you can hypothesize and test dynamics, recall significant statements or important interactions, and so forth, entirely for your own use as a therapist. This kind of record would be protected as a psychotherapy note under HIPAA (see Section 6.2 on psychotherapy notes).

# 4.6    The Fifth Path to Informed Consent: Consent to Treatment and Other Services

I use "consent-to-treatment forms" when a contract is too detailed or comprehensive, but agreement to participate in treatment must be documented for legal or therapeutic reasons. These consent forms leave out many of the goals, problem definitions, methods, and tactics, and they state only a few of the most critical items.

This section offers several different consent forms, covering the following:

- Generic consent to the treatment of an adult.

- Generic consent to the treatment of a minor child.

- Consent to counseling for a child whose parents are divorcing.

- Permission to make electronic recordings of sessions, and to make various uses of case material.

- Consent to psychological testing and evaluations.

No doubt other occasions would benefit from a written consent form. If you have developed such a form, please share it with me for the next edition (see the introduction to this book).

### Generic Consent to an Adult's Treatment

**FORM 14**    Form 14 is a brief form for obtaining generic consent to the treatment of an adult. As with all of the photocopiable forms in this book, you can use it "as is" or modify it to suit your own setting and practice.

### Generic Consent to a Minor Child's Treatment

**FORM 15**    Form 15 is a brief form for generic consent by a parent or legal guardian to the treatment of a child. Essentially, it certifies that you and the parent have had discussions on the issues relevant to the treatment.

## Consent to Treatment

I acknowledge that I have received, have read (or have had read to me), and understand the "Information for Clients" brochure and/or other information about the therapy I am considering. I have had all my questions answered fully.

I do hereby seek and consent to take part in the treatment by the therapist named below. I understand that developing a treatment plan with this therapist and regularly reviewing our work toward meeting the treatment goals are in my best interest. I agree to play an active role in this process.

I understand that no promises have been made to me as to the results of treatment or of any procedures provided by this therapist.

I am aware that I may stop my treatment with this therapist at any time. The only thing I will still be responsible for is paying for the services I have already received. I understand that I may lose other services or may have to deal with other problems if I stop treatment. (For example, if my treatment has been court-ordered, I will have to answer to the court.)

I know that I must call to cancel an appointment at least 72 hours (3 days) before the time of the appointment. If I do not cancel and do not show up, I will be charged for that appointment.

I am aware that an agent of my insurance company or other third-party payer may be given information about the type(s), cost(s), date(s), and providers of any services or treatments I receive. I understand that if payment for the services I receive here is not made, the therapist may stop my treatment.

My signature below shows that I understand and agree with all of these statements.

_____      _____
Signature of client (or person acting for client)          Date

_____      _____
Printed name          Relationship to client
(if necessary)

I, the therapist, have discussed the issues above with the client (and/or his or her parent, guardian, or other representative). My observations of this person's behavior and responses give me no reason to believe that this person is not fully competent to give informed and willing consent.

_____      _____
Signature of therapist          Date

❏ Copy accepted by client     ❏ Copy kept by therapist

*This is a strictly confidential patient medical record. Redisclosure or transfer is expressly prohibited by law.*

FORM 14. Form for generic consent to treatment of an adult. From *The Paper Office*. Copyright 2003 by Edward L. Zuckerman. Permission to photocopy this form is granted to purchasers of this book for personal use only (see copyright page for details).

# Consent to Treatment of a Child

Name of child client: _____

The therapist named below and I have discussed my child's situation. I have been informed of the risks and benefits of several different treatment choices. The treatment chosen includes these actions and methods:

1. _____

2. _____

3. _____

These actions and methods are for the purposes of:

1. _____

2. _____

3. _____

I have had the chance to discuss all of these issues, have had my questions answered, and believe I understand the treatment that is planned. Therefore, I agree to play an active role in this treatment as needed, and I give this therapist (or another professional, as he or she sees fit) permission to begin this treatment, as shown by my signature below.

_____          _____
Signature of parent/guardian                                              Date

I, the therapist, have discussed the issues above with the child's parent or guardian. My observations of this person's behavior and responses give me no reason, in my professional judgment, to believe that this person is not fully competent to give informed and willing consent to the child's treatment.

_____          _____
Signature of therapist                                                    Date

❏ Copy accepted by parent/guardian     ❏ Copy kept by therapist

*This is a strictly confidential patient medical record. Redisclosure or transfer is expressly prohibited by law.*

**FORM 15. Form for generic consent to treatment of a child.**     From *The Paper Office*. Copyright 2003 by Edward L. Zuckerman. Permission to photocopy this form is granted to purchasers of this book for personal use only (see copyright page for details).

## Consent to Counseling for a Child of Divorce

The children of divorcing parents often have an obvious need for treatment. Yet a therapist can easily stumble into a minefield of accusations. By definition, about half of the persons involved in a custody dispute will be dissatisfied with the outcome, and this area has been a very frequent source of ethics complaints and suits. Knapp and Tepper (1992) offer this preventative suggestion:

> If it appears that a child custody dispute may emerge, then the treating psychologist should inform the parent(s) that a court-appointed child custody evaluator, or an independent psychologist, may be a better person to provide psychological expert testimony. Treating psychologists may be accused of being biased since they have a therapeutic alliance with one of the parents. The psychologist also may fear that the courtroom testimony would jeopardize the quality of the needed psychotherapy. (p. 16)

**FORM 16**    Garber (1994) offers the agreement given below (Form 16), as a means of educating the parents and informing them about the role you will assume. Although the language of Garber's form may be a bit difficult for some parents, it does an admirable job of covering the important points. If the parents endorse this agreement beforehand, this should greatly reduce your risk exposure, in addition to supporting meaningful therapeutic interventions. I have modified numbered paragraph 4 to describe psychoeducational groups generically.

If it is too late to warn parents about the difficulties of a therapist's providing testimony in a custody case, Saunders (1993), in a very worthwhile article, offers these "practical steps a psychologist can take if he or she has been a therapist to one or more of the parties" (p. 55) to avoid additional problems:

1. Directly inform all parties of pertinent facts. E.g., the therapist, has no opinion on the matter before the Court; formulation of such an opinion may jeopardize the treatment relationship; the parties have had no opportunity for informed consent.

2. Suggest an independent evaluation of all parties, and make a referral where necessary.

3. Invoke the privileged communication statute if applicable in that state.

4. Have the existing record redacted by a trial judge, to exclude potentially harmful clinical material.

5. File a motion to quash the subpoena.

6. If called as a witness, withhold any expert opinion. (Serve only as a fact witness.) (p. 55)

## Authorization to Record Sessions and Use Case Materials

**FORM 17**    If you think you will ever use any of your clinical notes or cases in any future professional work, you should probably get Form 17 signed during treatment (but not at the beginning, because the client will not be able to give informed consent without knowing what will come up in therapy). For the same reasons, it is inadequate to ask for the client's consent as you are starting the recording; this is not likely to provide the client with sufficient information about what will be discussed or revealed to give informed consent. Use this form afterward.

# Agreement for Parents

Psychotherapy can be a very important resource for children of separation and divorce. Establishing a therapeutic alliance outside of the home can:

- Facilitate open and appropriate expression of the strong feelings which routinely accompany family transitions, including guilt, grief, sadness and anger.

- Provide an emotionally neutral setting in which children can explore these feelings.

- Help children understand and accept the new family composition and the plans for contact with each member of the family.

- Offer feedback and recommendations to a child's caregivers based on knowledge of the child's specific emotional needs and developmental capacities.

*However,* the usefulness of such therapy is extremely limited when the therapy itself becomes simply another matter of dispute between parents. With this in mind, and in order to best help your child, I strongly recommend that each of the child's caregivers (e.g., parents, stepparents, daycare workers, *guardian ad litem* [GAL]) mutually accept the following as requisites to participation in therapy.

1. As your child's psychotherapist, it is my primary responsibility to respond to your child's emotional needs. This includes, but is not limited to, contact with your child and each of his or her caregivers, and gathering information relevant to understanding your child's welfare and circumstances as perceived by important others (e.g., pediatrician, teachers). In some cases, this may include a recommendation that you consult with a physician, should matters of your child's physical health be relevant to this therapy.

2. I ask that all caregivers remain in frequent communication regarding this child's welfare and emotional well-being. Open communication about his or her emotional state and behavior is critical. In this regard, I invite each of you to initiate frequent and open exchange with me as your child's therapist.

3. I ask that all parties recognize and, as necessary, reaffirm to the child, that I am the child's helper and not allied with any disputing party.

4. I strongly recommend that all caregivers involved choose to participate in psychoeducational groups in which separating and divorced parents learn basic strategies for conducting a divorce in the best interests of the child. I can refer you to such programs.

5. Please be advised regarding the limits of confidentiality as it applies to psychotherapy with a child in these circumstances:

   - I keep records of all contacts relevant to your child's well-being. These records are subject to court subpoena and may, under some circumstances, be solicited by parties to your divorce, including your attorneys.

   - Any matter brought to my attention by either parent regarding the child may be revealed to the other parent. Matters which are brought to my attention that are irrelevant to the child's welfare may be kept in con-

*(cont.)*

---

**FORM 16. Agreement for parents regarding limitations and goal of psychotherapy with a child of divorce (p. 1 of 2).** Adapted from Garber (1994). Copyright 1994 by Division of Psychotherapy (29) of the American Psychological Association (APA). Adapted by permission. The APA grants purchasers of *The Paper Office* the right to make photocopies for personal use only. Further use of this material without the express written permission of the APA is strictly prohibited.—From *The Paper Office.*

fidence. However, these matters may best be brought to the attention of others, such as attorneys, personal therapists or counselors.

- **I am legally obligated to bring any concern regarding the child's health and safety to the attention of relevant authorities. When possible, should this necessity arise, I will advise all parties regarding my concerns.**

6. This psychotherapy will not yield recommendations about custody. In general, I recommend that parties who are disputing custody strongly consider participation in alternative forms of negotiation and conflict resolution, including mediation and custody evaluation, rather than try to settle a custody dispute in court.

7. Payment for my services is due, in full, at the time of service in a manner agreed to by all parties involved. Any outstanding balance accrued (for example, in conference with attorneys, the GAL, or teachers), must be paid promptly and in full. An initial retainer of $_____ will be required prior to commencing this therapy to be held against charges incurred and subject to reimbursement at the conclusion of this therapy, as appropriate.

Your understanding of these points and agreement in advance of starting this therapy may resolve difficulties that would otherwise arise and will help make this therapy successful. Your signature, below, signifies that you have read and accept these points.

_____     _____
Caregiver name                                                              Date

_____
Printed name

_____     _____
Caregiver name                                                              Date

_____
Printed name

_____     _____
Caregiver name                                                              Date

_____
Printed name

_____     _____
Caregiver name                                                              Date

_____
Printed name

_____     _____  _____
Child's name                                                     Date of birth          Age

_____     _____
Mental health professional                                         Date

❑ Copy accepted by client     ❑ Copy kept by therapist

*This is a strictly confidential patient medical record. Redisclosure or transfer is expressly prohibited by law.*

## Release and Permission to Record Sessions and to Use Case Materials

As a therapist, I naturally want to know more about how therapy helps people. To understand therapy better, I must collect information about clients before, during, and after therapy. Therefore, I am asking you to help by allowing me to record our sessions, and also perhaps by filling out some questionnaires about different parts of your life—relationships, changes, concerns, attitudes, and other areas. Video and audio recordings are sometimes used as aids in the therapy process, in the education of mental health professionals, and in research. I need to have your written permission to make and use these recordings and materials for these purposes.

I would also be grateful for your consent to use your case material in my other professional activities. Your material may help in the development of the mental health field or in the training of health care workers. It is possible that I could use your material in teaching, supervision, consultation with other therapists, publishing, or scientific research. For these purposes, I might use any of the following:

- Clinical or case notes I or other professionals have taken during or after our sessions.

- Psychological test responses and scores, questionnaires, checklists, and similar data collection forms.

- Electronic or other recordings (such as audiotape, videotape, video disc, transcriptions, case notes, physiological monitoring, or any other recording method) of any interview, examination, or treatment with me, my employees, or other professionals. These recordings may include clients, therapists, or others, and may be made in my office or in similar settings by other professionals.

- Other materials that are similar to those mentioned above but whose specifics I do not know at present.

- Observation of our meetings by professionals or student professionals, using videotapes or adjacent observation rooms.

For simplicity, everything listed above will be referred to as "materials" in the rest of this form.

When I use materials from my testing or therapy work, I do not want anyone who hears, reads, or sees it to be able to identify the clients involved. Therefore, I would conceal your identity by one of the following methods:

1. Reporting the results as grouped data (that is, publishing only numbers like averages, and not publishing any individual's scores or names).

2. Removing (or, if this is not possible, greatly changing) all names, dates, places, descriptions, or any other information by which you or anyone else involved could be identified. In particular, I will not use, or allow anyone else to use, your real name in any presentation of any of these materials.

3. Using any other methods for maintaining confidentiality appropriate to the medium, such as electronically concealing someone's face or altering his or her voice.

4. Using other methods (including those not yet available) that would be consistent with my professional code of ethics and professional guidelines for the maintenance of confidentiality.

*(cont.)*

---

**FORM 17. Release/permission form for recording sessions and using case materials in research, teaching, and professional publishing (p. 1 of 2).** From *The Paper Office.* Copyright 2003 by Edward L. Zuckerman. Permission to photocopy this form is granted to purchasers of this book for personal use only (see copyright page for details).

These materials will be presented only to other health care professionals and to their students. All of these persons are bound by federal and state laws and professional rules about clients' privacy. I will keep all these materials in a safe location, and destroy them as soon as they are no longer needed.

Therefore, I am asking you to read and sign the following:

I, the client (or his or her parent or guardian), consent to the recording of my sessions for the purposes described above. The purpose and value of recording have been fully explained to me, and I freely and willingly consent to this recording.

This consent is being given in regard to the professional services being provided by the therapist named below. I agree that I am to receive no financial benefit from the use of the materials. I understand that if I do not agree to the uses of these materials or the recording of meetings as indicated, I will not be penalized in any way, and it will not affect the care I am to receive in any way. I understand that I may ask for the recording to be turned off or erased at any time during my sessions. I also understand that within 5 days following a session, I may choose to request a viewing of the recording with the therapist. I further understand that I may then ask for the recording to be destroyed. If I choose to ask this, I will deliver a written statement to this effect to the therapist within 5 days following the viewing.

I understand that I am fully responsible for my own participation in any and all exercises and activities suggested by the therapist. I agree not to hold the therapist legally responsible for the effect of these exercises on me, either during the session or later.

I give the therapist named below my permission to use the materials for research, teaching, and advancing other professional purposes. I understand that they will be used as an aid in the process of improving mental health work or training health care workers. I agree that the materials may be sold or otherwise made available to health care professionals for educational, training, and/or research purposes. These professionals and their students are bound by state laws and by professional rules about clients' privacy.

I hereby give up my rights to any and all interests that I may have in the materials. I agree to let the therapist be the sole owner of all the rights in these materials for all purposes described above.

_____     _____
Signature of client (or parent/guardian)                                    Date


_____
Printed name


I, the therapist, have discussed the issues above with the client (and/or his or her parent or guardian). My observations of this person's behavior and responses give me no reason to believe that this person is not fully competent to give informed and willing consent.


_____     _____
Signature of therapist                                               Date

❏ Copy accepted by client   ❏ Copy kept by therapist

*This is a strictly confidential patient medical record. Redisclosure or transfer is expressly prohibited by law.*

Form 17 combines a consent-to-record form with a consent to use any materials for any professional purposes. Although separate forms are often offered to clients during treatment, a form combining these functions gives you more options for future use of case materials while addressing the confidentiality concerns of clients. In addition, the form includes patient education materials that explain how confidentiality will be maintained; these are designed to assist clients in giving their permission to allow you to use their clinical materials. Other points regarding this form are as follows:

- Most situations are covered through simply making identification impossible by altering the facts of the case, but sometimes these cannot be changed, and sometimes information slips through. So the use of this signed form may be double protection for little additional effort.

- According to the rules of the Federal Communications Commission (Rule 64, subpart E), you may record telephone conversations without using a beep tone every 15 seconds if you simply inform the other party that you are recording the conversation. There may be state or other regulations as well as the federal ones, however, and so you should check locally.

- If you are going to use videotape or show the client in such a way that he or she can be recognized, you will probably need to explain, in detail and in writing, exactly what is to be done with the materials (by whom, for what purposes, etc.). Form 17 can assist with that process.

Form 17 is based on ideas from the "Release and Permission to Tape Form" by Elizabeth A. Schilson, PhD, and from "Client Informed Consent for Videotaping." Both forms are in Piercy et al. (1989). Piercy et al.'s book also includes model release forms in legal language for the commercial use of photographs.

All of the above are very likely to continue to apply to your situation unless your state's laws or the regulations of your profession do not address these issues, in which case the HIPAA Privacy Rule would apply.

Under HIPAA you must distinguish PHI for use in treatment or training from PHI for use in research. The former does not require a separate authorization, because such use is covered under normal "treatment, payment, and health care operations" (TPO), and consent would have been obtained with the Notice of Privacy Practices (see Section 7.8) during the intake process. To use a recording in research you will need both the general consent for use of PHI in TPO and a signed research authorization, which goes beyond the core elements of the authorization described in Section 7.8 to addresses other issues raised by research participation. The authorization should include the following (from Section 164.508[f] of the HIPAA Privacy Rule).

- A description of each purpose of the use of the PHI in the research study. This can include how the PHI will be used in providing treatment to the participant and what PHI will *not* be used in the research.

- A statement that the participant may see and copy all PHI that is to be disclosed or used about him or her. The researcher may impose limitations regarding specific parts of the PHI and may insist that this inspection not occur until the study is completed.

- If the researcher is to be paid directly or indirectly by a third party for the use or disclosure, a statement to that effect.

- A statement that the participant may refuse to sign the authorization.

In addition:

- The authorization must be written in plain language.

- A copy of the authorization must be provided to the participant.

- The client *can* be excluded from the research program's treatment for not agreeing to the authorization for disclosure or use of his or her PHI. This is different from the protection in HIPAA that treatment cannot be "conditioned" upon an authorization.

- The authorization may be included in the same document as the more general consent to use or disclose PHI for TPO and with the Notice of Privacy Practices (see Section 7.8), and, in fact, those two documents are required to cover the participants' treatment (as part of the research project).

- The authorization process described can be waived or altered if the research is approved by and Institutional Review Board (see Section 164.512[i] of the Act).

- While HIPAA offers an alternative to seeking an authorization, namely, to "de-identify" the information, I cannot see how this procedure (removing names and other information; clustering data by, e.g., zip codes) would apply to video recording, and so cannot recommend it at present.

## Consent to Psychological Testing

The APA code of ethics (APA, 2002) specifically requires obtaining "informed consent for assessments, evaluations, or diagnostic services, . . . except when (1) testing is mandated by law or governmental regulation; (2) informed consent is implied because testing is conducted as a routine . . . organizational activity . . . or (3) one purpose of the testing is to evaluate decisional capacity" (Standard 9.03a). Neither Form 18 nor 19 refers to the confidentiality of the test materials and results such as protocols and scores. Their legal protection from disclosure resides with your state's laws and court decisions, because HIPAA does not specifically address these materials. However, one might argue that these should be included in "results of clinical tests" and thereby go into the general medical record rather than into psychotherapy notes (see Section 6.2).

Younggren (1995) reminds us:

> Patients have a right to know what a test is designed to measure, whether it is reliable and valid for the expected use, how the data will be used, how they will be stored and who will have access to the results. Psychologists who use scoring services and various electronic devices in conducting assessments should outline how these systems are constructed and what protections are provided. (p. 7)

On a related note, you should always ask clients you are testing whether they have been tested before, when, with what tests, by whom, and for what purposes. If a client is not very aware, delay these questions until the Wechsler Block Design subtest and then ask, "Have you seen these designs before?" In forensic and disability testing, you should expect that a client is likely to have been coached (sometimes extensively) by his or her lawyer or relatives, and so you should ask, "What have you been told about these tests, who told you, and what did they tell you?" Of course, the client does not have to tell the truth, but at least you can document what he or she says.

**FORM 18**    Form 18 is both a consent form for testing and an agreement to pay for such evaluations; it covers the most common and simplest cases. This form is based on one created by John M. Smothers, PhD, ABPP, of Bethesda, MD.

## Consent to Being Evaluated for a Third Party

Problems may arise when either a child or an adult is referred for an evaluation whose results are to be used by the referrer (such as a court or lawyer or agency) for its own purposes, which may not overlap with the client's preferences or even best interests. If you take such a case, you may be placed in a position where your obligations (to the client, to the referring agency, to the payer, to principles of beneficence, etc.) conflict. A form is needed that combines the elements of consent to be evaluated and release of the results of **FORM 19**    the evaluation; Form 19 does this. Some of the wording in this form has been provided by David A. Miller, PhD, of Kansas City, MO.

When evaluating a client sent by the courts, you must consider a different aspect of confidentiality—confessions. If guilt has been established in court, through conviction or an accepted plea bargain, then the client can feel free to discuss the crime and his or her role in it. However, if you are doing an examination before conviction, you must warn the client *at the start of the interview* specifically not to tell you what he or she did or did not do concerning the charges. Explain that if he or she were to tell you about this, you would have to include those statements in your report to the court; that this might be incriminating; and that, of course, he or she has a constitutional right not to make such admissions. Make it clear that if the client wishes to discuss any details of the case, this must be entirely voluntary, and it is likely to have consequences. You may need to clarify your role as employee or consultant to the court or to an attorney. In parallel, you should ask the defense attorney whether there are kinds of information he or she would like left out of your report. For example, you may—through reviewing records, gathering history, or interviewing the client—learn of previous convictions, which are not admissible in court. You can state that you read the records, but should not indicate this content.

If the attorney asks you to remove potentially damaging statements from your report, you will be in a potentially deep conflict. The proper way to deal with this is prevention. In any communication between you and the attorney, insert the phrase that the communication is "a work product, produced specifically for attorney–client activity, at the direction of the attorney." Such a "work product" can legitimately be omitted from any materials discoverable by the other side.

# Consent and Agreement for Psychological Testing and Evaluation

I,_____, agree to allow the psychologist named below to perform the following services:

❑ Psychological testing, assessment, or evaluation

❑ Report writing

❑ Consultation with school personnel

❑ Consultation with lawyers

❑ Deposition (that is, written testimony given to a court, but not made in open court)

❑ Testimony in court

❑ Other (describe): _____

This agreement concerns ❑ myself or ❑ _____

I understand that these services may include direct, face-to-face contact, interviewing, or testing. They may also include the psychologist's time required for the reading of records, consultations with other psychologists and professionals, scoring of tests, interpreting the results, and any other activities to support these services.

I understand that the fee for this (these) service(s) will be about $_____, and that this is payable in two parts: a deposit of $_____ payable before the start of this (these) services, and a second payment of the balance due on the completion and delivery of any report (or, for depositions, testimony, or other services, at the time these services take place). Though my health insurance may repay me for some of these fees, I understand that I am fully responsible for payment for these services.

I understand that this evaluation is to be done for the purpose(s) of:

1. _____

2. _____

I also understand the psychologist agrees to the following:

1. The procedures for selecting, giving, and scoring the tests, interpreting the results, and maintaining my privacy will be carried out in accord with the rules and guidelines of the American Psychological Association and other professional organizations.

2. Tests will be chosen that are suitable for the purposes described above. These tests will be given and scored according to the instructions in the tests' manuals, so that valid scores will be obtained. These scores will be interpreted according to scientific findings and guidelines from the scientific and professional literature.

3. Tests and test results will be kept in a secure place to maintain their confidentiality.

I agree to help as much as I can, by supplying full answers, making an honest effort, and working as best I can to make sure that the findings are accurate.

_____          _____
Signature of client (or parent/guardian)                                Date

I, the psychologist, have discussed the issues above with the client (and/or his or her parent or guardian). My observations of this person's behavior and responses give me no reason, in my professional judgment, to believe that this person is not fully competent to give informed and willing consent.

_____          _____
Signature of psychologist                                                Date

❑ Copy accepted by client     ❑ Copy kept by psychologist

*This is a strictly confidential patient medical record. Redisclosure or transfer is expressly prohibited by law.*

**FORM 18. Consent form and contract for psychological testing and evaluation.**     Adapted from a form devised by John M. Smothers, PhD, ABPP, of Bethesda, MD, and used by permission of Dr. Smothers.—From *The Paper Office*. Permission to photocopy this form is granted to purchasers of this book for personal use only (see copyright page for details).

# Consent to Evaluation

I agree to undergo (or I give consent for this person, _____, to undergo) a complete psychological/psychiatric/mental health/family evaluation at the direction of this third party: _____. I understand and agree that the results of this evaluation are to be the sole property of this third party. I agree that I will not hold this third party legally responsible for any events resulting from this evaluation or the records created by it.

I understand that the purpose(s) of this evaluation are:

1. _____

2. _____

3. _____

I understand and agree that no doctor–patient or therapist–client relationship exists or will be created between myself (or the person being evaluated) and the evaluator.

I understand that I may withdraw my consent to this evaluation and to the transfer of information at any time by means of a written letter. However, I also understand that my withdrawal will not be retroactive (that is, it will not apply to testing and information transfer that have already taken place). If I do not withdraw my consent, it will automatically expire in 90 days from the date I signed this form.

I agree that a photocopy of this form is acceptable, but that the photocopy must be individually signed by me and a witness. I understand I have the right to receive a copy of this form upon my request.

_____     _____
Signature of client (or custodial parent/guardian of young child)     Date

_____
Printed name

_____     _____
Signature of adolescent client     Date

_____
Printed name

I, the psychologist, have discussed the issues above with the client (and/or his or her parent or guardian). My observations of this person's behavior and responses gives me no reason to believe that this person is not fully competent to give informed and willing consent.

_____     _____
Signature of psychologist     Date

❑ Copy accepted by client     ❑ Copy kept by psychologist

*This is a strictly confidential patient medical record. Redisclosure or transfer is expressly prohibited by law.*

---

**FORM 19. Form for consent to being evaluated for a third party.** Adapted from a form devised by David A. Miller, PhD, of Kansas City, MO, and used by permission of Dr. Miller.—From *The Paper Office*. Permission to photocopy this form is granted to purchasers of this book for personal use only (see copyright page for details).

# CHAPTER 5

# Intake and Assessment Forms and Procedures

## 5.1    Creating the Client's Chart

Most clinicians dislike the burden of paperwork, but the keeping of clinical records is not optional. How, then, should It best be done? How can you be sure your records are legally and ethically adequate to protect you? How can you best document your effectiveness for supervisors or third-party payers?

### The Chronology of Record Keeping

This chapter and the next one offer standards for keeping clinical case records, and detailed suggestions for how to meet those standards. **They follow the natural chronology of recording a case.** I cover various types of records at the places in the chronology where you need to give them attention.

- I begin with a brief overview of what client records should contain.

- Then I start where you will start with a case—at the first telephone contact and the agreement to meet as therapist and client. I call this Phase 1 of the intake.

- Next, in Phase 2, I collect the basic intake information, or make other types of preappointment contact. I offer materials that can constitute a preappointment package, to be mailed before the first meeting. If time is short, these can be completed by the client in the office before the first meeting (Phase 3).

- Phase 3 occurs during the client's first office visit, just before I interview the client. This is the time for filling out informational forms (histories, financial data, reasons for seeking services) that must precede the face-to-face interview.

- Then, for the actual interview (Phase 4), I offer forms for structuring the collection of more detailed data. This information is often sensitive, and its collection requires face-to-face interaction with the client. Examples include information on suicide risk, physical or sexual abuse, and mental status. The interview should also include screening questions, where the client's reactions may suggest to the clinician that clinically significant information may be obtained by probing further.

- In Phase 5, the last phase of intake, the data collected are integrated and summarized. I offer forms for summarizing suicide risk, drug and alcohol use, and the formulation of the client's case. These form the basis for the next chapter, Chapter 6, which continues the chronology by looking at treatment planning, treatment progress notes, and termination.

## The Contents of the Record

I believe there are 10 categories of information we need to keep on each client. Each of these categories is described below.

### Intake and Assessment

1. *Intake forms.* The client's record should contain basic information on the client, the reasons for referral, and the client's chief concerns. This chapter offers three examples: the first-contact record and two client information forms.

2. *Histories.* The record can include personal and family histories, as well as histories of previous interventions or treatments. This chapter includes an interview guide and a form for parents to fill out on a child's developmental history.

3. *Evaluations and assessments.* The client record needs to include clinical assessments, previous evaluations, and any testing. This chapter offers two problem checklists (one for adults and one for children) and focused guides for the evaluation of chemical use, mental status, health information and medication, and suicide risk.

4. *Diagnoses and case formulations.* Each client record should include formal diagnoses and a case formulation. Offered here is an intake summary, which can help in case formulation and treatment planning.

### Treatment Planning, Progress, and Termination

5. *Treatment plan.* Each client's record should document the treatment plan. The plan should include the target problems, methods of intervention, reviews, and outcomes. Chapter 6 offers several plan formats.

6. *Progress notes.* These might include regular summaries of treatment sessions. See Section 6.2 for more possibilities for progress notes. Under the HIPAA Privacy Rule you can create a separate psychotherapy note as well as the regular progress note (see Section 6.2).

7. *Termination summary.* This should consist of a summary of treatment provided, the progress made, any remaining problems, the client's prognosis, the reasons for termination, and any clinical recommendations. (See Section 6.3.)

### Other Important Client Record Contents

8. *Correspondence.* This might include correspondence and records from past treaters and notes of nontrivial phone calls with the client or with other professionals about the client.

9. *Financial records.* These might include a signed agreement to pay; the dates of services; the charges, payments, bills, and collection phone calls; and notes to the client, insurance companies, and managed care organizations (MCOs) about bills and payments.

10. *Legal documents.* These would include any releases signed by the client and documentation of informed consent through contracts or the client information brochure (see Chapter 4).

It is a challenge to keep all of this information logically separated and yet easily accessible. See Section 1.4 for more on structures for organizing your records, and Section 6.2 for more on structuring the contents of what you record in your notes.

## 5.2    Phase I: The Initial Telephone Contact

> *Nobody, as long as he moves about among the chaotic currents of life, is without trouble.*
>
> —CARL JUNG

The client's record should begin at the beginning—with your first contact with him or her as a prospective client. This is almost always by telephone. But whether or not it takes place by telephone, this initial conversation should have the following goals:

- To assess whether you are an appropriate clinician to treat this person and problem.

- To discover whether there are reasons for refusing this person as a client (see below).

- If you discover no such reasons for refusal, to make efforts to increase the likelihood that the person will show up for treatment. (Section 5.3 discusses this in greater detail.)

- To begin the chart or record of your treatment so that it is professional, usable, and effective.

Your first contact with future clients can be a source of both satisfaction and income; do it right. Ideally, you should sound competent, efficient, and knowledgeable, as well as eager to listen. As the saying goes, you have only one chance to make a good first impression. Practice until you are comfortable, smooth, and confident when offering information and answering common questions. Be prepared to give information about office hours, insurance accepted, fees, and your credentials. Practice until your statements are anxiety-free and almost routine, so that your mind can attend to the clinical aspects of the call.

Remember, confidentiality extends to this first contact, so make sure no one can overhear you. If you suspect that some highly sensitive information is about to be revealed, make sure to defer it until you can meet with your caller and discuss the implications of its disclosure more fully.

## Reasons for Refusing a Caller as a Client

A caller may not be an appropriate client for you for a variety of reasons:

- You do not have the time available, and placing the caller on a waiting list is inappropriate or unacceptable.

- You and the caller are not able to establish a working relationship for some reason (e.g., your personalities or belief systems differ sharply).

- The caller is a relative, coworker, trainee, or the like. (See Section 3.8 on dual relationships.)

- The client cannot afford your fees (and your low-fee and *pro bono* hours are filled).

- The client may not be suitable for voluntary treatment because he or she has a significant or recent history of violence, is in an acute medical crisis, has active and severe substance abuse/dependence, is unable to consent to treatment, has repeatedly discontinued treatment against professional advice, or has refused prescribed treatments.

- The client has problems outside your area of expertise. Remember, you are not a master of every effective treatment, and therefore you are not competent to treat every problem or every person seeking treatment (because of his or her special needs, language skills, etc.).

## Getting the Essential Data

**FORM 20**

The simplest way to ensure the collection of basic data is to fill out the first-contact record (see Form 20, below) as you talk to the caller. You might keep blank copies in your briefcase or datebook, so as to have one available when you get a referral.

Form 20 will help you to cover these essential points:

1. Get the client's name, address, and phone number, spelled correctly (ask). Clarify the relationship to the identified patient if the caller is not the client, and get a practical telephone number. This is essential later if the client does not show or fails to keep the appointment, and you have to contact the client (or other person) to cancel, reschedule, or respond. (See Section 5.3.) Since confidentiality begins here, when you ask for a phone number, also ask whether it is all right to call that number and ask for the client by name. If the client wants to keep your appointments unknown by a coworker, boss, family member, or anyone else who might answer the phone, clarify this and make some arrangement (perhaps calling only during certain hours). Since you will be sending a preappointment package or letters or a bill for your services, confirm that the address is similarly confidential, or make alternative arrangements.

2. Identify the referrer by asking, "And how did you get my name?" This answer is needed for many insurance companies; more importantly, however, it tells you about your reputation and professional network, and perhaps the client's understanding of the problem. When appropriate later, you can ask for permission to send thanks to the

referrer and confirmation that the referral was completed (see Section 2.8). Having the caller offer a name may also increase the likelihood of his or her coming in. If the referrer is someone the client will see again, such as a physician, he or she may be likely to ask about the referral. If the client got your name from an advertisement or presentation you made to a group, it may be helpful to ask, "What most appealed to you? What moved you to call?" The answer to this question is central to your marketing efforts, but both this question and the referrer question are natural bridges to discussing the presenting problem.

3. Focus on the chief complaint or chief concern. This information is needed so that you can decide whether the client has reached the wrong helper, and you can then make a better referral. It also gives you insight into the level of the client's understanding of his or her difficulties, which can guide your interventions. Elicit this information by asking the caller, "Please tell me briefly what problem has caused you to call me," or "Please tell me about what is troubling you" or "Please try to tell me the problem in one sentence."

4. Determine the urgency of the problem. Get enough information about the situation so that you can decide how urgent the problem is, and can then set the first appointment, refer, or add other treatment resources.

5. Schedule the first appointment, and write its date and time in your appointment book. The longer the caller has to wait to see you, the less likely he or she is to come in (see the discussion of reducing dropout in Section 5.3). Less than 24 hours is ideal service (you would want that for yourself), but it does not allow enough time to mail out the preappointment package.

6. Tell the client you want to use the first meeting to get an understanding of his or her situation, history, and problem, and the ways the client has been coping with the situation. A useful phrasing is "This will be an opportunity for you to find out if I can understand your situation in a way that is useful to you." You can ask the client to bring a "list of issues" to provide some focus.

7. Tell the caller that "This time is set aside exclusively for you," and, that if he or she cancels it will be "impossible to fill this time." Indicate what a loss it would be to the caller (delay in resolving problems, getting clarity or relief, taking action, etc.) if this appointment is not kept.

8. Briefly tell the caller how to cancel, so you won't be waiting in your office at 10 P.M. You can try to charge the caller if he or she cancels or fails to show, but it won't usually work and it creates bad feelings.

9. Ask whether the caller needs directions to your office. Keep in mind the time of day (for light, landmarks, and safety), the parking situation, and public transportation specifics. You can easily produce either a general map of the area around your office, or even a map with driving directions from the client's home to your office, from your computer (use http://www.expedia.com) and mail this as part of your preappointment package (see Section 5.3).

10. Ask, "Do you have any questions?" The most usual question is about fees. Prepare a

short and simple explanation and rehearse it several times, *today*. Most of us are uncomfortable talking plainly about money.

11. Consider asking for the financial information indicated in Form 20. This is optional, but it can serve two purposes: (a) If you suspect that something is not quite right in this call or that there is unstable or insincere motivation for treatment, it is wise to gather this information as a means of screening the client, as well as to clearly state that you will charge the client the full fee if he or she does not show up for the appointment. (b) Raising these questions and making this statement will indeed enable you to charge for your (lost) time and effort if the client fails to keep the appointment.

12. If you see many people who are self-referred through the Yellow Pages, clinics, advertising, or unknown sources, you might try getting a credit card number to bill them or to "cover" the first appointment. Irvin P. R. Guyett, PhD, of Pittsburgh, PA, has successfully used this technique in a number of doubtful cases. This procedure is also a test of the client's motivation, which may be appropriate for some clients and some issues.

13. The bottom of Form 20 reminds you of what needs to be done before the first meeting. Make notes here and follow up immediately by making calls, sending your preappointment package, or whatever is most appropriate to each case.

After the first interview, in which the client information forms (see Forms 24, 25, and 26) are completed, place the first-contact record at the back of the new chart. The form has a place for entering a case number. If you file records by name, you don't need to use a number; however, if you want to keep all the records for members of a family together, or if the client's name changes, then an anonymous case number may be useful. If you need more room for responses, you can use the back of the form.

To recap, the purposes of Form 20 are to enable you to gather data (both demographic and clinical) for the initial appointment, and to support clinical decision making (triage) as early as possible. In addition, when completed, it can be used for "performance monitoring" of your practices at a later time. You can discover how long it takes to set up an appointment after an inquiry—information that MCOs believe to be important. You can also evaluate the distributions of your clients by age, gender, location, presenting problem, referral source, and so forth, in order to enhance or focus your practice.

## 5.3    Phase 2: The Preappointment Package and Other Types of Preappointment Contact

The purposes and functions of sending the client some paperwork (including forms to fill out) before the first appointment include the following:

- It provides material evidence of your response to the client's needs; it solidifies the relationship and demonstrates your caring.

- It confirms the existence of an appointment and the beginning of treatment.

# First-Contact Record

**Date:** _____  **Time:** _____ A.M./P.M.  **Case record #:** _____

## Identification

Name of caller: _____  Name of client: _____

Caller is  ❑ client  ❑ spouse/partner of client  ❑ parent  ❑ legal guardian  ❑ legal custodian

❑ other: _____  **Usable phone number** (day/eve/work): _____

**Client's address:** _____

_____

**Referral source** ("How did you get my name?"): _____

**Chief complaint** (in client's exact words): _____

_____

_____

**Urgency estimate:**  ❑ Emergency; immediate interventions  ❑ Serious disruption of functioning; act in next 24

hours  ❑ Treatment needed; act soon/routine  ❑ Wait for: _____

## Triage

❑ Referral to: _____  for: _____

❑ First appointment scheduled for: _____ at _____ A.M./P.M. at (location): _____

Given:  ❑ Goals for first meeting?  ❑ **Directions? Map?**  ❑ **Cancellation costs and method?**

**Any questions?** _____

_____

_____

## Financial information

Credit card:  Name on card: _____  Card #: _____  Exp. date: _____

Social Security #: _____  Driver's license #: _____

## Things to do before first appointment

Call: _____ at: _____ about: _____

❑ Send preappointment letter, client information brochure, and these forms:  ❑ Client demographic and clinical

information forms  ❑ Adult/child concerns checklist  ❑ Developmental history  ❑ Financial information form

❑ Agreement to pay  ❑ Other: _____

## Performance monitoring

Return call:  Date: _____  Time: _____ A.M./P.M.  Initials of call returner: _____

Call response latency:  Days: _____  Hours: _____

Appointment response latency:  Days: _____  Hours: _____

*This is a strictly confidential patient medical record. Redisclosure or transfer is expressly prohibited by law.*

**FORM 20. First-contact record.**  Boldface items are important to complete during first contact.—From *The Paper Office*. Copyright 2003 by Edward L. Zuckerman. Permission to photocopy this form is granted to purchasers of this book for personal use only (see copyright page for details).

- Because it provides this evidence, it is likely to reduce the rate of no-shows.

- It can present you in a very professional manner—as organized, attentive, responsive, and thorough.

- It can help you to collect the basic information you need about the client.

- The financial information form (Form 27) can get the client used to the idea of paying directly for your services, and can provide necessary information about insurance coverage. Other forms that are discussed in Section 5.4 could also be included in a preappointment package.

- Seeing how the client fills out the forms you send can give you information on motivation and competence for therapy.

- Sending your client information brochure (see Section 4.2) can help to socialize the client into the role of patient, answer unasked questions, and give him or her permission to express further concerns. It can also teach about informed consent, confidentiality, and your way of doing therapy.

However, not all therapists prefer to send new clients a preappointment package. Other ways of making preappointment contact are discussed next.

## Ways to Respond before the Initial Appointment

### The Appointment Card

**FORM 21**

The simplest response to a new client is to do nothing after the initial call. However, if there is time, confirming the appointment in some way has value. Even a simple card will maintain the connection. Appointment cards are available in many clever and functional formats from medical printers, including cards that clients can peel off and stick onto their own calendar, bulletin board, or appointment book. Form 21 is a sample card or slip. Note the possibility of appointments on Sunday, as well as the location blank for therapists with several offices.

### The Appointment Confirmation Letter

**FORM 22**

Confirming the appointment by means of a form letter allows you to add more information than is possible in a card. It can indicate how to cancel, how long to expect the appointment to take, and other possibilities. A letter also gives you the opportunity to give detailed instructions or to express your feelings. Form 22 is an appointment confirmation letter that you can use or modify for your practice. It includes language designed to prevent a no-show because of ambivalence and anxiety. It incorporates some ideas from Browning and Browning (as applied in a book of forms by Berk et al., 1994).

### A Personal Letter

You may want to use a more personal response to new clients than this form letter. Marc Andrews, ACSW, formerly of Pittsburgh, PA, does not schedule initial appointments dur-

_____ has an appointment

at _____ A.M./P.M. on the _____ (date) of _____ (month), which

is a   Monday   Tuesday   Wednesday   Thursday   Friday   Saturday   Sunday

with _____

at _____ (location).

    If you are unable to keep your appointment, please cancel it at least **48** hours

in advance by calling _____ (name)

at _____ (number). If you have an emergency,

call _____ (name)

at _____ (number).

**FORM 21.  Appointment card or slip.**    From _The Paper Office_. Copyright 2003 by Edward
L. Zuckerman. Permission to photocopy this form is granted to purchasers of this book for personal use
only (see copyright page for details).

ing the first phone contact. He tells callers, "I feel it is in your best interest if you first have
some information about who I am and how I conduct my private practice." He then sends
them a long letter, modeled on the client information brochure. It outlines questions that
might come up in the first several meetings. He feels that clients can make better decisions without the pressure to decide on the phone. He believes that this method has reduced his level of no-shows and increased the commitment of those who do follow
through.

### The Preappointment Package

Sending a confirmation letter can also allow the enclosure of other information to create a
package. Mention of any specific enclosures can be added to the letter. As noted earlier, the
client information brochure (see Section 4.2) may be useful to enclose, and several of the
preliminary assessment forms provided in Section 5.4 can also be included with instructions for the client. The HIPAA-required Notice of Privacy Practices and its related consent
could be included where needed (see Section 7.8).

For example, the letter might say, "In order to get a head start on our work, I would like
some information. Please complete the enclosed forms and bring them to our first meeting," or "Please read through the 'Information for Clients' brochure and note your questions on it." Specific enclosures might include the adult concerns checklist or the child
characteristics checklist, the financial information form, and the client demographic information form. If these forms are not sent in advance, they should be given at the first session. Again, see Section 5.4 for these forms and more detailed discussions of them.

Including a self-addressed stamped envelope with the package, or instructions to bring the
forms to the first meeting (if time is short), will increase the likelihood that the client will
complete the forms.

Dear _____,

First, let me thank you for choosing me for help with your problems. I intend and expect to provide you with high-quality professional services.

Your first appointment is scheduled as follows:

Day: _____    Date: _____    Time: _____ A.M./P.M.    With: _____.

Please note the location of your appointment: _____.

Your first appointment may take 2 hours or more, because my office staff and I will ask you to fill out some forms. So plan your schedule with this in mind.

If you are absolutely unable to keep this appointment, please reschedule it at least 72 hours in advance by calling _____.

It is common for those new to therapy to feel both eager to get going and uncomfortable about starting the process of therapy. Do not let some awkwardness keep you from beginning what you know will be in your long-term best interest. If you have some questions and you feel you need answers before this appointment, please call and let us discuss these. I hope that, as in most situations in life, you will find that if you forge ahead, your worries will soon lessen rapidly.

Over the years, my clients have found it very helpful to think about what they want to get from treatment or therapy. Please make some notes about your goals and what is most important to you, so that we can discuss these when we meet.

In order for us to serve you best, please bring *all* of your health insurance cards, so my staff and I can help determine your coverage, find out whom to bill, and give you some idea of what your costs will be.

The fee for this first visit will be $_____. My office policy is that payment must be made or insurance coverage must be arranged at the time of each visit. Even when you or the person legally responsible for the bill gives information about insurance coverage or other methods of payment, paying the charges for therapy is your responsibility.

I look forward to a productive and successful relationship.

Yours truly,

---

**FORM 22. Letter of appointment confirmation.**    From *The Paper Office*. Copyright 2003 by Edward L. Zuckerman. Permission to photocopy this form is granted to purchasers of this book for personal use only (see copyright page for details).

## Ways of Dealing with No-Shows and Early Dropouts

When patients drop out of treatment even before the first appointment, it wastes time and energy, depresses new therapists, limits the interpretation of therapy research, and (of course) fails to benefit the patients. Patients who do not show, or who drop out early, often can be encouraged to continue into therapy with appropriate interventions like those described below. Also, at a minimum, you need to protect yourself legally from complaints of abandonment. *(Note:* For issues of termination and procedures for managing it, see Section 6.3.)

### Following Up No-Shows

If a client does not show for a first appointment, there is not yet a treatment contract or a *strong* legal obligation upon the therapist. Making a phone call is better than sending a note. If you reschedule the initial appointment and the patient again fails to show, a simple note such as that below is all that is necessary; more than this may be seen by some patients as harassment.

Dear _____,

You, or your child, _____, did not keep your appointment on _____ or the rescheduled appointment you agreed to on _____. I believe you or your child can benefit from treatment. Because of my concern for your health and well-being, I will be available to you in the future. Or, if you like, I can refer you to another professional, therapist, or agency. If you no longer desire my services, and do not wish me to make a referral, I suggest you seek out another therapist immediately.

Yours truly,

_____

(Signature)

Although the following discussion goes somewhat beyond the preappointment context, I feel it is helpful and even essential to include it here. Of relevance at this point is Beckham's (1992) finding that missed and cancelled early sessions were highly predictive of treatment dropout. This suggests that therapists should make great efforts to build high rapport and to respond intensively to missed sessions.

Many therapists will not call a client who did not show for a regular appointment (or failed to keep or cancel an appointment), out of fear that they will hear complaints about their competence, helpfulness, or methods. Therapists should be more tough-skinned and realistic, and should follow up on every missed appointment. There are many reasons for doing this, including the ethical responsibility for continuity of care, and the need to avoid the possible abandonment of a patient. You can say, "I understood [or thought or believed] that we had an appointment at [date/time]. What happened?" Even though you are frustrated, if you express not hostility but acceptance of the client's anxiety, you will always be remembered fondly. Of course, you should not then try to solve large (or even medium-sized) problems on the phone. Lastly, calling is a way to practice your assertiveness (just what a therapist usually preaches) in the face of (fears of) rejection and overconcern with others' opinions, anger, or disappointment.

If the problem was not a simple mixup, ask why the client did not come in. If you sense some resistance, try using one of these responses:

- "Almost everyone would like to solve his or her problems without depending on someone else. This is the universal human need for independence. But there are times when you can't do it alone."

- "We therapists sometimes say that 'everyone wants to be happy but no one wants to change.' Change is always painful, no matter how desirable or necessary it may be. Perhaps this may be a reason why you missed our recent appointment."

- "Sometimes we think we're ready to start to change, but find we have underestimated the forces holding us back. What is true, however, is that if you face a fear, the fear shrinks. If you understand that it is the right thing to do but still feel afraid, pushing yourself to come to therapy can really work."

In my experience, about 50% of no-show cases can be attributed to a mix up in appointment times or some other easily resolvable or nonrecurring cause. A call is best for a missed appointment, and it should be made as soon as you realize a client hasn't shown—perhaps 20 minutes. Never wait more than 24 hours to make this important contact. If you call a no-show, he or she will usually come in, and the result will be a good course of treatment. The client may have had an attack of resistance or reactance, forgotten, "felt better," had an emergency, or simply been ashamed of not showing up and too embarrassed to call.

Research seems to indicate that the only predictor variables for treatment dropout are lower socioeconomic class, initial negative impression of the therapist, and therapist–client differences in understanding of the disorder and its therapy (Beckham, 1992). You can change all but the first of these. The following have *not* been found to be consistent predictors of dropout: age, sex, psychiatric diagnosis, level of education, patient–therapist racial similarity (Satler, 1977), Minnesota Multiphasic Personality Inventory variables (Walters et al., 1982), and therapist rating of patient motivation (Affleck & Garfield, 1961). For an earlier review of this literature, see Garfield (1986).

### Other Strategies for Preventing No-Shows and Dropouts

Getting clients to show up, to attend longer, or not to drop out can also be aided by the following methods (Pekarik, 1985; Kobayashi et al., 1998):

- Shortening the waiting time until an appointment or between appointments.

- Offering services at alternative hours or days (e.g., seeing clients on Sundays or at 7 A.M. or 10 P.M.).

- Using letters (not postcards—too public) and telephone calls as prompts for future appointments.

- Rapidly promoting a therapeutic alliance.

- Setting a focus of treatment.

- Writing contracts and treatment plans with a range of assignments.

- Contracting for a specific time limit to therapy (say, 12 sessions).

- Involving significant others in treatment efforts.

- Supporting and directing the self-monitoring of symptoms, contexts, responses, and so forth with checklists and diaries.

- Demonstrating greater therapist activity. Passivity, awaiting the best time to intervene, or using anxiety-arousing techniques may be counterproductive.

- Providing usable feedback (videotapes can demonstrate progress) and positive reinforcement for attendance.

- Providing pretherapy socialization or preparation through readings.

However, bear in mind that therapists and clients may view "dropping out" differently. Patients seem to expect significant improvement in only a few sessions. Some 40% of community mental health center patients attend only 1–2 visits, and less than a quarter attend even brief therapy's minimum of 10 visits (Ciarlo, 1979). In private practice, over half of the patients do not attend for 10 visits (Koss, 1979). Although those who attend for only 1–2 sessions have poor overall therapy outcomes (Gottschalk et al., 1967), a substantial percentage report being satisfied with the improvements gained in 4–6 sessions. Clients apparently expect therapy to last for fewer than 10 sessions, and anticipate improvement within 5 visits (Garfield & Wolpin, 1963).

# 5.4    Phase 3: The New Client's Arrival for a First Meeting

## Ways of Collecting Further Client Information

The initial telephone call with the new client should give you guidance for the additional information you need to gather. You can note the specific forms you want to have completed at the bottom of the first-contact form. If the client has not been mailed these forms in advance, they can be filled out in the waiting room before your first meeting. Using your notes, you or your receptionist can have the forms ready and waiting for the client on his or her arrival for the first appointment. The client can be asked to arrive 20 to 30 minutes before the interview "to complete some necessary paperwork while you wait for the therapist."

Having this information before you first meet the client face to face is very desirable. For example, without the financial information, you might start a relationship with a client whom you really cannot afford to see. Also, the client clinical information form (Form 24) will tell you whether you need to ask the client to fill out more detailed information on his or her drug/alcohol use or legal problems.

An alternative, but less reliable, procedure is to give these forms to the client after the first session and ask him or her to return them by mail the next day. Include a self-addressed stamped envelope, to increase the likelihood of return.

Information materials and forms suitable for completion by the client in the waiting room (or in the preappointment package) include the following:

- The client demographic information form (Form 23) which collects basic factual identifying information. It expands on and will replace the first-contact form.

- The client clinical information form (Form 24) is for more personal information, and so it may be better in some situations to offer it when the client is alone in the waiting room, or even to wait until the interview to give it.

- The brief health information form (Form 25) collects information on health problems, medications, and treatment sources. The chemical use survey (Form 26) collects more specific data on alcohol and drug use.

- The financial information form (Form 27) collects essential information about insurance and other resources.

- For those clients who do not use insurance, or for whom insurance will not cover the entire fee charged, the agreement to pay for professional services (Form 28) clarifies payment obligations.

- Problem checklists efficiently survey the client's functioning and understanding of problem areas; they also encourage the identification of difficulties, which the client may be reluctant to state during the initial call. I offer two forms—an adult checklist of concerns (Form 29) and a child checklist of characteristics (Form 30). For children, there is also a child developmental history record (Form 31). You could add to this package symptom checklists (e.g., the Symptom Checklist 90, or SCL-90), specialized questionnaires (say, for attention-deficit/hyperactivity disorder), or pre–post measures (e.g., the Beck Depression Inventory). However, do not give clients these standardized clinical questionnaires or other tests to take home, because of test security and ethical considerations.

- The Notice of Privacy Practices and the consent (see Section 7.8) should be included here.

Let us now look at each of these in more detail.

## Obtaining Client Demographic Information

**FORM 23**   When completed, the client demographic information form (Form 23) replaces the first-contact form, because it is more complete and can be placed first in the client's file, thus becoming the "face sheet." Again, it can be included in the preappointment package to be completed at home or given to the client in the waiting room at the first meeting. As its name implies, it is straightforward, is primarily demographic, and can easily be filled out by the client alone. By contrast, the client clinical information form (see Form 24, below)

# Client Information Form 1

**Today's date:** _____

*Note:* If you have been a patient here before, please fill in only the information that has changed.

## A. Identification

Your name: _____ Date of birth: _____ Age: _____

Nicknames or aliases: _____ Social Security #: _____

Home street address: _____ Apt.: _____

City: _____ State: _____ Zip: _____

Home/evening phone: _____ e-mail: _____

Calls or e-mail will be discreet, but please indicate any restrictions: _____

_____

## B. Referral: Who gave you my name to call?

Name: _____ Phone: _____

Address: _____

May I have your permission to thank this person for the referral? ❑ Yes ❑ No

How did this person explain how I might be of help to you? _____

_____

_____

## C. Your medical care: From whom or where do you get your medical care?

Clinic/doctor's name: _____ Phone: _____

Address: _____

If you enter treatment with me for psychological problems, may I tell your medical doctor so that he or she can be fully informed and we can coordinate your treatment? ❑ Yes ❑ No

## D. Your current employer

Employer: _____ Address: _____

_____

Work phone: _____ Calls will be discreet, but please indicate any restrictions: _____

_____

*(cont.)*

---

**FORM 23. Client demographic information form (p. 1 of 3).** From *The Paper Office.* Copyright 2003 by Edward L. Zuckerman. Permission to photocopy this form is granted to purchasers of this book for personal use only (see copyright page for details).

## E. Your education and training

| Dates | | Schools | Special classes? | Adjustment to school | Did you graduate? |
|---|---|---|---|---|---|
| From | To | | | | |
| | | | | | |

## F. Employment and military experiences

| Dates | | Name of military or employers | Job title or duties | Reason for leaving |
|---|---|---|---|---|
| From | To | | | |
| | | | | |

## G. Family-of-origin history

| Relative | Name | Current age (or age at death) | Illnesses (or cause of death, if deceased) | Education | Occupation |
|---|---|---|---|---|---|
| Father | | | | | |
| Mother | | | | | |
| Stepparents | | | | | |
| Grandparents | | | | | |
| Uncles/aunts | | | | | |
| Brothers | | | | | |
| Sisters | | | | | |

(cont.)

## H. Significant nonmarital relationships

|  | Name of other person | Person's age when started | Your age when started | Your age when ended | Reasons for ending |
|---|---|---|---|---|---|
| First |  |  |  |  |  |
| Second |  |  |  |  |  |
| Third |  |  |  |  |  |
| Current |  |  |  |  |  |

## I. Marital/relationship history

|  | Spouse's name | Spouse's age at marriage | Your age at marriage | Your age when divorced/widowed | Is spouse remarried? |
|---|---|---|---|---|---|
| First |  |  |  |  |  |
| Second |  |  |  |  |  |
| Third |  |  |  |  |  |

## J. Children (Indicate which are from a previous marriage or relationship with the letter P in the last column)

| Name | Current age | Sex | School | Grade | Adjustment problems? | P? |
|---|---|---|---|---|---|---|
|  |  |  |  |  |  |  |
|  |  |  |  |  |  |  |
|  |  |  |  |  |  |  |
|  |  |  |  |  |  |  |

*This is a strictly confidential patient medical record. Redisclosure or transfer is expressly prohibited by law.*

seeks more private and detailed information that may need your guidance, and it may be better to complete this form with the client during your first interview. Both of these forms are designed for those over 18 years of age.

The following are possible additions to Form 23. However, they may be seen as intrusive or irrelevant at this stage of the relationship, so decide whether you wish to include them.

---

### K. Emergency information

If some kind of emergency arises and we cannot reach you directly, or we need to reach someone close to you, whom should we call?

Name: _____     Phone: _____

Address: _____

Significant other/nearest friend or relative not residing with you: _____

_____

---

*Note:* If you include the following questions, it may be useful also to include here the "no discrimination" clause from the client information brochure (Section 4.2).

---

### L. Religious and racial/ethnic identification

Religious denomination/affiliation:   ❏ Protestant   ❏ Catholic   ❏ Jewish   ❏ Islamic   ❏ Buddhist
    ❏ Other (specify): _____

Involvement:   ❏ None   ❏ Some/irregular   ❏ Active

How important are spiritual concerns in your life? _____

Which (if any) church, synagogue, temple, or meeting are you involved with? _____

Ethnicity/national origin: _____ Race: _____

Or other similar way you identity yourself and consider important: _____

---

You might also add client information questions relevant to your setting or practice, such as language spoken in the home, sources of income, living situation, and so on.

## Obtaining Client Clinical Information

**FORM 24**

As noted earlier, the client clinical information form (Form 24) asks for more personal and detailed information, and so perhaps it should not be mailed to the client or completed when others are present. It should normally be completed during the first interview, but because it is useful to have this information *before* the first interview, it can be completed in the waiting room if you decide the client would not be uncomfortable doing so. I have seen forms like this one entitled "Application for Psychological Services."

Question 2 in section C of this form asks about medications because they can affect mental status. Barnett and Neel (2000) review core knowledge and strongly recommend that all psychologists and other mental health workers who are not physicians be conversant with the effects, side effects, and interactions of psychiatric medications, so that they can provide high-quality care. Rivas-Vazquez et al. (2000a, 2000b) offer summary information on

# Client Information Form 2

*Note:* **If you were a patient here before, please fill in only the information that has changed.**

## A. Identification

Name: _____ Date: _____

## B. Chief concern

**Please describe the main difficulty that has brought you to see me:** _____

_____

_____

_____

## C. Treatment

1. Have you ever received psychological, psychiatric, drug or alcohol treatment, or counseling services before?
   ❑ No ❑ Yes If yes, please indicate:

| When? | From whom? | For what? | With what results? |
|-------|-----------|-----------|--------------------|
|       |           |           |                    |
|       |           |           |                    |
|       |           |           |                    |
|       |           |           |                    |

2. Have you ever taken medications for psychiatric or emotional problems? ❑ No ❑ Yes If yes, please indicate:

| When? | From whom? | Which medications? | For what? | With what results? |
|-------|-----------|--------------------|-----------|--------------------|
|       |           |                    |           |                    |
|       |           |                    |           |                    |
|       |           |                    |           |                    |
|       |           |                    |           |                    |

*(cont.)*

**FORM 24. Client clinical information form (p. 1 of 4).** From *The Paper Office*. Copyright 2003 by Edward L. Zuckerman. Permission to photocopy this form is granted to purchasers of this book for personal use only (see copyright page for details).

**D. Relationships in your family of origin.** Please describe the following:

1. Your parents' relationship with each other: _____

_____

_____

_____

2. Your relationship with each parent and with other adults present: _____

_____

_____

_____

3. Your parents' physical health problems, drug or alocohol use, and mental or emotional difficulties: _____

_____

_____

_____

4. Your relationship with your brothers and sisters, in the past and present: _____

_____

_____

_____

**E. Abuse history:**  ❑ I was not abused in any way.  ❑ I was abused.  If you were abused, please indicate the following. For kind of abuse, use these letters: P = Physical, such as beatings. S = Sexual, such as touching/molesting, fondling, or intercourse. N = Neglect, such as failure to feed, shelter, or protect. E = Emotional, such as humiliation, etc.

| Your age | Kind of abuse | By whom? | Effects on you? | Whom did you tell? | Consequences of telling? |
|---|---|---|---|---|---|
|  |  |  |  |  |  |
|  |  |  |  |  |  |
|  |  |  |  |  |  |

**F. Present relationships**

1. How do you get along with your present spouse or partner? _____

_____

_____

_____

2. How do you get along with your children? _____

_____

_____

_____

*(cont.)*

3. Your important friends, past and present:

| Names | Good parts of relationship | Bad parts of relationship |
|-------|----------------------------|---------------------------|
|       |                            |                           |
|       |                            |                           |
|       |                            |                           |
|       |                            |                           |
|       |                            |                           |

## G. Chemical use

1. Have you ever felt the need to cut down on your drinking?  ❑ No  ❑ Yes

2. Have you ever felt annoyed by criticism of your drinking?  ❑ No  ❑ Yes

3. Have you ever felt guilty about your drinking?  ❑ No  ❑ Yes

4. Have you ever taken a morning "eye-opener"?  ❑ No  ❑ Yes

5. How much beer, wine, or hard liquor do you consume each week, on the average? _____

6. Are there times when you drink to unconsciousness, or run out of money as a result of drinking? _____

7. How much tobacco do you smoke or chew each week?

8. Have you ever used inhalants ("huffing"), such as glue, gasoline, or paint thinner?  ❑ No  ❑ Yes  If yes, which and when? _____

9. Which drugs (not medications prescribed for you) have you used in the last 10 years? _____

_____

_____

Please provide details about your use of these drugs or other chemicals, such as amounts, how often you used them, their effects, and so forth: _____

_____

_____

## H. Legal history

1. Are you presently suing anyone or thinking of suing anyone?  ❑ No  ❑ Yes  If yes, please explain:

_____

_____

2. Is your reason for coming to see me related to an accident or injury?  ❑ No  ❑ Yes  If yes, please explain:

_____

_____

3. Are you required by a court, the police, or a probation/parole officer to have this appointment?  ❑ No  ❑ Yes  If yes, please explain: _____

_____

_____

*(cont.)*

4. List all the contacts with the police, courts, and jails/prisons you have had. Include all open charges and pending ones. Under "Jurisdiction," write in a letter: F = federal, S = state, Co = county, Ci = city. Under "Sentence," write in the time and the type of sentence you served or have to serve (AR = accelerated or alternate resolution, CS = community service, F = fine, I = incarceration, Pr = probation, Po = parole, O = other, R = restitution).

| Date | Charge | Jurisdiction (F, S, C, Ci) | Sentence (AR, I, Pr, Pa) | Probation/parole officer's name | Your attorney's name |
|---|---|---|---|---|---|
| | | | | | |
| | | | | | |
| | | | | | |
| | | | | | |

5. Your current attorney's name: _____ Phone: _____

6. Are there any other legal involvements I should know about? _____

_____

_____

## I. Other

Is there anything else that is important for me as your therapist to know about, and that you have not written about on any of these forms? If yes, please tell me about it here or on another sheet of paper:

_____

_____

_____

_____

**Please do not write below this line.**

- - - - - - - - - - - - - - - - - - - - - - - - - - - - - - - - - - - - - - - - - - - - - - - - - -

## J. Follow-up by clinician

**Based on the responses above and on**  ❑ interview data   ❑ records I reviewed   ❑ other information
I have requested the client to complete and/or I have completed the following forms:

❑ Chemical use survey

❑ Suicide risk assessment summary and recommendations

❑ Mental status evaluation report

❑ Other: _____

*This is a strictly confidential patient medical record. Redisclosure or transfer is expressly prohibited by law.*

the newer "atypical" antipsychotics and SSRI (selective serotonin reuptake inhibitor) antidepressants; the latter have more intense and more common sexual dysfunctions as side effects than the older TCAs (tricyclic antidepressants) do.

In section G, questions 1–4 ask about the "CAGE" criteria for alcoholism, described by Ewing (1984). Depending on the client's answers, your observations, and any referral information, you may want to complete the chemical use survey (Form 26). These questions are widely used, but may not be the most sensitive measures of change or of dependence. Two 10-item tests are found in Zung (1979) and Skinner (1982); for more current and validated measures, the handbook by Allen and Columbus (1995) is recommended.

Some possible additional questions (the first two of which are from Eugene Snellings, CSW, ACP, of Baton Rouge, LA) are:

- List five things you like about yourself.

- List five things about yourself that you would like to change.

- What are your major strengths?

- Have any anniversaries of important or stressful events in your life occurred recently or are any due to occur soon?

- List any major problems or stressful events that other family members or close friends are currently dealing with.

- What solutions or efforts have you tried to solve the problems that bring you here?

Pediatricians and family practice physicians are being requested by their respective organizations to ask patients routinely whether they keep guns in the house, whether their friends do, and what safety precautions are being taken. Some may see this as intrusive and others as preventative of violence. You might add such questions to Form 24.

## Obtaining Client Medical Information

**FORM 25**   The purposes and functions of Form 25, the brief health information form, are as follows: (1) to gather basic information on the client's health status; (2) to document that this information was gathered; (3) to support consultation with the client's medical caregivers; and (4) to assess psychobiological conditions for intervention.

Gathering health-related and medical information about a client in psychotherapy has several goals:

- A key goal is making sure the client does not have an undiagnosed or untreated medical condition that is causing the psychological symptoms you observe; this presentation is called "psychiatric masquerade." (For a summary of medical conditions that may result in such "masquerade," see Zuckerman, 2000.) By being sensitive and informed about the psychological presentation of medical conditions, the competent therapist (medical as well as nonmedical) can make appropriate medical referrals for evaluation and treatment.

# Brief Health Information Form

## A. Identification

Client's name: _____ Case #: _____ Date: _____

## B. History

1. Starting with your childhood and proceeding up to the present, list *all* diseases, illnesses, important accidents and injuries, surgeries, hospitalizations, periods of loss of consciousness, convulsions/seizures, and any other medical conditions you have had. (Describe pregnancies in section E.)

| Age | Illness/diagnosis | Treatment received | Treated by | Result |
|-----|-------------------|--------------------|-----------|--------|
|     |                   |                    |           |        |
|     |                   |                    |           |        |
|     |                   |                    |           |        |
|     |                   |                    |           |        |

2. Describe any allergies you have.

| To what? | Reaction you have | Allergy medications you take |
|----------|-------------------|------------------------------|
|          |                   |                              |
|          |                   |                              |

3. List *all* medications, drugs, or other substances you take or have taken in the last year—prescribed, over-the-counter vitamins, herbs, and others.

| Medication/drug | Dose (how much?) | Taken for | Prescribed and supervised by |
|-----------------|------------------|-----------|------------------------------|
|                 |                  |           |                              |
|                 |                  |           |                              |
|                 |                  |           |                              |

*(cont.)*

**FORM 25. Brief health information form (p. 1 of 3).** From *The Paper Office*. Copyright 2003 by Edward L. Zuckerman. Permission to photocopy this form is granted to purchasers of this book for personal use only (see copyright page for details).

4. Have you done any kinds of work where you were exposed to toxic chemicals?

| Date | Kinds of chemicals | Kind of work | Effects |
|------|--------------------|--------------|---------|
|      |                    |              |         |
|      |                    |              |         |
|      |                    |              |         |

## C. Medical caregivers

1. Your current family or personal physician or medical agency:

| Name | Specialty | Address | Phone # | Date of last visit |
|------|-----------|---------|---------|--------------------|
|      |           |         |         |                    |
|      |           |         |         |                    |
|      |           |         |         |                    |

2. Other physicians treating you at present or in last 5 years:

| Name | Specialty | Address | Phone # | Date of last visit |
|------|-----------|---------|---------|--------------------|
|      |           |         |         |                    |
|      |           |         |         |                    |
|      |           |         |         |                    |

## D. Health habits

1. What kinds of physical exercise do you get? _____

_____

_____

2. How much coffee, cola, tea, or other sources of caffeine do you consume each day? _____

_____

_____

*(cont.)*

3. Do you try to restrict your eating in any way? How? Why? _____
_____
_____

4. Do you have any problems getting enough sleep? _____
_____
_____

### E. For women only

1. At what age did you start to menstruate (get your period): _____

2. Menstrual period experiences:

   a. How regular are they? _____

   b. How long do they last? _____

   c. How much pain do you have? _____

   d. How heavy are your periods? _____

   e. Other experiences during period? _____

3. Please list all of your pregnancies:

| Your age | What happened with this pregnancy? | | | Problems? |
| --- | --- | --- | --- | --- |
| | Miscarriage | Abortion | Child born | |
| 1. | | | | |
| 2. | | | | |
| 3. | | | | |
| 4. | | | | |
| 5. | | | | |
| 6. | | | | |

4. Menopause:

   a. If your menopause has started, at what age did it start? _____

   b. What signs or symptoms have you had? _____
   _____

### F. Other

Have you ever injected drugs?  ❑ Yes  ❑ No    Ever shared needles?  ❑ Yes  ❑ No

Have you had HIV testing in the last 6 months?  ❑ Yes  ❑ No   If yes, results: _____

Are there any other medical or physical problems you are concerned about? _____

_____
_____
_____
_____

*Note:* Significant aspects of family medical history should be recorded on "Client Information Form 2."

- Second, mental health clinicians can contribute to the psychological management of clients' medical conditions. For example, diabetes has painful and complex management needs that are often resisted, despite the well-known health and life threats its poor management presents. Psychological interventions can greatly facilitate patient compliance, and so can enhance both physical functioning and the quality of life.

- Through gathering health information, clinicians may also be able to discover and thus to treat psychophysiological disorders with specific interventions. For example, temperature biofeedback can be very effective for migraine and Reynaud's phenomenon. More general techniques, such as stress management or family therapy, can be helpful for hypertension and irritable bowel syndrome.

- Psychological techniques can lessen suffering from physiological conditions such as chronic pain, which often can be effectively managed with hypnosis or behavioral treatments.

- Depression and anxiety may be hidden in the presentation of medical complaints or frequent help-seeking patterns. When they are discovered their treatment becomes possible, and the reduced overutilization of medical resources (called "medical cost offset") becomes a very significant financial benefit.

There are other benefits of behavioral medicine for specific conditions; these are too numerous to describe here, but they are well worth the efforts of the professional therapist.

Many detailed checklists and forms for gathering health-related information about clients are available from the medical arts publishers. These ask clients to indicate their symptoms, histories, surgeries, and similar medical data. However, those who cannot interpret this data probably should not acquire it. The brief form offered here does not ask for details, but only for general problem areas (to be further investigated by both medical and psychological means), diagnoses that have been already established, and the name of the client's physician.

If you want a more formal assessment of symptoms or health, there are numerous instruments with empirical validation and norms based on large or varied populations. A commonly used questionnaire is the Cornell Medical Index Health Questionnaire (Broadman et al., 1949), which has 223 questions in 22 areas. A very complete form with 236 simple questions in eight areas is the Health Problems Checklist (Schinka, 1989), available from Psychological Assessment Resources (http://www.parinc.com). As noted above, there are many psychobiological conditions, which require careful analysis by those expert in both the mind and the body. Whether you are a physician or not, consultation with the client's primary care physician is appropriate both before and during your treatment. Of course, make certain not to make such a contact before getting the patient's agreement and a signed release.

A word about **medication** in particular is in order here. Is it proper for psychologists and other nonphysicians to discuss medications with clients? Littrell and Ashford (1995) argue that both ethically (there is a requirement for coordination of treatment) and legally (co-treating nurses and pharmacists already do it), nonphysician therapists can and should discuss medications with clients. Many prescription medications are taken by people who become therapy patients, and these may cause psychiatric symptoms, which may mislead the unwary professionals assessing or treating these persons. Meyer and Fink (1989) offer some helpful ideas for nonphysicians in obtaining a full and accurate medication history:

❑ Ask the patient to bring all current and recent medications to the introductory or intake session.

❑ Review with the patient all medications: prescribed, borrowed, over-the-counter, recently discontinued, recreational. For each drug obtain the dose, schedule (both prescribed and actual), source, side effects noted, efficacy, and other comments. Ask the patient to tell you of any future changes in medications.

❑ Review the possible psychiatric side effects of each medication. This is difficult, but Meyer and Fink (1989) offer a short list. However, no list is complete; effects are variable; and drugs interact. There is no substitute for a consulting relationship with a well-informed, sensitive psychiatric physician and/or pharmacist.

❑ Continually evaluate for the presence of these psychiatric conditions or symptoms.

❑ If a psychiatric condition is present, consider whether its onset appears to correlate strongly with the onset of or change in the medication.

❑ If such a correlation exists, obtain a release of information and contact the patient's physician or help the patient to do so.

❑ Seek out the consultation and provide the physician with a thorough evaluation of all the relevant factors (psychological, social, stress-related, developmental, etc.) that you are able to evaluate.

Again, Form 25 is designed to meet the documentation needs of the nonmedical psychotherapist, so it only asks about health status and records the medical resources available to the client. This form is not a substitute for a medical evaluation or any appropriate consultations with physicians.

## Assessing Chemical Use

FORM 26

The purposes and functions of Form 26, the chemical use survey, are as follows: (1) to screen all new clients for chemical use problems, such as dependence, abuse, or withdrawal; (2) to document that information on these issues was sought and obtained, and options were weighed; and (3) to assist with the formulation of the case in its full biopsychosocial context.

Chemical use is a complex biopsychosocial phenomenon, and so there is no checklist (no matter how large) that will substitute for a comprehensive evaluation by an experienced clinician. If you want interview questions, there is a very complete set of questions to evaluate most aspects of chemical use in Zuckerman (2000). Form 26 can be given to clients to complete when there is any indication—from the referrer, from your observations, or in responses to your screening interview questions—that chemical use may be a problem.

Because of the denial and shame centering around chemical use problems, it is especially important to get objective or confirmatory data beyond what the client tells you. Try to in-

# Chemical Use Survey

Name: _____ Date: _____

In order to treat you effectively, I need information about the ways you and your family have used alcohol, drugs, and/or other chemicals that can affect you psychologically. So please answer these questions fully.

## A. What have you used?

1. Think about any and all chemicals you have used, and indicate how much you used (amount) and how often. Then indicate all the effects it had on you (mental, physical, family, legal, etc.).

| Chemical | Age started | Last use | Over the last 30 days | | See question 3, below |
| --- | --- | --- | --- | --- | --- |
| | | | Amount and how often | Effects/consequences | |
| Caffeine | | | | | |
| Tobacco (smoked or chewed) | | | | | |
| Alcohol | | | | | |
| Marijuana/THC | | | | | |
| Cocaine/crack (snorted, injected, or smoked) | | | | | |
| Inhalants | | | | | |
| LSD | | | | | |
| Prescribed pills | | | | | |
| Others: Specify | | | | | |

2. Write "P" above next to your primary drug of choice.

3. For each chemical you currently use, what causes you to stop? Enter one or more of these letters in the last column above: A = The money runs out. B = I use up my supply. C = Personal choice. D = Unconsciousness. E = Achieved my purpose. F = Other reasons: _____

4. What are or were your sources of money for buying the chemicals you have used? _____

_____

_____

## B. Which of these have you had?  ❑ Blackouts  ❑ Bad reactions  ❑ Withdrawal symptoms

❑ Overdoses  ❑ Detoxification in a hospital  ❑ Other problems: _____

*(cont.)*

**FORM 26. Chemical use survey (p. 1 of 2).**    From *The Paper Office*. Copyright 2003 by Edward L. Zuckerman. Permission to photocopy this form is granted to purchasers of this book for personal use only (see copyright page for details).

## C. Family patterns of chemical use

Please describe the chemical(s) used by family members.

| | Name | Chemical | Age started | Last use | Over the last 30 days | |
| | | | | | Amount and how often | Effects |
|---|---|---|---|---|---|---|
| Father | | | | | | |
| Mother | | | | | | |
| Brothers/ sisters | | | | | | |
| Spouse/ partner | | | | | | |
| Other relatives | | | | | | |

Please add any other information you think is important: _____

_____

_____

## D. Treatment for chemical use

| Dates | | Agency/provider | Type of program* | Voluntary? (Yes or no) | Length of treatment | Methods used | Participation in aftercare programs (No/Which?) | Effects of treatment† |
| From | To | | | | | | | |
|---|---|---|---|---|---|---|---|---|
| | | | | | | | | |
| | | | | | | | | |
| | | | | | | | | |

*In the fourth column, use these codes: AA/NA = Alcoholics Anonymous/Narcotics Anonymous; O = Outpatient counseling; ID = Inpatient detoxification; IT = Inpatient treatment (e.g., 28-day); O = Other.

†In the last column, use these codes: W = made situation Worse; N = No change; U = better Understanding of addiction; R = Reduction of use; BA = Brief abstinence (up to a month); LA = Long-term abstinence (several months or more); O = Other effects: _____

## F. Self-description of use

1. Would you say you  ❑ are a social drinker  ❑ are a heavy drinker  ❑ have alcoholism or  ❑ have a drinking problem? Or how would you describe your use? _____

_____

2. Would you say you  ❑ are a recreational drug user  ❑ have an addiction or  ❑ have a drug problem? Or how would you describe your use? _____

_____

## G. Other

Has your drinking/drug use caused you any spiritual problems? _____

_____

_____

*This is a strictly confidential patient medical record. Redisclosure or transfer is expressly prohibited by law.*

terview a friend or family member of a person suspected of drug or alcohol misuse. Later in this chapter, Form 35, the chemical user's case formulation, is provided to aid you in summarizing all of your findings, formulating the case in a biopsychosocial context, and planning treatment for a client with a substance use problem.

Because chemical use problems can be understood from many perspectives, Form 26 offers several ways to document the findings; you can add or delete elements according to your preferences. (For example, you could add other chemicals to the list in section A.) Furthermore, the individual's patterns of use/overuse/misuse/abuse may change with availability, resources, setting, decision, treatment, and aging, and may involve cross-addictions, temporary substitutions or preferences, and many other factors, so a detailed and individualized history is desirable. Obviously, the central dynamic of denial will significantly affect your information gathering. Therefore, follow your clinical intuition and the client's lead (or avoidances) in history taking to get all the relevant facts.

## Obtaining Financial Information

**FORM 27**  The purposes and functions of Form 27, the financial information form, are as follows:

1. It collects all the essential data you need for evaluating the client's insurance benefits, and thus the true costs to you and to the client of your services.

2. It allows you to decide whether a client can afford your charges. If you do not use it before seeing the client, you should discuss fees and resources early in the interview, to avoid engaging anyone in a process and relationship that must then be disrupted. That is why it is best to mail this form to new clients or to give it to them while they wait for their first visit.

**Do not trust clients to understand their coverages or the technicalities of today's insurance marketplace.** When they come in, ask for and take photocopies of any insurance wallet cards they have. With those numbers and a Social Security number, you can call the insurer(s) to verify their coverage. Try not start therapy without such verification.

You may need to make some changes to this form. For example, if your state has a special name for its health insurance program, or you see a lot of patients covered by Tricare/CHAMPUS (Civilian Health and Medical Program of the Uniformed Services) or another specific carrier, you may need to change some of the wording of this form.

Sections F, G, and H of Form 27 are condensed legal statements addressing these issues, respectively: release of records to an insurer, accepting of financial responsibility, and assignment of benefits to you. If you are going to use other forms for these purposes (such as Form 52 about releasing records to an insurer, Form 28 about paying for services, or the letter in Section 2.7 about assignment of benefits), you do not need to include these three sections here.

Finally, the question asking for the secondary insurance company (question 2 in section D) is for "coordination of benefits," in which insurers set priorities about who will cover services first. Ideally, the secondary insurer will cover any remaining amount due you.

# Financial Information Form

I truly appreciate your choosing to come to me for psychological help. As part of providing high-quality services, we need to be clear about our financial arrangements.

- If you have health insurance, it may pay for a part of the cost of your treatment here. To find out if this is so, my staff and I need the information requested below. We will explain any part of this form that you do not understand.

- If you have no health insurance coverage, or do not intend to use it, please check here ❑ , complete sections A and E below, and return this form to me or my secretary.

**A.** Patient's name: _____ Birthdate: _____ Soc. Sec. #: _____

Address: _____ Home phone: _____

(If the patient is a dependent) Insured's/policy holder's name: _____ Occupation: _____

Employer: _____ Work phone: _____

Address of employer: _____

**B.** (If applicable) Spouse's name: _____ Birthdate: _____ Soc. Sec. #: _____

Occupation: _____ Employer: _____ Work phone: _____

Address of employer: _____

**C.** If you (or your spouse) have any of these kinds of insurance, please fill in the numbers and names for each one.

1. Blue Cross/Blue Shield

   Name of subscriber (if different from patient): _____

   Identification/agreement/policy #: _____ Group or enrollment #: _____

   Plan #/code or BS #: _____ Effective date: _____

   Location of plan: _____ Reciprocity #: _____

   Phone: _____ Provider's phone: _____

2. Commercial health insurance carrier/company

   Name of company: _____ Policy holder (if different from patient): _____

   Policy #: _____ Certificate #: _____

   Phone: _____ Provider's phone: _____

   Address to send claims: _____

3. Health maintenance organization (HMO)

   Name of HMO: _____ Policy holder (if different from patient): _____

   Authorization #: _____ Agreement #: _____

*(cont.)*

---

**FORM 27. Financial information form (p. 1 of 3).** From *The Paper Office.* Copyright 2003 by Edward L. Zuckerman. Permission to photocopy this form is granted to purchasers of this book for personal use only (see copyright page for details).

Phone: _____ Provider's phone: _____

Address to send claims: _____

4. Medical Assistance

List all numbers: _____

(*Note:* Copayments by you are required.)

5. Medicare

Agreement # with any letters: _____

Railroad Medicare/Mine Workers Medicare: _____

6. Workers' compensation insurance

Name of company: _____

Policy #: _____ Certificate #: _____

Address to send claims: _____

Phone: _____ Treatment authorized by: _____ Date of accident: _____

7. Do you or your spouse have any other insurance coverage that applies here (Tricare/CHAMPUS, motor vehicle insurance for an injury, etc.)? If yes, check here ❑ and fill in an empty section above.

**D.** For each kind of insurance you intend to use, you and I will have to make two decisions. First, we have to decide who will find the information to answer the questions below. Will you do this, or do you want this office to do it? The information will come either from your company's benefits office or from the insurance company. Then, when we have this information, we have to examine the treatment choices allowed by the coverage you have.

1. Company: _____ Effective date of coverage: _____

Deductible: $_____ ❑ per person or ❑ per family? ❑ per fiscal year or ❑ per calendar year or ❑ per policy year? ❑ per diagnosis?

How much of this deductible has been used so far? $_____

Benefit: _____% of ❑ charges ❑ Usual, customary, and reasonable (UCR) ❑ Maximum charge of $____ ❑ Other benefits: _____

Percent reduction, if any, for mental health? _____%

Limitations: Number of visits: _____ Monetary limits: $_____ per _____

Lifetime limits: $_____

Is outpatient group psychotherapy covered? ❑ Yes ❑ No

Must a physician refer the client? ❑ Yes ❑ No

Is psychological testing covered? ❑ Yes ❑ No

Does any rule about preexisting conditions apply here? ❑ No ❑ Yes: _____

Are there any other limitations (such as conditions not covered, service settings, maximum per-session charges, need for DSM or ICD diagnostic codes or CPT service codes)? _____

_____

_____

_____

*(cont.)*

277

2. Company:_____  Effective date of coverage:_____

    Deductible: $_____  ❑ per person or ❑ per family?  ❑ per fiscal year or ❑ per calendar year or

    ❑ per policy year?  ❑ per diagnosis?

    How much of this deductible has been used so far? $_____

    Benefit: _____% of  ❑ charges  ❑ Usual, customary, and reasonable (UCR)  ❑ Maximum charge of $____

        ❑ Other benefits: _____

    Percent reduction, if any, for mental health?  _____%

    Limitations: Number of visits: _____  Monetary limits: $_____  per _____

    Lifetime limits $_____

    Is outpatient group psychotherapy covered?  ❑ Yes  ❑ No

    Must a physician refer the client?  ❑ Yes  ❑ No

    Is psychological testing covered?  ❑ Yes  ❑ No

    Does any rule about preexisting conditions apply here?  ❑ No  ❑ Yes: _____

    Are there any other limitations (such as conditions not covered, service settings, maximum per-session

    charges, need for diagnostic codes or service codes)? _____

    _____

    _____

    _____

**E.** If you do not have insurance, how will you pay for services from this office? _____

_____

_____

_____

**F.** I give this office permission to release any information obtained during examinations or treatment of this patient that is necessary to support any insurance claims on this account and secure timely payments due to the assignee or myself.

**G.** I understand that I am responsible for all charges, regardless of insurance coverage.

**H.** Assignment of benefits

I hereby assign medical benefits, including those from government-sponsored programs and other health plans, to be paid to the therapist above. Medicare regulations may apply. A photocopy of this assignment is to be considered as good as the original.

_____       _____

      Client's (or parent/guardian's) signature,                 Date

    indicating agreement to all of the statements above

_____

             Printed name

## Assuring Financial Responsibility

**FORM 28**    The purpose of Form 28, the agreement to pay for professional services, is to formalize a client's (or someone else's) assumption of financial responsibility for therapy and other services. You may wonder "Isn't the client's stated promise to pay sufficient?" Simon (1992) indicates that an oral contract is valid and enforceable in simple circumstances where a client makes a simple promise such as "I will pay for his [or her] treatment," but where there is a condition such as "I will pay if he [or she] fails to pay," a written contract is needed. The client may harbor hidden assumptions—for example, that he of she will pay only if the problem is cured, or that he or she will need only a few sessions, or that psychotherapy services will be fully paid for by insurance or the government. Presenting this form (or the first paragraph as part of another form) brings these assumptions to the surface for resolution and clarification.

If any of the following situations apply, make certain to get a responsible person's signature before you become too involved in treatment:

- A noncustodial parent brings a child in for services. We must also get permission to treat (see Section 4.6).

- A divorcing spouse whose assets are likely to be in dispute or inadequate to pay for services comes for treatment.

- An adolescent without assets seeks your services.

- Treatment is going to be long or expensive, and you want someone besides the client to share the cost.

- You suspect that the client isn't sincere in offering to pay for your services.

- You feel that the client doesn't fully appreciate the responsibility involved.

Note that a statement indicating acceptance of financial responsibility is included at the end of the financial information form (Form 27, section G): "I understand that I am responsible for all charges, regardless of insurance coverage." It is always a good idea to repeat this point, and if you have any doubts about the client's full appreciation of this point, Form 28 can then be used.

Form 28 indicates that the client has read and agreed to the client information brochure (see Section 4.2), because the client cannot be expected to assume financial responsibility without knowing basic information about therapy (its duration, probable costs, etc.). It is best to include this form with the preappointment package; if it is offered in the waiting room before the first visit, it should be accompanied by the brochure.

## Problem Checklists

*It isn't that they can't see the solution. It's that they can't see the problem.*
—G. K. CHESTERTON

People come for "help" for many reasons (physician referral, threat of divorce, intolerable pain, desires for the cure of symptoms, need for answers or advice, support for their views, failure of previous efforts, etc.) and with many different understandings of the cause and

## Agreement to Pay for Professional Services

I request that the therapist named below provide professional services to me or to _____,

who is my _____, and I agree to pay this therapist's fee of $_____ per session

for these services.

I agree that this financial relationship with this therapist will continue as long as the therapist provides services or until I inform him or her, in person or by certified mail, that I wish to end it. I agree to meet with this therapist at least once before stopping therapy. I agree to pay for services provided to me (or this client) up until the time I end the relationship.

I agree that I am responsible for the charges for services provided by this therapist to me (or this client), although other persons or insurance companies may make payments on my (or this client's) account.

I have also read this therapist's "Information for Clients" brochure and agree to act according to everything stated there, as shown by my signature below and on the brochure.


_____          _____

Signature of client (or person acting for client)                                 Date


_____

Printed name


   I, the therapist, have discussed the issues above with the client (and/or the person acting for the client). My observations of the person's behavior and responses give me no reason to believe that this person is not fully competent to give informed and willing consent.


_____          _____

Signature of therapist                                                              Date


❑ Copy accepted by client     ❑ Copy kept by therapist


**FORM 28. Agreement to pay for professional services.**     From *The Paper Office*. Copyright 2003 by Edward L. Zuckerman. Permission to photocopy this form is granted to purchasers of this book for personal use only (see copyright page for details).

possible cure of their difficulties. It has been shown repeatedly that the more closely client and therapist agree on the nature, cause, and methods of relieving the presenting problem, the better the outcome of therapy. Yet the professional's role often involves relabeling or reformulating the "referral reason" into something he or she understands and has the skills to relieve.

The intent of problem checklists is to offer new clients the widest range of possible choices and ask them to select from among these. This allows the exploration of all concerns early in therapy. If you simply ask, "What brings you here today?", you will get an abridged list of items, probably emphasizing the most recent and most memorable events (critical incidents). Or you might get the "referral reason," which is simply the "problem" defined by another professional, or a request for a specific treatment method (such as hypnosis). Although clients may come seeking a particular kind of therapy, this should be a professional's well-considered decision.

**FORM 29**
**FORM 30**

The checklists offered here are labeled to avoid excessive pathologizing of the client's experience. The adult's version (Form 29) is called a checklist of "concerns" rather than "problems." The child's version (Form 30), called a checklist of "characteristics," offers both problematic and helpful behaviors so that you will have at least some positives to build upon, and is to be completed by parents or caregivers. As an alternative, a very simple yet quite large form with 208 questions in 12 areas is the Personal Problems Checklist (Schinka, 1984), available from Psychological Assessment Resources (http://www.parinc.com).

You can, of course, tailor these two lists to your own practice by adding some items; if you do so, I would also suggest removing some, so that the lists do not become burdensome for clients. (For example, if you do more behavioral health work, you can add "Headaches," "High blood pressure," "Pain management," etc., and delete less relevant items.) You can modify the format as well, by asking for a rating of severity or duration for each problem checked. Or you can ask patients to "Circle any of the following if they were a concern in the past, and underline those that are presently of concern to you."

Susan Lentulay, MA, of Erie, PA, suggests modifying the list of concerns to collect information on the intensity, frequency, duration, and impact of the symptomatic behaviors listed. Her format for recording these data uses vertical columns:

Instructions: Mark an × for each concern that applies to you and how it affects you.

| (Name of concern) | How severe is this? | | | Life areas affected: | | | How long has this lasted? | | |
|---|---|---|---|---|---|---|---|---|---|
| | Mild | Moderate | Severe | Work/ school | Home family | Social | 2 weeks or less | 3 weeks to 6–10 months | A year or longer |
| | | | | | | | | | |
| | | | | | | | | | |

Lentulay also adds two areas to the list of concerns: "personal traumas" and "health problems."

# Adult Checklist of Concerns

Name: _____ Date: _____

Please mark all of the items below that apply, and feel free to add any others at the bottom under "Any other concerns or issues." You may add a note or details in the space next to the concerns checked. (For a child, mark any of these and then complete the "Child Checklist of Characteristics.")

❑ I have no problem or concern bringing me here
❑ Abuse—physical, sexual, emotional, neglect (of children or elderly persons), cruelty to animals
❑ Aggression, violence
❑ Alcohol use
❑ Anger, hostility, arguing, irritability
❑ Anxiety, nervousness
❑ Attention, concentration, distractibility
❑ Career concerns, goals, and choices
❑ Childhood issues (your own childhood)
❑ Codependence
❑ Confusion
❑ Compulsions
❑ Custody of children
❑ Decision making, indecision, mixed feelings, putting off decisions
❑ Delusions (false ideas)
❑ Dependence
❑ Depression, low mood, sadness, crying
❑ Divorce, separation
❑ Drug use—prescription medications, over-the-counter medications, street drugs
❑ Eating problems—overeating, undereating, appetite, vomiting (see also "Weight and diet issues")
❑ Emptiness
❑ Failure
❑ Fatigue, tiredness, low energy
❑ Fears, phobias
❑ Financial or money troubles, debt, impulsive spending, low income
❑ Friendships
❑ Gambling
❑ Grieving, mourning, deaths, losses, divorce
❑ Guilt
❑ Headaches, other kinds of pains
❑ Health, illness, medical concerns, physical problems
❑ Housework/chores—quality, schedules, sharing duties
❑ Inferiority feelings

*(cont.)*

**FORM 29. Adult checklist of concerns (p. 1 of 2).** From *The Paper Office*. Copyright 2003 by Edward L. Zuckerman. Permission to photocopy this form is granted to purchasers of this book for personal use only (see copyright page for details).

- ❑ Interpersonal conflicts
- ❑ Impulsiveness, loss of control, outbursts
- ❑ Irresponsibility
- ❑ Judgment problems, risk taking
- ❑ Legal matters, charges, suits
- ❑ Loneliness
- ❑ Marital conflict, distance/coldness, infidelity/affairs, remarriage, different expectations, disappointments
- ❑ Memory problems
- ❑ Menstrual problems, PMS, menopause
- ❑ Mood swings
- ❑ Motivation, laziness
- ❑ Nervousness, tension
- ❑ Obsessions, compulsions (thoughts or actions that repeat themselves)
- ❑ Oversensitivity to rejection
- ❑ Panic or anxiety attacks
- ❑ Parenting, child management, single parenthood
- ❑ Perfectionism
- ❑ Pessimism
- ❑ Procrastination, work inhibitions, laziness
- ❑ Relationship problems (with friends, with relatives, or at work)
- ❑ School problems (see also "Career concerns . . . ")
- ❑ Self-centeredness
- ❑ Self-esteem
- ❑ Self-neglect, poor self-care
- ❑ Sexual issues, dysfunctions, conflicts, desire differences, other (see also "Abuse")
- ❑ Shyness, oversensitivity to criticism
- ❑ Sleep problems—too much, too little, insomnia, nightmares
- ❑ Smoking and tobacco use
- ❑ Spiritual, religious, moral, ethical issues
- ❑ Stress, relaxation, stress management, stress disorders, tension
- ❑ Suspiciousness
- ❑ Suicidal thoughts
- ❑ Temper problems, self-control, low frustration tolerance
- ❑ Thought disorganization and confusion
- ❑ Threats, violence
- ❑ Weight and diet issues
- ❑ Withdrawal, isolating
- ❑ Work problems, employment, workaholism/overworking, can't keep a job, dissatisfaction, ambition

Any other concerns or issues:

- ❑ _____
- ❑ _____

Please look back over the concerns you have checked off and choose the one that you most want help with. It is:

_____

*This is a strictly confidential patient medical record. Redisclosure or transfer is expressly prohibited by law.*

# Child Checklist of Characteristics

Name: _____     Date: _____

Age: _____     Person completing this form: _____

Many concerns can apply to both children and adults. If you have brought a child for evaluation or treatment, first please mark all of the items that apply to your child on the "Adult Checklist of Concerns." Then review this checklist, which contains concerns (as well as positive traits) that apply mostly to children, and mark any items that describe your child. Feel free to add any others at the end under "Any other characteristics."

- ❑ Affectionate
- ❑ Argues, "talks back," smart-alecky, defiant
- ❑ Bullies/intimidates, teases, inflicts pain on others, is bossy to others, picks on, provokes
- ❑ Cheats
- ❑ Cruel to animals
- ❑ Concern for others
- ❑ Conflicts with parents over persistent rule breaking, money, chores, homework, grades, choices in music/clothes/hair/friends
- ❑ Complains
- ❑ Cries easily, feelings are easily hurt
- ❑ Dawdles, procrastinates, wastes time
- ❑ Difficulties with parent's paramour/new marriage/new family
- ❑ Dependent, immature
- ❑ Developmental delays
- ❑ Disrupts family activities
- ❑ Disobedient, uncooperative, refuses, noncompliant, doesn't follow rules
- ❑ Distractible, inattentive, poor concentration, daydreams, slow to respond
- ❑ Dropping out of school
- ❑ Drug or alcohol use
- ❑ Eating—poor manners, refuses, appetite increase or decrease, odd combinations, overeats
- ❑ Exercise problems
- ❑ Extracurricular activities interfere with academics
- ❑ Failure in school
- ❑ Fearful
- ❑ Fighting, hitting, violent, aggressive, hostile, threatens, destructive
- ❑ Fire setting
- ❑ Friendly, outgoing, social
- ❑ Hypochondriac, always complains of feeling sick
- ❑ Immature, "clowns around," has only younger playmates
- ❑ Imaginary playmates, fantasy
- ❑ Independent
- ❑ Interrupts, talks out, yells
- ❑ Lacks organization, unprepared

*(cont.)*

---

**FORM 30. Child checklist of characteristics (p. 1 of 2).**     From *The Paper Office.* Copyright 2003 by Edward L. Zuckerman. Permission to photocopy this form is granted to purchasers of this book for personal use only (see copyright page for details).

❏ Lacks respect for authority, insults, dares, provokes, manipulates

❏ Learning disability

❏ Legal difficulties—truancy, loitering, panhandling, drinking, vandalism, stealing, fighting, drug sales

❏ Likes to be alone, withdraws, isolates

❏ Lying

❏ Low frustration tolerance, irritability

❏ Mental retardation

❏ Moody

❏ Mute, refuses to speak

❏ Nail biting

❏ Nervous

❏ Nightmares

❏ Need for high degree of supervision at home over play/chores/schedule

❏ Obedient

❏ Obesity

❏ Overactive, restless, hyperactive, overactive, out-of-seat behaviors, restlessness, fidgety, noisiness

❏ Oppositional, resists, refuses, does not comply, negativism

❏ Prejudiced, bigoted, insulting, name calling, intolerant

❏ Pouts

❏ Recent move, new school, loss of friends

❏ Relationships with brothers/sisters or friends/peers are poor—competition, fights, teasing/provoking, assaults

❏ Responsible

❏ Rocking or other repetitive movements

❏ Runs away

❏ Sad, unhappy

❏ Self-harming behaviors—biting or hitting self, head banging, scratching self

❏ Speech difficulties

❏ Sexual—sexual preoccupation, public masturbation, inappropriate sexual behaviors

❏ Shy, timid

❏ Stubborn

❏ Suicide talk or attempt

❏ Swearing, blasphemes, bathroom language, foul language

❏ Temper tantrums, rages

❏ Thumb sucking, finger sucking, hair chewing

❏ Tics—involuntary rapid movements, noises, or word productions

❏ Teased, picked on, victimized, bullied

❏ Truant, school avoiding

❏ Underactive, slow-moving or slow-responding, lethargic

❏ Uncoordinated, accident-prone

❏ Wetting or soiling the bed or clothes

❏ Work problems, employment, workaholism/overworking, can't keep a job

Any other characteristics:

❏ _____

Please look back over the concerns you have checked off and choose the one that you most want your child to be helped with. Which is it? _____

*This is a strictly confidential patient medical record. Redisclosure or transfer is expressly prohibited by law.*

If you have clients complete Form 29 or 30 before the first meeting, you can follow up those items checked to clarify exactly what is understood by each term and what difficulties are being presented.

Finally, I should note that under "Abuse" I have included cruelty to animals, which is both illegal in all states and highly correlated with violence against humans. For more information or resources, contact the American Humane Association (800-227-4645, http://www.americanhumane.org) or the Latham Foundation (http://www.latham.org).

### Obtaining Developmental Information

**FORM 31**

When the client is a child, collecting developmental history is essential. Much basic history information can be obtained on a form such as the one offered next (Form 31, the child developmental history record). However, more information will be required when there is a significant clinical problem with a child, and this additional and more detailed information is better acquired during an interview. When all the information has been collected, Form 37, the intake summary and case formulation, will help you integrate it. The purposes and functions of Form 31 are therefore (1) to gather and record information about major historical issues in development and (2) to support the later summarization of information to support treatment planning and initiation. Some items are adapted from a very complete set of forms by Robert E. McCarthy, PhD, of Myrtle Beach, SC.

## 5.5   Phase 4: First Meeting with a New Client

What is the best way to go about identifying a new client's problems? There is a continual struggle in the helping professions between using either broad or highly focused methods of collecting data. Sadly, you can't have both precision and comprehensiveness in data collection without expending enormous amounts of time. Should you use a questionnaire or checklist to ensure that you have missed nothing in the range of possible presenting symptoms, or should you rely on your interviewing skills ("clinical flags") and the conscientious patient to discover all of the important aspects of the case? Each approach has advantages and disadvantages, and so I have chosen to offer materials to support a combination approach, which is a multistep process.

*Step 1.* Use standard questionnaires to capture all the presenting problems, such as the two client information forms (Forms 23 and 24), the two checklists (Forms 29 and 30), and the child developmental history record (Form 31). At least some of these forms can be filled out by the client before the first meeting.

*Step 2.* Do an interview to follow up on the presenting problems in more detail, so that you and the client can come to a shared understanding of their nature and priority, and can establish a positive alliance.

*Step 3.* Because there may be other clinical issues that the client has not identified or was unwilling to indicate initially, do a survey interview with questions directed at some areas of known importance to all patients. The intake interview questions and guide (Form 32) provides structure when structure is desired, without imposing it.

# Child Developmental History Record

## A. Identifications

1. Child's name:_____ Birthdate:_____ Age:_____

   Person(s) completing this form: _____ Today's date: _____

2. Mother's name:_____ Birthdate:_____ Home phone:_____

   Address: _____

   Currently employed: ❑ No ❑ Yes, as: _____ Work phone: _____

3. Father's name:_____ Birthdate:_____ Home phone:_____

   Address: _____

   Currently employed: ❑ No ❑ Yes, as: _____ Work phone: _____

4. Parents are currently ❑ Married ❑ Divorced ❑ Remarried ❑ Never married ❑ Other:_____

   Child's custodian/guardian is: _____

5. Stepparent's name: _____ Birthdate:_____ Home phone:_____

   Address: _____

   Currently employed: ❑ No ❑ Yes, as: _____ Work phone: _____

## B. Development

Please fill in any information you have on the areas listed below.

1. Pregnancy and delivery

   Prenatal medical illnesses and health care: _____

   _____

   _____

   Was the child premature? _____ Weight and height at birth: _____ _____

   Any birth complications or problems? _____

   _____

   _____

2. The first few months of life

   Breast-fed? _____ If so, for how long? _____

   Any allergies? _____

*(cont.)*

---

**FORM 31. Child developmental history record (p. 1 of 3).** From *The Paper Office.* Copyright 2003 by Edward L. Zuckerman. Permission to photocopy this form is granted to purchasers of this book for personal use only (see copyright page for details).

Sleep patterns or problems: _____

_____

_____

Personality: _____

_____

_____

3. Milestones: At what age did this child do each of these?

Sat without support: _____  Crawled: _____

Walked without holding on: _____  Helped when being dressed: _____

Ate with a fork: _____  Stayed dry all day: _____

Didn't soil his or her pants: _____  Stayed dry all night: _____

Tied shoelaces: _____  Buttoned buttons: _____

4. Speech/language development

Age when child said first word understandable to a stranger: _____

Age when child said first sentence understandable to a stranger: _____

Any speech, hearing, or language difficulties? _____

_____

_____

## C. Health

List all childhood illnesses, hospitalizations, medications, allergies, head injuries, important accidents and injuries, surgeries, periods of loss of consciousness, convulsions/seizures, and other medical conditions.

| Condition | Age | Treated by whom? | Consequences? |
|-----------|-----|------------------|---------------|
|           |     |                  |               |

(cont.)

## D. Residences

### 1. Homes

| Dates | | Location | With whom | Reason for moving | Any problems? |
| From | To | | | | |
| --- | --- | --- | --- | --- | --- |
| | | | | | |

### 2. Residential placements, institutional placements, or foster care

| Dates | | Program name or location | Reason for placement | Problems? |
| From | To | | | |
| --- | --- | --- | --- | --- |
| | | | | |

## E. Schools

| School (name, district, address, phone) | Grade | Age | Teacher |
| --- | --- | --- | --- |
| | | | |

May I call and discuss your child with the current teacher?   ❑ Yes   ❑ No

## F. Special skills or talents of child

List hobbies, sports; recreational, musical, TV, and toy preferences; etc.: _____

_____

## G. Other

Is there anything else I should know that doesn't appear on this or other forms, but that is or might be important?

_____

_____

_____

*This is a strictly confidential patient medical record. Redisclosure or transfer is expressly prohibited by law.*

*Step 4.* Follow up any new concerns with detailed interviewing methods. A very complete list of questions, organized according to clinical symptoms or syndromes, can be found in the *Clinician's Thesaurus* (Zuckerman, 2000).

*Step 5.* Use very specialized and focused questionnaires, behavioral schedules, and checklists only when the presentation is very complex or detailed documentation is essential. These syndrome-specific materials are beyond the scope of this book.

*Step 6.* Summarize and organize your data, using the forms provided in Section 5.6 for suicide risk, chemical use, and overall case formulation.

## Preparing the Client for the Intake Interview

Some routine and some critical information has to be exchanged, and organizing this process is advantageous for both sides. You can streamline the process by specifying what information clients need to provide to you (by mailing your intake forms); giving them enough time to collect and record the information; encouraging the noting down of any questions and areas of uncertainty; and (during the first interview) complimenting them on the quality of their work and emphasizing that their efforts are both appreciated and augur well for the therapy enterprise.

Since most people get "nervous" in a professional's office, they will fail to disclose important material or to pursue answers to their questions. If you appear rushed, this will compound the problem—so make it clear to clients that you will not be interrupted by phone calls or by your staff members, and remind them how much time you have made available. For some clients, you might encourage them to take notes and support this with paper, pens, and a clipboard: "Write down what you think is most important in what we say today, the answers to your questions, and my recommendations and suggestions." If you have any doubts about the clarity and fullness of the communication, say, "I want to be sure we are understanding each other, so tell me what you remember about. . . ."

As you interview a client, having read over the forms, you may find it clarifying for both you and the client to record relevant information by constructing a genogram or family tree. A photocopy of this can be given to the client at the end of the interview, either as homework or as a way to assist with further history gathering.

The purposes and functions of the forms presented in this section and in Section 5.6 are as follows: (1) to enable you to identify and assess the client's problems in clinical terms and decide how to intervene; (2) to document your assessment so that it is concise, accessible, productive, and professional; and (3) to help you begin building a productive therapeutic alliance.

Another way to collect many of these data is to have the client write his or her own history using a comprehensive outline given by you. Joan Anderson, PhD, of Houston, TX, suggests that this is especially useful in any case you expect may go to court, because you will have the data in the client's own words (and usually his or her handwriting as well).

## Using the Intake Interview Questions and Guide

**FORM 32**

Rather than use a printed form (which always seems to have either too much or too little space) for recording the responses to interview questions, you can ask the questions from the intake interview questions and guide (Form 32) and record the client's responses, numbered to correspond to the question asked, on plain lined filler paper (see Section 1.4). As each question is answered, you can cross out its number on the form. Irvin P. R. Guyett, PhD, of Pittsburgh, PA, has used his laptop computer while interviewing patients and found that it is not as distracting as one might expect. It allows the answers to be placed under the questions, and wastes no space when the answers are printed out for the chart. Here are a few more suggestions about the use of Form 32:

- Just before "Introductory Questions," the form lists the item "Entered into birthday book." This pertains to the sending of birthday cards, which may be appropriate for some child clinicians.

- The introductory questions repeat some of those of the client information forms (Forms 23 and 24), and so it may not be necessary to ask these again. However, if it has been a while since the first contact, they can be asked as a way of reestablishing rapport and making sure you and the patient agree on the problems to be dealt with. You may also discover changes that have occurred since the earlier contact. Finally, if you have doubts or concerns about what the client indicated earlier, ask these questions again to gain more detailed information or check for inconsistencies.

- As always, you should add or delete questions to this form to suit your clientele or practice.

- If you prefer to use a written questionnaire, you can rephrase, reformat, and delete some of the questions in Form 32 for your clients to complete in writing.

## Collecting Information from Young Adults

**FORM 33**

Form 33 below is designed to be acceptable to and productive with adolescent clients, who are often reluctant to divulge information, unfamiliar with the ability to keep information confidential, hostile to seeing a "shrink," and otherwise resistant. It asks initial questions, which are then followed up during the interview for more detailed information. For example, the question "Do you party?" is a lead into alcohol consumption, sexual activity, use of contraception, and so forth. Alternate phrasings for the question "Why do you think you are here?" include: "Do you understand why you are coming here?", "Are you coming here because of a problem that is mainly someone else's?" If so, ask, "Whose?", or "What is the problem?" This form is based on one designed by Nora Fleming Young, PhD, of Mayer, AZ, and is adapted here with her kind permission. The confidentiality statement at the top may need to be modified for your state and the young person's age.

## Special Considerations for Interviewing a Child

During your interview of a child patient or his or her caregiver(s), you might want to consider collecting data and your impressions about these points:

## Intake Interview Questions and Guide

Client's name: _____   Date: _____   Interviewer's initials: _____

❏ OK to thank referrer?   ❏ Yes   ❏ No     ❏ Entered into phone book     ❏ Entered into birthday book

### Introductory questions

1. Who suggested that you come to see me? _____   Referral code: _____

2. What is the problem, in your own words? How do you see the situation? (Chief complaint/concern, presenting problem; symptoms—frequency, duration, intensity, latency, recurrence, course; distress caused, change efforts; why help is being sought *now*—precipitants, stressors, consequences; contexts, relevant history; needs, goals, strengths.)

### Essential information

3. Previous psychological episodes, treaters, and treatments.

   a. For what?

   b. Where/by whom?

   c. Treatment?

   d. When (from–to)?

   e. Outcome?

   f. Satisfaction/difficulties? (Especially follow up any hints of problems/abuse by therapists—e.g., dual relationships, sexual intimacies, litigation.)

   g. Release(s) for records signed?

4. History of abuse. (Interview partners separately: Disagreements and decisions; verbal, emotional, physical, sexual abuse; marital, elder, childhood, family-of-origin abuse; kinds of violence; coping and protections; actions taken against abuser; fears, danger.)

5. Follow-up of responses to client information forms.

   a. Health problems. (Injuries, illnesses, allergies, eating patterns, exercise, sleep, sex; all current medications; last exam by an MD?)

   b. Legal history. (Involvement with the law/police, arrests; charges lodged—civil and criminal, not paying bills, fraud, violence; consequences, sentences; litigation anticipated, pending or in past, especially against therapists; lawyer's name and phone number.)

*(cont.)*

---

**FORM 32. Intake interview questions and guide (p. 1 of 2).** From *The Paper Office*. Copyright 2003 by Edward L. Zuckerman. Permission to photocopy this form is granted to purchasers of this book for personal use only (see copyright page for details).

    c. Family of origin. (Make genogram. Parents: ages, health, education, etc. Sibs: number, ages, relationships, etc. Important friendships. For all relatives: issues of abuse, affection, control, discipline, expectations, aspirations, personalities, mental health, religion, schooling, occupations, marriages, legal issues.)

    d. Substance use history. (For client, family of origin, current family: Alcohol, drugs—street and prescription, chemicals, caffeine, tobacco; current and past use.)

    e. Current relationship/family situation. (How client met current partner; attraction, love; family's role; duration, transitions, stressors, and affectual tone of relationship; number and ages of children; problems with or concerns about children.)

## Optional questions

6. What changes do you hope therapy will lead to? (Realism, readiness to change, changes of self vs. others, consistency with therapist.)

7. What do you want to change about yourself? (Locus of responsibility, control.)

8. How will therapy help you make these changes? (Understanding, sophistication, dependence.)

9. What do you think a therapist should be like?

10. How long do you think these changes will take? (Realism of time frame.)

11. What are your major strengths? (Abilities, resources, education, employment, personality, feelings, habits, relationships.)

12. What have been your major crises of the last 1–5 years, and how have you handled them? (Precipitants, coping mechanisms/skills, defenses.)

13. What are your goals? (Ambitions, family situation and satisfaction, school/work situation and satisfaction.)

14. What persons, ideas, or forces have been most useful or influential to you in the past?

15. When are you happy? What are the positive factors in your life right now? (Hobbies? Sports? Family? Security?)

16. What spiritual or religious issues are important to you? How does your culture, heritage, etc., influence you?

17. Is there anything we haven't talked about that is relevant or important, or that you feel I should know about?

18. [Add other questions that seem called for or appropriate.]

19. Examiner's confidence in accuracy of information obtained (high, adequate, marginal, poor).

20. Quality and intensity of alliance (positive, meshing; positive, building; neutral, cautious; negative, distant/guarded; negative, hostile/suspicious).

# Young Adult Information Form

*Note:* Unless there is a serious risk of injury to you or someone else, the information on this form is confidential. It will not be discussed with your parents without your consent.

Your name: _____ Today's date: _____ Your age: _____

Your address: _____ Phone #: _____

## Health

How tall are you? _____ How much do you weigh? _____

What physical or medical problems do you have now, or have you had in the past? _____

_____

## Family

Birth parents' names: _____ and _____

Address: _____ Phone #: _____

Present parents'/guardians' names: _____ and _____

Address: _____ Phone #: _____

How would you describe your parents' relationship? _____

What kinds of problems are you having with:

Parents/stepparents/guardians?

Parents' live-in friends or boyfriends/girlfriends?

Brothers or sisters (or stepbrothers or stepsisters)?

*(cont.)*

**FORM 33. Information form for young adults (p. 1 of 3).**     Adapted from a form devised by Nora Fleming Young, PhD, of Mayer, AZ, and used by permission of Dr. Young.—From *The Paper Office*. Copyright 2003 by Edward L. Zuckerman. Permission to photocopy this handout is granted to purchasers of this book for personal use only (see copyright page for details).

**School**

Which school do you go to? _____ Grade level/year: _____

How are your grades? _____

Problems in school? _____

**Work**

Do you work? _____ If so, where? _____

Problems there? _____

**Friends**

Who are your close friends (names and ages)?

Do you have a serious one-on-one relationship now? _____

Do you party? _____ If so, when and where? _____

**Previous counseling**

1. With whom? _____ When? _____

   For what? _____

   With what results? _____

2. With whom? _____ When? _____

   For what? _____

   With what results? _____

**Concerns**

Would you like information or answers on:  ❑ Sex  ❑ Alcohol  ❑ Drugs  (If so, which? _____ )

  ❑ Birth control  ❑ Relationships  ❑ Other: _____

Is religion important to you and/or your family? _____ If so, in what ways? _____

_____

What worries or upsets you?

*(cont.)*

_____

What makes you happy?

Why do you think you are here? Please tell me in your own words.

What would you like to see happen or change because of this counseling?

What would you like me to let your parents know?

What else is important for me to know?

What would you like me to ask you about?

Signed: _____ Date: _____

*Social Context*

1. Relationship between this child and each parent or significant adult.

2. Ways affection is shown and emotions are expressed and controlled.

3. Parenting skills. (Empathy, appropriateness of expectations, methods of control/discipline, by whom.)

4. Chores expected and performance.

5. Autonomy. (Age-appropriateness; allowances; selection of clothes, friends, music; etc.)

6. Relationships with siblings, relatives.

7. Social skills. (Friendships, peers, older vs. younger playmates, skill level.)

8. Social context. (Cultural, ethnic, religious, economic, immigrant, etc.)

9. Other.

*Parental Understanding of Problem(s)*

1. Parent's view of child's main problem.

2. Parental efforts to handle, change, or cure the child's problems.

3. Parental ideas of what the school or consultant can do for the child.

## The Evaluation of Mental Status

**FORM 34**  The purposes of Form 34, the mental status evaluation and report, are as follows: (1) to record observations about the customarily noted aspects of cognitive functioning in a systematic way; (2) to document the client's current mental status for baseline and treatment planning; and (3) to help a treating therapist, who may not be a clinician experienced in comprehensive and precise mental status evaluations, document later observations.

There is no paper substitute for a comprehensive evaluation by an experienced clinician, because mental status is a complex biopsychosocial phenomenon. There are more formal brief mental status tests, such as the Folstein et al. (1975) Mini-Mental State, and clinical neuropsychological evaluation instruments, such as the Halstead-Reitan.

This form does not offer the interview questions that would produce the data it summarizes, because there are so many possibilities. It is reprinted from Zuckerman (2000), which contains detailed resources for evaluating and describing mental status: a large collection of mental status questions under all headings, and 20 pages of words and phrases describing all aspects of cognitive functioning commonly evaluated in a mental status evaluation.

# Mental Status Evaluation and Report

*Directions:* Rate current observed performance, not reported, historical, or projected. Circle the most appropriate descriptive terms in part C, and feel free to write in others. If an aspect of mental status was not assessed, cross out the heading. Write additional observations, clarifications, and quotations in part D.

Client: _____ Date: _____ Evaluator: _____

**A. Informed consent** was obtained about:

❑ The recipient(s) of this report  ❑ Confidentiality  ❑ Competency  ❑ Other: _____

**B. Evaluation methods**

1. The information and assessments below are based on my observation of this client during:

   ❑ Intake interview  ❑ Psychotherapy  ❑ Formal mental status testing  ❑ Group therapy

   ❑ Other: _____

2. We interacted for a total of _____ minutes.

3. Setting of the contact:  ❑ Professional office  ❑ Hospital room  ❑ Clinic  ❑ School  ❑ Home  ❑ Work

   ❑ Jail/prison  ❑ Other: _____

**C. Mental status descriptors** (Circle all appropriate items)

1. **Appearance and self-care**

| | | | | | | |
|---|---|---|---|---|---|---|
| *Stature* | Average | Small | Tall | (For age, if a child) | | |
| *Weight* | Average weight | Overweight | Obese | Underweight | Thin | Cachectic |
| *Clothing* | Neat/clean | Careless/inappropriate | Meticulous | Disheveled | Dirty | |
| | Appropriate for age, occasion, weather | | Seductive | Inappropriate | Bizarre | |
| *Grooming* | Normal | Well-groomed | Neglected | Bizarre | | |
| *Cosmetic use* | Age-appropriate | Inappropriate for age | Excessive | None | | |
| *Posture/gait* | Normal | Tense | Rigid | Stooped | Slumped | Bizarre | Other:_____ |
| *Motor activity* | Not remarkable | Slowed | Repetitive | Restless | Agitated | Tremor |

Other notable aspects: _____

2. **Sensorium**

| | | | | | | | |
|---|---|---|---|---|---|---|---|
| *Attention* | Normal | Unaware | Inattentive | Distractible | Confused | Persistent | Vigilant |
| *Concentration* | Normal | Scattered | Variable | Preoccupied | Anxiety interferes | | |
| | Focuses on irrelevancies | | | | | | |
| *Orientation* | ×5 | Time | Person | Place | Situation | Object | |
| *Recall/memory* | Normal | Defective in: Immediate/short-term | Recent | Remote | | | |

*(cont.)*

**FORM 34. Mental status evaluation and report (p. 1 of 2).**    From Zuckerman (2000). Copyright 2000 by Edward L. Zuckerman. Reprinted by permission.—From *The Paper Office*. Permission to photocopy this form is granted to purchasers of this book for personal use only (see copyright page for details).

3. **Relating**

| | | | | | | |
|---|---|---|---|---|---|---|
| *Eye contact* | Normal | Fleeting | Avoided | None | Staring | |
| *Facial expression* | Responsive | Constricted | Tense | Anxious | Sad | Depressed | Angry |

*Attitude toward examiner*    Cooperative    Dependent    Dramatic    Passive    Uninterested    Silly
Resistant    Critical    Hostile    Sarcastic    Irritable    Threatening
Suspicious    Guarded    Defensive    Manipulative    Argumentative

4. **Affect and mood**

*Affect*    Appropriate    Labile    Restricted    Blunted    Flat    Other:_____

*Mood*    Euthymic    Pessimistic    Depressed    Hypomanic    Euphoric
Other:_____

5. **Thought and language**

*Speech flow*    Normal    Mute    Loud    Blocked    Paucity    Pressured    Flight of ideas

*Thought content*    Appropriate to mood and circumstances    Personalizations    Persecutions
Suspicions    Delusions    Ideas of reference    Ideas of influence    Illusions

*Preoccupations*    Phobias    Somatic    Suicide    Homicidal    Guilt    Religion    Other:_____

*Hallucinations*    Auditory    Visual    Other:_____

*Organization*    Logical    Goal-directed    Circumstantial    Loose    Perseverations

6. **Executive functions**

*Fund of knowledge*    Average    Impoverished by:_____

*Intelligence*    Average    Below average    Above average    Needs investigation

*Abstraction*    Normal    Concrete    Functional    Popular    Abstract    Overly abstract

*Judgment*    Normal    Common-sensical    Fair    Poor    Dangerous

*Reality testing*    Realistic    Adequate    Distorted    Variable    Unaware

*Insight*    Uses connections    Gaps    Flashes of    Unaware    Nil    Denial

*Decision making*    Normal    Only simple    Impulsive    Vacillates    Confused    Paralyzed

7. **Stress**

*Stressors*    Money    Housing    Family conflict    Work    Grief/losses    Illness    Transitions

*Coping ability*    Normal    Resilient    Exhausted    Overwhelmed    Deficient supports
Deficient skills    Growing

*Skill deficits*    None    Intellect/educ.    Communication    Interpersonal    Decision making
Self-control    Responsibility    Self-care    Activities of daily living

*Supports*    Usual    Family    Friends    Church    Service system
Needed:_____

8. **Social functioning**

*Social maturity*    Responsible    Irresponsible    Self-centered    Impulsive    Isolates

*Social judgment*    Normal    "Street-smart"    Naive    Heedless    Victimized    Impropriety

**D. Other aspects of mental status**

_____

_____

*This is a strictly confidential patient medical record. Redisclosure or transfer is expressly prohibited by law.*

*This report reflects the patient's condition at the time of consultation or evaluation. It does not necessarily reflect the patient's diagnosis or condition at any subsequent time.*

# 5.6   Phase 5: Summarizing the Intake Information

During the previous phases of the intake process, you have collected data about the client from the client, your observations, forms and perhaps other sources. Now it is time to review, sift, and integrate those data. This section offers three forms to assist with this process.

## Summarizing Chemical Use and Suicide Risk Data

**FORM 35**
**FORM 36**

The processes of assessing clients' chemical use and suicide risk have already been discussed in Sections 5.4 and 3.11, respectively. Form 35, the chemical user's case formulation, and Form 36, the suicide risk assessment summary and recommendations, are designed to assist you in summarizing and integrating all the relevant information in cases where one or the other of these factors plays a significant role.

## Formulating the Whole Case

When the information presented by a new client has been collected, the data must be organized for the making of clinical decisions. If treatment is appropriate, what should be the goals, and what methods should be used? A treatment plan is needed. Also, what should be the disposition of the case: Should the client be referred elsewhere, be sent for further assessments or consultations, receive treatment from you, or be sent to a specialized treatment program?

**FORM 37**

The purposes and functions of Form 37, the intake summary and case formulation, are to gather and formulate the findings so as to (1) prioritize the client's most important and immediate problems; (2) facilitate all appropriate referrals for evaluation or treatment; (3) support consultations and coordination with other professionals; (4) document the need for services to funding sources (e.g., health insurers and MCOs); (5) concentrate the data needed to develop a treatment plan; and (6) provide for continuity and comprehensiveness of care. Completion of this form should precede treatment of any patient. If your patient requires MCO approval, complete this first and then see Form 38, the individualized treatment plan for MCOs, at the end of Section 6.1.

Section D, part 1, of Form 37 offers checkoffs for the assessment of risks. Some of the items can be expanded if your setting needs greater precision, as in these examples:

---

a. *Suicide*:   ❑ Not assessed   ❑ No indications   ❑ Passive death wish   ❑ Ideation without plan

❑ Threat   ❑ Preoccupation   ❑ Plan   ❑ Gesture   ❑ Prior attempt

❑ Plan without means   ❑ Access to means

b. *Homicide*:   ❑ Not assessed   ❑ No indications   ❑ Ideation without plan   ❑ Threat

❑ Specific victim   ❑ No identifiable victim   ❑ Preoccupation   ❑ Plan

❑ Prior attempt   ❑ Plan without means   ❑ Access to means

---

Or other categories of risk can be added:

---

*Self-injury*: ❑ Not assessed  ❑ No indications  ❑ Ideation without plan  ❑ Threat

❑ Preoccupation  ❑ Plan  ❑ Prior injuries: _____  ❑ Access to means

*Isolation*: ❑ Self-preoccupation  ❑ Avoidance  ❑ Seclusion  ❑ Self-neglect  ❑ Refuses supports

❑ Harm or injury from neglect

---

In the "self-injury" category, you may need to distinguish acts of suicidal intent from body modification (tattooing, piercing, scarification), sexual or power exchange activities (knife play, slave and master, etc.), and acts motivated by psychopathology (relief or psychic pain through self-cutting and blood).

Another revision you could make is that you could add or substitute a visual scale for each of the risks in Section D, part 1:

---

When compared with this practice's/agency's typical patient population, the risk this client presents is judged at this time to be:

| | | | | |
|---|---|---|---|---|
| Very low | Low | Medium | High | Very high |

---

Among other changes you might make to this form, DSM-IV (American Psychiatric Association, 1994) has proposed three axes for future study; it may be useful to start using these now, so that outcome changes on these can be scored in the future. They should go at the end of section D, part 3 ("Diagnoses").

---

Social and Occupational Functioning Assessment Scale (SOFAS: 0–100): Currently: _____ Past year: _____

Global Assessment of Relational Functioning (GARF) Scale (0–100): Currently: _____ Past year: _____

Defensive Functioning Scale (DFS): List up to seven defenses, most prominent first:

_____

_____

Predominant current defense level: ❑ High adaptive  ❑ Mental inhibitions  ❑ Minor image-distorting

❑ Disavowal  ❑ Major image-distorting  ❑ Action  ❑ Defensive dysregulation

---

# Chemical User's Case Formulation

Based on the data collected during this evaluation process, here are my conclusions. (The best descriptors are checked.)

**A. Identification**

Name: _____ Date: _____ Case #: _____

**B. Observations**

| | | | | | |
|---|---|---|---|---|---|
| Client was intoxicated at interview | ❑ Not at all | ❑ Possibly | ❑ Mildly | ❑ Clearly | ❑ Hung over |
| Consumption history was | ❑ Acknowledged | ❑ Minimized | ❑ Denied, | ❑ but confirmed | |
| Legal consequences were | ❑ Acknowledged | ❑ Minimized | ❑ Denied, | ❑ but confirmed | |
| Financial consequences were | ❑ Acknowledged | ❑ Minimized | ❑ Denied, | ❑ but confirmed | |
| Health consequences were | ❑ Acknowledged | ❑ Minimized | ❑ Denied, | ❑ but confirmed | |
| Spiritual consequences were | ❑ Acknowledged | ❑ Minimized | ❑ Denied, | ❑ but confirmed | |
| Vocational consequences were | ❑ Acknowledged | ❑ Minimized | ❑ Denied, | ❑ but confirmed | |
| Familial consequences were | ❑ Acknowledged | ❑ Minimized | ❑ Denied, | ❑ but confirmed | |

What brought the patient in now? _____

_____

The patient's goals (realism, comprehensiveness, resources needed): _____

_____

_____

**C. Degree of identification/denial as having alcoholism/addiction**

❑ Denies any intemperate use; denies need for treatment

❑ Minimizes consequences of drinking/use

❑ Is "treatment-wise" or "just going through the motions"

❑ Identifies self as "alcoholic/addicted," "in recovery"; has made sobriety his or her first priority

❑ Is willing to and did do whatever is necessary to maintain sobriety, has a positive and optimistic attitude toward the future

**D. Stage in the progression of the disease (for alcoholism only)**

❑ None  ❑ Prealcoholism  ❑ Prodromal  ❑ Crucial  ❑ Chronic  ❑ Periodic excessive drinking

❑ Blackouts  ❑ Sneaking drinks  ❑ Loss of control over drinking  ❑ Remorse and rationalization

❑ Changing the pattern of drinking  ❑ Morning drinking  ❑ Benders/binges  ❑ Defeat

*(cont.)*

**FORM 35. Chemical user's case formulation (p. 1 of 2).** From *The Paper Office*. Copyright 2003 by Edward L. Zuckerman. Permission to photocopy this form is granted to purchasers of this book for personal use only (see copyright page for details).

## E. Personal variables

Gender/sex role training    ❑ Not relevant   ❑ Minimal   ❑ Important   ❑ Crucial

Social class    ❑ Not relevant   ❑ Minimal   ❑ Important   ❑ Crucial

Ethnicity    ❑ Not relevant   ❑ Minimal   ❑ Important   ❑ Crucial

Self-esteem/sense of efficacy    ❑ Normal   ❑ Control in other life areas   ❑ Helpless/passive/defeated   ❑ Blames others/denial   ❑ Self-destroying

Impact of abuse    ❑ None   ❑ Mild   ❑ Significant   ❑ Severe/prolonged

Attitude toward treatment    ❑ Eager for   ❑ Hopeful   ❑ Neutral   ❑ Pessimistic

Other: _____

## F. Social variables

Residence    ❑ Comfortable, stable   ❑ Unstable   ❑ None/illegal

Employment    ❑ Regular, consistent   ❑ Irregular or inconsistent   ❑ High-risk

Friends    ❑ No friends   ❑ No abusers   ❑ Some abusers   ❑ Only abusers

Addiction of spouse/significant other    ❑ None   ❑ Minimal   ❑ Important   ❑ Crucial

Addiction of close relatives    ❑ Not relevant   ❑ Minimal   ❑ Important   ❑ Crucial

Spouse/significant other    ❑ Supportive   ❑ Uncooperative   ❑ Not involved   ❑ In denial   ❑ Enabling   ❑ Codependent   ❑ Addicted

Family involvement    ❑ None   ❑ In denial   ❑ Cooperative   ❑ Exhausted   ❑ Punitive

Support system for sobriety    ❑ Excellent, stable, broad   ❑ Some   ❑ Minimal   ❑ Counterproductive

Other factors: _____

## G. Diagnosis (DSM-IV or ICD diagnosis is on intake summary)

❑ Abstaining   ❑ In recovery   ❑ Social drinking/controlled drinking   ❑ Heavy drinking   ❑ Problem drinking

❑ Alcoholism   ❑ Uncontrolled drinking/alcohol addiction/compulsive drinking   ❑ Terminal alcoholism

❑ "Dry drunk" syndrome   ❑ At risk   ❑ Addiction   ❑ Cross-addiction   ❑ Controlled use   Other: _____

## H. Additional assessments needed

❑ Mental status exam   ❑ Neuropsychological   ❑ Neurological   ❑ Medical

❑ Diagnostic evaluations for presence of concurrent psychiatric disorders

❑ Assessment of relationship/marital/sexual difficulties   ❑ Assessment of risk for suicide, homicide, abuse, violence

## I. Prognosis

The prognosis, with treatment as specified in the individual treatment plan, is considered to be as follows:

1. For participation in and benefit from treatments: ❑ Optimistic   ❑ Good   ❑ Guarded   ❑ Poor   ❑ Negative

2. For improvement of symptoms:   ❑ Optimistic   ❑ Good   ❑ Guarded   ❑ Poor   ❑ Negative

3. For recovery to previous level of functioning: ❑ Optimistic   ❑ Good   ❑ Guarded   ❑ Poor   ❑ Negative

4. For growth and wellness:   ❑ Optimistic   ❑ Good   ❑ Guarded   ❑ Poor   ❑ Negative

*This is a strictly confidential patient medical record. Redisclosure or transfer is expressly prohibited by law.*

*This report reflects the patient's condition at the time of consultation or evaluation. It does not necessarily reflect the patient's diagnosis or condition at any subsequent time.*

## Suicide Risk Assessment Summary and Recommendations

Client's name: _____ Date: _____

This assessment is based on information collected from the following:

❑ My interview(s) with these persons:          On these dates:

   ❑ The client

   ❑ Family members: _____ _____

   ❑ Friends: _____ _____

   ❑ Other people: _____ _____

❑ Reading of records (specify): _____

❑ Knowledge of the risk factors this client and situation present

❑ Other sources: _____

It is my professional judgment that this person currently presents the following risk of suicide:

❑ Almost nonexistent   No direct or indirect evidence for suicidal ideation, rumination, or behaviors from client or others. (It is against strongly held beliefs; the client has many or valued reasons for living.)

❑ Low   Only passive/death wishes (tired of living/pain; fleeting ideation).

❑ Moderate   Ideation without plan, means, motivation (ambivalence, wondering, considering).

❑ Significant/likely   Persistent ideation, making plans, acquiring means. (The client has made statements, rehearsals, threats, gestures or low-lethality/symbolic/ineffective attempts. The client has discussed suicide.)

❑ Very high   Serious/high-lethality attempt is likely in near future. (The client has arranged some affairs, has acquired some means, and has some plan of action and privacy.)

❑ Acute and immediate   Persistent and preoccupying thoughts, continual efforts. (The client has acquired high-lethality means and is deliberate and focused. The client has one or more effective plans of action and the necessary privacy.)

*(cont.)*

**FORM 36. Suicide risk assessment summary and recommendations (p. 1 of 2).** From *The Paper Office.* Copyright 2003 by Edward L. Zuckerman. Permission to photocopy this form is granted to purchasers of this book for personal use only (see copyright page for details).

Therefore, I recommend the following interventions:

❑ No intervention is needed at present.

❑ Reevaluate by this date: _____

❑ Consultation with these people or organizations:

   ❑ Relatives: _____

   ❑ Other professionals: _____

   ❑ Mental health authorities: _____

   ❑ Law enforcement authorities: _____

   ❑ Other: _____

❑ Changes to therapy or new therapeutic interventions:

   ❑ Confrontation and concerned discussion by client's therapist to explore issues and motives

   ❑ No-suicide contracting

   ❑ More intensive psychotherapy

   ❑ Changes in medications

   ❑ Intensive family interventions and support

   ❑ Crisis intervention team

   ❑ Partial hospitalization with intensive treatment

   ❑ Psychiatric inpatient hospitalization:   ❑ Voluntary   ❑ Involuntary

   ❑ Contacts with police or other authorities

   ❑ Other recommendations: _____

   _____

   _____

   _____


_____     _____
                    Signature                                      Date

_____
                  Printed name


A copy of this form should now be sent to: _____


*This is a strictly confidential patient medical record. Redisclosure or transfer is expressly prohibited by law.*

*This report reflects the patient's condition at the time of consultation or evaluation. It does not necessarily reflect the patient's diagnosis or condition at any subsequent time.*

# Intake Summary and Case Formulation

Where space is insufficient, use an asterisk and write the information on the back of the last page.

## A. Basic information

Client: _____ Date: _____ ID #: _____

*Purpose of this intake:* ❑ New client evaluation ❑ Readmission; previous intake on _____

❑ Consultation; copy to be sent to _____ ❑ Reevaluation or review

❑ Other purpose: _____

*Documents reviewed*

| Name | Date created | Source/organization | Signed by | Date reviewed |
|------|--------------|---------------------|-----------|---------------|
|      |              |                     |           |               |
|      |              |                     |           |               |
|      |              |                     |           |               |
|      |              |                     |           |               |

## B. Dynamics of difficulties

1. Risk factors/vulnerabilities/diatheses: a._____

   b. _____ c. _____

2. Stressors and precipitants:

   Acute: a. _____ b. _____

   Enduring: a. _____ b. _____

3. Contributors to relapse (e.g., cognitions, moods, interactions, situations): a._____

   b. _____ c. _____

4. Resources/support systems/coping skills available (describe and then write "Yes" or "No" in right-hand column to indicate whether it is currently being used):

   a. In the client (motivations, resilience, own efforts for change): _____

   _____

   b. Other persons: _____

   _____

   c. Organizations: _____

   _____

*(cont.)*

**FORM 37. Intake summary and case formulation (p. 1 of 5).** From *The Paper Office.* Copyright 2003 by Edward L. Zuckerman. Permission to photocopy this form is granted to purchasers of this book for personal use only (see copyright page for details).

**C. Present level of functioning/limitations/impairment** (describe specific impairments at left, and rate degree of functional impairment at right with GAF number [100 = none, 70 = little, 30 = significant, 10 = incapacitated] or use descriptors):

| Area of functioning | GAF rating |
|---|---|
| 1. School/work functioning: _____ | _____ |
| 2. Intimate relationship/marriage: _____ | _____ |
| 3. Family/children: _____ | _____ |
| 4. Social relationships: _____ | _____ |
| 5. Psychological/personal functioning: _____ | _____ |
| 6. Other areas: _____ | _____ |

**D. Assessment conclusions**

1. Assessment of currently known **risk factors**:

   a. *Suicide:* ❏ Not assessed  ❏ No known behaviors  ❏ Ideation only  ❏ Plan
   ❏ Intent without means  ❏ Intent with means

   b. *Homicide:* ❏ Not assessed  ❏ No known behaviors  ❏ Ideation only  ❏ Plan
   ❏ Intent without means  ❏ Intent with means

   c. *Impulse control:* ❏ Not assessed  ❏ Sufficient control  ❏ Moderate  ❏ Minimal  ❏ Inconsistent

   d. *Compliance with treatments:* ❏ Not assessed  ❏ Full compliance  ❏ Minimal noncompliance
   ❏ Moderate noncompliance  ❏ Variable  ❏ Little or no compliance

   e. *Substance abuse/dependence:* ❏ Not assessed  ❏ None/normal use  ❏ Overuse  ❏ Abuse
   ❏ Dependence  ❏ Unstable remission of abuse

   f. *Current physical or sexual abuse:* ❏ Not assessed  ❏ No  ❏ Yes  Legally reportable? ❏ Yes ❏ No

   g. *Current child/elder neglect:* ❏ Not assessed  ❏ No  ❏ Yes  Legally reportable? ❏ Yes ❏ No
   If yes, client is  ❏ Victim  ❏ Perpetrator  ❏ Both  ❏ Neither, but abuse exists in family

   h. *If risk exists:* Client ❏ can ❏ cannot meaningfully agree to a contract not to harm ❏ self ❏ others ❏ both

   i. *History* that may affect current level of risk or impairment of functioning:
   _____
   _____

   j. *Other concerns:* _____

*(cont.)*

2. **Urgency** estimate ❏ Emergency; immediate interventions ❏ Serious disruption of functioning; act in next 24 hours ❏ Treatment needed; act soon/routine ❏ Wait for: _____

3. **Diagnoses**—Current best formulation

| Name (indicate which is primary diagnosis with "P") | Code #<br>❏ DSM-IV or<br>❏ ICD? |
|---|---|
| **Axis I** _____ | _____ |
| _____ | _____ |
| _____ | _____ |
| **Axis II** _____ | _____ |
| _____ | _____ |
| _____ | _____ |

"Rule-outs" (other possible diagnoses to be evaluated over time): _____

_____

_____

**Axis III**—Significant and relevant medical conditions, including allergies and drug sensitivities:

| Condition | Treatment/medication (regimen) | Provider | Status |
|---|---|---|---|
|  |  |  |  |
|  |  |  |  |
|  |  |  |  |

**Axis IV**—Psychosocial and environmental problems in last year; overall severity rating: _____

❏ Problems with primary support group ❏ Problems related to the social environment

❏ Educational problems ❏ Occupational problems

❏ Housing problems ❏ Economic problems

❏ Problems with access to health care services

❏ Problems related to interaction with the legal system/crime

Other psychosocial and environmental problems (specify): _____

_____

_____

**Axis V**—Global Assessment of Functioning (GAF) Rating:  Currently: _____  Highest in past year: _____

**V Codes**—Other problems that may be a focus of clinical attention: _____

_____

_____

(cont.)

**E. Treatment plan** (if additional problems are to be addressed, use copies of this page):

Significant improvement is to be expected, with treatment as specified, for:

Problem 1: _____

- Behaviors to be changed: _____
  _____
  _____

- Interventions (who does what, how often, with what resources; modality, frequency, duration): _____
  _____
  _____

- Observable indicators of improvement (behaviors, reports):      ■ Expected number of visits to
  _____         achieve each indicator: _____
  _____
  _____

- Discharge level of problem behaviors: _____    ■ Review date: _____
  _____

Problem 2: _____

- Behaviors to be changed: _____
  _____
  _____

- Interventions (who does what, how often, with what resources; modality, frequency, duration): _____
  _____
  _____

- Observable indicators of improvement (behaviors, reports):      ■ Expected number of visits to
  _____         achieve each indicator: _____
  _____
  _____

- Discharge level of problem behaviors: _____    ■ Review date: _____
  _____

Problem 3: _____

- Behaviors to be changed: _____
  _____
  _____

- Interventions (who does what, how often, with what resources; modality, frequency, duration): _____
  _____
  _____

- Observable indicators of improvement (behaviors, reports):      ■ Expected number of visits to
  _____         achieve each indicator: _____
  _____
  _____

- Discharge level of problem behaviors: _____    ■ Review date: _____
  _____

*(cont.)*

**F. Recommended program of coordinated liaisons, consultations, evaluations, and services**

1. Psychotherapy: ❑ Cognitive ❑ Behavioral ❑ Family/systems ❑ Insight-oriented ❑ Play therapy
   ❑ Support/maintenance ❑ Environmental change ❑ Focal group ❑ Clinical hypnosis ❑ Biofeedback
   ❑ Other: _____
   CPT code(s) to be used: _____

2. Support groups:  Twelve-Step program: ❑ AA ❑ NA ❑ Overeaters ❑ Gamblers ❑ Other
   ❑ Other community support groups: _____
   Psychoeducational groups: ❑ Parenting skills/child management ❑ Communication skills
   ❑ Stress management ❑ Assertiveness ❑ Women's issues ❑ Other: _____
   Ancillary services: ❑ Pain clinic ❑ Back school ❑ Physical therapy ❑ Other: _____

3. Legal services: ❑ Offender program ❑ Sex ❑ Substance abuse/dependence ❑ Other: _____
   ❑ Victim support ❑ Referral to emergency services/advocates: _____

4. **Referrals for continuing services**

| Referred to | For (kind of service) | Date of referral |
|---|---|---|
|  | Psychotropic medications<br>Physical medical care<br>Psychiatric evaluation<br>Patient education<br>Nursing care<br>Educational/vocational services<br>Occupational/physical therapy<br>Other: _____ |  |

5. **Further assessments,** based on current clinical evaluation, are needed to answer these concerns or rule out these possible coexisting conditions:

   ❑ Psychological presentation/symptoms of medical condition
     Likely possible sources:  ❑ Thyroid ❑ Diabetes ❑ Alcohol/drug misuse ❑ Circulatory problem
     ❑ Neurological problem ❑ Poor nutrition ❑ Medication interactions ❑ Toxin exposure
     ❑ Other: _____

   ❑ Sexual dysfunctions  ❑ Factitious disorders  ❑ Substance abuse/dependence

   ❑ Psychophysiological disorders  ❑ Learning disabilities  ❑ Genetic disorders/counseling

   ❑ Other: _____

6. **Documents to be obtained** (have requests for records completed and signed, photocopied, and placed in client's file so that receipt can be assured):

| Type of record | Source | Date of first request |
|---|---|---|
| ❑ Medical/physician/hospital |  |  |
| ❑ School |  |  |
| ❑ Agency |  |  |
| ❑ Other: _____ |  |  |

7. **Other needed resources and services:** _____

_____

# CHAPTER 6

# Planning and Then Documenting Treatment

After intake and assessment have been completed and recorded, planning treatment, documenting its progress, and finally case termination are the next clinical and record-keeping tasks. This chapter of *The Paper Office* covers these aspects in detail.

## 6.1  Treatment Planning

*A good plan today is better than a perfect plan tomorrow.*
—GENERAL GEORGE S. PATTON

The whole subject of treatment planning is in flux. There is neither a widely accepted set of essentials for a plan, nor any universally accepted format in use. The following general guidelines, as well as the forms and formats offered in this chapter, are intended to provide ideas and a framework rather than to be prescriptive or final.

### Issues

Many therapists working today resist the planning of treatment, because they believe it interferes with the immediacy and spontaneity they value in therapy. It also seems to require the prediction of what they see as unpredictable—the evolving, branching dance of client and therapist, problem and intervention.

The research has not resolved the question of whether a planful or a spontaneous approach is better, and it may never. Funding sources, manualized treatment methods, and clinical experience all suggest that at least some degree of organization is beneficial. However, as Hare-Mustin et al. (1979) point out, goal setting is extraordinarily difficult for some situations: when a client is unable to be specific; when children do not conform to their parents' goals (e.g., obedience); when spouses/partners have conflicting goals; when the client's goals stem from an ineffective conceptualization of the problem; when the client's symptomatic behaviors seem understandable or even socially acceptable to the therapist; and so forth.

Developing a treatment plan jointly with each client requires the kind of thoughtful, comprehensive, insightful effort that ensures successful therapy. It can be a productive focusing of therapeutic time. This process can be used cooperatively to involve the client in planning, homework/self-monitoring, revision of methods, and overall evaluation. Such a model of joint decision making strengthens the connections among consultation, planning, treatment, and evaluation. It also implements beliefs in mutuality and equality.

In addition, a treatment plan serves to limit distractions from the central goals. Without a plan, sequence, or map, both you and your client can easily be distracted from what is most important. You can both easily lose your "vision" in the welter of data, intercurrent events, levels of analysis, and so on, and fail to integrate the immediate into the important. As the saying goes, when we are up to our ears wrestling alligators, it is hard to remember that we came here to drain the swamp.

## Guidelines for Treatment Planning

Typically, a client comes in with complaints or problems, some ideas of their causes, and some desired outcomes. His or her presentation is reformulated by the therapist within a framework that allows for intervention and change. The therapist's favorite (or even just familiar) methods are offered to the client, and change is assessed irregularly and mainly unreliably. A more systematic and yet realistic sequence for treatment planning would proceed as follows:

- **Identify and assess** all the current problematic or symptomatic behaviors, affects, or cognitions. First, list, with the client, the major problems and related effects of these problems on his or her life. Review all areas of functioning. Prioritize these concerns. Chapter 5's forms support this process, and formats for problem list are offered in Section 6.2.

- **Define the outcomes desired**—both long-term "goals" and short-term "objectives." Some view the relationship between goals and objectives as analogous to strategic and tactical efforts in military terms. One way to seek objectives is to ask, "If we are to achieve this long-term goal by this specific date [such as next year], what smaller steps would have to be accomplished and by when [such as next month]?" These smaller steps, or objectives, are usually more behavioral, measurable, and concrete than goals. For a simple and yet reliable and valid way of assessing the accomplishment of goals, see the discussion of goal attainment scaling later in this section.

- **Consider the interventions and resources needed** to achieve the goals. The selecting and sequencing of interventions is the responsibility of the therapist.

- **Provide reliable ways to evaluate** the client's current status, progress, and outcomes.

These steps are considered in more detail below.

## Systems and Formats of Treatment Planning

If you are seeking a comprehensive system of planning treatment, consider the following models. Some are more comprehensive or more detailed than others, and some will suit your setting or needs better. They are presented here roughly in the order of their complexity.

### The PIC Treatment Plan

A simple, practical, and unique format is described by Levenstein (1994a). It has the advantages of coordinating treatment plans and progress notes, and of addressing obstacles to the progress of treatment. After a comprehensive evaluation, the clinician does the following:

1. Identifies the primary issues, and formulates a tentative explanation of how the problems occurred.

2. Gives a formal diagnosis (DSM-IV).

3. Creates the goal plan (in essence, the treatment plan).

4. Assigns a target date for each goal.

The format for the goal plan uses the acronym "PIC":

- P is for the problem (current behavior) or goal (desired end state).

- I is for the intervention(s).

- C is for the indicators of change (specific, overt behaviors to be tracked, how they will be assessed, and by whom).

With the addition of R for resistance or obstacles (Levenstein, 1994b), this format can be easily adapted for progress notes. See Section 6.2 for various types of progress notes.

### The Problem-Oriented Record

The problem-oriented record (POR) is a comprehensive and logical method that is widely used in medicine. It is discussed in detail in Section 6.2.

### The Expanded Problem-Oriented Record

The expanded POR is simple, flexible, and comprehensive, and is readily accepted in medical settings. It can be written in paragraphs devoted to these topics:

1. The problem.

2. The outcome or goal sought; foci of treatment (immediate and long-term issues); measurable performances or operationalizations of levels of progress.

3. The client's strengths or assets.

4. The client's liabilities, or the barriers to change in the client or elsewhere.

5. The treatment(s)/methods used: What, when, by whom? (Include interventions/ methods/means/modalities, resources required, staff members and others involved, frequency of contacts, expected dates of achievement, dates of review.)

6. The means and dates of evaluation.

### Individualized Treatment Plan for Managed Care Organizations

Managed care organizations (MCOs) require that an individualized treatment plan be developed the first or second session. Form 38 (see below) will assist you in developing such a plan.

### Impairment Profile

Goodman et al. (1992) cleverly suggest using a patient impairment profile to document and communicate treatment needs, to develop a rationale for treatment and a treatment plan, and to predict outcome of care. The list of impairments (in their Appendix A) becomes a common language for helpers from different disciplines. When combined with a severity rating, it suggests an appropriate level of service or care. They add outcome objectives, selections from a list of interventions (their Appendix B), and progress measures to assess the effectiveness of treatment (basically, changes in the ratings of severity). Their system is neat and complete, but requires a new model—that of impairments.

As another example of an impairment-based approach, the World Health Organization has been working on an *International Classification of Functioning, Disability and Health* (ICFDH). This is likely to substantially replace the DSM for most psychotherapy and rehabilitation, so it is well worth your monitoring and support. It can be searched, browsed, and downloaded at http://www3.who.int/icf/icftemplate.cfm.

## Other Points in Planning Treatment

### Taking Account of Resistance

> *Everybody wants to be happier. No one wants to change.*
> —Anonymous

If a treatment plan is to be truly effective, it must anticipate and respond to the obstacles to change. A great deal of the elegance and effectiveness of psychotherapy is found in its sophistication about handling "resistance." Here are some questions I like to ask a client in the course of planning treatment; the client's responses to these questions can be built into the plan, and can thus increase the chances of a successful outcome.

- "What would happen if you were to make the changes you say you want? How would these changes affect your partner, family, and friends? What would be the negative consequences?" (This question identifies demotivators, obstacles, and blind spots.)

- "What are the blockages/obstacles to change?" (This lets you see how the client conceptualizes the problem.)

- "What has not worked in the past?" (This might keep you from repeating unsuccessful approaches.)

- "What *has* been helpful in the past in dealing with these problems?" (You can then build on these.)

- "When were there situations like this, but you were able to manage them successfully?" (This is a solution-focused approach.)

- "Who are your best allies in helping you deal with problems like these?" (This question identifies the client's social and other supports.)

- "Who do you know who has successfully dealt with these same problems?" (This identifies potential role models.)

- "What do you think is necessary to make things better, and how long might each of these take?" (This question explores the client's conceptualization of treatment, so that you can blend into it or work to change it. Carl Whitaker called this "learning the family's dance; teaching them some new steps.")

## Coordinating Treatment Efforts

If treatments must be simultaneous, you will need to communicate the relevant information among providers. Traditionally, case and team conferences have borne this function; however, unless they are very well organized (see, e.g., Doyle & Straus, 1993; Kelsey & Plumb, 1999), they have been demonstrated to make poor decisions (Meehl, 1973) and waste everyone's time and a lot of money. Consider alternatives like a client-oriented newsletter, with a title such as "Nancy's News," which could be circulated by e-mail and posted to a password-protected Web site. PORs (see Section 6.2) are a paperwork improvement, but there is no reason not to be creative.

## Evaluating Outcomes with Goal Attainment Scaling

How can you evaluate the changes a client makes? The methods of planning described earlier generally use symptom reduction as the criterion of change. However, alternative, more flexible models exist. The best-known one is "goal attainment scaling," which is a very simple but powerful method of documenting progress toward goals (Kiresuk & Sherman, 1968; Kiresuk et al., 1994). It consists of the following components:

1. Specifying at least five goals. Goals can be described in *any* terms or areas; this is a major strength of this method.

2. Specifying a date in the future when progress toward the goals is to be evaluated.

3. Defining possible outcomes, in observable terms, at five levels for each goal. These five levels are as follows (slightly reworded):

   −2 = The worst outcome that is likely to occur.

   −1 = An outcome less successful than expected.

    0 = An outcome that achieves the expected level of success.

   +1 = An outcome more successful than expected.

   +2 = The most favorable outcome thought likely.

4. At the previously decided point or points in time, the level of attainment of each goal is scored.

5. Statistical tests can be applied to this score to determine whether it happened by chance. Scores can be compared over time, across clients, or across programs.

Some difficulties will arise if expectations are low and the true cause of the change cannot be determined. But the method is simple, easily learned (as by a client), and widely applicable. Its greatest advantage is that it can be applied to almost any kind of goal, and is thus independent of any theory or orientation.

## Formulating Treatment Plans for Managed Care Organizations

We should not let the current and substantial differences between the objectives of MCOs (see Section 3.12) and those of clinicians obscure the commonalities. Thoughtful planning of treatment interventions is always desirable and in the patient's best interest.[1]

Keeping an eye on treatment plans is managed care's preferred method for tracking "quality and appropriate care," says Scott Harris, PhD, codirector of the Center for Behavioral Health Care in Los Angeles. "It provides a structured mechanism for periodic review and authorization, monitoring providers for appropriateness, competence, and effectiveness."

Harris provides the following guidelines for writing a treatment plan (with special attention to the expectations of MCOs):

1. **Comprehensive overview.** Provide a full profile of the patient. Outline both the nature of the crisis and the focus of treatment.

2. **Goals and progress.** State treatment goals in measurable, behavioral terms. Indicate specific progress to be made within a given time period. Link clinical improvement to specific interventions and detail a predischarge level of progress.

3. **Action.** [The plan should] reflect the thinking, planning, and actions taken by

---

[1]The following passage, including the remarks and guidelines by Scott Harris, PhD, is reprinted from "Ten Steps to Create a Successful Treatment Plan" (1993). Copyright 1993 by Ridgewood Financial Institute. Reprinted by permission.

the therapist with the patient. Interventions must promote change and movement through the therapy.

4. **Timeliness.** Treatment planning must correspond with the [MCO's] authorization as well as the clinician's billing. Without coordinated documentation, a delay in claims processing and reimbursement may result. That means frustrating phone calls and, perhaps, filing the claim a second or third time.

5. **Benefit awareness.** Know the limits and structure of the specific benefit being administered by the managed care firm. Some benefits may include only 3 to 5 sessions, while others allow as many as 50.

6. **Alternative services.** Show that you are aware of, and willing to refer to, other levels of care such as day treatment, hospitalization, etc., as well as other resources that complement and reinforce treatment goals. This may mean specifying patient involvement in 12-step programs, support groups, parenting classes, or medication consultations with a psychiatrist.

7. **Professional liaisons.** Specifically state the role of other professionals essential to the outcome of the case.

8. **Crisis and other potential red flags.** Understand, identify, and plan for potential crisis situations. Responses and steps for crisis intervention need to be clearly detailed for cases involving potential suicide or child abuse. Use case managers as resources.

9. **Chemical dependency.** Address and plan treatment for potential or existing chronic chemical dependency problems.

10. **Copies.** Always keep copies of treatment plans and authorizations. This prevents multiple frustrations when you learn that a plan has not been received, or received and then lost.

**FORM 38**   Form 38 is an individualized treatment form for MCOs that will enable you to follow these guidelines. Its purposes and functions are (1) to serve as a checklist to assure that all evaluations and treatments have been considered; (2) to document the recommendations for treatment; (3) to support consultation with MCO reviewers to assess needed level of care and "medical necessity"; and (4) to enable you to initiate the first phase of treatment.

To simplify record making, this form is nearly identical to Form 36: it has a different first page and an additional last page. Thus, after summarizing your understanding of a case and developing a treatment plan on Form 37, you can easily reuse that material to create a treatment plan suitable for MCOs. Simply fill out the first and last pages of Form 38, photocopy pages 2–5 of Form 37, and insert those pages into Form 38. Your letterhead must contain any additional identifying information that the MCO requires (provider number, supervisor, credentials, license number, etc.).

You can make various changes to Form 38. For example, see the suggestions in Section 5.6 for changes to Form 37. In addition, you can elaborate on crisis management with this under heading D:

# Individualized Behavioral/Mental Health Treatment Plan

This is for ☐ Preauthorization for initial certification   ☐ Concurrent review for reauthorization of care

Date current episode of treatment began: _____   Date last plan created: _____

## A. Identification

Client's name:_____ Soc.Sec.#:_____ ID #:_____

Membership #:_____ Date of birth:_____ Sex:_____

Group name/#:_____ Certificate #:_____

Name of subscriber/member, and address (if other than client):_____

Release-of-records form(s) signed:  ☐ Yes  ☐ Not yet

## B. Case formulation/overview

1. Presenting problem(s)/reason(s) for seeking treatment:

| Problem | Impair-ment* | Duration |
|---|---|---|
| a. | | |
| b. | | |
| c. | | |

   *Code impairment as follows (per GAF Scale): 80–90 = mild, 60–70 = moderate, 40–50 = severe, 30 or less = very severe.

2. History of presenting problem(s) and current situation (precipitants, motivations, stressors, resources/coping skills, comorbid conditions, living conditions, relevant demographics): _____

_____

_____

_____

_____

3. Summary of mental status evaluation results: _____

_____

_____

*(cont.)*

**FORM 38. Individualized treatment plan for managed care organizations (p. 1 of 6).**   From *The Paper Office*.

Copyright 2003 by Edward L. Zuckerman. Permission to photocopy this form is granted to purchasers of this book for personal use only (see copyright page for details).

**C. Present level of functioning/limitations/impairment** (describe specific impairments at left, and rate degree of functional impairment at right with GAF number [100 = none, 70 = little, 30 = significant, 10 = incapacitated] or use descriptors):

| Area of functioning | GAF rating |
|---|---|
| 1. School/work functioning: _____ | ____ |
| 2. Intimate relationship/marriage: _____ | ____ |
| 3. Family/children: _____ | ____ |
| 4. Social relationships: _____ | ____ |
| 5. Psychological/personal functioning: _____ | ____ |
| 6. Other areas: _____ | ____ |

**D. Assessment conclusions**

1. Assessment of currently known **risk factors**:

   a. *Suicide*: ❑ Not assessed    ❑ No known behaviors    ❑ Ideation only    ❑ Plan
        ❑ Intent without means    ❑ Intent with means

   b. *Homicide*: ❑ Not assessed    ❑ No known behaviors    ❑ Ideation only    ❑ Plan
        ❑ Intent without means    ❑ Intent with means

   c. *Impulse control*: ❑ Not assessed    ❑ Sufficient control    ❑ Moderate    ❑ Minimal    ❑ Inconsistent

   d. *Compliance with treatments*: ❑ Not assessed    ❑ Full compliance    ❑ Minimal noncompliance
        ❑ Moderate noncompliance    ❑ Variable    ❑ Little or no compliance

   e. *Substance abuse/dependence*: ❑ Not assessed    ❑ None/normal use    ❑ Overuse    ❑ Abuse
        ❑ Dependence    ❑ Unstable remission of abuse

   f. *Current physical or sexual abuse*: ❑ Not assessed    ❑ No    ❑ Yes     Legally reportable? ❑ Yes ❑ No

   g. *Current child/elder neglect*: ❑ Not assessed    ❑ No    ❑ Yes     Legally reportable? ❑ Yes ❑ No
        If yes, client is   ❑ Victim    ❑ Perpetrator    ❑ Both    ❑ Neither, but abuse exists in family

   h. *If risk exists*: Client ❑ can ❑ cannot meaningfully agree to a contract not to harm ❑ self ❑ others ❑ both

   I. *History* that may affect current level of risk or impairment of functioning:
        _____

   j. *Other concerns*: _____

*(cont.)*

2. **Urgency** estimate ❑ Emergency; immediate interventions ❑ Serious disruption of functioning; act in next 24 hours ❑ Treatment needed; act soon/routine ❑ Wait for: _____

3. **Diagnoses**—Current best formulation

| Name (indicate which is primary diagnosis with "P") | Code #<br>❑ DSM-IV or<br>❑ ICD? |
|---|---|
| **Axis I** _____ | _____ |
| _____ | _____ |
| _____ | _____ |
| **Axis II**_____ | _____ |
| _____ | _____ |
| _____ | _____ |

"Rule-outs" (other possible diagnoses to be evaluated over time): _____
_____
_____

**Axis III**—Significant and relevant medical conditions, including allergies and drug sensitivities:

| Condition | Treatment/medication (regimen) | Provider | Status |
|---|---|---|---|
| | | | |
| | | | |
| | | | |

**Axis IV**—Psychosocial and environmental problems in last year; overall severity rating: _____

❑ Problems with primary support group ❑ Problems related to the social environment

❑ Educational problems ❑ Occupational problems

❑ Housing problems ❑ Economic problems

❑ Problems with access to health care services

❑ Problems related to interaction with the legal system/crime

Other psychosocial and environmental problems (specify): _____
_____
_____

**Axis V**—Global Assessment of Functioning (GAF) rating: Currently: _____ Highest in past year: _____

**V Codes**—Other problems that may be a focus of clinical attention: _____
_____
_____

*(cont.)*

**E. Treatment plan** (if additional problems are to be addressed, use copies of this page):

Significant improvement is to be expected, with treatment as specified, for:

Problem 1: _____

- Behaviors to be changed: _____

_____

_____

- Interventions (who does what, how often, with what resources; modality, frequency, duration): _____

_____

_____

- Observable indicators of improvement (behaviors, reports):  •  Expected number of visits to achieve each indicator: _____

_____

_____

- Discharge level of problem behaviors: _____  •  Review date: _____

_____

Problem 2: _____

- Behaviors to be changed: _____

_____

_____

- Interventions (who does what, how often, with what resources; modality, frequency, duration): _____

_____

_____

- Observable indicators of improvement (behaviors, reports):  •  Expected number of visits to achieve each indicator: _____

_____

_____

- Discharge level of problem behaviors: _____  •  Review date: _____

_____

Problem 3: _____

- Behaviors to be changed: _____

_____

_____

- Interventions (who does what, how often, with what resources; modality, frequency, duration): _____

_____

_____

- Observable indicators of improvement (behaviors, reports):  •  Expected number of visits to achieve each indicator: _____

_____

_____

- Discharge level of problem behaviors: _____  •  Review date: _____

_____

*(cont.)*

321

## F. Recommended program of coordinated liaisons, consultations, evaluations, and services

1. Psychotherapy:  ❏ Cognitive  ❏ Behavioral  ❏ Family/systems  ❏ Insight-oriented  ❏ Play therapy
   ❏ Support/maintenance  ❏ Environmental change  ❏ Focal group  ❏ Clinical hypnosis  ❏ Biofeedback
   ❏ Other: _____
   CPT code(s) to be used: _____

2. Support groups:  Twelve-Step program: ❏ AA  ❏ NA  ❏ Overeaters  ❏ Gamblers  ❏ Other
   ❏ Other community support groups: _____
   Psychoeducational groups:  ❏ Parenting skills/child management  ❏ Communication skills
   ❏ Stress management  ❏ Assertiveness  ❏ Women's issues  ❏ Other: _____
   Ancillary services:  ❏ Pain clinic  ❏ Back school  ❏ Physical therapy  ❏ Other: _____

3. Legal services:  ❏ Offender program  ❏ Sex  ❏ Substance abuse/dependence  ❏ Other: _____
   ❏ Victim support  ❏ Referral to emergency services/advocates: _____

4. **Referrals for continuing services**

| Referred to | For (kind of service) | Date of referral |
|---|---|---|
|  | Psychotropic medications |  |
|  | Physical medical care |  |
|  | Psychiatric evaluation |  |
|  | Patient education |  |
|  | Nursing care |  |
|  | Educational/vocational services |  |
|  | Occupational/physical therapy |  |
|  | Other: _____ |  |

5. **Further assessments,** based on current clinical evaluation, are needed to answer these concerns or rule out these possible coexisting conditions:

   ❏ Psychological presentation/symptoms of medical condition
   Likely possible sources:  ❏ Thyroid  ❏ Diabetes  ❏ Alcohol/drug misuse  ❏ Circulatory problem
   ❏ Neurological problem  ❏ Poor nutrition  ❏ Medication interactions  ❏ Toxin exposure
   ❏ Other: _____

   ❏ Sexual dysfunctions          ❏ Factitious disorders          ❏ Substance abuse/dependence
   ❏ Psychophysiological disorders    ❏ Learning disabilities
   ❏ Genetic disorders/counseling    ❏ Other: _____

6. **Documents to be obtained** (have requests for records completed and signed, photocopied, and placed in client's file so that receipt can be assured):

| Type of record | Source | Date of first request |
|---|---|---|
| ❏ Medical/physician/hospital |  |  |
| ❏ School |  |  |
| ❏ Agency |  |  |
| ❏ Other: _____ |  |  |

7. **Other needed resources and services:** _____
   _____

*(cont.)*

## G. Administrative

1. Case manager's additional suggestions for treatments and resources:

| Date | Name | Suggestions |
|------|------|-------------|
|      |      |             |

2. Services:

| Sessions requested* | Date of request | Start of sessions | Number of sessions authorized | Date of authorization | Date of next review |
|---------------------|-----------------|-------------------|-------------------------------|-----------------------|---------------------|
|                     |                 |                   |                               |                       |                     |

*Code sessions with a number (number of sessions) and letter: C = Collateral contacts, E = Evaluation, F = Family therapy, G = Group therapy, I = Individual therapy.

## H. Additional comments and information _____

_____

_____

_____

_____

_____

## I. Cooperative treatment planning

Our signatures below mean that we have participated in the formulation of this treatment plan, understand and approve of it, and accept the responsibility to carry out our parts of the plan fully.

_____    _____

Signature of client (or person acting for client)                          Date

_____    _____    _____

Signature of service provider                          Provider number          Date

*This is a strictly confidential patient medical record. Redisclosure or transfer is expressly prohibited by law.*

*This report reflects the patient's condition at the time of consultation or evaluation. It does not necessarily reflect the patient's diagnosis or condition at any subsequent time.*

Plans for possible crises:

| Crisis | Risk level (1–10) | Intervention | Resources |
|---|---|---|---|
| ❑ Suicide | | | |
| ❑ Homicide | | | |
| ❑ Violence | | | |
| ❑ Substance abuse | | | |
| ❑ Child or other abuse | | | |
| ❑ Impulse dyscontrol | | | |
| ❑ Noncompliance | | | |
| ❑ Other: _____ | | | |

Under each problem in section E ("Behaviors to be changed," "Interventions," "Observable indicators of improvement," "Expected number of visits to achieve each indicator," and "Discharge level of problem behaviors"), you can substitute one of a number of alternative formats:

- "Goal," "Interventions," "Observable indicators of improvement," and "Time frame."

- "Target symptoms," "Target date," and "Expected outcome."

- "Diagnosis-related symptoms," "Symptom-related goals," "Interventions," and "Target date."

- "Short-term objectives," "Target date," "Long-term goals," and "Target date."

For the present section F, you could substitute a statement or checklist with options of the services you have available, in order of intensity of service/need:

**F. Recommended level of care**
   ❑ Emergency/immediate psychiatric hospitalization
   ❑ Regular psychiatric hospitalization
   ❑ Residential treatment center
   ❑ Inpatient medical detoxification
   ❑ Inpatient substance abuse/dependence program
   ❑ Specialized inpatient program for: _____
   ❑ Group or supported housing
   ❑ Partial hospitalization/day treatment program
   ❑ Structured/intensive outpatient program for: _____

Or, depending on the likely needs of your clientele, you can add these to the present section F:

---

Residential care: ❑ Shelter   ❑ Partial hospitalization   ❑ Inpatient 24-hour hospitalization
  ❑ Group home   ❑ Family support   ❑ Other: _____

Educational/vocational services: ❑ Agency evaluation   ❑ GED classes   ❑ Work hardening
  ❑ Sheltered workshop   ❑ Special school services   ❑ Other: _____

Economic supports: ❑ Welfare/AFDC   ❑ Soc. Sec. Disability   ❑ Other: _____

---

## About Managed Care Organizations' Own Checkoff Forms

Several of the large MCOs now use their own checkoff-type forms at least for reauthorizations. Although this reduces the MCOs' processing costs (compared to having a human read and understand a narrative), they may increase your vulnerability, for several reasons:

1. You have to reduce complex issues and judgments to only a few options.

2. The choices presented by these forms may not fit your interventions very well. For example, the form from Magellan (TRF 3/16/2000; available as an Adobe PDF file at http://www.magellanprovider.com/supplements.trf_formp2.pdf) offers exactly six kinds of therapy and their combinations. You may "target" only five of the symptoms recorded "at the beginning of this course of treatment" for "improvement." Is this the way you think of the therapy you do?

3. The choices presented may not fit a client very well. The forms do not allow more than two Axis I diagnoses. When you are seeking more treatment sessions, each symptom has to be neatly rated as either "worse," "same," "improved," or "resolved." What degree of progress are you agreeing to with "improved," and are you ever sure a symptom is cleanly "resolved"?

4. The data can more easily be entered into computerized data bases and sold, shared with other organizations, and used for profiling providers.

5. The choices may not be mutually exclusive or accurate. For example, doesn't the intended use of a selective serotonin reuptake inhibitor as an "antidepressant," "mood stabilizer," or "other" depend on the patient's situation and not the drug's "class"?

In light of these risks, I suggest not only the usual thoughtfulness and attempts to foresee the consequences, but also recording comments and qualifications in your case notes.

A form titled "Outpatient Treatment Report Form—Confidential," which addresses confidentiality and treatment concerns much better than most MCOs' forms do, has been developed by the American Psychiatric Association. It is available as a download at http://www.psych.org/pract_of_psych/otrform.pdf.

# 6.2   Documenting Treatment's Progress

*Change is certain. Progress is not.*
—E. H. CARR

After treatment has been planned and initiated, records of its implementation need to be kept. The interactions between you and the client that result in progress (or its absence) must be noted. The treatment planning formats offered earlier in this chapter often include ways to monitor the progress of the case. This section discusses those and other options in more detail. Specifically, it discusses the following options for keeping treatment records:

- Note taking, including guidelines for when and how to take notes.

- The problem-oriented record (POR), including a POR progress note form.

- Structured progress notes for individual and for group therapy.

- Client-generated records.

## Note Taking: Guidelines and Suggestions

Most clinicians write without a guiding framework for recording, and so their notes only partially describe the important facts of their therapy. Such notes will not protect these therapists or support understanding of their therapy. If this description applies to you, find or invent a system you can live with—one that makes sense for your way of working, helps you do your job, and protects you. The following ideas may help.

### When to Write Notes

Writing notes during a treatment session saves time, but may lead to incompleteness and (because of lack of reflection or excess brevity) later incomprehensibility. It also reduces eye contact and rapport with the client. One position is to "Never take notes when an individual is talking about his feelings, or discussing matters which are sensitive, emotionally laden or difficult to express" (Wilson, 1980, p. 7). Other therapists find that taking notes uses little time, is seen as thoroughness, and gives them time to weigh what is happening and to consider their responses carefully. However, saying "Let me just make a note of that," or even the minimal cue of writing after a client says something, may reinforce that topic, mood, or pattern even when you don't want to increase symptomatic behavior; If a client becomes uneasy, discontinue your note taking and offer to share the notes with him or her.

Two additional possibilities for taking notes during a session are as follows:

- Take notes about the major issues in a "headline" or "telegraphic" format, leaving space. As soon as the session is over, write in the details and your well-considered formulations. You can certainly use a shorthand method or Speedwriting™, which essentially omits all vowels. However, notes that are illegible or too telegraphic will not serve to defend you by demonstrating your clinical judgments, thought processes, and decision making, and will not support any of the other functions of clinical notes.

- Take real-time notes of things you suspect you will forget or any factual data that you may not remember accurately without a reminder (Wilson, 1980, p. 7).

Taking notes immediately after a session allows for perspective on the whole session, as well as for the identification of themes and the most important events. Make certain to schedule enough time and to include this time in your charge to the client.

The problem with taking notes at the end of the day is that writing so far removed from the experience leads to contamination of your memories of one client by those of other clients or events, as well as to other errors or distortions in your recollections. This is not fair to you or your clients.

By the way, *not* keeping notes is not an option; you are ethically required to have such records. (See Section 1.4 for information on record-keeping obligations.) And, whatever note-taking schedule you adopt, always keep you notes current. Periodically, or at case closing, you can revise your working notes into formal records and destroy the notes.

## The Confidentiality of Psychotherapy Notes

Traditional lore suggested that a clinician could keep personal notes (often called "process notes"); that these need not be included in the patient's chart; and therefore that these need not be revealed to anyone, even in a legal battle. This concept was generally not supported by the courts (especially in the contexts of reporting abuse, self-protection for therapists, providing needed continuity of treatment, and similar social obligations), but states' laws varied. However, this changed with the promulgation of regulations by the U.S. Department of Health and Human Services concerning the implementation of the 1996 Health Insurance Portability and Accountability Act (HIPAA) (see http://www.hhs.gov/ocr/hipaa for the HIPAA text).

These HIPAA regulations create a category of protected health information (PHI) called psychotherapy notes, which receives special privacy protection: "psychotherapy notes . . . are not part of the medical record and [were] never intended to be shared with anyone else." A response in the regulations notes that "any notes that are routinely shared with others, whether as part of the medical record or otherwise, are, by definition, not psychotherapy notes, as we have defined them." This specifically means other treaters or members of a treatment team.

The regulations go on to indicate that

> the rationale for providing special protection for psychotherapy notes is not only that they contain particularly sensitive information, but also that they are the personal notes of the therapist, intended to help him or her recall the therapy discussion and are of little or no use to others not involved in the therapy. Information in these notes is not intended to communicate to, or even be seen by, persons other than the therapist. Although all psychotherapy information may be considered sensitive, we have limited the definition of psychotherapy notes to only that information that is kept separate by the provider for his or her own purposes. It does not refer to the

medical record and other sources of information that would normally be disclosed for treatment, payment, and health care operations.

Also,

> These notes are often referred to as "process notes," distinguishable from "progress notes," "the medical record," or "official records." These process notes capture the therapist's impressions about the patient, contain details of the psychotherapy conversation considered to be inappropriate for the medical record, and are used by the provider for future sessions. . . . Process notes are often kept separate to limit access, even in an electronic record system, because they contain sensitive information relevant to no one other than the treating provider. These separate "process notes" are what we are calling "psychotherapy notes."

To consider creating them, we first need to clarify what would be entered into versus excluded from psychotherapy notes, and thus what would be included in what I will call routine progress notes. Under HIPAA Section 164.508(a)(3)(iv)(a), psychotherapy notes are defined "as notes recorded (in any medium) by a health care provider who is a mental health professional documenting or analyzing the contents of conversation during a private counseling session or a group, joint, or family counseling session." The regulations go on to specifically exclude the following information and thus place these into routine progress notes: "medication prescription and monitoring, counseling session start and stop times, the modalities and frequencies of treatment furnished, results of clinical tests, and any summary of the following items: diagnosis, functional status, the treatment plan, symptoms, prognosis, and progress." It does not appear to me that this distinction protects much that a client would prefer to keep confidential.

The HIPAA regulations also say the following:

- "Furthermore, we stated in the preamble of the proposed rule that psychotherapy notes would have to be maintained separately from the medical record." The meaning of the word "separate" is not given. Certainly they should be on different pages from the routine progress notes, but need they be in separate files, filing systems, or departments? Separate computer files or even systems, separate security methods (e.g., different passwords and encryption keys)? It seems reasonable that the implementation of "separate" should be based on the rationale that only the therapist will access them for his or her own purposes as a therapist.

- The format of the notes—written by hand versus on a word processor—does not alter their privacy protection, which is based on the *information* contained. Therefore, if the same information is moved to or also maintained in a different location, such as into the medical record, it is no longer protected.

- A different authorization is required to release psychotherapy notes for use in TPO as well as a few other situations. However, the response opines that such an authorization will only rarely be needed because psychotherapy notes do not include information that covered entities typically need for TPO.

- Indeed, there are a host of situations in which an authorization is *not* required to disclose these psychotherapy notes:

An authorization is not required for use or disclosure of psychotherapy notes when required for enforcement purposes, in accordance with subpart C of part 160 of this subchapter; when mandated by law, in accordance with § 164.512(a); when needed for oversight of the health care provider who created the psychotherapy notes, in accordance with § 164.512(d); when needed by a coroner or medical examiner, in accordance with § 164.512(g)(1); or when needed to avert a serious and imminent threat to health or safety, in accordance with § 164.512(j)(1)(i).

Also, the notes can be disclosed without authorization for use in training programs or supervision for any kind of counseling or therapy and to defend the therapist in a legal action brought by the client. (This is a complex situation and, should you find yourself in this position, consult a lawyer familiar with your state laws as well as HIPAA.) As you can see, there are many areas where these notes can and will be disclosed and many areas open to interpretation, which would likely lead to more disclosures.

- Clients do not have a right of access to psychotherapy notes under HIPAA (see Section 164.524[a]), although perhaps they do under your state's rules. HIPAA says you may *allow* access.

### Should You Create Psychotherapy Notes?

Here are some relevant points:

- Very little important information is protected when included in such notes.

- They must be kept "separate" from other clinical information, which is burdensome.

- You cannot share the notes or the information in the notes with other treaters or a treatment team (per HIPAA Section 164.508), or with family or friends of the patient (Section 164.510[b]), unless you obtain a special authorization (Section 164.508). However, because "health care operations" is so broad, it is not possible to know in advance the ramifications of such a disclosure.

- If the information is disclosed to any "non-covered entities," the HIPAA regulations are not able to prevent their redisclosure.

- The authorization cannot be combined with other authorizations to simplify paperwork procedures.

Based on the above, it is my recommendation that you do not create psychotherapy notes, at least until these regulations are modified by court decisions. Rely instead on the privacy protections of your state laws and legal decisions and be guided by your profession's code of ethics.

For more on HIPAA as it develops, see http://www.hipaadvisory.com and http://www.apa.org/practice. For more on the legal aspects of privacy in psychotherapy, see "The Psychotherapist–Patient Privilege [*Jaffee v. Redmond*, 518 U.S. 1]: History, Documents, and Opinions" page at http://www.psa-uny.org/jr; see also DeBell and Jones (1997) and Knapp and VandeCreek (1997a).

## How to Write Notes: Formats

*Progress versus Process Notes.* Some authorities recommend keeping progress notes separate from process notes because they differ so much. Progress notes are the official "chart" and are available to the client and others. They usually include the following:

- Dates of appointments.

- Problems addressed.

- Treatment efforts.

- Contents of interviews.

- Referrals.

- Homework assignments.

- Objective data.

Process or working notes contain the following:

- Sensitive information.

- The therapist's reactions, fantasies, feelings, speculations, hypotheses, reflections, and so on.

- Notes to the therapist by the therapist.

- Notes on process that would make no sense to anyone outside the session.

Some therapists think it best not to include these working notes in the client's regular record; however, this is controversial and risky. (See "What to Write Down: Guidelines," below.)

Various formats for recording both process and progress notes follow.

*Progress Recording in Social Work.* According to Kagle (1991, p. 18), a progress-oriented record in social work must contain the following logical elements: (1) the client, the situation, and the available resources, which form the basis for (2) service decisions and actions, including (3) the purpose, goals, plan, and process of service, and (4) the effects service is expected to have upon the client, the situation, and the available resources. She offers this set of headings (p. 124):

- What happened during the session.

- New problems/issues/needs that surfaced.

- Interventions used.

- New referrals, plans (e.g., for the next session), or recommendations made.

To this list can be added:

- Session goals.

- Homework plan.

*Process Recording in Social Work.* Social workers are often trained in the use of process recording, which includes the following:

- An almost verbatim record of what each person said, in a format like C (Client): . . . and W (Social Worker): . . .

- Notes on the client's nonverbal behaviors.

- The worker's feelings and reactions to the client.

- Observations and analytical thoughts about the client's internal processes and the events of the interview.

- A section headed "Diagnostic Summary" or "Worker's Impressions," which summarizes the worker's analytical thoughts and understandings.

- A section headed "Social Service Plan," "Casework Plan," "Comprehensive Service Plan," or (more recently) just "Treatment Plan."

This format is helpful with a confusing case or for documentation for training and supervision.

*Process versus Progress Recording in Family Therapy.* Should you record process or record progress/content for family therapy? Brock and Barnard (1988) have this to say:

> Historically, clinical case notes have been more content oriented than process oriented. Process notes are more specific regarding systemic notions such as the family's rules, roles, evident communications styles, and patterns that appear to be operational: Attending to the organization and structure of a family in notes lends itself to the development of direction, goals, and possible interventions, for the therapist. Merely recording the content of who said what and where the session left off ignores such systemic information and may, in fact, get in the way of the therapist's appropriately conceptualizing the family in systemic fashion. We can all be entranced and diverted by stories. (pp. 139–140)

More is said later in this section about keeping notes in family or couple therapy.

*The Individual Psychotherapy Session Note.* A process-focused format designed for individual dynamic therapy, modified from that of Presser and Pfost (1985), calls for the following:

A.  A brief, narrative summary of the session.

B.  The therapist's observations of:

1a. The client's behaviors

2a. The therapist's behaviors

3a. The client–therapist interaction

Items 1a, 2a, and 3a are paralleled by the therapist's interpretations, questions, and hypotheses about each of these (which could be called 1b, 2b, and 3b). A new heading, C, could be considered the therapist's interventions for change, their rationales, and their predicted effects. One could also include D, the trends of the session in light of previous sessions, and E, the trends in relation to the problem list.

### How to Write Notes: A Checklist of Tips

Although notes should be concise, they must also be coherent, accurate, current, relevant, and handled in ways to assure and maintain confidentiality.

❏ All entries should be dated, sometimes timed, and signed. A signature may be unnecessary when the notes are in your handwriting, but initials should indicate where a particular note ends.

❏ Make subheadings of the session's notes for clarity. <u>Underline important information if you will have to search for it later.</u> (See how well it works?) Number issues and subjects in your notes. You can also circle some numbers. If you use a problem list, you can cross-reference each entry to a problem (by its number P1, P2, etc.). See the discussion of the POR, below.

❏ Write paragraphs giving full explanations, which are better than phrases or cryptic notations.

❏ Use words that help the reader visualize; make your words a camera. Terms such as "No change" or "Improving" are too open to varying interpretations.

❏ Ignore set lengths as required on a printed form. Write as complete a note as necessary to achieve the record's purpose (Wilson, 1980, p. 113).

❏ The sources of all information recorded should be indicated. Never state as fact what a client reported. Use direct quotations whenever possible to indicate the client's experiences and thought processes. Separate your judgments and conclusions from the facts and observations. A simple and practical notation scheme is as follows:

All unmarked notations are the client's ideas and reports.

Quotes from the client can be indicated by standard double quotation marks: " ".

Statements from others reported to you by the client can be indicated by both double and single quotes " ' ' ".

Words in parentheses are (your statements to the client).

Words in square brackets are [your unspoken hypotheses or conclusions].

Also, you can use HW for homework assignments and Rx for topics to cover in the future.

❏ Never alter any notations you have already made. If corrections are made to the record, it should be clear that they were made later than the entry being corrected, because not to make this clear is misleading and suspicious. For very small changes, it is best to draw one line through the error and to date and initial the correction. For larger changes make a notation at the earlier date, such as "See also entry of [today's date]"; then indicate in the later note that "My present recall differs, in that . . . " or "I was misinformed at that time, and now believe . . . ". If you later recall something you did not record earlier, you can write it with a notation that it is "Prior knowledge [or understanding or recollection] presently recorded."

❏ Do not add comments near a previously recorded entry in your notes. This may also appear to be tampering with the record. Instead, write notes at the end with today's date and cross-reference them to the original location in your notes (Gutheil, 1980). For example, "August 1: In rereading my notes of July 4, I note that neglected to mention the fireworks, which . . . ".

## What to Write Down: Guidelines

There are legal risks to be considered in excluding anything form your notes (Fulero & Wilbert, 1988). For example, omitting material on sex may leave you with little defense against an accusation of impropriety during a session. Releasing records with premature diagnoses or speculations could be the basis of a malpractice claim. This is why some therapists have kept dual records—one set not to be released, in order to protect both themselves and their clients, and a second or redacted set to be released upon request or court order. However, keep in mind that **there can no longer be secret records,** even as the obligation remains to try to keep information private. If you work in a setting covered by federal law, the Privacy Act of 1974 (Public Law 93-579) and the Freedom of Information Act of 1974 (Public Law 93-502) give clients rights of access to all your notes about them. Furthermore, state law or case law, or just filing a suit against you, will also give them access (Fulero & Wilbert, 1988). Obviously these laws and decisions will have to be integrated with the *Jaffee vs. Redmond* (1996) decision and the evolving HIPAA rules (see above), which effectively deny patients access to your "psychotherapy notes," although they may be discoverable. The best advice is the most cautious: Create records with the expectation that they will be read by someone else and should be clear when read years later. Your clients may someday see your notes, so consider their psychological and legal implications. The best policy may be to write your records so that all will be well when a client or a client's parents read your notes.

Since you can't record everything, you need to choose what to note while bearing in mind the purpose of the record. I suggest the following priorities.

First, make a record of your clinical decision making for your own later review. Ask yourself, "Will I need to know this later? For the next session? Later in treatment or after treatment, for another purpose?" If having this information will not change some aspect of treatment, do not bother to record it. In particular, record any event or decision that precedes a change in the patient's condition (a new problem develops or is recognized, there is a response or a lack of response to adequate treatment, etc.).

Klein et al. (1984) (as summarized in Soisson et al., 1987) recommend the documentation of *all* significant decisions during therapy. Specifically, the record should include the following:

1. What the treatment choice is expected to accomplish (goals, objectives).

2. Why you believe it will be effective (a rationale).

3. Any risks involved and why they are justified.

4. Which alternative treatments were considered.

5. Why they were rejected or delayed.

6. Any steps taken to improve the effectiveness of the chosen treatments.

7. Evidence of informed consent provided by the client's statements or your own observations supporting the client's consent.

8. The rationales for any referrals made.

Second, make a record of your clinical decision making for self-defense. A useful rule of thumb may be "If it might make a mess, make a note." In a similar vein, Gutheil (1980, p. 482) intelligently suggests that when taking any risky actions, you should "think out loud for the record" so that if the unfortunate happens, it can be traced only to an error in judgment and not to negligence. The following specific pointers may be helpful:

- Explicitly note where information isn't clear.

- Document all clinically significant events, such as nonroutine calls, missed sessions, and consultations with other professionals (Soisson et al., 1987).

- When forensically significant events or possible malpractice situations are anticipated, the record should be written from the perspective of future readers (Gutheil & Appelbaum, 2000), especially unfriendly readers. An example of such a situation might be a suicidal patient.

- Emergency treatment situations are responsible for a disproportionately large share of malpractice claims, and so should be documented with extra care (Gutheil & Appelbaum, 2000). Get full consultations, and document any resistance from significant others, so that responsibility can be placed accurately (Cohen, 1979).

- Your statements about the limitations of a treatment should be noted; its success should not be guaranteed, and excessive optimism should be shunned to avoid responsibility for a failure (Gutheil & Appelbaum, 2000).

- Do not hesitate out of modesty to record a client's statements of appreciation for your work or successes and improvements during therapy. Similarly, regularly asking about any concerns clients might have and recording their comments on the progress of treatment will both allow you to refer to these comments when things are not going well and can serve as a defense against a complaint.

### What Not to Write Down: Guidelines

Do not record anything that is unnecessary for or irrelevant to treatment. I suggest that you generally exclude the following:

- Excessive detail.

- Gossip and hearsay.

- Emotional statements, editorializing, or hunches.

- Moral or personal value judgments (especially negative ones) about the client or others (e.g., "fat," "lazy," "weak," or "stupid").

- The client's political religious, or other personal beliefs.

- Difficulties you had with other professionals or agencies in this client's case.

- Names of paramours (use initials?) or specific indicators of affairs.

- Reports of most illegal activity in the past.

- Incriminating information about illegal activity in the present (e.g., details of drug use).

- Medical diagnoses or other judgments that your training and experience do not qualify you to make.

- Most sexual practices.

- Sensitive, embarrassing, or harmful statements.

### Special Considerations for Keeping Notes in Family or Couple Therapy

If you see several members of a family, or a couple, you will have particularly complex decisions to make about record keeping.

You can keep separate records (separate pages) on each person involved in a conjoint session, so that you do not have to release all the records when just one client is involved.

Confidentiality can then be maintained. Margolin (1982) offers an extensive and thoughtful discussion of the privacy issues in marriage and family therapy. On the other hand, separate records create a fiction that there were not several interacting people in the room. Because the family members' issues involve each other, separate notes on each person cannot be considered truly independent and so cannot logically be read separately.

The suggestion that all participating members must give permission for the release of the record seems logical. However, this must be implemented before the therapy is begun, by means of a paragraph in your client information brochure and paragraphs in your release-of-records forms. Two problems arise: You are initially asking family members to agree to conditions for the release of records whose content they do not know, because the therapy and the records of it have not happened yet. This cannot be considered informed consent. Second, problems may arise when one member does not consent to the release that another member seeks.

### Other Ideas about Documenting Treatment

For some purposes (clinical, research, protective, forensic, or administrative), recording sessions on audiotapes or videotapes may make sense. Tapes can be given to the client for review or kept privately. You will need permission to make such recordings, since they are not usual and have the potential to breach confidentiality. See Section 4.6 for a discussion and a permission-to-record form.

Client-created records (which are discussed at the end of this section) may be another way of getting around some of these issues. Although certainly the clients know what is in such records, they may not understand the implications of their release.

## The Problem-Oriented Record

When you are documenting the progress of a case, the challenge is to record treatment-relevant information in an accessible form. However, clinicians, because of their differing training and interests, may record such diverse topics as the process of therapy, the symptoms of a disorder, the relationship with the client, the contents of interactions and outside events, the goals of recovery or growth, or many other possibilities.

In this diversity, the word "problem" has become a label acceptable to clinicians of many disciplines and backgrounds. Lawrence Weed (1971) invented a new record-keeping method because he found that the information necessary to treat a patient was being recorded in medical charts in too many places to be useful. Instead of being entered under arbitrary topical or discipline-based headings ("Intake," "Diagnoses," "Social History," "Psychological Evaluations," "Nursing Notes," "Consultant's Reports," etc.), all notes must be keyed to numbered problems. This method is called the "problem-oriented record" (POR), the "problem-oriented medical record," the "Weed system," or "SOAP notes." It is widely used in medicine and has been adapted to the psychotherapy setting.

As slightly modified for the psychotherapy context (see Grant & Maletzky, 1973, and Sturm, 1987), the format consists of four main components: (1) the problem list, which remains on top of the chart and which serves as a table of contents to it; (2) the data base of history and findings; (3) the initial treatment plan; and (4) progress notes, or the continuing record of the clinician's observations and understanding of the patient. Each progress note entry is recorded in the "SOAP" format (see below) and is cross-referenced to a problem on the problem list by number. Therefore, all the information in the chart is organized around problems. All evaluations and their results are thus tied to their sources and their implications for treatment. To find all of the information in the chart about a concern, the reader has only to look for its problem number on all pages.

## The Problem List

**FORM 39** The problem list is simply a numbered listing of all problems identified by you or the client and used as a guide to the POR system. Forms 29, 30, and 31 offer several ways to identify problems. Once created, the list is placed on top of the chart to serve as a table of contents for the continuing record. Problems are defined at their current level of understanding, and are rewritten and renumbered as they become better or differently understood. Problems can be added and, when resolved, closed by making an entry and by not reusing that number. Added to this listing should be a psychiatric diagnosis with all axes considered; an evaluation of difficulties with activities of daily living; and a description of all functional impairments. Form 39 permits you to create a problem list for a POR.

## The Data Base

The data base consists of the following usual and expected psychological topics, with each entry tied to the list of problems:

- Chief complaint.

- Mental status examination results.

- Social situation—personal, familial, environmental factors.

- Personal and social history.

- History of other medical and psychological conditions and their treatments.

- Records obtained from other treaters.

- Results of testing, or other relevant data.

*The Paper Office* does not provide separate forms for all of these, because they can be recorded in whatever format and size you may prefer. However, Chapter 5 includes forms and guides for recording most of this information.

## The Initial Treatment Plan

Psychological interventions usually require the consideration of many dimensions simultaneously, and so a treatment plan is necessary. See Section 6.1 for suggested treatment plan formats and essentials. The POR treatment plan is simply a listing of therapeutic responses to each currently recognized and defined problem. It is the starting point for treatment, and is modified or added to through changes in the progress notes as the case progresses.

## Problem List for a Problem-Oriented Record (POR)

Client: _____ Page #: _____

| Problem number | Date problem recognized | Problems currently active — Problem title/formulation | Problems now inactive — Prob. # where problem is now included, *or* → | Date problem resolved |
|---|---|---|---|---|
| | | | | |

*This is a strictly confidential patient medical record. Redisclosure or transfer is expressly prohibited by law.*

**FORM 39. Problem list for a problem-oriented record (POR).**    From *The Paper Office*. Copyright 2003 by Edward L. Zuckerman. Permission to photocopy this form is granted to purchasers of this book for personal use only (see copyright page for details).

The plan may include every kind of treatment by anyone (patient education, collection of more information, treatment of and by others, etc.), as well as the usual therapies.

### Progress Notes Using the SOAP Format

"SOAP" is an acronym for four kinds of information that needs to be documented for each problem addressed during each client meeting. This is where the POR shines. Every note begins with the problem number for cross-reference and completeness, and continues as follows:

- S is for subjective data—the client's reports of complaints, symptoms, efforts made, problems, changes, and difficulties. S also includes notes of the statements of others.

- O is for objective data—your observations and the observations of others; measurable signs (especially changes); the results of psychological testing of the client; and his or her observable behaviors, appearance, and social situation.

- A is for assessment—your conclusions, diagnoses, interpretations, impressions, judgments, case formulations, and analyses of the meaning of the data.

- P is for the plan of treatment (both immediate and future), as created by you and by the others concerned. Diagnostic studies, patient education, and follow-up would also be placed here.

**FORM 40**   Form 40 is a photocopiable form for making POR progress notes according to the SOAP format, and Figure 5 is a completed example of this form. Of course, you can make various changes both to the SOAP format and to Form 40. First, progress notes can be made "SOAPIER," which is well suited for the current direction of psychotherapies. Use the SOAP format as described above, and then add the following:

- I is for intervention or implementation of the plan—what you have done to, for, or with the patient relative to this problem. In this version you would put the longer-term goals into the plan (P), and use implementation (I) for the shorter-term objectives.

- E is for evaluation/effectiveness of the intervention—that is, the outcomes of intervention, positive or negative. These, of course, could be recorded under S and O, but in this framework they are separated for greater specificity.

- R is for revisions of the plan if it was ineffective. Again, these could be recorded under P as a new plan, but using this new heading makes the changes more salient.

An alternative to the SOAP format is to use a "DAR" format:

- D is for data.

- A is for the action you take based on this data.

- R is for the response of the patient or other.

# POR Progress Note Form

Client: _____ Page #: _____

| Problem number | Date of note | Problem status$^*$ | Progress notes$^{**}$ |
|---|---|---|---|
| | | | |

$^*$Problem status codes: C = continuing focused treatment; R = problem resolved; I = inactive problem; IT = inactive due to ongoing treatment; D = treatment deferred; N = newly identified problem; ReDf to # = problem redefined or combined with another problem whose number is indicated.

$^{**}$Each entry must be related to a problem number; coded S for subjective, O for objective, A for assessment, or P for plan; and signed.

*This is a strictly confidential patient medical record. Redisclosure or transfer is expressly prohibited by law.*

**FORM 40. POR progress note form.**     From *The Paper Office*. Copyright 2003 by Edward L. Zuckerman. Permission to photocopy this form is granted to purchasers of this book for personal use only (see copyright page for details).

Galactic Health Care Organization
Wellness Plaza
New Hope, PA 12345

## POR Progress Note Form

Client: ___Last name, First name_____ Page #: ___1___

| Problem number | Date of note | Problem status* | Progress notes** |
|---|---|---|---|
| 1. Depression | 9/9/02 | C | S: No suicidal thoughts this week<br>More energy— started painting project<br>Fears of being fired<br>Spouse confirms more optimism<br><br>O: Increased facial expressions, more hand and arm gestures, faster movements<br>BDI score = 9<br><br>A: Lessened depression<br><br>P: Maintain or add treatments as follows:<br>—Spousal reinforcement for activities as scheduled<br>—Cognitive therapy 1/week<br>—Continue meds<br>—Consider adding new group activity  9/23/02<br>—Reevaluate medication— 10/9/02<br><br><br>                              Anna F. Therapist |

*Problem status codes: C = continuing focused treatment; R = problem resolved; I = inactive problem; IT = inactive due to ongoing treatment; D = treatment deferred; N = newly identified problem; ReDf to # = problem redefined or combined with another problem whose number is indicated.

**Each entry must be related to a problem number; coded S for subjective, O for objective, A for assessment, or P for plan; and signed.

FIGURE 5. Completed sample of a POR progress note form.

*Advantages of the POR*

- The POR is a complete record. It is logical and tidy. The information in it is accessible to other care providers, supervisors, or reviewers, and is easily defended in court.

- The POR is a means of keeping the focus of treatment on the client's larger concerns ("keeping your eye on the ball"). It is all too easy to go along with the client's desire to avoid change; to be distracted by interesting and possibly relevant side paths; or to avoid doing the hard work of being a therapist ("It's not fun any more"). The POR can help you keep such distractions to a minimum.

- The POR can keep both of you focused when the going gets confusing or slow, by keeping the horizon in view and allowing you to mesh the immediate and lively with the long-term and important.

- At another level, the problem list, treatment plan, and SOAP notes are the map of the territory of the client's life situation.

*Disadvantages of the POR*

- The POR format tends to oversimplify the complexity of psychotherapy's understandings and interventions.

- It can lessen the attention paid to the client's strengths and resources.

- Because it is person-focused, rather than focused on the person in his or her situation, context, or system, it may underemphasize the client's relationships. Environmental and case management interventions may be overlooked as a result.

- Its weakest point is defining what exactly is a problem. The good news, however, is that problems can be described at whatever level of understanding is currently available, and redescribed when they are understood differently. Simply close a problem entry with a cross-reference to the newer definition.

## Two Structured Progress Note Forms

### A Structured Form for Individual Clients

**FORM 41**    The form presented below, the structured progress note form (Form 41), is an efficient way of recording a client's progress when you do not use the POR system described above. The purposes of this form are (1) to document the progress of your treatment and the client's response to it; (2) to enable you to do this with as little time and effort as possible; and (3) to support evaluation of the treatment by you, the client, and other interested parties.

Form 41 is designed to be rather broadly useful for many kinds of treatment; it offers choices that may fit many practices, but you can enter specifics to fit your practice under the headings. This form is based loosely on an excellent one from Ronnie M. Hirsch, PhD, of New York, NY. If you need a more elaborate form, the "Professional Progress Notes"

# Progress Note

If a checkbox (❏) is inappropriate or insufficient, enter a letter and write additional comments on a separate page.

## A. Client and meeting information

Client:_____ Date:_____

Meeting #:_____ of _____ authorized on this date _____ with provider # _____

Meeting was:   ❏ Scheduled   ❏ Emergency    Others present:_____

Meeting lasted:   ❏ 15   ❏ 30   ❏ 45–50   ❏ 60   ❏ 90   ❏ ____ minutes

Client:   ❏ Was on time   ❏ Was late by ____ min.   ❏ Did not show   ❏ Cancelled and was rescheduled for _____

Meeting took place at:   ❏ Office   ❏ By phone   ❏ Clinic   ❏ Hospital   ❏ Client's home   ❏ Workplace

Mode of treatment:   ❏ Individual therapy   ❏ Family   ❏ Group   ❏ Couple   ❏ Consultation

## B. Topics/themes discussed                                    **Notes**

❏ Homework assignments        _____

❏ Relationship(s)        _____

❏ Stressors        _____

❏ Identity/role        _____

❏ Work problem        _____

❏ Alcohol/drug problem        _____

❏ Childhood/fam. of origin        _____

❏ Sexual problem        _____

❏ Parenting        _____

❏ Dream(s)        _____

❏ Other        _____

## C. Treatments/interventions/techniques

❏ Insights        _____

❏ Behavioral        _____

❏ Cognitive        _____

❏ Homework given        _____

❏ Family        _____

❏ Relationship        _____

❏ Problem solving        _____

❏ Support        _____

*(cont.)*

**FORM 41. Structured progress note form (p. 1 of 2).**    From *The Paper Office*. Copyright 2003 by Edward L. Zuckerman.
Permission to photocopy this form is granted to purchasers of this book for personal use only (see copyright page for details).

## D. Assessments

### 1. Symptoms

| Symptom/concern/complaint | Current severity rating* | Change since last evaluation (enter a check mark) | | | | | |
|---|---|---|---|---|---|---|---|
| | | No change | Less severe | Much improved | Resolved/ absent | More severe | Much worse |
| | | | | | | | |

*Rate from 0 to 10 as follows: 0 = not a problem/resolved; 5 = distressing/limiting; 10 = very severe distress, disruption, harm/risk.

### 2. Stressors and coping

| Stressor | Current severity rating* | Changes in severity? | Current level of coping/functioning† | Changes in coping level? | Coping skills employed |
|---|---|---|---|---|---|
| | | | | | |

*Rate from 0 = not a problem to 10 = very severe, continuous, omnipresent, preoccupying.

†Rate from 0 to 10 as follows: 0 = much less able to cope; 5 = no change from last meeting/evaluation; or 10 = much improved level of coping.

3. Mood: ❏ Normal/euthymic ❏ Anxious ❏ Depressed ❏ Angry ❏ Euphoric
   Affect: ❏ Normal/appropriate ❏ Intense ❏ Blunted ❏ Inappropriate ❏ Labile

4. Mental status: ❏ Normal ❏ Lessened awareness ❏ Memory deficiencies ❏ Disoriented ❏ Disorganized ❏ Vigilant ❏ Delusional ❏ Hallucinating ❏ Other: _____

5. Suicide/violence risk: ❏ None ❏ Ideation only ❏ Threat ❏ Gesture ❏ Rehearsal ❏ Attempt

6. Sleep quality: ❏ Normal ❏ Restless/broken ❏ Delayed ❏ Nightmares ❏ Oversleeps

7. Participation level: ❏ Active/eager ❏ Variable ❏ Only responsive ❏ Minimal ❏ None ❏ Resistant

8. Treatment compliance: ❏ Full ❏ Partial ❏ Low/noncompliant ❏ Resistant ❏ Denial of disorder

9. Response to treatment: ❏ As expected ❏ Better than expected ❏ Much better ❏ Poorer ❏ Very poor

10. Global Assessment of Functioning (GAF) rating from 100 to 0 is currently: _____

11. Other observations/evaluations: _____

## E. Changes to diagnoses: ❏ None or _____

## F. Changes to treatment plan: ❏ None or _____

If treatment was changed, indicate rationale, alternatives considered/rejected/selected in notes.

## G. Follow-ups

❏ Next appointment is scheduled for next ❏ week ❏ month ❏ 2 months ❏ 3 months ❏ as needed.

❏ Referral/consultation to: _____ For: _____

❏ Call/write to: _____ For: _____

## H. Clinician's signature: _____ Date: _____

*This is a strictly confidential patient medical record. Redisclosure or transfer is expressly prohibited by law.*

form from Psychological Assessment Resources (http://www.parinc.com) is similar, but more elaborate in its coverage and evaluation of such risk areas as suicide potential, referrals needed, health problems, and allegations of sexual improprieties. In addition, its manual is a very thorough resource regarding record keeping and the use of good records as a malpractice risk reduction method. It is recommended.

To tailor Form 41 even more specifically to your practice, you might want to delete the "Next appointment . . . " or "Symptoms" items and add "Instructions, suggestions, directions" under Treatments (as suggested by Muriel L. Golub, PhD, of Tustin, CA). If you work in an agency setting, you might want to add such options as "Chart reviewed," "Case consultation," "Treatment team meeting attended," or "Aftercare planning meeting." Specific target symptoms taken from Form 33 or elsewhere can be added to the listing, as well as a section on medications.

### A Structured Form for Group Therapy

**FORM 42**

In keeping notes about the progress of individual clients in a therapy group, a simple checklist reduces the paperwork burden. You can use either Form 41, which contains several sections not in this one, or Form 42, which records more information about interventions, interactions, and participation in the group. You can, of course, add items from Form 41 to Form 42—for example, the "Symptoms," "Stressors," "Level of functioning," and/or "Changes to diagnoses" items.

## Client-Generated Records

When clients take notes, or make drawings or flow charts of their problems' causes and interactions, they bring additional cognitive resources to bear on their issues. These can be especially valuable activities; when accompanied by at-home review, they should be encouraged.

- Diaries of associations, dreams, and relationship interactions in dynamic therapies help the client to see connections. Similar records are called "client memoranda" in social work, and "diaries," "logs," and "frequency counts" in behavioral therapies.

- There are many kinds of affect and behavior checklists to help identify situations for clinical interventions. In rational–emotive behavior therapy, the use of antecedent–behavior–consequence analyses will reinforce teaching in the session and build a pattern for approaching stressful situations.

- I have asked some patients to keep their notes in a three-ring binder, which they may call "The Book of My [or Our] Therapy" and use for many purposes. The binder can also house handouts; notes the patients have made from assigned readings; notes taken and questions raised during reviews of audiotapes of their therapy sessions; observations of their family members, friends, or television characters; self-study and journal writings; poetry and artwork; and many other items. When such materials are collected in one place, they are much more likely to be reviewed (and therefore to generate awareness and change) than if they are scattered in space and time.

# Group Therapy Progress Note

## Client and group information

Client: _____ Date: _____ Meeting attended is #: ____ for this client.

Group's name: _____ Time: _____ A.M./P.M.

Location: _____ # present: _____

Leader(s): _____ Signature(s): _____

_____ _____

## Assessment of client

1. Participation level: ❑ Active/eager ❑ Variable ❑ Only responsive ❑ Minimal ❑ None

2. Participation quality: ❑ Expected ❑ Supportive ❑ Sharing ❑ Attentive ❑ Intrusive ❑ Monopolizing
   ❑ Resistant ❑ Other: _____

3. Mood: ❑ Normal/euthymic ❑ Anxious ❑ Depressed ❑ Angry ❑ Euphoric ❑ Other: _____
   Affect: ❑ Normal ❑ Intense ❑ Blunted ❑ Inappropriate ❑ Labile ❑ Other: _____

4. Mental status: ❑ Normal ❑ Lessened awareness ❑ Memory deficiencies ❑ Disoriented
   ❑ Disorganized ❑ Confused ❑ Vigilant ❑ Delusional ❑ Hallucinating ❑ Other: _____

5. Suicide/violence risk: ❑ None ❑ Ideation only ❑ Threat ❑ Gesture ❑ Rehearsal ❑ Attempt

6. Change in stressors: ❑ Less severe/fewer ❑ Different stressors ❑ More/more severe ❑ Chronic stressors

7. Change in coping ability/skills: ❑ No change ❑ Improved ❑ Less able ❑ Much less able

8. Change in symptom severity: ❑ Same ❑ Less severe ❑ Resolved ❑ More severe ❑ Much worse

9. Other observations/evaluations: _____
   _____

## Modes of interventions/treatments

❑ Support ❑ Clarification ❑ Education ❑ Exploration ❑ Problem solving ❑ Limit setting
❑ Socialization ❑ Orientation ❑ Reminiscence ❑ Reality testing ❑ Activity ❑ Confrontation
❑ Other: _____

## Topics/themes/critical incidents

❑ Relationship(s) ❑ Work problems ❑ Alcohol/drug problems ❑ Parenting ❑ Abuse
❑ Childhood/fam. of origin ❑ Sexual ❑ Homework assignments ❑ Process ❑ Logistics/structure
❑ Other: _____

## Further comments: _____

_____

*This is a strictly confidential patient medical record. Redisclosure or transfer is expressly prohibited by law.*

**FORM 42. Structured progress note form for group therapy.** From *The Paper Office*. Copyright 2003 by Edward L. Zuckerman. Permission to photocopy this form is granted to purchasers of this book for personal use only (see copyright page for details).

- One of the most intriguing options is described by Albeck and Goldman (1991): The client and therapist coauthor a progress note after each session—a process these authors call "codocumentation." By reviewing each other's views and experiences, both parties benefit, and a supervisor who reads both could be of great assistance to the therapy.

- There are guides for diary writing as therapy, usually called "journal keeping" (e.g., Baker, 1988) or just "journaling."

### Evaluating Each Therapy Session

**FORM 43**

When the rapport is not strong, or you suspect the client has some unarticulated reservations, or you believe that the client lacks the social skills to address these issues face to face, you can use the questions in Form 43 to collect immediate feedback. Such a questionnaire can be offered at any point in treatment and can be used repeatedly—for example, after the 3rd, 8th, 15th, and 20th sessions. It can be distributed (perhaps mailed, with a stamped, self-addressed return envelope) every 5 sessions, but if you start doing this with a patient you must continue, because he or she will expect it and may hold comments for the form.

Review the four sets of questions offered here; revise, edit, and select from them to suit your practice and style; decide on and consistently use a first- or third-person pronoun to refer to yourself as the therapist; and then try it with your next three clients. When it is satisfactory, incorporate it into your routines for every patient, examine your data, and you will become a scientist/practitioner.

## 6.3   Case Termination

*If we can turn neurotic pain into normal misery we have done a lot.*
—SIGMUND FREUD

A lack of clear goals may prevent both client and therapist from knowing whether therapy is finished. However, therapy should have a distinct ending even if its goals have not been accomplished. The absence of a message of closure is not only confusing to both parties, but can expose you legally. For example, if you agree to a client's decision for a premature termination or terminate a client for nonpayment of fees, it may be legally seen as negligent unless the client's welfare is protected. By far the most important point in termination, regardless of reason, is the client's welfare. The American Psychological Association's code of ethics (APA, 2002, Standard 10.10) addresses the termination of professional relationships.

### Reasons for Terminating or Transferring a Patient

First, **you simply cannot terminate a patient in crisis or at high risk.** On the other hand, you can terminate a patient for any of the following reasons:

- The patient has failed to pay fair and negotiated fees. Termination in such a case is often therapeutic as well.

- The patient is not cooperating with treatment. You must first try to work through the

## Session Evaluation Questionnaire

Initials of client: _____     Initials of therapist: _____     Date: _____

**A. These questions focus on the benefits and the communications of the session.**

Please list what you got out of this session.

What was the best part?

What suggestions do you have?

What points do you want to have considered in our next session?

What did I miss or underconsider?

What didn't you tell me?

What did you want to tell me or do today that we didn't get to?

What will you take with you?

Therapist's response to the comments/feedback above:

*(cont.)*

---

**FORM 43. Session evaluation questionnaire for clients (p. 1 of 3).**     From *The Paper Office.* Copyright 2003 by Edward L. Zuckerman. Permission to photocopy this form is granted to purchasers of this book for personal use only (see copyright page for details).

**B. These questions focus on the therapeutic behaviors and qualities of the relationship.**

Please rate each of these aspects of my behavior during this session on a 7-point scale where 1 means "not at all" and 7 means "very much," and feel free to add any comments or explanations.

| | Rating | Comments |
|---|---|---|
| Asked the right questions. | ___ | |
| Basically grasped/understood my situation. | ___ | |
| Tuned in to where I needed help. | ___ | |
| Was there for me/I felt supported. | ___ | |
| Used me for his or her own problems/needs. | ___ | |
| Coerced me until I backed up. | ___ | |
| Worked well with my reluctances, fears, defenses. | ___ | |
| Encouraged me to go further. | ___ | |
| I felt close to him or her. | ___ | |
| Was warm/caring. | ___ | |
| Accepted me as I am. | ___ | |
| Supported hope and change. | | |
| Confronted me when I needed it. | ___ | |
| Didn't panic when I felt confused or overwhelmed. | ___ | |
| Helped me clarify my feelings, goals, needs. | ___ | |
| Made constructive use of problems/negatives. | ___ | |
| His or her self-disclosure was helpful. | ___ | |
| I want to work with him or her again. | ___ | |

This was a positive experience for me because:

This was a negative experience for me because:

Additional comments, please.

(cont.)

**C. These questions focus on "learning" from the session.**

1. How did you feel (for example, anxious, relaxed, tense, angry, afraid, excited—use single-word emotions, though you can use more than one)?

    a. Before the session: _____

    b. During the session: _____

    c. After the session: _____

2. What did you learn about yourself that was new and that you believe will aid you in dealing with your problems?

    a.

    b.

    c.

3. What did you relearn or have reinforced that you believe will aid you in dealing with your problems?

    a.

    b.

    c.

4. If you are able to implement these plans at this time, what specific short-term changes would occur in your life? What long-term ones?

**D. These questions focus on the therapist's assisting the client to achieve benefits.**

Using the 1–7 scale where 1 means "not at all" and 7 means "very much," please write a number next to each benefit and feel free to add explanations or anything else you think would be beneficial to our relationship.

| | Rating | Comments |
|---|---|---|
| During this session you helped me to . . . | | |
| Clarify my thoughts and feelings. | ____ | |
| Understand what I was feeling and why. | ____ | |
| Approach some difficult and scary issues. | ____ | |
| Overcome depression. | ____ | |
| Resolve problems in my relationships. | ____ | |
| Relate better to my spouse/partner or children. | ____ | |

I really appreciate the time and effort you put into answering these questions, and I promise that I will consider your answers and will review these points at the start of our next meeting. Thank you.

patient's resistance to treatment and document these efforts, but failure to follow an agreed-upon and appropriate treatment plan is very important.

- There are conflicts of interests, disruptive romantic thoughts, countertransference, or similar issues that you have not been able to resolve.

- The APA ethics code (APA, 2002) says that you are ethically obligated to terminate when there has been little progress. (See "No-Improvement Terminations," below.)

- Although this is not explicit in the code, you should terminate and transfer when another, and incompatible, therapist or therapy appears to be in the patient's best interest. The patient may need services you cannot offer, such as medical interventions, inpatient care, or neuropsychological rehabilitation.

- Your own needs may require you to terminate the patient (e.g., you are leaving the area).

Termination issues are best dealt with early and continually in treatment. Remember that they are a major focus in the quite successful time-limited therapies. Be alert to your possible reluctance to terminate a successfully treated and functional patient who pays his or her bills reliably, is not difficult, and perhaps is pleasant to see. Being a responsible professional can be bittersweet.

## How to Terminate Treatment in Different Situations

The options offered below are designed for five kinds of termination situations. The section on dealing with premature or early terminations is based upon ideas from the Philadelphia Society of Clinical Psychologists' Committee on Ethics (1988) and from Ewing (1990) and Barnett et al. (2000), both of whose discussions are brief and highly recommended. O'Leary and Norcross (1998) offer excellent guidance on making successful referrals. Kramer (1990) has written a thorough book on "bringing meaningful closure" to therapy.

### Appropriate Terminations

When the therapy is finished and the termination is mutually agreed upon, document the following:

- The reasons for termination. (Ideally, the goals of therapy have been met and the client no longer needs your services.)

- The client's reactions.

- Any continuity-of-care needs.

- Any referrals.

- Any other unfinished details.

Although it's not necessary, you can send **a follow-up note** to each appropriately terminated patient, either 1 month after the end of treatment or 3, 6, or 12 months later. If you do so, keep a copy. Some therapists may see such a note as purely self-promotional; you could, of course, deal with all these points in the final interview(s) instead of sending a note. It can be argued, however, that using the patient's paid time is more manipulative than using your (unpaid) time to construct the note. A note could include the following:

- Your hope that all is going well for the patient.

- A summary of treatment—progress, successes, high points, any unfinished work, or recommendations. You might include lessons learned, if doing so does not seem too preachy; it all depends on the relationship.

- A statement that "The door is always open" for additional work or for "checkups" or "booster sessions." Indicate that the patient only has to call, and that you will be pleased to see him or her again (if this is true).

- A reminder that you are most pleased to accept referrals from former patients, as these are almost always appropriate and successful.

- Your best wishes.

This note is not the place to indicate any unpaid balances due to you or difficulties with insurance reimbursement.

### Premature or Early Terminations

Premature or early terminations are ethically complex. When you feel the therapy is not finished but the patient declines to continue, the decision should be made jointly if at all possible. Handle termination therapeutically, working through the patient's issues; also, document these points, your efforts, and the outcomes.

Here are some suggestions for the last few therapy sessions (or, if the patient cannot be dissuaded, just the last visit):

- Do not argue or defend any perceived attack on your abilities.

- Assert your concern for the patient/family.

- Affirm the patient's right to choose to terminate.

- Express your regret, respect for the patient's decision, and acceptance (not agreement).

- Specify the factual bases for your recommendation to continue therapy at this point. Indicate why you think it may be harmful to stop now, and describe any negative consequences you foresee.

- Encourage the continuation of therapy. You can point out the "honeymoon" or "flight into health" effects and describe how they don't last.

- Offer to resume therapy at any time in the future.

- Offer your assistance in finding another therapist. Perhaps make a referral to an agency, or provide the traditional three referral names. When you do refer or transfer a patient to someone else, ethically you must make sure the professional to whom you are sending the patient is qualified (by training, credentials, experience, licensure status, etc.) or you could be vulnerable to an ethics charge ("negligent referral").

- Offer your services for emergencies in the interim before the patient finds a new therapist.

- Offer to send your records, with the patient's signed consent, to another therapist.

- Record all this in your notes.

- If you think there is some risk involved in termination at this time, you may prefer to have the patient sign a release indicating that the termination is against your advice. This formality may also encourage the patient to reconsider. If the patient refuses to sign, note this too. (See Section 3.11.) Consider sending a letter by certified mail, with an even stronger recommendation to continue treatment somewhere.

### Necessary Terminations

In some cases, you may feel that the therapy is not finished, but you are discharging or transferring the client for one or more of the following reasons: Your own needs require it (e.g., you are leaving the area); the client requires services you are not competent to provide (e.g., medications, inpatient admission); financial noncooperation or limitations exist; or the relationship has deteriorated into counterproductivity. Perhaps you or the client have not been able to maintain a schedule or intensity of contacts that would support significant work and change, or the client has not performed or refused his or her responsibilities as specified in the agreed-to treatment plan and its revisions.

When any of these situations exists, one of your concerns is not being negligent. To assure that you are not, do the following:

- Give the client a list of the reasons for termination, and make a note of the fact that you have done this.

- Give reasonable notice of the end of treatment, and enter this into your notes as well.

- If the client fails to show for his or her last scheduled appointment, make at least one call or send one letter to discover the reasons for the no-show. Record these reasons or your attempts to terminate properly. Offer to meet at least once more to "wrap things up," but not to "look at where we were and where we are now," as this is an invitation to continue in therapy.

It is usually better to discuss the reasons for termination in person, but a call or letter may be your only possibility. Even when there is a face-to-face discussion, it is best to send a letter as well. Keep a copy. A "discharged from treatment" letter can include any of the points above, as well as a number of the following suggestions:

- Describe what you have done (such as evaluate the client, discuss diagnoses and treatments, read records, initiate treatment, make referrals, etc.).

- List some of the successes and high points, if possible.

- Indicate that the purpose of the letter is to confirm your final conversations, if you had such.

- Give the client your reasons for discharging him or her.

- Express your regret at the ending of an important relationship. List some of the successes and high points, if possible.

- Recommend continuance of therapy, if clinically appropriate: "Since your condition requires treatment . . . " or "I believe you can benefit from continued treatment." Encourage the client to seek services without delay (Simon, 1992).

- Indicate that the client should now consider "our" treatment over, and that you are not, in any continuing sense, the client's therapist.

- Indicate your availability during a specific transitional period. This not only is clinically and ethically appropriate, but will protect you from a charge of abandonment. You can say, "Because your condition requires treatment (or monitoring or follow up) I will continue to be available to you only for essential clinical services for a brief transitional period. You must make such arrangements immediately, because I will only provide care for a period of _____ (1 week, 1 month, etc)." Current opinion suggests that to be safe, you should continue to be available. "Only when another licensed professional has accepted the patient (and vice versa) does the original therapist's responsibility end" (Meyer et al., 1988, p. 50).

- Offer recommendations for treatment by someone else. As indicated above, giving three referral names is traditional (but not essential). You have an ethical obligation to know that these care providers are competent to help the client. It may be appropriate to say that you will make a suitable referral if one is desired.

- Indicate that when written consent has been given for doing so, you will send your records or a summary of their treatment to another therapist with whom the client enters treatment.

- Remind the client that any balance due must be paid. Enclosing the bill makes this clearest, but sending it separately serves to separate the two issues if you want to.

- Offer your "best wishes"—the generic, can't-be-misread closing.

You should make an appropriate effort to follow up with the client, to ensure that you have done all you could to make a transfer go smoothly and cause no harm to the client.

### No-Improvement Terminations

When there has been little or no improvement despite appropriate treatment, you must terminate (see APA, 2002, Standard 10.10a). After you have done your best, including having reevaluated, reconsidered, and made extra efforts to get things moving forward again, you should do the following:

- Consult a colleague. Be sure, though, that you have honestly prepared the case, recognized and dealt with your ego involvements, and can listen openly. Document this consultation. Modify treatment as suggested by the consultation.

- Try a different approach, with the client's permission.

- If there is still no improvement, you must terminate and refer. You must also terminate when the client is being harmed by the relationship, such as in irresolvable transference issues.

- Send a "discharged from treatment" letter as described above.

### Reluctant Terminators

When you feel that a client is ready to terminate but the client is apprehensive or resistant, you can encourage termination by recounting improvements. If you have discussed progress and options as you went along in therapy or labeled your treatment as "time-limited," then your pushing for termination will not come as a surprise. Depending on the length and qualities of the therapy, this may take several sessions. Consider the process of termination very carefully and make a plan.

- Expect emotional reactions (relapses, development of "new problems needing immediate treatment," "wanting to be friends/business partners afterward," etc.) and process them. See Section 3.8 on dual relationships.

- Clearly indicate the reasons for termination, so that it cannot be seen as a result of the client's deficiencies. Say that termination is for the client's long-term good, that it is necessary because of managed care requirements, or whatever the truths are.

- When it is appropriate to do so, offer the client the names of up to three other therapists if he or she wishes to continue therapy.

## 6.4    The Case Closing Summary

It is best to set aside time after the last session with a client, to compose a summary while the case is still fresh in your mind. You might consider dictating a summary using the headings below, and not having it typed unless you need it, in order to save some costs. A complete narrative on each patient at the end of treatment is better. But just reviewing your notes and adding to them at the end, in the form of a summary, will be valuable.

I strongly recommend that you also send (with the client's permission, of course) a termination note to the case manager or reviewer at any MCO involved in the case and to the referral source when appropriate. Both of these have moral if not legal involvement, and everybody wants closure and likes to hear good news, even if only some of the goals were achieved.

## Outline for Dictation

The following outline is very comprehensive and assumes that you have *not* been using the forms provided in this book.

A. Client information.

   1. Client's name and some other basic information (e.g., date of birth, Social Security number).

   2. Referral source and reason.

   3. Dates of initial and final contacts, consultations, hospitalizations, referrals.

   4. Presenting problems (e.g., problem list) and severity ratings; levels of functioning.

B. Treatments.

   1. Planned treatments.

   2. Services you actually provided; perhaps a sentence or paragraph about each session by date, specifying:

      a. Problems presented/addressed, homework.

      b. Relationship qualities.

      c. Process, motivations.

C. Narrative summary of therapy, including critical incidents, unresolved problems.

D. Status of each problem at discharge/termination and severity ratings; levels of functioning.

E. Information about termination.

   1. Reasons/rationale for termination.

   2. Was treatment prematurely discontinued? (If yes, indicate why.)

   3. Originator of the decision to terminate.

4.   Recommendations and suggestions of continuing care, if any.

5.   Did the patient accept your recommendations at discharge?

F.   Optional: Lessons you have learned.

## A Termination Summary Form

**FORM 44**    Form 44 is quite different from but based on a form in Piercy et al. (1989) called "Family Termination Summary," by Larry Constantine, LCSW.

# 6.5   Assessing Client Satisfaction and Outcomes

Much has been made, especially by MCOs, of the value of satisfying the consumers of health care services. Consumers' answers to simple questions about the distance from the office to a bus stop or the furniture in the office apparently have been used to remove or "disenroll" physicians from MCOs' panels of providers.

For therapists, such measures do not have great clinical import. Summarizing eight studies, Pekarik and Wolff (1996) concluded. "Research has indicated that the correlations between satisfaction and other outcome measures are low to modest, with correlations generally ranging approximately from zero to .40" (p. 202). Pekarik and Guidry (1999) again found no significant relationship for those treated by private practitioners. Examining a different group of studies, Lambert et al. (1998) came to the same conclusion.

However, "Satisfaction measures have several virtues, including ease of administration, high face validity, and appeal as indexes of treatment acceptability" (Pekarik & Wolff, 1996, p. 202) and so there may be advantages to your collecting this information. First, it can help you present your practice to MCOs as caring and well liked by your clients; second, such data could be an alternative to having the MCOs impose their generic questionnaires on you and your clients; finally, a questionnaire tailored to your way of working and the kinds of problems you typically address could be part of a continual quality improvement program for your services.

## Client Satisfaction Measures

The most widely used form for medical practices is the Client Satisfaction Questionnaire (CSQ-8; Larsen, Attkisson, Hargreaves, & Nguyen, 1979).

> The CSQ-8 evaluates many dimensions of service delivery that are primary targets of satisfaction ratings by clients: (a) physical surroundings; (b) kind or type of service; (c) treatment staff; (d) quality of service; (e) amount, length, or quantity of service; (f) outcome of service; (g) general satisfaction; and (h) procedures. There are four response choices for each question, scored 1 through 4 so scores range from 8 to 32, with higher scores reflecting higher satisfaction with treatment. (Sabourin et al., 1989, p. 353)

# Termination Summary

Client: _____ Date: _____

Signature(s) of therapist(s) : _____ _____

## A. Main reason for termination

❑ The planned treatment was completed. ❑ The client refused to receive or participate in services.

❑ The client was unable to afford continued treatment or did not pay bills on time. ❑ Client moved.

❑ There was little or no progress in treatment. ❑ This is a planned pause in treatment.

❑ The client needs services not available here, and so was referred to: _____

❑ Other:_____

## B. Source of termination decision

The decision to terminate was: ❑ Client-initiated ❑ Therapist-initiated ❑ A mutual decision ❑ MCO-affected ❑ Other: _____

## C. Treatment sessions

Referred on date: _____ Date of first contact: _____ Date of last session: _____

Number of sessions: Scheduled: _____ Attended: _____ Cancelled: _____ Did not show: _____

## D. Kinds of services rendered

❑ Individual psychotherapy, for _____ sessions ❑ Couple/family therapy, for _____ sessions

❑ Group therapy, for _____ sessions ❑ Other: _____

## E. Treatment goals and outcomes (code outcomes as follows: N = no change, S = some or slight [about 25% to 35%], M = moderate [about 50%], V = very good [about 75% to 100%], E = exceeded expectation)

| Goal | Outcome |
|---|---|
| | |
| | |
| | |

Other notable aspects of treatment outcome, change, or progress: _____

_____

_____

*This is a strictly confidential patient medical record. Redisclosure or transfer is expressly prohibited by law.*

**FORM 44. Termination summary form.** From *The Paper Office*. Copyright 2003 by Edward L. Zuckerman. Permission to photocopy this form is granted to purchasers of this book for personal use only (see copyright page for details).

Analyses indicate that the CSQ-8 has quite high reliability and validity and measures only one factor.

Based on their review of the literature, Pekarik and Wolff (1996) decided that a simpler set of four questions was sufficient:

> The client was asked, (a) "Overall, how satisfied are you with the services you received?"; (b) "Would you recommend this agency to others seeking help?"; (c) "If you were to seek help again, would you return to this agency?"; and (d) "How would you rate your therapist?" Ratings were obtained on 5-point Likert scales.

You could easily adapt or expand these questions to your practice. A 39-question version, developed for MCOs' uses, is available in Eisen et al. (1999).

**FORM 45**

If you design a client satisfaction measure of your own, make it one page long and completable in 5 minutes or less; enclose a stamped envelope addressed to you; and use a code to make it anonymous. Ask some colleagues to review your work and pilot-test it. If you wish to use instruments with research support, the Association for Ambulatory Behavioral Healthcare (1997) offers a very useful list of these and tells how to obtain them. Form 45, below, contains a more detailed set of questions, but these do not have any research support.

## Outcome Assessment Questionnaires

**FORM 46**

Clinicians in private practice have almost never done outcome evaluations. This is unfortunate both because it leaves the responsibility for the improvement of clinical work to distant researchers, and because it denies clients the benefits of systematic, data-based, tailored clinician self-improvement. To address this issue, Clement (1999) offers his own experiences and methods, which can be easily implemented by even the busiest practitioner. Form 46, below, is a set of questions exploring your ex-client's views of the changes brought by treatment rather than the setting of treatment (which is explored in Form 45).

## Cover Letters for These Questionnaires

One of the following two cover letters can be used for mailing both satisfaction and outcome questionnaires to clients. Although your clients deserve the use of their names, anonymity has its benefits. If you choose to use the client's name on the cover letter and a code number on the questionnaire, make sure they are on different sheets of paper. Or, as in the first letter below, you can use a "Dear Client" form of address.

*Version A*

Dear Client,

Would you please help us to improve our work by answering some questions about the services you received from us? We are interested in your honest opinions (whether they are positive or negative), and we welcome your comments and suggestions.

All your answers are completely confidential, because your name will not be used on this form. We will use only an ID number (not a Social Security number). To ensure confidentiality, please do not write your name on the questionnaire. None of your responses will be included in your treatment records. Returning this questionnaire will be regarded as giving your informed consent to participate in the survey. You can choose to withdraw from this research at any time and refuse to answer any questions. Doing this will not affect the care you might receive in the future from us. If answering any of these questions makes you uncomfortable, please skip the question.

Thank you for taking the time to provide us with your feedback; we really appreciate your help.

Sincerely,

_____

(Signature)

*Version B*

Dear _____:

As you may recall, when we first met I requested your permission to ask you some questions about your treatment after it was completed. You can help me to provide better services to my clients by taking just a few minutes to answer these questions about how you were treated by me and my office. Please be totally honest, because only realistic feedback will allow me to improve my services. I will carefully consider everything you write.

Thank you.

_____

(Signature)

Forms 45 and 46 are designed for use by groups or agencies, and so they include both space for a letterhead and the name of the treatment provider. If you are in solo practice, omit the "Therapist." Before sending out either questionnaire, enter the date of the client's last session and the therapist's name. The use of "6 12 24 ____" is to code the number of months after the end of treatment this letter is being sent. "Today's date" is to allow for the client's not completing and returning the form promptly.

## Follow-Up Questionnaire 1

ID #: _____

Therapist's name: _____     Today's date: _____

Date of last session: _____     6  12  24  _____

What is your gender?    ❏ Male   ❏ Female   How old are you? _____ years

For each question, please circle a number to show how much you agree with the statement. Use a scale from 1 = "I completely **disagree**" to 7 = "I completely **agree**." If the statement does not apply to you or your experience, please circle NA.

|  |  | Disagree    Agree |  |
|---|---|---|---|
| 1. | I was treated with courtesy and respect by the secretary/receptionist and other staff. | 1 2 3 4 5 6 7 | NA |
| 2. | I was treated with courtesy and respect by the therapist. | 1 2 3 4 5 6 7 | NA |
| 3. | I felt the therapist was appropriately concerned about my problem. | 1 2 3 4 5 6 7 | NA |
| 4. | The therapist seemed well trained and skilled in helping me with my concerns. | 1 2 3 4 5 6 7 | NA |
| 5. | The therapist helped me to be comfortable enough to express what I was thinking and/or feeling most of the time. | 1 2 3 4 5 6 7 | NA |
| 6. | I felt there were too many forms to fill out on my first appointment. | 1 2 3 4 5 6 7 | NA |
| 7. | The amount of time I had to wait for the first appointment was too long. | 1 2 3 4 5 6 7 | NA |
| 8. | The amount of time I had to wait between appointments was too long. | 1 2 3 4 5 6 7 | NA |
| 9. | I felt the fees for service were affordable. | 1 2 3 4 5 6 7 | NA |
| 10. | The hours for appointments were convenient. | 1 2 3 4 5 6 7 | NA |
| 11. | The location and accessibility of the office were convenient. | 1 2 3 4 5 6 7 | NA |
| 12. | I received the kind of service I wanted when I came for therapy. | 1 2 3 4 5 6 7 | NA |
| 13. | I received helpful information about resources in the community. | 1 2 3 4 5 6 7 | NA |
| 14. | I believe that any information I revealed will be treated confidentially. | 1 2 3 4 5 6 7 | NA |
| 15. | If the need to speak to someone arises again, I would return to this therapist. | 1 2 3 4 5 6 7 | NA |
| 16. | I would recommend therapist to others. | 1 2 3 4 5 6 7 | NA |
| 17. | I felt that the visit(s) were useful. | 1 2 3 4 5 6 7 | NA |
| 18. | I experienced improvement in the condition or problems for which I sought services. | 1 2 3 4 5 6 7 | NA |
| 19. | In an overall, general sense, I was very satisfied with the services I received. | 1 2 3 4 5 6 7 | NA |

20. How many therapy/counseling sessions did you have?  _____

Please add any other comments you wish about your experience with us. Use additional sheets if you wish. Thank you very much for your time and efforts.

**FORM 45. Client satisfaction follow-up questionnaire.**   From *The Paper Office*. Copyright 2003 by Edward L. Zuckerman. Permission to photocopy this form is granted to purchasers of this book for personal use only (see copyright page for details).

## Follow-Up Questionnaire 2

Therapist's name: _____     Today's date: _____

Date of last session: _____     6   12   24   ____

What is your gender?   ❑ Male   ❑ Female   How old are you? _____ years

Please feel free to add further comments about each question (use the back of this form if necessary).

1. What was the main problem that caused you to seek treatment?


2. When this therapist's treatment ended, was this problem:
   ❑ Resolved, no longer a problem?   ❑ Better?   ❑ About the same?   ❑ Worse?

3. If this problem was not completely resolved, have you gotten treatment from anyone else?
   ❑ No.   ❑ Yes.   If you have, whom have you seen? _____

4. Are these problem now   ❑ Resolved, not a problem?   ❑ Better?   ❑ About the same?   ❑ Worse?

5. Did any other problems come up during this therapist's treatment?     ❑ No or not really.   ❑ Yes.

   a. If yes, what were these?


   b. Is this problem now   ❑ Resolved, not a problem?   ❑ Better?   ❑ About the same?   ❑ Worse?

6. What did the therapy or therapist do that was most helpful to you?


7. What have you learned (in therapy or from anyone or anywhere) about your original problems that has been helpful to you?


8. What did the therapist do that was not helpful to you?


9. What could the therapist have done that he or she did not do or did not do enough of?


10. Has your therapy helped your performance at work?


11. Has your therapy helped you deal with any family problems?


12. Has your therapy helped you deal with any problems with friends or social organizations?


13. Do you have other comments and suggestions?


14. How many therapy/counseling sessions did you have? _____


Thank you very much for your time and efforts.

**FORM 46. Client outcome follow-up questionnaire.**     From *The Paper Office*. Copyright 2003 by Edward L. Zuckerman. Permission to photocopy this form is granted to purchasers of this book for personal use only (see copyright page for details).

# CHAPTER 7

# Confidentiality and Releasing Records

## 7.1   Understanding Confidentiality

> *Whatever, in connection with my professional service, or not in connection with it, I see or hear, in the life of men, which ought not to be spoken of abroad, I will not divulge, as reckoning that all such should be kept secret. While I continue to keep this Oath unviolated, may it be granted to me to enjoy life and the practice of the art, respected by all men, in all times. But should I trespass and violate this Oath, may the reverse be my lot.*
> —HIPPOCRATES (translated by Francis Adams, available at
> http://classics.mit.edu/Hippocrates/hippooath.html)

Over the course of Chapters 5 and 6, we have considered what client records need to be created from the first contact to the ending of therapy. Now one important issue remains concerning the maintenance of this paperwork: confidentiality.

Confidentiality seems to be crucial for meaningful psychotherapy, and its actual practice is complex. Rubanowitz (1987) found that 80% of patients believe that all information (including financial data for insurers) is confidential. Since this is not true, you must explain what is confidential and what will be released. Yet Baird and Rupert (1987) found that about half of the psychologists they surveyed either said nothing to patients about confidentiality or indicated that everything is confidential—neither of which is realistic. Later studies have confirmed this pattern, although more therapists now discuss confidentiality and get a form signed. The methods of obtaining informed consent in Chapter 4 include detailed explanations of this issue. Because confidentiality is an almost universal concern, you have the responsibility to discuss it, and especially its limits, with every patient.

### Basic Definitions

"Confidentiality" is related to the concepts of "privacy" and "privileged communication." It can be seen as lying between the other two concepts in terms of narrowness.

**Privacy** is frequently considered a basic right granted, by implication, through the Fourth and Ninth Amendments and other sections of the U.S. Constitution. It is understood as the right of an individual to decide which of his or her thoughts, feelings, or other personal data will be shared with others. This right protects attitudes, beliefs, behaviors, and opinions. The individual can decide to divulge or to withhold; can decide when, how, and under what circumstances to share information; and can do so with regard to which particular others.

**Confidentiality** is a concept that exists within many professions. "Confidentiality is an ethical concept that prohibits the physician from discussing his patient with anyone except under compelling legal circumstances" (Sadoff, 1988, p. 41). In all states it has legal recognition, but it is not primarily a legal concept. It is an ethic based on a recognition of the potentially damaging nature of some of the information we therapists collect and record (Wilson, 1980), and on respect of the client's right to privacy.

**Privileged communication** (or just privilege) is a legal term for a right that belongs to the client, not to the therapist. However, it can be asserted by the therapist to protect the client (as when the therapist does not want to release the client's records) until the issues are discussed with a client, and the client then may assert the privilege. It is granted by state rather than federal laws and by state as well as federal court decisions (*Jaffee v. Redmond*, 518 U.S. 1996; see http://www.psa-uny.org/jr). It restricts a clinician or other person from disclosing, in an open court, or in other legal proceedings, information that was given with assumed confidentiality. The restriction can apply to spouses, attorneys, priests, and physicians, as well as to many psychotherapists. The legal bases for privileged communication are extensions of the state statutes concerning attorney–client privilege, which vary from state to state.

In summary, **all privileged communications are confidential, but not all confidential communications are necessarily privileged.** A Venn diagram would show three concentric circles—the largest being privacy, the middle confidentiality, and the smallest privilege. Gutheil (quoted in Reid, 1999, p. 91) offers this clever mnemonic: "PRivilege is the Patient's Right, while COnfidentiality is the Clinician's Obligation."

The rules protecting confidentiality are confused, confusing, and ambiguous, because they may vary depending on the following circumstances:

- The topics communicated. The abuse of children, and serious threats of harm, are generally not protected; sexual affairs, actions that ended a long time ago, or actions that were situation-specific are generally protected.

- The legal status of those present. Some of these are protected in different situations: spouse, boyfriend or girlfriend, public employee, child, employee, and cotherapist.

- Your credentials, discipline, and licensure.

- The state in which you practice. Credentialing laws, case law, legislation, regulations, and legal climate vary with jurisdiction. For example, Massachusetts law denies privilege to non-doctoral-level psychologists.

- Whether you are doing individual, couple, marital, family, or group therapy.

- A judge's discretion, evolving case law, and court decisions.

- Whether civil or criminal actions will be involved.

- Whether the legal actions are in federal or state courts.

- Whether HIPAA regulations have preempted your state's rules because they were less protective than HIPAA's, or whether HIPAA applies because your state had no previous rules applicable to the situation.

- Other factors unknown at present.

## Exceptions to Confidentiality

The common exceptions to the rules of confidentiality, according to Stromberg et al. (1988, p. 371 ff.) and Koocher and Keith-Spiegel (1998), are as follows:

1. **When a patient requests his or her own records.** The law about this may vary from state to state. The main concerns are (a) whether the patient would be harmed through too full a disclosure, and (b) the patient's inability to understand the record's wording or ideas. The options include providing a summary rather than the full records, or disclosure to a third party (a mental health professional competent to understand and explain the records' contents) agreed upon by the patient and the therapist. Most authorities believe that the therapist should review the records' contents with the patient, explaining and answering questions, and that this will result in increased trust and prevent the misuse of the information. Patient "requests often reflect clinical issues, such as patients wondering 'What is wrong with me?' or, 'What does my therapist think of me?' Usually it is sufficient to deal with these issues directly within psychotherapy without having to show patients their records" (Knapp, VandeCreek, & Tepper, 1998, p. 19).

2. **The patient may also consent to the release of records.** To truly consent, the patient must have been fully informed of all aspects and consequences of what is to be released. This is discussed in Chapter 4, and the client's understanding can be documented by a highly specific release form, such as Form 47 or 48. Problems may arise if the client does not know all of what is in a record. If you suspect that anything you are asked for should not be released, discuss the situation with the client. If the client agrees, he or she can revoke the release or sign a revised, more limited version.

   If the request is from a lawyer (e.g., it is a subpoena) and appears inappropriately broad, you can write a letter to both parties (the defense and the prosecution) saying that you need a more specific release or a court order, and let them decide what to do. If you or your clients are involved in a dispute and you are not comfortable with a subpoena you receive, seek a court ruling on the limits of what to disclose. You can ask the court to decide and can discuss it with the judge.

3. **Certain laws require disclosure.** Child abuse or neglect, suspected or proven, is the most common situation legally requiring disclosure. The first fact that you must know is this: Are you a "mandated" reporter of abuse? Not all citizens or providers of

services are, and state rules vary. Are those you supervise, who may have different credentials or be in a different relationship with a child, mandated reporters? Does the child or the suspected perpetrator have to be your client, or is a spouse's/partner's report to you sufficient to trigger your required reporting? Does your state require the reporting of the abuse of an elderly or disabled person? You must know exactly what your state laws require, because you must act immediately (usually within 24 hours). Besides your state association, the National Clearinghouse on Child Abuse and Neglect (http://www.calib.com/nccanch/catalog/statutes.cfm) has tables of information on definitions, immunity, penalties, and procedures by state. These documents must be downloaded but are very accessible. For further guidance, you can call your state reporting agency's hotline and discuss a "hypothetical" situation for advice.

As you consider your own state's rules about reporting child abuse, bear in mind the following key questions. Let me use myself as a psychologist licensed in Pennsylvania as an example. First, **what is my relationship with the child?** Psychologists must have direct contact with a child who "comes before them in their professional or official capacity" [23 Pa. Cons. Stat. Anon. § 6311]. In other states, you must simply learn about the abuse. Second, **who is the perpetrator?** I must report abuse by a parent, paramour, responsible person, or household resident, but need not if the perpetrator is a teacher, neighbor, or stranger, as these are simply criminal assaults. (I do still have some a moral obligation as a citizen to protect others.) Third, **what is abuse?** It includes "a. non-accidental physical injury; b. neglect of supervision, shelter, clothes, food or medical care and not due to conditions the parent had no control over; c. sexual abuse or exploitation; d. emotional abuse" (per Child Protective Services Fam. in PA.). This last must be severe. Fourth, **when did it occur?** For a physical injury, it has to have been within the last 2 years, but the other types of abuse do not have time limits. Fifth, what if I am unclear about what has happened? **How much proof do I need to have before I report abuse?** The answer is none. I must report if I have a "reason to believe" or "reasonable cause to suspect" (per Child Protective Serices Fam. in PA.). This is a very low threshold, because the laws were deliberately written to protect the greatest number of children, and so they disregard my professional judgment or need for evidence. I should not do any exploring, questioning, or therapy. The state agency will do the investigation. Sixth, **whom should I report to and when?** I can phone 24 hours a day to a toll-free number. The law does not say when, but if the danger is high, I must call immediately. If the danger is past, I may take a day or so, but I cannot put it off too long. Seventh, **what if I am wrong?** In Pennsylvania, I have immunity for making a report in "good faith" [23 Pa. Cons. Stat. Ann. § 6318(a–b) (West Supp. 1998)]. Eighth, **what if I don't make the report?** The first violation is a summary offense, and later ones are misdemeanors of the third degree [23 Pa. Cons. Stat. Ann. § 6319 (West 1991)]. Anything else? Yes. Immediately consult with one or more colleagues and document everything you heard, saw, and did; what actions you considered; and why you chose the ones you did. This is especially important if you have decided not to report.

Laws differ, but these requirements on reporting abuse seem typical:

a. You usually must have seen an allegedly abused child, but many states require you to make a disclosure if you have reason to trust an adult client's report of his or her abusive behaviors. Even where you are not legally required to report this abuse (because the perpetrator, not the child, is your patient), you may have the ethical or civic duty to make a report in order to protect the child or to prevent violence.

b.  Even professional students and your assistants may be required to make such reports.

c.  Proof of abuse is not needed to make a report; generally, you have no discretion about investigating and do not need to investigate. This is a sticking point for many therapists, because they do not want to serve as "police," would prefer to make a decision in what they see as the best interests of the child or family, and do not trust an agency to make good decisions. In the area of child abuse, Taube and Elwork (1990) found that disclosing the mandatory reporting issue to patients led to fewer self-reports of child neglect and punishment behaviors by caregiver clients. Similarly, the legal obligation for psychiatrists to report child sexual abuse in Maryland was counterproductive: The number of self-referrals for child abuse and the self-disclosure rate during therapy both went to zero, and the number of children identified as abused did not increase (Berlin et al., 1991). It appears that we mental health professionals have failed to make our need for options clear to our legislators.

d.  You generally must report even abuse that occurred some time ago, if the victim is still under 18 and thus is considered vulnerable.

e.  Bear in mind, however, that a duty to report is not a release of information; the patient's privilege still holds, and you may have to assert it when the patient has not, even when your patient is the suspected perpetrator. To provide more than the information your state authorities legally require will require a release from the client.

Some states, such as Pennsylvania, require you to report impaired drivers as well. These may include drivers with epilepsy, hallucinations, disorientation, homicidal tendencies, or a history of accidents or near-misses (Knapp et al., 1998, pp. 70–73).

4.  **When the patient is a litigant and sues you.** Privilege cannot be used as "both a shield and a sword." That is, the client cannot waive privilege and have only some facts supportive of his or her case opened to view (the sword), while protecting himself or herself from the import of other facts (the shield). Once privilege is waived, it is generally waived completely. These situations are, however, negotiated between lawyers and the court, and some material can be excluded if it is of no relevance and is potentially damaging to the client. However, if you have been formally accused of malpractice, you may generally reveal *only* the information necessary to defend yourself—not everything you were told or recorded or received as records from others.

In regard to lawsuits or ethics complaints, be careful about what you reveal to whom. It is natural to want to complain to or seek support from friends, colleagues, or a trusted supervisor. But these are *not* privileged conversations, and these people can be subpoenaed to testify about what you told them. Similarly, although ethical complaints to professional organizations and licensing boards are evaluated in confidence, the information revealed is also not privileged. The amount of material revealed depends on the attorneys and investigators and on the local procedures.

5. **When therapy or evaluations are court-ordered.** In this situation, the results of your evaluation or records of your therapy will be sent to both sides, so you must fully inform the client of this before you perform these services. It would be a good idea to make a note that you have informed the client that anything he or she says during an evaluation may be included in your report (American Psychiatric Association, 1987). Interestingly, examinations done at the request of a client's attorney may be protected by attorney–client privilege, and so may be suppressed if they are unfavorable to the client. (See Section 4.6.)

6. **Any legal proceeding where a client's mental status could be an issue.** Lawsuits over head injuries, custody battles, adoptions, or disability claims can bring the records you created into court. This can include allegations of emotional pain and suffering or having been involuntarily psychiatrically hospitalized. In addition, your testimony may be required by a judge.

7. **Parents have rights to information about the diagnosis and treatment of their minor children.** See Section 4.5 and below.

8. **If your client seriously threatens an identifiable person or persons.** This is future criminal behavior, and you may have the "duty to warn or protect" (see Section 3.10 for clarification of this). Note that except in South Dakota, therapists are not required to report past criminal behavior if it is not ongoing.

9. **You must disclose in emergencies**—for example, when a "patient's health is seriously or imminently at stake" (Stromberg et al., 1988, p. 400). Keep the information disclosed to a minimum—that is, what a competent patient would agree would be necessary. In an emergency, a patient's oral consent to disclose is acceptable, but the details should be carefully documented. If the patient is unable (not unwilling) to provide the information or to consent, break confidentiality only if withholding it would endanger the patient and if the local law permits or does not forbid such disclosure.

10. **Nonlicensed therapists do not have privilege.** This includes intern psychologists, most "counselors," and those in training whom you may supervise. In general, students (including psychology interns, trainees, or supervisees) are not specifically covered by statutes granting privilege (Koocher & Keith-Spiegel, 1998). Note two points if the HIPAA regulations apply to you. First, they specifically allow the sharing of PHI with students and supervisees and would, I suppose, by extension, require such students to maintain privilege. Second, as to other professions, the regulations are extremely broadly worded, and apply HIPAA to all those included in the Medicare regulations (Title XI, 42 U.S.C. 1301, Section 1861[u]). As such they seem to include just about any of the "various licensed/certified health care practitioners," and this may conflict with your state's rules or profession's codes.

## Other Points about Confidentiality and Its Limitations

To obtain reimbursement with Medicare and Medicaid clients, providers are required to disclose more than basic identifying data. Managed care organizations' (MCOs') reviewers ask for lots of clinical information, and a client has almost always (and without any awareness of its implications) signed a blanket release for an MCO when applying for coverage. If the HIPAA regulations apply in this situation, the "minimum necessary" disclosure of

PHI (see Section 164.5029[b]) may apply. These rules require the MCO to identify exactly what information each level of their organization needs and to seek only that information; they may not request the entire medical record. It even appears that workers' compensation insurers routinely expect release of *all* records you create; this may be quite problematic when a client's employer is self-insured, and so the company's benefits staff can see records and may have few safeguards for maintaining their confidentiality. Clients need to know what will be revealed before they use their insurance, and they usually expect to use it from the beginning. Therefore you must inform them of this at the start of treatment. The client information brochure (see Section 4.2) covers this, as does Handout 3.

The sharing of information among members of a treatment team or care providers within an agency is generally acceptable without a release when the client has consented to treatment that he or she understands to involve several persons or departments within the agency (American Psychiatric Association, 1987). The HIPAA regulations specifically support the sharing of patient information among members of the treatment team and any others providing treatment with no more than the basic consent obtained during notification of privacy rights (see Section 7.8). Again, it would be best to include this point in the efforts you make to inform the client. Be especially careful about nonclinical personnel's access to agency records.

When you talk to a consultant about a client, do not add details that might enable the consultant to identify the client (American Psychological Association [APA], 2001, Standard 4.06). This is especially important if the consultant may know the client personally or by reputation, or if a case involves sensitive disorders (e.g., child or drug abuse, sexual difficulties). The consultant rarely needs detailed knowledge, it cannot be unlearned; and it becomes a burden to the other that he or she does not need to carry. The courts call this "guilty knowledge" and it is a very useful concept in doing psychotherapy.

Unless it is very sensitive, you do not need specific permission to share information with a consultant from whom you are seeking professional advice when this relationship was explained to and approved by the client. If you want to be careful—perhaps because you do not know the contents of what will be revealed—you might get a consent signed at the first meeting with the client, or document the absence of consent. This does not cover informally discussing a case with several peers, and this kind of consultation is not usually privileged, so don't do it. It is best to share clinical information only when doing so benefits the client, or else you are on thin ice.

In most states, the fact that a person is a client is itself not privileged information (although you should certainly treat it as confidential). Similarly, the dates and number of appointments, as well as billing information, are accessible to the courts (Knapp, 1994). Turning a case over to a collection agency or going to small-claims court is not a breach of confidentiality if the client is notified that it may occur. This notification is best included in your client information brochure. However, the information shared with the court should be minimal, given simply to establish the debt's legitimacy (client's identity, dates of service, fees) (APA, 2002, Standard 4.05b). Moreover, communications, reports, and observations made for purposes other than treatment are not covered by privilege; these include communications for employment or insurance purposes (American Psychiatric Association, 1987).

Confidentiality rules apply even after the death of the client involved. The privilege passes to the executor or legal representative of the client.

Finally, claims of "that's confidential" cannot be used to protect the therapist, only the client. Such claims cannot be used to conceal harmful practices, protect the autonomy of the therapist, avoid the scrutiny of peers, or defend a need to be "right" (Sweet, 1990, p. 7).

## Confidentiality and Children

With a competent adult, the person seeking services and the recipient of those services are the same; however, when the recipient of assessment or treatment services is a child, there are two "clients." In this situation, to whom does the therapist owe the duty of confidentiality? Even when the ethical duty is to the child, the legal duty may be to the parents. The best resolution can be found by looking for the local answers to the following questions suggested by Morris (1993, p. 11):

1. Is a child in psychotherapy accorded legally-protected privileged communication in your state?

2. If yes, what are the exceptions to privileged communications for a child in your state?

3. Is there a common usage lower age limit for children legally granting them privileged communication?

4. Is there legal precedent in your state that has tested the constitutionality of the privileged communication granted to children and adolescents?

The therapist should, of course, inform the child of all the limitations of confidentiality. For example, the child should be told that the therapist will be discussing the contents of each interview (in general ways) with his or her parents, and that nothing can be kept secret. If the therapist will be consulting with school or hospital personnel, the child should be told that as well. Morris (1993) recommends putting these points in writing and obtaining the dated signatures of parents and child. Obviously, the wording of both oral and written statements must suit the child's understanding and reading levels. (See Form 12 of this book for a written statement suitable for an older child or an adolescent.) In general, the approach to an older or "emancipated" adolescent is like that to an adult.

Parental access to information and records varies a great deal. State laws usually do not address this issue, but logic suggests that if you need parental consent to provide treatment, the parents have the right to access the records of that treatment, and vice versa. The most common exceptions to the need for parental consent to treatment are emergencies and cases in which minors have graduated from high school or are married. You could try to discuss the issues of confidentiality in the first session with both adolescent and parent present. Goldberg (1995) suggests, at least, reassuring the parents that you will inform them if their child is in imminent danger.

## Confidentiality and HIV-Positive Clients

There are many benefits of confidentiality for HIV-positive clients (including reduced risk of discrimination), but these must be weighed against its possible social costs (such as the infection of third parties). The APA's position as of July 1992 is that no legal duty should be imposed. If it is, however, disclosure should be permitted only "when (a) the provider knows an identifiable third party who the provider has compelling reason to believe is at significant risk of infection; (b) the provider has reasonable belief that the third party has no reason to suspect that he or she is at risk; and (c) the client/patient has been urged to inform the third party, and has either refused or is considered unreliable in his/her willingness to notify the third party" (Fox, 1992, p. 912). Fox goes on to suggest respect for local laws and encouraging (through therapy, teaching, consulting, or referring) HIV-infected persons to reduce the risk of further infection. Some states, such as Pennsylvania, have passed laws specifically prohibiting the warning of potential victims. See also Section 3.10.

## A Handout on the Limits of Confidentiality

**HANDOUT 8**

Issues concerning confidentiality have been incorporated into the client information brochure (see Section 4.2), because the APA ethics code (APA, 2002, Standard 4.02b) requires a discussion of confidentiality's limits before therapy begins. The same section requires discussion of limits as new circumstances warrant it. If and when you believe your clients need more specific information, the handout offered below (Handout 8) covers confidentiality issues in greater detail than does the brochure. I recommend offering this handout only to those who raise concerns after reading the more general brochure, or to those whose referral (e.g., by the courts) or history suggests its need. The issues can then be discussed in a therapy session. Another way to use it is to make it available with other client education materials in a three-ring binder in your waiting room, perhaps entitled "For Your Information."

Like the other handouts and forms in this book, Handout 8 can be photocopied and distributed to your clients. It has been written to be generic enough to be applicable to most practices, and addresses issues relevant to adult, child, and family therapy. However, it does not fully address the issue of secrets between spouses in marital therapy. See Margolin (1982) for a discussion of this thorny topic.

Before using this handout, check on alterations you may need to make because of your locality, your profession or credentials, or your preferred methods of practice:

- If you treat older children, you might consider amplifying what is said here about what you have to reveal to parents or guardians.

- Weigh what you have to reveal to third-party payers with whom you have contracts in your state. Handout 3 is a more specific informed consent handout for MCO patients. In addition, review the current rules on releasing records of Medicare patients.

- If you do group therapy, consider its confidentiality limitations. (See Form 13.)

- Adapt section 1d to your state's rules about the basis for reporting abuse. States differ in requiring a "suspicion" standard or a "reasonable belief" standard. The suspicion standard requires a lower level of certainty to trigger the mandated reporting requirement. Also, states differ in their definitions of elder abuse. Usually elder abuse is defined more broadly than child abuse and includes financial exploitation (Sam Knapp, personal communication, October 2, 1996).

# What You Should Know about Confidentiality in Therapy

I will treat what you tell me with great care. My professional ethics (that is, my profession's rules about moral matters) and the laws of this state prevent me from telling anyone else what you tell me unless you give me written permission. These rules and laws are the ways our society recognizes and supports the privacy of what we talk about—in other words, the "confidentiality" of therapy. But I cannot promise that everything you tell me will *never* be revealed to someone else. There are some times when the law requires me to tell things to others. There are also some other limits on our confidentiality. We need to discuss these, because I want you to understand clearly what I can and cannot keep confidential. You need to know about these rules now, so that you don't tell me something as a "secret" that I cannot keep secret. These are very important issues, so please read these pages carefully and keep this copy. At our next meeting, we can discuss any questions you might have.

1. **When you or other persons are in physical danger,** the law requires me to tell others about it. Specifically:

   a. If I come to believe that you are threatening serious harm to another person, I am required to try to protect that person. I may have to tell the person and the police, or perhaps try to have you put in a hospital.

   b. If you seriously threaten or act in a way that is very likely to harm yourself, I may have to seek a hospital for you, or to call on your family members or others who can help protect you. If such a situation does come up, I will fully discuss the situation with you before I do anything, unless there is a very strong reason not to.

   c. In an emergency where your life or health is in danger, and I cannot get your consent, I may give another professional some information to protect your life. I will try to get your permission first, and I will discuss this with you as soon as possible afterwards.

   d. If I believe or suspect that you are abusing a child, an elderly person, or a disabled person I must file a report with a state agency. To "abuse" means to neglect, hurt, or sexually molest another person. I do not have any legal power to investigate the situation to find out all the facts. The state agency will investigate. If this might be your situation, we should discuss the legal aspects in detail before you tell me anything about these topics. You may also want to talk to your lawyer.

   In any of these situations, I would reveal only the information that is needed to protect you or the other person. I would not tell everything you have told me.

2. In general, **if you become involved in a court case or proceeding,** you can prevent me from testifying in court about what you have told me. This is called "privilege," and it is your choice to prevent me from testifying or to allow me to do so. However, there are some situations where a judge or court may require me to testify:

   a. In child custody or adoption proceedings, where your fitness as a parent is questioned or in doubt.

*(cont.)*

---

**HANDOUT 8. Patient handout on the limits of confidentiality (p. 1 of 3).**    From *The Paper Office*. Copyright 2003 by Edward L. Zuckerman. Permission to photocopy this form is granted to purchasers of this book for personal use only (see copyright page for details).

b. In cases where your emotional or mental condition is important information for a court's decision.

c. During a malpractice case or an investigation of me or another therapist by a professional group.

d. In a civil commitment hearing to decide if you will be admitted to or continued in a psychiatric hospital.

e. When you are seeing me for court-ordered evaluations or treatment. In this case we need to discuss confidentiality fully, because you don't have to tell me what you don't want the court to find out through my report.

3. There are a few other things you must know about confidentiality and your treatment:

a. I may sometimes consult (talk) with another professional about your treatment. This other person is also required by professional ethics to keep your information confidential. Likewise, when I am out of town or unavailable, another therapist will be available to help my clients. I must give him or her some information about my clients, like you.

b. I am required to keep records of your treatment, such as the notes I take when we meet. You have a right to review these records with me. If something in the record might seriously upset you, I may leave it out, but I will fully explain my reasons to you.

4. Here is what you need to know about confidentiality **in regard to insurance and money matters:**

a. If you use your health insurance to pay a part of my fees, insurance companies require some information about our therapy. Insurers such as Blue Cross/Blue Shield or managed care organizations ask for much information about you and your symptoms, as well as a detailed treatment plan.

b. I usually give you my bill with any other forms needed, and ask you to send these to your insurance company to file a claim for your benefits. That way, you can see what the company will know about our therapy. It is against the law for insurers to release information about our office visits to anyone without your written permission. Although I believe the insurance company will act morally and legally, I cannot control who sees this information at the insurer's office. You cannot be required to release more information just to get payments.

c. If you have been sent to me by your employer's Employee Assistance Program, the program's staffers may require some information. Again, I believe that they will act morally and legally, but I cannot control who sees this information at their offices. If this is your situation, let us fully discuss my agreement with your employer or the program before we talk further.

d. If your account with me is unpaid and we have not arranged a payment plan, I can use legal means to get paid. The only information I will give to the court, a collection agency, or a lawyer will be your name and address, the dates we met for professional services, and the amount due to me.

5. **Children and families create some special confidentiality questions.**

a. When I treat children under the age of about 12, I must tell their parents or guardians whatever they ask me. As children grow more able to understand and choose, they assume legal rights. For those between the ages of 12 and 18, most of the details in things they tell me will be treated as confidential. However, parents or guardians do have the right to *general* information, including how therapy is going. They need to be

(cont.)

able to make well-informed decisions about therapy. I may also have to tell parents or guardians some information about other family members that I am told. This is especially true if these others' actions put them or others in any danger.

b. In cases where I treat several members of a family (parents and children or other relatives), the confidentiality situation can become very complicated. I may have different duties toward different family members. At the start of our treatment, we must all have a clear understanding of our purposes and my role. Then we can be clear about any limits on confidentiality that may exist.

c. If you tell me something your spouse does not know, and not knowing this could harm him or her, I cannot promise to keep it confidential. I will work with you to decide on the best long-term way to handle situations like this.

d. If you and your spouse have a custody dispute, or a court custody hearing is coming up, I will need to know about it. My professional ethics prevent me from doing both therapy and custody evaluations.

e. If you are seeing me for marriage counseling, you must agree at the start of treatment that if you eventually decide to divorce, you will not request my testimony for either side. The court, however, may order me to testify.

f. At the start of family treatment, we must also specify which members of the family must sign a release form for the common record I create in the therapy or therapies. (See point 7b, below.)

6. **Confidentiality in group therapy is also a special situation.**

In group therapy, the other members of the group are not therapists. They do not have the same ethics and laws that I have to work under. You cannot be certain that they will always keep what you say in the group confidential.

7. Finally, here are a few other points:

a. I will not record our therapy sessions on audiotape or videotape without your written permission.

b. If you want me to send information about our therapy to someone else, you must sign a "release-of-records" form. I have copies you can see, so you will know what is involved.

c. Any information that you also share outside of therapy, willingly and publicly, will not be considered protected or confidential by a court.

The laws and rules on confidentiality are complicated. Please bear in mind that I am not able to give you legal advice. If you have special or unusual concerns, and so need special advice, I strongly suggest that you talk to a lawyer to protect your interests legally and to act in your best interests.

The signatures here show that we each have read, discussed, understand, and agree to abide by the points presented above.

_____          _____
Signature of client (or person acting for client)                              Date

_____
Printed name

_____          _____
Signature of therapist                                                          Date

- Section 3a states that anyone you seek consultation from is "required by professional ethics to keep your information confidential." This is an ethical but not likely a legal requirement; you, the person seeking consultation, are not the consultant's client.

- Adapt section 3b to your state's rules and preferred practices about clients' access to records. This section says, "You have a right to review these records with me; however, reading them with you may not be possible or may be too costly." The exact means of a client's access to his or her records varies with states and regulations. Sending actual copies allows for misinterpretation and risks revelations to other parties. Sending them to another mental health professional for interpretation may be safest.

  If HIPAA regulations on patient access to your records (Section 164.524) apply in your state, the patient does not have a right to read your psychotherapy notes (if you created them), although you may allow such inspection. Patients do not have the right to "access, inspect, and copy" information related to legal proceedings, research, or some other areas. You can limit access when you decide that access is "reasonably likely to endanger the life or physical safety" of the patient or another person or when access might similarly harm another person identified in the record. If you do allow access the regulations specify timely access and procedures for review of such denials of access. You should modify the wording in section 3b to these rules.

- If the HIPAA Privacy Rule applies in your state, you should modify section 4a to explain what will be in the routine office notes that the client's insurer will access. See Section 6.2 on the content of these notes as well as psychotherapy notes.

- Section 4b says, "I usually give you my bill . . . ". This may not be your policy, so adapt the wording.

- You could expand the policy stated in sections 5d and 5e on your becoming a witness in custody or divorce proceedings. Incorporate some possible alternatives:

  "I will not serve as a witness or provide records for such matters, and I ask you to agree that if such a situation arises, you will accept my policy. If you go to court, you will have to ask another professional to do any evaluations of yourselves, your children, and your relationship."

  "I ask you to agree that my records will not be requested in court by either party, and to keep this in mind during our therapy."

  "I will provide a summary, but not the actual records, to the court. My charge for this summary is $100 per hour of preparation time."

- Section 5f covers the question of which family members sign a release-of-records form. The safest method of release for a family's or couple's records is to require the consent of all adults or participants, although this is also the most complex solution.

Because of the litigious and "paranoid" flavor of our times, you might add wording like this:

"I do not sell or in any way make available your name or any of the information you provide to me to anyone without your permission. I will not even acknowledge that you are a client of my practice without your specific permission."

The general rule is this: **Make certain that the client is informed about all the likely implications and consequences of confidentiality.** A handout like Handout 8, and your detailed notes, should show that you have told the client what he or she needs to know to act in his or her own best interest.

# 7.2 Maintaining Confidentiality

## Guidelines for Maintaining Confidentiality

- Encourage clients to ask questions about confidentiality concerns when they arise in therapy, and to resolve them before they make any risky revelations. When answering questions, be careful to promise very little specific protection; you cannot know how confidential you can keep a client's specific situation until you are told, and then it may be too late. Clients have rarely formulated their situations within the ethical or legal frameworks you are bound to live by.

- Many clinicians worry that disclosing the limits of confidentiality will inhibit the freedom of discussion necessary for effective therapy. Nowell and Spruill (1993), surveying rather naive college students, found that disclosing exceptions to total confidentiality did result in some inhibition of self-disclosure. However, they also found that offering a complete description of the limitations did not result in more inhibition than a brief, cursory description, which is now seen as essential. Standard 4.02 of the APA ethics code (APA, 2002) requires that the limits of confidentiality be communicated explicitly and in advance. The client information brochure (see Section 4.2) incorporates these kinds of notifications.

- If in doubt, consult. By itself, making this effort offers you some malpractice protection and you may learn how to protect your client. Document these consultations.

- Avoid giving legal advice on confidentiality, and refer complex questions to the client's attorney.

- You must assure the confidentiality of your computerized client records. (See also Section 1.6.) Your records could be read and copied by any of the following: your own staff; cleaning persons in your office when you are not present; anyone on your local or larger network (unless you have blocked access to client files); those entering through your always-on Internet high-speed digital subscriber line (DSL) or cable modem connection, or secretly sending you a program that sends your files to them (a "Trojan Horse" virus); a thief who steals your computer; a repair person if it needs service or upgrading; legal wiretappers; those using video monitoring "security cameras"; and probably others.

    In my opinion, passwords are insufficient protection, burdensome, and likely to be misused by being changed too infrequently or used on too many accounts. Also, there are easily available programs for breaking passwords.

    At the very minimum, immediately download and use one of the free programs that make designated files or folders invisible. These can be cracked by a knowledgeable person, but are suitable for basic protection. A better solution is to encrypt all your text files with the encryption built into most word-processing programs. The liability is that you will be using a password to decrypt these files. For those programs without an encryption option (such as billing or data base programs), use any of the free (e.g., Pretty Good Privacy) or more convenient moderately priced encryption programs that you can download. If you use DSL or a cable modem, use and keep current a "firewall" program. You can find all these at Shareware.com, Download.com, and others. For privacy tools for all kinds of electronic communication, see http://www.epic. org/privacy/tools.html, or do a google.com search for the latest tools.

- Do not gossip or otherwise talk lightly or casually about your patients. Famous patients, fascinating clinical phenomena, bragging, making the irresistible joke—all these are tempting conversational topics. We may try to gain points for ourselves at the expense of our patients, trusting that no one will figure out their identity or use the information. The best rule is *never* to discuss your patients or your work with your spouse, friends, or even other therapists, but only with a consultant or in a carefully prepared presentation. With such a rule, you won't have to keep deciding what to reveal, or feel the anxiety of uncertainty.

- Leave nothing with a client's name on it lying around anywhere—no folders, no letters, no phone notes, no unusable photocopies. Arrange your office and office procedures to prevent the viewing of charts, appointment books, telephone messages, computer screens, and the like by clients, salespersons, cleaning people, visitors, and other staff members. Lock your door, desk, and cabinet when you are out of the office. If you share an office, each therapist will need a locked record storage area.

- To be safest, develop a rule of never using a client's name in any conversation with anyone outside your consulting room. Never discuss clients, even for consultation or supervision, in any place (whether public or professional) where anyone not bound by your professional code could *possibly* overhear. Certainly do not do so in an elevator or taxi. Make the time for consultation and do it right. Words cannot be unsaid, and lawsuits are depressing.

- Train all members of your staff in all aspects of the maintenance of confidentiality. Make it clear to your staff that any kind of client information must not be casually or carelessly discussed (over lunch, in rest rooms, in elevators, etc.), including in the office. If other staff members, employees, or even other clinicians bound by confidentiality are present when you need to communicate, write the client's name down and point to it for your conversation. Similarly, do not allow your staff or office mates to refer to clients who phone or otherwise come up in conversation, except as "this client" or "he" or "she." Finally, make clear your intention to dismiss immediately anyone who breaks any of the rules of the office.

- Be careful when you replay the answering machine, so that no one else can overhear. Instruct your staff to do the same. Use password-protected "mailboxes" for your voice mail.

- Assure yourself that your answering service also understands these rules and obeys them. Ask about the staff's training, offer some hypothetical situations, and perhaps call as someone else to test the service.

- Do not use a client's name in the waiting room unless you and the client are alone. It may seem odd, but you can just make eye contact and say, "Won't you please come in?" without mentioning the client's name. If it is a first appointment, saying "I'm Dr. Doe. Are you here to see me?" will serve the same purpose in a busy waiting area. If the office is used by professionals of other disciplines, such as dentists, they are likely to use clients' names freely; do not be swayed.

- In some cases, just revealing information in the presence of a third party (such as another therapist, an uninvolved professional, or perhaps even an employee) may void the legal protection of confidentiality. This also applies to your clients, so discourage them from saying private things when others (such as family or friends) are around. There is no privilege if the patient tells other people about the session, because that, too, means it is no longer actually confidential.

  1. Did the patient intend the session to be confidential? The answer to this question often lies in the original reason for the session. If the patient has a regular, long-term relationship with the therapist (e.g., is being treated for a disorder), then the reason for the sessions are solely for the patient's private benefit, and clearly are intended to be confidential. However, many people contact psychologists in connection with some particular legal rather than psychological problem. Perhaps they are in the process of or contemplating divorce, are being evaluated as parents for custody or adoption purposes, have been raped or abused and are pressing charges, are fulfilling a condition of probation, or the like. In these cases, the courts are likely to find that the patient intended immediately or in the future to disclose the fact that he or she was undergoing treatment, in which case there is no evidentiary privilege.

  2. Was the session in fact confidential? There is no privilege if the FBI is lawfully wiretapping the session, or an undercover police officer is actually present in the room.

- *Never* discuss any kind of confidential matter on a wireless or cellular phone. Be aware that they are broadcasting devices and do not have the same protections (legal or technical) for confidentiality that wired phones do. Encryption programs for wireless phones are available.

- Make sure you have sufficient sound muffling in your office. You can achieve this with white-noise generators, an air deflector in the air conditioning ductwork, double-studded and double-wallboarded walls, a radio with several speakers (set fairly loud and not under the control of the clients in the waiting room), and heavily weather-stripped or carpeted doors.

- Even if a client's spouse is in therapy with the client, it is not appropriate to discuss the client's treatment in detail with the spouse. The law is frequently silent on the issue of the privileged status of what is said to spouses in marriage counseling, or to a therapist's assistants, staff, and employees, so you may not have protection. Court-ordered marriage counseling may be an exception to confidentiality, but check your local rules.

- Make explicit in your client information brochure how you will handle the confidentiality issues of family therapy.

■ Keep separate sets of group therapy records. That is, keep a record for each individual in which other members are not identified, and a separate record for the group as a whole. See Form 13, the group therapy contract.

■ Develop a clear plan to dispose of your records without breaking confidentiality. See Section 1.6.

## A Checklist for Staff Training in Confidentiality

Since you can be held responsible for the unethical actions of your office staff, training them in your rules and procedures is essential. Below is a checklist of the issues of greatest concern and likelihood (and the sections of this book where you will find some guidance). It is presented here as an example only; you should add items to fit your practice and revise the contents over time. It can be used to organize your training of employees (permanent or temporary, part- or full-time), answering service personnel, or anyone else with access to your records. It can also be used as an employee agreement to maintain confidentiality. A few sentences are based on a form devised by Ginger Blume, PhD, of Middletown, CT. The HIPAA Privacy Rule specifies that you must train your staff in these issues (Section 164.530[b]) and must "have in place appropriate administrative, technical, and physical safeguards to protect the privacy of protected health information" (Section 164.530[c]). The forthcoming Security Rule will add more detail for electronic records.

### Checklist for Staff Training in Confidentiality

First, you should assume that *everything* is confidential in this office and treat it accordingly. Because you wish to work in this office, you must agree to the following points about confidentiality and privacy.

A checkmark below indicates that this topic was discussed with those present on this date: _____.
I, _____, conducted this training.

❑ The codes of ethics and guidelines of my profession.

❑ The main malpractice and ethics issues and risks—confidentiality, dual relationships, billing, and _____.

❑ Procedures and limitations on releasing any kind of records.

❑ Procedures for copying any kind of records.

❑ Responding to phone calls about clients (Section 7.3).

❑ The organization, handling, and storing of all material with patients' names—charts, forms, photocopies, faxes, voice mail boxes, computer screens, appointment books, phone messages and books, and so forth.

❑ Not using patients' names on the phone, in the waiting area, or elsewhere.

❑ Privately playing the answering machine or calling the answering service.

❑ Casual conversations and gossip about patients, in and out of the office.

❑ Computer security—passwords and encryption (Sections 1.5 and 7.2), backups, off-site storage, and the like.

❑ The fact that the confidentiality of a patient's information extends after the death of the patient or the professional, after my leaving this employment, and into the future indefinitely.

❑ The breaking of confidentiality rules as grounds for immediate dismissal.

❑ How to handle questions of ethics, confidentiality, access, and so forth raised by clients, by other professionals, or by situations.

My signature below indicates the following:

❑ I have read and discussed:

   ❑ The "Information for Clients" brochure (Section 4.2) or the other routes to informed consent (Section 4.3–4.6).

   ❑ The handout on limits of confidentiality (Handout 8).

   ❑ The handout on managed care (Handout 3).

   ❑ Other patient education handouts, and information, consent, and release forms, as appropriate.

❑ I have been informed about the issues and guidelines above, have had the opportunity to raise any questions, and have had my questions answered. I believe I understand the issues and concerns about confidentiality and related issues, and will ask _____ when any questions or concerns arise for me.

❑ I agree not to disclose any patient information to third parties, persons outside this practice/office/organization, other patients, or anyone else unless authorized to do so in writing by a patient (or patient's guardian) and approved by my employing professional.

❑ If a breach of this agreement or the confidentiality of any records should occur, I agree to notify my employer immediately or within 24 hours of its discovery.

❑ I understand that any material breach of this agreement shall constitute good cause of my discharge from this employment. In addition, such breach may subject me to liability and legal damages.

---

_____        _____
Signature of employee                 Printed name of employee


_____        _____
Signature of employee                 Printed name of employee


_____        _____
Signature of employee                 Printed name of employee

---

## Creating Confidential Records

There are three methods of increasing the likelihood of confidentiality of your records:

1. Always abridge as much as possible. This means limiting the client information collected, recorded, retained, and reported. Do not put information of a sensitive nature

into a report if it is not *clearly* necessary to the purposes of that report. For example, do not repeat a client's history from earlier reports or the reports of others, unless this is essential. If you do incorporate others' information, you are in effect releasing information sent to you in confidentiality—presumably with a limited and legal release—but without a legal release from the client. Simple as this rule is, it is broken frequently. You cannot control the destinies of your reports, and your primary responsibility is to your client. If the information is crucial and very sensitive, consider telling the referral source or other concerned persons orally.

2. Ensure the client's access to his or her records. (The rules about this access should be indicated in your client information brochure.) Access can further protect clients' privacy by (a) informing them of what information has been collected and how it is interpreted and used; (b) allowing them the opportunities to correct errors; and (c) allowing them to make informed decisions before releasing information. All of this is empowering to clients and thus protects them in a larger sense. It is also supported by federal law and perhaps by your local laws.

3. If a client is at risk from the information, write it in a protecting, discreet, thoughtful way.

## A Quick Test

1. A physician you know calls to ask: "This is Dr. Jones. Did my patient, Joe Smith, whom I referred to you, come in?" How should you answer?

2. An attorney asks: "Did my client, Joe Smith, come in to see you?" How should you answer?

3. A caller asks: "Did my brother, Joe Smith, get to your office OK?" How should you answer?"

One or more of the following may run through your mind:

- "I don't want to be rude to this caller."

- "My first duty is to conceal my patient's identity by protecting his privacy."

- "All three of us know Joe was supposed to be here, so where is the risk?"

- "Is there anyone who can overhear this conversation?"

- "Am I certain this is indeed Dr. Jones/Ms. Brown/Joe's sister?"

However mixed your reactions may be, unless you know the caller and are willing to take the risk of breaking confidentiality, the only acceptable answer to all three of these queries is this: "I'm sorry, but I cannot give you that information. If you will have the person [don't even use Joe Smith's name, as it could signal that he is known] sign a consent form releasing the information you want, I will check to see if he is known to us, and then I will be able to talk further with you or send you the information you want." Instruct the members of your staff today that they are never to take the risk of responding in any other way. As a way to soften the pain of refusal, you should explain the need for privacy, and you can offer to send the caller a copy of your release form.

# 7.3   Releasing Clients' Records

*Note:* See also Chapter 4 on informed consent.

The balance of this chapter offers a variety of more specific guidelines to help you answer questions such as these:

- How can you decide whether or not to honor a request for a client's records?

- How can you best protect the client's confidentiality when you do release your records?

- What legal elements must a request for the records of another professional contain?

The first of these questions is addressed here. Later sections include sample forms for requesting records from and releasing records to different requesters. The forms are designed to meet important legal and ethical guidelines.

## A Pretest

How sophisticated are you in weighing the relevant issues in releasing records? Pope (1988e) offers the following fictional case history.[1] A 17-year-old married father of a 1-year-old child, living with his parents, comes in complaining of headaches. He is a full-time employee with insurance to pay for your testing. This is an unusual and complicated case, but not entirely unlikely. After you do the evaluation, you receive six requests for your records, from the following:

(a) the boy's physician, an internist.

(b) the boy's parents, who are concerned about his depression.

(c) the boy's employer, in connection with a worker's compensation claim filed by the boy.

(d) the attorney for the insurance company that is contesting the worker's compensation claim.

(e) the attorney for the boy's wife, who is suing for divorce and for custody of the baby.

(f) the attorney [for the boy], who is considering suing you for malpractice since he doesn't like the results of the tests.

----

[1]The passage below is reprinted, and the case history is taken, from Pope (1988). Copyright 1988 by Division 42 of the American Psychological Association. Used by permission.

Each of the requests asks for: (a) the full formal report, (b) the original test data, and (c) copies of each of the tests you administered (e.g., instructions and all items for the MMPI).

To which of these people are you legally or ethically obligated to supply all information requested? Partial information? A summary of the report? No information at all? (Pope, 1988e, p. 24)

Again, this is admittedly a complex situation, and Pope does not offer answers. Before reading further, take a pencil and paper and try to indicate which records you would send out and which you wouldn't, and to whom you would send them. My answers can be found at the end of this section (see pp. 394–395).

We still have to act in the real world. Records must often be shared among professionals for the benefit of clients, but breaches of confidentiality can destroy the trust essential for intimate work. The professions have therefore developed procedures for protecting the privacy of records. The following discussion shows how to evaluate a request for your client's records. In general, as in the case above, you need to weigh the needs of the requester against the ethical and legal requirements. These are described next.

## Ethical Considerations in Releasing Records

A release that authorizes you to "release and disclose all information and to discuss anything pertaining to this client and the client's progress" appears to be illegally vague and broad, and is prohibited by HIPAA regulations concerning the "minimal necessary" disclosure rules (see Section 164.502).

The HIPAA Privacy Rule is much less restrictive about the confidentiality of your records. However, wherever your state's laws and court decisions are more stringent, it will not apply, and it does not remove the necessity for your complying with your profession's ethics codes. Therefore, I have inserted some information where it is most applicable, and have clustered a discussion of the HIPAA changes and required procedures at the end of this chapter (see Section 7.8).

The basic rule is that consent to release records must be *informed* and *voluntary*, and must be obtained from a *competent* person. These requirements are discussed in Chapter 4. Informed consent to release records requires that the client know and agree to the following:

- Which specific person wants the records (name, position, affiliation, function).

- What the records sought contain. Knowledge can come from the client's reading the materials, or from having the materials read and explained to him or her.

- Exactly what information is sought.

- Why this information is sought and exactly how it will be used. What decision(s) will be based on it?

- How the information in the records can be corrected or amended.

- Whether the requester can share this information with anyone else (e.g., consultants, treatment team members).

- What repercussions would follow from granting or withholding permission.

- That the client's consent is time-limited (often 60 days).

- That the client's consent is revocable except for information already released.

- What procedures are available for revoking such consent.

- That the consent and revocation must be given in writing.

Finally, this may seem obvious, but the client must believe that it is in his or her long-term best interest to release the records. For fuller comprehension, your release-of-records form should be available for the client to read; anything the client does not understand must be explained at his or her level of comprehension, and in his or her native language if necessary.

## Legal Requirements for a Release of Records

According to the Code of Federal Regulations (42 C.F.R. Part 2, Public Law 93-282, Sections 2.31(a) and 2.33, governing the confidentiality of alcohol and drug abuse patients' records), a valid release form must address all of the following:

- Name of client. Date of birth is also usually sought, as is Social Security number, because names are not unique.

- The name or title of the person or organization requesting disclosure of the record.

- Either the name or general designation of the program from which or person from whom the records are to be released.

- The extent or nature of the information to be disclosed. (A request for "any and all information" should never be made or honored.)

- The purpose of the request, or why these records are needed. (You may receive a request by error that was created for another proceeding.)

- The consequences of refusing to release the records (e.g., loss of reimbursement for medical costs or of disability benefits).

- The signature of the client (or his or her representative) and the date signed. (The signature must usually be given within 90 days of the time you receive the form.)

- Verification that the person signing is of legal age, or documentation of his or her "emancipation."

- Verification that the signature belongs to this person, or is validly witnessed.

■ A notice that the consent is revocable at any time. (If your suspicions are raised, check—perhaps by calling the client—to see whether the request may have been revoked.)

■ When, how, or on what condition upon which the consent will expire if not revoked earlier.

For clarification about how some of these ideas are carried out, see the release forms in Sections 7.4 and 7.5. Additional criteria may be required by your state.

## Eight Variations on the Theme of "Please Send Your Records"

Many different people may request your records in many different ways. Each request needs to be considered from an ethical perspective. The following discussion evaluates eight of these variations.

### I. A Third Party's Routine Written Request for Records

Consider these usual bases for releasing information to a third party:

■ A competent patient has requested release. The disclosure is necessary for the patient's continuing or comprehensive care by another provider or institution, for reimbursement, or for a needed consultation.

■ A *surrogate* consent is received for a minor, for someone adjudicated incompetent, or for a dead person.

■ A law requires disclosure (e.g., Medicare, mandatory child abuse reporting). See variation 2, below.

Now consider these possible bases against releasing information to a third party:

■ The release form sent to you is faulty. It is missing some of the necessary contents of a proper release as listed above. As a courtesy, you could, if you are still in contact with the patient, use one of your releases (perhaps Form 47) to construct a proper release.

■ The requester is someone you don't recognize, and you know nothing about the intended uses for this information. "Verify the requester's identity and official capacity" before proceeding, say Stromberg et al. (1988, p. 394).

■ The information in your possession is not relevant to the request (e.g., it may not pertain to the request's purposes, the decisions to be made, the time period in question, or even the patient named in the request).

■ Confidentiality law or privilege protects against release, and your general duty to protect confidentiality is not overcome by any recognized exception (see Section 7.1 for a list of exceptions).

- In family therapy, the "family" or "couple" cannot have legal confidentiality; only individual members have this privilege. Thus you will have to clarify and negotiate rules for release with each family member. Ideally, you have specified in your introductory materials that all members must sign a release.

- Is it completely clear that the patient is fully informed about all the information in the record and the effects of passing on all this information? If not, contact the patient directly to clarify the release. In one case in Pennsylvania, a patient sued (successfully at first) the psychologist whom she had specifically requested to write a letter to her employer seeking a less stressful job for her, after she had signed a release form. She sued for invasion of privacy and infliction of emotional distress. The psychologist probably would have received a dismissal (before going to the Court of Appeals) if he or she had had the patient see and authorize the release of the exact letter. It is best to have all records released be seen by the patient, or at least to have their release specifically approved by him or her.

- Can you withhold records if you have not been paid for your services? The APA ethics code (APA, 2002) says in Standard 6.03 that "Psychologists may not withhold records . . . that are requested and needed for a client's/patient's emergency treatment solely because payment has not been received." Notice the qualifiers "emergency" and "solely." I believe the message is that you can indeed withhold records for nonpayment in nonemergency situations. You certainly would not withhold records in an emergency with serious consequences, but what if the request is being made only for the convenience of the patient (e.g., in support of a school transfer) and he or she is fully capable of paying you?

One last point: Should you type up your notes to make them actually readable? No, just send copies of your records in whatever shape they are in. Typing them up is not what you were asked for, and it would tempt you to make minor revisions (for clarification), which would create doubts about your veracity and integrity.

## 2. A Patient's Request to See His or Her Own Records

Who actually *owns* a patient's records? Hirsh (1978) says that "records are considered to be the property of the health care provider [who created them] or his or her employing agency [who paid the creator]. Generally, the consumer controls the dissemination of the records, but the right of patients to have direct access to their records varies from state to state."

When a patient asks to see his or her own records, consider these points:

- What disclosure does the applicable state law require? Applicable laws may concern workers' compensation, disabilities acts, dual-diagnosis clients, substance abuse/dependence, your specific discipline, relationships with other mental health professions, and so forth.

- Consider why the patient wants these records and work from there. The request may conceal other needs, which can be resolved better through different methods.

- In general, offer to review the records with the patient, or offer a *précis* of the record. The issues are the impact on the patient of the disclosure of a diagnosis (which will require explanation and guidance for the patient to understand productively) and the impact of other information (see variation 3, below).

- What if a couple wants the records of couple therapy? It is best to establish a policy on this and to put it into your client information brochure. Since the records reflect both partners' actions, both must agree to the release.

- Consider whether there may be errors in the record, which the patient has a right to see, correct, or amend. The client also has the right to add a statement of agreement or disagreement. These rights come from the Privacy Act of 1974 (Public Law 93-579), the HIPAA regulations, and, for drug and alcohol clients, the Drug Abuse Office and Treatment Act of 1972 (Public Law 92-255).

### 3. A Patient's Request to See His or Her Own Records, Which Contain Potentially Harmful Information

An example of a patient who could be harmed by information in his or her records is an adult with a history of childhood sexual or physical abuse where the patient may be unaware of or deny the abuse, but it is supported by records released to you.

Your plan in such a case should depend on the circumstances, your understanding of the patient, and the impact of the information. You could sidestep the issue by refusing to release to the patient records generated by someone else. This is perfectly legitimate and would require the patient to seek those records from their creators. However, you might not be acting in the patient's best interest because those records would have to be released to someone, and this someone might not do as sensitive a presentation of the distressing information as you could. If you think the information will harm the patient, you can withhold it; this is called "therapeutic privilege." You may not have heard of this privilege, because it is getting rarer and should be invoked only in extraordinary circumstances (Stromberg & Dellinger, 1993). However, the recent HIPAA regulations have revived this concept and do allow you to restrict the information a client can access (see Section 164.524[a][3][ii]). In such a situation you are asking the patient to understand that some information would be upsetting, and to agree that he or she should be kept ignorant of this information (which seems to go against informed consent). You are also asking that if the information is presented to the patient, he or she will not hold you responsible for any damages (which seems to ask the patient to waive recourse from a harm he or she cannot anticipate—this again seems unfair). If the situation is touchy, go slowly and carefully; give full attention to maintaining the best possible relationship with the patient; document the issues, rationales, and choices made; and get consultation.

The following are some suggestions for proceeding:

- Decide whether it is "advisable and feasible to discuss the records with the patient prior to making them available in order to clarify matters" (Stromberg et al., 1988, p. 422).

- Then decide "which portions of the records should be revealed and which portions (if any) should not be" (Stromberg et al., 1988, p. 422).

- If the patient might be harmed, is there someone else (an advisor or family member) who can then represent the patient for the purpose of reviewing the record?

- If you decide that releasing certain information would not be in the patient's best interest if he or she were to read it, Woody (1988, p. 210) suggests that you should (1) obtain a release for that specific information, or (2) obtain a waiver from the patient of his or her right to have access to this report. You could also write a letter to the requester justifying your refusal to release damaging information, and base it on your local regulations. Here is an example:

  > The regulations of the Pennsylvania Department of Health govern a patient's access to his or her records: "The hospital shall provide the patient, upon request, access to all information contained in his (or her) records, unless access is specifically restricted by the attending physician for medical reasons" (Pa. Code 103.22 (b) (15)).
  >
  > I have discussed the release of these records with my attorney, and in my considered professional opinion, this patient should not have access to the following parts of the records that are attached:
  >
  > 1.
  >
  > 2.
  >
  > 3.
  >
  > I believe that the patient's coming to know the information contained in these parts will cause him or her to suffer mental anguish and pain without any balancing productive or beneficial effects. It is also, in my opinion, likely that reading this information will interfere with further treatment or cause the patient to lose gains already achieved.
  >
  > Because of these likely negative effects upon the patient, I strongly recommend that the information contained in these parts of the record not be disclosed to the patient. If you believe a situation arises in which it is absolutely necessary to disclose this information to the patient, I strongly recommend that this be done only by myself or a professional whom I designate, and not by you or any other person, professional, or organization who may obtain these records.

Prepare in advance for this possibility by adding language to your client information brochure. Section 4.2 includes this statement: "I may temporarily remove parts of your records before you see them. This would happen if I believe that the information will be harmful to you, but I will discuss this with you." Ideally, you have avoided using any language in the record that might exacerbate the emotional state of the client.

*Clients' Access to Their Records under HIPAA.*  In the past, patients have had little real ability to examine their own medical records. HIPAA has given them some ability to "access, inspect, and copy protected health information" (under Section 164.524).

A patient has the right to access, inspect, and obtain a copy of the PHI that you created unless one or more of the following applies:

- The information was collected for use in a legal proceeding (civil, criminal, or administrative).

- The information is in your psychotherapy notes.

- The patient was an inmate of a correctional institution for which you work.

- The information was generated as part of a research project that is still ongoing, and prior to entering the research the client agreed to delay access.

- The information was collected by a health care provider who was promised anonymity, and the information would reveal the identity of this person.

Denial of access for any of the above reasons is not a reviewable decision.

Access can also be denied it if it might harm the client. If, as a licensed health care provider, you come to believe that allowing the patient access to his or her PHI is likely to endanger the life, safety, or health of the patient or someone else, you can deny access. This denial can be appealed and reviewed by an additional licensed health care professional (see HIPAA Section 164.524[d][4]).

Access requests must be in writing and must be acted on within 30 days (for records on-site, and 60 days for those off-site) or formally extended for another 30 days. If you wholly or partly deny the request, you have to provide the denial in writing, in plain language, containing the basis for the denial, explaining the rights and procedures for a review of the denial, and explaining how, if he or she chooses to do so, the patient can complain to you or the Secretary of Health and Human Services (HHS) with names and phone numbers.

While the information would usually be in photocopied or printed form, it can be otherwise if the patient is amenable. You can provide a summary or explanation of the information if the patient agrees to this and to your fees for such a version. You can assess charges for copying and postage.

If you don't have the information sought by the patient but know who does, you must direct the patient there.

*Amending a Client's Record.* The HIPAA regulations (Section 164.526) describe how a patient may seek to amend, not "correct" records with PHI. You will provide a link, in the record, to the newer information.

You can refuse to amend your records (per HIPAA Section 164.526[d]) if one of the following is true:

- You didn't create the record. However, you may still amend it if you believe that the originator of the record is no longer available.

- The record would not otherwise be available for the patient to "access, inspect, and copy" it (see above).

- You believe the record is accurate and complete.

You should tell clients that they may be able to amend their records if they have good reason and make a request in writing. You will have to act on such a request within 60 days and either amend the record or deny the request in whole or in part. In either case you must inform the patient. If you agree to amend, you must make efforts to provide this amended record to others who the patient has identified or others who "may have relied, or could foreseeably rely, on such information to the detriment of the [patient]." If you deny the request you must explain in plain language, in writing, the basis for the denial; the client's right to and the procedure for submitting a written disagreement; a statement that you will, if the client requests it, include in future disclosures the client's request for amendment and the denial you made; and an explanation, including names and phone numbers, of how the patient can complain to the covered entity or the Secretary of HHS. The regulations allow you to limit the size of the client's request and to substitute a summary of the issues. Your records must indicate all of these exchanges and their outcome.

## 4. A Parent or Guardian's Request for Records

Parents and guardians have a right to know about minor children's status and progress. This is a right to *information* about the children's treatment, not full access to all their *records*. Remember, you own (or your agency owns) the actual records.

Minors, however, have few rights; so unless your state laws give them privilege, be careful what you write, and be diplomatic and therapeutic with the parents. (See also the forms for consent to treatment of children in Section 4.6.) Young children cannot claim confidentiality, but teens have "rights" to be respected. Be frank in advising children of their lack of these guarantees. You may also be able to negotiate with the parents to accept less information than they desire. Whether a parent is custodial or noncustodial usually makes no legal difference (Stromberg, Lindberg, Mishkin, & Baker, 1993).

If parents or guardians seem to be seeking more information than you think they or others need, try educating them before releasing the data. For example, explain that by their very nature, reports tend to focus on negatives or weaknesses (Sweet, 1990, p. 8). You can also explore the adults' motivations for seeking the records. Take into account parents' legal obligation to know in order to protect their children, as well as their emotional concerns for their children. If there is a difference of opinion about treatment, clarifying this through discussion, or perhaps sending records to another therapist for a "second opinion," may serve the parents' needs.

In custody cases, privilege may be overridden by the "best interests of the child." Try to get permission, at intake, to prevent your notes from being subpoenaed by one party if the other objects. The client information brochure (in Section 4.2) addresses this issue. And see Form 53 for a consent form for releasing information to family members.

## 5. A Subpoena[2]

If you receive a subpoena, do not release everything (or anything precipitously) just to be done with it. "A subpoena, which is a request for documents, is authorized by a court but actually is filled out and served by the attorney seeking the information" (Tepper et al., 1991, p. 14). You have to *respond* to a subpoena, but you do not have to *comply* with it. Your options include sending the requested information, challenging the relevance or validity of the subpoena by seeking to "quash" it, or refusing to comply on legal or ethical grounds

---

[2]Most of the quotations in this subsection are taken from Tepper, Rinella, and Siegel (1991). Copyright 1991 by the Pennsylvania Psychological Association. Reprinted by permission.

(e.g., privileged communication or local laws, regulations, or precedents). You may also negotiate sending a summary, or revealing information only in a private meeting with the judge. If you are reluctant to comply immediately, contact the attorney who has requested your records and find out "what type of legal action is pending, and why these materials are being requested. Let the attorney know that you are not attempting merely to avoid complying with the request, but, rather, that you yourself have certain ethical and legal obligations you must satisfy before releasing any patient information" (Tepper et al. 1991, p. 14). If you are still reluctant, "After obtaining the written consent of your patient, contact [the patient's] attorney, explain the situation, and see if the two attorneys can come to an agreeable resolution" (Tepper et al., 1991, p. 14).

What happens if you do not comply with a subpoena? Tepper et al. (1991, p. 14) continue: "Since a subpoena is a court authorized request, non-compliance technically puts you in contempt of court. However, the requesting attorney still must go to a judge to seek further compliance with the subpoena. If you have outlined the grounds for your initial refusal, you later will be able to argue that you acted in a reasonable fashion." If the court orders you to provide the information, you can either comply or appeal to a higher court:

> A court order is a document signed by a judge, requesting that certain materials be provided to a party named in the order. A court order may follow a subpoena or may be issued on its own. By its very nature, a court order indicates that a judge has already authorized the request. You may or may not agree with what you are being requested to do; however, failure to respond to the court order may result in a contempt hearing in which you will be required to explain your behavior before the issuing judge. Nonetheless, if you continue to have questions regarding the court order, such inquiries also may be directed to the requesting attorney, the opposing attorney, or the Court itself. At this stage, a consultation with your own attorney [will] also become necessary. (Tepper et al., 1991, p. 14)

Woody (1991) suggests placing a specific statement in your client information brochure. Because it is so specialized, it has not been included in the brochure in this book (Section 4.2), but it may suit your practice. Woody's statement is as follows:

> Notice: In the event that a subpoena for records or testimony is received, the policy will be that (1) the client will be notified in writing and provided with a copy of the subpoena; (2) the client must either provide the practitioner with a written waiver of objection to the subpoena (an authorization form for honoring the subpoena will be provided) or indicate that an objection will be filed with the court (with a copy send to the practitioner); and (3) if an objection to that subpoena is to be filed, it is the responsibility of the client to have it filed with the court. (p. 126)

The APA's Committee on Legal Issues (1996) has recently offered guidance on coping with subpoenas and the releasing of client records and test data. Some further suggestions for dealing with a subpoena are as follows:

- Make sure that any request you receive, even a subpoena, is valid and complete (see above). A subpoena is just a request and does not carry the weight of a court order.

- If you release any subpoenaed information, you can charge for it and for your time to prepare it.

- Harry Corsover, PhD, of Evergreen, CO, suggests that when you receive a subpoena, you negotiate with the lawyer and offer him or her some report choices like these: (1) a full mental health treatment report for the whole treatment or a part of it; (2) responses to specific questions; or (3) a detailed, session-by-session summary. The fee for each depends on the time it takes to prepare.

## 6. A Request to Which the Patient Does Not Consent

If the patient has not given his or her consent to a request for records (e.g., a subpoena from opposing counsel), discuss the issues fully with him or her to lessen any feelings of distrust and lower the risk of a suit for improper disclosure. Discuss the implications of the request and your planned response with the patient; he or she may then decide to give consent. Knapp (1994) also suggests that you encourage the patient to consult an attorney for advice. Here are some other suggestions:

- If you do not get consent or a disposition of the request agreed to by the requester, obtain a court ruling on whether the release is proper. Let the judge be your guide.

- In the absence of consent or a court order to release the records, verify that there is a basis for the release.

- Perhaps the patient cannot give consent. He or she may be a minor or may be ruled incompetent because of a variety of factors (significant mental retardation; dementia; intoxication on drugs, alcohol, or medications; etc.). The person seeking your records must seek "substitute consent" from the patient's parent or guardian, or from the court of jurisdiction.

## 7. A Request for Test Materials, Raw Data, or Protocols of Evaluation

There are few if any laws about the release of records of evaluations (as opposed to the release of treatment records), but it is likely to be treated similarly by the courts (Stromberg, Lindberg, Mishkin, & Baker, 1993). The APA Committee on Psychological Tests and Assessment (1996) has issued guidelines on disclosing test data, accessing records, and providing feedback to the test taker. In these situations, your ethical responsibility is to maintain "test security" for the valid evaluation of future patients. The APA ethics code (APA, 2002, Standard 9.04) prohibits the release of raw test results and data to unqualified persons such as judges and attorneys; your local codes of professional conduct may also prevent you from releasing raw data or test materials. Tranel (1994, p. 35) suggests a simple strategy: Advise the attorney or other to hire a psychologist consultant "who is qualified by virtue of licensure, training, and experience, to receive the data" and send the data to this psychologist, with the patient's consent. Tranel also points out that this consultant "must operate under the same rules and standards of ethics and confidentiality" as you do. (See also Form 53.)

## 8. The Need to Share Records with a Consultant or Referrer

The principle about sharing records with a consultant or referrer is that if the patient has approved of the consultation or has accepted the referral to you or to another professional, you do not need a signed release (American Psychiatric Association, 1987). If you are operating under the HIPAA regulations, the client's initial consent allows full sharing of all relevant information among all treaters. However, if you have any doubts because of the kind or amount of material to be discussed or about the patient's understanding, get a signed release. (See APA, 2002, Standard 4.06.)

## Guidelines and Considerations in Sending Records

- It bears repeating: Never send the originals of your records anywhere. The only exception might be a legal copying service arranged by your lawyer. And, speaking of lawyers, never let a patient's lawyer do any copying of your records.

- If you decide to release records, consider the extent of necessary disclosure, and ways to continue to protect confidentiality as much as possible.

- Never copy and send your whole record, because it may contain material irrelevant to the issues at hand. Ideally, you will be able to discuss the issues, costs and benefits, and implications of releasing records with a client. Hamberger (2000) offers many specific topics and language for such a discussion, and reports that about 60% of clients who originally asked to have their entire records released changed their minds after full discussions.

- Consider the possibility that the patient may read the records, reports, or materials you are sending.

- Weigh the best way to organize and present the necessary information. For example, send written records instead of discussing the contents of the records over the telephone, because this will make it clearer what has and has not been disclosed. If a release must be oral, confirm in writing the contents released as soon as possible. Use fax only when you are sure of confidentiality (see Section 7.6).

- Prepare and retain careful documentation on the following:

  Your discussions with the patient and the patient's responses to the issues involved in the release, such as the content of your records and the nature of confidentiality.

  The information ultimately released, the release date, and the person or agency to whom or which it is provided. Record on the release before making copies (see below) which pages are included; what forms, letters, or notes are enclosed; and so on.

  Either the release signed by the patient (or his or her legal representative), or the response why a duty to disclose without consent seems to exist.

- Both release forms and requests for records to be released by another provider (see Section 7.4) should be prepared in triplicate—an original and two photocopies, each signed in ink (preferably blue so that it is clear that the signature has not been photocopied). These should be distributed as follows: one for the patient or his or her guardian; one for the party releasing the information; and one for the party receiving the information.

- Notifying the recipient that this is sensitive material is important and can be accomplished in several ways. You can use the more specific notices provided in Section 7.7; use your computer's printer to print them as labels on peel-off paper, or have your word processor put the notice in a "header" or "footer" on every page. Some therapists have had a rubber stamp made up with one of the confidentiality notices from Section 7.7, which they then stamp on each page released. But note that a stamp for each page that says simply "Do not copy" or "Confidential" or "Personal and confidential" is probably not legally sufficient notification. In addition, enclose an explanatory, cautioning, and educational cover letter with all records you send. Form 49 can be used for this purpose.

- If you are asked to send the record to anyone whose credentials you don't know or recognize, write or speak to him or her and suggest that you could send the records directly to a different and more appropriately qualified professional for interpretation (with, of course, a new release form).

- Although discretion and sensitivity to the client's wishes in releasing information are appropriate (as in providing selective disclosure), providing false information (e.g., a different diagnosis than in the records) is unethical (Stromberg et al., 1988, p. 392).

- You can certainly charge for copying your records and sending them. A charge of $10 to $15 seems to be common, but do charge more if your efforts justify the cost. Make certain to include and clearly mark your federal tax identification number or Social Security number on your bill or you will waste a lot of time on the phone when requesters want to pay you. It seems fair to charge for records requested by non-health-care professionals who will make a profit from the record (e.g., lawyers, insurance companies). I would not charge for a record sent to the patient or his or her face-to-face health care provider (not an agency). If a patient requests that I send copies to several providers, I might send a single copy to the patient and let him or her arrange things.

- In summary, "the overriding rule is *'When in doubt, don't give it out!'* (The next rule, of course, is *'If still in doubt, call your redoubtable lawyer'*)" (Stromberg et al., 1988, p. 389; emphasis in original).

The HIPAA regulations greatly simplify the above procedures for obtaining consent to share information (see Section 7.8), but the issues discussed above are still relevant and must be considered.

## Comments on the Pretest

At the beginning of this section (pp. 382–383), I offered a case example from Pope (1988e) that raises many of the issues just examined. Would your answers now be different from your earlier responses? Here is my best understanding of this situation.

First, I would not send the tests' data or copies of the tests to anyone, citing in my cover letter both the inability of nonpsychologists (all of the requesters) to interpret the tests' data, and the ethical and professional need to maintain the security of the tests. I would also mention in this letter that if the requesters, after reading my letter or report, believed they had a need for the raw data or for test copies, I would consider releasing these to another sufficiently qualified psychologist who could interpret them for the requesters. I would add that they should arrange this.

Second, I would contact the young man and tell him of the requests I had received. The issue to be dealt with is the degree to which this man understood the content and implications of my report's contents. If he did not, he could not informedly release the report. I would suggest that he and I meet (at his expense) to discuss the contents, and that he consult his lawyer about the report's consequences in regard to each of the intended recipients, especially his own and the other attorneys.

Third, I would indicate to each requester that I would be willing to create a version of my report that might answer specific questions each might raise, but that since I did not know the requester's needs, I would be very reluctant to release a full report containing a great deal of material that was likely to be irrelevant to the requester's needs, might easily be misunderstood, and could embarrass my client. I would offer to produce these revised reports at my usual per-hour fee, to be paid by the requesters, in advance. As the requesters would probably not initially accept this proposal, I would telephone each one, attempt to clarify his or her needs for information, and discuss (in a general way) whether or not my report might contain information to meet their needs.

There are, to be sure, other concerns and responses.

# 7.4    Forms for Requesting and Releasing Information

Both the briefer form (Form 47) and the longer form (Form 48) provided in this section give you the option of using them either to have a client release your records, or to request records from another provider.

## A Briefer Request/Release Form

**FORM 47**  The following form (Form 47) is a simple and multipurpose one-page document and should meet most of your needs. It can be used for a child or an adult; it can be used either to obtain or to release records; and it leaves spaces to write in some specifics.

## A More Comprehensive Request/Release Form

**FORM 48**  I use the following form (Form 48) when I have little confidence in the ethical sophistication of the professional to whom I am sending it. It contains formal and legal language that may impress its recipient, and it cites all the regulations; it may thus educate (or intimidate) the recipient into following ethical practices, such as fully informing the client about what is to be released and what will be done with the information. This longer form has some useful additions and advantages over typical request/release forms:

- It meets the special standards for requesting/releasing drug and alcohol treatment records (see part C).

- It allows telephone contacts (see part D), which is a convenience.

- It includes a release of liability (see part H).

- It adds an authorization to make photocopies for sending multiple records or keeping some copies for later use (see part J).

# Request/Authorization to Release Confidential Records and Information

I hereby authorize:

Person or facility: _____

_____

Address: _____

_____ Phone: _____

to release information from records about _____, born on _____,

and whose Social Security number is_____, for the following purpose(s):

❏ Further mental health evaluation, treatment, or care  ❏ Rehabilitation program development or services

❏ Treatment planning  ❏ Research  ❏ Other: _____

These records concern the time between _____ and _____.

The information to be disclosed is marked by an × in the boxes below, and the items not to be released have a line drawn through them. Page numbers are indicated when appropriate. Written dates indicate when those records were mailed to the requester.

❏ Intake and discharge summaries _____  ❏ Medical history and evaluation(s) _____

❏ Mental health evaluations _____  ❏ Developmental and/or social history _____  ❏ Educational records _____

❏ Progress notes, and treatment or closing summary _____  ❏ Other: _____

Select only one:

❏ Please forward the records to the address in the letterhead at the top of this form.

❏ Please forward the records to the address written above.

HIV-related information and drug and alcohol information contained in these records will be released under this consent unless indicated here:  ❏ Do not release.

I have had explained to me and fully understand this request/authorization to release records and information, including the nature of the records, their contents, and the consequences and implications of their release. This request is entirely voluntary on my part. I understand that I may take back this consent at any time within 90 days, except to the extent that action based on this consent has already been taken. This consent will expire automatically after 90 days from the date on which it is signed, or upon fulfillment of the purposes stated above.

| _____ | _____ | _____ |
| Signature of client | Printed name | Date |

| _____ | _____ | _____ | _____ |
| Signature of parent/ guardian/representative | Printed name | Relationship | Date |

I witnessed that the person understood the nature of this request/authorization and freely gave his or her consent, but was physically unable to provide a signature.

| _____ | _____ | _____ |
| Signature of witness | Printed name | Date |

❏ Copy for patient or parent/guardian  ❏ Copy for source of records  ❏ Copy for recipient of records

---

**FORM 47. Briefer form for requesting/releasing confidential records and information.** From *The Paper Office.*
Copyright 2003 by Edward L. Zuckerman. Permission to photocopy this form is granted to purchasers of this book for personal use only (see copyright page for details).

# Request/Authorization to Release Confidential Records and Information

**A.** Person or facility: _____

_____

Address: _____

_____ Phone: _____

**B.** Identifying information about me/the patient

Name: _____

Address: _____

_____

Phone: _____ Birthdate: _____ Social Security #: _____

Parent/guardian (if applicable): _____

Address and phone of parent/guardian: _____

_____

**C.** I hereby authorize the source named above to send, as promptly as possible, the records listed below marked by an × in the boxes below. (The items not to be released have a line drawn through them.) Page numbers are indicated where appropriate. Written dates (other than those regarding inpatient admission/outpatient treatment) indicate when those records were mailed to the requester.

❑ Inpatient or outpatient treatment records for physical and/or psychological, psychiatric, or emotional illness or drug or alcohol abuse:

Date(s) of inpatient admission: _____ Date(s) of outpatient treatment: _____

Other identifying information about the service(s) rendered: _____

❑ Psychological evaluation(s) or testing records, and behavioral observations or checklists completed by any staff member or by the patient.

❑ Psychiatric evaluations, reports, or treatment notes and summaries.

❑ Treatment plans, recovery plans, aftercare plans.

❑ Admission and discharge summaries.

❑ Social histories, assessments with diagnoses, prognoses, recommendations, and all similar documents.

❑ Information about how the patient's condition affects or has affected his or her ability to complete tasks, activities of daily living, or ability to work.

❑ Workshop reports and other vocational evaluations and reports.

❑ Billing records.

❑ Academic or educational records.

❑ Report of teachers' observations.

❑ Achievement and other tests' results.

❑ A letter containing dates of treatment(s) and a summary of progress.

❑ HIV-related information and drug and alcohol information contained in these records will be released under this consent unless indicated here: ❑ Do not release.

❑ Other: _____

*(cont.)*

---

**FORM 48. Requesting or releasing confidential records and information (p. 1 of 2).** From *The Paper Office*.

Copyright 2003 by Edward L. Zuckerman. Permission to photocopy this form is granted to purchasers of this book for personal use only (see copyright page for details).

**D.** Select only one:

❑ Please forward the records to the address in the letterhead at the top of this form.

❑ Please forward the records to the address written above.

**E.** I authorize the source named above to speak by telephone with the therapist identified in part N about the reasons for my/the patient's referral, any relevant history or diagnoses, and other similar information that can assist with my/the patient's receiving treatment or being evaluated or referred elsewhere.

**F.** I understand that no services will be denied me/the patient solely because I refuse to consent to this release of information, and that I am not in any way obligated to release these records. I do release them because I believe that they are necessary to assist in the development of the best possible treatment plan for me/the patient. The information disclosed may be used in connection with my/the patient's treatment.

**G.** This request/authorization to release confidential information is being made in compliance with the terms of the Privacy Act of 1974 (Public Law 93-579) and the Freedom of Information Act of 1974 (Public Law 93-502); and pursuant to Federal Rule of Evidence 1158 (Inspection and Copying of Records upon Patient's Written Authorization). This form is to serve as both a general authorization, and a special authorization to release information under the Drug Abuse Office and Treatment Act of 1972 (Public Law 92-255), the Comprehensive Alcohol Abuse and Alcoholism Prevention, Treatment and Rehabilitation Act Amendments of 1974 (Public Law 93-282), the Veterans Omnibus Health Care Act of 1976 (Public Law 94-581), and the Veterans Benefit and Services Act of 1988 (Public Law 100-322). It is also in compliance with 42 C.F.R. Part 2 (Public Law 93-282), which prohibits further disclosure without the express written consent of the person to whom it pertains, or as otherwise permitted by such regulations.

**H.** In consideration of this consent, I hereby release the source of the records from any and all liability arising therefrom.

**I.** This request/authorization is valid during the pendency of any claim or demand made by or in behalf of me/the patient, and arising out of an accident, injury, or occurrence to me/the patient. I understand that I may void this request/authorization, except for action already taken, at any time by means of a written letter revoking the authorization and transfer of information, but that this revocation is not retroactive. If I do not void this request/authorization, it will automatically expire in 90 days from the date I signed it.

**J.** I agree that a photocopy of this form is acceptable, but it must be individually signed by me, the releaser, and a witness if necessary.

**K.** I have been informed of the risks to privacy and limitations on confidentiality of the use of electronic means of information transfer, and I accept these.

**L.** I affirm that everything in this form that was not clear to me has been explained. I also understand that I have the right to receive a copy of this form upon my request.

**M.** Signatures:

| | | |
|---|---|---|
| _____ | _____ | _____ |
| Signature of client | Printed name | Date |

| | | | |
|---|---|---|---|
| _____ | _____ | _____ | _____ |
| Signature of parent/<br>guardian/representative | Printed name | Relationship | Date |

I witnessed that the person understood the nature of this request/authorization and freely gave his or her consent, but was physically unable to provide a signature.

| | | |
|---|---|---|
| _____ | _____ | _____ |
| Signature of witness | Printed name | Date |

**N.** I, a mental health professional, have discussed the issues above with the patient and/or his or her parent or guardian. My observations of behavior and responses give me no reason to believe that this person is not fully competent to give informed and willing consent.

| | | |
|---|---|---|
| _____ | _____ | _____ |
| Signature of professional | Printed name | Date |

❑ Copy for patient or parent/guardian  ❑ Copy for source of records  ❑ Copy for recipient of records

- It documents the client's acceptance of the inevitable and not foreseeable risks of transferring information by electronic means, such as fax, e-mail, and other methods not yet common (see part K). Informed consent to this is an ethical responsibility (see APA, 2002, Standard 4.02c).

- It offers your opinion that the signer is competent (see part N).

As always, you can tailor this form to your needs in various ways. You may want to add any other specific records you regularly request to the list in part C.

Other changes you can make to Form 48 include the following:

- If you are not doing treatment, you might want to change the wording at the end of part F to indicate your need and the uses or purposes of the disclosure of the records.

- Releases must have time limits. The one in part I says "90 days," but if that is insufficient, you can replace it with a longer time or this sentence: "It shall be valid no longer than is reasonably necessary to meet the purposes stated above, and not to exceed 1 year."

- You can add one or both of these sentences to part L: "I further understand that I have the right to inspect and copy any of the information I request/authorize for release," and/or "This therapist and I have explored the likely consequences of waiving the privilege of confidentiality."

- In the signatures section (part M), you might want to consider that the older a child is, the more his or her wishes should be considered and honored. So even if your state does not legally give power to an adolescent, you might want to make him or her a participant by having him or her sign the form.

Forms 47 and 48 can even be made interactive by inserting language like that below. (However, I do not know whether this has been tested in a legal setting.)

---

I, _____ request and authorize the two parties listed below to release to each other all information and records either party may have created (about my history, symptoms, diagnoses, functioning, treatments, prognoses, etc.). These parties are:

_____ and _____

---

## 7.5    More Specific Forms for Releasing Information

### A Release-of-Records Cover Letter

It is standard practice to provide a cover letter to accompany any records you sent to another professional or organization; this informs the recipient of his or her legal and ethical responsibilities. Or, if for some reason you cannot release a patient's records as requested, you must, of course, write a letter to explain the reason for the refusal.

**FORM 49**  The form letter provided below (Form 49) can serve either of these purposes. Its thoroughness can save you effort and impress medical record sophisticates (such as registered record librarians, some physicians, and defense lawyers). However, you may have to modify it to suit your setting, local laws, and practice. For example, if you operate in Pennsylvania, you can add the following protected-information disclosure notices after the one provided for drug and alcohol disclosure. If you work elsewhere, substitute your local versions.

---

*Psychiatric disclosure—55 Pa. Code Section 5100.34.* This information has been disclosed to you from records whose confidentiality is protected by state law. State regulations prohibit you from making any further disclosure of this information without the prior written consent of the person to whom it pertains.

*HIV disclosure—the Confidentiality of HIV-Related Information Act (1990).* This information has been disclosed to you from records protected by Pennsylvania law. Pennsylvania law prohibits you from making any further disclosure of this information unless further disclosure is expressly permitted by the written consent of the person to whom it pertains or is authorized by the Confidentiality of HIV-Related Information Act. A general authorization for the release of medical or other information is not sufficient for this purpose.

---

The information in records can become outdated, inaccurate, and misleading, and releasing it can be harmful to the client's interests. The APA's record-keeping guidelines (APA, Committee on Professional Practice and Standards, 1993) and the ethics code (APA, 2002, Standard 9.08) require that when this is the case, you clearly indicate their limited utility or invalidity.

Also, if you don't keep records for a prolonged period, you could substitute the following for the current first option under "I am unable to comply ... ":

---

❑ My office policy is to retain patients' records for 12 years and then destroy them. In accord with this policy, the records you have asked for no longer exist. I can state only that this person was treated by me between the dates of _____ and _____.

---

## Releasing Psychological Test Results

Psychologists have resisted allowing the public, lawyers, or anyone untrained in their interpretation to see raw test data, such as protocols of answers given to test questions and the questions themselves. There are three rationales for maintaining such "test security":

1.  The data would be misunderstood by anyone not trained in their use. The same would apply to X-rays or laboratory test results; only those qualified to interpret the client's responses or the conclusions drawn from them should have access. In fact, the publishers of all high-quality tests restrict who can purchase their materials, to ensure that only those who have the training to understand the tests' appropriate clients and limitations can buy them.

2.  If the test questions became widely known, they would lose their discriminant validity. People seeking to present themselves as ill or incapable would learn how to "fake

Re: the following patient: _____ Date of birth: _____

Dear Sir or Madam:

Regarding the information you requested in a request-for-information form or consent-to-release-records form dated
_____:

❏ Please find attached the records or information you requested on the above-named patient. The charge for copying these records is $_____. Please forward this amount with the same courtesy, trust, and dispatch as my staff and I have used in collecting and providing this information to you. Thank you.

Also, please note the following points:

1. *Protected-information disclosure notice: Drug and alcohol disclosure.* This information has been disclosed to you from records whose confidentiality is protected by state and federal law. Federal regulations (42 C.F.R. Part 2, Sections 2.31(a) and 2.33) and state regulations prohibit you from making any further disclosure of it without the specific written consent of the person to whom it pertains, or as otherwise permitted by such regulations. A general authorization for the release of medical or other information is not sufficient for this purpose. These regulations provide for a fine of up to $500 for the first offense and up to $5,000 for each subsequent offense.

2. This is strictly confidential material and is for the information of only the person to whom it is addressed. I can accept no responsibility if it is made available to any other person, *including the patient.* Redisclosure or retransfer of these records is expressly prohibited, and such redisclosure may subject you to civil and criminal liability.

3. Federal and state rules restrict use of this information to criminally investigate or prosecute any alcohol or drug abuse patient.

❏ I have completed the form or forms you sent and have enclosed them.

❏ You have sent a form for me to complete, which will take some of my professional time. If you wish this done, please forward, in the next 10 days, the sum of $_____ to pay for the additional service.

❏ According to my records, this information was sent to you on _____. If you have not received it, please call this office and send another copy of your Request for Information Form.

❏ Enclosed are the remaining records you requested. The other records were sent to you on _____.

❏ I am unable to comply with your request for these records, because:

   ❏ All records are destroyed after 7 years following the date of the last visit. Records of minor patients (14 years and younger) are retained for 7 years after they are no longer minors. Enclosed is the only available information.

   ❏ The records you are seeking are not complete at this time. I will send the records as soon as they are completed.

   ❏ No authorization or release was enclosed with your request. I cannot release records without such an authorization or release.

*(cont.)*

---

**FORM 49. A release-of-records form letter (p. 1 of 2).** From *The Paper Office.* Copyright 2003 by Edward L. Zuckerman. Permission to photocopy this form is granted to purchasers of this book for personal use only (see copyright page for details).

❏ After a thorough search of the records, my staff and I are unable to locate any record on this person with the information you provided. Please check to see whether he or she may have used another name when treated by me, or provide additional information to help us locate the records, such as date of birth, Social Security number, or dates of service.

❏ I am sure that I have not provided service to this person.

❏ I have not provided service to this person during the time period covered by the release.

❏ I did not originate the records you requested, and so cannot release them.

❏ The information you requested is not available here. You might try contacting: _____.

❏ The authorization enclosed was deficient because it is or was:

    ❏ Not dated, or not dated after treatment ended.

    ❏ Dated more than 6 months prior to the receipt of your request.

    ❏ Not sufficiently specific. Please indicate exactly what information is needed.

    ❏ Not legally adequate.

    ❏ For a minor patient, but had no signed authorization by one or both parents or a guardian. (If the latter is the case, proof of guardianship is also required.)

    ❏ For an emancipated minor, and so a parent's or guardian's signature is not acceptable.

    ❏ Signed by someone other than the patient. Such authorizations must be signed by the patient unless the patient is physically or mentally unable to do so.

    ❏ Signed illegibly, and so I am unable to verify that it is the signature of the patient.

❏ Your request/authorization/consent-to-release records form does not conform to the requirements of state/federal regulations covering the release of confidential records. Because of the nature of the information contained in this record, a general medical consent form cannot be accepted. Specifically, it _____
_____.

    ❏ I have enclosed a form for you to execute.

❏ The patient is deceased, so an authorization must be signed by the next of kin or the administrator of the estate, and appropriate documentation is required (i.e., death certificate/short form, proof of being the executor of the patient's estate, letters of administration, or power of attorney).

❏ This information is not released directly to patients or families because of the potential for its misinterpretation, misuse, or misunderstanding. Because it may have been generated to address psychological distress and psychopathology, there may be only slight or no attention paid to strengths and positive characteristics of the client. Statements in it require interpretation and explanation by an appropriately trained and licensed professional. If you want this information released, please send the name and address of a professional who would understand this information and a suitable request-for-information form or consent-to-release records form.

❏ Other reason: _____.

If you have any questions, please do not hesitate to contact me. If you need additional information, please return this letter with your second request for information or records.

Sincerely yours,

bad," and those wishing to conceal deficits and disorders would be able to "fake good." Disability evaluations, forensic testing, and academic assessments would lose the capability of distinguishing between people with and without psychological problems. Thus the tests' ability to provide useful information to society would be crippled.

3. The test materials are copyrighted by their creators, and so they may not be given away or made public in a way that would lessen their sales. The tests' authors have legal control over their distribution.

These three reasons are incorporated into the ethical prohibition in Standards 9.04 and 9.11 of the APA's code of ethics (APA, 2002). However, this standard recognizes the complexities of releases made with client approval. Do consult and keep abreast of developments in this area.

*Note:* Forms for permission to test or evaluate a person are provided in Chapter 4 (Forms 18 and 19).

**FORM 50**    Sometimes you will be specifically requested to send the results of a psychological evaluation to another professional or agency. Form 50 can be used as an authorization form for this purpose. This form is modified from one by Ruth H. Sosis, PhD, of Avondale, OH, and is adapted with her kind permission. (Note that, like Forms 47 and 48 but unlike the other forms in this section, Form 50 can also be used to *request* information.)

## Releasing Information to an Attorney

**FORM 51**    The sending of records or reports to a client's attorney should be accompanied by the same consent elements as the sending of records to anyone else. In addition, the release form, offered here as Form 51 authorizes your deposition, testimony, and other ways of sharing information. It also adds wording designed to protect you and to assure payment in a legal case where deferring (part of) your payment may be necessary but is not contingent on the outcome of the case.

When lawyers have sought raw test data and test materials for their own psychologist consultants to examine, there are often few problems, because both psychologists are more or less equally trained and bound by the same code of ethics. However, lawyers have often sought such materials to cross-examine psychologists, test by test, question, by question and even interpretation by interpretation.

The proper procedure is to release such materials (with the written consent of the client) only to those qualified to interpret them. Ask the attorney for the name and qualifications of his or her psychologist consultant, and ask that this person sign a statement such as "I agree to protect the test materials in accordance with the principles set forth in the APA Ethical Principles of Psychologists and Code of Conduct." For all other cases, such as a subpoena signed by a judge or a court order, you will have to explain your concerns to the judge and try to negotiate a release that maintains the test security. Excellent initial guidance can be found at http://www.nanonline.org/paid/security.shtm.

Incidentally, you should not accept contingency fees, in which you will get paid only if the client wins a judgment. That arrangement could prejudice your professional opinion, make it appear worthless, and compromise your reputation. You can be certain that opposing

# Request/Authorization for Release of Evaluation Information

Client: _____

Address: _____

Phone: _____ Birthdate: _____ Social Security #: _____

Regarding the administration of psychological tests, I give my permission to (select only one):

   ❑ the professional named in the letterhead at the top of this form, or

   ❑ _____

   of _____

   _____

to release the results of the tests taken by me/the patient, in order to:

   ❑ Assist with treatment planning

   ❑ Document a need for services

   ❑ Support an application for _____

   ❑ Other: _____

and to send these records to (select only one):

   ❑ the professional named in the letterhead, or to

   ❑ _____

   of _____

   _____

I hereby release the person or organization sending these records and results from any liability associated with administering, scoring, interpreting, evaluating, reporting, or transmitting the results of these tests.

I understand that the records, information, or results will not be given to me by the evaluator.

| _____ | _____ | _____ |
| Signature of client | Printed name | Date |

| _____ | _____ | _____ | _____ |
| Signature of parent/ guardian/representative | Printed name | Relationship | Date |

I witnessed that the person understood the nature of this request/authorization and freely gave his or her consent, but was physically unable to provide a signature.

| _____ | _____ | _____ |
| Signature of witness | Printed name | Date |

❑ Copy for client or parent/guardian  ❑ Copy for source of records  ❑ Copy for recipient of records

**FORM 50. Request/authorization for release of evaluation information.** Adapted from a form devised by Ruth H. Sosis, PhD, of Cincinnati, OH, and used by permission of Dr. Sosis.—From *The Paper Office*. Permission to photocopy this form is granted to purchasers of this book for personal use only (see copyright page for details).

## Authorization to Release Confidential Information to an Attorney

I do hereby authorize you, the clinician named in the letterhead above, to furnish to _____,
my attorney, at _____,
with a full report of your examination, diagnosis, treatments, prognosis, and any other records concerning me/the
patient named _____ in regard to the accident/incident/condition
for which I/the patient sought your services, which began on _____.

I authorize you, the clinician, to answer any and all questions or other requests for information from my attorney
regarding my/this patient's treatment by you, and to appear and to testify regarding my/this patient's treatment and records at depositions or in court or any administrative proceedings.

I completely waive and release any rights of confidentiality I may have concerning these records and information,
and agree to hold the clinician harmless and to indemnify him or her from any and all claims made against him or her in
connection with the release or transfer of these records and information as here authorized.

I understand and accept that I am directly and fully responsible to you, the clinician, for all bills submitted for services you render to me/this patient, and that this agreement is made solely for your additional protection and in consideration of your awaiting payment. I understand that submission of your reports or other written materials may be contingent upon settlement of this account. And I further understand that such payment is not contingent on any
settlement, judgment, or verdict by which I/this patient may eventually recover monies, and that I am responsible for
this payment.

I hereby authorize and direct my attorney to pay directly to you such sums as may be due and owing to you for
mental health/psychological/counseling services rendered to me/this patient, by reason of any other settlement, judgment, or award that may be paid to you, my attorney, or me/the patient as the result of the injuries/incident/condition
for which I have/the patient has been evaluated or treated, or any other litigation on my/the patient's behalf. I hereby
state my intention and desire that you be paid at the time you provide services, no matter what is common practice or
the legal decisions made.

I affirm that everything in this form that was not clear to me has been explained to my satisfaction.

A photocopy of this release is to be considered as valid as the original.

| | | |
|---|---|---|
| _____ | _____ | _____ |
| Signature of client | Printed name | Date |
| _____ | _____ | _____ |
| Signature of parent/ | Printed name | Relationship    Date |
| guardian/representative | | |

I witnessed that the person understood the nature of this request/authorization and freely gave his or her consent,
but was physically unable to provide a signature.

| | | |
|---|---|---|
| _____ | _____ | _____ |
| Signature of witness | Printed name | Date |

**For the Attorney:**

The undersigned, being attorney of record for the above-named patient, does hereby agree to observe all the
terms described above, and also agrees to withhold such sums from any settlement, judgment, or award as may be necessary to adequately protect the above-named clinician or otherwise to guarantee reimbursement.

| | | |
|---|---|---|
| _____ | _____ | _____ |
| Signature of attorney | Printed name | Date |

**Please date, sign, and return one copy to the clinician's office and keep one copy for your records.**

❏ Copy for client or parent/guardian    ❏ Copy for clinician    ❏ 2 copies for attorney

---

**FORM 51. Authorization to release confidential information to an attorney.** From *The Paper Office*. Copyright
2003 by Edward L. Zuckerman. Permission to photocopy this form is granted to purchasers of this book for personal use only (see copyright page for details).

counsel will ask you whether your fee is contingent. If so, this will be used as a means of disparaging your findings. The number of similar evaluations and testimonies you have done can also be used to present you either as inexperienced or as a possible "hired gun" if you do a lot of testifying.

The third paragraph of this form waives confidentiality and requires discussion with the client and his or her attorney. The general principle is that confidentiality cannot be waived partially, so once it is waived, all contents of the record are available to both sides. As noted earlier in this chapter, confidentiality cannot be used as "both a shield and a sword"; that is, you cannot release only the evidence that favors your client's side. (However, courts frequently will suppress irrelevant information when asked to do so.) Therefore, all the contents of the record and the implications of those contents should be fully explored before the decision to release is made.

### Releasing Records to an Insurance Company or Other Third-Party Payer

You will probably be sending various kind of information to insurance companies, MCOs, government agencies, and similar programs to support reimbursement or payments from health insurance policies. In most cases the information is routine and nonthreatening, and usually a release signed by the person insured is attached to or part of the form requesting the information. Form 52 specifically reminds the recipient of the applicable federal confidentiality laws, and so may add some protection for both you and your patient.

**FORM 52**

### Releasing Information to the Patient's Family

What should a therapist tell the patient's family about the patient? There is always the potential for conflict between a family's legitimate right to information about its members and the therapist's obligation to keep information confidential (Zipple et al., 1990). For example, the spouse of a patient may ask a question, or the adult child of an older patient may inquire. Unless the issue of who has a right to know is clarified, staff members may refuse to provide simple and nondisruptive information about a patient to an appropriate family member, because "We do not reveal patient information" (Marsh, 1995). Getting a form such as Form 53 signed early in treatment can lessen problems. If you intend to release significantly different information to different persons/relatives, use several versions of this form.

**FORM 53**  Form 53, adapted from Marsh (1995), can empower both the patient and family by making the process and content of family communications more explicit and informed. It sets boundaries, specifies contact persons, and then allows you to negotiate the exact information to be supplied with all parties.

## 7.6   Confidentiality When Faxing Records or Sending E-Mail

If you send clinical information by facsimile machine, you risk compromising its confidentiality. It could be mistakenly sent to the wrong person or department by misdialing; It could be seen by inappropriate people at the receiving end; and/or it could be read by

[The third party's name and address should go here.]

Re: _____

Birthdate: _____

SS #: _____

# Authorization to Release Confidential Information to a Health Insurer or Other Third-Party Payer

**A.** This form authorizes the provider named in the letterhead above to release information from the patient's/my records maintained while the patient/I was treated by this provider during _____ or from _____ to _____.

**B.** The information to be disclosed is marked by an × in the boxes below, and any items not to be released have a line drawn through them. Dates written in blanks at the ends of lines indicate when those records were mailed to the requester.

❑ Intake forms, clinical records, summaries, treatment plans, and similar clinical documents. _____

❑ Psychological evaluation(s) or testing records, and behavioral observations or checklists completed by any staff member or by the patient/myself. _____

❑ Psychiatric evaluations, reports, or treatment notes and summaries. _____

❑ Treatment plans, recovery plans, aftercare plans. _____

❑ Admission and discharge summaries. _____

❑ Social histories, assessments, with diagnoses, prognoses, recommendations, and all similar documents. _____

❑ Information about how the patient's/my condition affects or has affected the patient's/my ability to complete tasks and activities of daily living, or about how the patient's/my condition affects or has affected the patient's/my ability to work. _____

❑ Workshop reports and other vocational evaluations and reports. _____

❑ Billing records. _____

❑ Academic or educational records. _____

❑ Reports of teachers' observations. _____

❑ Achievement and other tests' results. _____

❑ A letter containing dates of treatment(s) and a summary of progress. _____

❑ Other: _____

**C.** HIV-related information and drug and alcohol information contained in these records will be released under this consent unless indicated here:  ❑ Do not release. _____

**D.** This information is to be sent to the third-party payer or its agents named above, and is needed for the following purpose(s):

❑ Receiving health insurance benefits, reimbursements, payments for related services, or other similar decisions.

❑ Applying for life, disability, or other insurance.

❑ Other: _____

*(cont.)*

FORM 52. **Authorization to release confidential information to a health insurer or other third-party payer (p. 1 of 2).** From *The Paper Office.* Copyright 2003 by Edward L. Zuckerman. Permission to photocopy this form is granted to purchasers of this book for personal use only (see copyright page for details).

**E.** I understand that, by law, I need not consent to the release of this information. This information is not required for my/the patient's treatment. However, I willingly choose to release it for the purpose(s) specified above. I understand that I may revoke this release at any time within 90 days, except to the extent that action has been taken in reliance on my consent.

**F.** Also, **please note the following points:**

1. This information has been disclosed to you from **records whose confidentiality is protected by state and federal law.** Federal regulations (42 C.F.R. Part 2, Sections 2.31(a) and 2.33) and state regulations prohibit you from making any further disclosure of it without the specific written consent of the person to whom it pertains, or as otherwise permitted by such regulations.

2. This is **strictly confidential material** and is for the information of only persons who are professionally capable of understanding, appreciating, and acting upon it according to their specific and advanced professional training in the mental health field. Please restrict the availability of these records to those persons in your employ who have the training and experience to interpret and understand the information contained in them. These ethical and legal responsibilities are yours. No responsibility can be accepted by the provider or author of these records if this material is made available to any other person or persons who lack such training, or who would not treat it in a professionally responsible manner, or who otherwise should not have access to it, *including the patient.*

3. Redisclosure or retransfer of these records is expressly prohibited, and such redisclosure may subject you to civil and criminal liability.

4. Federal and state rules restrict any use of the information to criminally investigate or prosecute any alcohol or drug abuse patient.

**G. Assignment of health insurance benefits:** My signature below authorizes the payment, directly to the above-named provider, of benefits payable under my policy. I understand that such payments will be credited to my account with this provider. I further understand that I am financially responsible to this provider for charges not covered or reimbursed by my policy, up to the fee the provider has agreed to accept.

**H. For Medicare patients only:** I request that payment of authorized benefits be made to the provider listed above on my behalf. I authorize any holder of medical information about me to release to the Centers for Medicare and Medicaid Services and its agents any information needed to determine those benefits or the benefits payable for related services.

**I.** I affirm that everything in this form that was not clear to me has been explained to my satisfaction.

**J.** A photocopy of this release is to be considered as valid as the original.

**K.** Signatures:

| | | |
|---|---|---|
| _____ | _____ | _____ |
| Signature of client | Printed name | Date |

| | | | |
|---|---|---|---|
| _____ | _____ | _____ | _____ |
| Signature of parent/ guardian/representative | Printed name | Relationship | Date |

I witnessed that the person understood the nature of this request/authorization and freely gave his or her consent, but was physically unable to provide a signature.

| | | |
|---|---|---|
| _____ | _____ | _____ |
| Signature of witness | Printed name | Date |

❑ Copy for client or parent/guardian     ❑ Copy for provider     ❑ Copy for third-party payer

## Authorization to Release Confidential Information to Family Members

Name of patient: _____ Date of birth: _____ Social Security #: _____

I understand that the purpose of this release is to assist with my/this patient's treatment by improving communication between professional service providers or agencies and the important individual(s) in my/the patient's life. To further this goal, I authorize this specific service provider, therapist, case manager, or _____, to release the below-specified information regarding me/the patient to the individual(s) listed below, and to receive information from them. I have been informed of the risks to privacy and limitations on confidentiality of the use of electronic means of information transfer, and I accept these.

The information to be disclosed is marked by an × in the boxes below, and any items not to be released have a line drawn through them:

❑ Name of therapist   ❑ Name of case manager   ❑ Name(s) of treatment program(s)

❑ Admission/discharge information   ❑ Treatment plan   ❑ Scheduled appointments   ❑ Progress notes

❑ Compliance with treatment   ❑ Discharge plans   ❑ Treatment summary

❑ Psychological evaluation   ❑ Medications   ❑ Other: _____

This information is to be disclosed to these persons, who have the indicated relationship to me/the patient:

| _____ | _____ |
|---|---|
| Name of person | Relationship |
| _____ | _____ |
| Name of person | Relationship |
| _____ | _____ |
| Name of person | Relationship |

I understand that I may revoke this release at any time, except to the extent that it has already been acted upon. This release will expire on ❑ I year from this date, ❑ upon my discharge from treatment by this agency or by the person specified above, or ❑ under these circumstances: _____

| _____ | _____ | _____ |
|---|---|---|
| Signature of client | Printed name | Date |

| _____ | _____ | _____ | _____ |
|---|---|---|---|
| Signature of parent/ guardian/representative | Printed name | Relationship | Date |

I witnessed that the person understood the nature of this request/authorization and freely gave his or her consent, but was physically unable to provide a signature.

| _____ | _____ | _____ |
|---|---|---|
| Signature of witness | Printed name | Date |

| _____ | _____ | _____ | _____ |
|---|---|---|---|
| Signature of witness (a second witness is needed if person is unable to give oral consent) | Printed name | Relationship | Date |

❑ Copy for patient or parent/guardian   ❑ Copy for provider/therapist/case manager   ❑ Copy for family member

**FORM 53. Authorization to release confidential information to family members.**   Adapted from Marsh (1995). Copyright 1995 by the Pennsylvania Psychological Association. Adapted by permission.—From *The Paper Office*. Permission to photocopy this form is granted to purchasers of this book for personal use only (see copyright page for details).

those at your end who should not have access, such as untrained workers. You should make the rules of confidentiality (see Section 7.1) part of the orientation of *all* new hires in your practice. For those whose services you use on a shared or part-time basis, some refresher training should be provided. You, the professional, are the only one who will be held responsible for violations.

In 1992, Barton Bernstein, an attorney in Dallas, TX, suggested adding a paragraph to your intake forms to let clients know that you may be faxing clinical data to their MCOs ("Legal Issues," 1992). A warning like this has been included in the client information brochure in this book (see Section 4.2) and is part of the APA code of ethics (APA, 2002, Standard 4.02c). Many fax machines have ways to send this kind of warning as part of their built-in "cover sheet." Here is a warning in ordinary language that can be added to your fax cover sheet:

---

Confidentiality Warning!!

This communication may be **confidential and legally privileged.** If you are not the person to whom it is addressed, do not read, copy or let anyone else besides the addressee see it. Please respect the confidentiality of this personal information and respect the federal and state laws that protect its confidentiality. If this has been transmitted to you by mistake, we ask you to extend the courtesy of calling us back at the voice number listed above and telling us what went wrong.

Thank you very much.

---

The following more legalistic version is based on the article cited above ("Legal Issues," 1992).

---

Confidentiality Warning!!

The information contained in this fax message is intended only for the personal and confidential use of the designated recipient or entity named above. As such, this communication is **privileged, confidential, and exempt from disclosure under applicable law.** If the reader or actual recipient is not the intended recipient or an agent or employee responsible for delivering it to the intended recipient, you are hereby notified that you have received this document in error, and that any review, dissemination, distribution, or copying of this message is strictly prohibited by federal and state laws with civil and criminal penalties. If you have received this communication in error, we apologize for any inconvenience. We would appreciate your notifying us immediately by phone and then return the original to us by the U.S. Postal Service at the address listed above.

Thank you.

---

The sending of information from or to clients by e-mail will no doubt increase in the future. There have already been errors in such transmissions (e.g., a physician accidentally posted a confidential message in a public area on a large online service). Here are some guidelines:

- Until you have fully electronic records, print out all exchanges and place them in a client's chart.

- Ask the client whether his or her e-mail address is confidential, and ask for permission to use it for confidential messages. Document this permission in the client's chart.

- Inform clients of possible risks in the use of e-mail, such as having messages read by others because of being (1) misaddressed, (2) duplicated and forwarded, or (3) preserved at the sites of their Internet service providers or sites supplying their e-mail addresses (e.g., aol.com, hotmail.com, bigfoot.com, yahoo.com).

- Explain the following to clients:

  - How you will verify their and your identities in each e-mail. Code words may be sufficient, but electronic signature guarantees and public key encryption technology are ideal.

  - What your encryption methods are for all e-mail. Offer these to clients.

  - How long you will preserve their e-mail and electronic documents, and how you will protect their confidentiality; allow legal release; use them in supervision, consultation, research, or legal proceedings; and so on.

  - How often you will pick up your messages. Offer procedures if clients need to contact you sooner, or if there is a failure of the e-mail technology (lost or erased messages, changes in e-mail addresses, etc.).

  - How the lack of the usual contextual information acquired in face-to-face meetings can lead to misunderstanding, and how to cope with this.

# 7.7    Confidentiality Notifications

I believe that a stamped note on each page of a report warning "Do not make copies," "Do not redistribute," or merely "Confidential" does not provide enough information for the reader to make decisions about how to store and use the pages. As a simple and inexpensive alternative, I suggest notices like those given below. These notices include explicit rationales and warnings, so records are less likely to be misused and their confidentiality breached. You can edit one of the notices below or create your own version; you can then place it on the paper in various different ways:

- You can type it onto each page of every document you send out.

- If you use a word processor, it can be printed on every page of reports you create by adding it, from a "glossary" entry, as a "header" or "footer" on each page.

- You can photocopy it onto a sheet of labels, and then stick a label onto each page or onto the first page of records or reports you send out.

- You can make a rubber stamp with the notice's text and use it on each page of records you release.

The sample notices follow; as indicated below, many are from Zuckerman (2000). (*Note:* Your state may have additional requirements for the release of HIV information or drug and alcohol information, as Pennsylvania does. If so, you may need to add the exact phrasing or citation of the appropriate laws to your releases.)

Permission to send these records to you/the addressee has been given to me in writing by the concerned patient or his or her guardian. You do not have the legal right to share these records with any other person, agency, organization, or program unless you first obtain written permission to do so from the subject of these records or his or her guardian.

CONFIDENTIAL PATIENT INFORMATION

WARNING: This report may contain sensitive client information. You must protect this document as confidential medical information. Please handle, store, and dispose of properly.

This is privileged and confidential patient information. Any unauthorized disclosure is a federal offense. Not to be duplicated. (Zuckerman, 2000, p. 85)

This information has been disclosed to you from records protected by federal confidentiality rules (42 C.F.R. Part 2, P.L. 93-282) and state law (e.g., Pennsylvania Law 7100-111-4). These regulations prohibit you from making any further disclosure of this information unless further disclosure is expressly permitted by the written consent of the person to whom it pertains or as otherwise permitted by 42 C.F.R. Part 2. A general authorization for the release of information is not sufficient for this purpose. The federal rules restrict any use of the information to criminally investigate or prosecute any alcohol or drug abuse patient. (Zuckerman, 2000, p. 85)

This report may contain client information. Release only to professionals capable of ethically and professionally interpreting and understanding the information it contains. (Zuckerman, 2000, p. 85)

It is inappropriate to release the information contained herein directly to the client or other parties. If this information is released to interested individuals before they are afforded an opportunity to discuss its meaning with a trained mental health professional, it is likely that the content of the report may be misunderstood, leading to emotional distress on the part of the uninformed reader. (Zuckerman, 2000, p. 86)

This information is not to be used against the interests of the subject of this report. (Zuckerman, 2000, p. 86)

Persons or entities granted access to this record may discuss this information with the patient only insofar as necessary to represent the patient in legal proceedings or other matters for which this record has been legally released. (Zuckerman, 2000, p. 85)

## For a Child:

The contents of this report have/have not been shared with the child's parent(s)/guardian. She/he/they may review this report with the evaluator or his/her specific designee. Copies of this report may be released only by the evaluator or his/her departmental administrator, or in accord with the school district's policy. (Zuckerman, 2000, p. 86)

The information contained in this report is private, privileged, and confidential. It cannot be released outside the school system except by the examining psychologist/evaluator/creator of this report, upon receipt of written consent by the parent or guardian. Not to be duplicated or transmitted. (Zuckerman, 2000, p. 86)

# 7.8 Overview of HIPAA

The Health Insurance Portability and Accountability Act of 1996 (August 21), or Public Law 104-191, was designed to improve the efficiency of health care services by standardizing electronic data, and to protect privacy of this data by imposing procedures and standards across the country. The full text of the Act can be found at http://www.hhs.gov/ocr/hipaa.

HIPAA, though large and detailed, can be divided into three sections, each with a number of rules and standards.

1. The Electronic Health Transactions Standards concern health insurance programs, eligibility for benefits, claims, coordination of benefits, payments, and so forth. These require the adoption of "Standard Code Sets" for each kind of transaction to describe disorders and interventions. Your billing service, billing program's developers, and the insurers you deal with will develop and provide these for you.

2. The Security and Electronic Signature Standards concern verification of identity and accuracy of electronically transferred data. Again, your billing service or billing program's developers will handle this for you.

3. The Security and Privacy Standards concern the maintenance of confidentiality and the access to an individual's "protected health information" (PHI). You are responsible for becoming compliant to these standards by April 14, 2003.

HIPAA applies to many kinds of organizations, but our concern is with "covered entities" which includes all health care providers, health plans, and clearinghouses, because they collect, store, and transmit health care information. While technically you may not be covered if you are a small practice and do not bill electronically at present for your services, for all practical purposes, you should assume that you will have to conform to HIPAA. Also, HIPAA calls for severe civil and criminal penalties for noncompliance and has deadlines for compliance.

## Health Information and Its Uses

The regulations of relevance to therapists concern PHI, which is individually identifiable health information that "relates to the past, present, or future physical or mental health or condition of an individual; the provision of health care to an individual; or the past, present, or future payment for the provision of health care to an individual" (HIPAA Section 164.501) and that is maintained or transmitted by a "covered entity" (CE), whether in electronic form, paper form, or as an oral discussion. Covered entities are health plans (HMOs, managed care organizations, insurers, etc.), health care clearinghouses (who process claims), and you, the health care provider. For all practical purposes this means all providers of all kinds.

The regulations concern how the information is kept private when it is collected, created, stored in your office, shared with other treaters, used in training or research, and sent to insurers. It is the *information* in the record that is protected by this law, and so not only electronic records (word processor, fax, data entry), but paper records, and even oral communications such as conversations, telephone calls, and messages, as well as most consultations and teaching, are covered.

A client's PHI is used in "treatment, payment, or health care operations" or TPO. Exact definitions can be found in HIPAA Section 164.501, but here are some simplified versions.

**Treatment** is when a provider offers or manages health care or related services, consults with other providers, or makes a referral.

**Payment** includes what a health care plan does to obtain premiums, determine eligibility, coverage, and provide reimbursement. These can include activities such as coordination of benefits with other insurance, assessment of the patient's health, determining the medical necessity of care, and reviewing utilization.

**Health care operations** means any of the following activities conducted by the CE or the CE's organization: quality assessment and improvement activities; review of the performance, competence, or qualifications of health care or non-health-care professionals; training of students or practitioners; accrediting, licensing, or credentialing of health care professionals; activities relating to health insurance or health benefits; medical review, legal services, and auditing functions, including fraud and abuse detection and compliance programs; as well as a variety of actions to support business administration, planning, customer service, grievance resolution, due diligence, and so forth.

As you can see, almost every kind of activity is covered, and thus a client's consent to participate allows a great deal of freedom to share information about the individual.

## HIPAA and Privacy

HIPAA creates a kind of universal "floor" of very basic privacy rights that does not replace (preempt) more stringent state laws. Sorting out the interaction between HIPAA and state laws will require years of argument, litigation, and legislation.

Procedurally, a simple notification to a patient during intake is needed to allow you to share his or her PHI among CEs such treaters, treating agencies, those in training, health insurers, managed care organizations, and others (see Section 164.506). For psychotherapists, once notified of his or her rights, the client signs a "consent," and treatment by you or your organization may begin. PHI can be used within the organization and disclosed to other participants in the patient's TPO. No accounting of such disclosures and uses is required. Generally, you can refuse to treat anyone who does not consent to these uses and disclosures.

If the PHI ever needs to be used for other than TPO or disclosed to anyone outside the organization, a written release (authorization) is required. You must keep a record of these releases. Besides the forms described below, you will need to have a written set of policies for implementing the procedures. Also, activities for fundraising or marketing, which we used to consider unethical and a misuse of our authority, are usually permissible under HIPAA.

In the regulations there are so many exceptions and exclusions to these requirements for control over a patient's PHI that the result is a very, very basic level of privacy protection.

In reality, most of the methods you currently use for consent and release will still be needed (over and above the HIPAA procedures), because your state's laws take precedence if they more stringently protect the patient's privacy.

## Becoming "HIPAA Compliant"

1. Select someone in your practice to be the "privacy official" for implementing HIPAA. First, his or her task is to become informed about the Act; second, to understand how PHI is currently created, used, accessed, disclosed, and stored in your practice; and third, to discover, from reading, consultation, and continuing education programs from your state professional organizations or commercial sources, how much of HIPAA you will actually have to implement, considering that your local laws are likely to be more stringent.

2. As needed, develop the following paperwork:

   a.  A "Notice of Privacy Practices."

   b.  A consent form for disclosure of PHI for TPO.

   c.  An authorization form for disclosures of PHI not covered by the general consent, for example, for research, marketing, or release of psychotherapy notes.

   d.  A business associate contract. Business associates are non-CEs who perform non-TPO services (such as billing services) on your behalf and to whom you may disclose PHI. They must agree, in a contract, to respect the HIPAA privacy rules regarding PHI. This is a developing and legally complex area beyond the scope of this book.

3. Develop policies and procedures concerning PHI to allow patients to do the following:

   a.  Request their PHI be released to others.

   b.  Access, inspect and copy their PHI.

   c.  Amend their PHI.

You will need to have all this in place before April 14, 2003, but you will not need to use it retroactively.

## Notice of Privacy Practices

You will need to create a Notice of Privacy Practices (NPP) form, written in plain language, which you can give to clients to inform them of their rights and how their PHI will be used.

It must be headed with this statement: "THIS NOTICE DESCRIBES HOW MEDICAL INFORMATION ABOUT YOU MAY BE USED AND DISCLOSED AND HOW YOU CAN GET ACCESS TO THIS INFORMATION. PLEASE REVIEW IT CAREFULLY."

The NPP must contain statements that do the following:

- Describe all the uses and disclosures of PHI that you are permitted or required to make for TPO without authorization, including those uses or disclosures subject to the consent requirements, such as law enforcement and public health. You must include at least one example of the types of uses and disclosures you can make in terms of TPO.

- List the client's rights, including the right to:

  - Request restrictions on certain uses and disclosures, including the statement that you are not required to agree to a requested restriction.

  - Receive confidential communications of PHI. This means he or she can arrange for you to send mail or bills to certain addresses or limit phone calls to retain privacy.

  - Inspect and copy his or her PHI.

  - Amend his or her PHI.

  - Receive an accounting of disclosures of PHI beyond that used for TPO.

- Assure the client's right to a paper copy of the NPP upon request.

- Explain your legal duty and practices to maintain the privacy of the client's PHI and inform the client that you will abide by the terms of the current NPP.

- Describe how the client can lodge a complaint if he or she comes to believe his or her privacy rights have been violated.

- State that you will not disclose the PHI for any other purposes without his or her authorization (see below).

- Inform the client that your business associates will comply with the HIPAA regulations and procedures.

- Show the date on which the NPP became effective.

You will need to customize the NPP for yourself, but some sample Notice of Privacy Practices forms are available at:

http://www.apapractice.org/hipaa/index.html
http://www.ama-assn.org/ama/pub/category/6669.html (for physicians)
http://www.nchica.org/HIPAAResources/Samples/EVpDocuments.htm
http://www.mh.state.oh.us/hipaa/hipaa.policies.index.html

## Documenting Consent

The HIPAA regulations do not provide a model consent but do specify some of the rules about the use and disclosure of the client's PHI to be included (in Section 164.506[c]):

- The client's PHI may be used and disclosed by the CE to carry out TPO. Actually you have to specify which uses and which disclosures your office requires to perform specific parts of TPO.

- For more information on uses and disclosures the client is referred to the NPP.

- The client has a right to review the NPP before signing the consent.

- You should say that you have the option to change the terms of the NPP, and then explain how the client may obtain a revised NPP.

- The client has a right to request restrictions on uses and disclosures of PHI for TPO (see below). The client must be told that you do not have to agree to these requests but if you do, the agreement is binding.

- The client can revoke the consent in writing but not retroactively.

- The consent should be signed and dated.

Other points about consents:

- Consents do not have a specified duration, and generally will be effective for the duration of an episode of treatment. Also, they can be revoked.

- You must keep a copy of the consent for 6 years after it was obtained or 6 years from the time it was last in effect, whichever is later.

- The consent must be written in plain language.

- The consent may not be combined with the NPP but can be combined with other releases, for example, for the assignment of benefits or for research that includes treatment. You may do this so long as the consent is both visually and organizationally separate, and separately signed and dated.

Some sample consent forms, which you should customize for your own purposes, are available at:

http://www.ama-assn.org/ama/pub/category/6913.html (for physicians)
http://www.mh.state.oh.us/hipaa/hipaa.policies.index.html

## The Right to Object or Agree to Uses and Disclosures

Clients must be given the "opportunity to agree to or prohibit or restrict the disclosure" of PHI. You can disclose PHI to family members and close friends who are involved in the client's treatment or payment for treatment (per HIPAA Section 164.510[b]), if the client agrees. You should then document in your notes whether the client agreed or objected to such disclosure. You should use your professional judgment about what to tell those who are not close relatives or friends. The regulations are rather broad and incomplete about how one can limit disclosures.

## The Right to Limit Disclosure of One's PHI

As indicated in the NPP, clients have a right to request restrictions on the uses and disclosures of their PHI for TPO, and you (the CE) must accommodate "reasonable" limitations. However, you do not have to agree to the request, and if you do agree (with a written agreement) and then violate the agreed limitations on disclosure, there is no method of redress under HIPAA. Furthermore, you can, without the patient's consent, terminate this agreement and begin releasing information acquired after the date of informing the patient of the agreement's termination. Lastly, you can release information in an emergency, despite such an agreement. See HIPAA Section 164.522 for details.

## An Authorization to Send or Receive Records

An authorization is required for use and disclosure of PHI for purposes other than TPO or purposes not otherwise permitted by the HIPAA Privacy Rule, as in, for example, for potential health insurers to determine the client's insurability (underwriting).

Technically, there should be three forms for authorizations: for internal (but not TPO) use of PHI, for requesting PHI from others, and for handling PHI in a research treatment context. In general, authorizations must be in plain language and must contain these elements (per HIPAA Section 164.508):

- A description of the information to be disclosed or used.

- A description of how the information will be used for TPO if this is a request for others' records.

- Identification of the person or organization who is to make the disclosure.

- Identification of the person to whom the information will be disclosed.

- An expiration date or event after which the authorization will no longer be valid.

- A statement that the participant has the right to revoke, in writing, this authorization; a description of the means for doing so; and the exceptions to such revocation (e.g., that it is not retroactive and thus won't apply to what has already been disclosed, that the participant will no longer receive treatment as part of the research project, etc.).

- A notice that after the PHI is disclosed it may be redisclosed and thus no longer protected by HIPAA regulations.

- A statement that the client does not have to sign the authorization. If this authorization is for your (the CE's) use, you need to state that your providing treatment, payment, enrollment, and so forth is not contingent (or "conditioned") upon their agreeing to the release of your or others' records. Note that agreement *is* required for treatment in a research program, obtaining health insurance, and some other situations.

- An indication that you will be paid directly or indirectly for this disclosure, if that is true.

- The date and signature of the client or representative.

You will need very few of these authorizations (requests for and releases of records), even in states where only HIPAA applies, because therapists send and receive records almost exclusively to and from other treaters or treating organizations, and such disclosures are exempt because they are for TPO.

Procedurally, you can combine this authorization with the Notice of Privacy Practices and consent to use or disclose PHI for TPO. A copy must be provided to the patient and one must be kept by you, probably for 6 years.

Sample draft authorization forms can be found at:

> http://www.nchica.org/HIPAAResources/Samples/EVpDocuments.htm
> http://www.mh.state.oh.us/hipaa/hipaa.policies.index.html
> http://www.ama-assn.org/ama/pub/category/6900.html  (for physicians)

Sample draft "request for records" forms can be found at:

> http://www.nchica.org/HIPAAResources/Samples/EVpDocuments.htm
> http://www.ama-assn.org/ama/pub/category/6696.html  (for physicians)

## Keeping an Accounting of Disclosures You Made

Although you are unlikely to make many authorized disclosures, the HIPAA regulations (Section 164.528) require you to keep a record of them for 6 years—a kind of audit trail. You do not need to record disclosures you have made for purposes of TPO, to the client, to those involved in the patient's care (like family members), to law officers, for lawsuits, or before April 14, 2003, but you do need to record disclosures made to or by your business associates. No form for this record is provided in the regulations.

When an account of disclosures is requested by HHS or the client, you will have up to 90 days to provide it and, after the first such accounting, you can charge a fee. The accounting must include the following information: the date of the disclosure; the name and address, if known, of the entity or person who received the PHI; a brief description of the PHI disclosed; and a brief statement of the purpose of the disclosure or a copy of the individual's authorization of the disclosure.

## When Consent, Authorization, or Opportunity to Object Are Not Required

There are many circumstances in which PHI can be used and disclosed without any control by the client: when required by law, such as in cases of rape, abuse, neglect, or domestic violence; for almost any judicial or administrative proceeding, such as a subpoena or discovery; for any law enforcement official's request; to a coroner after the individual's death; for research approved by an Institutional Review Board or even to prepare for such research; to workers' compensation and similar programs; and finally

> if the covered entity, in good faith, believes the use or disclosure: (i)(A) Is necessary to prevent or lessen a serious and imminent threat to the health or safety of a person or the public; and (B) Is to a person or persons reasonably able to prevent or lessen the threat, including the target of the threat; or (ii) Is necessary for law enforcement authorities to identify or apprehend an individual: (A) Because of a statement by an individual admitting participation in a violent crime that the covered entity reasonably believes may have caused serious physcial harm to the victim, or . . . (HIPAA Section 164.512[j])

As you can see, the client has very little control over his or her health information under HIPAA.

# APPENDICES

# Resources

## Appendix A.
## Books on Practice Development and Marketing

Ackley, D. C. (1997). *Breaking free of managed care*. New York: Guilford Press.

Although Ackley explains the poisonous consequences of managed care with precision, the best parts of the book are those identifying and challenging the thoughts and assumptions of therapists that keep them from leaving managed care dependence. He demonstrates the value of psychology to clients and to businesses, and inspires us to follow him.

Barnes, D., & Kaye, J. (1999). *Independent practice for the mental health professional: Growing a private practice for the 21st century*. New York: Brunner/Mazel.

Grodzki, L. (2000). *Building your ideal private practice: A guide for therapists and other healing professionals*. New York: Norton.

Grodzki discusses developing a framework for practice, creating a business vision, attracting clients, avoiding pitfalls, learning strategies, and staying successful over time.

Heller, K. M. (1997). *Strategic marketing: How to achieve independence and prosperity in your mental health practice*. Sarasota, FL: Professional Resource Exchange.

If you shy away from "marketing" but know you need to do something, Heller will help you understand, design, and implement a strategy that will enhance your work.

Kolt, L. (1999). *How to build a thriving fee-for-service practice: Integrating the healing side with the business side of psychotherapy*. New York: Academic Press.

Kolt combines exercises in awareness and attitude change with tools for surveying community needs, developing specialty practices, marketing ideas, presenting public seminars, and using financial data.

Lawless, L. (1997). *Therapy, Inc.: A hands-on guide to developing, positioning, and marketing your mental health practice in the 1990s*. New York: Wiley.

Lawless, L., & Wright, J. (1999). *How to get referrals: The mental health professional's guide to strategic marketing*. New York: Wiley.

More narrowly focused than Lawless's earlier book, but with lots of excellent ideas for this essential activity.

# Appendix B.
# Readings in the Law, Ethics, and Malpractice

Anderson, B. S., & Hopkins, B. R. (1990). *The counselor and the law* (4th ed.). Alexandria, VA: American Association on Counseling and Development.

The laws and guidelines that apply especially to counselors.

Bernstein, B. E., & Hartsell, Jr., T. L. (2000). *The portable ethicist for mental health professionals: An A–Z guide to responsible practice.* New York: Wiley.

Very readable and practical guidance.

Bersoff, D. N. (Ed.). (1999). *Ethical conflicts in psychology* (2nd ed.). Washington, DC: American Psychological Association.

Excerpts of more than 100 articles from many sources and perspectives, with well-considered commentary. Very instructive.

Bongar, B. (2002). *The suicidal patient: Clinical and legal standards of care* (2nd ed.). Washington, DC: American Psychological Association.

Realistic standards of care, sophisticated risk management strategies, risk estimators, legal action guidelines, postvention methods, and a review of the literature.

Canter, M., Bennett, B. E., Jones, S. E., & Nagy, T. F. (1994). *Ethics for psychologists: A commentary on the APA ethics code.* Washington, DC: American Psychological Association.

Thoughtful commentaries on each section of the 1992 code revision by the authors of the code.

Gutheil, T. G., & Appelbaum, P. S. (2000). *Clinical handbook of psychiatry and the law* (3rd ed.). Philadelphia: Lippincott Williams & Wilkins.

Haas, L. J., & Malouf., J. L. (1995). *Keeping up the good work: A practitioner's guide to mental health ethics* (2nd ed.). Sarasota, FL: Professional Resource Exchange.

Comprehensive, readable, full of practical advice and a usable model for ethical decision making—all in 200 small pages. Very highly recommended.

Jacob-Timm, S., & Hartshorne, T. (1998). *Ethics and law for school psychologists* (3rd ed.). New York: Wiley.

Very thorough coverage of the special areas and considerations of school practice.

Koocher, G. P., & Keith-Spiegel, P. (1998). *Ethics in psychology: Professional standards and cases* (2nd ed.). New York: Oxford University Press.

A standard text in ethics. Lots of cases, addressing all the areas of concern, and highly readable.

Nagy, T. F. (1999). Ethics in plain English: An illustrative casebook for psychologists. Washington, DC: American Psychological Association.

Lots of cases make understanding the issues much easier.

Nurcombe, B., & Partlett, D. F. (1994) Child mental health and the law. New York: Free Press.

Pope, K. S., & Vasquez, M. J. T. (1998). *Ethics in psychotherapy and counseling: A practical guide for psychologists* (2nd ed.). San Francisco: Jossey-Bass.

Highly recommended. It is up-to-date, well reasoned and integrated, very comprehensive, readable, and practical. Written by experts in the field.

Rave, E. J., & Larsen, C. C. (Eds.). (1995). *Ethical decision making in therapy: Feminist perspectives*. New York: Guilford Press.

> At least two experts respond to each dilemma using the Feminist Therapy Institute's code of ethics and more traditional ethical approaches.

Reid, W. H. (1999). *A clinician's guide to legal issues in psychotherapy, or proceed with caution*. Phoenix, AZ: Zeig, Tucker.

> Reid combines a lively style with his contentions and advice based on "the standard of practice" and stable and durable ethical principles. Highly recommended.

Woody, R. H. (2000). *Child custody: Practice standards, ethical issues, and legal safeguards for mental health professionals*. Sarasota, FL: Professional Resource Exchange.

Zobel, H. B., & Rous, S. N. (1993). *Doctors and the law: Defendants and expert witnesses*. New York: Norton.

> Advice and insights into the processes of malpractice litigation.

# Appendix C.
# Professional Liability Insurance Resources

## General Information

Margaret A. Bogie is a licensed property and casualty insurance consultant who has worked with mental health professionals for years. She has written an extremely informative paper on professional insurance topics, which are available at http://www.americanprofessional.com/shopping.htm.

The APAIT Web site (see "Sellers of Insurance," below) has some very terse information.

You may find a list of insurance terms to help you understand policies not written in "plain English" at http://www.aishealth.com/ehealthbusiness/ehealthterms.html.

*Forum* is a bimonthly newsletter from the Risk Management Foundation of the Harvard Medical Institutions, Tillinghast Financial Center, Suite 600, 695 East Main Street, Stamford, CT 06901-2138; 203-326-5400.

Last but not least, **read your policy carefully.** Know and understand it. Call and ask the agent or agency any questions. Pay special attention to the many important exclusions.

## Sellers of Insurance

This list is current as of November 2002.

American Professional Agency, 95 Broadway, Amityville, NY 11701; 516-691-6400 or 800-421-6694; http://www.americanprofessional.com.

> Coverage is available for students and for members of all the mental health professions. Do read Margaret A. Bogie's "Shopping" section on the Web site (see above).

American Psychological Association Insurance Trust (APAIT), 750 First Street, N.E., Suite 605, Washington, DC 20002-4242; 800-447-1200. www.apait.org.

> The APAIT offers many kinds of insurance besides professional liability, but only to APA members. It stands as an intermediate and marketing organization.

American Psychotherapist Professional Liability Insurance Program (APPLIP), http://www.applip.com.

> Besides occurrence policies, the APPLIP offers directors' and officers' insurance and coverage for just about any kind of organization. The plan administrator is J. J. Negley Associates, P.O. Box 206, Cedar Grove, NJ 07009; 973-239-9107 or 800-845-1209; http://www.jjnegley.com.

Benham Insurance Associates, P.O. Box 369, Sylvania OH, 43560; 419-882-7117 or 800-472-7549.

> This company is very experienced with and knowledgeable about psychologists.

CPH and Associates, 727 S. Dearborn, Suite 312, Chicago, IL 60605; 800-875-1911; http://www.cphins.com.

> This company offers occurrence policies, a "loss assistance hotline," and the usual components.

Princeton Insurance Company, P.O. Box 5322, Princeton, NJ 08543-9955; 877-743-2792; http://www.pinsco.com/psych.html.

> This company serves mainly East Coast states and offers an occurrence policy with level rates. The plan administrator is the Harjes Agency, 800-942-7537.

Rockport Insurance Associates, P.O. Box 1809, Rockport, TX 78381-1809; 800-423-5344 or 361-790-9043; http://www.rockportinsurance.com.

> Rockport's liability policy includes premises liability. Sexual misconduct coverage is available, with a limit of $25,000.

# Appendix D.
# Practice Guidelines from Professional Organizations

American Association for Counseling and Development. (1995). *Ethical standards for the American Association for Counseling and Development.* Alexandria, VA: Author.

> Also available online at http://www.counseling.org/resources/codeofethics.htm.

American Association for Marriage and Family Therapy (AAMFT). (2000). *AAMFT code of ethical principles for marriage and family therapists.* Washington, DC: Author.

> This revision became effective July 1, 2001. It can be found online at http://www.aamft.org/about/revisedcodeethics.htm.

American Psychiatric Association. (1985). *Opinion of the Ethics Committee on the principles of medical ethics.* Washington, DC: Author.

American Psychiatric Association. (1986). *The principles of medical ethics with annotations especially applicable to psychiatry.* Washington, DC: Author.

American Psychiatric Association. (1987). Guidelines on confidentiality. *American Journal of Psychiatry, 144,* 1522–1526.

American Psychological Association. (1997). *Standards for providers of psychological services.* Washington, DC: Author.

American Psychological Association. (1981a). Ethical principles of psychologists. *American Psychologist, 36*(6), 633–638.

American Psychological Association. (1981b). Specialty guidelines for the delivery of services by clinical (counseling, industrial/organizational, and school) psychologists. *American Psychologist, 36*(6), 639–681.

American Psychological Association. (1982). *Ethical principles in the conduct of research with human participants.* Washington, DC: Author.

American Psychological Association. (1985). *Standards for educational and psychological tests.* Washington, DC: Author.

American Psychological Association. (1986). *Guidelines for computer-based tests and interpretations.* Washington, DC: Author.

American Psychological Association. (1987). General guidelines for providers of psychological services. *American Psychologist, 42,* 712–723.

American Psychological Association. (1990). Ethical principles of psychologists. *American Psychologist, 45,* 390–395.

American Psychological Association. (1992a). Ethical principles of psychologists and code of conduct. *American Psychologist, 47,* 1598–1611.

Also available at www.apa.org/ethics/code.html.

American Psychological Association. (1992b). *Consent agreement with the Federal Trade Commission.* Washington, DC: Author.

American Psychological Association. (1993). *Guidelines for ethical conduct in the care and use of animals.* Washington, DC: Author.

Also available at www.apa.org/science/anguide.html.

American Psychological Association. (1994). Guidelines for child custody evaluations in divorce proceedings. *American Psychologist, 49,* 677–680.

American Psychological Association. (1997a). Guidelines for psychological evaluations in child protection matters. *American Psychologist, 54*(8), 586–593.

Also available online at http://www.apa.org/practice/childprotection.html.

American Psychological Association. (1997b). Services by telephone, teleconferencing, and Internet: A statement by the Ethics Committee of the American Psychological Association. Washington, DC: Author.

Also available online at http://www.apa.org/ethics/stmnt01.html).

American Psychological Association. (2001, October 21). *Ethical principles of psychologists and code of conduct: Draft 6 for Comment* [Online]. Available: http://www.apa.org/ethics [2002, April 2].

American Psychological Association, Committee on Ethical Guidelines for Forensic Psychologists. (1991). Specialty guidelines for forensic psychologists. *Law and Behavior, 15,* 655–665.

American Psychological Association, Committee on Professional Practice and Standards. (1993). Record keeping guidelines. *American Psychologist, 48,* 984–986.

American Psychological Association, Office of Minority Affairs. (1993). Guidelines for providers of psychological services to ethnic, linguistic, and culturally diverse populations. *American Psychologist, 48*, 45–48.

Division 44/Committee on Lesbian, Gay, and Bisexual Concerns Joint Task Force on Guidelines for Psychotherapy with Lesbian, Gay, and Bisexual Clients. (2000). Guidelines for psychotherapy with lesbian, gay and bisexual clients. *American Psychologist, 55*(12), 1440–1451.

National Association of School Psychologists. (1992a). *Principles of professional ethics.* Silver Spring, MD: Author.

National Association of School Psychologists. (1992b). *Standards for the provision of school psychological services.* Silver Spring, MD: Author.

National Association of School Psychologists. (1992c). *Professional conduct manual.* Silver Spring, MD: Author.

National Association of Social Workers. (1999). *Code of ethics of the National Association of Social Workers.* Washington, DC: Author.

    Also available online at http://www.naswdc.org/code/ethics.htm.

National Board for Certified Counselors (NBCC). (1997, October 31). *NBCC's code of ethics* [Online]. Available: http://www.nbcc.org/ethics/index.htm [2002, February 12].

National Board for Certified Counselors (NBCC). (2001, November 3). *The practice of Internet counseling* [Online]. Available: http://www.nbcc.org/ethics/webethics.htm [2002, February 12].

# Appendix E.
# Dealing with Managed Care Organizations

## Multimedia Resources

The National Coalition of Mental Health Professionals and Consumers, P.O. Box 438, Commack, NY, 11725; 888-SAY-NO-MC (888-729-6662) or 631-424-5232; http://www.nomanagedcare.org/foyer.htm.

The major anti-managed care organization, with a history of successful advocacy and ingenious alternatives.

- Under "Helpful Resources" on the Web site is a superb set of links to national and other organizations for consumers and professionals.

- The National Coalition has also published a *Mental Health Consumer Protection Manual: A Guide to Solving Problems with Insurance and Managed Care.* "Many consumers are finding that the strategies in the manual are useful for dealing with managed care problems within all of healthcare. Those who cannot afford the cost may obtain a copy at no cost." (See the address above.)

## Newsletters

*Psychotherapy Finances*, 13901 U.S. Highway 1, Suite #5, Juno Beach, FL 33408; 800-747-869-8450; http://www.psychotherapyfinances.com.

> Not anti-managed-care. The publishers of this excellent newsletter now have a second one, *Managed Care Strategies: Building Quality and Profits in Behavioral Health Practice*.

> The Web site offers several dozen articles from both newsletters on marketing and practice issues (click on the "Articles" box at the top) and many useful links.

*Open Minds: The Behavioral Health Industry Analyst*, 4465 Old Harrisburg Road, Gettysburg, PA 17325; 717-334-1329; http://www.openminds.com.

> This newsletter offers information from and addressed to the MCO side. The Web site offers about 10 articles.

## Books

Ackley, D. (1997). *Breaking free of managed care*. New York: Guilford Press.

> See Appendix A.

Browning, C. H., & Browning, B. J. (1996). *How to partner with managed care: A "do-it-yourself kit" for building working relationships and getting steady referrals*. New York: Wiley.

> Very comprehensive, clear, positive, and practical advice on dealing with MCOs.

Chambliss, C. H. (1999). Psychotherapy and managed care: Reconciling research and reality. Boston: Allyn & Bacon.

> Chambliss accepts the reality of managed care and the challenge to use research findings to improve care.

Clement, P. W. (1999). *Outcomes and incomes: How to evaluate, improve, and market your psychotherapy practice by measuring outcomes*. New York: Guilford Press.

> This is a book of measures that will enable those in private practice to evaluate their outcomes; it explains how to use this information for marketing and for dealing with MCOs.

Corcoran, K., & Vandiver, V. (1996). *Maneuvering the maze of managed care: Skills for mental health practitioners*. New York: Free Press.

> Heavily researched and clearly written, it offers background and direction, as well as forms and procedures.

Davis, S. R., & Meier, S. R. (2000). *The elements of managed care: A guide for helping professionals*. Belmont, CA: Wadsworth.

> A very brief (110-page) introduction to managed care.

Frager, S. (2000). *Managing managed care: Secrets from a former case manager*. New York: Wiley.

> Clearly written and solid strategies for dealing with MCO representatives, writing treatment plans, and getting claims paid.

MacKenzie, K. R. (Ed.). (1995). *Effective use of group therapy in managed care*. Washington, DC: American Psychiatric Press.

> Just what the title says.

Poynter, W. L. (1994). *The preferred provider's handbook: Building a successful private therapy practice in the managed care marketplace*. New York: Brunner/Mazel.

> This book mainly concerns how to market your private practice to MCOs.

Poynter, W. L. (1998). *The textbook of behavioral managed care: From concept through management to treatment*. New York: Brunner/Mazel.

> This book helps clinicians to evaluate and restructure their practices in the managed care context. It covers assessment, goal setting, treatment, reauthorization, and patient satisfaction.

Winegar, N., & Hayter, L. M. (1998). *Guidebook to managed care and practice management terminology*. New York: Haworth Press.

> This is a middle-level book for those not expert yet on the contract terms, financial arrangements, and other internal workings of MCO.

Zieman, G. L. (1998). *The handbook of managed behavioral healthcare: A complete up-to-date guide for students and practitioners*. San Francisco: Jossey-Bass.

> The author says that this book includes "the history of managed care, annotated samples of a provider contract and a credentialing application with a managed care company, and extensive appendices including a glossary and resources regarding managed care information."

# Appendix F.
# Resources for Supervision and Consultation

Brantley, A. (2000). A clinical supervision documentation form. In L. VandeCreek & T. L. Jackson (Eds.), *Innovations in clinical practice: A sourcebook* (Vol. 18, 301–307). Sarasota, FL: Professional Resource Exchange.

> If you wish to use a structured format for documenting supervision, Brantley offers a clever and efficient two-page form that should cover all bases.

> There are also two journals: *The Clinical Supervisor* from The Haworth Press (http://www.haworthpressinc.com) and *Counselor Education and Supervision* from the American Counseling Association (http://www.counseling.org).

Campbell, J. (2000). *Becoming an effective supervisor: A workbook for counselors and psychotherapists*. Philadelphia: Accelerated Development.

> This is a workbook that integrates theory and research across disciplines and offers many practical resources.

Haber, R. (1996). *Dimensions of psychotherapy supervision: Maps and means*. New York: Norton.

> Haber offers both a metaphor (maps) and consideration of the practical matters and methods of psychotherapy supervision, all from a family systems perspective.

Hamilton, J. C., & Spruill, J. (1999). Identifying and reducing risk factors related to trainee–client sexual misconduct. *Professional Psychology: Research and Practice, 30*(3), 318–327.

> In terms of ethics, these authors specifically address how supervisors can reduce the likelihood of trainee–client sexual misconduct.

Todd, T. C. (Ed.). (1997). *The complete systemic supervisor: Context, philosophy, and pragmatics.* Boston: Allyn & Bacon.

> This is a very nice package for the supervisor, with background, strategies, objectives, ethical guidelines, and lots of resources.

Williams, A. (1995). *Visual and active supervision: Roles, focus, technique.* New York: Norton.

> Williams covers the roles inherent in the supervision process, and encourages being both systematic and creative.

# References

Ackley, D. C. (1997). *Breaking free of managed care: A step-by-step guide to regaining control of your practice.* New York: Guilford Press.

Adams, S., & Orgel, M. (1975). *Through the mental health maze.* Washington, DC: Health Research Group.

Affleck, D. C., & Garfield, S. L. (1961). Predictive judgements of therapists and duration of stay in psychotherapy. *Journal of Clinical Psychology, 17,* 134–137.

Alabama Psychological Association. (n.d.). *Client–therapist intimacy: Appropriate and inappropriate conduct.* Montgomery: Author.

Albeck, J. H., & Goldman, C. (1991). Patient–therapist co-documentation: Implications of jointly authored progress notes for psychotherapy practice, research, training, supervision, and risk management. *American Journal of Psychotherapy, 3*(3), 317–334.

Allen, I. P., & Columbus, M. (Eds.). (1995). *Assessing alcohol problems: A guide for clinicians and researchers.* (NIAAA Treatment Handbook Series 4). Bethesda, MD: National Institute on Alcohol Abuse and Alcoholism.

Allen, M. H., Serper, M. R., & Elfenbein, C. (1994). Psychiatric principles. In L. R. Goldfrank, N. E. Flomenbaum, N. A. Lewin, et al. (Eds.), *Goldfrank's toxicologic emergencies.* Norwalk, CT: Appleton & Lange.

American Medical Association. (2002). *Physicians' current procedural terminology* (CPT 2002). Washington, DC: Author.

American Professional Agency. (1992). *Important information concerning your professional liability claim.* Amityville, NY: Author.

American Psychiatric Association. (1987). APA guidelines on confidentiality. *American Journal of Psychiatry, 144,* 1522–1526.

American Psychiatric Association. (1994). *Diagnostic and statistical manual of mental disorders* (4th ed.). Washington, DC: Author.

American Psychological Association. (APA). (1981). Specialty guidelines for the delivery of services by clinical (counseling, industrial/organizational, and school) psychologists. *American Psychologist, 36*(6), 639–681.

American Psychological Association (APA). (1992). *Consent agreement with the Federal Trade Commission.* Washington, DC: Author.

American Psychological Association (APA). (1993). Guidelines for providers of psychological services to ethnic, linguistic, and culturally diverse populations. *American Psychologist, 48,* 45–48.

American Psychological Association (APA). (2002). *Ethical principles of psychologists and code of conduct* [Online]. Available: http://www.apa.org/ethics/code2002.html.

American Psychological Association (APA), Committee on Ethics. (1988). Trends in ethics cases, common pitfalls and published resources. *American Psychologist, 43,* 564–572.

American Psychological Association (APA), Committee on Legal Issues. (1996). Strategies for private practitioners coping with subpoenas or compelled testimony for client records or test data. *Professional Psychology: Research and Practice, 27*(3), 245–251.

American Psychological Association (APA), Committee on Professional Practice and Standards. (1993). Record keeping guidelines. *American Psychologist, 48,* 308–310, 984–986.

American Psychological Association (APA), Committee on Professional Practice and Standards. (1996). Twenty-four questions (and answers) about professional practice in the area of child abuse. *Professional Psychology: Research and Practice, 26*(4), 377–385.

American Psychological Association (APA) Committee on Professional Practice and Standards. (1998). *Guidelines for psychological evaluations in child protection matters* [Online]. Available: http://www.apa.org/practice/childprotection.html [2002, April 1].

American Psychological Association (APA), Committee on Psychological Tests and Assessment. (1996). Statement on the disclosure of test data. *American Psychologist, 51*(6), 644–648.

American Psychological Association (APA), Committee on Women in Psychology. (1989). If sex enters the psychotherapy relationship. *Professional Psychology: Research and Practice, 20,* 112–115.

Anderten, P., Staulcup, V., & Grisso, T. (1980). On being ethical in legal places. *Professional Psychology: Research and Practice, 11,* 764–773.

Appelbaum, P. S. (1993). Legal liability and managed care. *American Psychologist, 48*(3), 251–257.

Appelbaum, P. S. (1996). Suits against clinicians for warning of patients' violence. *Psychiatric Services, 47*(7), 683–684.

Appelbaum P. S. (2001). Third party suits against therapists in recovered-memory cases. *Psychiatric Services, 52*(1), 27–28.

Association for Advancement of Behavior Therapy. (1977, May 22). *Professional consultation and peer review* [Pamphlet]. New York: Author.

Association for Ambulatory Behavioral Healthcare. (1997). A protocol for measuring outcomes and a client satisfaction survey. In L. VandeCreek, S. Knapp, & T. L. Jackson (Eds.), *Innovations in clinical practice: A source book* (Vol. 15, pp. 215–225). Sarasota, FL: Professional Resource Exchange.

Baird, K. A., & Rupert, P. A. (1987). Clinical management of confidentiality: A survey of psychologists in seven states. *Professional Psychology Research and Practice, 18*(4), 347–352.

Baker, E. K. (1988). Use of journal writing for psychologists. In P. A. Keller & S. R. Heyman (Eds.), *Innovations in clinical practice: A sourcebook* (Vol. 7, pp. 269–282). Sarasota, FL: Professional Resource Press.

Barge, B. N., & Fenalason, K. I. (1989). *Dealing effectively with malpractice litigation.* (Available from Human Factors Department, Risk Management Services Division, St. Paul Companies, 385 Washington St., St. Paul, MN 55102)

Barnett, J. E., Hillard, D., & Lowery, K. (2001). Ethical and legal issues in the treatment of minors. In L. VandeCreek & T. L. Jackson (Eds.), *Innovations in clinical practice: A source book* (Vol. 19, pp. 257–272). Sarasota, FL: Professional Resources Press.

Barnett, J. E., MacGlashan, S. G., & Clarke, A. J. (2000). Risk management and ethical issues regarding termination and abandonment. In L. VandeCreek & T. L. Jackson (Eds.), *Innovations in clinical practice: A source book* (Vol. 18, pp. 231–245). Sarasota, FL: Professional Resource Exchange.

Barnett, J. E., & Neel, M. L. (2000). Must all psychologists study psychopharmacology? *Professional Psychology: Research and Practice, 31*(6), 619–627.

Barnett, J. E., & Polakoff, N. (2000). Maintaining professional competence for working with culturally diverse and aging clients. In L. VandeCreek & T. L. Jackson (Eds.), Innovations in clinical practice: A sourcebook. (Vol. 18, 257–272). Sarasota, FL: Professional Resource Exchange.

Barnett, J. E., & Porter, J. E. (1998). The suicidal patient: Clinical and risk management strategies. In L. VandeCreek, S. Knapp, & T. L. Jackson (Eds.), *Innovations in clinical practice: A source book* (Vol. 16, pp. 95–107). Sarasota, FL: Professional Resource Exchange.

Barnett, I. E., & Yutrzenka, B. A. (1994). Nonsexual dual relationships in professional practice, with special applications to rural and military communities. *Independent Practitioner, 14*(5), 243–248.

Bates, C., & Brodsky, A. (1993). *Sex in the therapy hour: A case of professional incest.* New York: Guilford Press.

Beahrs, J. O., & Gutheil, T. G. (2001). Informed consent in psychotherapy. *American Journal of Psychiatry, 158*(1), 4–10.

Beck, A. T. (1986). Hopelessness as a predictor of eventual suicide. *Annals of the New York Academy of Sciences, 487,* 90–96.

Beck, A. T., Kovacs, M., & Weissman, A. (1979). Assessment of suicidal intention: The Scale for Suicide Ideation. *Journal of Consulting and Clinical Psychology, 47,* 343–352.

Beck, A. T., Schuyler, D., & Herman, I. (1974). Development of suicide intent scales. In A. T. Beck, H. L. P. Resnik, & A. I. Lettieri (Eds.), *The prediction of suicide.* Bowie, MD: Charles Press.

Beck, I. C. (1982). When the patient threatens violence: An empirical study of clinical practice after Tarasoff. *Bulletin of the Academy of Psychiatry and the Law, 10,* 189–201.

Beck, I. C. (1990). The potentially violent patient: Clinical, legal, and ethical implications. In E. A. Margenau (Ed.), *The encyclopedic handbook of private practice* (pp. 697–709). New York: Gardner Press.

Beckham, E. E. (1992). Predicting patient dropout in psychotherapy. *Psychotherapy, 29,* 177–182.

Beeman, D. G., & Scott, N. A. (1991). Therapists' attitudes toward psychotherapy informed consent with adolescents. *Professional Psychology Research and Practice, 22*(3), 230–234.

Bennett, B. E., Bryant, B., VandenBos, G. R., & Greenwood, A. (1990). *Professional liability and risk management.* Washington, DC: American Psychological Association.

Berk, M., Rubin, R., & Peck, S. (1994). *Super-pak practice builders: Forty forms for psychotherapists.* Island Park, NY: Private Practitioners Group.

Berkowitz, S. (1995). Common questions and answers regarding process notes. *Massachusetts Psychologist Quarterly, 39*(2), 4–12.

Berlin, F. S., Malin, H. M., & Dean, S. (1991). Effects of statutes requiring psychiatrists to report suspected sexual abuse of children. *American Journal of Psychiatry, 148*(4), 449–453.

Bindrim, P. (1980, July). Group therapy: Protecting privacy. *Psychology Today,* pp. 24–28.

Blumenthal, S. J., & Kupfer, D. J. (Eds.). (1990). *Suicide over the life cycle: Risk factors, assessment and treatment of suicidal patients.* Washington, DC: American Psychiatric Press.

Boedecker, A. L. (1995). Practicing with integrity: Responding to a malpractice suit. *Networker: Newsletter of the New Hampshire Psychological Association, 7*(7), 2–3.

Bogie, M. (2002). *Shopping tips* [Online]. Available: http://www.americanprofessional.com/shopping.htm.

Bongar, B. (1992). Effective risk management and the suicidal patient. *Register Report, 18*(6), 1–26.

Bongar, B., Harris, E., Maris, R. W., Silverman, M. M. Packman, W., & Berman, A. L. (1998). *Risk management with suicidal patients.* New York: Guilford Press.

Branscomb, L. (1996, Winter). Clinical advantages of the extended psychotherapy disclosure form: A feminist ethical perspective. *Georgia Psychologist,* pp. 46–49.

Bratten, E. B., & Handelsman, M. M. (1997). Client preferences for informed consent information. *Ethics and Behavior, 7,* 311–328.

Bratten, E. B., Otto, S., & Handelsman, M. M. (1993). What do people want to know about psychotherapy? *Psychotherapy, 30*(4), 565–570.

Bouhoutsos, J., Holroyd, J., Lerman, H., Forer, B. R., & Greenberg, M. (1983). Sexual intimacy between psychotherapists and patients. *Professional Psychology: Research and Practice, 14,* 185–196.

Broadman, K., Erdmann, A. J., Jr., & Wolff, H. G. (1949). *Manual: Cornell Medical Index Health Questionnaire.* New York: Cornell University Medical College.

Brock, G. W., & Barnard, C. P. (1988). *Procedures in marriage and family therapy* (2nd ed.). Boston: Allyn & Bacon.

Brodsky, S. L., & Schumacher, J. E. (1990). The impact of litigation on psychotherapy practice: Litigation fears and litigaphobia. In E. A. Margenau (Ed.), *The encyclopedic handbook of private practice* (pp. 664–676). New York: Gardner Press.

Brown, L. (1998). Psychotherapy with clients recovering memories of childhood trauma. In G. P. Koocher, J. C. Norcross, & S. S. Hill III (Eds.), *Psychologists' desk reference* (pp. 343–348). New York: Oxford University Press.

Caldwell, C. B., & Gottesman, I. I. (1990). Schizophrenics kill themselves too: A review of the risk factors for suicide. *Schizophrenia Bulletin, 16*(4), 571–584.

Cannella, M. (1995, Summer). Resident's column. *New Jersey Psychiatric News.*

Canter, M., Bennett, B. E., Jones, S. E., & Nagy, T. F. (1994). *Ethics for psychologists: A commentary on the APA ethics code.* Washington, DC: American Psychological Press.

Cantor, D. (1999). Ensuring the future of professional psychology. *American Psychologist, 54*(11), 922–930.

Cervantes, N. (1992). Ethical responsibility of therapists: Spousal abuse cases. *Psychotherapy Bulletin, 26*(4), 12–15.

Charles, S. C. (1985). Doctors and the litigation process: Going against the grain. *Child and Adolescent Psychotherapy, 3,* 219–222.

Charles, S. C., Warnecke, R. B., Nelson, A., & Pyskoty, C. E. (1988). Appraisal of the event as a factor in coping with malpractice litigation. *Behavioral Medicine, 14*(4), 148–155.

Charles, S. C., Wilbert, J. R., & Franke, K. J. (1985). Sued and non-sued physicians' reactions to malpractice litigation. *American Journal of Psychiatry, 142*(4), 437–440.

Chenneville, T. (2000). HIV, confidentiality, and duty to protect: A decision-making model. *Professional Psychology: Research and Practice, 31*(6), 661–670.

Ciarlo, J. A. (1979). Awareness, use, and consequences of evaluative data in a community mental health center. *Community Mental Health Journal, 15*(1), 7–16.

Claiborne, C. D., Berberoglu, L. S., Nerison, R. M., & Somberg, D. R. (1994). The client's perspective: Ethical judgements and perceptions of therapist practices. *Professional Psychology: Research and Practice, 25*(3), 268–274.

Clement, P. W. (1999). *Outcomes and incomes: How to evaluate, improve, and market your psychotherapy practice by measuring outcomes.* New York: Guilford Press.

Cohen, R. J. (1979). *Malpractice: A guide for mental health professionals.* New York: Free Press.

Cohen, R. J. (1990). The professional liability of behavioral scientists. In E. A. Margenau (Ed.), *The encyclopedic handbook of private practice* (pp. 651–663). New York: Gardner Press. (Original work published 1983)

Confidentiality of HIV-Related Information Act, 35 P.C.S.A. 7601 et seq. (1990).

Corey, G. (1984). Ethical issues in group therapy. In P. Keller & L. G. Ritt (Eds.), *Innovations in clinical practice: A source book* (Vol. 3, pp. 406–418). Sarasota, FL: Professional Resource Exchange.

Cross, H., & Deardorff, W. M. (1987). Malpractice in psychotherapy and psychological evaluation. In J. R. McNamara & M. Appel (Eds.), *Critical issues, developments, and trends in professional psychology* (Vol. 3, pp. 55–79). New York: Praeger.

Cull, J. G., & Gill, W. S. (1988). *Suicide Probability Scale.* Los Angeles: Western Psychological Services.

Dattilio, F. M. (2002). Board certification in psychology: Is it really necessary? *Professional Psychology: Research and Practice, 33*(1), 54–57.

Dauser, P. J., Hedstrom, S. M., & Croteau, J. M. (1995). Effects of disclosure of comprehensive pretherapy information on clients at a university counseling center. *Professional Psychology: Research and Practice, 26*(2), 190–195.

DeBell, C., & Jones, R. D. (1997). Privileged communication at last?: An overview of *Jaffee v. Redmond. Professional Psychology: Research and Practice, 28*(6), 559–566.

Doverspike, W. F. (1997). Informed consent forms. In L. VandeCreek, S. Knapp, & T. L. Jackson (Eds.), *Innovations in clinical practice: A source book* (Vol. 15, pp. 201–214). Sarasota, FL: Professional Resource Exchange.

Downey, D. L. (2001). Therapeutic touch in psychotherapy. *Psychotherapy Bulletin, 36*(1), 35–39.

Doyle, M., & Straus, D. (1993). *How to make meetings work.* New York: Berkley.

Durana, C. (1998). The use of touch in psychotherapy: Ethical and legal guidelines. *Psychotherapy, 35*(2), 269–280.

Eichelman, B. S., & Hartwig, A. C. (1995). *Patient violence and the clinician.* Washington, DC: American Psychiatric Press.

Eidetics. (1988). *The malpractice suit: A survival guide for physicians and their families* [Videotape]. Boston: Author.

Eimer, B. (1988). A patient's guide to psychotherapy. In P. Keller & S. Heyman (Eds.), *Innovations in clinical practice: A source book* (Vol. 7, pp. 499–501). Sarasota, FL: Professional Resource Exchange.

Eisen, S. V., Shaul, J. A., Claridge, B., Nelson, D., Spink, J., & Cleary, P. D. (1999). Development of a consumer survey for behavioral health services. *Psychiatric Services, 50*(6), 793–798.

Elwork, A. (1993, April). Adolescents and informed consent: Facts and fictions. *Pennsylvania Psychologist Update*, pp. 1–3.

Employee Retirement Income Security Act. 29 U.S.C. § 1001 *et seq.*, 29 C.F.R. § 2509 *et seq.* (1974).

Epstein, R. S., & Simon, R. I. (1990). The Exploitation Index: An early warning indicator of boundary violations in psychotherapy. *Bulletin of the Menninger Clinic, 54*(4), 450–465.

Everstine, L., Everstine, D. H., Heyman, G. M., True, R. H., Prey, D. H., Johnson, H. G., & Seiden, R. H. (1980). Privacy and confidentiality in psychotherapy. *American Psychologist, 35*(9), 828–840.

Ewing, C. P. (1983). Ethical issues in clinical practice. In P. Keller & L. G. Ritt (Eds.), *Innovations in clinical practice: A source book* (Vol. 2, pp. 399–410). Sarasota, FL: Professional Resource Exchange.

Ewing, C. P. (1990). Legal issues in terminating treatment. In E. A. Margenau (Ed.), *The encyclopedic handbook of private practice* (pp. 720–236). New York: Gardner Press.

Ewing, J. A. (1984). Detecting alcoholism: The CAGE questionnaire. *Journal of the American Medical Association, 252*, 1905–1907.

Fine, M. A., & Kurdek, L. A. (1993). Reflections on determining authorship credit and authorship order on faculty–student collaborations. *American Psychologist, 48*(11), 1141–1147.

Folman, R. (1990). *Legislative action on therapist misconduct: Implications for clinical training and treatment.* Address presented at the annual convention of the American Psychological Association, Boston.

Folstein, M. F., Folstein, S. E., & McHugh, P. R. (1975). Mini-Mental State: A practical method for grading the cognitive state of patients for the clinician. *Journal of Psychiatric Research, 12*, 189–198.

Foster, S. (1996, January). The consequences of violating the "forbidden zone." *Counseling Today*, pp. 25–53.

Fox, R. E. (1992). Proceedings of the American Psychological Association, Incorporated, for the year 1991. *American Psychologist, 47*(7), 912–913.

Freud, S. (1958). Further recommendations on the technique of psychoanalysis: On beginning the treatment. In J. Strachey (Ed. and Trans.), *The standard edition of the complete psychological works of Sigmund Freud* (Vol. 12, pp. 121–144). London: Hogarth Press. (Original work published 1913)

Fulero, S. M. (1988). Tarasoff: Ten years later. *Professional Psychology: Research and Practice, 19*(2), 184–190.

Fulero, S. M., & Wilbert, J. R. (1988). Record-keeping practices of clinical and counseling psychologists: A survey of practitioners. *Professional Psychology Research and Practice, 19*(6), 658–660.

Garber, B. D. (1994). Practical limitations in considering psychotherapy with children of separation and divorce. *Psychotherapy, 31*(2), 254–261.

Garfield, S. L. (1986). Research on client variables in psychotherapy. In S. L. Garfield & A. E. Bergin (Eds.), *Handbook of psychotherapy and behavior change* (3rd ed., pp. 213–256). New York: Wiley.

Garfield, S. L., & Wolpin, M. (1963). Expectations regarding psychotherapy. *Journal of Nervous and Mental Disease, 137*, 353–362.

Geissler, E. (1998). *A pocket guide to cultural assessment* (2nd ed.). St. Louis, MO: Mosby.

Goldberg, R. (1995, October). Ethical dilemmas in working with children and adolescents. *Pennsylvania Psychologist Update*, pp. 7–9.

Glassman, J. B. (1998). Preventing and managing board complaints: The downside of custody evaluation. *Professional Psychology: Research and Practice, 29*(2), 121–124.

Gonsiorek, J., & Brown, L. (1989). Post-therapy sexual relationships with clients. In G. Schoener, J. Milgrom, J. Gonsiorek, E. Luepker, & R. Conroe (Eds.), *Psychotherapists' sexual involvement with clients* (pp. 289–301). Minneapolis, MN: Walk-In Counseling Center.

Goode, T. D. (2000). *Promoting cultural diversity and cultural competency: Self-assessment checklist for personnel providing services and supports to children with special health needs and their families* [Online]. Available: http://gucdc.georgetown.edu/nccc7.html [2001, April 20].

Goodman, M., Brown, J., & Deitz, P. (1992). *Managing managed care: A mental health practitioner's survival guide.* Washington, DC: American Psychiatric Press.

Gottlieb, M. C. (1993). Avoiding exploitative dual relationships: A decision-making model. *Psychotherapy, 30*(1), 41–48.

Gottschalk, L. A., Mayerson, P., & Gottlieb, A. A. (1967). Prediction and evaluation of outcome in an emergency brief psychotherapy clinic. *Journal of Nervous and Mental Disease, 144*, 77–96.

Grant, R. L., & Maletzky, B. M. (1973). Application of the Weed system to psychiatric records. *Psychiatry in Medicine, 3,* 119–129.

Graziano, A. M., & Fink, R. S. (1973). Second order effects in mental health treatment. *Journal of Consulting and Clinical Psychology, 40,* 356–364.

Grisso, T., & Appelbaum, P. S. (1998). *Assessing competence to consent to treatment: A guide for physicians and other health professionals.* New York: Oxford University Press.

Grosch, W. N., & Olsen, D. C. (1994). *When helping starts to hurt.* New York: Norton.

Group for the Advancement of Psychiatry (GAP). (1990). *Casebook in psychiatric ethics.* New York: Brunner/Mazel.

Grunder, T. M. (1980). On the readability of surgical consent forms. *New England Journal of Medicine, 302,* 900–902.

Gustafson, K. E., & McNamara, J. R. (1987). Confidentiality with minor clients: Issues and guidelines for therapists. *Professional Psychology: Research and Practice, 18,* 503–515.

Gustafson, K. E., McNamara, J. R., & Jensen, J. A. (1994). Parents' informed consent decisions regarding psychotherapy for their children: Consideration of therapeutic risks and benefits. *Professional Psychology: Research and Practice, 25*(1), 16–22.

Gutheil, T. G. (1980). Paranoia and progress notes: A guide to forensically informed psychiatric recordkeeping. *Hospital and Community Psychiatry, 31,* 479–482.

Gutheil, T. G. (1992). Approaches to forensic assessment of false claims of sexual misconduct by therapist. *Bulletin of the American Academy of Psychiatry and the Law, 20,* 289–296.

Gutheil, T. G. (1993). Letter to the editor. *Hospital and Community Psychiatry, 44*(10), 1005.

Gutheil, T. G., & Appelbaum, P. S. (2000). *The clinical handbook of psychiatry and the law* (3rd ed.). Philadelphia: Lippincott Williams & Wilkins.

Gutheil, T. G., & Gabbard, G. O. (1993). The concept of boundaries in clinical practice: Theoretical and risk management dimensions. *American Journal of Psychiatry, 150,* 188–196.

Gutheil, T. G., & Simon, R. I. (1997). Clinically based risk management principles for recovered memory cases. *Psychiatric Services, 48*(11), 1403–1407.

Guy, J. K., Brown, C. K., & Poelstra, P. L. (1992). Safety concerns and protective measures used by psychotherapists. *Professional Psychology: Research and Practice, 23*(5), 421–423.

Haas, L. J., & Malouf, J. L. (1995). *Keeping up the good work: A practitioner's guide to mental health ethics* (2nd ed.). Sarasota, FL: Professional Resource Exchange.

Haas, L. J., Malouf, J. L., & Mayerson, N. H. (1986). Ethical dilemmas in psychological practice: Results of a national survey. *Professional Psychology: Research and Practice, 17,* 317–321.

Hamberger, L. K. (2000). Requests for complete record release: A three-step response protocol. *Psychotherapy, 37*(10), 89–97.

Handelsman, M. M. (1990). Do written consent forms influence clients' first impressions of therapists? *Professional Psychology: Research and Practice, 21*(6), 451–454.

Handelsman, M. M., & Galvin, M: D. (1988). Facilitating informed consent for outpatient psychotherapy: A suggested written format. *Professional Psychology: Research and Practice, 19*(2), 223–225.

Handelsman, M. M., Kemper, M. B., Kesson-Craig, P., McLain, I., & Johnsrud, C. (1986). Use, content, and readability of written informed consent forms for treatment. *Professional Psychology: Research and Practice, 17,* 514–518.

Hansen, I. C., Green, S., & Kutner, K. B. (1989). Ethical issues facing school psychologists working with families. *Professional School Psychology, 4,* 245–255.

Hansen, N. D., & Goldberg, S. G. (1999). Navigating the nuances: A matrix of considerations for ethical–legal dilemmas. *Professional Psychology: Research and Practice, 30*(5), 495–503.

Hare-Mustin, R. T., Marecek, I., Kaplan, A. G., & Liss-Levinson, N. (1979). Rights of clients, responsibilities of therapists. *American Psychologist, 34,* 3–16.

Haspel, K. C., Jorgenson, L. M., Wincze, J. P., & Parsons, J. P. (1997). Legislative intervention regarding therapist sexual misconduct: An overview. *Professional Psychology: Research and Practice, 28*(1), 63–72.

Hawkins, I. L., & Bullock, S. L. (1995). Informed consent and religious values: A neglected area of diversity. *Psychotherapy, 32*(2), 293–300.

Health Insurance Portability and Accountability Act (HIPAA) of 1996, Pub. Law No. 104-191, 110 Stat. 1936 (1996).

Herron, W. G., & Sitkowski, S. (1986). Effect of fees on psychotherapy: What is the evidence? *Professional Psychology: Research and Practice, 17*(4), 347–351.

Higuchi, S. A. (1994). Recent managed care legislative and legal issues. In R. L. Lowman & R. I. Resnick (Eds.), *The mental health professional's guide to managed care* (pp. 83–118). Washington, DC: American Psychological Association.

Hillard, J. R. (1995). Predicting suicide. *Psychiatric Services, 46*(3), 223–225.

Hines, P., & Hare-Mustin, R. (1978). Ethical concerns in family therapy. *Professional Psychology, 9,* 165–171.

Hirsh, H. L. (1978). Will your medical records get you into trouble? *Legal Aspects of Medical Practice, 6,* 46–51.

Hirshfeld, R., & Davidson, L. (1988). Risk factors for suicide. In A. I. Frances & R. E. Hales (Eds.), *American Psychiatric Press review of psychiatry* (Vol. 7, pp. 307–333). Washington, DC: American Psychiatric Press.

Hulteng, R. J., & Goldman, E. B. (1986). Potential liability in outpatient practice: A primer for psychotherapists. In L. G. Ritt & S. R. Heyman (Eds.), *Innovations in clinical practice: A source book* (Vol. 5, pp. 233–242). Sarasota, FL: Professional Resource Exchange.

Hurvitz, N. (1976). Marital problems following psychotherapy with one spouse. *Journal of Consulting Psychology, 31,* 38–47.

Hussey, W. R. (1986). How to use small claims court for collections. In L. G. Ritt & S. R. Heyman (Eds.), *Innovations in clinical practice: A source book* (Vol. 5, pp. 245–256). Sarasota, FL: Professional Resource Exchange.

Interstate Insurance Group. (1994, October). *Psychologists professional liability claims-made insurance policy* [Form No. PLI-2008]. (Available from Chicago Insurance Company, 55 E. Monroe St., Chicago, IL 60603)

Jaffee v. Redmond, 518 U.S. 1 (1996).

Jensen, J. A., McNamara, J. R., & Gustafson, K. E. (1991). Parents' and clinicians' attitudes toward the risks and benefits of child psychotherapy: A study of informed-consent content. *Professional Psychology Research and Practice, 22*(2), 161–170.

Jones, W. H. S. (Trans.). (1923). *Hippocrates* (Vols 1 & 2). New York: Putnam.

Kachorek, J. (1990). Record keeping. In E. A. Margenau (Ed.), *The encyclopedic handbook of private practice* (pp. 96–112). New York: Gardner Press.

Kagle, J. D. (1991). *Social work records* (2nd ed.). Belmont, CA: Wadsworth.

Kalichman, S. C. (1995). *Understanding AIDS: A guide for mental health professionals.* Washington, DC: American Psychological Association.

Kalichman, S. C. (1998). Preventing AIDS: A sourcebook for behavioral interventions. Mahwah, NJ: Erlbaum.

Kaplan, A. I. (1990). Nonsexual dual relationships: Protecting the psychologist. *Illinois Psychologist, 28*(3), 25, 30.

Keith-Spiegel, P. (1977, September). *Sex with clients: Ten reasons why it is a very stupid thing to do.* Paper presented at the annual convention of the American Psychological Association, Washington, DC.

Kelsey, D., & Plumb, P. (1999). *Great meetings!: How to facilitate like a pro.* Portland, ME: Hanson Park Press.

Kertay, L., & Reviere, S. (1993). The use of touch in psychotherapy: Theoretical and ethical considerations. *Psychotherapy, 30*(1), 32–40.

King, J. H. Jr. (1977). *The law of medical malpractice.* St. Paul, MN: West.

Kiresuk, T., & Sherman, R. (1968). Goal attainment scaling: A general method for evaluating comprehensive mental health programs. *Community Mental Health Journal, 4,* 443–453.

Kiresuk, T., Smith, A., & Cardillo, J. E. (Eds.). (1994). *Goal attainment scaling: Applications, theory, and measurement.* Hillsdale, NJ: Erlbaum.

Kirkland, K., & Kirkland, K. L. (2001). Frequency of child custody evaluation complaints and related disciplinary action: A survey of the Association of State and Provincial Boards. *Professional Psychology, 32*(2), 171–174.

Kleespies, P. M., Deleppo, J. D., Gallagher, P. L., & Niles, B. L. (1999). Managing suicidal emergencies: Recommendations for the practitioner. *Professional Psychology: Research and Practice, 30*(5), 454–463.

Klein, J., Macbeth, J., & Onek, J. (1984). *Legal issues in the private practice of psychiatry.* Washington, DC: American Psychiatric Press.

Knapp, S. (1992a, April 16). *Record keeping.* Handout presented at workshop, Practicing Safely and Ethically in the 1990s, Pittsburgh, PA.

Knapp, S. (1992b, April). Medicare update. *Pennsylvania Psychologist Update*, p. 7.

Knapp, S. (1994). *Pennsylvania law and psychology.* Harrisburg: Pennsylvania Psychological Association.

Knapp, S., & Tepper, A. M. (1992, May). Caught in the middle: The parent, child and psychologist triangle. *Pennsylvania Psychologist Quarterly*, p. 16.

Knapp, S., & VandeCreek, L. (1981). Behavioral medicine: Its malpractice risks for psychologists. *Professional Psychology: Research and Practice, 12*, 677–683.

Knapp, S., & VandeCreek, L. (1983). Malpractice risks with suicidal patients. *Psychotherapy: Theory, Research, and Practice, 20*, 274–280.

Knapp, S., & VandeCreek, L. (1997a). *Jaffee v. Redmond*: The Supreme Court recognizes a psychotherapist–patient privilege in federal courts. *Professional Psychology: Research and Practice, 28*(6), 567–572.

Knapp, S., & VandeCreek, L. (1997b). *Treating patients with memories of abuse: Legal risk management.* Washington, DC: American Psychological Association.

Knapp, S., VandeCreek, L., & Tepper, A. (1998). *Pennsylvania law and psychology* (3rd ed.). Harrisburg: Pennsylvania Psychological Association.

Kobayashi, M., Smith, T. P., & Norcross, J. C. (1998). Enhancing adherence. In G. P. Koocher, J. C. Norcross, & S. S. Hill III (Eds.), *Psychologists' desk reference* (pp. 2360). New York: Oxford University Press.

Koocher, G., & Keith-Spiegel, P. (1998). *Ethics in psychology: Professional standards and cases* (2nd ed.). New York: Oxford University Press.

Koss, M. P. (1979). Length of psychotherapy for clients seen in private practice. *Journal of Consulting and Clinical Psychology, 47*, 210–212.

Kovacs, A. L. (1987). Insurance billing: The growing risk of lawsuits against psychologists. *Independent Practitioner, 7*, 21–24.

Kramer, S. A. (1990). *Positive endings in psychotherapy: Bringing meaningful closure to therapeutic relationships.* San Francisco: Jossey-Bass.

Kremer, T. G., & Gesten, E. L. (1998). Confidentiality limits of managed care and client's willingness to self-disclose. *Professional Psychology: Research and Practice, 29*(6), 553–558.

Lamb, D. H., Clark, C., Drumheller, P., Frizzell, K., & Surrey, L. (1989). Applying Tarasoff to AIDS-related psychotherapy issues. *Professional Psychology, 20*(1), 37–43.

Lambert, W., Salzer, M. S., & Bickman, L. (1998). Clinical outcome, consumer satisfaction, and ad hoc ratings of improvement in children's mental health. *Journal of Consulting and Clinical Psychology, 66*(2), 270–279.

Larsen, D. L., Attkisson, C. C., Hargreaves, W. A., & Nguyen, T. D. (1979). Assessment of client/patient satisfaction: Development of the general scale. *Evaluation and Program Planning, 2*, 197–207.

Legal issues: How to avoid problems with cellular phones and fax machines. (1992). *Psychotherapy Finances, 18*(2), 3.

Levenstein, J. (1994a). Treatment documentation in private practice: I. The PIC treatment plan. *Independent Practitioner, 14*(4), 181–185

Levenstein, J. (1994b). Treatment documentation in private practice: II. PIRC progress notes. *Independent Practitioner, 14*(5), 233–237.

Ley, P. (1982). Studies in recall in medical settings. *Human Learning, 1*, 223–233.

Liberman, B. (1990). Letter to the editor. *Independent Psychologist, 10*(4), 5.

Lidz, C. W., Meisel, A., Zerubavel, E., Carter, M., Sestak, R. M., & Roth, L. H. (1984). *Informed consent: A study of decisionmaking in psychiatry.* New York: Guilford Press.

Lipman, A. J. (1995). Treating borderline personality disorder. *Contemporary Psychology, 40*(10), 996–997.

Littrell, J., & Ashford, J. B. (1995). Is it proper for psychologists to discuss medications with clients? *Professional Psychology: Research and Practice, 26*(3), 238–244.

Lobes, D. A., & Berman, A. L. (1993). Suicide and malpractice liability: Assessing and revising policies, procedures, and practice in outpatient settings. *Professional Psychology: Research and Practice, 24*(1), 91–99.

LoVerde, M. E., Prochazka, A. V., & Byyny, R. L. (1989). Research consent forms: Continued unreadability and increasing length. *Journal of General Internal Medicine, 4*(5), 410–412.

Mallory, S. D., Gert, B., & Culver, C. M. (1986). Family coercion and valid consent. *Theoretical Medicine, 7*, 123–126.

Maltsberger, J. T. (1986). *Suicide risk: The formation of clinical judgement.* New York: New York University Press.

Margolin, G. (1982). Ethical and legal considerations in marital and family therapy. *American Psychologist, 37*(7), 788–801.

Marine, E. C., & Caudill, O. B. (1996, Winter). What have we learned about false memory cases? *New Mexico Psychologist,* pp. 11–12.

Marine, E. C. (n.d.). [Online]. Available: http://www.americanprofessional.com/risk_html [2002, April 1].

Marsh, D. T. (1995, January). Confidentiality and the rights of families: Resolving possible conflicts. *Pennsylvania Psychologist Update,* pp. 1–3.

McGoldrick, M., Giordano, J., & Pearce, J. K. (Eds.). (1996). *Ethnicity and family therapy* (2nd ed.). New York: Guilford Press.

Meehl, P. E. (1973). Why I do not attend case conferences. In P. E. Meehl (Ed.), *Psychodiagnosis: Selected papers.* Minneapolis: University of Minnesota Press.

Meek, C. (1987). Suggestions on the collection of fees. In P. A. Keller & S. R. Heyman (Eds.), *Innovations in clinical practice: A source book* (Vol. 6, pp. 271–276). Sarasota, FL: Professional Resource Exchange.

Meek, C. (1990). Parent/guardian responsibility for a child in treatment. In L. G. Ritt & S. R. Heyman (Eds.), *Innovations in clinical practice: A source book* (Vol. 9, pp. 265–270). Sarasota, FL: Professional Resource Exchange.

Meek, C., Keller, P. A., & Ritt, L. G. (1985). A collection of office forms. In P. A. Keller & L. G. Ritt (Eds.), *Innovations in clinical practice: A source book* (Vol. 4, pp. 345–360). Sarasota, FL: Professional Resource Exchange.

Meisel, A., Roth, L. H., & Lidz, C. W. (1977). Toward a model of the legal doctrine of informed consent. *American Journal of Psychiatry, 134,* 285–289.

Meiselman, K. C. (1990). *Resolving the trauma of incest.* San Francisco: Jossey-Bass.

Melchert, T. P., & Patterson, M. M. (1999). Duty to warn and interventions with HIV-positive clients. *Professional Psychology: Research and Practice, 30*(2), 180–186.

Meyer, J. D., & Fink, C. (1989). Psychiatric symptoms from prescription medications. *Professional Psychology: Research and Practice, 20*(2), 90–96.

Meyer, R. G., Landis, E. R., & Hays, J. R. (1988). *Law for the psychotherapist.* New York: Norton.

Miller, I. J. (1998). *Eleven unethical managed care practices every patient should know about (with emphasis on mental health care)* [Online]. Available: http://www.nomanagedcare.org/foyer.htm [2001, March 10].

Miller, I. J. (2000). *Dealing with insurance refusal to pay for couples therapy* [Online]. Available: http://www.psychotherapistguild.com/refusal.html [2002, April 1].

Miller, I. J. (2001). Protecting privacy with the absence of records. *Independent Practitioner, 21*(2), 78–79.

Miller, M. C., Jacobes, D. G., & Gutheil, T. G. (1998). Talisman or taboo: The controversy of the suicide-prevention contract. *Harvard Review of Psychiatry, 6*(2), 78–87.

Monahan, J. (1981). *The clinical prediction of violent behavior.* Washington, DC: U.S. Government Printing Office.

Monahan, J. (1993). Limiting therapist exposure to Tarasoff liability: Guidelines for risk containment. *American Psychologist, 48*(3), 242–250.

Monahan, J., & Stedman, H. J. (Eds.). (1994). *Violence and mental disorder: Developments in risk assessment.* Chicago: University of Chicago Press.

Moline, M. E., Williams, G. T., & Austin, K. M. (1998). Documenting psychotherapy: Essential for mental health practitioners. Thousand Oaks, CA: Sage.

Montgomery, L. M., Cupit, B. E., & Wimberley, T. K. (1999). Complaints, malpractice, and risk management: Professional issues and personal experiences. *Professional Psychology: Research and Practice, 30*(4), 402–410.

Moreland, K. L., Eyde, L. D., Robertson, G. J., Primoff, E. S., & Most, R. B. (1995). Assessment of test user qualifications: A research-based measurement procedure. *American Psychologist, 50*(1), 14–23.

Morris, R. J. (1993). Ethical issues in the assessment and treatment of children and adolescents. *Register Report, 19*(1), 4–12.

Morrison, J. K., Fredrico, M., & Rosenthal, H. J. (1975). Contracting confidentiality in group psychotherapy. *Journal of Forensic Psychology, 7,* 1–6.

Nagy, T. F. (1994, July–August). Guidelines and direction when treating clients with repressed memories. *National Psychologist,* pp. 8–9.

National Center for Health Statistics. (1988). *Vital statistics mortality data: Multiple cause-of-death detail.* Hyattsville, MD: U.S. Department of Health and Human Services.

Negley, E. T. (1985). Malpractice prevention and risk management for clinicians. In P. A. Keller & L. G. Ritt (Eds.), *Innovations in clinical practice: A source book* (Vol. 4, pp. 243–251). Sarasota, FL: Professional Resource Exchange.

Newman, R. (2002, April 24). *APA comments: Proposed rule providing modifications to standards for privacy of individually identifiable health information* [On-line]. Available: http://www.apa.org/practice/privacy_302.html

Norris, M. P., Molinari, V., & Rosowsky, E. (1998). Providing mental health care to older adults: Unraveling the maze of Medicare and managed care. *Psychotherapy, 35*(4), 490–497.

Nowell, D., & Spruill, J. (1993). If it's not absolutely confidential, will information be disclosed? *Professional Psychology: Research and Practice, 24*(3), 367–369.

Okun, B. F. (1996). *Understanding diverse families: What practitioners need to know.* New York: Guilford Press.

O'Leary, B. J., & Norcross, J. C. (1998). Making successful referrals. In G. P. Koocher, J. C. Norcross, & S. S. Hill III (Eds.), *Psychologists' desk reference* (pp. 524–526). New York: Oxford University Press.

Orlandi, M. A., Weston, R., & Epstein, L. G. (1992). *Cultural competence for evaluations: A guide for alcohol and other drug abuse prevention practitioners working with ethnic/racial communities.* Rockville, MD: U.S. Department of Health and Human Services.

Ownby, R. L. (1991). *Psychological reports: A guide to report writing in professional psychology* (2nd ed.). Brandon, VT: Clinical Psychology.

Pargament, K. I. (1997). *The psychology of religion and coping: Theory, research, and practice.* New York: Guilford Press.

Paniagua, F. A. (1998). *Assessing and treating culturally diverse clients: A practical guide* (2nd ed.). Thousand Oaks, CA: Sage.

Parsons, I. P., & Wincze, I. P. (1995). A survey of client–therapist sexual involvement in Rhode Island as reported by subsequent treating therapists. *Professional Psychology: Research and Practice, 26*(2), 171–175.

Patten, C., Barnett, T., & Houlihan, D. (1991). Ethics in marital and family therapy: A review of the literature. *Professional Psychology: Research and Practice, 22,* 171–175.

Pearlman, L. A., & Saakvitne, K. W. (1995). *Trauma and the therapist.* New York: Norton.

Pekarik, G. (1985). Coping with dropouts. *Professional Psychology: Research and Practice, 16*(1), 114–123.

Pekarik, G., & Guidry, L. L. (1999). Relationship of satisfaction to symptom change, follow-up adjustment, and clinical significance in private practice. *Professional Psychology: Research and Practice, 30*(5), 474–478.

Pekarik, G., & Wolff, C. B. (1996). Relationship of satisfaction to symptom change, follow-up adjustment, and clinical significance. *Professional Psychology: Research and Practice, 27*(2), 202–208.

Peterson, M. R. (1992). *At personal risk: Boundary violations in professional–client relationships*. New York: Norton.

Philadelphia Society of Clinical Psychologists, Committee on Ethics. (1988, January–February). Ethical issues in psychotherapy termination. *Pennsylvania Psychologist*, p. 10.

Piercy, F., Lasswell, M., & Brock, G. (1989). *AAMFT forms book*. Washington, DC: American Association for Marriage and Family Therapy.

Polythress, N. G. (1992). Expert testimony on violence and dangerousness: Roles for mental health professionals. *Forensic Reports, 5*(1), 135–150.

Pope, K. S. (1987). Preventing therapist–patient sexual intimacy: Therapy for a therapist at risk. *Professional Psychology: Research and Practice, 18*(6), 624–628.

Pope, K. S. (1988a). Dual relationships: A source of ethical, legal and clinical problems. *Independent Practitioner, 8*(4), 17–25.

Pope, K. S. (1988b). How clients are harmed by sexual contact with mental health professionals: The syndrome and its prevalence. *Journal of Counseling and Development, 67*, 222–226.

Pope, K. S. (1988c). Fee policies and procedures: Causes of malpractice suits and ethics complaints. *Independent Practitioner, 8*(4), 24–29.

Pope, K. (1988d). Avoid malpractice in the area of diagnosis, assessment, and testing. *Independent Practitioner, 8*(3), 18–25.

Pope, K. (1988e). More on avoiding malpractice in the area of diagnosis, assessment, and testing. *Independent Practitioner, 8*(4), 23–24.

Pope, K. S. (1989a). Malpractice suits, licensing disciplinary actions and ethics cases: Frequencies, causes, and costs. *Independent Practitioner, 9*(1), 22–26.

Pope, K. S. (1989b). Therapists who become sexually intimate with a patient: Classification, dynamics, recidivism and rehabilitation. *Independent Practitioner, 9*(3), 28–34.

Pope, K. S. (1992). Responsibilities in providing psychological test feedback to clients. *Psychological Assessment, 1*(3), 268–271.

Pope, K. S. (1995). What psychologists better know about recovered memories, research, lawsuits, and the pivotal experiment. *Clinical Psychology: Science and Practice, 2*(3), 304–315.

Pope, K. S. (1996). Memory, abuse, and science: Questioning claims about the false memory syndrome epidemic. *American Psychologist, 51*(9), 957–974.

Pope, K. S. (1997). Science as careful questioning: Are claims of a false memory syndrome epidemic based on empirical evidence? *American Psychologist, 52*(9), 997–1006.

Pope, K. S. (1998). Pseudoscience, cross-examination, and scientific evidence in the recovered memory controversy. *Psychology, Public Policy, and Law, 4*(4),1160–1181.

Pope, K. S. (2000). Therapists' sexual feelings and behaviors: Research, trends, and quandaries. In L. Szuchman & F. Muscarella (Eds.), *Psychological perspectives on human sexuality* (pp. 603–658). New York: Wiley.

Pope, K. S., & Bouhoutsos, I. (1986). *Sexual intimacy between therapists and patients*. New York: Praeger.

Pope, K. S., Sonne, J. L., & Holroyd, J. (1993). *Sexual feelings in psychotherapy: Explorations for therapists-in-training*. Washington, DC: American Psychological Association.

Presser, N. R., & Pfost, K. S. (1985). A format for individual psychotherapy session notes. *Professional Psychology: Research and Practice, 16*(1), 11–16.

Pressman, R. M., & Siegler, R. (1983). *The independent practitioner: Practice management for the allied health professional*. Homewood, IL: Dow Jones-Irwin.

Psychiatrists' Risk Retention Group. (1996). *Description of coverage*. Arlington, VA: Author.

Quinn, V. (n.d.). *Professional therapy never includes sex*. (Available from California Department of Consumer Affairs, 1020 N Street, Sacramento, CA 95814; single copies available at no charge)

Ragusea, S. A. (2002). A professional living will for psychologists and other mental health professionals. In L. VandeCreek & T. L. Jackson (Eds.), *Innovations in clinical practice: A source book* (Vol. 20). Sarasota, FL: Professional Resource Exchange.

Reid, W. H. (1999). *A clinician's guide to legal issues in psychotherapy or proceed with caution*. Phoenix, AZ: Zeig, Tucker.

Repressed memory claims expected to soar. (1996, May–June). *National Psychologist*, p. 7.

Reynolds, W. M. (1991). *Adult Suicidal Ideation Questionnaire*. Odessa, FL: Psychological Assessment Resources.

Rivas-Vazquez, R. A., Blais, M. A., Rey, G. J., & Rivas-Vazquez, A. A. (2000a). Atypical antipsychotic medications: Pharmalogical profiles and psychological implications. *Professional Psychology: Research and Practice, 31*(6), 628–640.

Rivas-Vazquez, R. A., Blais, M. A., Rey, G. J., & Rivas-Vazquez, A. A. (2000b). Sexual dysfunction associated with antidepressant treatment. Professional Psychology: Research and Practice, 31(6), 641–651.

Rosenthal, M. B. (2000). Risk sharing and the supply of mental health services. Journal of Health Economics, 19, 1047–1065.

Rosenthal, V. A. (1976, Spring). A bare branch with buds. *Voices*, pp. 2–10.

Roth, L. (Ed.). (1987). *Clinical treatment of the violent person.* New York: Guilford Press.

Rubanowitz, D. (1987). Public attitudes toward psychotherapist–client confidentiality. *Professional Psychology: Research and Practice, 18*, 613–618.

Rudd, M. D., Dahm, P. F., & Rajab, M. H. (1993). Diagnostic comorbidity in persons with suicidal ideation and behavior. *American Journal of Psychiatry, 150*, 928–934.

Sabourin, S., Laferrière, N., Sicuro, F., Coallier, J.-C., Cournoyer, L.-G., & Gendreau, P. (1989). Social desirability, psychological distress, and consumer satisfaction with mental health treatment. *Journal of Counseling Psychology, 36*(3), 352–356.

Sadoff, R. L. (1988). Record keeping in private practice. In F. Flach (Ed.), *Psychiatric risk management.* New York: Directions in Psychiatry.

Sahid, J. R. (1998). *Practice Strategies, 4*(11).

Satler, J. M. (1977). The effects of therapist–client racial similarity. In A. S. Gurman & A. M. Razin (Eds.), *Effective psychotherapy: A handbook of research* (pp. 250–288). Elmsford, NY: Pergamon Press.

Saunders, T. R. (1993). Some ethical and legal features of child custody disputes: A case illustration and applications. *Psychotherapy, 30*(1), 49–58.

Schinka, J. (1984). *Personal Problems Checklist.* Odessa, FL: Psychological Assessment Resources.

Schinka, J. (1989). *Health Problems Checklist.* Odessa, FL: Psychological Assessment Resources.

Schlosser, B., & Tower, R. B. (1991). Office policies for assessment services. In P. A. Keller & S. R. Heyman (Eds.), *Innovations in clinical practice: A source book* (Vol. 10, pp. 393–405). Sarasota, FL: Professional Resource Exchange.

Schoenfeld, L. S., Hatch, J. P., & Conzalez, J. M. (2001). Responses of psychologists to complaints filed against them with a state licensing board. *Professional Psychology: Research and Practice, 35*(5), 491–495.

Sederer, L. I., & Libby, M. (1995). False allegations of sexual misconduct: Clinical and institutional considerations. *Psychiatric Services, 46*(2), 160–163.

Shafranske, E. P. (Ed.). (1996). Religion and the clinical practice of psychology. Washington, DC: American Psychological Association.

Simon, R. I. (1992). *Clinical psychiatry and the law* (2nd ed.). Washington, DC: American Psychiatric Press.

Skinner, H. A. (1982). The Drug Abuse Screening Test (DAST). *Addictive Behaviors, 7*, 363–371.

Small, R. F. (1993). *Maximizing third-party reimbursement in your mental health practice* (2nd ed.). Sarasota, FL: Professional Resource Exchange.

Simon, R. I. (1999). The suicide prevention contract: Clinical, legal, and risk management issues. *Journal of the American Academy of Psychiatry and Law, 27*(3), 445–450.

Small, R. F., & Barnhill, L. R. (Eds.). (1998). Practicing in the new mental health marketplace: Ethical, legal, and moral issues. Washington, DC: American Psychological Association.

Small, R. F., & Barnhill, L. R. (Eds.). (1998). *Practicing in the new mental health marketplace: Ethical, legal, and moral issues.* Washington, DC: American Psychological Association.

Smith, D., & Fitzpatrick, M. (1995). Patient–therapist boundary issues: An integrative review of theory and research. *Professional Psychology: Research and Practice, 26*(5), 499–506.

Smith, E. W. L., Clance, P. R., & Imes, S. (Eds.). (1998). *Touch in psychotherapy: Theory, research, and practice.* New York: Guilford Press.

Smith, M. L., & Glass, G. V. (1977). Meta-analysis of psychotherapy outcome studies. *American Psychologist, 32,* 752–760.

Soisson, E., VandeCreek, L., & Knapp, S. (1987). Thorough record keeping: A good defense in a litigious era. *Professional Psychology: Research and Practice, 18,* 498–502.

Sommers-Flanagan, I., & Sommers-Flanagan, R. (1995). Intake interviewing with suicidal patients: A systematic approach. *Professional Psychology: Research and Practice, 26*(1), 41–47.

Sonne, J. L. (1994). Multiple relationships: Does the new ethics code answer the right questions? *Professional Psychology: Research and Practice, 25*(4), 336–343.

Soreff, S. M., & McDuffee, M. A. (1993). *Documentation survival handbook for psychiatrists and other mental health professionals: A clinician's guide to charting for better care, certification, reimbursement, and risk management.* Seattle, WA: Hogrefe & Huber.

Spayd, C. S., & Wiley, M. O. (2001, April). Closing a professional practice: Clinical and practical considerations. Pennsylvania Psychologist Update, p. 8.

Staal, M. A., & King, R. E. (2000). Managing a multiple relationship environment: The ethics of military psychology. *Professional Psychology: Research and Practice, 31*(6), 698–705.

Stout, C. E., Levant, R. F., Reed, G. M., & Murphy, M. J. (2001). Contracts: A primer for psychologists. *Professional Psychology: Research and Practice, 32*(1), 88–91.

Stromberg, C. D., & Dellinger, A. (1993, December). Malpractice and other professional liability. In *The psychologist's legal update, 3.* Washington, DC: National Register of Health Service Providers in Psychology.

Stromberg, C. D., Haggarty, D. I., Mishkin, B., Liebenluft, R. F., McMillan, M. H., Rubin, B. L., & Trilling, H. R. (1988). *The psychologist's legal handbook.* Washington, DC: National Register of Health Service Providers in Psychology.

Stromberg, C. D., Lindberg, D., Mishkin, B., & Baker, M. (1993, April). Privacy, confidentiality, and privilege. In *The psychologist's legal update, 1* (p. 8). Washington, DC: National Register of Health Service Providers in Psychology.

Stromberg, C. D., Schneider, J., & Joondeph, B. (1993, August). Dealing with potentially dangerous patients. In *The psychologist's legal update, 2* (p. 10). Washington, DC: National Register of Health Service Providers in Psychology.

Stuart, R. B. (1975). *Treatment contract.* Champaign, IL: Research Press.

Sturm, I. E. (1987). The psychologist and the problem-oriented record (POR). *Professional Psychology: Research and Practice, 18,* 155–158.

Sue, D., & Sue, D. W. (1999). *Counseling the culturally different: Theory and practice* (3rd ed.). New York: Wiley.

Sullivan, T., Martin, W. L., & Handelsman, M. M. (1993). Practical benefits of an informed-consent procedure: An empirical investigation. *Professional Psychology: Research and Practice, 24*(2), 160–163.

Sweet, J. J. (1990). Further considerations of ethics in psychological testing: A broader perspective on releasing records. *Illinois Psychologist, 28*(4), 5–9.

Tarasoff v. Regents of the University of California, 131 Cal. Rptr. 14, 551 P.2d 334 (1976).

Taube, D. O., & Elwork, A. (1990). Researching the effects of confidentiality law on patients' self-disclosures. *Professional Psychology Research and Practice, 22*(1), 72–75.

Taylor, L., & Adelman, H. S. (1989). Reframing the confidentiality dilemma to work in children's best interests. *Professional Psychology: Research and Practice, 20,* 79–83.

Teisman, M. (1980). Convening strategies in family therapy. *Family Process, 19,* 393–400.

Ten steps to create a successful treatment plan. (1993, August). *Managed Care Strategies, 1*(6), 5–6.

Tepper, A. M., Rinella, V. J., Jr., & Siegel, A. M. (1991, November). Subpoenas and court orders in the everyday practice of psychology. *Pennsylvania Psychologist Quarterly,* pp. 14–15.

Thorn, B. E., Shealy, R. C., & Briggs, S. D. (1993). Sexual misconduct in psychotherapy: Reactions to a consumer-oriented brochure. *Professional Psychology: Research and Practice, 24*(1), 75–82.

Tips from an attorney on how to handle lost, stolen or damaged records. (1998). *Practice Strategies, 4*(3), 2, 7.

Tracy, M. (n.d.). *An ounce of prevention now will pay off later for psychiatrists, their practices* [Online].

Available: http://www.prmsva.com/risk_management/An_ounce_of_prevention.htm [2001, October 24].

Tranel, D. (1994). The release of psychological data to nonexperts: Ethical and legal considerations. *Psychotherapy: Theory, Research, and Practice, 25*(1), 33–38.

Truscott, D., Evans, J., & Mansell, S. (1995). Outpatient psychotherapy with dangerous clients: A model of clinical decision making. *Professional Psychology: Research and Practice, 26*(5), 484–490.

Vaccarino, J. M. (1978). Consent, informed consent, and consent forms. *New England Journal of Medicine, 298,* 455.

Vinson, J. S. (1987). Use of complaint procedures in cases of therapist–patient sexual contact. *Professional Psychology: Research and Practice, 18*(2), 159–164.

Wagner, L., Davis, S., & Handelsman, M. M. (1998). In search of the abominable consent form: The impact of readability and personalization. *Journal of Clinical Psychology, 54*(1), 115–120.

Walters, G. C., Solomon, G. S., & Walden, V. R. (1982). Use of the MMPI in predicting persistence of male and female patients. *Journal of Clinical Psychology, 38,* 80–83.

Weed, L. L. (1971). *Medical records, medical education and patient care: The problem-oriented record as a basic tool.* Chicago: Yearbook Medical.

Weiner, B. A., & Wettstein, R. M. (1993). *Legal issues in mental health care.* New York: Plenum Press.

Weiner, I. (1989). On competence and ethicality in psychodiagnostic assessment. *Journal of Personality Assessment, 53,* 827–831.

Wendorf, D., & Wendorf, R. (1985). A systemic view of family therapy ethics. *Family Process, 24,* 443–353.

Werth, J. L., & Carney, J. (1994). Incorporating HIV-related issues into graduate student training. *Professional Psychology: Research and Practice, 25*(4), 458–465.

Widiger, T. A., & Rorer, L. G. (1984). The responsible psychotherapist. *American Psychologist, 39,* 503–515.

Wilbert, J. R., Charles, S. C., Warnecke, R. B., & Lichtenbert, R. (1987). Coping with the stress of malpractice litigation. *Illinois Medical Journal, 17*(1), 23–27.

Wilcoxon, A., & Fenell, D. (1983). Engaging the non-attending spouse in marital therapy through the use of therapist-initiated written communication. *Journal of Marital and Family Therapy, 9,* 199–203.

Wilkinson, A. P. (1982). Psychiatric malpractice: Identifying areas of liability. *Trial, 18*(10),73–77, 89–90.

Willbach, D. (1989). Ethics and family therapy: The case management of family violence. *Journal of Marital and Family Therapy, 1,* 43–52.

Williams, M. (1992). Exploitation and inference: Mapping the damage from therapist–patient sexual involvement. *American Psychologist, 47*(3), 412–421.

Wilson, S. J. (1980). *Recording guidelines for social workers.* New York: Free Press.

Wollersheim, I. P. (1974). The assessment of suicide potential via interview methods. *Psychotherapy, 11,* 222–225.

Woody, R. H. (1988). *Fifty ways to avoid malpractice: A guidebook for mental health professionals.* Sarasota, FL: Professional Resource Exchange.

Woody, R. H. (1991). *Quality care in mental health: Assuring the best clinical services.* San Francisco: Jossey-Bass.

Woody, R. H. (1999). Bartering for psychological services. *Professional Psychology: Research and Practice, 29*(2), 174–178.

Woody, R. H. (2000). *Child custody: Practice standards, ethical issues, and legal safeguards for mental health professionals.* Sarasota, FL: Professional Resource Exchange.

Wright, R. H. (1981a). Psychologists and professional liability (malpractice) insurance. *American Psychologist, 36,* 1485–1493.

Wright, R. H. (1981b). What to do until the malpractice lawyer comes: A survivor's manual. *American Psychologist, 36,* 1535–1541.

Younggren, J. N. (1995). Informed consent: Simply a reminder. *Register Report, 21*(2), 6–7.

Younggren, J. N. (2002, May). *Ethical decision-making and dual relationships* [On-line]. Available: http://kspope.com/younggren.html

Zipple, A. M., Landle, S., Spaniol, L., & Fisher, H. (1990). Client confidentiality and the family's need to know: Strategies for resolving the conflict. *Community Mental Health Journal, 26,* 553–545.

Zhu, S., & Pierce, J. P. (1995). A new scheduling method for time-limited counseling. *Professional Psychology: Research and Practice, 26*(6), 624–625.

Zuckerman, E. L. (2000). *Clinician's thesaurus* (5th ed.): *The guidebook for writing psychological reports.* New York: Guilford Press.

Zung, B. I. (1979). Psychometric properties of the MAST and two briefer versions. *Journal of Studies on Alcohol, 40,* 845–859.

# Index

*Note.* The titles of figures, forms, and handouts are shown in **boldface**.

# Feedback Form

Dear Fellow Clinician,

This book is the result of many therapists' efforts to assist their peers in coping with the rapid and complex ethical and legal developments in the independent practice of psychotherapy. Continuing changes will make parts of *The Paper Office* obsolete in a few years, and so I intend to revise it to meet the evolving needs of therapists for ethical and legal forms and procedures. Please help me keep it useful and relevant by sending me your suggestions and modifications. You will receive credit in the revised editions, as well as a **free copy of the next edition,** for a significant contribution.

Edward L. Zuckerman, PhD
P.O. Box 222
Armbrust, PA 15616-0222
http://thepaperoffice.com

**First,** would you please tell me about your professional life?

Name: _____

Mailing address: _____
_____

Highest relevant credential(s): ❑ Licensed ❑ Registered ❑ Certified ❑ National Register ❑ ABEPP
❑ ACSW ❑ NBCC ❑ MFCC ❑ Other: _____

Member of this (these) national associations: ❑ AACD ❑ AAMD ❑ AAMFT/MSCC ❑ ACSW ❑ ANA
❑ APsychologA ❑ APsychiatA ❑ APsychNurseA ❑ ACS ❑ NASP ❑ None ❑ Other: _____
❑ Division(s) of this national association: _____

Member of your state's professional association: ❑ Yes ❑ No ❑ No state association

Your professional title: _____ Degree(s): _____ Areas of practice
you specialize in: _____

Years in private practice when you bought this book: Full-time: _____ years. Part-time: _____ years.

What were the biggest obstacles to your entering private practice? _____
_____

What have been your biggest problems in private practice? _____
_____

Which ethical or legal problems or questions seem most pressing to *you* right now? _____
_____

**Now,** please tell me about *The Paper Office:*

What is your overall evaluation of the book? _____
_____
_____

What specific changes would you suggest?

Increase: _____
_____

Decrease or eliminate: _____

What forms not included were most useful to you? _____
_____
_____

What forms do you still need? _____
_____

# Instructions for Installing *The Paper Office's* Forms onto Your Computer

## For Windows Computers (98 or Higher)

Insert the CD-ROM, open Windows Explorer, and select your CD drive under "Folders" on the left side of the directory by clicking on the drive letter once. The contents of the CD will be shown on the right side of the directory, under "Name." You will see four folders; double-click on the one entitled "Windows," and then on the file inside entitled "Install.exe." Follow the on-screen directions to install the forms into a folder, which you should name as you see fit. When you are done, go to the new folder in Explorer and open it with a double-click. You will see two folders: "RTFforms" and "PDFforms." One set is in RTF (Rich Text Format) which can be opened by all word processors and modified by you. The other set is in PDF (Portable Document Format) for viewing and printing with the Adobe's Acrobat Reader program.

### Installing Adobe Acrobat Reader on a Windows Computer

If you do not have Reader or have an earlier version and would like to upgrade to version 5, open Windows Explorer and select your CD drive under "Folders" on the left side of the directory by clicking on it once. The contents of the CD will be shown on the right side of the directory. You will see four folders; double-click on the one entitled "AR Installers," and then on the file entitled "Setup.exe." This will install the latest version of Adobe Acrobat Reader onto your computer. Older and different versions can be downloaded from http://www.adobe.com/products/acrobat/readstep2.html.

## For Macintosh Computers

Insert the CD-ROM, and when the icon for the CD appears on the desktop, double-click to open its directory. Copy the whole folder entitled "Forms for Mac" to your desktop by clicking on it once, dragging the folder's icon to the desktop (or another location if you prefer), and releasing the mouse button. The computer will tell you which files it is copying. Inside the new folder, "Forms for Mac," which is now on your hard disk, are the forms in two versions, each in a separate folder: the forms in RTF (Rich Text Format) are for all word processors, so you can modify them, and the forms in PDF (Portable Document Format) are for viewing and printing in Adobe's Acrobat Reader program.

### Installing Adobe Acrobat Reader on a Macintosh Computer

If you do not have Reader or have an earlier version and would like to upgrade to version 5, go to this Web site: http://www.adobe.com/products/acrobat/readstep2.html. Here you will find various versions for downloading.

## Using the Forms

You will find that the forms and handouts from the book are offered in two formats, PDF and RTF. Only some of the forms (those that you will most likely have need of changing or customizing) have been included in RTF format. RTF retains the formatting seen in the printed version (such as bold and italic, tabs, check boxes, etc.), but not always exactly as it appears in the book. RTF files can be opened by all current Macintosh word-processing programs, such as Nisus (my favorite), and Windows programs such as Corel WordPerfect and Microsoft Word (all versions), as well as various "works," "office," or "suite" programs. PDF versions can't be modified but will print just like the forms in the book.

To use a form, simply double-click on its name, and the appropriate application will open the file (your word processor or Adobe Acrobat Reader). You are then ready to work.